solutions@syngress.com

With more than 1,500,000 copies of our MCSE, MCSD, CompTIA, and Cisco study guides in print, we continue to look for ways we can better serve the information needs of our readers. One way we do that is by listening.

Readers like yourself have been telling us they want an Internet-based service that would extend and enhance the value of our books. Based on reader feedback and our own strategic plan, we have created a Web site that we hope will exceed your expectations.

Solutions@syngress.com is an interactive treasure trove of useful information focusing on our book topics and related technologies. The site offers the following features:

- One-year warranty against content obsolescence due to vendor product upgrades. You can access online updates for any affected chapters.

- "Ask the Author"™ customer query forms that enable you to post questions to our authors and editors.

- Exclusive monthly mailings in which our experts provide answers to reader queries and clear explanations of complex material.

- Regularly updated links to sites specially selected by our editors for readers desiring additional reliable information on key topics.

Best of all, the book you're now holding is your key to this amazing site. Just go to **www.syngress.com/solutions**, and keep this book handy when you register to verify your purchase.

Thank you for giving us the opportunity to serve your needs. And be sure to let us know if there's anything else we can do to help you get the maximum value from your investment. We're listening.

www.syngress.com/solutions

SYNGRESS®

HACK PROOFING™

Linux: A Guide to Open Source Security

The Only Way to Stop a Hacker Is to Think Like One

James Stanger
Patrick T. Lane

SYNGRESS®

KEY	SERIAL NUMBER
001	NFKA4UR934
002	DFTGEGHFG6
003	9456VMPDSP
004	MKC8EWR535
005	ZL94V343BB
006	AS56J89HGE
007	MJTY3D29H6
008	ADQW9UU6NN
009	5TGBXDQ7TN
010	KRF4W2F6P9

PUBLISHED BY
Syngress Publishing, Inc.
800 Hingham Street
Rockland, MA 02370

Hack Proofing Linux: A Guide to Open Source Security

Printed in the United States of America

1 2 3 4 5 6 7 8 9 0

ISBN: 1-928994-34-2

Technical Editors: Edgar Danielyan and Larry Karnis
Co-Publisher: Richard Kristof
Acquisitions Editor: Catherine B. Nolan
Developmental Editor: Kate Glennon
CD Production: Michael Donovan

Freelance Editorial Manager: Maribeth Corona-Evans
Cover Designer: Michael Kavish
Page Layout and Art by: Shannon Tozier
Copy Editor: Beth A. Roberts and Darren Meiss
Indexer: Jennifer Coker

Distributed by Publishers Group West in the United States.

Acknowledgments

We would like to acknowledge the following people for their kindness and support in making this book possible.

Richard Kristof and Duncan Anderson of Global Knowledge, for their generous access to the IT industry's best courses, instructors, and training facilities.

Ralph Troupe, Rhonda St. John, and the team at Callisma for their invaluable insight into the challenges of designing, deploying and supporting world-class enterprise networks.

Karen Cross, Lance Tilford, Meaghan Cunningham, Kim Wylie, Harry Kirchner, Bill Richter, Kevin Votel, and Kent Anderson of Publishers Group West for sharing their incredible marketing experience and expertise.

Mary Ging, Caroline Hird, Simon Beale, Caroline Wheeler, Victoria Fuller, Jonathan Bunkell, and Klaus Beran of Harcourt International for making certain that our vision remains worldwide in scope.

Anneke Baeten, Annabel Dent, and Laurie Giles of Harcourt Australia for all their help.

David Buckland, Wendi Wong, Daniel Loh, Marie Chieng, Lucy Chong, Leslie Lim, Audrey Gan, Charlotte Chan, and Joseph Chan of Transquest Publishers for the enthusiasm with which they receive our books.

Kwon Sung June at Acorn Publishing for his support.

Ethan Atkin at Cranbury International for his help in expanding the Syngress program.

Joe Pisco, Helen Moyer, Paul Zanoli, Alan Steele, and the great folks at InterCity Press for all their help.

Philip Allen at Brewer & Lord LLC for all his work and generosity.

Contributors

Patrick T. Lane (MCSE, MCP+I, MCT, Network+, i-Net+, CIW) is a Content Architect for ProsoftTraining.com, a leading Internet skills training and curriculum development company. He is the author of more than 20 technical courses and is the Director of the CIW Foundations and CIW Internetworking Professional series. While at ProsoftTraining.com, Patrick helped create the Certified Internet Webmaster (CIW) program and the i-Accelerate program for Intel, Novell, and Microsoft professionals.

Patrick consults as a mail, news, FTP, and Web Administrator for several organizations, including jCert Initiative Inc. and ProsoftTraining.com. He is also a network security consultant and writer who specializes in TCP/IP internetworking, LAN/WAN solutions, network and operating system security, and the Linux and Windows NT/2000 platforms. He has consulted for the University of Phoenix/Apollo Group, Novell, Intel, NETg, WAVE technologies, KT Solutions, SmartForce, and Futurekids. Patrick is a member of the CompTIA Network+ Advisory Committee, and co-author of Syngress Publishing's *E-mail Virus Protection Handbook* (ISBN: 1-928994-23-7). His work has been published in eight languages and he has been a featured speaker for the SmartForce Seminar Series on E-Business, the Internet World PING Series on Internet Protocol version 6, and the Information Technology Association of America (ITAA). He holds a master's degree in education.

James Stanger (Ph.D., MCSE, MCT) directs the Linux, Security, and Server Administrator certification tracks for ProsoftTraining.com. Since receiving his Ph.D. in 1997, he has focused on auditing Internet servers and writing courseware, books, and articles about administering and securing Internet servers. James has consulted for IBM, Symantec, Evinci (www.evinci.org), Pomeroy (www.pomeroy.com), Securify (www.securify.com), Brigham Young University, and California State, San Bernardino. He specializes in troubleshooting firewalls, intrusion detection, DNS, e-mail, and Web server implementations.

James was the Technical Editor of Syngress Publishing's *E-mail Virus Protection Handbook* (ISBN: 1-928994-23-7) and has been an instructional designer of security and A+ courses for NetG, Thompson/WAVE learning, and ComputerPREP. Active in the Linux community, James sits on the Linux Professional Institute (www.lpi.org), SAIR (www.linuxcertification.org), and CompTIA Linux+ (www.comptia.org) advisory boards, each of which is dedicated to creating and maintaining industry-respected certifications. As the Vice Chair of the Linux Professional Institute (LPI) Advisory Council, he acts as liaison between the LPI and companies such as IBM, Compaq, and Intel.

Technical Editors

Edgar Danielyan (CCNA) is a self-employed developer specializing in GCC, X Window, Tcl/Tk, logic programming, Internet security, and TCP/IP; as well as having with BSD, SVR4.2, FreeBSD, SCO, Solaris, and UnixWare. He has a diploma in company law from the British Institute of Legal Executives as well as a paralegal certificate from the University of Southern Colorado. He is currently working as the Network Administrator and Manager of a top-level Armenian domain. He has also worked for the United Nations, the Ministry of Defense of the Republic of Armenia, and Armenian national telephone companies and financial institutions. Edgar speaks four languages, and is a member of ACM, IEEE CS, USENIX, CIPS, ISOC, and IPG.

Larry Karnis (RHCE, Master ACE, CITP), is a Senior Consultant for Application Enhancements, a Unix, Linux, and Internet consulting firm located in Toronto, Canada. His first exposure to Unix was over 20 years ago where he used Unix Version 6 while completing a bachelor's degree in computer science and mathematics. Larry deploys and manages Linux-based solutions such as Web and file and print servers, and Linux firewalls.

About the CD

This book is accompanied by a CD containing files and open source programs used throughout the book. The files include configuration examples, packet captures, and additional resources. We have included the specific open source programs used in the book so you can follow the chapter demonstrations step-by-step on your own systems.

Each file on the CD is discussed in detail and referenced throughout the book with the CD icon below. When a specific file or program is required, it directs you to the accompanying CD. The book also directs you to the Web site where you can download the most current version, and find additional resources relating to that program. For instance, you can download Free Secure Wide Area Network (FreeS/WAN) at www.freeswan.org, or use the version located on the CD. It is recommended that you use the version included on the CD because this will increase the chances that the book demonstrations will be successful, as some of the programs may have changed since this book was printed.

The book is written to Red Hat Linux 7.x. Therefore, most of the CD files are Red Hat Package Manager (.rpm) files. There are also many Tape Archive (.tar) files and GNU Zip (.gzip) files. Instructions for unpacking and installing these files are included in their respective locations throughout the book. To mount the CD onto your Linux system, you would issue the following command (for Red Hat systems):

```
mount -t iso9660 /dev/cdrom /mnt/cdrom
```

And to unmount:

```
umount /mnt/cdrom
```

It is recommended that you copy the CD files to your hard drive before working with them. If you use other versions of Linux, you may need to modify the demonstrations, or download a portable version of the open source programs to work with your version of Linux.

 Look for this CD icon when obtaining files used in the book demonstrations.

Contents

Using the GNU General Public License

The GNU General Public License (GPL) is the basis of the open source movement. This license is provided by the Gnu is Not Unix (GNU) organization, which develops various software packages. The most important element of this license is that instead of protecting a particular person or company, it protects the software code that creates the application.

**Determining Which
Ports to Block**

When determining which
ports to block on your
server, you must first
determine which services
you require. In most cases,
block all ports that are not
exclusively required by
these services. This is tricky,
because you can easily
block yourself from
services you need,
especially services that use
ephemeral ports. If your
server is an exclusive e-mail
server running SMTP and
IMAP, you can block all TCP
ports except ports 25 and
143, respectively. If your
server is an exclusive HTTP
server, you can block all
ports except TCP port 80.

**Learn How to Set
Preferences For
TkAntivir**

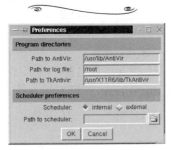

SECURITY ALERT!

Although Tripwire has a "file integrity mode," Tripwire is not really an integrity checker in the classic sense. It does not, for example, test the file's stability or inode number or any other aspect in regards to file storage. Tripwire simply compares a file's new signature with that taken when the database was created. Other tools may be used to check the integrity of a file's permissions and ownership information.

Chapter 5 Troubleshooting the Network with Sniffers   261

Chapter 6 Network Authentication and Encryption   299

Learn the Flags Used in TCP Connections

Flag	Description
SYN	Synchronize sequence numbers. Used for connection establishment.
FIN	The sender is finished with the connection. Used for connection termination.
RST	Reset the connection.
PSH	Push the data.
ACK	Acknowledgment
URG	Urgent

**Answer Your
Questions about
Kerberos**

Q: I wish to remove a
principal from the
keytab of one of my
Kerberos clients. How
do I do this?

A: Enter kadmin as an
administrative user on
the Kerberos client
(not the KDC) and use
the **ketremove** option.
For example, if you
wanted to remove the
principal for the user
named *james*, you
would do the
following:

```
terminal$/usr/
  kerberos/sbin/kadmin
kadmin: ktremove
  -p james
kadmin: quit
terminal$
```

Chapter 7 Avoiding Sniffing Attacks through Encryption   353

Secure E-Commerce Transactions

If hackers were alerted to an unsecure server, they could capture packets going in and out of the server to gain the data they sought. For example, if an e-commerce server does not use any type of network encryption for transactions, there is a great deal of data to be gained by a hacker. Unfortunately, many small companies or entrepreneurs set up their own Web servers, unaware of potential security problems, and set up simple scripts to process payment forms.

Secure Tunneling with Virtual Private Networks (VPNs)

VPNs provide a private data network over public telecommunication infrastructures, such as the Internet, by providing authentication and encryption through a data "tunnel" between devices. All data transmitted between the devices through the tunnel is secure, regardless of what programs the devices are running.

**Understand Essential
Linux Firewall
Functions**

- IP address conservation
  and traffic forwarding
- Network differentiation
- Protection against
  denial-of-service,
  scanning, and sniffing
  attacks
- IP and port
- Content filtering
- Packet redirection
- Enhanced
  authentication and
  encryption
- Supplemented logging

**Configure Squid
with the /etc/squid/
squid.conf file**

Chapter 11 Maintaining Firewalls   543

See How to Use the Firelogd Program

Firelogd (Firewall Log Daemon) is a relatively simple program that can either be run as an application or (you might have guessed) as a daemon. It does two things:

- It reads the kernel log entries and passes them into a "first in, first out" (FIFO) pipe, which Firelogd can then process.

- Once its buffer is full, it e-mails a report of suspicious traffic to an account of your choosing. You can have it mailed to a local account, or to a remote system of your choice.

Preface

Hack Proofing Linux: A Guide to Open Source Security is designed to help you deploy a Linux system on the Internet in a variety of security roles. This book provides practical instructions and pointers concerning the open source security tools that we use every day.

First, we show you how to obtain the software; and then, how to use the Bastille application to "harden" your Linux operating system so that it can function securely as it fulfills a specific role of your choice (e.g., as a Web server, as an E-mail server, and so forth). You will also learn how to use your Linux system as an auditing tool to scan systems for vulnerabilities as well as create an Intrusion Detection System (IDS), which enables your Linux system to log and respond to suspicious activity. From virus protection to encrypting transmissions using Gnu Privacy Guard and FreeSWAN, you will be able to configure your system to secure local data as well as data that will be passed along the network. After reading this book, you will be able to identify open source and "for-fee" tools that can help you further secure your Linux system.

We have also included chapters concerning ways to sniff and troubleshoot network connections and how to implement strong authentication using One Time Passwords (OTP) and Kerberos. Tools such as Squid proxy server and Ipchains/Iptables will help you use your Linux system so that it can act as a firewall. With the tools on the accompanying CD as well as the advice and instructions given in this book, you will be able to deploy your Linux system in various roles with confidence.

We decided to focus on profiling the most commonly used security tools found on the Linux platform. We also decided to emphasize the real-world implementation of these tools, as opposed to just providing conceptual overviews. Finally, we decided to describe the steps you should take when things go wrong. As a result, we have created a book that is a valuable resource that helps you use your Linux system as efficiently as possible.

One of the most exciting things about this book is that it provides hands-on instructions for implementing security applications. From Gnu Privacy Guard (GPG) and Bastille to FreeSWAN, Kerberos, and firewall troubleshooting utilities, this book shows you how to use your Linux skills to provide the most important security services such as encryption, authentication, access control, and logging.

While writing the book, we had the following three-part structure in mind:

- Locking Down the Network (Chapters 1 through 4)

- Securing Data Passing Across the Network (Chapters 5 through 8)

- Protecting the Network Perimeter with Firewalls (Chapters 9 through 11)

Each of these sections is designed to help you find the best solution for your particular situation. Although the book itself isn't explicitly divided into sections, as you are reading remember this rough division because it will help you to implement security measures in your own environment.

Chapter 1 discusses open source concepts, including the GNU General Public License, as presented by the www.gnu.org people (the Free Software Foundation), and then moves on to showing how you can use GPG and Pretty Good Privacy (PGP) to encrypt transmissions and also to check the signatures of files that you download from the Web. It also provides information concerning the steps to take when auditing a network.

Chapter 2 shows you how to lock down your operating system so that it provides only those Internet services that you desire. Chapter 3 shows you how to use applications such as AntiVir, Gnome ServiceScan, Nmap, Rnmap, and Nessus to scan for vulnerabilities. In Chapter 4, you will learn about host and network-based IDS applications such as Snort, Tripwire, and PortSentry. Chapter 5 explains how to use network sniffers such as Tcpdump, Ethereal, and EtherApe to their full advantage. With this knowledge, auditing a network and truly understanding what is going on "beneath the hood" will make you a much more effective network security administrator.

By the time you finish Chapter 6, you will know how to deploy One Time Passwords and Kerberos, and in Chapter 7, you will understand how to avoid sniffing attacks, and in Chapter 8, you will enable IPSec by deploying FreeSWAN. Chapter 9 empowers you to create personal firewalls as well as packet filtering firewalls using either Ipchains or Iptables. Chapter 10 shows you how to implement Squid so that you can more carefully monitor and process packets. Finally, Chapter 11 provides you with tools that test your firewall implementation.

The open source community has fulfilled the need for a powerful, free system that allows you to conduct audits, serve up Web pages, provide e-mail services, or any other Internet service you wish to provide. Once you are able to take advantage of the security software provided by the open source community, you will receive the benefit of having a huge pool of developers working for you. You will gain more freedom because you will be able to choose widely tested security tools provided by a variety of skilled developers. You can even choose (at your own risk) to use rather obscure tools that have been recently created. It is up to you.

Open source operating systems and security tools are both a blessing and a curse: You are blessed with (usually) free software, but you are then cursed with having to spend time working with the software's idiosyncrasies. By reading this book and implementing the tools and practices we've described, you should be able to minimize the "curse." It is also our hope that as you read this book you will also become further involved in the open source software movement, which has begun to fulfill its promise of creating powerful, useful software.

—James Stanger, Ph.D., MCSE, MCT

## Chapter 1

Introduction to Open Source Security

Solutions in this chapter:

- Using the GNU General Public License
- Soft Skills: Coping with Open Source Quirks
- Should I Use an RPM or Tarballs?
- Obtaining Open Source Software
- A Brief Encryption Review
- Public Key and Trust Relationships
- Auditing Procedures

☑ Summary

☑ Solutions Fast Track

☑ Frequently Asked Questions

Introduction

In spite of the ups and downs of the dot-com industry, open source software has become a viable alternative to commercial companies such as Microsoft, Sun, and IBM. Although open source software has its quirks and its problems, the open source movement has made its niche in the networking market. As a networking professional, it is in your best interest to understand some of the more important security applications and services that are available.

This book is designed to provide experienced systems administrators with open source security tools. Although we have made every effort to include as many people and as many skill sets as possible, this book assumes a fundamental knowledge of Linux. This book focuses on open source Linux applications, daemons, and system fixes. In the book's first chapters, you will learn how to lock down your network. Chapter 2 discusses ways to secure and monitor the operating system, and ways to scan local and remote networks for weaknesses. You will receive detailed information on how to ensure that your system's services and the root account are as secure as possible.

In Chapter 3, you will learn how to deploy antivirus and scanning programs for your local system. By using these scanning programs, you will be able to mitigate risk and learn more about the nature of services on your network. Scanners such as nmap and nessus will help you learn about the open ports on your network, and how these open ports might pose a threat to your system. Chapter 3 gives you detailed information about practical ways to implement intrusion detection on your local system and on your network. Using applications such as Tripwire, Portsentry, and Snort, you will be able to precisely identify system anomalies and detect inappropriate logins. Chapter 5 shows how you can use open source tools such as tcpdump, Ethereal, EtherApe, and Ntop to inspect and gauge traffic on the network.

The second part of the book focuses on ways to enhance authentication using open source software. In Chapter 6, you will learn about One Time Passwords (OTP) and Kerberos as ways to ensure that malicious users won't be able to obtain your passwords as they cross the network. Chapter 7 discusses ways to use Secure Shell (SSH) and Secure Sockets Layer (SSL), which are ways to enable on-the-fly encryption to protect data. In Chapter 8, you will learn about how to enable IPSec on a Linux system so that you can implement a virtual private network (VPN). As you learn more about the primary VPN product called Free Secure Wide Area Network (FreeS/WAN), you will see how it is possible to protect network traffic as it passes through your own network, and over the Internet.

The final part of the book focuses on ways to create an effective network perimeter. Chapter 9, shows how to install and configure Ipchains and Iptables on a Linux system. Kernels earlier than 2.3 can use Ipchains, whereas kernel versions 2.3 and later use Iptables. Regardless of the way you do it, you will learn to filter traffic with these two packet filtering tools.

In Chapter 10, you will learn how a proxy server can further enhance your control over your network perimeter. Specifically, you will use the Squid proxy server to control client access to the Internet. You will also learn how to configure Linux clients to access the proxy server. Finally, Chapter 11, shows how to troubleshoot and counteract problems with your network perimeter. You will learn how to maintain, test, and log the firewall so that you have a functional barrier between you and the outside world.

It is our intention to create a book that gives you practical information and advice about the most common open source security tools.

The Tools Used in This Book

This book was written using version 7.0 of the Red Hat Linux operating system. Although it may not be the "best" Linux distribution (there are at least 100 versions in the world), it is the most popular. We have tried to ensure that the skills and tools you obtain in this book will be portable to other Linux versions, and even other open source operating systems such as FreeBSD (www.freebsd.org). However, each Linux flavor has its own quirks, and you may find it necessary to deviate from some of the instructions in this book.

Using the GNU General Public License

The GNU General Public License (GPL) is the basis of the open source movement. This license is provided by the Gnu is Not Unix (GNU) organization, which develops various software packages. Begun in 1984 by Richard Stallman, GNU has worked to create a license designed to ensure that the open source movement continues to thrive. You can learn more about GNU at the www.gnu.org Web site, shown in Figure 1.1.

The most important element of this license is that instead of protecting a particular person or company, it protects the software code that creates the application. Traditionally, copyrights have enabled individuals to lay claim to a particular piece of software and then sell it for profit. In addition, the copyright enables that individual to then take action against anyone else who uses that code to create similar functionality. For better or for worse, Richard Stallman, Eric Raymond, and others helped found and popularize the concept of an open software license called the Gnu General Public License (often referred to as the *GPL*). You can read the GPL at www.gnu.org/copyleft/gpl.html.

Figure 1.1 The GNU Web Site

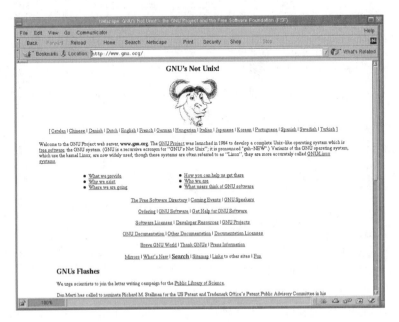

This license is part of the "copyleft" movement, which considers itself an alternative to traditional copyright laws. The GPL essentially allows anyone who develops code to ensure that the code remains open, meaning that GPL-licensed code can be taken and improved upon by anyone, as long as the improved code is given to the original writer and the software writing community. Consequently, a piece of code protected by the GPL will, by law, always remain accessible by anyone who wants to read or modify it. Without the GPL license, another person can take the code that you invent, and make it closed and proprietary.

The GNU GPL is not the only free software license in existence. Figure 1.2 shows the GNU page dedicated to understanding additional licenses. If you wish, you can read about additional licenses that are similar to the GPL at www.gnu.org/philosophy/license-list.html.

For more information about the open source movement, one of the more revealing books is Erik Raymond's *The Cathedral and the Bazaar* (O'Reilly &

Associates, 2001). Although somewhat overly enthusiastic, it is a very helpful book in understanding the mindset of many open source code writers.

Figure 1.2 Viewing GNU's Licenses Comment Section

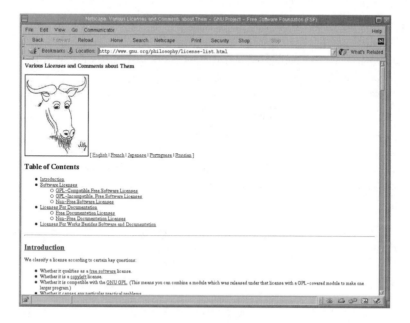

Fee-Based GPL Software

Contrary to what you might think, open source code protected by the GPL is not necessarily free. Under the terms of the GPL, any person or corporation can take GPL software, modify it, and then package it for sale. However, this person or corporation must make this software freely available for anyone to read or modify.

Can I Use GPL Software in My Company?

The GNU GPL does not ask companies to supply licensing agreements or otherwise register the programs. However, other licenses, which you can read at GNU's comparative forum, may invoke restrictions that you may have to consider as you implement the software. The software covered in this book is, in one way or another, open software, which means it can be used by any organization.

Soft Skills: Coping with Open Source Quirks

You should consider, however, that open source software can present challenges. Consider them before you delve into the open source world. It is likely that using open source software will require you to use your "soft skills," such as how to overcome objections and manage constant change. The more important challenges to your soft skills are discussed in the following sections.

General Lack of Installation and Configuration Support

Although many of the applications you will use are written by clever, knowledgeable coders, most of these people create this code on their own time. Thus, no formal support structure exists for the software you use. As a result, you will be forced to rely on knowledgeable individuals to implement and maintain your open source applications.

Infrequent or Irregular Update Schedules

Many closed-source companies update their software at regular periods. Usually, a for-profit company's desire to keep sales high by requiring constant for-fee upgrades is tempered by its need to maintain the product's reputation for stability, ease of use, and longevity. Thus, upgrades will happen at regular intervals. However, the open source community is not held in check by this desire. Generally, software is frequently upgraded. You may, therefore, find that you will have to spend considerable time upgrading the open source products you use.

It is also quite unlikely that you will be notified of any problems that have been discovered in the specific version of your application. For example, many for-profit companies spend time publicizing problems and even contacting licensed users to notify them of a security problem. If you use an open source security application, the burden is placed on you: it is assumed that you will take the time to keep current about any developments concerning the application you are using.

Command-Line Dominance

Many open source applications use command-line interfaces. In the past several years, the trend has been to create a graphical user interface (GUI) for command-line applications. Generally, however, these GUI interfaces are not as portable between operating systems. In some cases, the GUI interface, unless superbly written, does not provide the same functionality (that is, you can't do the same thing with the GUI that you can at the command line).

Lack of Backward Compatibility and No Regular Distribution Body

When you upgrade an operating system, it is possible that the applications you have been using no longer work, or behave differently. Although the open source community is remarkably well coordinated, you should consider this possibility.

Furthermore, it is possible that the software you use may become unavailable, or may become fee based. While discovering that a Web site URL has changed is inconvenient, discovering that an upgrade for your favorite application will now cost you money can raise serious issues about your continued use of the product.

Inconvenient Upgrade Paths

Many open source applications change their coding rather radically. As a result, a previous version may not be upgradeable, and you may have to reinstall it. Even then, it is possible that a simple reinstallation is not possible. Many open source applications provide their own versions of a Windows-style configuration wizard, but when you upgrade, you may have to install the new files manually.

Conflicts in Supporting Libraries and Limited Platform Support

Even though you find a piece of software that you really find interesting, it is possible that you will have to take rather intricate steps to make your operating system ready for the application. Most of these steps involve updating system libraries, which are sets of routines and helper applications. Examples of libraries include the Tool Command Language/Tool Kit (tcl/tk) and the Gnome libraries (gnome-lib).

Often, steps for upgrading these libraries are poorly documented and rather difficult to follow. Additionally, operating systems such as Linux are loosely integrated, which means that no central "brain," such as a Windows 2000 registry, exists to coordinate library usage. So, even though you may be able to enable your system to accept your cool new application, you may end up causing incompatibilities that cause other applications to fail.

Another problem with software that isn't quite "ready for prime time" is that it may be developed for only one Linux flavor, or even only one version of a specific Linux flavor. If you upgrade your system (or one of the libraries), it is possible that the application will stop working

Interface Changes

Coders and end users rarely want radical changes in a GUI interface to occur. Changing an interface requires more coding work on the part of coders, and it could result in an application losing popularity. However, due to changes in the open source libraries and in coding practices, you may find that commands and interfaces are radically changed from one version to the next.

Partially Developed Solutions

Sometimes, the code you want to use promises to do things it just can't deliver. Some expected or advertised features may be missing, or may not be implemented yet. Sometimes, this happens because the open source application's development team has the best of intentions and is working to complete the project. Other times, the development team runs out of gas, and you end up wishing that the application had delivered on its potential.

In such cases, your options are rather limited, unless you have the means at your disposal to deploy your own development team and take up the project where your predecessors left off.

Developing & Deploying…

Open Source as Malware?

Thus far, you have learned about technical issues concerning open source software. However, there are business and security issues as well. If you are a manager, make sure you carefully consider the use of open source software. There may be times when open source software is not appropriate for a certain task. Consider the following questions:

- Aren't these hacker programs?
- Do I have time to train my employees on this software?

Continued

- Is the software stable enough to use?
- Have I had the code reviewed to ensure it is safe?
- How will I explain the use of open source software to my management?
- How will I explain the use of open source software to customers and business partners?

The first question is significant. Many open source security applications have been written as *proof of concept* exploits. A proof of concept exploit is basically an application meant to prove that a theoretical or much-discussed weakness in an operating system really does exist. Other applications are provided to allow hackers to gain information about a network or network host. However, just because an application was created for malicious intent does not necessarily mean that it has to be used maliciously. In fact, many open source applications have been created with the best of intentions, only to have them used to cause problems. Therefore, as a manager, you should ensure that all parties involved in maintaining your network understand that simple use of a particular application does not necessarily mean that the user has become a hacker.

As you choose the software, make sure that you actually take some time to educate your IT employees so that they use it properly. Have them consider how using the application can affect the network. If used at certain times, using a network probing application may cause too much network traffic and thus impact end-user communication. In addition, when you choose this application, consider that it may still be in beta development, and that certain features are bound to change.

Because it is difficult to verify that this code is in fact safe, take the time to review it. If you cannot do it yourself, contact a reliable source to verify that the code does not contain an element, such as a Trojan horse, that can erode your network's security.

Finally, it is possible that you may have to explain why your company uses open source applications. Increasingly, business partners and insurance companies are interested in knowing exactly how you audit your systems. In some situations, you may find yourself having to explain why using open source applications is appropriate. In other cases, you may find that using open source software is wholly inappropriate.

Should I Use an RPM or Tarballs?

In regard to Linux, open source software generally comes in three flavors: source tarball, Red Hat Package Manager (RPM), and Debian. A source tarball is a group of files and directories that usually must be compiled. Generally, tarballs come with a special file called a *makefile*, which contains instructions that tell the source code where the supporting libraries are for the application you are installing. Many will argue passionately that one is better than the other (or, that one operating system—such as the Debian operating system—is better than all the rest). The best approach to take is to use the right tool for the right job. In some cases, tarballs will work best. In other cases, using RPMs is the best way, as long as the RPM was created by a person who really understands the operating system, and that you have chosen the correct RPM for your operating system version.

Tarball

When using source tarballs, the most portable and extensible format, the code usually comes in packages that are first run through the tar application, which creates archives of files and directories that can then be easily transported from one system to another. Sometimes, the tarball contents are precompiled binaries, which means that all you have to do is decompress and install the application. Other times, the code comes as C or (less often) C++ "source code," which must then be compiled using, for example, the makefiles and the Gnu CC (gcc) or Gnu C++ gc++ compilers. These tarball packages are then compressed by using any number of applications. The most common (de)compression programs are GNU Zip (**gzip**, **gunzip**, **gzcat**) programs, which create compressed tarball archives with a tar.gz, .tgz, or tar.Z ending. The **gzip** command creates the tar.gz ending. The .tgz extension is also created in **gzip** by those who know that their files may be downloaded by Microsoft-oriented browsers, which often have difficulty downloading files with the tar.gz ending. The .Z extension is created by the Unix command called **compress**. Slackware systems often use the .tgz tarball ending. The **bzip** program has also become popular. Compressed bzip files have a .bz ending. Generally, you install a gzipped tarball by using the **tar -zxvf** command.

The source code that comes in source code tarballs can be edited to conform to your own system. Perhaps more importantly, source tarballs allow you to specify compile options that can greatly extend the usefulness of the application or daemon you wish to install. You will be given explicit instructions whenever this is necessary. Also note that tarballs can contain pre-compiled binary applications and supporting files rather than source code.

Tarballs often require editing of a special file called a *makefile*. However, this is not necessarily all that difficult. It simply requires that you know where your supporting applications and libraries are. In addition, most open source software will contain instructions concerning how to edit the makefile. Most well-known operating systems, such as Red Hat Linux and Slackware, do not require makefile modification.

Red Hat Package Manager

Originally developed by Red Hat, Red Hat Package Manager (RPM) files have become more universal. TurboLinux, Mandrake, and Kondara, for example, all support this format. RPMs come in either precompiled binary format, or as source RPMs. Make sure that you obtain the correct RPM for your distribution and hardware. You can then install an RPM (barring library and resource conflicts) by using the **rpm –ivh** command. These packages usually contain precompiled binary files, but it is possible to install *source RPMs* (.srpm) that will deposit source code that you must then compile using **make** and the appropriate gcc and g++ compilers.

RPMs are installed using the RPM utility. To install an RPM, you could enter the following command:

```
host# rpm -ivh packagename.versionnumber.i386.rpm
```

This command uses the **–I** option, which simply means *install*. The **–vh** options have the RPM utility go into *verbose* mode and report the installation progress using hash marks. You can learn more about the RPM facility by consulting the rpm man page. As you will see in later sections, tarball, RPM, and Debian packages can pose threats to your system—after all, they are designed to automatically place code onto your system. Many times, this code is precompiled and "ready to go." It is possible for malicious users to place code into these packages. You must be extremely careful whenever installing any of these packages. Later in this chapter, you will see how you can at least partially protect yourself by using digital signatures.

Debian

Debian (.deb) Linux uses .deb packages in a similar way that Red Hat, for example, uses RPMs. Debian packages are installed by using the **dpkg –i** command. As with tarballs and RPM files, these packages can also contain source files, rather than precompiled binaries.

Obtaining Open Source Software

Now that you have considered some of the more pressing open source issues, it's time to learn where to get open source security software. As you might suspect, there is no single source. Some of the best Web sites for open source security software include the following (many other sources exist):

- **SourceForge** www.sourceforge.com

- **Freshmeat** www.freshmeat.net

- **Packetstorm** http://packetstorm.securify.com

- **RPMFind** www.rpmfind.net

- **LinuxLinks** www.linuxlinks.com

- **Tucows** www.tucows.com

- **Startplaza** www.startplaza.nu

- **SecurityFocus** www.securityfocus.com

- **AtStake** www.atstake.com

SourceForge

SourceForge, shown in Figure 1.3, is an especially rich source for security content. From here, you can download applications such as EtherApe, Ethereal, and many others.

One of the primary benefits of obtaining software from SourceForge is that you can learn about the development history, learn about the developers of an application, and even send the developers e-mail (good luck getting answers!). You can also learn about what language the program was developed in, and what operating systems the application was specifically developed for. In many ways, this site does much of the research for you.

Finally, SourceForge provides a login feature that allows you to:

- Participate in open discussions concerning software.

- Register an open source project.

- Learn about top projects.

- Obtain information about various topics, including the latest Linux kernel development updates.

Figure 1.3 The SourceForge Web Site

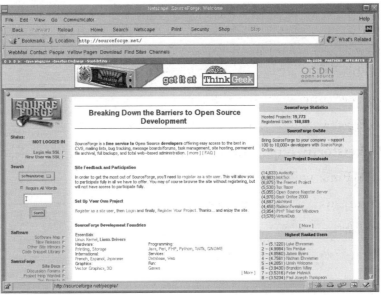

Freshmeat

The Freshmeat Web site, shown in Figure 1.4, derives its name from its primary function, which is to provide the latest and greatest software from the open source community. Like SourceForge, this site is not completely devoted to security. Nevertheless, you should spend time at this site to learn about the latest applications, most of which are created for Linux. By just typing **security** in the search field, you can learn about the latest applications meant to increase security, as well as those meant to defeat existing security measures.

This site also provides a login feature. One of the benefits of logging in is the ability to catch up on the latest projects that have been registered on the site. In less than a week, several hundred new projects can be registered, many of them having to do with security. Another benefit is the ability to search for articles written about the applications in which you are interested. The search feature includes filtering mechanisms designed to help you drill down to the most relevant information.

Figure 1.4 The Freshmeat Web Site

Figure 1.5 The Packetstorm Web Site

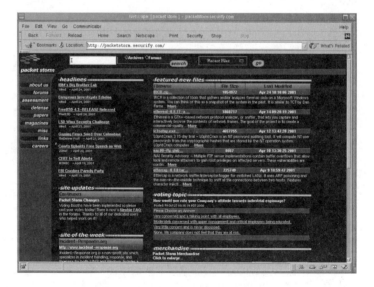

Packetstorm

Packetstorm is specifically devoted to security, and has an extensive collection of files. At this site, shown in Figure 1.5, you can download both "white hat" and "black hat" applications; in other words, you can download applications that help detect and/or stop intrusions, or you can download applications specifically designed to break into systems. The developers of the site spend a great deal of time surfing the top Internet sites (including SourceForge and Freshmeat) for the "latest and greatest" files.

One of the many convenient features of this site is its listing of the most recent tools, exploits, and warnings the site has obtained. Another is its Forums feature, which allows you to converse with others interested in security. The site also lists the most current advisories, so you can see if anyone has discovered a problem in any of the open source applications you are using.

SecurityFocus

The SecurityFocus site is a well-organized repository of security files. Its home page is shown in Figure 1.6. As well organized as it is, its collection of files, found in the Tools section, is not as extensive. Still, the site provides informative news about the latest security developments, and does a good job archiving the latest security files.

Figure 1.6 The SecurityFocus Web Site

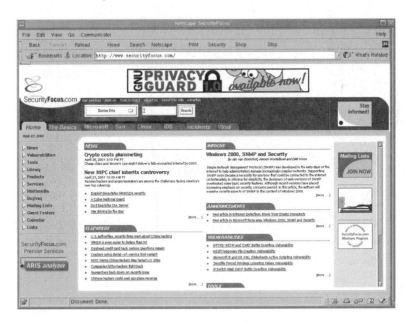

Is That Download Safe?

Another problem with open source code is that you spend a great deal of time downloading files from untrusted sites. As a security professional, you have to consider the possibility that some of these files may have been tampered with. Many in the open source community have encountered files that contain *Trojan horses*, which are stealthy programs meant to thwart security. Trojan code hides legitimate code. Sometimes, the Trojan can wait to activate, or it can activate itself when you install what appears to be a perfectly legitimate program. Examples of Trojan horses include:

- **Illicit servers** Hidden servers that open ports that allow a malicious user (usually) root access to the server.

- **Root kits** Programs, such as **ps**, **ls**, or **su**, which will still work, but also thwart security by, for example, key logging the administrator's password and then sending it to an anonymous FTP. The malicious user can then download the password and log in to the system.

So, how can you determine if this download is secure? One of the best ways is to obtain a *digital signature* for the software package. A digital signature is a small piece of code generated by an encryption algorithm. A signature allows you to determine two things. First, you can learn if the file has been tampered with in any way. Second, you can use the key to verify that the software was in fact authored by the person who claims authorship. Before you learn more about checking signatures, it is important that you first understand the basic encryption principles involved.

A Brief Encryption Review

One of the most important things you can understand in terms of open source security is how encryption operates on networks. Feel free to skip this section if you already understand these terms. If you don't, then read on. They will be implied throughout this book.

Why is encryption important? At one time, Microsoft's old LANmanager product (a precursor to Windows NT and 2000) did not encrypt its passwords as it communicated with other hosts. As a result, this particular operating system fell out of favor, forcing Microsoft to improve its product. One of those improvements was the use of encrypted transmissions. Encryption is not a foolproof solution. It is possible to misconfigure your encryption tools, and even properly encrypted transmissions are not completely safe. Nevertheless, encryption does tend to raise the bar enough to make most hackers search for other systems to attack.

Before we continue, it is important to understand the three types of encryption in general use:

- **Symmetric** The use of one key to encrypt and decrypt information. This is a common type of encryption, but can be easily defeated if you misplace the key, or if a malicious user intercepts the key in transit. If a malicious user is able to intercept the key, he or she can then use it to decrypt your secret messages.

- **Asymmetric** This type of encryption uses a mathematically related *key pair* to encrypt and decrypt information. It is commonly used on the Internet and on LANs, because it reduces the likelihood that the key can be learned by a malicious user, and aids in authentication.

- **One way** The use of an algorithm to encrypt information so that it is, mathematically speaking, impossible to unencrypt it. One-way encryption is also used to read a file and then create a *hash* of that file. The resulting hash value is said to be mathematically unrecoverable.

You should understand that in regard to networking, the "information" discussed in this section can include a file, or a series of network packets emanating from a network host. Many encryption applications, such as GNU Privacy Guard (GPG) and Pretty Good Privacy (PGP) employ all three of these types of encryption, as you will see later.

Symmetric Key Encryption

Your car key is a crude, although helpful, example of symmetric encryption. Consider that most people use the same physical key to lock, unlock, and start their cars. If you lose your key, anyone who finds it can locate your car, insert your key in the door and the ignition, and then drive it away. Suppose, now, if you tried to pass this key to another person in a crowded room, and someone you do not trust was to intercept it. You would probably then have a problem: the only thing keeping this untrusted person out of your car is that person's honesty and his or her knowledge of what your car looks like. If that person wanted to, he or she could find your car, open it, and drive away.

The use of symmetric encryption across an untrusted network such as the Internet (or, really, your LAN or enterprise network) presents the same problem as the use of a single car key: anyone who intercepts your symmetric key with a packet sniffer can decrypt your messages. This type of attack is a *sniffing* attack. A sniffing attack is a type of man-in-the-middle attack, where a host that resides in the middle of a connection is able to obtain and then manipulate data. You will learn more about this type of attack in Chapter 7.

The obvious response to this analogy and the threat of sniffing attacks would be, "Well, I guess I just won't send my passwords across the Internet or my network." However, it has traditionally been very difficult to get your job done without sending passwords across the Internet. The ability to communicate securely is the backbone of e-commerce and network communication. So, how will you get that password to a person? Even if you use a telephone (a very slow, awkward option), you are not guaranteed safety. After all, your friend who receives this password could write it down on a sticky note, exposing it to anyone passing by. Besides, what if you needed to get a password not to a person, but to a network host?

Another problem with the use of symmetric encryption is that if someone sniffs your symmetrically encrypted message, it is possible for this person to use a password-cracking program to guess the password (the key) you used to encrypt the message. This type of application effectively reverse-engineers the password creation process by taking multiple guesses to try and find the answer. Such applications include L0phtCrack (www.atstake.com/research/redirect.html) and John the Ripper (available at various sites, including http://packetstorm.securify.com). Using such applications, a suitably powerful computer, and enough time, a person can guess the right password. This type of attack is called a *brute-force* attack.

Asymmetric Key Encryption

One of the answers to sniffing and brute-force attacks is the use of a pair of keys. Asymmetric encryption allows you to do two things:

- Encrypt transmissions
- Authenticate users and hosts

For example, suppose that the car key you had in the earlier example concerning symmetric encryption was only part of the key necessary to unlock and start the car. Suppose further that this physical key, which you can now publicly distribute, was related to another key locked in your car, and that this locked key then had a way to ask any holder of your public key to further authenticate himself before he gained access to use your car. This is basically how asymmetric key encryption works.

The public key can be distributed to anyone. It can be placed on public key servers all over the Internet or to anyone you know (or don't know, for that matter). However, the private key must be kept, as you might have already guessed, private. The easiest way to understand public key encryption is to understand the relationship between each key pair. Each pair is generated at the same time. The algorithm that creates the key pair ensures that this pair is so related that one half of this pair can decrypt the other half.

Public Key and Trust Relationships

Let's say that you have generated a key pair. The private key is (hopefully) stored safely on your hard drive, and you are ready to distribute your public key. Your friend has done the same: she has created her private key and is ready to give you her public key. Before both of you can use asymmetric key encryption, you must give each other your public keys.

Giving your public key to another person (or host) is often called establishing a *trust relationship*. Once you have given each other your public keys, you both can then engage in asymmetric key encryption. How? You compose a message, and then you encrypt this message to your friend's public key. Once this message is encrypted, no one but your friend can read this message. Even though you created the message, you cannot read it either, because you encrypted it to your friend's public key.

So, all you have to do now is find a way to get this message to your friend. Once you use e-mail or FTP to do this, your friend receives a bunch of garbled text that means nothing. This is the encrypted message. Your friend can then take this message and then decrypt it using her private key. Once this message is decrypted, your friend can read it. With any luck, your friend won't still think that she received a bunch of garbled text that means nothing. Figure 1.7 illustrates this process.

In Figure 1.7, User A on System A encrypts his message to User B's public key. In order to encrypt the message to User B's public key, User A must first enter a password to use his public key to sign the message. The encrypted and signed message is then sent across the Internet, where User B uses her private key to decrypt the message.

How has this process solved the symmetric encryption problem? First, the only way that your message can be unencrypted is by using your friend's private key.

Figure 1.7 Using Public Keys to Encrypt Transmissions

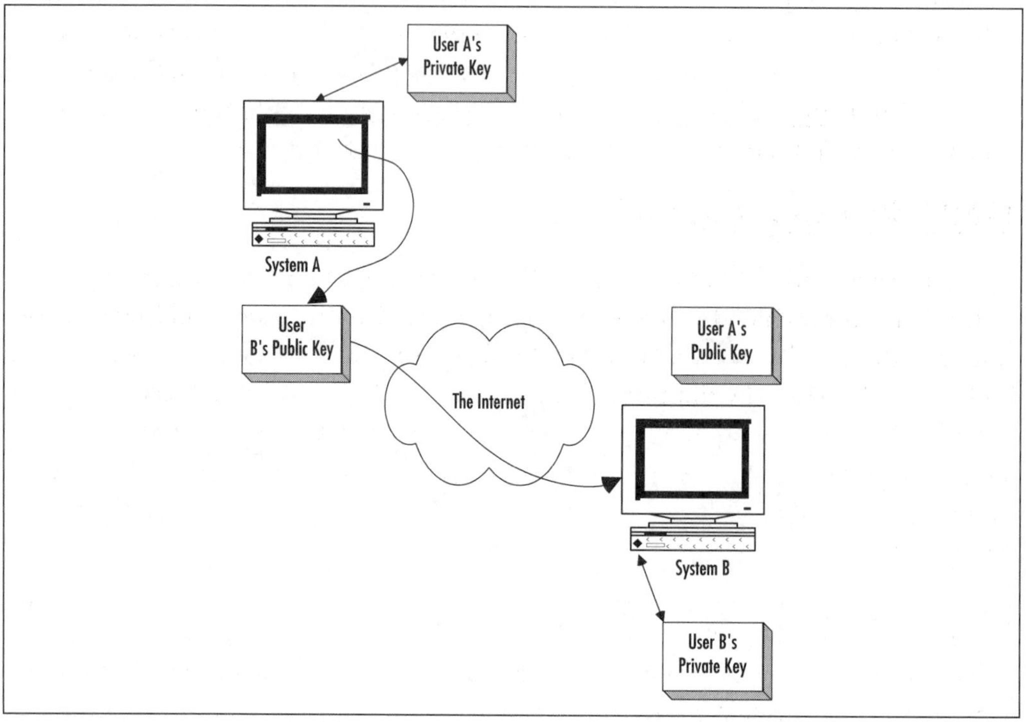

As long as this key remains private, then chances are, so will your letter. Second, notice that you and your friend did not have to distribute the whole password in some way. You only distributed half of the password (the public key). And, usually, it is extremely difficult to guess the private key from the public key. It is, of course, mathematically possible to use the public key to guess the private key, but it would take many million-dollar-plus supercomputers several months to do this. Only state-run organizations such as Scotland Yard and the CIA are likely to devote such resources to your little old message.

As far as authentication is concerned, asymmetric encryption accomplishes this by verifying the owner of the public key. You will learn more about this as you learn about IPSec and VPNs later in this book.

One-Way Encryption

You may ask yourself why anyone would want to irretrievably encrypt a piece of information. After all, doing this makes the information, well, *irretrievable*—it can't be used anymore. One-way encryption is not useful for encrypting and unencrypting files. It is, however, useful for obtaining a file's signature. A signature is obtained by running a one-way encryption algorithm on the file. The resulting value, called a *hash*, is closely related to the contents of the file. This value is so related that if even the slightest change is made to the file's contents, the hash value will not match. Many applications use one-way encryption to ensure that information is not altered as it passes over the network.

GNU Privacy Guard

GNU Privacy Guard (GPG) is one of the primary open source tools in use today. You can download it from www.gnupg.org. You can download binaries and source code for all Unix versions. For Linux, g-zipped archives and RPM files are both available. Most distributions (TurboLinux, Red Hat, Caldera, Slackware, etc.) include GPG in their source files. Using GPG, you will be able to encrypt files and e-mail messages. You will also be able to import and export public keys in order to verify PGP- and GPG-generated keys from the tarballs and RPM files you download.

Deploying GNU Privacy Guard

Although many GUI interfaces are in the planning stage for GPG, the following steps focus on using GPG with the command line. The steps assume that you already have GPG installed on your system. Verify this by using the **whereis** command:

```
whereis gpg
gpg: /usr/bin/gpg
```

If you do not have GPG installed, you can download GPG from www.rpmfind.net, from www.gnupg.org/download.html, or from the CD that accompanies this book (gnupg-1.0.4-11.i386.rpm or the equivalent gnupg-1.0.5.tar.gz).

Now that you know the program is installed, your first step is to secure how it allocates memory to nonroot users. GPG requires that most Linux systems run it as SUID root. Any application allocates pages of memory from the system, and GPG wants this memory to be secure. Otherwise, an illicit user could capture this memory and then gain access to the information you are going to encrypt. In order to secure these memory pages, GPG locks this memory before using it. It needs to run as root to lock the memory. As soon as this is done, GPG then runs under the permissions of the owner.

> **NOTE**
>
> Running an application as SUID root means that the application is run as root, even though the owner who starts it is a nonroot user.

By default, however, GPG is not installed as SUID root. To make it setuid root, do the following:

1. Find the application (in Red Hat Linux, GPG is at /usr/bin/gpg).

2. If you are not already root, become root with the command **su**.

3. Issue the command **chmod u+s /usr/bin/gpg**.

If you cannot do this on your own system for some reason, or do not wish to, you can enter the following line into the **~/.gnupg/options** file of any non-root user:

```
/usr/bin/gpg --gen-key
```

This command will create the necessary directories and files for GPG to work. Once you create these directories, generate a key pair for the user you are logged in as. You do this by issuing the **gpg --genkey** command again.

GPG will then ask you to select a key type. You will have the option of choosing **Digital Signature Algorithm (DSA)** and **ElGamal (the default) DSA**, or **ElGamal (sign and encrypt)**. Each of these options defines different types of signature and encryption algorithms. The first uses both the standard ElGamal key distribution method and the DSA, which is used to sign and encrypt data. DSA is a nonproprietary algorithm, unlike the RSA algorithm, which was previously used. If you only wish to sign and encrypt documents, you can just use DSA. Most people use the first option, which is to both sign and encrypt information. Traditionally, the first choice (the default) is the best.

You are then given the choice of the keysize. The default keysize of 1024 bits is actually quite sufficient for most purposes. Selecting anything higher can significantly slow your application. So, select **1**, and then press **ENTER**.

Enter **1y** to make your key expire one year from now, and then press **ENTER**. Press **y** to confirm this choice.

Enter your name in the *Real name:* field.

> **W**ARNING
>
> You should write down the e-mail address that you use. You will use this address to refer to your public and private key often, when using GPG or PGP.

Next, enter your e-mail address. In the *Comment:* field, enter **GPG signature**, or any text you wish, and then press **ENTER**.

You will then be asked to confirm your settings. If you are happy with what you entered, press **O** (that's the letter O, not the digit 0), and then press **ENTER**.

Enter a passphrase for your private key. This passphrase should be sufficiently long (at least six passwords), but should also be something you will remember. Press **ENTER**, confirm the passphrase, and press **ENTER** again. After doing this, GPG will generate a new key. Move your mouse and/or enter text into the keyboard so that the machine has enough entropy to generate a good private key. Once GPG is finished, you will receive a message that your key is created and signed.

Now, verify that GPG correctly created and signed keys for your account with the following commands:

```
gpg --list-secret-key
gpg --list-public-key
gpg --list-sig
```

These commands list your secret key, your public key, and your signature, respectively. Once you do this, you should create a revocation certificate in case you need to publish the fact that your private key is no longer valid. You do this by following the sequence outlined here:

```
gpg --output revoke.asc --gen-revoke james@root.test.com
sec   1024D/3B386145 2000-07-01    jamesroot (root) <james@root.test.com>
Create a revocation certificate for this key? y
Please select the reason for the revocation:
  1 = Key has been compromised
  2 = Key is superseded
  3 = Key is no longer used
  0 = Cancel
(Probably you want to select 1 here)
```

```
Your decision? 1
Enter an optional description; end it with an empty line:
> For my keats system root account
>
Reason for revocation: Key has been compromised
For my keats system root account
Is this okay? y
You need a passphrase to unlock the secret key for user: "jamesroot
(root) <james@root.test.com>"
1024-bit DSA key, ID 3B386145, created 2000-07-01
ASCII armored output forced.
Revocation certificate created.
Please move it to a medium which you can hide away; if Mallory gets
access to this certificate he can use it to make your key unusable.
It is smart to print this certificate and store it away, just in case
your media become unreadable.  But have some caution:  The print system
of your machine might store the data and make it available to others!
```

After verifying that you have keys and a revocation certificate, you are now able to import and export keys. To export your key, use the following command:

```
gpg --export --armor > yourname.asc
```

This command will create a file that contains your public key. You can then distribute this key to anyone and establish a trust relationship.

With this capability, you now can use the RPM command to check the signatures and public keys generated by others. For example, suppose you wish to update your version of Red Hat Linux due to a security alert. To help you verify that this package has not been tampered with, and that it has truly originated from Red Hat, you can obtain Red Hat's signature. Go to www.redhat.com and obtain the public key for the site and the RPM-based download you want. Figure 1.8 shows Red Hat's public key. As of this writing, the key is located at www.redhat.com/about/contact/redhat2.asc.

Now that you have created your own key ring, which is where you will store the public keys of the people with whom you wish to communicate, you can now import the Red Hat public key into GPG using the following **GPG** command:

```
gpg --import redhat2.asc
```

Figure 1.8 The Red Hat Linux Public Key

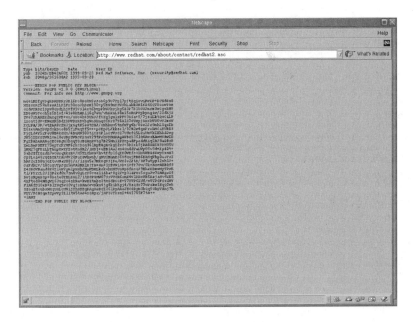

It is possible that the public key you wish to import has a different extension. Now, sign this key. Failure to sign this key will cause it to return error messages when you try to use it. Make sure that you have made absolutely no changes to this key file. Once this key is imported, you need to sign it. Remember, you just downloaded it from a trusted source, and are reasonably sure that you can trust this key. You can sign it using the **gpg --sign** command, or you can use GPG's interactive mode, shown in the following sequence:

```
gpg --edit-key security@redhat.com
gpg (GnuPG) 1.0.2; Copyright (C) 2000 Free Software Foundation, Inc.
This program comes with ABSOLUTELY NO WARRANTY.
This is free software, and you are welcome to redistribute it
under certain conditions. See the file COPYING for details.
pub   1024D/DB42A60E   created: 1999-09-23 expires: never       trust: -/f
sub   2048g/961630A2   created: 1999-09-23 expires: never
(1)   Red Hat, Inc <security@redhat.com>
Command> sign
Are you really sure that you want to sign this key
with your key: "yourkey (key) <yourkey@yoursystem.domain.com>"
```

Really sign? y

```
You need a passphrase to unlock the secret key for
user: "jamesroot (root) <james@root.test.com>"
1024-bit DSA key, ID 3B386145, created 2000-07-01
```

Command> q

Save changes y

Now, you can issue the following command to check the latest GNU GPG RPM file:

```
rpm -Kv your_rpm.i386.rpm
```

You will receive a message that both the MD5 signature and the PGP signature are acceptable:

```
rpm -Kv your_rpm.i386.rpm
your_rpm.i386.rpm:
MD5 sum OK: fc28444c7c7dee7d59671ac5e27b2ad0
gpg: Signature made Wed 30 Aug 2000 03:16:54 PM PDT using DSA key
    IDDB42A60E
gpg: Good signature from "Red Hat, Inc <security@redhat.com>"
```

NOTE

Two major ways exist to create and verify signatures. The open source alternative is GPG. The older, but now proprietary, method is through the use of Pretty Good Privacy (PGP). The latest versions of GPG are compatible with PGP versions 5.0 and later. However, if a signature was made using PGP 2.6 or earlier, GPG will not be able to read it. PGP version 2.6 and earlier used the IDEA algorithm, which is patented.

If you do not find a message similar to this, but instead find a message that reads *public key not found*, then you know that this public key is not valid for this RPM. You will either have to find the right public key, or find another RPM. You can, of course, use GPG to verify any public key you wish. You have now configured and used GPG to help ensure that the file you are installing is safe.

> **NOTE**
>
> If, while working with GPG, you receive a message that reads *gpg: waiting for lock*, then a previous instance of GPG had a problem while working with either the public or the private key. As a result, the public and/or private key ring in the hidden ~./.gnupg directory is locked. Go to the ~./.gnupg directory and remove any file that ends in a .lock extension.

Installing PGP

Although GPG has become a standard, you can also use the PGP program, which behaves rather differently. You can download PGP from the Massachusetts Institute of Technology Web site at http://web.mit.edu/network/pgp-form.html. You will then have to repeat many of the earlier steps to create a public and private key, and then import the site's key. Because PGP (and GPG, for that matter) enables powerful encryption, MIT will ask you questions concerning your intentions for PGP. Answer these according to your intentions. If you enter the right answers, you will be able to download PGP. Choose the correct file for your distribution.

1. MIT uses gzip to compress the RPM files. If you are using Red Hat Linux, the RPM package works best. Use tar to unzip and un-tar the RPM package: **tar –zxvf pgprpmfile.tar.gz**.

2. This process will deposit an RPM file. Run RPM to install it: **rpm –ivh pgprpmfile**.

3. Once you have installed PGP, issue the following command to create a key pair: **pgp –kg**.

4. Choose the **DSS/DH** option, which is the default.

5. Choose **1** to generate a new signing key.

6. You will be asked to choose the size of your key. Enter **1024**, and then press **ENTER**.

7. Enter a user ID for your public key. Enter your name and e-mail address. *This will become your PGP username.* This is important, as you will see later when it comes time to edit the RPM configuration file.

8. Enter **0** to keep the key forever. Don't worry, you can revoke it and generate a new key pair later.

9. Enter a passphrase. Make sure this is a solid passphrase (over eight char-
    acters, containing at least one capital letter and one nonstandard char-
    acter), but also one that you can remember. Confirm your password by
    entering it again.

10. You will be asked if you need an encryption key. Press **y**, and then press
    ENTER.

11. The choice of key size is up to you. Just remember that the larger the
    key size, the slower information will be processed. Most people choose
    either **1024** or **2048**.

12. Enter **0** as the "validity period." As before, this value means that the key
    is valid forever.

13. PGP will ask you to press random keys on the keyboard so that it can
    generate enough entropy.

14. When PGP is finished, it will ask you if you want to make this key the
    default signing key. Press **y** to indicate *yes*.

15. Now, you need to enter the public key of the GNU GPG RPM. You
    do this with the following command: **pgp --ka gnugpg.publickey**.

16. You will see a list of keys. Indicate that you wish to add these keys to
    your key ring by pressing **y**.

17. You will see that several new keys and signatures have been added.

18. Now, you must edit the macros file for your version of RPM. In Red
    Hat 7.0, this file is in //usr/lib/rpm/macros. Find the following values
    and change the values according to your own information:

    ```
    %_pgp_name your PGP user name

    %_pgp_path The path to your public key. For example, /root/.pgp/
    ```

    Instead of taking this second step, you can set the PGPPATH vari-
    able in your bash_profile file.

19. You can now use RPM to verify your RPM:

    ```
    rpm -Kv your_rpm.i386.rpm

    your_rpm.i386.rpm:

    MD5 sum OK: fc28444c7c7dee7d59671ac5e27b2ad0

    gpg: Signature made Wed 30 Aug 2000 03:16:54 PM PDT using DSA
        key IDDB42A60E
    ```

```
gpg: Good signature from "Red Hat, Inc <security@redhat.com>"
```

If you want to learn more about PGP, read the man pages, or issue the following commands:

```
pgp -h
pgp -k
```

This book focuses on using GPG.

> **NOTE**
>
> Thus far, you have learned how to use GPG with the RPM package. Of course, GPG has many other uses. Once you have engaged in a trust relationship with the recipient, you can encrypt files to this person. The following command can encrypt a file named *managerreport.txt*: **gpg --encrypt --r public_keyname_of_recipient managerreport.txt**.
> You will have to enter the password of your private key. Hopefully, you can remember it; otherwise, you will have to generate a new private/public key pair. After you enter your passphrase, GPG will create a file named *managerreport.txt.gpg*.
> You can then send this key to the intended recipient, who can then decrypt it with the following command: **gpg --decrypt managerreport .txt.gpg > managerreport.txt**.
> The recipient will, of course, have to enter his or her passphrase to decrypt the message and read it.
> To create a signature file, you can create an empty file named *yourname*, and then enter the following command: **host# gpg --clearsign yourname**.
> You will then be asked to enter your password. After this sequence is completed, you will see a new file named *yourname.asc*, which has your signature in it.

Skipping Public Key Verification

If you want to check a signature to ensure that the contents haven't been changed, and don't really wish to verify the original author's public key, enter the following command:

```
rpm -K --nopgp rpmfile.i386.rpm
rpmfile.i386.rpm: md5 gpg OK
```

Using GPG to Verify Signatures on Tarball Packages

Follow these steps to verify the signature of a gzipped tarball:

1. Add the public key of the person or organization that created the package.

2. Sign the public key using GPG. You can either use GPG's **--sign** command, or you can enter GPG's interactive mode.

3. Once you have added and signed the public key of the person who owns the package, enter the following command: **gpg --verify signaturefile.tar.gz taballpackage.gz**.

You will then receive a message either that the signature is good, or that the public key cannot be found. If the public key cannot be found, you must obtain another public key, or you will not be able to verify who owns the package.

Using Md5sum

Sometimes, a developer will use the **md5sum** command to generate a hash of the file. You can use this hash and the **md5sum** command to ensure that the file has not been altered. The easiest way to do this is to read the hash that the developer generated, download the binary in question, and then run **md5sum** against it.

For example, suppose that you learn that the wu-ftpd daemon (the daemon responsible for providing FTP on many sites) has a security problem. You wish to install the latest secure version. After downloading it, you run **md5sum** against the file:

```
md5sum wu-ftpd-2.8.1-6.i386.rpm

t412cfhh5bf1376cia9da6c5dd86a463   wu-ftpd-2.6.1-6.i386.rpm
```

However, you notice that the developer's **md5sum** value for the same program reads as follows:

```
y415cfgz5bf1356cib8da6c5dd8da0k5
```

You should then delete the file and find another source where you can verify the **md5sum** hash.

Auditing Procedures

As you use the software discussed in this book, you will generally be deploying it assuming three major roles, which we discuss in the next sections:

- Locking down your network
- Securing data across the network
- Protecting the network perimeter

Locking Down Your Network Hosts

As you lock down your network, you will have to focus on individual hosts. As shown in Figure 1.9, you will audit the daemons that this host runs. For example, you will use scanners to determine what ports are open, and if those daemons present a danger to your system. An auditor also seeks to enhance login security, to enhance logging, and to discover what, if any, virus protection measures are present.

Figure 1.9 System Aspects to Audit

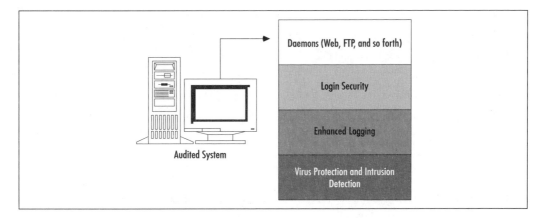

Another part of scanning local systems is enabling ways to detect unauthorized login. As you approach your systems using the open source tools in this book, you will find that many are geared to help you enhance the security in each of these areas.

Securing Data across the Network

Figure 1.10 shows how it is possible to create an auditing station on a network. This station can monitor the transmissions from other hosts. The auditing host has the following responsibilities:

- Obtain relevant data concerning the network without affecting the performance of the network.

- Provide remote administration capabilities.

- Generate logs so that information can be carefully scanned.

Figure 1.10 Auditing Network Transmissions

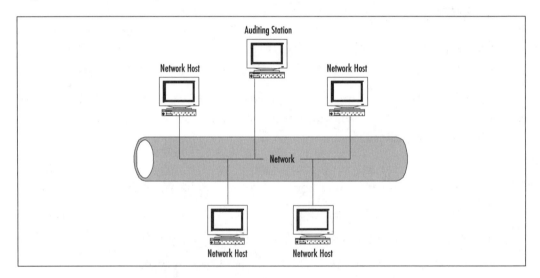

Intrusion detection systems can use this structure, although structures that are more complex exist. For example, it is possible to divide the tasks of the auditing host among multiple hosts. The chief benefit of dividing tasks is redundancy—if one element of the network goes down, the network can still be monitored and protected.

The structure outlined previously can be responsible for *passive monitoring* or *active monitoring*. Passive monitoring is simply the ability to listen to network traffic and log it. Active monitoring involves the ability to either:

- Monitor traffic and then send alerts concerning the traffic that is discovered.
- Actually intercept and forbid this traffic.

You will learn more about intrusion detection in later chapters.

Protecting the Network Perimeter

As you configure your firewall to establish a network perimeter, you will have to take the following actions:

- Logging
- Firewall reconfiguration
- Troubleshooting
- Enabling and disabling traffic emanating from inside the network
- Enabling and disabling traffic emanating from outside the network

Figure 1.11 shows two networks communicating over the Internet. Each uses a firewall to monitor, log, and forbid traffic. As you audit, you will have to perform the following tasks:

- Use tools to send packets that traverse the firewall. These packets will help you determine just how well your firewall limits traffic.
- Determine which internal services require access outside of the firewall.
- Redirect packets from a proxy server to your firewall.
- Scan logs to determine if any break-ins have occurred.

Figure 1.11 Auditing a Firewall

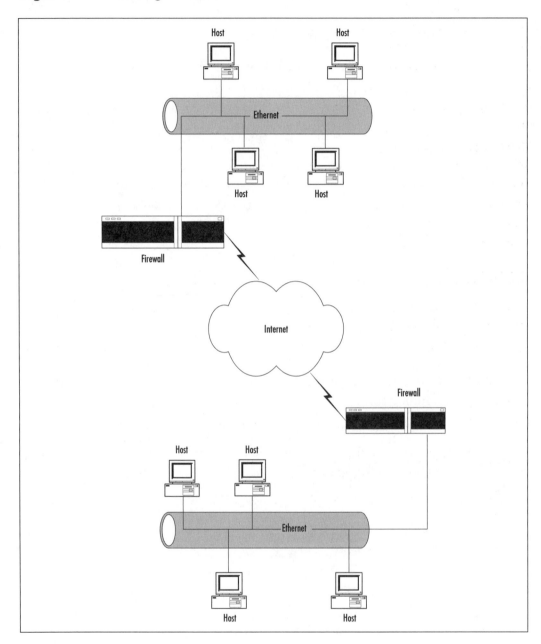

Summary

This introduction provided practical knowledge of the open source community, and how it can help you with your security concerns. You learned about several key open source sites, how the open source movement protects software instead of individuals and corporations, and you reviewed your knowledge of encryption.

You learned how to verify the integrity of the files you download from people you don't know. Using GPG (and, if you wish, PGP), you can verify RPM and tarball packages.

This book is designed to deploy open source tools in three key areas (host security, network security, and perimeter security). We hope that this book will be of practical importance to you. It is designed to give you advice concerning troubleshooting Linux using open source tools.

Solutions Fast Track

Using the GNU General Public License

☑ The GPL protects the software code, not a corporation or an individual.

☑ Protecting code rather than individuals is a radical change, because it allows code to be improved upon without being made completely proprietary.

☑ Open source code does not necessarily have to be free. For example, companies such as Red Hat and Caldera sell their products, which are based on the open source Linux kernel.

Soft Skills: Coping with Open Source Quirks

☑ As you use open source code, remember that this code may represent a work in progress.

☑ Sometimes, open source code changes radically, forcing you to retrain users. You may find that updates happen irregularly, and that it is sometimes more challenging to update open source code. Furthermore, once you upgrade the code, you may be presented with an application that behaves very differently, or has a radically different interface.

☑ Before installing open source software, make sure that your operating system contains all of the necessary supporting applications and libraries.

Should I Use an RPM or Tarballs?

☑ RPMs sometimes offer convenience. However, precompiled RPMs often do not have all of the features necessary to implement a truly useful product.

☑ Tarballs often require editing of a special file called a *makefile*. However, this is not necessarily all that difficult. It simply requires that you know where your supporting applications and libraries are. Also, most open source software will contain instructions concerning how to edit the makefile. Most well-known operating systems, such as Red Hat Linux and Slackware, do not require makefile modification.

☑ RPMs often contain useful startup scripts that are not found elsewhere. Sometimes, it is useful to install the RPM, then the tarball version, and then combine elements from the two for a complete solution.

Obtaining Open Source Software

☑ Sites such as SourceForge (www.sourceforge.com), RPMFind (www.rpmfind.net), and SecurityFocus (www.securityfocus.com) are valuable software sources.

☑ Be especially careful when downloading any source code, regardless of format. Digital signatures can help you determine the author of a package, as well as whether a package has been altered.

☑ The Gnu Privacy Guard (GPG) and Pretty Good Privacy (PGP) packages are available to help you verify signatures. They do not stop the execution of malicious code, however. They simply inform you about the nature of the code's author, and of any changes that may have occurred to the code.

A Brief Encryption Review

☑ Symmetric encryption is the use of one key to encrypt and decrypt information. If a malicious user is able to intercept the key, he or she can then use it to decrypt your secret messages.

☑ Asymmetric encryption uses a mathematically related *key pair* to encrypt and decrypt information. This type of encryption is commonly used on the Internet and on LANs, because it reduces the likelihood that the key can be learned by a malicious user, and aids in authentication.

☑ One-way encryption is the use of an algorithm to encrypt information so that it is, mathematically speaking, impossible to unencrypt. One-way encryption is also used to read a file and then create a *hash* of that file. The resulting hash value is said to be mathematically unrecoverable. Hash code is often used to compare one value to another during the login process: the person logging in enters a username and password, and the authentication mechanism creates a hash of these two values and compares it to the hash values generated from the /etc/passwd and /etc/shadow databases. If the values match, access is allowed.

Public Key and Trust Relationships

☑ You must generate a key pair to begin using your public key to authenticate yourself or to encrypt network transmissions.

☑ Establishing a trust relationship involves exchanging public keys. Sometimes, individual users must give public keys. At other times, public keys are exchanged between network hosts.

☑ Never reveal your private key. If your private key is made available to a third party, this person will be able to read all of your encrypted files.

Auditing Procedures

☑ As an auditor, your job is to lock down your network, which means that you must consider the security of each host using tools that allow you to determine changes in files and directories, and who has scanned and accessed your system. You must also monitor network transmission and

configure your firewall to establish an effective network perimeter that
separates your network from all others.

☑ An Intrusion Detection System (IDS) acts as an auditing host or series of
auditing hosts that allow you to monitor and secure data as it passes
across the network.

☑ Protecting the network perimeter involves proper firewall and proxy
server configuration, logging, and monitoring.

Frequently Asked Questions

The following Frequently Asked Questions, answered by the authors of this book,
are designed to both measure your understanding of the concepts presented in
this chapter and to assist you with real-life implementation of these concepts. To
have your questions about this chapter answered by the author, browse to
www.syngress.com/solutions and click on the **"Ask the Author"** form.

Q: Copyright has been around a long time. I don't understand all of the fuss
people are making about the GPL. Can't people just create code and not provide a license at all?

A: The GPL protects the source code of an application so that it always remains
public. No one person can then patent this code and make it his or her own.
If you were to create a piece of software and not license it, then very quickly,
this code could become proprietary. The creators of the GPL hope that as
more and more people view the same piece of code, it will improve, and
everyone will benefit.

Q: When verifying a signature with GPG, I keep getting a message that the
public key can't be found, even though I know that I loaded the public key
into GPG. What is wrong with RPM and/or PGP?

A: Nothing. There is something wrong with the package you downloaded.
Either that, or you somehow made an inadvertent change to the public key
before you imported it.

Q: The BSD version of Unix existed before Linux. Why has Linux become so
popular?

A: One reason is because Linux follows the GNU GPL, which has allowed the open source community to embrace it and develop many, many applications and daemons for it. Also, the Regents of the University of California held the copyright for all of the BSD developed code. It was not always available in source. One of the reasons for that is that until BSD 4.4, there was still proprietary AT&T source code in the BSD distributions. One of the specific objectives of BSD 4.4 was to eliminate any AT&T property. Therefore, while BSD was still license encumbered, Linux was freely available (in source and binary).

Q: In your auditing discussion, you discuss the idea of passive and active auditing. Don't intrusion detection applications also do signature-based and anomaly-based detection?

A: Yes, they do. You will learn more about these two intrusion detection methods in later chapters. Signature-based detection means that you predefine what an attack looks like, and then configure your network monitoring software to look for that signature. Anomaly-based detection requires the intrusion detection system to actually listen to the network and gather evidence about "normal" traffic. Then, if any traffic occurs that seems different, the intrusion detection system will respond by, for example, sending out an alert to the network administrator.

## Chapter 2

Hardening the Operating System

Solutions in this chapter:

- **Updating the Operating System**
- **Handling Maintenance Issues**
- **Manually Disabling Unnecessary Services and Ports**
- **Locking Down Ports**
- **Hardening the System with Bastille**
- **Controlling and Auditing Root Access with Sudo**
- **Managing Your Log Files**
- **Using Logging Enhancers**

- ☑ **Summary**
- ☑ **Solutions Fast Track**
- ☑ **Frequently Asked Questions**

Introduction

Linux is capable of high-end security; however, the out-of-the-box configurations must be altered to meet the security needs of most businesses with an Internet presence. This chapter shows you the steps for securing a Linux system—called *hardening* the server—using both manual methods and open source security solutions. The hardening process focuses on the operating system, and is important regardless of the services offered by the server. The steps will vary slightly between services, such as e-mail and Hypertext Transfer Protocol (HTTP), but are essential for protecting any server that is connected to a network, especially the Internet. Hardening the operating system allows the server to operate efficiently and securely.

This chapter includes the essential steps an administrator must follow to harden a Unix system; specifically, a Red Hat Linux system. These steps include updating the system, disabling unnecessary services, locking down ports, logging, and maintenance. Open source programs allow administrators to automate these processes using Bastille, sudo, logging enhancers such as SWATCH, and antivirus software. Before you implement these programs, you should first understand how to harden a system manually.

Updating the Operating System

An operating system may contain many security vulnerabilities and software bugs when it is first released. Vendors, such as Red Hat, provide updates to the operating system to fix these vulnerabilities and bugs. In fact, many consulting firms recommend that companies do not purchase and implement new operating systems until the first update is available. In most cases, the first update will fix many of the problems encountered with the first release of the operating system. In this section, you will learn where to find the most current Red Hat Linux errata and updates.

Red Hat Linux Errata and Update Service Packages

The first step in hardening a Linux server is to apply the most current errata and Update Service Package to the operating system. The Update Service Package provides the latest fixes and additions to the operating system. It is a collection of fixes, corrections, and updates to the Red Hat products, such as bug fixes, security advisories, package enhancements, and add-on software. Updates can be downloaded individually as errata, but it is a good idea to start with the latest Update Service Package, and then install errata as necessary. However, you must pay to receive the Update Service Packages, and the errata are free. Many errata and Update Service Packages are not required upgrades. You need to read the documentation to determine if you need to install it.

The Update Service Packages include all of the errata in one package to keep your system up to date. After you pay for the service, you can order Update Service Packages on CD, or download them directly from the Red Hat Web site. To find out more about the Update Service Packages, visit www.redhat.com/support/services/update.html (Figure 2.1). You will learn more about errata in the maintenance section of this chapter.

Figure 2.1 Red Hat Errata and Updates

Handling Maintenance Issues

You should apply the latest service pack and updates before the server goes live, and constantly maintain the server after it is deployed to make sure the most current required patches are installed. The more time an operating system is available to the public, the more time malicious hackers have to exploit discovered vulnerabilities. Vendors offer patches to fix these vulnerabilities as quickly as possible; in some cases, the fixes are available at the vendor's site the same day.

Administrators must also regularly test their systems using security analyzer software. Security analyzer software scans systems to uncover security vulnerabilities, and recommends fixes to close the security hole. (These tools are discussed in detail in Chapter 3.)

This section discusses the maintenance required to ensure that your systems are safe from the daily threats of the Internet.

Red Hat Linux Errata: Fixes and Advisories

Once your Red Hat system is live, you must make sure that the most current required Red Hat errata are installed. These errata include bug fixes, corrections, and updates to Red Hat products. You should always check the Red Hat site at www.redhat.com/apps/support/updates.html for the latest errata news. The following list defines the different types of errata found at the Red Hat Updates and Errata site.

- **Bug fixes** Address coding errors discovered after the release of the product, and may be critical to program functionality. These Red Hat Package Manager tools (RPMs) can be downloaded for free. Bug fixes provide a fix to specific issues, such as a certain error message that may occur when completing an operating system task. Bug fixes should only be installed if your system experiences a specific problem. Another helpful resource is Bugzilla, the Red Hat bug-tracking system at http://bugzilla.redhat.com/bugzilla.

- **Security advisories** Provide updates that eliminate security vulnerabilities on the system. Red Hat recommends that all administrators download and install the security upgrades to avoid denial-of-service (DoS) and intrusion attacks that can result from these weaknesses. For example, a security update can be downloaded for a vulnerability that caused a memory overflow due to improper input verification in Netscape's Joint Photographic Experts Group (JPEG) code.

- **Package enhancements** Provide updates to the functions and features of the operating system or specific applications. Package enhancements are usually not critical to the system's integrity; they often fix functionality programs, such as an RPM that provides new features.

Here are the steps for accessing Linux bug fixes, security advisories, and package enhancements:

1. To download bug fixes, point your browser to **www.redhat.com/ apps/support/updates.html**. Under the "Errata: Fixes and Advisories" section, click the **Red Hat Linux Bug Fixes** link. The latest bug fixes are available for download on this page. Click each bug to learn more, and determine whether it affects your system. Some fixes do not include software downloads, such as RPMs; instead, they explain how to configure your system to fix the problem.

2. To download security advisories, point your browser to **www.redhat .com/apps/support/updates.html**. Under the "Errata: Fixes and Advisories" section, click the **Red Hat Linux Security Advisories** link. The available security fixes are listed as shown in Figure 2.2. For example, one download contains three security hole fixes, as well as additional support for Pentium 4 processors. This affects Red Hat 6.*x* and 7.0 users. It is imperative for Linux administrators to check this Web site on a regular basis, determine if the changes are necessary, and implement the vulnerability fix.

Figure 2.2 Available Security Fixes for Red Hat Linux

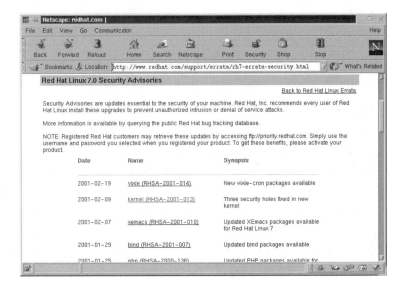

3. To download package enhancements, point your browser to **www.redhat.com/apps/support/updates.html**. Under the "Errata: Fixes and Advisories" section, click the **All Red Hat Linux Errata** link, and then the **Package Enhancements** link. A Red Hat Linux

Package Enhancements link may also exist on the main Errata page. The available package enhancements are listed. Check the list to see if any enhancements affect your operating system or applications. If an enhancement exists, and installing it would benefit your system, download and install the corresponding package.

Bug Fix Case Study

In a production environment, a problem may exist if a system has an i810 chipset and is running Red Hat Linux 6.2. The correct amount of system RAM may not be available to the system. Consequently, the system cannot maximize RAM usage, and may not run certain programs because it thinks it does not have enough RAM. A fix for this problem is available at the Red Hat Updates and Errata Web site.

According to the bug fix, an administrator needs to manually enter the amount of RAM for the system. To check if the problem exists on a system, the administrator must log on as root and enter:

```
cat /proc/meminfo
```

If the memTotal value is not within a few MB of the actual system RAM, the administrator needs to manually enter the correct amount of system RAM. To accomplish this task, the administrator must have root access and edit the /etc/lilo.conf file by entering:

```
vi /etc/lilo.conf
```

The administrator must locate the current kernel image and add a new line by pressing **i** (to enter vi's insert mode) and entering the following:
```
append="mem=[total amount of ram (in MB)]"
```
Figure 2.3 displays an edited lilo.conf file for a system that has 256MB of RAM. One MB should be subtracted from the total because the final megabyte is not available on all systems.

The administrator must write and quit the lilo.conf file by pressing **Esc** (to exit vi's insert mode) and entering:

```
:wq
```

Then he or she must load the updated lilo.conf file into memory by entering:

```
/sbin/lilo
```

Figure 2.3 Editing the Lilo.conf File to Fix a Bug

The administrator must reboot the machine. Afterward, he or she must check the RAM allocation by entering:

```
cat /proc/meminfo
```

If it is within a few MB of the actual RAM, the bug has been fixed. If not, the administrator must repeat the case study steps to ensure that the correct amount of RAM is allocated to the OS.

Manually Disabling Unnecessary Services and Ports

To harden a server, you must first disable any unnecessary services and ports. This process involves removing any unnecessary services, such as the Linux rlogin service, and locking down unnecessary Transmission Control Protocol/User Datagram Protocol (TCP/UDP) ports. Once these services and ports are secure, you must then regularly maintain the system.

This section shows you how to manually disable several vulnerable services. Later in this lesson, you learn how to disable unnecessary services and ports using the open source program Bastille.

Services to Disable

Linux, by nature, is more secure than most operating systems. Regardless, there are still uncertainties to every new Linux kernel that is released, and many security vulnerabilities that have not been discovered. Most Linux services are not vulnerable to these exploits. However, an administrator can reduce the amount of risk by removing unnecessary services. Red Hat Linux includes many services, so it makes sense that an administrator customize the system to suit the company needs. Remember, you are removing risk when you remove unnecessary services.

The xinetd.conf File

The /etc/xinetd.conf file (previously the inetd.conf file) controls many Unix services, including File Transfer Protocol (FTP) and Telnet. It determines what services are available to the system. The xinetd (like inetd) service is a "super server" listening for incoming network activity for a range of services. It determines the actual nature of the service being requested and launches the appropriate server. The primary reason for the design is to avoid having to start and run a large number of low-volume servers. Additionally, xinetd's ability to launch services on demand means that only the needed number of servers is run.

The etc/xinted.conf file directs requests for xinetd services to the /etc/xinetd.d directory. Each xinetd service has a configuration file in the xinetd.d directory. If a service is commented out in its specified configuration file, the service is unavailable. Because xinetd is so powerful, only the root should be able to configure its services.

The /etc/xinetd.d directory makes it simple to disable services that your system is not using. For example, you can disable the FTP and Telnet services by commenting out the FTP and Telnet entries in the respective file and restarting the service. If the service is commented out, it will not restart. The next section demonstrates how to disable the Telnet, FTP, and rlogin services.

Telnet and FTP

Most administrators find it convenient to log in to their Unix machines over a network for administration purposes. This allows the administrator to work remotely while maintaining network services. However, in a high-security environment, only physical access may be permitted for administering a server. In this case, you should disable the Telnet interactive login utility. Once disabled, no one can access the machine via Telnet.

1. To disable Telnet, you must edit the /etc/xinetd.d/telnet file. Open the **Telnet file**, as shown in Figure 2.4, using vi or an editor of your choice.

2. Comment out the **service telnet** line by adding a number sign (#) before **service telnet**:

   ```
   #service telnet
   ```

3. Write and quit the file.

Figure 2.4 Disabling Telnet Using the /xinetd.d/telnet File

4. Next, you must restart xinetd by entering:

```
/etc/rc.d/init.d/xinetd restart

Stopping xinetd:                                    [OK}

Starting xinetd:                                    [OK}
```

5. Attempt to log on to the system using Telnet. You should fail.

6. Note that commenting out the service line in the respective xinetd.d directory can disable many services.

7. Disable the FTP service using the same method (e.g., edit the /xinetd.d/wu-ftpd file by commenting out the `service ftp` line and restarting xinetd).

8. Attempt to access the system via FTP. You should be unable to log in to the server.

The Rlogin Service

The remote login (rlogin) service is enabled by default in the /etc/xinetd.d/ rlogin file. Rlogin has security vulnerabilities because it can bypass the password prompt to access a system remotely. There are two services associated with rlogin: login and RSH (remote shell). To disable these services, open the **/xinetd.d/ rlogin file** and comment out the **service login** line. Then, open the **/etc/ xinetd.d/rsh file** and comment out the **service shell** line. Restart xinetd to ensure that your system is no longer offering these services.

Locking Down Ports

TCP/IP networks assign a port to each service, such as HTTP, Simple Mail Transfer Protocol (SMTP), and Post Office Protocol version 3 (POP3). This port is given a number, called a port number, used to link incoming data to the correct service. For example, if a client browser is requesting to view a server's Web page, the request will be directed to port 80 on the server. The Web service receives the request and sends the Web page to the client. Each service is assigned a port number, and each port number has a TCP and UDP port. For example, port 53 is used for the Domain Name System (DNS) and has a TCP port and a UDP port. TCP port 53 is used for zone transfers between DNS servers; UDP port 53 is used for common DNS queries—resolving domain names to IP addresses.

Well-Known and Registered Ports

There are two ranges of ports used for TCP/IP networks: well-known ports and registered ports. The well-known ports are the network services that have been assigned a specific port number (as defined by /etc/services). For example, SMTP is assigned port 25, and HTTP is assigned port 80. Servers listen on the network for requests at the well-known ports. Registered ports are temporary ports, usually used by clients, and will vary each time a service is used. Registered ports are also called ephemeral ports, because they last for only a brief time. The port is then abandoned and can be used by other services.

The port number ranges are classified, as shown in Table 2.1, according to Request for Comments (RFC) 1700. To access RFC 1700, go to ftp://ftp.isi.edu/in-notes/rfc1700.txt.

Table 2.1 Port Number Ranges for Various Types

Type	Port Number Range
Well-known	1 to 1023
Registered	1024 to 65535

NOTE

Connections to ports number 1023 and below are assumed to run with root-level privileges. This means that untrusted services should never be configured with a port number below 1024.

You will see how well-known ports work with registered ports shortly. Table 2.2 is a list of well-known TCP/UDP port numbers.

Table 2.2 Commonly Used Well-Known TCP/UDP Port Numbers

Protocol	Port Number
FTP (Default data)	20
FTP (Connection dialog, control)	21
Telnet	23
SMTP	25
DNS	53
DHCP BOOTP Server	67
DHCP BOOTP Client	68
TFTP	69
Gopher	70
HTTP	80
POP3	110
NNTP	119
NetBIOS Session Service	139
Internet Message Access Protocol (IMAP), version 2	143

To explain how well-known ports work with registered ports, let's look at a typical Web site connection from a Web browser to a Web server. The client sends the HTTP request from a registered TCP port, such as port 1025. The request is routed across the network to the well-known TCP port 80 of a Web server. Once a session is established, the server continues to use port 80, and the client uses various registered ports, such as TCP port 1025 and 1026, to transfer the HTTP data.

Figure 2.5 is a packet capture that displays the establishment of a TCP session between a client and server, and the transmission of HTTP data between them.

In frame 2 of the packet capture, the source address (24.130.10.35) is the client computer requesting the Web page. The destination address (192.0.34.65) is the Web server, which hosts the Internet Corporation of Assigned Names and Numbers (ICANN) Web site. In the Info field, the 1025 > 80 indicates that the source TCP port is 1025. The 80 indicates that the destination TCP port is 80. The first three frames display the TCP handshake, which establishes a TCP connection between the client and server. In the frames that follow, the client requests HTTP data from the server. The request determines the HTTP version that the client and server will use. The client then requests and downloads the contents of the Web page.

Figure 2.5 Port Usage in a Client/Server HTTP Session

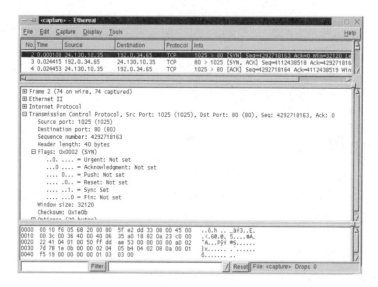

Determining Ports to Block

When determining which ports to block on your server, you must first determine which services you require. In most cases, block all ports that are not exclusively required by these services. This is tricky, because you can easily block yourself from services you need, especially services that use ephemeral ports, as explained earlier.

If your server is an exclusive e-mail server running SMTP and IMAP, you can block all TCP ports except ports 25 and 143, respectively. If your server is an exclusive HTTP server, you can block all ports except TCP port 80. In both cases, you can block all UDP ports since SMTP and IMAP all use TCP services exclusively. However, if you want to use your server as an HTTP client (i.e., for accessing operating system updates) or as an e-mail client to a remote mail server, you will restrict the system. Clients require registered UDP ports for DNS, as well as registered TCP ports for establishing connections with Web servers.

If you open only the corresponding UDP ports 25, 80, and 143, DNS requests are blocked because DNS queries use UDP port 53, and DNS answers use a UDP registered port (e.g., the response stating that www.syngress.com= 205.181.158.215). Even if you open port 53, a different registered port may be assigned each time for the answer. Attempting to allow access to a randomly assigned registered port is almost impossible and a waste of time. The same problem applies with TCP connections that require ephemeral ports.

Therefore, you should either open all TCP/UDP registered ports (so you can use your server as a client), or block them (except for the services you require) and access resources, such as operating system updates, another way. Many administrators order the Red Hat Linux Update CDs, which are re-mastered every eight weeks, that contain all current updates (www.redhat.com/products/software/linux/updatecd/). You can also simply download the updates from another computer.

Blocking Ports

To block TCP/UDP services in Linux, you must disable the service that uses the specific port. The following section discusses disabling ports using xinetd, and disabling ports assigned to stand-alone services.

Xinetd Services

Many services are disabled by their respective files in the /etc/xinetd.d directory by commenting out the service that uses the port. You learned how to comment out xinetd services earlier in this chapter. For example, to disable port 79 (used for finger services, which gives out user data that can be used by malicious hackers), you would comment out the **service finger** entry in /etc/xinetd.d/ finger file. Refer to Table 2.2 to view other ports you may wish to block. It lists common ports blocked by firewalls. However, these ports can also be blocked at the server itself. Follow these steps to disable port 79:

1. To disable port 79, you must edit the /etc/xinetd.d/finger file. Open the **finger file** and locate the service finger line.

2. Comment out the finger service line, and then write and quit the file.

3. Next, you must restart xinetd by entering:

    ```
    /etc/rc.d/init.d/xinetd restart
    ```

4. If you have a finger program installed on your system, or access to a finger gateway, attempt a finger request to your system. You should fail. Note that you can use xinetd to disable many other ports.

Stand-Alone Services

To disable ports whose corresponding services are not included in the
/etc/xinetd.d directory, you must kill the service's process and make sure that service does not automatically restart upon reboot. These services are called stand-alone services. For example, port 111 is assigned a stand-alone portmapper service not required for most e-mail servers. The portmapper service, which is technically part of the Sun Remote Procedure Call (RPC) service, runs on server machines and assigns port numbers to RPC packets, such as NIS and NFS packets. Because these RPC services are not used by most e-mail services, port 111 is not necessary. To disable port 111, you must disable the portmapper service as follows:

1. To disable the portmapper service, identify the process identifier (PID) for portmap by entering:

   ```
   ps aux | grep portmap
   ```

2. The second column lists the PID number. The last column lists the process using that PID. To stop the portmapper service, identify the PID number and enter:

   ```
   kill -9 [PID NUMBER]
   ```

3. To make sure the service does not restart during reboot, enter:

   ```
   ntsysv
   ```

4. Scroll down to the portmap service and uncheck the check box next to the service. Click **OK**. The portmap service will no longer restart at bootup.

NOTE

Some ports, such as port 80, are not activated unless the service is installed. For example, if you have not installed Apache server, then port 80 is not used. There is no need to block the port because it is already disabled.

Hardening the System with Bastille

Bastille is an open source program that facilitates the hardening of a Linux system. It performs many of the tasks discussed in this chapter, including downloading operating system updates and disabling services and ports that are not required for the system's job functions. The program also offers a wider range of additional services, from installing a firewall (ipchains) to implementing secure shell (SSH).

Bastille is powerful and can save administrators time from configuring each individual file and program throughout the operating system. Instead, the administrator answers a series of "Yes" and "No" questions through an interactive text-based interface. The program automatically implements the administrator's preferences based on the answers to the questions.

Bastille is written specifically to Red Hat Linux and Mandrake Linux, but can be easily modified to run on most Unix flavors. The specific Red Hat/Mandrake content has been generalized, and now the hard-code filenames are represented as variables. These variables are set automatically at runtime.

Bastille Functions

The following list highlights the security features offered by Bastille to secure your system. You will choose which feature you want to implement on your system during the question–and–answer period. For example, many servers do not need to provide firewall or Network Address Translation (NAT), so you may not need to configure ipchains. This list may vary as new versions of Bastille are released and the program becomes more powerful. More information about each of these features is explained in the program.

- **Run the ipchains script** You can configure your system as a packet filter. This allows your system to perform NAT, serve as a small firewall, and deny certain connection types to your server.

- **Download and install RPM updates** The most recent versions of the RPMs used on your system are downloaded and installed. These RPM downloads are obtained from the Red Hat Errata page (www.redhat.com/support/errata).

- **Apply restrictive permissions on administrator utilities** Allows only the root to read and execute common Administrator utilities such as ifconfig, linuxconf, ping, traceroute, and runlevel). It disables the SUID root status for these programs, so nonroot users cannot use them.

- **Create a second root account** A second UID 0 (root) account allows administrators to track the original root account. This is helpful for tracking hackers because Bastille notifies the second account to original account logins. If you always use the second account, then you know when a security breach may have occurred.

- **Disable r-protocols** The r-protocols allow users to log on to remote systems using IP-based authentication. IP-based authentication permits only specific IP addresses to remotely log on to a system. Because this authentication is based on the IP address, a hacker who has discovered an authorized IP address can create *spoofed* packets that appear to be from the authorized system.

- **Implement password aging** Default Red Hat Linux systems allow passwords to expire after 99,999 days. Because this is too long in a secure environment, Bastille offers to change the password expiration time to 180 days. These configurations are written to the /etc/login.defs file, as shown in Figure 2.6.

Figure 2.6 The /etc/login.defs File Configured for 180-Day Password Expiration

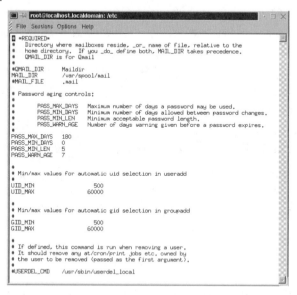

- **Password protect the LILO prompt** Allows users with the correct password to add arguments to the LILO prompt. Otherwise, only the default value (usually *linux*) is allowed. Be careful to implement this

change if you have a dual-boot system, because the name of the operating system, such as *dos*, is often typed at the LILO prompt to access other operating systems.

- **Disable CTRL-ALT-DELETE rebooting** This disallows rebooting the machine by this method.

- **Password protect single-user mode** If a user gains access to your physical system, he or she can enter single-user mode by typing init 1. Once in single-user mode, that user has root access, and no one else can access the machine. By placing a password on single-user mode, run-level 1 is protected (the password is the root password).

- **Optimize TCP Wrappers** This choice modifies the inetd.conf (pre-Red Hat Linux 7 versions only) and /etc/hosts.allow files so that inetd must contact TCP Wrappers whenever it gets a request, instead of automatically running the requested service. TCP Wrappers will determine if the requesting IP address is allowed to run the particular service. If the request is not allowed, the request is denied and the attempt is logged. Although IP-based authentication can be vulnerable, this optimization adds a layer of security to the process.

- **Add Authorized Use banners** These banners automatically appear whenever anyone logs on to the system. Authorized Use banners are helpful in prosecuting malicious hackers, and should be added to every system on your network that allows access to the network. An information bulletin from the U.S. Department of Energy's Computer Incident Advisory Capability can be found at http://ciac.llnl.gov/ciac/bulletins/ j-043.shtml.

  The bulletin is titled "Creating Login Banners" and explains what is required within login banners for government computers. It also includes how to create banners and provides the text from the approved banner for Federal Government computer systems. Bastille uses a modified version of this login banner. If you choose to create a login banner, it will resemble Figure 2.7. You can modify the banner text to suit your security needs in the etc/motd file.

- **Disable the compiler** Most hackers access systems through regular user accounts. Once they have access to the system, they compile malicious programs to attack the system and other systems. Disabling the compiler denies users from compiling programs, which reduces the security risk. This step is recommended for dedicated servers and fire-walls, but may be too strict for workstations used by employees who require use of the compiler for their job tasks.

Figure 2.7 The etc/motd File Displaying Banner Text

- **Limit system resource usage** If you limit system resource usage, you can reduce the chances of server failure from a DoS attack. If you choose to limit system resource usage in Bastille, the following changes will occur:

  - Individual file size is limited to 40MB.

  - Each individual user is limited to 150 processes.

  - The allowable core files number is configured to zero. Core files are used for system troubleshooting. They are large and exploitable if a hacker gains control of them: they can grow and consume your file system.

  These limits are written to the /etc/security/limits.conf file, as shown in Figures 2.8 and 2.9.

- **Restrict console access** Anyone with access to the console has special rights, such as CD-ROM mounting. Bastille can specify which user accounts are allowed to log on via the console.

Figure 2.8 The /etc/security/limits.conf File

Figure 2.9 The /etc/security/limits.conf File Configured to Limit the Allowable Core Files, User File Sizes, and User Processes

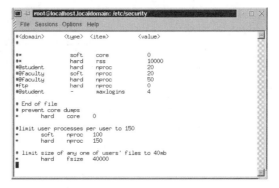

- **Additional and remote logging** Two additional logs can be added to /var/log/:

  - **/var/log/kernel** (kernel messages)

  - **/var/log/syslog** (error and warning severity messages)

    You can also log to a remote logging host if one exists.

- **Process accounting setup** Allows you to log the commands of all users. It also records when the commands were executed. This log file is helpful in retracing a hacker's steps into your system, but the file can become large quickly. If the hacker has root access, the hacker can remove this accounting log.

- **Disable unnecessary daemons** As discussed earlier in this chapter, only the required services should run on a system. All other services should be removed. Bastille allows you to disable daemons that are often unnecessary and pose potential security risks. If you performed a custom Red Hat installation with "everything," you will be asked if you want to disable the services shown in Table 2.3.

Table 2.3 Disabling Unnecessary Daemons

Service	Description	Reason for Disabling
Ampd	Monitors battery power on laptop computers	Often unnecessary
Network File System (NFS) and Samba	Unix network file systems used for sharing files	Potential security risk
Atd	At daemon used for scheduling commands	Potential security risk
PCMCIA services	Used for laptop computers	Often unnecessary
Dynamic Host Configuration Protocol (DHCP) daemon	Used by DHCP servers	Often unnecessary
News server daemon	Used by news servers	Often unnecessary
Routing daemon	Used by routers	Often unnecessary
Network Information System (NIS) server and client programs	Unix network naming and administration system	Potential security risk and often unnecessary
Simple Network Management Protocol (SNMP) daemon	Used to manage network devices	Potential security risk and often unnecessary
Sendmail daemon mode	Used by sendmail servers	Often unnecessary

- **Download and install Secure Shell (SSH)** A standard for securely logging on to remote systems. SSH encrypts usernames, passwords, and all information between hosts as they communicate across the network. Standard telnet connections send the information in clear text. Therefore, you should always use SSH to ensure secure remote connections.

- **Deactivate and chroot named** Similar to other services, named should be deactivated if the service is not required (e.g., if the server will

not answer DNS queries). Bastille also offers to change the root directory of named to a child node on the directory tree, which is
/home/dns. This new directory is considered a "chroot'ed prison"
because the daemon is limited to only part of the file system and can
only access the required files needed to function. These prisons are not
entirely secure, but they do offer another layer of security to fend off a
would-be hacker. This change is transparent, except that all configuration
files and editing must occur in /home/dns. In addition, if you control
named with ndc, you must enter: **ndc -c /home/dns/var/run/ndc**.

NOTE

The chroot() system call makes the current working directory act as if it
were /. Consequently, a process that has used the chroot() system call
cannot cd to higher-level directories. This prevents anyone exploiting the
service from general access to the system.

- **Harden Apache Web server** httpd should be deactivated if the service
  is not required. If you decide to use Apache, you can perform the steps
  shown in the "Hardening the Apache Web Server" sidebar in Bastille to
  run the service.

Damage & Defense...

Hardening the Apache Web Server

Bastille has a reputation for being unable to secure the Apache Web
server. If you implement the following steps for hardening Apache, be
aware that security issues may still arise.

1. **Run Apache as localhost only** This action is especially
   helpful for Web designers and programmers because it allows
   them to work on their code and view their progress without
   opening the Web server to others network users. They access
   their local Web server by entering http://localhost.

Continued

2. **Bind the Web server to a specific interface** Allows you to bind the Web server's IP address to an interface, such as an Ethernet network interface card (NIC). The option overrides the previous localhost-only action.

3. **Disable symbolic links** Symbolic links are "pointers" to other files in a file system. They are capable of allowing Web site visitors to access files outside of the Web server directories. If you disable symbolic links, you limit the files accessible to visitors on the Web server.

4. **Deactivate server-side includes** Server-side includes (SSIs) are interpreters or programs on a Web server that are activated by a client. SSIs can create HTML on the fly, which reduces bandwidth usage. SSIs are HTML directives to run programs on the server and add the programs' output to the page being returned to the client. The problem is that crackers could cause the program to run in an insecure way, and in some cases could even cause other programs to run. Consequently, SSIs are considered insecure and have fallen out of favor. If you do not use SSIs on your Apache Web server, you should deactivate them.

5. **Disable CGI scripts** Common Gateway Interface (CGI) scripts allow a Web server to communicate with an application, such as a database, and then return that data to a client. CGI scripts should be limited to certain users, depending on the CGI scripts. For example, many scripts are used to process Web page forms, which are available to the public. Some scripts may be used to access private databases, which require limited access. If you do not use CGI scripts on your Apache Web server, you should deactivate them.

6. **Disable indexes** A world-readable file or directory allows Web site visitors access to files or directories. An automatically generated index file will list the contents of these files and directories. Listing them is usually a bad idea unless you want the files to be listed for HTTP downloads (Web-based file archives) or similar uses.

■ **Disable printing** Printing should only be enabled if your system needs to print. If printing is not required, Bastille removes SUID root on lpr, and disables lpr and lpd. As stated in the configuration script, if you disable SUID root on lpr and need to print, you must undo the setting by entering the following:

```
/bin/chmod 06555 /usr/bin/lpr /usr/bin/lprm
/sbin/chkconfig lpd on
```

- **Disable FTP daemon user privileges** By default (in the wu-ftpd configuration file), FTP clients cannot connect anonymously and upload files via FTP. Users with accounts on the system can still access the FTP server. This is dangerous if they access the server over a public network because the FTP passwords are sent as clear text, which can be captured by anyone with a packet sniffer. Anyone who has upload privileges can compromise the FTP daemon, because uploading files cause most attacks that allow root access.

- **Disable anonymous download** Allows anyone to download files from your FTP server without a unique username and password. Instead, it is recommended that you use an Apache Web-based file archive to allow the public to download files.

Bastille Versions

Bastille 1.1.0 and later incorporates several important changes that make the program even more powerful and easy to use. The examples in this book use Bastille 1.1.1. It is recommended that you implement at least version 1.1.0 because of the following enhancements:

- **Nonvirgin system install** Bastille runs on systems that are already in production. Previous versions only allowed Bastille to run on systems with a new install only.

- **Multiple runnings** Bastille can be run many times on the same system. Therefore, administrators can change settings as needed.

- **Log-only feature** Administrators can run Bastille without actually implementing the changes. Instead, the changes are written to a log file. This is helpful because it allows an administrator to decide what will work best for his or her system without being forced to commit to the changes. One wrong choice in Bastille can restrict the system's functionality, and not allow the server to perform its job (hence, the all-important

Undo feature).To run the program in log-only mode, enter the following at the prompt when using interactive mode:

```
./InteractiveBastille.pl -v
```

- **Distribution support** Bastille is written specifically to Red Hat Linux and Mandrake Linux.The specific Red Hat/Mandrake content has been generalized, and hard-code filenames are now represented as variables. These variables are set automatically at runtime.

- **Undo feature** Administrators can undo settings through various methods that are listed at the end of this section.

Implementing Bastille

Bastille is available for free download at www.bastille-linux.org.This tarball is also on the CD accompanying this book (Bastille-1.1.1.tar.gz).The program is offered in tarball format and must be installed by a root user in his or her root directory (a tarball is a collection of archived files that have been archived using the Unix tar program and have the .tar extension). Because Bastille is actually a collection of Perl scripts, you must also ensure that Perl 5.0 or later is installed on your system.

The program automatically implements the administrator's preferences based on the answers to the questions, and saves them in the /root/Bastille/config file, as shown in Figure 2.10.

Figure 2.10 Bastille Configuration File

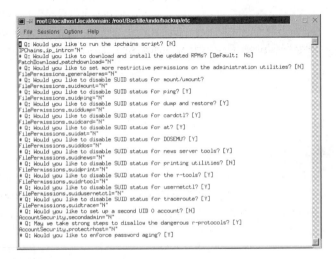

Bastille allows the same configuration to be implemented on other systems. To do this, administrators need to install Bastille on that machine, copy the config file and the BackEnd.pl file to the new system's ~/Bastille directory, and then run the command:

```
./BackEnd.pl
```

Damage & Defense...

Logging Your Configurations in Bastille

As with many security programs, Bastille is relatively simple to implement, but it's easy to lose track of the changes you implemented. This can be a problem if you are unable to perform a typical operation on the system, or are denied access to a command or service. Many times, it is because you locked down part of the system by mistake, or misjudged the impact of a particular Bastille choice.

It is always a good idea to create a hard-copy log of the options you select in Bastille, or any security configurations you implement on your system. When you configure Bastille on your systems, use the Bastille log included in Appendix A of this book. It includes each configuration question and an area for your manual input. Make copies of the Appendix A, fill out the table during configuration, and keep the hard copies in a safe place.

If your system goes down, you can access the hard copies and recreate your Bastille configurations. Of course, if your system became unusable due to Bastille, it will help you determine what went wrong. This is especially helpful if you are unable to access the /root/Bastille/ config file, which saves the administrator's preferences based on the answers to the Bastille questions.

Follow these steps to install and configure Bastille:

1. Log in as root.

2. Copy the Bastille tarball to your root directory. You can access the tarball from the CD accompanying this book (Bastille-1.1.1.tar.gz), or from www.bastille-linux.org. This lab is written for version 1.1.1, so we recommend that you use the version on the CD. The filename will resemble:

```
Bastille-1.1.1.tar.gz
```

3. In the root directory, decompress the image by entering:

```
tar -zxvf Bastille-1.1.1.tar.gz
```

4. Access the newly created Bastille directory in your root directory.

```
cd Bastille
```

5. To run the Perl configuration scripts in the interactive text-based mode, enter the following in the Bastille directory:

```
./InteractiveBastille.pl
```

The opening Bastille screen appears, as shown in Figure 2.11.

Figure 2.11 Interactive Bastille Opening Screen

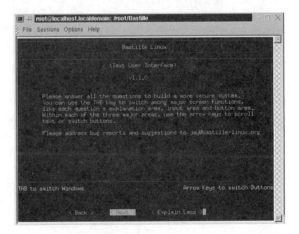

6. All choices you implement in Bastille are logged to the /root/Bastille/ config file. If you want to log your choices without implementing them, you can append the **-v** option. Your choices are still logged to the /root/Bastille/config file, which is the same file to which the actions are logged. Therefore, we strongly recommend that you make a backup of the config file before running Bastille and keep a manual log.

7. The opening screen appears, identifying how to navigate through the Bastille configuration process. Select **Next** to access the first configuration screen, as shown in Figure 2.12.

Figure 2.12 Bastille Linux Question-and-Answer Script

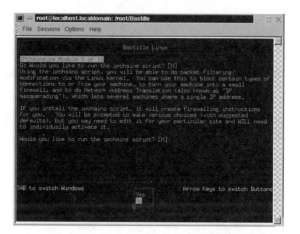

8. Table 2.5 leads you through the configuration process. The configuration used in this example performs a few basic hardening techniques on a Red Hat Linux 7.0 system with a custom installation with everything installed. The main purpose is to show you what Bastille offers and how to use it. You can use Bastille to secure a system based on your system's services and needs, which will vary from the example. The bolded sections in the Choice column are choices you will skip for this example. The default answers are displayed for your interest. You will install many of these services later in this book, such as SSH.

Table 2.5 Simple Bastille Configurations

Question	Choice
Module 1: IPChains.pm	
1. Would you like to run the ipchains script? (Choosing "No" will skip to Module 2; you will implement ipchains later in this book.)	No
2. Do you need the advanced networking options?	**No**
3. DNS servers	**0.0.0.0/0**

Continued

Table 2.5 Continued

Question	Choice
4. Public interfaces	eth+ ppp+ slip+
5. TCP services to audit (name or port number).	telnet ftp imap pop-3 finger sunrpc exec login linuxconf ssh
6. UDP services to audit (name or port number); the "Back Orifice" port number on Microsoft clients is listed by default.	31337
7. ICMP services to audit (name or port number); an example is the Microsoft "echo-request" service (Microsoft ping and tracert commands).	(Blank)
8. TCP service names or port numbers to allow on public interfaces (typical workstations should not allow any services).	(Blank)
9. UDP service names or port numbers to allow on public interfaces (typical workstations should not allow any services).	(Blank)
10. Force passive mode (i.e., for clients connecting to an FTP server).	No
11. TCP services to block (if you force passive mode, you can skip this step).	1024 2049 2065:2090 6000:6020 7100
12. UDP services to block.	1066 2049 6770
13. ICMP allowed types.	Destination-unreachable echo-reply time-exceeded
14. Enable source address verification.	Yes
15. Reject method.	DENY
16. Interfaces for DHCP queries.	(Blank)
17. NTP servers to query.	(Blank)
18. ICMP types to disallow outbound.	Destination-unreachable time-exceeded

Continued

Table 2.5 Continued

Question	Choice
Module 2: PatchDownload.pm	
1. Would you like to download and install the updated RPMs?	No
Module 3: FilePermissions.pm	
1. Would you like to set more restrictive permissions on the administration utilities?	Yes
2. Would you like to disable SUID status for mount/ umount?	No
3. Would you like to disable SUID status for ping?	Yes
4. Would you like to disable SUID status for dump and restore?	No
5. Would you like to disable SUID status for cardctl?	No
6. Would you like to disable SUID status for at?	No
7. Would you like to disable SUID status for DOSEMU?	No
8. Would you like to disable SUID status for news server tools?	No
9. Would you like to disable SUID status for printing utilities?	No
10. Would you like to disable SUID status for the r-tools?	No
11. Would you like to disable SUID status for usernetctl?	No
12. Would you like to disable SUID status for traceroute?	Yes
Module 4: AccountSecurity.pm	
1. Would you like to set up a second UID 0 account?	No
1a. What should we name the second UID 0 account?	**admin**
2. May we take strong steps to disallow the dangerous r-protocols?	No
3. Would you like to enforce password aging?	Yes
4. Would you like to create a nonroot user account?	Yes
4a. What should we name your nonroot account?	dave
5. Would you like to restrict the use of cron to adminis-trator accounts?	No
	No

Continued

Table 2.5 Continued

Question	Choice
Module 5: BootSecurity.pm	
1. Would you like to password protect the LILO prompt?	No
1a. Enter LILO password, please.	**(Blank)**
2. Would you like to reduce the LILO delay time to zero?	No
3. Do you ever boot Linux from the hard drive?	Yes
4. Would you like to write the LILO changes to a boot floppy?	No
4a. Floppy drive device name.	**fd0**
5. Would you like to disable CTRL-ALT-DELETE rebooting?	No
6. Would you like to password protect single-user mode?	Yes
Module 6: SecureInetd.pm	
1. Would you like to modify inetd.conf and /etc/hosts .allow to optimize use of Wrappers?	No
2. Would you like to set sshd to accept connections only from a small list of IP addresses?	No
2a. IP addresses to accept SSH from:	**(Blank)**
3. Would you like to make Authorized Use banners?	Yes
Module 7: DisableUserTools.pm	
1. Would you like to disable the compiler?	No
Module 8: ConfigureMiscPAM.pm	
1. Would you like to put limits on system resource usage?	Yes
2. Should we restrict console access to a small group of user accounts?	No
2a. What accounts should be able to log in at console?	**root**
Module 9: Logging.pm	
1. Would you like to add additional logging?	No
2. Do you have a remote logging host?	No
2a. What is the IP address of the machine you want to log to?	**127.0.0.1**

Continued

Table 2.5 Continued

Question	Choice
3. Would you like to set up process accounting?	No
Module 10: MiscellaneousDaemons.pm	
1. Would you like to disable apmd?	No
2. Would you like to deactivate NFS and Samba?	No
3. Would you like to disable atd?	No
4. Would you like to disable PCMCIA services?	No
5. Would you like to disable the DHCP daemon?	No
6. Would you like to disable GPM?	No
7. Would you like to disable the news server daemon?	No
8. Would you like to deactivate the routing daemons?	No
9. Would you like to deactivate NIS server and client programs?	No
10. Would you like to disable SNMPD?	No
Module 11: Sendmail.pm	
1. Do you want to leave sendmail running in daemon mode?	Yes
2. Would you like to run sendmail via cron to process the queue?	No
3. Would you like to disable the VRFY and EXPN send-mail commands?	No
Module 12: RemoteAccess.pm	
1. Would you like to download and install SSH?	No
Module 13: DNS.pm	
1. Would you like to chroot named and set it to run as a nonroot user?	No
2. Would you like to deactivate named, at least for now?	No
Module 14: Apache.pm	
1. Would you like to deactivate the Apache Web server?	No
2. Would you like to bind the Web server to listen only to the localhost?	No

Continued

Table 2.5 Continued

Question	Choice
3. Would you like to bind the Web server to a particular interface?	No
3a. Address to bind the Web server to?	**127.0.0.1**
4. Would you like to deactivate the following of symbolic links?	No
5. Would you like to deactivate server-side includes?	No
6. Would you like to disable CGI scripts, at least for now?	No
7. Would you like to disable indexes?	No

Module 15: Printing.pm

1. Would you like to disable printing?	No

Module 16: FTP.pm

1. Would you like to disable user privileges on the FTP daemon?	No
2. Would you like to disable anonymous download?	No

9. Bastille asks if you wish to implement these changes, as shown in Figure 2.13.

Figure 2.13 Implementing Bastille Changes

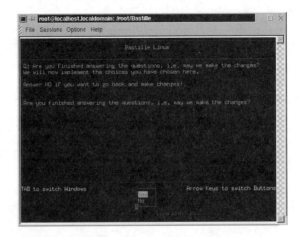

10. Select **Yes**. The credits will appear. Press **TAB** to return to the prompt.

11. To test the changes you made to your system, enter the following **ping** and **traceroute** commands as root. The commands should run successfully.

```
ping www.bastille-linux.org
traceroute www.bastille-linux org
```

12. Create a password for the dave account you created in Bastille by entering:

```
passwd dave
Changing password for user dave
New UNIX password:
Retype new UNIX password:
passwd: all authentication tokens updated successfully
```

13. Log in as user *dave*. The "NOTICE TO USERS" authorization banner will appear (the etc/motd file), warning that the computer system is for authorized use only. The banner will appear when any user, including users with SUID status, log on to the system.

14. Enter the **ping** and **traceroute** commands again as *dave*. The commands should fail, because only users with SUID status are allowed to run these commands. The error messages will appear as follows:

```
ping www.bastille-linux.org
/bin/ping: Permission denied
traceroute www.bastille-linux.org
traceroute: command not found
```

15. You also implemented password aging to 180 days. Observe the changes you made to the login.def file by entering:

```
cat /etc/login.defs | less
```

   Press any key to display the next page. Press **q** to access the prompt.

16. You applied limits to system resources by limiting individual file size to 40MB, limiting individual users to 150 processes, and configuring the allowable core files number to zero. Observe the changes you made to the limits.conf file by entering:

```
cat /etc/security/limits.conf | less
```

Press any key to display the next page. Press **q** to access the prompt.

17. Log in as root so you can add an account in the next step.

18. You password protected single-user mode. If a user gains access to your physical system, he or she must enter a password to enter single-user mode. This will keep anyone from accessing single-user mode, giving him or her root access and no one else access to the machine. The password is the root password. To test this action, follow these steps:

19. Reboot the system.

20. At the lilo prompt, enter:

```
linux init 1
```

21. The following instructions will appear. Enter your root password as requested:

```
Telling INIT to go to single user mode.
INIT: Going single user
Give root password for maintenance
(or type Control-D for normal startup): ********
```

22. You will access single-user mode, but only if you enter the root password. Access run-level 3 by entering:

```
init 3
```

Undoing Bastille Changes

At the time of this writing, a reliable automatic undo feature did not exist in Bastille. To undo the changes, you can run through the configuration questions again and select different answers. There are two other options. There is a Perl script named Undo.pl in the Bastille directory that is designed to undo all changes except for RPM installations. There is also a backup directory located at /root/Bastille/undo/backup that contains all the original system files that Bastille modified. The backup directory structure is the same as the system's directory, so you can manually replace the files fairly easily.

You cannot undo your Bastille configurations by simply removing Bastille. If you do this, your changes will still be written to their specific files. If you want to remove the program and your settings, you must undo your changes, and then remove the Bastille directory.

The following steps demonstrate three ways to undo the changes that you implemented in Table 2.5.

1. One method to undo Bastille configurations is to run through the configuration questions again and select different answers. If you choose this method, access the **Bastille directory** and enter:

```
./InteractiveBastille.pl
```

2. Run through the selection from Table 2.5 again, but replace several of the "Yes" configurations with a "No" answer, as shown in Table 2.6.

Table 2.6 Undoing Bastille Configurations

Question	Choice
Module 3: FilePermissions.pm	
1. Would you like to set more restrictive permissions on the administration utilities?	No
3. Would you like to disable SUID status for ping?	No
12. Would you like to disable SUID status for traceroute?	No
Module 4: AccountSecurity.pm	
3. Would you like to enforce password aging?	No
4. Would you like to create a nonroot user account?	No
Module 5: BootSecurity.pm	
6. Would you like to password protect single-user mode?	No
Module 6: SecureInetd.pm	
3. Would you like to make Authorized Use banners?	No
Module 8: ConfigureMiscPAM.pm	
1. Would you like to put limits on system resource usage?	No

3. Bastille asks if you wish to implement these changes. Select **Yes**. The credits will appear. Press **TAB** to return to the prompt.

4. The dave account you created will not be deleted because you only specified that you did not want to create a new account during the undo process. To delete the dave account, enter:

```
userdel -r dave
```

The command will remove all entries for dave in the system account files and the dave account's home directory.

5. The Authorized Use banner may still appear at logon. To manually delete the Authorized Use banner, delete the banner text in the /etc/motd file, or replace the motd file with the backup file. The location of the backup file is explained in step 7.

6. A second method to undo Bastille configurations is to run the automated Perl script that will undo the changes. The script is named Undo.pl, and is designed to undo all changes except for RPM installations. To run the Undo.pl script, access the **Bastille directory** and enter:

```
./Undo
```

7. A third method to undo Bastille configurations is to manually remove the changes. This can be done by replacing each file that was changed with the backup files in the Bastille directory. The backup directory is located at:

```
/root/Bastille/undo/backup
```

The backup files contain the original files before they were changed, so the original configurations are intact. Bastille makes a backup file of each file before the file is modified. A Bastille backup directory is shown in Figure 2.14.

Figure 2.14 Bastille Backup Directory Example

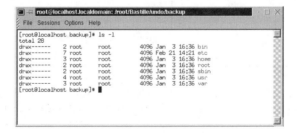

8. For example, to change password aging back to its default 99,999 days, replace the login.defs file with the backup file. Enter the following:

```
cd /root/Bastille/undo/backup/etc/login.defs
cp logindefs /etc/login.defs
cp: overwrite '/etc/login.defs'? y
```

The backup file replaces the current file, thus returning the password expiration configuration to its default setting.

As you can see, Bastille is a powerful security tool that helps you harden your system. It is relatively simple to use, and can save administrators a great deal of time because it automatically configures the required files for each selection. Administrators do not have to manually write to each file, or disable services individually. Bastille is recommended for any Unix system that offers services, whether it is a LAN or Internet server.

Controlling and Auditing Root Access with Sudo

Superuser Do (sudo) is an open source security tool that allows an administrator to give specific users or groups the ability to run certain commands as root or as another user. The program can also log commands and arguments entered by specified system users. The developers of sudo state that the basic philosophy (www.courtesan.com/sudo/readme.html) of the program is to "give as few privileges as possible but still allow people to get their work done." Sudo was first released to the public in the summer of 1986, and Todd Miller of Courtesan Consulting currently maintains the program and distributes it freely under a BSD-style license. The Sudo Main Page is located at www.courtesan.com/sudo, as shown in Figure 2.15.

The program is a command-line tool that operates one command at a time. Table 2.7 lists several important features of sudo.

Table 2.7 Sudo Features

Feature	Description
Command logging	Commands and argument can be logged. Commands entered can be traced to the user. Ideal for system auditing.

Continued

Table 2.7 Continued

Feature	Description
Centralized logging of multiple systems	Sudo can be used with the system log daemon (syslog) to log all commands to a central host.
Command restrictions	Each user or group of users can be limited to what commands they are allowed to enter on the system.
Ticketing system	The ticketing system sets a time limit by creating a ticket when a user logs on to sudo. The ticket is valid for a configurable amount of time. Each new command refreshes the ticket for the predefined amount of time. The default time is five minutes.
Centralized administration of multiple systems	The sudo configurations are written to the /etc/sudoers file. This file can be used on multiple systems and allows administration from a central host. The file is designed to allow user privileges on a host-by-host basis.

Figure 2.15 Sudo Home Page

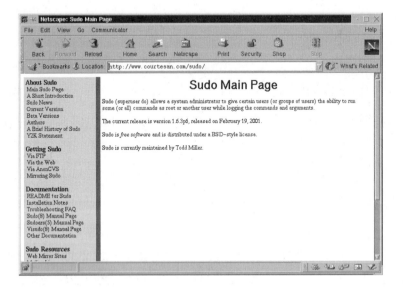

Because sudo logs all commands run as root (or specified otherwise), many administrators use it instead of using the root shell. This allows them to log their own commands for troubleshooting and additional security.

The ticketing system is ideal because if the root user walks away from the system while still logged in (a very bad idea), another user cannot access the system simply because he or she has physical access to the keyboard.

After the ticket expires, users must log on to the system again. A shorter time is recommended, such as the default five minutes. The ticketing system also allows users to remove their ticket file.

System Requirements

To install and run sudo from the source distribution, you must have a system running Unix. Almost all versions of Unix support the sudo source distribution, including almost all flavors of POSIX, BSD, and SYSV. You must also install the C compiler and the make utility.

Sudo is known to run on the following Unix flavors: Auspex, SunOS, Solaris, ISC, RISCos, SCO, HP-UX, Ultrix, IRIX, NEXTSTEP, DEC Unix, AIX, ConvexOS, BSD/OS, OpenBSD, Linux, UnixWare, Pyramid, ATT, SINIX, ReliantUNIX, NCR, Unicos, DG/UX, Dynix/ptx, DC-Osx, HI-UX/MPP, SVR4, and NonStop-UX. It also runs on MacOSX Server. To see if your OS version is compatible, visit www.courtesan.com/sudo/runson.html. In the following examples, the Linux 2.2.16 kernel (included with Red Hat Linux 7) will be used on an i586 system.

The Sudo Command

The **sudo** command allows a user to execute a command as a superuser or another user. All configurations for sudo are written to the /etc/sudoers file. The sudoers file specifies whether that command is allowed by that particular user.

In order to use sudo, the user must have already supplied a username and password. If a user attempts to run the command via sudo and that user is not in the sudoers file, an e-mail is automatically sent to the administrator, indicating that an unauthorized user is accessing the system.

Once a user logs in to sudo, a ticket is issued that is valid by default for five minutes. A user can update the ticket by issuing the **−v** flag, which will validate the ticket for another five minutes. The command is entered as follows:

```
sudo −v
```

If an unauthorized user runs the **-v** flag, an e-mail will not be sent to the administrator. The **-v** flag informs the unauthorized user that he or she is not a valid user. If the user enters command via sudo anyway, an e-mail will then be sent to the administrator.

Sudo logs login attempts, successful and unsuccessful, to the syslog(3) file by default. However, this can be changed during sudo configuration. Some of the command-line options listed in Table 2.8 are used by sudo.

Table 2.8 Selected Sudo Command Options

Option	Option Name	Description
-V	Version	Prints version number and exits.
-l	List	Lists the commands that are allowed and denied by current user.
-h	Help	Prints usage message and exits.
-v	Validate	Updates the user's ticket for a configured amount of time (default is five minutes). If required, the user must re-enter the user password.
-k	Kill	Expires the user's ticket. Completing this option requires the user to re-enter the user password to update the ticket.
-K	Sure kill	Removes the user's ticket entirely. User must log in with username and password after running this option.
-u	User	Runs the specific command as the username specified. The user specified can be any user except root. If you want to enter a uid, enter **#uid** instead of the username.

Downloading Sudo

Sudo can be downloaded from multiple sites, all specified at the sudo Web site (www.courtesan.com/sudo). For this demonstration, I used version 1.6.3p6, which is included on the companion CD (sudo-1.6.3p6.tar.gz). Other versions should be similar. For sudo download locations (many exist) via FTP and HTTP, visit the following Web addresses:

- **FTP** www.courtesan.com/sudo/ftp.html
- **HTTP** www.courtesan.com/sudo/www.html

The master FTP and HTTP sites for sudo are located and maintained by Courtesan Consulting at:

- **FTP** ftp://ftp.courtesan.com/pub/sudo
- **HTTP** www.courtesan.com/sudo/dist

Many distributions exist for the different Unix flavors. Download the version specific to your system. For example, follow these steps to download sudo for Red Hat Linux:

1. Access the sudo master http download site at www.courtesan.com/sudo/dist.

2. Download the latest version of sudo displayed at the bottom of the directory. For example, in Figure 2.16, you will select **sudo-1.6.3p6.tar.gz**. Later versions will function in this example.

Figure 2.16 Downloading Sudo

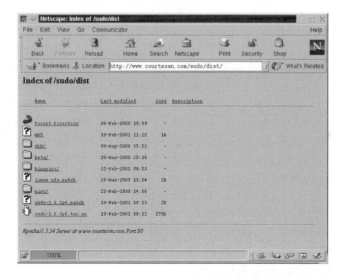

3. Download the tarball to any directory you choose. Unlike Bastille, you are not required to run the program in the root directory only. Sudo has been downloaded to the /root directory for this example.

Installing Sudo

To install sudo, you must first download the specific sudo tarball. After download, locate the directory where you downloaded sudo and follow these steps:

1. Access the directory where you downloaded sudo, and decompress the tar file (your sudo version number will vary depending on the version of sudo that you downloaded) by entering:

   ```
   tar -zxvf sudo-1.6.3p6.tar.gz
   ```

2. A directory will be created, such as sudo-1.6.3p6.

3. Access the sudo directory by entering:

   ```
   cd sudo-1.6.3p6
   ```

4. To creates a makefile and config.h file that will allow you to configure sudo, enter:

   ```
   ./configure
   ```

5. You can add options to the **./configure** command to customize your sudo installation. Simply append the options listed in Table 2.9 to your **./configure** command. The entire list of options is available in the /sudo/INSTALL file.

Table 2.9 Sudo ./**configure** Options

Option	Description	Default (if applicable)
--bindir=DIR	Sudo installed in DIR.	EPREFIX/bin
--sbindir=DIR	Visudo installed in DIR.	EPREFIX/sbin
--sysconfdir=DIR	Sudoers file installed in DIR.	/etc
--mandir=DIR	Man pages installed in DIR.	PREFIX/man
--with-skey	Support S/Key One Time Password (OTP).	n/a
--with-SecurID=DIR	Support SecurID. DIR is the directory where sdiclient.a, sdi_athd.h, sdconf.h, and sdacmvls.h will be located.	n/a

Continued

Table 2.9 Continued

Option	Description	Default (if applicable)
--with-fwtk=DIR	Support TIS Firewall Toolkit (FWTK) 'authsrv'. DIR is the base directory where the compiled FWTK package will be located.	n/a
--with-kerb4	Support Kerberos v4. Cygnus Network Security (CNS) is the only tested package.	n/a
--with-kerb5	Support Kerberos v5. For authentication, Kerberos passphrases are used, not the Kerberos cookie scheme. MIT Kerberos V, release 1.1 (will not work with versions earlier than 1.1) is the only test package, but CNS should also work.	n/a
--disable-shadow	Disable shadow passwords.	Supported. Shadow password used if it exists.
--with-sudoers-uid	Defines the UID (User ID) that owns the sudoers file. Actually configured in the makefile.	0
--with-sudoers-gid	Defines the GUI (Group ID) that owns the sudoers file. Actually configured in the makefile.	n/a
--without-passwd	Disables authentication using the passwd or shadow file. Do not disable this authentication method unless you are using another authentication method.	n/a

Continued

www.syngress.com

Table 2.9 Continued

Option	Description	Default (if applicable)
--with-logging=TYPE	Defines logging method. The types include *syslog*, *file*, or both. syslog allows centralized logging and is recommended.	syslog
--with-logpath=PATH	Defines the location of the sudo log file.	Default is /var/log/sudo. If your system does not have this directory, it defaults to /var/adm/sudo.log or /usr/adm/sudo.log.
--with-mailto	Defines the user account that sudo mail will be sent. Mail usually indicates an alert.	root
--with-mailsubject	Defines the subject of the sudo mail.	"*** SECURITY information for *hostname***"
--with-runas-default=USER	Defines the default user for the **sudo** command. By default, sudo gives root privileges if the –u flag is not specified.	root
--with-passwd-tries=TRIES	Defines the number of password attempts given to a user.	Three tries
--with-timeout=MINUTES	Defines the number of minutes before another sudo password is required	Five minutes. Configure minutes to zero and sudo will always request a password.
--with-password-timeout=MINUTES	Defines the number of minutes that sudo waits before the sudo password prompt times out.	Five minutes. Configure minutes to zero for no password timeout.

Continued

Table 2.9 Continued

Option	Description	Default (if applicable)
--with-editor=PATH	Defines the default editor path used by visudo. You can also list several editors in a colon-separated list. visudo checks the USER environment variable and selects the defined one. It can also select the first editor that is installed on the list.	vi system path

6. You can also edit makefile to change the default paths for installation, as well as the other configurations listed in Table 2.8. If you require this change, open **makefile** in a text editor. For example, enter:

```
vi Makefile
```

7. Locate the "Where to install things..." section of makefile, as shown in Figure 2.17.

Figure 2.17 Sudo Makefile

8. Change the default paths if necessary. For this example, we recommend that you use the default paths.

9. Quit the file. If you use the vi text editor, enter:

   ```
   :q
   ```

10. (Optional) You can also change the default installation paths when you run the **./configure** command (you ran the **configure** command in a previous step). To do this, enter an option after the command. For example, by default the sudoers file is installed in the /etc directory. You can change this location by entering:

    ```
    ./configure --sysconfdir=DIR
    ```

    where DIR is the new installation directory.

11. To compile sudo, run the **make** command by entering:

    ```
    make
    ```

12. (Optional) You will probably need GNU if you install sudo in a directory other than the source file directory. If you have errors during installation, read the TROUBLESHOOTING and PORTING files.

13. To install sudo, you must be the root user. Run the **make install** command to install the man pages, visudo, and a basic sudoers file by entering:

    ```
    make install
    ```

NOTE

Any existing sudoers file will not be overwritten.

14. You have installed sudo. The next section explains how to configure it to suit your system's needs.

Configuring Sudo

To configure sudo, you must edit the %/sudo-1.6.3p6/sudoers file. The sudoers file defines which users are allowed to execute what commands. Only the root user is allowed to edit the file, and it must be edited with the **visudo** command. A sample.sudoers file is included in the sudo directory, and is shown in Figure 2.18.

Figure 2.18 Sample.Sudoers File

```
root@we-24-130-10-205.we.mediaone.net: /root/sudo-1.6.3p6

File  Sessions  Options  Help

# Sample /etc/sudoers file.
#
# This file MUST be edited with the 'visudo' command as root.
#
# See the sudoers man page for the details on how to write a sudoers file.
#

##
# User alias specification
##
User_Alias      FULLTIMERS = millert, mikef, dowdy
User_Alias      PARTTIMERS = bostley, jwfox, crawl
User_Alias      WEBMASTERS = will, wendy, wim

##
# Runas alias specification
##
Runas_Alias     OP = root, operator
Runas_Alias     DB = oracle, sybase

##
# Host alias specification
##
Host_Alias      SPARC = bigtime, eclipse, moet, anchor:\
                SGI = grolsch, dandelion, black:\
                ALPHA = widget, thalamus, foobar:\
                HPPA = boa, nag, python
Host_Alias      CUNETS = 128.138.0.0/255.255.0.0
Host_Alias      CSNETS = 128.138.243.0, 128.138.204.0/24, 128.138.242.0
Host_Alias      SERVERS = master, mail, www, ns
Host_Alias      CDROM = orion, perseus, hercules

##
# Cmnd alias specification
##
Cmnd_Alias      DUMPS = /usr/sbin/dump, /usr/sbin/rdump, /usr/sbin/restore, \
"sample.sudoers" 129L, 3966C
```

The **visudo** command opens the sudoers file, by default, in the vi text editor. The **vi** commands are used to edit and write the file. You can change the default text editor used by visudo using the compile time option. Visudo uses the EDITOR environment variable. The **visudo** command performs the following tasks when editing the sudoers file:

- **Checks for parse errors** Visudo will not save any changes if a syntax error exists. It will state the line number of the error and prompt you for guidance. You will be offered a "What Now?" prompt and three choices: "e" to re-edit the file, "x" to exit without saving, and "Q" to quit and save changes. A syntax error result is shown in Figure 2.19.

NOTE

If a syntax error exists in the sudoers file and you choose **Q** to quit and save the visudo changes, sudo will not run until the problem is corrected. You must run visudo again, fix the problem, and save the file again. It is recommended that you select **e** to attempt to fix the problem, or **x** to exit without saving (if you are not sure of what went wrong).

- **Prevents multiple edits to the file simultaneously** If you attempt to run visudo while the sudoers file is being edited, you will receive an error message informing you to try again at a later time.

Figure 2.19 Visudo Parse Error

The sudoers file consists of two different types of entries, *user specifications* and *aliases*. The following examples show you how to use user specifications, which define which user is allowed to run what commands. Aliases are basically variables.

The sudoers file contains a root entry. The default sudoers file is shown in Figure 2.20. The user privilege specification is listed as:

```
root    ALL=(ALL) ALL
```

This configuration allows the root user to issue all commands.

Figure 2.20 Default Sudoers File Allowing the Root User Access to All Commands

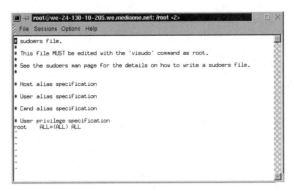

To allow other users to run commands as root, you must enter those users in the sudoers file. You must also list the host on which they are allowed to run the commands. Last, you must list the specific commands that those users are allowed to run as root. In the following steps, you will create user *bob* and allow him to run several commands as root using sudo on your system.

1. Open the sudoers file by entering:

```
visudo
```

2. The sudoers file opens in vi. Locate the "User privilege specification" section. After the root entry, enter the following (press **i** to insert text):

```
bob   your-hostname = /sbin/ifconfig, /bin/kill, /bin/ls
```

This line allows user bob to run the **ifconfig**, **kill**, and **ls** commands as root. Your screen should resemble Figure 2.21 (except the host name).

Figure 2.21 User Privilege Specification in Sudoers File

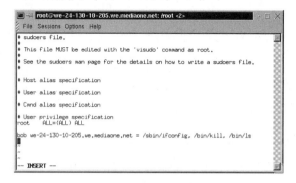

3. Press **Esc** to write and quit the file. Then, enter:

```
:wq
```

This command writes and quits the file using vi.

4. Now you must create user bob. Enter:

```
useradd bob
```

5. Create a password for user bob by entering:

```
passwd bob
Changing password for user bob
New UNIX password:
Retype new UNIX password:
passwd: all authentication tokens updated successfully
```

NOTE

By default, all commands you list in sudoers will run as root unless you specify otherwise. For example, bob could run commands as user *bugman* if desired. You would enter:

```
bob your-hostname = (bugman) /sbin/ifconfig
```

In this case, the **ifconfig** command will run as user bugman. You can allow bob to enter commands as several different users.

```
bob your-hostname = (bugman) /sbin/ifconfig, (root) /bin/kill,
    /bin/ls
```

The **kill** and **ls** commands will run as root, while the **ifconfig** command runs as bugman. At the command line, bob will enter:

```
sudo -u bugman /sbin/ifconfig
```

Running Sudo

You have configured sudo to allow user bob root privileges for the **ifconfig**, **kill**, and **ls** commands. When bob wants to run these commands, he must first enter the **sudo** command, and then his password.

1. Log on as user bob.

2. To find out what commands bob has root access to, enter the following:

   ```
   sudo -l
   ```

3. If this is your first time running sudo as user bob, a warning will display:

   ```
   We trust you have received the usual lecture from the local
   System Administrator. It usually boils down to these two things:
   #1) Respect the privacy of others.
   #2) Think before you type
   ```

4. A password prompt appears. Do *not* enter the root password. Enter bob's password.

   ```
   Password:
   ```

5. The commands that bob is allowed to run on this host are listed, as shown in Figure 2.22.

Figure 2.22 Commands That User bob Can Run as Root

6. To test your sudo configurations, run an ifconfig option that requires root permission without using sudo. Enter:

```
/sbin/ifconfig eth0 down
```

Permission is denied because bob is not allowed to deactivate the system's interface.

7. To deactivate the interface, bob must use sudo. Enter:

```
sudo /sbin/ifconfig eth0 down
```

You will be successful. Please note that sudo will ask for the bob's password if bob's ticket has expired (the default is five minutes). If you run this command within five minutes from the last, you will not be prompted for a password.

8. Reactivate the interface. Enter:

```
sudo /sbin/ifconfig eth0 up
```

9. Next, restart one of the httpd processes using the **kill** command by entering:

```
ps aux | grep httpd
```

10. Choose an Apache PID from the list that appears. (If Apache is not installed, select a different service process to restart.) Enter:

```
kill -HUP [PID NUMBER]
```

11. You are not allowed to restart the httpd process because you are not root. You will receive the following result:

```
bash: kill: (PID NUMBER) - Not owner
```

12. Instead, use sudo to run the command as root by entering:

```
sudo kill -HUP (PID NUMBER)
```

You should be successful.

13. Next, you will list the root user directory as user bob using the **ls** command. Enter:

```
ls /root
```

Permission is denied because you are not root.

14. Again, use sudo to run the command as root:

```
sudo ls /root
```

Permission is granted and the root user's directory is displayed.

15. To expire bob's timestamp, enter the command **sudo –k**. Bob will have to enter a password the next time he uses sudo.

No Password

In some situations, entering a password each time sudo is run is redundant because the user has already logged on to the system. Sudo offers a way around this monotonous task by using the NOPASSWD tag in the sudoers file.

1. To remove the password requirement in the sudoers file, log on as *root* and enter:

```
visudo
```

2. The sudoers file opens in vi. Modify bob's user privilege specification to match the following (press **i** to insert text):

```
bob    your-hostname = NOPASSWD: /sbin/ifconfig, /bin/kill, /bin/ls
```

3. Press **Esc**. Enter **:wq** to write and quit the file.

4. Log on as bob. Deactivate the interface using sudo:

```
sudo /sbin/ifconfig eth0 down
```

You will not be prompted for your password and the command will run as root.

5. Reactivate the interface. Enter:

```
sudo /sbin/ifconfig eth0 up
```

Sudo Logging

As mentioned previously, sudo logs which users run what commands. Logging does not occur automatically. You must set up sudo and syslogd to log commands. This involves two steps. First, you must create a sudo logfile in /var/log. Second, you must configure syslog.conf to log sudo commands. The following steps show you how to configure sudo logging.

1. Log on as root. Create a sudo log file in /var/log/. Enter:

```
touch /var/log/sudo
```

2. Next, you must add a line in the syslog.conf file to direct logging to your sudo logging file. Open syslog.conf by entering the following:

```
vi /etc/syslog.conf
```

3. Enter the following line at the end of the syslog.conf file (press **i** to insert text). If you installed Bastille earlier in this lesson, insert the line before or after the Bastille insert. The white space must be created using the **TAB** key, not the **SPACEBAR**.

```
local2.debug                        /var/log/sudo
```

4. This syslog.conf entry logs all successful and unsuccessful sudo commands to the /var/log/sudo file. You can also log to a network host by indicating the network host instead of a local directory. The syslog.conf file is shown in Figure 2.23.

5. Press **ESC** to write and quit the file. Then, enter:

```
:wq
```

6. Since you have modified the syslog.conf file, you need to restart syslogd. To send a HUP signal to syslogd, you must first know the syslogd process identifier (PID). To identify the syslogd PID, enter:

```
ps aux | grep syslogd
```

Figure 2.23 Editing the Syslog.conf File for Sudo Logging

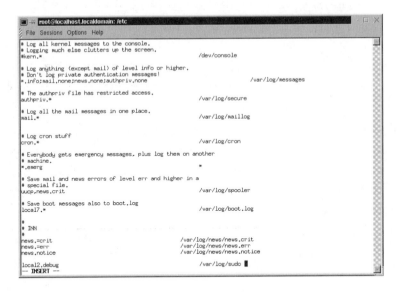

7. The second column lists the PID number. The last column lists the process using that PID. To restart syslogd, identify the PID number and enter:

    ```
    kill -HUP [PID NUMBER]
    ```

8. First, you will generate log entries for user bob. Log on as user bob.

9. Enter the following **ifconfig** commands while logged on as user bob:

    ```
    sudo -l
    sudo /sbin/ifconfig eth0 down
    sudo /sbin/ifconfig eth0 up
    ```

10. Restart one of the httpd processes (or another process) using the **kill** command by entering:

    ```
    ps aux | grep httpd
    ```

11. Choose an Apache (httpd) PID from the list that appears. Enter:

    ```
    sudo kill -HUP [PID NUMBER]
    ```

12. Now list the root user directory as user bob. Enter:

    ```
    sudo ls /root
    ```

13. Log on as root and view the sudo log file. All the sudo commands that bob entered are listed, as shown in Figure 2.24.

Figure 2.24 Sudo Log File Displaying User bob's Commands

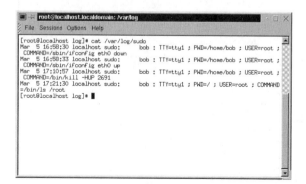

14. You can log any root commands by simply typing **sudo** before each command. For example, make sure that you are logged on as root and enter the following commands (or any commands you choose):

```
sudo useradd susan
sudo passwd susan
sudo vi /hosts
```

15. Access and view the sudo log file by entering:

```
sudo cat /var/log/sudo
```

All root user entries are logged, including the **cat** command you just entered, as shown in Figure 2.25.

Figure 2.25 Sudo Log File Displaying Root User Commands

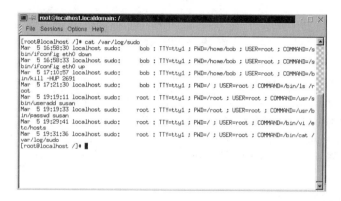

As you can see, sudo is extremely helpful for controlling and auditing root access. It allows a system administrator to distribute root system tasks without distributing the root password. An administrator can control what root access is needed for each user, and can customize system access based on those needs.

Sudo is used almost entirely by system administrators, and is a great way to train new system administrators. New administrators can be given a new account with only selected root privileges. The master administrator can then review the work of the administrator in training.

This section discussed one of the many ways to use sudo; it focused primarily on user specifications in the sudoers file. For more information on extending sudo, such as using aliases, please consult the sudoers man file.

Managing Your Log Files

Another aspect of system security is managing your log files. By default, Linux offer modest logging so that administrators can see who and what has accessed their system. More logging is available (both more detail and logging on more services), but Linux keeps it brief so that you don't fill your hard disk with log information. This section briefly discusses helpful commands and programs that provide access to system logs.

Linux offers commands that allow administrators to access useful log files. Two commands of interest are **last** and **lastlog**. The message file also offers useful data for determining possible security breaches on your system.

The **last** command displays data such as who is logged on to the system, who recently logged on, and when the system has rebooted. For example, you may receive data such as the following:

```
root    tty1                         Fri May 25 13:53    still   logged on
frank   pts/0         209.113.84.112 Fri May 25 12:13 - 14:36   (02:22)
reboot system boot 2.2.12-20         Fri May 25 12:06           (04:18)
```

The **lastlog** command displays the users and services that have accounts on your machine. It lists the last time each account logged in to the system, or if the account has ever logged in. Each service in Linux is given an account. This is very helpful because if a service logged in without your knowledge, a hacker may be responsible. This would indicate that the hacker controls your system and is currently exploiting it. It could also mean that another administrator started the service without telling you.

The messages file is a log file that displays a list of recent activity on the system. For example, it lists if a password was changed and who changed it. It identifies when a user session opens and closes. It also lists the time and data each event took place. It can be viewed by entering the following command:

```
tail /var/log/messages
```

If you prefer a GUI to view your log files, a program called *SWATCH* (not installed by default) allows an instant and real-time display for various log files. It can view any log files you specify and is discussed in the next section.

The Linux logs should be checked frequently to determine if any security violations have occurred on your system. Logs do not offer solutions, so you must analyze the data and decide how to counteract the attack.

Using Logging Enhancers

Logging enhancers are tools that simplify logging by allowing logging information to be filtered and often displaying logs in simplified formats. Many open source logging programs exist to make system administration much easier. Viewing text-based files with hundreds or thousands of entries can be burdensome, especially if you are only looking for one specific error entry. Logging enhancers can make logging a much more user-friendly experience, and greatly expand and customize the information you need to log.

The next sections explain three popular logging services used by administrators: SWATCH, scanlogd, and the next generation of syslogd (syslogd–ng).

SWATCH

Simple WATCHer or Simple WATCHdog (SWATCH) is an open source package that allows administrators to efficiently monitor system activity. It can monitor events on a system, or a large number of systems, by monitoring system logs for specified events. SWATCH'S main function is to monitor messages actively as they are written to a log files through the Unix syslog utility. SWATCH requires Perl 5 to function.

SWATCH is efficient because it allows administrators to modify the SWATCH configuration file (/etc/swatchrc) to filter logging entries and respond to certain events. For example, SWATCH can monitor the system for bad login attempts, and e-mail the administrator whenever this failed authentication event occurs. It can monitor and alter when system halts and reboots occur, when a user upgrades to root using the **su** command, when the file system is full, and when someone is sniffing the system. It can monitor anything desired from the log files.

To learn about SWATCH and download the program, you need to visit the SWATCH home page (Figure 2.26) at www.stanford.edu/~atkins/swatch or at www.engr.ucsb.edu/~eta/swatch. This RPM is also available on the accompanying CD (swatch-3.064-1.noarch.rpm).

Figure 2.26 SWATCH Home Page

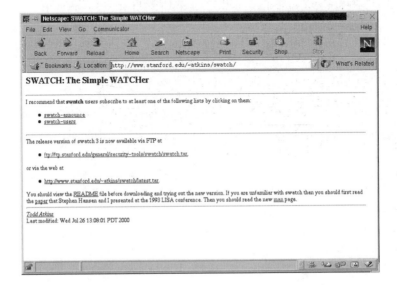

NOTE

At the time of this writing, version 3 of SWATCH was available for download. It has a different configuration file format than previous versions, and much of the code has been rewritten to take advantage of Perl 5. If you use previous configuration files, you must use the **--old-style-config** switch during configuration.

SWATCH uses two required fields: *pattern(s)* and *action(s)*.

- **Patterns** The SWATCH configuration file looks for *patterns* in logging entries. For example, bad login attempts display a "Failed Authentication" error.

- **Actions** Whenever a pattern is discovered, SWATCH seeks an *action*, such as e-mailing the administrator of the failed login attempt.

Two optional fields are used to further customize the configuration file:

- **Throttle** Throttle determines the amount of time that SWATCH will ignore repeated logged entries before listing the entry again. This saves administrators time from viewing 300 identical "Failed Authentication" errors. However, a secure system should limit the number of login attempts. The throttle entry is defined as HH:MM:SS, where H represents hours, M represents minutes, and S represents seconds.

- **Timestamp** Timestamp defines the length and location of the timestamp. The timestamp entry is defined as start:length.

The following are two examples from the SWATCH configuration file. SWATCH will actively watch for these messages as they are written to their respective log files through the syslog utility. The first example monitors logging for failed login attempts and e-mails root when a failed login attempt occurs.

```
#Failed login attempts
watchfor        /failed/
                echo bold
                mail addresses=root,subject=Failed Authentication
```

The second example monitors your log files and e-mails root when a user sued to gain root access.

```
#Users sued to gain root access
watchfor        /su:/
                echo bold
                mail addresses=root,subject=User sued to root
```

SWATCH filters logging files so that administrators only receive the information they require. It saves a lot of time and trouble once configured and is recommended for system administrators who are overwhelmed by log files (and perhaps do not use them for that reason). To download an RPM version of SWATCH, visit www.rpmfind.net.

Scanlogd

Scanlogd is an open source program that detects and logs TCP-port scanning on a system. For example, it can detect nmap scans. Nmap is a program used by hackers to create a "map" of your network. It is often the first step a hacker takes once he or she has access to your network to determine which system to hack. Nmap lists the systems and the services on the network. Scanlogd can alert an administrator when the network is being mapped, but it cannot stop the intrusion.

SECURITY ALERT!

Scanlogd was originally designed to illustrate attacks, not to fix them. Therefore, even though it is safe to run on your system, it does not prevent hacking attacks. You must read the system log to discover what happened to your system, and then determine the appropriate solution.

Scanlogd writes one line per scan using the syslog(3) mechanism. It also logs when a source address sends many packets to several different ports in a short amount of time. You can learn about scanlogd and download the program at www.openwall.com/scanlogd. The scanlogd home page is shown in Figure 2.27.

Figure 2.27 Scanlogd Home Page

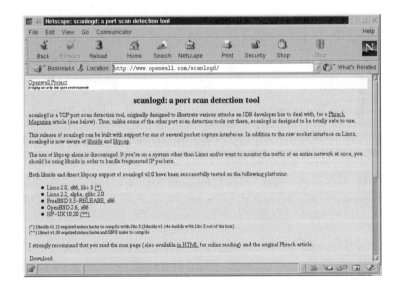

Because scanlogd is only meant to detect scans, it is totally safe to run on your system. It must have access to raw IP packets to function, and can capture packets coming in and out of the system interface, or across the network to which the system is attached. In addition, scanlogd v2 supports the raw socket interface on libnids, libpcap, and Linux.

Syslogd-ng

Syslogd-ng is a logging daemon that is the replacement for the traditional syslogd. The "ng" is an acronym for "next generation." The original syslogd was the general Unix logging daemon that handled requests for syslog services, but was difficult to configure. Syslogd-ng is easier to configure and offers additional logging features, such as more configurations. For example, syslogd-ng allows administrators to filter messages based on priority, as well as the content of the messages. You can also forward logs on TCP, sort logs to different destinations, and create a direct log stream to various hosts. It will eventually support log files that are protected with hash encryption. The syslog-ng home page is shown in Figure 2.28 and is located at www.balabit.hu/en/products/syslog-ng.

Figure 2.28 Syslog-ng Home Page

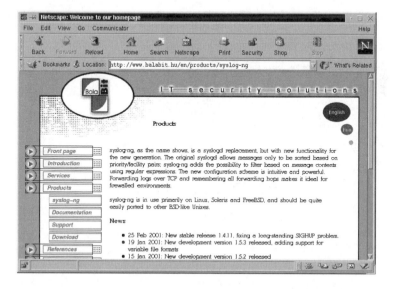

The basic problem with system logs is that they contain a lot of unimportant information. This information is often called *noise*. Many events are lost because they are buried in the noise. Syslogd made it difficult to choose only the important messages.

The reason this occurs is that messages are sent to different destinations depending on the assigned facility/priority pair. These destinations are very broad, and include general facilities such as mail, news, auth, and so forth, and priorities ranging from alert to debug. Many programs use the facilities, so many unneeded messages are written to their logs. In many cases, the message and the facility are not even related. Syslogd-ng filters messages based on message content in addition to the facility/priority pair. Using this method, only the messages that are needed are logged.

Syslogd-ng has been tested on Linux, BSDi, and Solaris. At the time of this writing, the latest stable version was 1.4.10. You can learn more about syslog-ng and download it from the Balabit site at www.balabit.hu/en/products/syslog-ng/downloads. The site also contains information on installing and configuring the service.

Summary

This chapter covered the basics of hardening a server to avoid security vulnerabilities using Linux. The main sections covered disabling unnecessary services, locking down ports, Bastille, sudo, and logging enhancers.

It is extremely important to install the latest service pack or updates to the operating system, which fix many security vulnerabilities and bugs before you install any programs. Many services provided with operating systems are not required and can be removed. The key to remember is that the fewer services running, the less potential vulnerability. TCP/UDP ports were covered in this chapter, and how each port is used by specific services. If you block ports on your server, you block the services that use those ports. Locking down ports is an excellent way to reduce exploitations of your system.

Maintaining your server involves downloading service packs and updates, and requires regularly installing bug fixes, security patches, and software updates. These items are available through the operating system vendors, as well as the specific vendors that created the software that you implement.

Bastille is an open source program that facilitates the hardening of a Linux system. It performs many of the tasks listed previously, including downloading operating system updates and disabling services and ports that are not required for the system's job functions. Bastille is powerful and can save administrators time from configuring each individual file and program throughout the operating system. Instead, administrators answer a series of "Yes" and "No" questions through an interactive text-based interface. The program automatically implements the administrators' preferences based on the answers to the questions.

Superuser Do (sudo) is an open source security tool that allows an administrator to give specific users or groups the ability to run certain commands as root or as another user. The program can also log commands and arguments entered by specified system users. The developers of sudo state that the basic philosophy (www.courtesan.com/sudo/readme.html) of the program is to "give as few privileges as possible, but still allow people to get their work done."

Logging enhancers are tools that simplify logging by allowing logging information to be filtered and often displaying logs in simplified formats. Many open source logging programs exist to make system administration easier. You were introduced in this chapter to SWATCH, scanlogd, and syslog-ng.

SWATCH is an open source package that allows administrators to efficiently monitor system activity. It can monitor events on a system, or a large number of systems, by monitoring system logs for specified events. SWATCH's main function is to monitor messages actively as they are written to log files through the Unix syslog utility.

Scanlogd is an open source program that detects and logs TCP-port scanning on a system. Scanlogd can alert an administrator when the network is being mapped, but it cannot stop the intrusion.

Syslogd-ng is a logging daemon that is the replacement for the traditional syslogd. The "ng" is an acronym for "next generation." The original syslogd was the general Unix logging daemon that handled request for syslog services, but was difficult to configure. Syslogd-ng is easier to configure and offers additional logging features, such as more configurations. For example, syslogd-ng allows administrators to filter messages based on priority, as well as the content of the messages.

Solutions Fast Track

Updating the Operating Systems

☑ Operating system releases usually contain software bugs and security vulnerabilities.

☑ Operating system vendors or organizations offer fixes, corrections, and updates to the system. For example, Red Hat offers this material at its Web site, which includes Update Service Packages and the Red Hat Network.

☑ You should always ensure your system has the latest necessary upgrades. Many errata and Update Service Packages are not required for every system. You should always read the associated documentation to determine if you need to install it.

Handling Maintenance Issues

☑ After your system goes live, you must always maintain it by making sure the most current patches and errata are installed, which include the fixes, corrections, and updates to the system, as well as the applications running on it.

☑ You should always check the Red Hat site at www.redhat.com/apps/support/updates.html for the latest errata news.

☑ For example, Red Hat security advisories provide updates that eliminate security vulnerabilities on the system. Red Hat recommends that all administrators download and install the security upgrades to avoid denial-of-service (DoS) and intrusion attacks that can result from these weaknesses.

Manually Disabling Unnecessary Services and Ports

☑ You should always disable vulnerable services and ports on your system that are not used. You are removing risk when you remove unnecessary services.

☑ The /etc/xinetd.d directory makes it simple to disable services that your system is not using. For example, you can disable the FTP and Telnet services by commenting out the FTP and Telnet entries in the respective file and restarting the service. If the service is commented out, it will not restart.

Locking Down Ports

☑ When determining which ports to block on your server, you must first determine which services you require. In most cases, block all ports that are not exclusively required by these services.

☑ To block TCP/UDP services in Linux, you must disable the service that uses the specific port.

Hardening the System with Bastille

☑ The Bastille program facilitates the hardening of a Linux system. It saves administrators time from configuring each individual file and program throughout the operating system.

☑ Administrators answer a series of "Yes" and "No" questions through an interactive text-based interface. The program automatically implements the administrators' preferences based on the answers to the questions.

☑ Bastille can download and install RPM updates, apply restrictive permissions on administrator utilities, disable unnecessary services and ports, and much more.

Controlling and Auditing Root Access with Sudo

☑ Sudo (Superuser Do) allows an administrator to give specific users or groups the ability to run certain commands as root or as another user.

☑ Sudo features command logging, command restrictions, centralized administration of multiple systems, and much more.

☑ The **sudo** command is used to execute a command as a superuser or another user. In order to use the **sudo** command, the user must supply a username and password. If a user attempts to run the command via sudo and that user is not entered in the sudoers file, an e-mail is automatically sent to the administrator, indicating that an unauthorized user is accessing the system.

Managing Your Log Files

☑ Logging allows administrators to see who and what has accessed their system. Many helpful Linux log files are located in the /var/log directory.

☑ Linux offers commands that allow administrators to access useful log files. Two commands of interest are *last* and *lastlog*. The message file also offers useful data for determining possible security breaches on your system.

☑ The Linux logs should be checked frequently to determine if any security violations have occurred on your system. Logs do not offer solutions, so you must analyze the data and decide how to counteract the attack.

Using Logging Enhancers

☑ Logging enhancers are tools that simplify logging by allowing logging information to be filtered and often displaying logs in simplified formats.

☑ Viewing text-based files with hundreds or thousands of entries can be burdensome, especially if you are only looking for one specific error entry.

☑ Three popular logging services used by administrators are SWATCH, scanlogd, and the next generation of syslogd (syslogd-ng).

Frequently Asked Questions

The following Frequently Asked Questions, answered by the authors of this book, are designed to both measure your understanding of the concepts presented in this chapter and to assist you with real-life implementation of these concepts. To have your questions about this chapter answered by the author, browse to **www.syngress.com/solutions** and click on the **"Ask the Author"** form.

Q: I have a server that is strictly a mail server and uses SMTP and POP3. However, I want to download security patches from my vendor's Web site directly to the server. Even though I open the TCP/UDP port 80 (HTTP) and port 53 (DNS), I am unable to download the patches on the mail server.

A: If security is a priority, you should order update CDs through your vendor, such Red Hat's Update Service Packages, and install them via your CD drive. You can also simply download your updates from another system on your network.

Q: Should I place my e-mail server behind the firewall, or in a service network (that is, a "demilitarized zone")?

A: Standard practice is to place the e-mail server in the DMZ. A DMZ is usually comprised of a screening router that blocks most attacks (denial-of-service, system scanning, attacks against Microsoft NetBIOS ports, etc.), and a firewall device that authoritatively blocks incoming traffic, effectively separating the internal network from the world. The DMZ exists between the screening router and the firewall. However, it is often a best practice to place the e-mail server behind the firewall itself. If you do this, however, you must make sure your firewall is configured correctly. Otherwise, a malicious user can take advantage of a misconfigured firewall and gain access to your internal network.

Q: When I install Bastille and run configure, why does the program report that the C compiler cannot create an executable?

A: This error most likely indicates that your system does not have a functioning compiler. If often occurs because you do not have a license, or part of the compiler suite cannot be located. Access and view the config.log to determine the cause. Many compiler components are found in /usr/css/bin. This path may not be identified in the environment variable PATH.

Q: By default, sudo uses syslog(3) for logging. Since I did not change this default during setup, why am I not generating any logging messages?

A: In order to generate sudo log files, you need to create a /var/log/sudo file, and add an entry to the syslog.conf file. Since the default log facility is local2, you must add the following line with TAB keys separating the facility (local2.debug) from the destination (a local logging file).

```
local2.debug                              /var/log/sudo
```

You must then restart syslogd to ensure that it re-reads the file.

Q: I am tired of entering my password in sudo each time my ticket expires. How can I avoid this hassle?

A: Use the NOPASSWD tag in sudoers for specific users and commands by inserting the tag before the command list. If you want to disable all sudo passwords, there are two methods. You can run configure with the **--without-passwd** option, or you can add **!authenticate** to the Default line in sudoers. Finally, you can disable passwords to users and hosts in sudoers by adding specific user or host Defaults entries. See the sudo man file for specifics on disabling sudo password prompts.

## Chapter 3

System Scanning and Probing

Solutions in this chapter:

- **Scanning for Viruses Using the AntiVir Antivirus Application**

- **Scanning Systems for DDoS Attack Software Using a Zombie Zapper**

- **Scanning System Ports Using the Gnome Service Scan Port Scanner**

- **Using Nmap**

- **Using Nmapfe as a Graphical Front End**

- **Using Remote Nmap as a Central Scanning Device**

- **Deploying Cheops to Monitor Your Network**

- **Deploying Nessus to Test Daemon Security**

- ☑ Summary

- ☑ Solutions Fast Track

- ☑ Frequently Asked Questions

Introduction

You now have hardened your system using open source tools. Changes are constantly made to production systems. In addition, malicious users are constantly discovering and exploiting new weaknesses. This chapter discusses ways to scan your systems for weaknesses that may already exist or may develop. You will learn how to scan your hard drive, and then scour running processes to determine if any problems exist.

Finally, you will learn how to deploy the Nessus scanner to test for common server weaknesses. By the end of this chapter, you will have a system that is reasonably secure, and can actually test additional servers for vulnerabilities.

Scanning for Viruses Using the AntiVir Antivirus Application

The AntiVir for Servers binary is a truly impressive command-line virus scanner sold by H+BDEV. It is capable of searching for the latest Linux viruses, and once you purchase the product, you can obtain daily virus definition updates. Although AntiVir is not part of the GNU GPL, it is nevertheless free to use. You can obtain AntiVir from either of the following locations:

- **www.hbedv.com** The main distribution site.
- **www.freshmeat.net** This site has only information about the daemon and links to the AntiVir site.

Understanding Linux Viruses

You may be thinking to yourself, "Come on, who ever heard of a Linux virus?" It is true that Linux viruses are far less common than those in the Windows world are, but in fact, Linux viruses are becoming increasingly common.

For example, the Linux/Bliss virus (also known as the "Bliss" or simply as the "Linux virus," can infect standard Linux Executable and Linking Format (ELF) binaries. It can also spread to other systems all by itself, which means that it is acts like a *worm*, a program that can replicate itself from system to system without any user intervention. Understand, however, that the way this virus replicates itself is by searching for /etc/hosts.equiv files and then exploiting them. If you have deployed Bastille, you likely will not have any problem.

NOTE

Executable and Linking Format (ELF) is a binary executable file format standardized by commercial Unix systems and adopted by Linux. In Linux, executable files are called ELF-style files. Other link formats that may be supported by your kernel include common object file format (COFF) and the now deprecated a.out format.

This virus can actually replace the ELF binaries that allow write access with its own binaries. When the hapless user (or system) tries to execute these infected binaries, it will not be able to do so. Consequently, elements of the system will crash. Additional viruses and Trojans exist, including Loadable Kernel Module (LKM) root kits. LKM root kits work by installing hidden Linux modules and replacing legitimate applications with those designed to ignore Trojan processes. Your updated version of AntiVir should capture many of these Trojans. LKM-based root kits such as Adore (available at various sites, including http://packet-storm.securify.com) are particularly powerful and difficult to find, however. In many cases, a system reinstall is necessary to ensure that the compromised system is again secure.

Linux viruses do exist, and the very presence of Linux viruses and virus scanners such as AntiVir and others suggests that Linux could stand to do some more maturing as a product. However, management can now take Linux seriously, now that you can answer "yes" to the question, "Can you protect this system against viruses?" After all, what good manager would really believe that your Linux system is magically impervious to virus attacks? For example, AntiVir will find (and, if so ordered, delete) the following virus types:

- **Macro viruses** Viruses that exist in complex documents, such as Word and StarOffice files.

- **Boot sector viruses** Small programs that infect system initialization files (that is, the files that the system uses to boot up).

- **E-mail viruses** AntiVir scans for all of the latest e-mail viruses, including the Anna Kournikova virus.

- **Distributed denial-of-service (DDoS) daemons** AntiVir scans for DDoS daemons, such as Tribe Flood Network 2000.

You can learn more about the currently available antivirus products at www.cn.is.fh-furtwangen.de/~link/security/av-linux_e.txt. As of this writing, the Packetstorm site has an extensive collection of antivirus applications at http://packetstorm.securify.com/viral-db/avp-linux.

Using AntiVir

As with any other virus scanner, AntiVir can do the following:

- Check the system's boot record.
- Search directories and subdirectories.
- Automatically delete infected files.
- Save scans into a log file.
- Use an internal scheduler, or an external scheduler, such as at or cron.
- Scan NFS-mounted drives.
- Delete infected files.
- Move infected files to a central "quarantine" area of your own choosing.

AntiVir scans the files you specify using its virus definition file, which is located at /usr/lib/AntiVir/antivir.vdf. Run without arguments, AntiVir will scan only the current directory. For a more extensive scan, you must specify arguments to change this default behavior. For example, to have AntiVir scan the /var/log/ directory, you would have to issue the following command:

```
antivir /var/log -s -allfiles -s -nolnk -r4
```

You can review all of the command-line options by issuing the **antivir -h** command, which is handy when you have forgotten exactly how to use the program. Figure 3.1 shows all of the command-line options available to you.

Table 3.1 lists some of the more relevant arguments to AntiVir.

Table 3.1 AntiVir Options

Argument	Description
-allfiles	Scans all files in the directory.
-z	Scans archived files.
-onefs	Scans only locally mounted drives (does not scan NFS-mounted drives).

Continued

Table 3.1 Continued

Argument	Description
-del	Removes infected files.
-r4	Places AntiVir into verbose mode, which means that you will be able to see extensive output. If you choose to save logs of the scan, your logs will also contain this information.
-ro	Overwrites the existing log file.
-ra	Appends new scan information to the existing log file.
-rf	Allows you to specify the location and name of the log file (e.g., /root/antivirlog.txt).
-s	Recursively scans all subdirectories.

Figure 3.1 Command-Line Arguments

Key Mode and Non–Key Mode

AntiVir is sold by a for-profit company, and it gives you some licensing options when running the program. First, you can run the program without any license at all. This will place the program into "non-key mode," which limits the program so that the **-s**, **–nolnk**, and **–onefs** options will not work. Consequently, you will not be able to, for example, tell AntiVir to search the entire drive by issuing the following command:

```
antivir / -s -allfiles -s -nolnk -r4
```

Licensing AntiVir

If you plan to use this application for private use, you can download and install the program, and then apply for a private license at www.antivir.de/order/privreg/order_e.htm.

Eventually, you will receive a license file named hbedv.key. Once you have this license, you must place it in the /usr/lib/AntiVir directory. Once you start (or restart) AntiVir, you can use all of the options the program has to offer.

Exercise: Updating AntiVir

An antivirus application is only as useful as its virus definition file. If you are running in non-key mode, you cannot install any updates for AntiVir. Those who legally obtain and use the private license are entitled to one update every two months. If you purchase AntiVir, you can obtain daily updates.

To obtain an update, go to www.hbedv.com/download/download.htm and download the appropriate .vdf file for your application. Once you obtain a key, place it in the /usr/lib/AntiVir/ directory.

Installing version 6.6.0.0 of AntiVir is simplicity itself. This exercise assumes that you have already downloaded and registered AntiVir.

1. Create a directory named *antivir*.

2. Obtain the file named avlxsrv.tgz from the CD that accompanies this book and place it in the antivir directory. Normally, when a tarball is unzipped, the package will create its own directory. However, this isn't the case with AntiVir. You can also install the Red Hat Packet Manager (RPM) if you wish.

3. Issue the following command: **tar –zxvf avlxsrv.tgz**.

4. Several files will be generated, including the install.sh script. Issue the following command, exactly as shown:

```
./install.sh
```

5. The preceding command tells the system to run the install.sh script. Upon doing so, you will see that the program creates the /usr/lib/ AntiVir directory. You will be asked if you want to create a symbolic link (the program uses the word *symlink*. Press **y** to indicate yes. The symbolic link this creates is from the /usr/lib/AntiVir/antivir directory to the /usr/bin directory. Establishing this symbolic link allows AntiVir to start without you having to enter the entire path (e.g., /usr/bin/antivir).

NOTE

A symbolic link is similar to a Windows shortcut, although more powerful. It is a reference to another file system object on any file system (on the local system or on another network) supported by Linux. In Unix, you can create a symbolic link that leads to a binary by using the **ln -s** command:

```
ln -s existingItem newItem
```

6. You have now installed AntiVir. However, you still cannot use all of AntiVir's options. Now, open a browser and go to www.antivir.de/ order/privreg/order_e.htm.

7. Enter the relevant information, and then order your key. The key will be sent to you in a few minutes.

8. Once you obtain the key, copy it to the /usr/lib/AntiVir/ directory. Now, scan your local directory for a virus by issuing the following command:

```
antivir
```

9. The system will load its file (/usr/lib/AnviVir/antivir.vdf), and then scan the directory. In all likelihood, it will find nothing. Now, scan all files and all subdirectories in your home directory:

```
antivir /root -allfiles -s
```

10. Thus far, AntiVir hasn't been very forthcoming about what it finds. Also, notice how all output goes onto the screen, rather than to a log file. You can change this by issuing the following command:

```
antivir ~ -allfiles -s -r4 -rf/log.txt -ro
```

This command has AntiVir go into verbose mode, and then deposit all of its standard output into a file in your current directory named log.txt. The **-ro** command will erase any file named log.txt and replace it with what it finds. If you want to append information to the end of the log.txt file, instead of overwriting it, use the **-ra** option.

11. The following command, for example, searches the var/spool/ directory, which can contain mail files:

```
"/var/spool/*" -s -rf/log.txt -ro
```

12. Now, change to the /etc/cron.daily directory.

13. Using a text editor such as vi or pico, create a file named antivir.cron, and enter the following code:

```
#!/bin/sh
antivir / -allfiles -s -r4 -rf/root/log.txt -ro
```

This command has crontab run AntiVir so that it scans the entire hard drive for viruses, and then creates a log file named log.txt in the /root directory. Because you have created this cron entry in the /etc/cron.daily/ directory, the job will be run every day.

To learn more about AntiVir options, consult the README file that comes with the program. You can also learn more about the program by typing **antivir -h** and scrolling through the options.

Using TkAntivir

The command-line interface is very useful when you want to administer the system quickly, or when you have to remotely administer a system using SSH or Telnet. However, a rather elegant GUI front end called TkAntivir is available for free at the Geiges Software Training and Consulting Web page at www.geiges.de/tkantivir or from the accompanying CD (tkav.gz or the equivalent tkantivir-1.30-1.i386.rpm.

When you download TkAntivir, make sure that you obtain the version that supports your language. The program was developed in Germany, and if you are not careful, you will install the German language version, rather than the English version.

Required Libraries and Settings

Before you try to install TkAntivir, you must have the following libraries and settings:

- **Tcl/Tk version 8.x or higher** Most systems already have Tcl/Tk installed, but you may have to upgrade the version on your system. A default installation of Red Hat 7.0 has adequate versions of this library already installed.

- **A resolution of at least 800 x 600** You may have to run Xconfigurator or XF86Setup to reconfigure your X settings.

NOTE

Although TkAntivir is designed to run in any X-Windows environment, it runs best in KDE, which is not surprising, since the KDE interface was first developed in Germany. The application runs on the Gnome desktop as well. You can download Gnome at www.gnome.org. If you are running certain versions of the Blackbox window manager, TkAntivir will go through the loading procedure, but will not run. Try running KDE or Gnome to solve this problem.

You have the option of installing TkAntivir using tarball or RPM packages. In this particular instance, Red Hat systems seem to respond better to the RPM.

Scanning Systems for Boot Sector and E-Mail Viruses

The TkAntivir interface, shown in Figure 3.2, is relatively intuitive and allows you to concentrate on what you want AntiVir to do, as opposed to getting the command-line syntax correct. The *Scanning options* section allows you to specify the path you wish to search. You can also use this section to search only for certain file types, which is useful when scanning e-mail spooling directories for suspect attachments. The *Options* section allows you to skip checking the system boot record and symbolic links, which helps the scan finish faster, because it won't have to scan the same file repeatedly. This section also allows you to specify whether you want to search for compressed files (e.g., files compressed by zip or gzip). Verbose scan mode allows you to receive more information in your log file.

Figure 3.2 The TkAntivir Interface

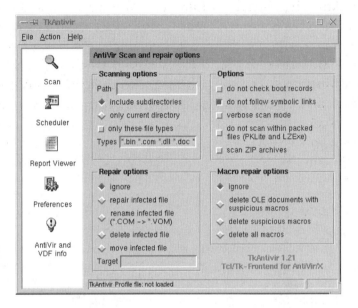

The *Repair options* section allows you to determine what AntiVir will do when it finds a virus. Notice that it is set to *ignore* by default, which is wise. Virus applications, like any scanning or monitoring application, are susceptible to false positives, which are instances when an application identifies a perfectly benign file, process, or activity as somehow threatening. If you tell AntiVir to delete any file that it thinks is defective, and AntiVir makes a mistake, you may end up deleting an important system file, or removing a user's important report. Either way, you could cause problems for yourself if you automate file removal.

Finally, the *Macro repair options* section allows you to determine what will be done with macros created by various applications, including Microsoft Word. If, for example, you have a Linux server acting as a file and print server, you may want to consider some of these options. Again, remember that mistakenly deleting files can cause serious problems because Unix/Linux has no native undelete facility.

The Scan icon, at the upper-left portion of the interface, allows you to activate the settings you enter. The Scheduler icon brings up the Scheduler interface, shown in Figure 3.3. From here, you can:

- **Choose the path that a particular job will scan.** You can also include subdirectories.

- **Tell AntiVir when it should run.** You can schedule a one-time event, or schedule AntiVir to run every day, every week, or after a certain number of days. Figure 3.3 shows that a job is scheduled to run at 2:00 A.M. each week. The job will run on Monday of each week. If you click **Single Events**, you will be able to configure AntiVir to run at a certain time on the same day, or the next day, or after a certain number of days. Once you are finished configuring the time, you can then click **Add a Job**. You can also review and update existing jobs, simply by highlighting the existing job and then clicking either **Job Info** or **Update**.

Figure 3.3 Scheduling a Scan

The Report Viewer icon allows you to view reports generated earlier, or reports generated on other systems. Once you click this icon, you will see the

Open dialog box, shown in Figure 3.4. Once this dialog box opens, you can then navigate to the log file you want to read, and then open it.

Figure 3.4 The Open Dialog Box in TkAntivir

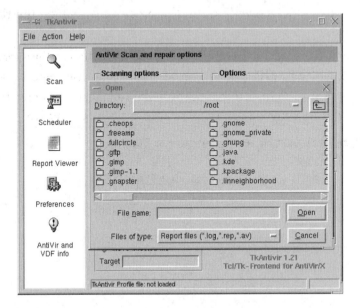

Additional Information

The Preferences tab allows you to change the location of AntiVir binary, the TkAntivir files, or the log file. The AntiVir and VDV info file allows you to determine when it is time to download and install a new .vdf file. Now that you are familiar with the requirements for TkAntivir, it is time to install and use it.

Exercise: Using TkAntivir

1. Make sure that you have all of the required libraries. Review this section for more details.

2. Verify that you have 800 x 600 resolution. Consult your man pages for Xconfigurator or XF86Setup. You can also directly edit your X-Windows configuration file (XF86Config).

3. Download and install TkAntivir from www.geiges.de/tkantivir. Although your situation may vary, the RPM file works best on Red Hat systems. Once you obtain the RPM file, check its MD5 signature, and then install it using the **rpm –ivh** command.

4. Enter the following command to create a log file directory off of the /usr/lib/AntiVir/log/ directory:

```
mkdir /usr/lib/AntiVir/log/
```

5. Once you install TkAntivir, run the program by issuing the **tkantivir** command.

6. You will see a dialog box informing you that the configuration is not complete. Click **OK** to bring up the configuration window. Enter the information shown in Figure 3.5. Make sure that you enter this text exactly as shown—Linux systems are always case sensitive.

Figure 3.5 Setting Preferences for TkAntivir

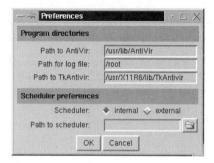

7. Click **OK**. You will see the splash screen shown in Figure 3.6.

Figure 3.6 The TkAntivir Splash Screen

8. You will then see the main interface. If you do not see this interface, either you need to use KDE or Gnome, or you need to change your monitor resolution.

9. Once the interface appears, scan your entire directory. Make the changes shown in Figure 3.7.

Figure 3.7 Configuring TkAntivir to Scan the Entire Home Directory

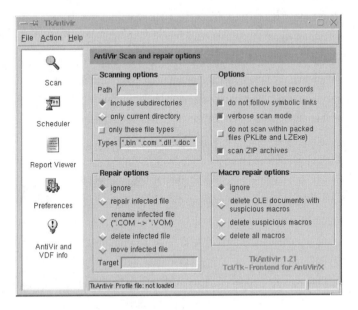

10. Click the **Scan** icon. You will see a pop-up window similar to that shown in Figure 3.8 asking you if you are ready to issue this command.

Figure 3.8 Confirming a Disk Scan with TkAntivir

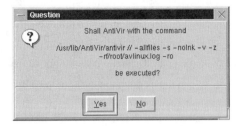

11. Click **Yes**. You will then see a window informing you that the scan is taking place. If the scan takes place very quickly, you likely have not downloaded and properly installed your key. The scan may take some time, depending on the speed of your system's processor and the size of your hard drive. Once the scan finishes, TkAntivir will generate a report. Scroll down the report to view all of the files. In the results shown in

Figure 3.9, AntiVir was able to find two viruses. Your system is now protected against Linux viruses.

Figure 3.9 Viewing TkAntivir Scanning Results

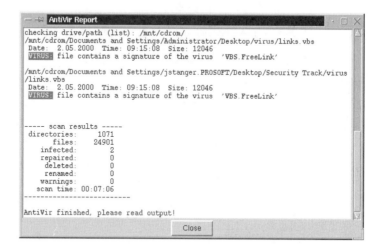

Scanning Systems for DDoS Attack Software Using a Zombie Zapper

Since late 1999, many sites have become the victims of devastating *denial-of-service* (DoS) attacks. A DoS attack is basically where an attacker finds a way to disable the services (in this case, the network's Web sites) so that they cannot be provided to anyone. In February 2000, a series of attacks against Web sites such as www.cnn.com, www.ebay.com, and www.amazon.com caused these sites to be knocked off the Internet.

The specific type of attack waged against the preceding Web sites was unique, because it involved multiple attacking machines controlled by one attacker. Because of these attacks, a new security term, a *distributed denial of service* (DDoS) attack was born. In a DDoS attack, an attacker instructs several compromised systems to flood a target system with service requests. The resulting attack can bring down almost any Web site, or generate so much traffic that an entire network can no longer communicate with the rest of the Internet.

Attackers are able to wage these DoS attacks by first finding and hacking into insecure systems on the Internet. Then, they install programs such as Tribe Flood Network 2000 (Tfn2k), stacheldraht, and others. The compromised systems now have illicit programs, called *zombies*, installed on them. Traditionally, zombies have been Unix/Linux systems (because it is easy to program network services on these systems). Prime targets for zombies are computers used by colleges and universities. There are several reasons for this:

- These systems typically have a large number of users—students. Consequently, it is easy to hide a rogue account/program.

- These systems have user populations that change regularly. Again, this makes it easy to hide zombie programs. In addition, due to the turnover of students and courses, university networks often do not employ stringent security techniques.

- Computers in academic environments typically have access to very high-speed Internet connections. This makes it possible for the zombie to blast the system under attack with an especially high volume of traffic.

For additional information about DDoS attacks, consult www.cert.org/incident_notes/IN-99-07.html.

How Zombies Work and How to Stop Them

Once a zombie is commanded to attack a victim, it will generally continue the attack until it is forced to stop. This is where *zombie zapper* utilities become useful. Such programs are able to act as clients to the DDoS servers that are sending packets to victim hosts. Zombie zapping utilities are useful when you suspect that your system is acting as a zombie, and you wish to quickly disable the illicit zombie server (that is, stop it from generating the DOS packets) without shutting down your entire system.

Rather than trying to learn how to use, say, the Tfn2k client, you can use a zombie zapper to shut down the zombie. However, you should understand that most zombie zappers are somewhat limited in what they can do:

- Zombie zappers are programmed to shut down only certain DDoS servers. If a malicious user has created a new one that uses a different port, your zombie zapper will likely not work.

- If the malicious user has changed the password of the illicit server that has turned one of your hosts into a zombie, then it is likely that your zombie zapper software will not work. For example, the installation process for Tfn2k requires the malicious user to create a new password. Thus, most zombie zappers won't work against this product. Still, zombie zappers are useful for other DDoS servers, because most people who install them are either relatively inexperienced, or are in too much of a hurry to change the password.

■ If you try to use a zombie zapper against a remote computer, it is possible that a firewall that lies between you and the remote computer will block the packets you send. DDoS attacks have been widely publicized, and many systems administrators have created firewall rules that will block out all DDoS traffic, including that sent by your application.

■ Because DDoS attack servers spoof packets, you may be using your zombie zapper against the wrong host.

■ Your attempt to disable a zombie computer on someone else's network may be misconstrued as an attack—you may get some interesting calls from that system administrator.

When Should I Use a Zombie Zapper?

In spite of the reasons why you should be careful, installing and using a zombie zapper is useful in a number of situations. You can configure your intrusion detection service (IDS) devices to automatically run a zombie zapper against an offending system. This way, the problem is automatically solved. You will learn about how IDS applications and firewalls can respond automatically to threats in Chapters 9 and 11.

If you notice large amounts of unknown traffic when you monitor your network or network perimeter, you can use a zombie zapper against the host or hosts generating this traffic. Chapter 4 will show you how an IDS application can help you scan for problem traffic. In Chapter 5, you will learn how to use packet sniffers to check the complexion of traffic on your LAN.

You should understand that although DDoS attacks are not new, it is likely that they will continue. After all, the Melissa, I Love You, and Anna Kournikova e-mail viruses are all very similar to the 1989 Robert Morris worm attack (the first large-scale attack of Internet connected servers).

What Zombie Zapper Should I Use?

Many different utilities exist for disabling zombies. You can learn about these at various sites, including http://packetstorm.securify.com, by doing a search for *zombie* and *zapper*. One of the more useful utilities is Zombie Zapper, available at the Bindview site (www.bindview.com). As of this writing, the URL is http://razor.bindview.com/tools/ZombieZapper_form.shtml. The utility is also available on the CD accompanying this book (zombie-1.2.tgz).

Zombie Zapper Commands

When compiled, Zombie Zapper is designed to be run by using the **./** command. If you enter **./zz** without any arguments, you will receive the following:

```
./zz
Zombie Zapper v1.2 - DDoS killer
Bugs/comments to thegnome@razor.bindview.com
More info and free tools at http://razor.bindview.com
Copyright (c) 2000 BindView Development


=== You must specify target(s) or a class C to send to
USAGE:
./zz [-a 0-5] [-c class C] [-d dev] [-h] [-m host] [-s src] [-u udp]
    [-v] hosts


    -a antiddos type to kill:
         0   types 1-4 (default)
         1   trinoo
         2   tfn
         3   stacheldraht
         4   trinoo on Windows
         5   shaft (requires you use the -m option)
    -c class C in x.x.x.0 form
    -f time in seconds to send packets (default 1)
    -d grab local IP from dev (default eth0)
    -h this help screen
    -m my host being flooded (used with -a 5 above, only one host)
    -s spoofed source address (just in case)
    -u UDP source port for trinoo (default 53)
    -v verbose mode (use twice for more verbosity)
    host(s) are target hosts (ignored if using -c)
```

Table 3.2 provides a brief overview of some of the more common commands.

Table 3.2 Common Zombie Zapper Commands

Command	Definition
-a	Allows you to specify the address to where you will send the packets.
-c	You can specify an entire class C address when sending stop packets.
-s	Allows you to spoof your own address. This and the **-u** option allow you to defeat some firewall rules when trying to disable zombies on remote networks.
-u	Allows you to change the default UDP port for sending stop packets.
0-5	Each number enables Zombie Zapper to imitate a specific DDoS client. If, for example, you think you have found a tfn client, you would issue a command with the number 2 in it.

What Does Zombie Zapper Require to Compile?

You will need the following to install Zombie Zapper:

- A standard Linux system.

- **Libnet** This set of supporting libraries allows your system to generate packets for use on a network. You need these libraries because the creators of Zombie Zapper used them in development, and the program will not compile properly unless you have them installed on your system. These libraries are popular, and are often used by other developers. You can download the Libnet libraries at www.canvasnet.com/libnet.

Exercise: Using Zombie Zapper

1. Obtain the Zombie Zapper source code from the accompanying CD or at www.bindview.com. Once you have unzipped and untarred the file using the **tar -zxvf** command, you are ready to compile. See the preceding URLs for obtaining Zombie Zapper.

    Before you can compile this code, you must first obtain and install the Libnet libraries. A version of Libnet (libnet-0.10.8.tar.gz) is available on the accompanying CD. Once you have obtained Libnet, unzip and untar it using the **tar -zxvf** command. The ./configure script will install Libnet into the directories appropriate to your system.

2. Install Libnet by changing to the Libnet.x.x directory, and then using the configure script:

```
./configure
```

3. When the configure script is finished, type **make**.

4. Type **make install**.

5. Although optional for installing Zombie Zapper, you can now install the supplemental and utility libraries by typing **make supp** and then **make util**.

6. Now that you have installed Libnet, you can compile Zombie Zapper. Because the code for Zombie Zapper relies on this library, you must tell the GCC compiler that the Libnet library exists. Issue the following command:

```
gcc 'libnet-config -defines' -o zz zz.c -lnet
```

7. This command tells the GCC compiler to use the libnet-config file, which is found in the /usr/bin/ directory for most Linux systems. You will not have to edit this file. When you type this command, make sure that you use the "backtic" character, which is the character above the **TAB** key on your keyboard. Do not use an apostrophe. If you do not use the backtic character, GCC will not search for libnet-config, and Libnet will give you a message informing you that you need to define some values in the libnet-config script. Ignore this message, and type the correct character.

8. Now that zz is compiled, you can use it. Issue the following command:

```
./zz
```

9. You will see a Help menu informing you how to use the program. This confirms that you have compiled the program correctly.

10. Now, suppose that you notice that your internal network of 192.168.5.0 has several hosts on it that are sending tfn packets. As long as the tfn server is using a default password, the following command will stop the server:

```
./zz -c 192.168.5.0
```

11. The servers that a malicious hacker has turned into zombies on this particular class C subnet should stop immediately. You cannot use the **-c** command with class A or class B network addresses. To do this, you would have to specify the IP address, along with the type of server you wish to shut down. For example, if you suspected the server at 207.192.45.2 to be attacking you with the stacheldraht DDoS server, you would issue the following command:

    ```
    ./zz -a 3 207.192.45.2
    ```

12. To learn more about the nature of the packets you are sending, you can use the **-vv** command:

    ```
    ./zz -a 3 -vv 207.192.45.2
    ```

13. If you wish to spoof your own address so that the malicious user can't learn who deactivated his or her zombies, you would use the **-s** command, followed by an IP address of your choosing:

    ```
    ./zz -a 3 -vv 207.192.45.2 -s 10.1.2.3
    ```

Scanning System Ports Using the Gnome Service Scan Port Scanner

Gnome Service Scan (GSS) is a simple port scanner. It is quite fast, and has a GUI interface. It is also easy to install, and uses the same libraries as the Gnome (that is, Ximian) desktop. The main GserviceScan window is shown in Figure 3.10.

You can download the source code for GSS at www.gnome.org/applist/view.php3?name=Gnome%20Service%20Scanner. The Preferences section, shown in Figure 3.11, allows you to further customize GSS.

Setting longer TCP and UDP timeout values may ensure that you obtain results that are more accurate. Longer timeout values, however, mean longer, more time-consuming scans, so strike a balance. A good idea would be a default of 7 and 10 seconds for the TCP and UPD timeout values, respectively. In addition, if your network is experiencing DNS problems, you can disable DNS so that you at least learn the IP address and the open ports of the remote host.

Figure 3.10 The Main GserviceScan Screen

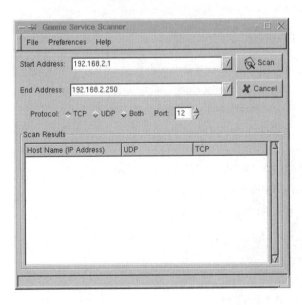

Figure 3.11 Customizing GSS

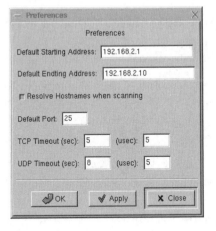

Required Libraries

To install GserviceScan, you must have the Gnome desktop installed, complete with all packages from the www.gnome.org site. If you don't have Gnome installed, log on to your Linux system and issue the following command:

```
lynx -source http://go-gnome.com/ | sh.
```

Of course, you can install the appropriate RPMs from the Red Hat distribution CDs. However, if you install Gnome from the Gnome site, the latest Gnome updates and features become available to you.

This command tells Lynx, a text-based Web browser, to contact the http://go-gnome.com site and download a shell program. After the small program downloads, a graphical wizard will guide you through the rest of the process. You can customize the packages you wish to install; you do not have to install the packages relating to software development. You can then install the GSS by obtaining the gservicescan-0.8.tar.gz file from the accompanying CD, or from the Gnome home page (www.gnome.org), which will have the latest version.

> **NOTE**
>
> The command for checking for the presence of an RPM is **rpm -qa | grep text_string**, where *text_string* is part of the package name for which you are searching.

Why Use a Port Scanner?

Systems administrators find port scanners useful when auditing their own systems. Although a simple port scanner such as GSS does not actually test for flaws in binaries and Web applications, a good port scanner can help you isolate which ports are open, and then take any action that is necessary.

Port scanning a machine may set off an alarm for the system's administrator, who might take a dim view of your actions. Be extremely careful using any of the applications in this chapter. Improper use of these applications could lead to a strong reprimand, dismissal, or telephone calls from irate systems administrators. You should conduct port scans only on systems that you administer. Even then, you should scan them only if you have explicit permission, as your scan can set off triggers and alerts that can cause many people a great deal of work. Unless you have explicit (sometimes, even written) permission from the system administrator, you may cause a serious violation of your security policy.

Exercise: Using Gnome Service Scanner

1. If necessary, open the Lynx browser and issue the command given earlier to download and install the necessary Gnome libraries. If you do not have Lynx installed, download it from www.rpmfind.net.

2. In the Start Address field, enter the beginning host IP address for your particular network or network segment.

3. In the End Address field, enter the last host IP address of this network or network segment. Remember, you should not conduct port scans on systems that are not yours.

4. In the Protocol section, make sure that the TCP button is selected. Using the arrow, select **110** (the port for POP3 e-mail).

5. Click **Scan**. You will see a list of several hosts, some of which will have open ports. See Figure 3.12.

Figure 3.12 Viewing Gnome Service Scanner Results

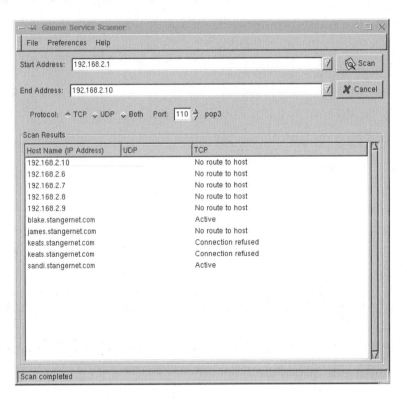

You now know that various hosts in your network are up ("Connection refused"), which are not responding ("No route to host"), and which are acting as POP3 e-mail servers.

Using Nmap

Nmap is an advanced port scanner. It is also capable of identifying the version of an operating system. You can download Nmap, shown in Figure 3.13, at www.insecure.org. Perhaps the best thing about Nmap is that its developer, Fyodor, is extremely talented, active, and a good collaborator. He and his colleagues update Nmap often, and the updates usually bring desirable new features and improvements.

Figure 3.13 Nmap

```
[root@keats /root]# nmap -h
nmap V. 2.53 Usage: nmap [Scan Type(s)] [Options] <host or net list>
Some Common Scan Types ('*' options require root privileges)
  -sT TCP connect() port scan (default)
* -sS TCP SYN stealth port scan (best all-around TCP scan)
* -sU UDP port scan
  -sP ping scan (Find any reachable machines)
* -sF,-sX,-sN Stealth FIN, Xmas, or Null scan (experts only)
  -sR/-I RPC/Identd scan (use with other scan types)
Some Common Options (none are required, most can be combined):
* -O Use TCP/IP fingerprinting to guess remote operating system
  -p <range> ports to scan.  Example range: '1-1024,1080,6666,31337'
  -F Only scans ports listed in nmap-services
  -v Verbose. Its use is recommended.  Use twice for greater effect.
  -P0 Don't ping hosts (needed to scan www.microsoft.com and others)
* -Ddecoy_host1,decoy2[,...] Hide scan using many decoys
  -T <Paranoid|Sneaky|Polite|Normal|Aggressive|Insane> General timing policy
  -n/-R Never do DNS resolution/Always resolve [default: sometimes resolve]
  -oN/-oM <logfile> Output normal/machine parsable scan logs to <logfile>
  -iL <inputfile> Get targets from file; Use '-' for stdin
* -S <your_IP>/-e <devicename> Specify source address or network interface
  --interactive Go into interactive mode (then press h for help)
Example: nmap -v -sS -O www.my.com 192.168.0.0/16 '192.88-90.*.*'
SEE THE MAN PAGE FOR MANY MORE OPTIONS, DESCRIPTIONS, AND EXAMPLES
[root@keats /root]#
```

Tools & Traps...

Nmap: A Tool for Hackers or Security Professionals?

You may be wondering whether Nmap is actually a "hacker tool" meant to help compromise the security of a network. Nmap was first introduced as a hacking tool, but has been quickly adopted by IT professionals. It provides excellent information concerning hosts on your network. It also allows your IT professionals to:

- **Audit your network** Using this application, your employees can quickly scan a network for hosts that have unsecured ports.

Continued

- **Test firewall configurations** Nmap will help to ensure that the firewall blocks as many packets as it can, without compromising your ability to communicate with the outside world.

- **Identify the nature of suspicious remote systems** Although scanning a host that has scanned you may be considered bad etiquette, doing so can help your employees quickly size up a threat.

- **Test your router and switch configuration** TCP/IP has built-in testing features that allow one echo request to cause an entire network of hosts to respond to a host. While this feature may be useful in determining if all hosts can traverse the default gateway, it can also have disastrous effects if exploited by a malicious user. Using readily available software, a malicious user can use your network to attack other networks.

While it is true that you would not want any stranger to use Nmap against your hosts, it is a valuable tool in the hands of someone who knows how to use the information it presents to help secure your network.

Isn't Nmap Just Another Port Scanner?

Nmap is essentially a network host scanner, like GSS. However, it has additional features that make it the most popular Unix-based scanner, including:

- **Fast ping and port scan capabilities** You can find out if systems are up, and what ports are open.

- **Operating system fingerprinting** Nmap has the ability to guess the operating system of the host it is scanning. Although Nmap must make a guess, it is a very well informed one. This is because Nmap contains an extensive database of TCP-, UDP-, and IP-based responses from hundreds of different operating systems. Nmap can query your system, and then compare its responses to this database. Vendors are required to make their versions of TCP/IP compliant to technical specifications found in documents called Request for Comments (RFCs). These files are available at various places on the Internet, including www.faqs.org/rfcs/index.html. However, each vendor implements TCP/IP in a slightly different fashion, and Nmap is able to compare these differences and then inform you about the operating system.

- **Sequence prediction** All TCP-based communications require each system to establish a pattern to which it will conform when sending TCP packets. This pattern is established during the three-way TCP handshake. Nmap is able to determine elements of this pattern. In some systems, such as all versions of Windows NT 4.0 before Service Pack 5, these sequences are not sufficiently randomized, and are easy to predict. In the past, hackers have been able to identify such simple TCP sequences, and use them to hijack connections. Nmap provides this information. Most Internet-ready operating systems, such as modern versions of Linux, have truly random sequencing, and are much more difficult to predict.

- **Ability to imitate all different aspects of a TCP-based connection** When a TCP connection begins, it takes some modest amount of time (a few milliseconds) to establish the connection, a process called the *handshake*. Many firewalls are configured to drop initial SYN packets for certain systems, because network administrators do not want anyone in the outside world to establish contact to the system (without going through a firewall). Most scanners use the SYN packet, and will thus be dropped. Nmap is able to generate packets that many firewalls will allow, and thus Nmap can traverse through a firewall to map remote hosts and networks.

- **Spoofing features** Many network administrators will try to learn exactly who conducted a scan of their network. Using Nmap's spoofing feature, it is possible for a malicious user to imitate another host. Consequently, the systems administrator may be led to believe that some innocent third party initiated a scan; IT professionals can use the spoofing feature to test firewall configurations.

- **The ability to control scan speed and sequence** Many Intrusion Detection System (IDS) applications will generate alerts if they notice that a network's hosts are being scanned sequentially. An IDS will also report an attack if it notices that a series of hosts has been scanned quickly. Using Nmap, you can slow an attack. Whereas a malicious user would use Nmap to thwart security, IT professionals can use it to help audit a firewall.

- **The ability to save output to text files** This feature makes it possible to use Nmap output in other programs, or to save output for future reference.

- **The ability to read input information from text files** This feature makes is possible to read input information from text files.

Acquiring and Installing Nmap

Nmap is self-contained, and can thus be run on many Unix systems. Generally, installing the RPM is more reliable than the tarball on Red Hat systems. In this particular case, there are no compilation options as of yet, so there is no reason not to use the RPM file if your distribution supports it (available on the CD accompanying this book: nmap-2.53-1.i386.rpm). You can verify your installation with:

```
rpm -qa | grep nmap
```

Common Nmap Options

One of the exciting things about Nmap is its sheer versatility. You can use it as a basic port scanner for a system on your internal network, or you can have it identify the operating system version of a remote system on another firewall-protected network. You can use it to run a single scan, or use it in interactive mode to run multiple scans from the same system at the same time.

The two scan options given in the next section are common in various scanning applications. However, they are less effective because many firewalls are configured to reject a SYN connection that is first initiated from the outside world. These scans will also appear on the logs of your firewall or IDS applications:

- **P0** By default, Nmap sends an ICMP message to each remote host. This option turns off this default behavior. This option is useful when scanning systems that do not appear to be up, because they do not respond to ICMP ping packets. If you use this option, you should understand that the information Nmap provides may not be accurate.

- **-sP** Has Nmap use only ICMP to conduct a standard ping scan. Nmap options preceded with the **-s** option are considered "stealth" options that help Nmap conduct less obvious scans.

- **-PT** Tells Nmap to use a TCP packet to ping the host instead of an ICMP packet. This option is useful when testing a firewall to see if it can block both ICMP and TCP packets intelligently. When you use the **–PT** option, Nmap will send out a TCP ACK packet, and then wait for hosts to send back an RST packet. Many firewalls will allow ACK and RST packets to traverse the firewall, and thus you can scan the entire network.

- **–sT** Conducts a full TCP connection to each port on the remote system.

- **–sS** Uses the SYN feature of TCP. When TCP begins a connection, it will send a SYN packet to the remote host to tell it to begin a connection. When Nmap sends a SYN packet, it essentially creates a half-open connection. Even if the remote computer doesn't want to communicate with your host, Nmap is still able to gather sufficient information from this scan to learn the open ports.

- **–0** Tells Nmap to guess the operating system version. This is a much-touted feature of Nmap, because it allows illicit users to quickly determine the type of operating system in use so that they can then research vulnerabilities associated with it. Nmap uses a database of operating system signatures. Once the application conducts the scan, it compares the information it obtains from the scanned host and compares it to its database. The creators of Nmap spend a great deal of time trying to keep this feature as up to date as possible by making sure that Nmap's signature database is current. One of the ways that Nmap accomplishes operating system guessing is that it understands how each particular operating system implements specific TCP/IP applications.

- **–v** Has Nmap go into verbose mode so that you can gain more information about what Nmap is pumping out to a remote host, and what the remote host is sending back. If you specify **–v –v**, Nmap will give you even more information, depending on your scan.

Applied Examples

Suppose you just want to conduct a ping scan of your local network to see what hosts are currently up. Suppose further that your network address is 10.100.100.0 with a subnet mask of 255.255.255.0. You would issue the following command:

```
nmap -sP 10.100.100.0/24
```

If you add the **-v** option, you will also see a list of systems that are down. Using the **-sT** option is useful when pinging remote hosts over routers or firewalls that do not allow ICMP packets.

The following command will conduct a "half open" TCP scan, give you Nmap's best guess concerning the operating system, and not ping the host beforehand:

```
nmap -sS -O -P0 host.
```

If you specify the **-v** option, you will see further details concerning how Nmap operates.

Scanning Entire Networks and Subnets

If you want to scan an entire network, Nmap supports wildcards and Classless Internet Domain Routing (CIDR) notation. Nmap uses the standard wildcard of "*.". CIDR notation is where you use **/24** to indicate a standard class C subnet mask of 255.255.255.0, which indicates that we want 24 bits of subnet mask starting from bit 1. The remaining 8 bits are used as the node number for our network. The 172.16.0.0/18 subnet uses 2 bits of subnet mask to divide the single class B network number (172.16) into four additional, separate subnets (172.16.0, 172.16.64, 172.16.128, and 172.16.192). Each subnet would then have 14 bits of node number addressing:

```
nmap -P0 -oN output.txt 172.16.0.0/18 ."*.*"
nmap -P0 -oN output.txt 192.168.0.0/24
```

You should use quotation marks around wild cards, such as those used in the preceding code. Otherwise, Linux may interpret the commands as the filename wildcard, resulting in the rewriting of any files in the current directory that match the pattern. You can also use single quotes, if you wish.

These commands would scan all of the hosts, making sure to save the results in the file named output.txt. Using CIDR notation allows you to scan networks that use custom subnet masks. For example, suppose that you have a network address of 172.16.0.0/8, and a subnet mask of 255.0.0.0. To properly scan this subnet, you would use the following command:

```
nmap -P0 -oN output.txt 172.16.0.0/8
```

The 172.16.0.0/18 subnet uses 2 bits of subnet mask to divide the single class B network number (172.16) into four additional, separate subnets (172.16.0,

172.16.64, 172.16.128, and 172.16.192). Each subnet would then have 14 bits of node number addressing.

Selective Scanning

Suppose, now, that you want to scan only certain ports on the hosts that belong to an entire subnet. Doing this can help you selectively scan for only a specific service on a network, such as a Web and DNS server, as shown here:

```
nmap -sX -p 22,53 -oN syngress.txt 192.168.0.0/24
```

NOTE

The following operating systems do not respond accurately to "Xmas" scans, because they do not follow standard RFCs:
Microsoft
CISCO
All BSD systems that are not FreeBSD or NetBSD
IRIX
HP/UX

Adding More Stealth

You have already seen how Nmap is capable of manipulating aspects of TCP to hide its scans from firewalls. Additional stealth options include:

- **-sF** Using a TCP packet with the FIN bit sent, Nmap can send out packets to all ports on a host.

- **-sX** Called the "Xmas Tree" packet argument, if you specify this argument, the FIN, URG and PUSH flags will all be set.

- **-sN** Called the "Null scan," this argument turns off all flags, sending out an essentially empty bit. If the system responds, Nmap knows that the host is up, and can deduce information it derives from the remote system's return packet. Microsoft systems do not reply to this packet, and if you are careful in your network scans, you can use Nmap to help distinguish Microsoft systems from all others.

- **–D** This option allows you to specify several additional hosts who will appear as originators of the scan. Hackers often use this option to confuse systems administrators, who will usually not be able to tell from where the scan truly came. As a systems administrator, you can use it to test your intrusion detection systems and firewalls to see how well they find and log all scans of your network. When using the **–D** option, you would separate each bogus host with a comma:

```
nmap -sF -v 192.34.35.0/24 -D bogushost1, bogushost2,
    bogushost3
```

  If you specify the ME option, you will increase the likelihood that your system will be hidden from all IDS logs.

To scan the 192.15.3.10/24 network protected by a firewall that denies all SYN packets, issue the following command:

```
nmap -sF -v 192.15.3.0/24
```

The following command would conduct the same scan and specify bogus scanning hosts:

```
nmap -sF -v 192.15.3.0/24 -D www.yourwebserver.com,www
    .yoursecondwebserver.com,www.yourftpserver.com,ME,www
    .youre-mailserver.com
```

As you use Nmap, experiment with the **–sX** and **–xN** arguments to see if they are useful in your particular situation. It is important to understand that you can specify only one TCP option at a time. This means that you cannot use both the **–sF** and **–sS** arguments in the same command.

Saving to Text and Reading from Text

You may have already noticed that some of these scans can be quite lengthy. For example, if you do a detailed scan of all ports on an entire network of 253 hosts, you may not be able to see all of them on your display, no matter how long you can scroll your terminal. Nmap provides the following options to save output into a text file:

- **–oN filename** Places the scan results in a text file that you can read later.

- **–oM filename** Places the scan into machine-readable format. If, for example, you scan a network, you can then use this file with another application, such as Cheops or an IDS to generate a network map. See later in this chapter and Chapter 4 for more information.

- **–iL** Allows Nmap to read information from a text file. For example, if you already have a text file that contains the IP addresses or host names of a text file, you can specify this filename rather than an IP or host range.

For example, if you wished to save Nmap output into a file named file.txt, you would issue the following command:

```
nmap -v -oN file.txt -O host.yourcompany.com
```

Testing Firewalls and Intrusion Detection Systems

You may wish to use Nmap in a network that uses a well-configured firewall or an IDS). If so, you may want to conduct scans that cannot be easily detected, or are actually able to traverse a firewall without being blocked. The following options are effective in these cases:

- **–f** Has Nmap break up its scans into smaller IP packets. This way, a firewall will not be able to capture and log the packets as easily.

- **–S Address** Allows you to specify the originating address of the scan. Originally meant to allow Nmap to work with various operating systems that would not report the IP address to Nmap, it is possible to use this feature to spoof the source address of the scan. Generally, if you use this argument to spoof the source of the attack, you will also need to use the **–e –P0** options. The **–e** option allows you to specify the interface to use (usually eth0). The **–P0** option, as you have already learned, tells Nmap not to conduct a ping scan. The **–D** option is quite similar to this option, as it provides disinformation to any target host that may be recording your scan.

- **–g port** By default, Nmap will open an ephemeral port (i.e., one above 1024) to begin a scan. Many firewalls are configured to block these ports. However, firewalls are often configured to allow incoming traffic through certain well-known port address (such as ports 80, 110, 53). By specifying a port the firewall allows, you (or a malicious user) can find a way through the firewall to conduct your scans.

Example: Spoofing the Source Address of a Scan

Suppose that your system actually has the IP address of 192.168.3.4, but you wish all of the Nmap packets your system issues to be marked with the IP address of 20.20.20.20. You would issue the following command against a system named sandi:

```
nmap -S 20.20.20.20 -e eth0 -P0 -sS -v sandi
```

The **-P0** (no ping) and **-sS** (TCP SYN stealth port scan) enable Nmap to conduct a TCP-based scan that does not first send out a ping packet. The **-sS** option helps the scan get past firewalls, which will often filter out initial SYN packets.

To have your system use port 53 to originate packets to conduct the same scan, you would issue the following command:

```
nmap -g 53 -S 20.20.20.20 -e eth0 -P0 -sS -v sandi
```

Timing Your Scan Speeds

Many intrusion detection systems will send alerts if a large scan occurs. You can use Nmap to test these IDS applications by using the **-T** argument, which allows you to have Nmap wait a certain interval between sending packets. The idea behind this option is that if a scan is spread out over time, the IDS will not be able to find it as quickly. This argument takes six options:

- **paranoid** Has Nmap send a packet only after five minutes have passed. You can specify the number 0, instead of paranoid, if you wish.

- **sneaky** Nmap will wait 15 seconds to send another packet. You can specify the number 1, instead of sneaky, if you wish.

- **polite** Waits 0.4 seconds to send packets. You can specify the number 2, instead of polite, if you wish.

- **normal** The default setting that has Nmap send another packet as soon as the target host sends a reply. You can specify the number 3, instead of normal, if you wish.

- **aggressive** and **insane** These options actually speed up the scan, and are useful only if you want to conduct quick ping and port scans. Be careful with these settings, as they may negatively affect network performance by generating a large amount of network traffic. Numbers 4 and 5 represent aggressive and insane, respectively.

Example: Conducting a Paranoid Scan

To conduct a paranoid scan against a host, you would issue the following command:

```
nmap -S 20.20.20.20 -e eth -P0 -sS -v -T paranoid sandi
```

Remember however, that this scan will take some time to complete, because the paranoid setting has Nmap wait five minutes between sending packets.

NOTE

As you run Nmap, you may find that it takes considerable time to complete the scan. Usually, this is because some of the options you specify may cause Nmap to wait for some time before it can process the packets it generates. Sometimes, the scan is slowed by the firewalls or routers that exist between you and the host you are scanning. If you use multiple arguments, or scan multiple remote systems, you may find that the scan will take several minutes to complete.

Exercise: Using Nmap

1. Copy nmap-2.53-1.i386.rpm from the accompanying CD, or go to www.insecure.org and download the Nmap RPM.

2. Install the RPM using the following command:

```
rpm -ivh RPM_File
```

3. Now, issue the following command to a system running any Microsoft product:

```
nmap -O -sS host
```

You should see a list of the open ports, as well as Nmap's guess concerning the operating system. Now, issue the same command on a Linux system. You will see a listing of the open ports, as well as a guess concerning the system kernel. Notice that it will not return information concerning whether this system is a Red Hat or Caldera system. This is because Nmap focuses on the kernel used, rather than any other feature. Now, save your query into a log file:

```
nmap -O -sS host -v -oN file.txt hostname
```

4. You will see that the scan is reported to standard output, as well as sent to the text file. Open file.txt to view your scan. Now, use Nmap to issue a ping scan of your entire network, but also have Nmap spoof the source IP address.

5. Although this will take some time, use the Nmap paranoid feature to conduct a scan of a host. Be prepared to come back after several hours to view the results.

Using Nmap in Interactive Mode

Thus far, you have used Nmap to issue single commands. Nmap's "interactive mode" allows you to do two things that you should be aware of as a systems administrator:

- It can conduct multiple Nmap sessions/.

- It can disguise the fact that it is running on your system. Using the "spoof" feature, it is possible to make Nmap appear as an innocuous program, such as vi, or a daemon such as named (for DNS) or sendmail.

To run Nmap interactively, you would issue the following command:

```
nmap --interactive
```

You will then see the following command prompt: **nmap>**. From here, you can issue Nmap commands. Figure 3.14 shows a sequence where the user starts Nmap, issues a simple scan of the entire 192.168.2.0/24 network, and then scans a system named Jacob. Notice how both requests go into the background, and that the second request finishes after the first request. All of these questions are answered later.

Consider the usefulness of interactive mode when using the paranoid flag. You could, for example, issue several paranoid scans that could take days to complete. You could walk away, and then return and read the text file after the scan is complete. Because such scans can take several days to complete, it has become necessary for hackers to try to hide the process that spawns these scans. As a systems administrator, you would likely not use this feature. However, you should be aware that seemingly benign processes may, in fact, be instances of Nmap.

Figure 3.14 Viewing Nmap's Interactive Mode

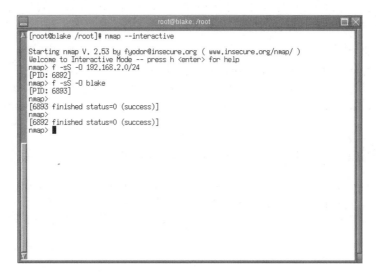

```
[root@blake /root]# nmap --interactive

Starting nmap V. 2.53 by fyodor@insecure.org ( www.insecure.org/nmap/ )
Welcome to Interactive Mode -- press h <enter> for help
nmap> f -sS -O 192.168.2.0/24
[PID: 6892]
nmap> f -sS -O blake
[PID: 6893]
nmap>
[6893 finished status=0 (success)]
nmap>
[6892 finished status=0 (success)]
nmap>
```

Exercise: Using Nmap in Interactive Mode

1. Begin an interactive Nmap session:

   ```
   nmap --interactive
   ```

2. Scan a remote system using the following command:

   ```
   nmap> n -sF -O -v hostname
   ```

3. You will see that this scan did not go into the background. This is because you did not use the **f** command. Do so now, making sure to save your scan into a text file (otherwise, you will not be able to view the scan):

   ```
   nmap> f -sF -O -v hostname -oN scan.txt
   ```

4. You should immediately see the prompt again and a PID number, such as [PID: 9034]. Just about as quickly, you will notice that this process finishes. This is because you launched a scan as a background process, and this background process is complete. Open a second terminal to view the scan.txt file. Close the file when you are finished.

5. Now, issue the following command to begin a paranoid scan of the same host. This time, disguise this scan as a process named /var/syngress:

   ```
   nmap> f -spoof "/"/var/syngress" " -sF -O -v hostname -oN -T 0
       scanparanoid.txt
   ```

6. Now, go to the second terminal and issue the following command:

   ```
   ps aux | grep syngress
   ```

7. You will see that the syngress process is running; actually, it is the Nmap scan taking place. You just as easily could have named this process named, httpd, sendmail, or any other daemon. As a systems administrator, consider the usefulness of carefully documenting the role of each of your servers so that if you see a suspicious service running, you can shut it down.

Now that you are familiar with Nmap, consult the Nmap man page, as well as additional information at www.insecure.org.

Using NmapFE as a Graphical Front End

You are not limited to a command-line interface. The Nmap Front End (NmapFE) provides a well-written, stable GUI that allows you to control almost every aspect of Nmap. You can download NmapFE at www.insecure.org. It is available in both a tarball and an RPM (the RPM is available on the CD accompanying this book: nmap-frontend-0.2.53-1.i386.rpm). As with Nmap, the latter works best in Red Hat systems. Figure 3.15 shows the NmapFE interface after it has issued a FIN Stealth scan, in fast mode, using only a TCP ping that has been fragmented.

Figure 3.15 The NmapFE Interface

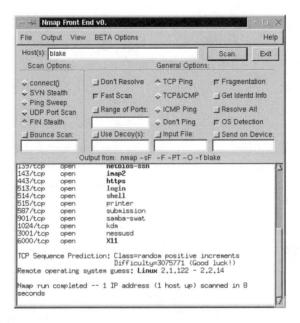

Exercise: Using NmapFE

1. Copy nmap-frontend–0.2.53–1.i386.rpm from the accompanyiong CD, or go to www.insecure.org and download the latest stable version of NmapFE.

2. Install it using the **rpm –ivh** command.

3. The GUI is quite intuitive. Issue commands at will. Notice, however, that although you can specify decoys and fragment, you cannot specify paranoid scans.

NOTE
___

You should note, however, that this interface is somewhat unstable, and given to faults that lead to complete crashes (core dumps). This is especially the case in systems that have been upgraded (say, from Red Hat version 7.0 to 7.1). It is possible that upgrades create conflicts in some of the supporting libraries.

Using Remote Nmap as a Central Scanning Device

Thus far, you have used your local copy of Nmap to scan remote systems. Remote Nmap (Rnmap) enables a client system to connect to a central Nmap server. Developed by Tuomo Makinen, it is designed to allow network administrators a central Nmap source that is easy to administer and update. It is currently in beta, but both the client and the server are quite strong. Rnmap has the following features:

-   User authentication

-   A command-line and GUI client

-   Available encryption (still in beta form)

You can download Rnmap from http://rnmap.sourceforge.net. Rnmap is written in the Python scripting language, which means that your Linux system must have Python installed. Standard installations usually have Python installed, but you can check for its presence using the following RPM command:

```
rpm -qa pyth
```

If you do not see any references to Python, download it from www.rpmfind .net, or obtain it from your installation disks. If you do not use RPM, you can search for the file using the **find** command:

```
find / -name python
```

Usually, the python interpreter is located at /usr/bin/python. Once Python is installed, you can then use the client and the server after unzipping them from their tarfile. No compilation is necessary, because the scripts for the server and the front end use the python interpreter. Because Python is portable between various operating systems, Rnmap is equally as portable.

Exercise: Scanning Systems with Rnmap

1. Copy rnmap_0.5.2-beta.tar.gz from the accompanying CD. Alternatively, go to http://rnmap.sourceforge.net and obtain version 0.5-beta of Rnmap. You must also have the Nmap application on the machine that will act as the server. If you wish to install a more current version of Rnmap, do so. However, the steps of this exercise are written for version 0.5-beta.

2. Once you have downloaded Rnmap, unzip and untar the file using the following command:

   ```
   tar -zxvf Rnmapfile.tar.gz
   ```

3. Unzipping and untarring this file creates the Rnmap directory. Change to it now.

4. Make sure that you have Nmap installed. The server uses the standard Nmap binary to make queries and then provide access to the client.

5. Once you have verified that Nmap is installed and have uncompressed the Rnmap files, you are ready to go. Remember, because Rnmap is written in Python, you do not have to compile anything. Remember, though, that Rnmap supports user-based access. In the server subdirectory, issue the following command to add a user:

   ```
   ./rnmap-adduser
   ```

6. You will be asked for a username. Enter your username of choice.

7. Enter a password. You will be asked to confirm it.

8. When you confirm your password, you may receive several error messages. This is because you have not yet started the server. Generally, it is best to add a user first, because the server tends to not re-read the users.list file, which contains the username and password information. Once you start (or restart) Rnmapd, it will then correctly read the file.

9. Now that you have added a user, change to the server subdirectory, and begin the server as shown:

```
./rnmapd
```

10. You are now ready to use the client to connect to this server. Change to the client subdirectory. If you are in the server subdirectory, all you have to do is enter the following command:

```
cd ../client
```

11. List the directory. You will see that two files are in it. The file named grnmp.py is the GUI client, and the file named rnmpa.py is the command-line client. The GUI client is useful when using Rnmap interactively (i.e., when you are sitting in front of the computer). The command-line client is useful when using Telnet or SSH. To use the GUI client, issue the following command:

```
./grnmap.py
```

You will see the client shown in Figure 3.16.

12. Enter the name of the host you wish to scan.

13. Enter the Login ID and password you created in steps 6 and 7.

14. Select **OS Detect**, **Verbose**, **Fragment IP**, and **FIN scan**, and then click **Scan**. If you have entered the right password and the server is running, the scan will complete. If you receive a message that reads "Can't connect to remote host," then the server is not running. If you receive an "Access denied" message, then you have used the wrong password. Verify your username and password information in the client, and then retry the connection. If this doesn't work, add a new username and password, and kill and restart the server if necessary. When you are successful, you will see a screen similar to Figure 3.17.

15. Now that you have verified the server is running, transfer the grnmap.py file to a remote Linux host and use it to contact your server. As long as this remote Linux host is using Python, it will work. Notice that this file is extremely small, and is thus quite handy. You can keep it on any system, or even on a floppy, along with several other files. Finally, you could use this file on a Windows system, if you wish, because Windows systems support the Python language and interpreter. For more information, go to www.python.org.

Figure 3.16 The Rnmap GUI Client

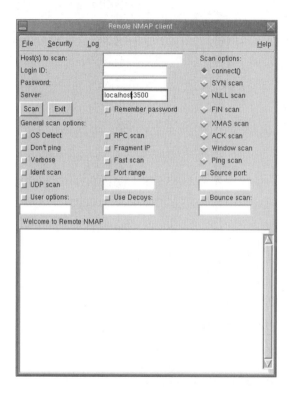

Figure 3.17 A Completed Rnmap Scan

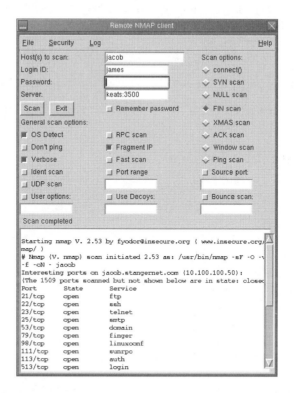

Deploying Cheops to Monitor Your Network

Cheops, developed by Mark Spencer, is intended as a network management tool. Its chief functioning features include:

- Automatic network scans to add all hosts present on the network
- A graphical network map of each host that shows the default gateway for the network
- The ability to provide crude port scans for each host
- Operating system identification
- Active monitoring of remote systems to see if the host is up, or if a particular service is up and running
- The ability to manually add or delete a host from the map

- The ability to add an entire IP network or DNS domain to the map, and then have Cheops automatically add new hosts to the map

- The use of the Simple Network Management Protocol (SNMP) to query hosts

- Resolution of DNS names (including reverse DNS lookup)

- Use of ping or traceroute on each host on the map

- Ability to access the network services (e.g., FTP, Telnet, and SSH) provided by a host on the map

NOTE

The most impressive feature that Cheops offers is scalability. You can configure Cheops to launch any application you wish to further help you determine the nature of a host. You will learn how to do this in the exercise later in this section.

Billed as a graphical network neighborhood, Cheops is related to applications such as HP OpenView. HP OpenView is a sophisticated, expensive graphical front end that uses SNMP, a protocol that allows you to monitor remote systems. Both Cheops and HP OpenView allow you to create a graphical map of the network, and then manage any host on that map. Although Cheops is not nearly as sophisticated, it still allows you to quickly learn which hosts are up on a particular network segment.

The Simple Network Management Protocol (SNMP) helps you gain information from remote systems. It can also be used to set operating system values. It is commonly used on routers, as it can be used to change routing values, IP addresses, and any element of the operating system. SNMP requires that the remote system install small daemons, called *agents*, that accept commands from an application commonly called a "Network Management Station" (NMS). Examples of NMS applications include snmpwalk, snmpget, and Scotty. In the Windows world, the HP OpenView application is especially popular. Using NMS applications, it is possible to issue queries to agents to learn information such as:

- The configuration of the operating system, including IP addresses, active interfaces, and defined users.

- Processes currently running on the operating system.

- The amount of IP, ICMP, TCP, and UDP traffic that has passed through an interface.

- A count of the number of routers a packet is supposed to travel through before it reaches a particular network. This number is often known as a *hop count*.

If the system agents are allowed to write values to the operating system, it is possible to have these agents actually change the configuration of the operating system. For example, agents can change the IP address on some operating systems. For more information about how SNMP works, install the UCD SNMP tools (discussed later in this chapter), and consult the snmpwalk and snmpget man pages. You can also learn more about SNMP at the Research Web site (www.snmp.org).

How Cheops Works

Cheops issues network broadcasts, and then processes these replies to discover remote hosts. Some older versions of Cheops use an application called Queso to read the replies of remote systems. Queso is similar to Nmap, although not as sophisticated or recent. Still, like Nmap, Queso uses stack fingerprinting to guess the operating system of a remote server. Once Cheops makes a guess as to the remote operating system, it will provide an icon that represents that remote host's operating system. Although Queso is quite old, it is still remarkably accurate for today's systems. Newer versions of Cheops use Nmap. However, some of the newer betas do not work as well on Linux systems, so it is recommended that you use Cheops version 0.59a-1 which can be found on the accompnying CD. An equivalent RPM version is also on the CD. You will see how it is possible to use Nmap with Cheops later in this chapter.

NOTE

Cheops also issues standard ping scan and port scan techniques to learn about a host's available systems. One of its more useful features is the ability to specifically listen to remote system SNMP ports (161 and 162).

Obtaining Cheops

You can obtain Cheops from any Red Hat 7.0 Power Tools CD, or from www.marko.net/cheops. Although the site provides a tarball file, the RPM works best for Red Hat systems.

Required Libraries

Cheops will run well on most Linux systems (we tested Cheops on Caldera, TurboLinux, Red Hat, and SuSE). You must, however, have the following gtk, glib, and SNMP packages installed first:

- gtk+10-1.0.6-9 or higher.

- glib10-1.x

- ucd-snmp

- ucd-snmp-devel

- ucd-snmp-utils

- All libraries associated with a graphics editing application called "The Gimp" (www.gimp.org), especially the gimp-devel package. Any package for Red Hat 6.2 or later, for example, will work, if you are using Red Hat Linux. Once you have installed GIMP and the additional libraries mentioned previously, you then have the libraries necessary to run Cheops.

Open source applications often require that you spend time adjusting supporting libraries on your system. Sometimes, adjusting one supporting library requires you to adjust other libraries, because of dependencies. Sometimes, this can be very frustrating. The following is a list of all gtk libraries installed on a Red Hat 7.0 and Red Hat 7.1 system, respectively:

- gtkglarea-1.2.1-1

- pygtk-libglade-0.6.6-4_helix_2

- rep-gtk-gnome-0.15-0_helix_2

- gtk+-devel-1.2.8-7_helix_1

- gtk-engines-0.10-9_helix_1

- gtk+10-1.0.6-9

- pygtk-0.6.6-4_helix_2
- rep-gtk-libglade-0.15-0_helix_2
- gtkmm-1.2.1-8
- gtk+-1.2.8-7_helix_1
    - rep-gtk-0.15-0_helix_2
- pygtk-0.6.6-4
- rep-gtk-libglade-0.13-3
- gtk+-1.2.8-7
- gtk-engines-0.10-9
- pygtk-libglade-0.6.6-4
- rep-gtk-gnome-0.13-3
- gtk+10-1.0.6-9
- gtk+-devel-1.2.8-7
- rep-gtk-0.13-3
    - gtkmm-1.2.1-8

Other combinations are possible; your system's supporting libraries may vary. You can obtain the gtk+ and glib libraries either from your distribution disk, or www.rpmfind.net. The SNMP packages are important only for their libraries. You do not have to run the SNMP daemon in order to use Cheops, because the application simply uses the libraries, not the actual daemon. Most Linux distributions include these SNMP packages, although you can obtain these at www.rpmfind.net as well.

The Cheops Interface

When you first start Cheops, you will see the Cheops Auto-scan dialog box, shown in Figure 3.18. If you click **Yes**, Cheops will begin to scan your network.

Figure 3.18 The Cheops Initial Scan Dialog Box

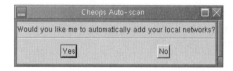

Once Cheops finishes processing replies from remote hosts, the main Cheops interface will appear, as shown in Figure 3.19.

Figure 3.19 Viewing a Small LAN in Cheops

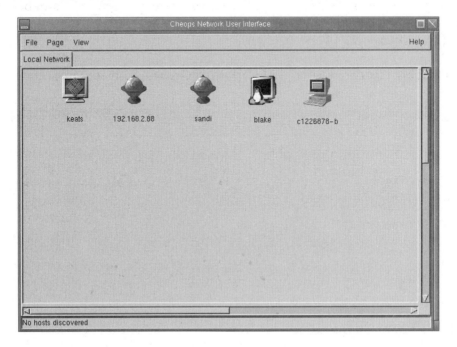

Of course, it is possible to map much larger networks. In fact, Cheops has been used to map hundreds of hosts, as well as trace the routers between hosts all across the Internet.

NOTE

As with many applications, Cheops works best on a nonswitched LAN. However, it is possible for it to obtain valid responses in switched environment.

Cheops refers to the default screen as a *page*. You can create additional pages for additional networks or hosts, if you wish. You can then right-click on individual hosts to conduct simple port scans.

Mapping Relations between Computers

Nmap allows you to determine routing in your network. You can do this by right-clicking on the actual page, and then select the Map | Map option. Mapping the network will cause Cheops to automatically generate lines between each host. These lines, shown in Figure 3.20, show how each host is related to the network's default gateway.

Figure 3.20 Viewing a Small Network Map Generated by Cheops

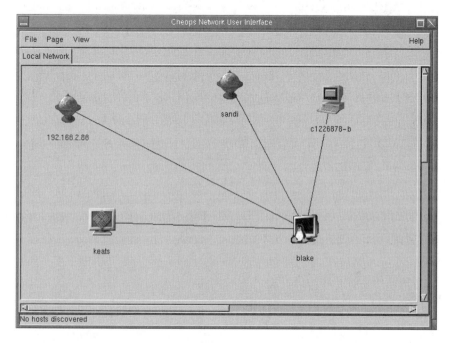

Cheops Monitoring Methods

Cheops is capable of two types of monitoring. First, it can have your Linux system issue simple ping requests to see if a remote host is up. If the host is up and responding, it receives a green icon. If a host does not respond, the network host will appear red. You should understand, of course, that a host is not necessarily down just because a host does not respond to ping requests. It is possible, for example, that an intervening firewall is blocking ping requests between your host and the remote system . It is also possible that the host you are monitoring has been configured to not respond to ping requests.

The second type of monitoring at least partially solves this problem. Instead of relying on a crude ping request, Cheops allows you to pick a specific service offered by the remote host. If, for example, you wish to monitor Apache Server on a remote Solaris host, you can configure the monitor daemon to test that port.

To enable monitoring for a specific host, all you have to do is right-click on its icon, and then select the **Monitoring?** option. Figure 3.21 shows monitoring being enabled on the FTP and Web servers for the machine named sandi.stangernet.com.

Figure 3.21 Monitoring Systems Using Cheops

Once you click **Save** or **Close** (available in version 0.59 of Cheops), you will then be able to monitor if and when the Web and FTP server goes down by seeing the icon turn from green to red. You can also view past alerts by going to View | Event log to bring up the General Event Log, shown in Figure 3.22. You can then acknowledge an individual message, or all messages. Acknowledging the messages clears them from the log.

Figure 3.22 The General Event Log

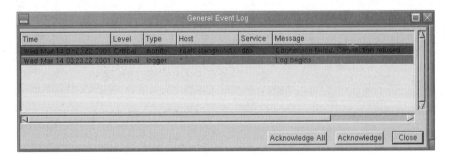

Connectivity Features

You can use Cheops to connect to remote systems. If their services, such as Web, FTP, SSH, and Telnet, are up and running, all you have to do is right-click on the icon, and then select the service you want to use. When you right-click on the icon, the resulting menu is context sensitive for each system. This list will contain only those services that are currently running on this system. If, for example, system A is running SSH and a Web server, and system B is running a Telnet and an FTP server, the menu will be different for each system.

However, two menu items will always be the same: ping and traceroute. You can specify different "helper" applications with this interface. For example, when you indicate that you want to use traceroute, Cheops will automatically open a terminal. You may not like the looks of this default terminal. In some cases, the default terminal may not appear correctly in your X session. You can change the default terminal by going to the File | Options menu and selecting the Helpers tab. You can then use the drop-down box to specify another terminal emulator, or you can enter your own command.

Notes from the Underground…

Cheops-ng

Cheops-ng is a more recent version of Cheops. It uses an agent-manager structure. However, when it comes to Linux systems, Cheops-ng is not as stable as Cheops is. At your own risk, you can download Cheops-ng at http://sourceforge.net/projects/cheops-ng. If you use a Linux system, using the RPM is highly recommended. Version 0.0.1.3 does not compile properly on Red Hat 7.0 when installing it from a tarball.

You must also install Nmap. However, the OS detection feature currently does not work properly in Cheops-ng version 0.1.1 (the RPM version), because it searches for Nmap in the wrong location. Additional required libraries for Cheops-ng include adns (www.gnu.org/software/adns), gnome, and libpcap (libpcap is on the accompanying CD). All but adns are installed by default in Red Hat 7.0 systems, and all of the RPM packages are available at www.rpmfind.net.

Once you install Cheops-ng, you first run the /usr/sbin/cheops-agent daemon. You can then use the cheops-ng client to access the agent to

Continued

map the network. One of the exciting things about Cheops-ng (when it works) is that you can use the Cheops-ng client to contact remote agents. These agents can then scan your system. The connection is encrypted, so any transmissions you make are relatively secure. This chapter does not focus on Cheops-ng because it is not stable at this point. Cheops-ng is, however, a promising project. Check its home page over time to see if it becomes truly stable.

Now that you have learned about the most salient features of Cheops, it's time to investigate how the program works. Although many different Cheops features vary from version to version, one of the more stable versions is 0.59a, and it is used in the following exercise.

Exercise: Installing and Configuring Cheops

1. Install Cheops and all supporting libraries.

2. Start Cheops by issuing the following command: **cheops &**.

3. Indicate that you do want to automatically scan for network hosts. What did you find?

4. If you did not find anything, go to **Page | Edit**. This menu allows you to configure the networks that Cheops will scan and report. If necessary, remove any entries that are not appropriate for your network by clicking **Remove Host/Network**. Now, click **Add Host/Network**.

5. Add the network address, followed by the subnet mask. Remember, a network address does not contain the host portion of your particular IP address. When you are finished, click **OK**.

6. Click **Update**.

7. Now, quit and restart Cheops. Have Cheops rescan your network to discover hosts.

8. You may have to add a few more hosts that were not scanned. You can do this by going to **Page | Add host**, and then entering the name or IP address of the host you want.

9. Now, go to **Page | Map** to see how well Cheops maps the topology of your network. It is possible that Cheops will see your system as a router, even if it is not. This is a quirk of Cheops, because sometimes it will

identify the computer from which it is run as the router. Remember, this is open source code, after all.

10. The default setting is to use large icons to represent the hosts. Right-click on an empty part of the page, then select the **View | List** option, and then select the **View | Small Icons** option. You can return to the default view by selecting **View | Icons**.

11. Now, enable monitoring for a remote system. Ping the host to make sure it is up and responding to ping requests.

12. Instead of having to ping the system yourself, have Cheops do it for you. Highlight the system, and then right-click it.

13. Select the **Monitoring?** option.

14. First, do a simple monitoring test. Select the **Availability** (Ping) option. Change the frequency to 1 minute by changing the **every** entry to **1**.

15. Click **Save**.

16. The icon for the host you are monitoring should be green. Now, shut down the remote system.

17. The icon for that host will turn red after a short time, because it has been configured to report the remote server's condition. Now, open the Event log and view the alert.

18. Now, restart the remote system. You will see that the icon automatically turns green. Edit this setting so that it is more reasonable.

19. Next, right-click on this server and select the **Scan?** option. Cheops will conduct a scan, and when it is finished, Cheops will generate a report. Now, click **More**, and you will see a report similar to that shown in Figure 3.23.

20. Notice that the bottom window gives you more information about the daemons running on the remote system. Cheops 0.59a-1 uses a program called Queso to learn the operating system type. Because Cheops is a TCP/IP fingerprinting application, it is somewhat effective, but it is not maintained as actively as is Nmap. Configure Cheops to offer Nmap as a plug-in. Go to **File | Options**, and then select the **Services** tab.

21. You will see a list of predefined services. This window allows you to configure applications to contact different systems or ports. If, for example, you enter **0** in the Port field, and Cheops recognizes this

remote system as a responding system, Cheops will provide this option when you right-click on a host. You can then launch the application specified in the Command text box. If you enter an actual port, such as port 80, then this option will be presented only if that particular port is open. You can also use macros to make your commands more context specific. The **%i** macro, for example, allows you to specify the remote system's IP address. Cheops will fill this value in automatically. The **%h** macro allows you to specify the remote system's host name. Additional macros exist, and are explained in the interface. Now, click **Add** and enter Nmap in the **Name** field.

Figure 3.23 Viewing a System Scan in Cheops

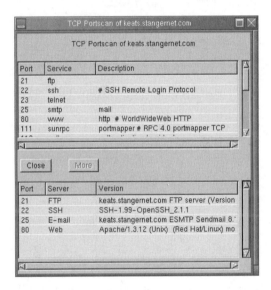

22. In the **Port** field, enter **0**.

23. In the **Command** field, enter the following text string:

```
%x -T 'We are going to Nmap %h' -e sh -c '/usr/bin/nmap -sS -O
    -P0 %I && read a'
```

Make sure there is no space between the two ampersand characters, &&. In addition, make sure you use the standard apostrophe character (the one below the double quotes character to the right of your keyboard) to enclose the Nmap command.

This text string has Cheops launch a terminal with the title of 'We are going to Nmap *hostname*', and then execute a shell, which then launches Nmap to conduct a stealth scan, an operating system identification. The host will not be pinged during the scan. The final part of the command has the terminal remain on the screen so you can read it. Otherwise, the terminal would completely disappear as soon as Nmap finished, making it impossible to read the output. Figure 3.24 shows the completed command.

Figure 3.24 Creating an Entry for Nmap in Cheops

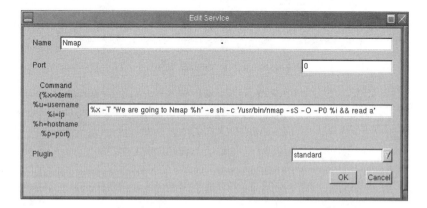

24. Click **OK**.

25. When you are finished, you will see your entry among all of the others, as shown in Figure 3.25.

Figure 3.25 Viewing Cheops Command Entries

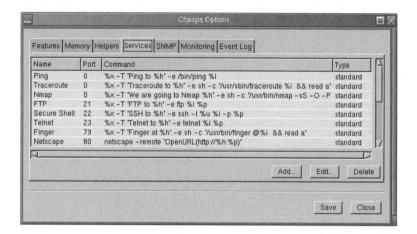

26. Click **Save** to return to the Cheops main interface.

27. Right-click a functioning host. You will see your new entry appear.

28. Select your new Nmap entry and note the scan.

29. You have now configured Cheops to conduct a useful scan of your network hosts using a current piece of software.

30. Consider additional commands you could configure, including dig, snmpwalk, and any other application that can help you further monitor your network.

31. Now, create another plug-in option by entering the following command:

```
%x -t 'SNMPWALK of %h' -e sh -c 'snmpwalk %i publicname |less
    && read a'
```

32. This command has the program named snmpwalk query the system using the public name of "publicname." Any system that has SNMP installed, and uses the public name of "publicname" will respond. You should, of course, change the public name to the one used on your systems and routers.

33. Consider additional plug-ins. You can configure plug-ins to use commands such as **snmpget**, **snmpset**, **host**, **GSS**, or any others you wish you use. In addition, consider the different types of systems you wish to scan. For example, what applications would you want to configure if you used Cheops to monitor a DNS server, as opposed to monitoring a collection of routers and switches?

34. Cheops can send you its log messages by e-mail. This is an excellent way to check Cheops logs without first having to log in to the server. Go to **File | Options**, then select the **Event Log** tab. Enter the host name or IP address of the e-mail server you normally check every day to get your e-mail. Each event that Cheops logs, such as when your Web server goes down or comes back up, will be sent to you as it happens.

You can now monitor systems and gather information about the services they are offering from a central console. You will find that such software significantly increases your ability to monitor the network and determine if any hosts have been brought down by attacks.

NOTE

Cheops may crash and lose all of the service plug-ins you have defined, as well as the default plug-ins. You will find out that you have lost all of these services when you right-click an icon and are unable to choose any. Remember that Cheops creates the .cheops directory in your home directory. If you lose your services, search for the ~/.cheops/services file. If it is empty, but present, delete the file. You will then get at least your default services back. However, you will lose all of the plug-ins you have configured. The best way to protect yourself against losing these plug-ins is to create a backup of the ~/.cheops/services file. If it is lost, you can then recopy the backup file in the place of the original.

Deploying Nessus to Test Daemon Security

Thus far, you have learned how to use port scanning and monitoring devices. These applications are quite effective in determining if your server is up and running. They are perfect tools if you want to find out what type of service is listening. However, using vulnerability detection software, you can find out exactly what specific application is listening on that port. A good hacker is well informed concerning the popular servers on the Internet, and can quickly take advantage of a specific daemon that has a security problem.

Nessus allows you to proactively scan your systems to determine its weaknesses. Nessus is comprised of a server and a client. The server runs only on Linux systems, whereas clients exist for Linux, Windows, and Macintosh systems. The Nessus home page is shown in Figure 3.26.

Although no scanner can offer you a 100-percent solution, this scanner is updated often, and is in wide use. It will scan for the following types of problems:

- Old daemon and service versions that have known security issues (including sendmail, Finger, NIS, and NFS)

- Writeable anonymous FTP directories

- Open X Windows ports. X Windows ports can allow unauthorized users easy access to the system.

www.syngress.com

Figure 3.26 The Nessus Home Page

- CGI issues concerning Web servers

- Backdoors, Trojans, and DDOS daemons, such as TFN2k

- Extraneous services that have been activated and left running on a system. Just because you have deactivated a service using Bastille, doesn't mean that the service will remain deactivated.

- Backdoors, which are daemons and applications that defeat your system's authentication measures by opening ports that are tied directly to a login shell.

Nessus uses special files, called plug-ins, to provide the "brains" for Nessus. You will learn how to update these plug-ins later in this chapter. Current versions of Nessus use port 1241. Older versions of Nessus (anything earlier than version 1.0) used port 3001.

SECURITY ALERT!

Like many scanners, Nessus contains various plug-ins that simulate attacks. Some of these plug-ins simulate attacks so effectively that they can crash systems. Although Nessus cannot destroy information on a remote system, it can:

- Issue an attack against the system so that it crashes. In other words, Nessus can conduct a DoS attack on your system while testing its ability to withstand DoS attacks.
- Generate vast amounts of network traffic that can affect end users on the network.

It is a good idea to schedule your Nessus scans for off-peak hours. Be prepared to restart various servers. Most importantly, make sure that any server you scan with Nessus can be brought offline for a short period of time. The last thing you want to do is bring about an unplanned crash to a production server in the middle of the business day.

The Nessus Client/Server Relationship

The Nessus client, shown in Figure 3.27, allows you to connect to the Nessus daemon, which is usually on a remote server. Several different clients exist, including those for Windows, Macintosh, and Unix/Linux systems. You will learn more about the Windows client shortly. You can configure your Nessus daemon to expect encrypted (called "cipher") or plaintext authentication. The wisest course of action is, of course, to choose cipher authentication, because it is more secure and because Nessus defaults to cipher mode.

When you launch the client for the first time, it will take some time to create a public key pair, which will be used to authenticate with any Nessus daemon.

In Figure 3.27, the Linux Nessus client has logged in to the host named Keats, using the username of *nessusremote*. It is very important that you understand that you must first log in to the Nessus server. Here are some addition things to remember when using any Nessus client:

- When the client first launches after compilation, it will ask you to create a password. This password has nothing to do with authenticating with the server. It is simply there to prevent an unauthorized user from accessing the client.

Figure 3.27 The Nessus Client

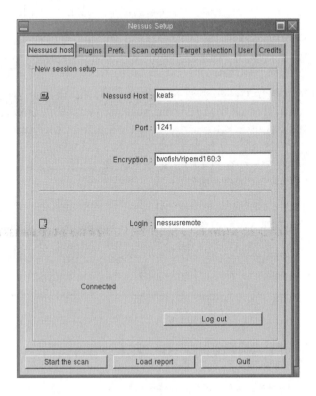

- Whenever you launch any Nessus client, the client is not logged on to any Nessus daemon. You will have to enter the Nessus host name, port, and login name, and then click **Log In** to connect. You must, of course, have the correct account created on the Nessus host, or authentication will fail. You will learn more about creating usernames for remote hosts later in this chapter.

- Once you log in, you will be presented with a list of plug-ins. You can then choose and configure them according to your preferences. If you are not logged in, the plug-ins menu will be blank.

- When you have logged in and chosen the plug-ins you wish to use, you must then click the **Target Selection** tab to choose a target host.

Once you have completed a scan, you will see a report similar to that shown in Figure 3.28. When you have finished a scan, Nessus will do one of two things—either finish and inform you that no errors were found, or issue a reports summary. You can double-click on the left-hand pane to see the individual alerts. As shown in Figure 3.28, you can then expand these alerts to learn more about the nature of the problem and how to solve it.

Figure 3.28 Viewing a Report Generated by the Linux Nessus Client

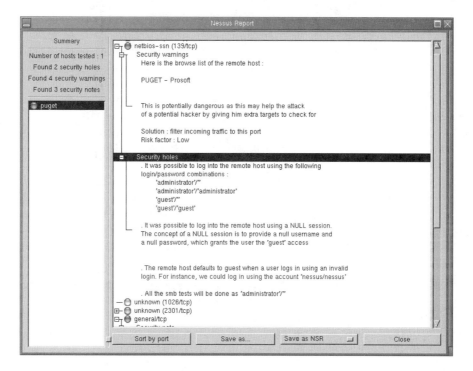

Windows Nessus Clients

Several Windows clients exist, although WinNessus is the most reliable. As you can see in Figure 3.29, its interface is almost identical to the Linux client.

Required Libraries

Nessus requires the following libraries and applications:

- **GTK** The Gimp Toolkit, available at www.gimp.org, or at www.rpmfind.net.

- **Nmap** Available at www.insecure.org.

- **m4** A macro utility used by many applications and daemons. It is standard equipment for most systems. You can obtain it from www.rpmfind.net.

Figure 3.29 The WinNessus Client

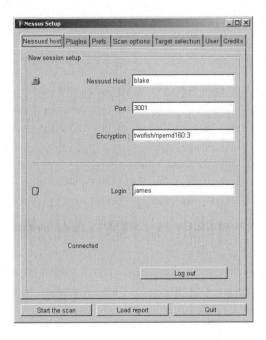

In short, if you have installed the Graphics Image Manipulation Program (GIMP), you can install Nessus.

Order of Installation

Although the prebuilt RPM packages are useful, they do not provide additional features that allow you to conduct unattended and partial scans. You will learn more about these shortly. Thus, you should install Nessus from the tarball format.

Regardless of the Nessus version you install, you must install the following tarball files in the following order, as root:

1. nessus-libraries-1.0.7a.tar.gz
2. libnasl-1.0.7a-1.tar.gz
3. nessus-core-1.0.7a-1.tar.gz
4. nessus-plugins-1.0.7a-1.tar.gz

These files are all available at www.nessus.org and on the CD accompanying this book. Compiling these individual libraries is straightforward.

1. Once you run gunzip against the nessus-libraries tarball, the tarball will create the nessus-libraries directory. Change to this directory, and then run the following commands:

   ```
   ./configure
   make
   make install
   ```

2. Make sure that /usr/local/bin is in your system path If you install Nessus using RPMs, all files are installed in /usr/bin. You can verify your system path by entering the following command:

   ```
   echo $PATH
   ```

3. Repeat these steps for the libnasl package.

4. Once you get to the nessus-core package, you have one compilation option available to you. The following command and argument allows Nessus to conduct differential, detached, and continuous scans (you will learn more about these, later):

   ```
   ./configure --enable-save-kb --enable-save-sessions
   ```

5. Once you have compiled the nessus-core package, repeat the **./configure**, **make**, and **make install** steps for the nessus-plugins.

6. Then, using a text editor, enter the following line into the /etc/ld.so.conf file:

   ```
   ./usr/local/lib
   ```

7. To make sure these changes take effect, enter the following command, still as root:

   ```
   ldconfig
   ```

What If I Don't Want to Use X?

If you want your server to act as a Nessus daemon, and not support the X client, you can disable gtk support by issuing the following argument to the ./configure script when installing the nessus-core package:

```
./configure --disable-gtk ; make && make install
```

RPM-Based Installations

If you wish to install Nessus by using the RPMs, you would install the files in the following order:

1. nessus-common-1.0.7a-1.i386.rpm

2. nessus-server-1.0.7a-1.i386.rpm

3. nessus-plugins-1.0.7a-1.i386.rpm

4. nessus-devel-1.0.7a-1.i386.rpm

5. nessus-client-1.0.7a-1.i386.rpm

Each of these files is available at the www.nessus.org site and on the CD accompanying this book. Look for a special link at www.nessus.org that takes you directly to the RPM files. Understand, however, that most RPM binary installations have not been compiled with the --enable-save-kb feature, which allows you to conduct detached and differential scans. If you do not want to use the X client when installing with RPMs, do not install the nessus-client package.

NOTE

When you first create a remote user using nessus-useradd, this remote user will use a one-time password that is passed across the network. Although the password is encrypted, it is still never a good idea to allow even encrypted passwords to regularly cross a network. Nessus, however, does this only once, because as soon as a Nessus user authenticates using the one-time password, the public keys are exchanged, and all subsequent authentication occurs using your public key. No password information will ever cross over the network, at least as far as this Nessus client and server are concerned.

You can learn about a particular nessusd's configuration, including its ability to conduct differential and detached scans, by issuing the following command:

```
/usr/local/sbin/nessusd -d
```

The resulting output will inform you about the server version, as well as its ability to enter KB saving mode.

Configuring Plug-Ins

Some of the plug-ins require you to enter additional settings in order to run effectively. For example, FTP, e-mail, and login checks often require you to enter default user account information. It is also possible to configure the FTP plug-in to actually store a file in the FTP directory to prove that it is writeable. Additional options exist, including those for Nmap. Figure 3.30 shows some of the options that you can configure.

Figure 3.30 Configuring Nessus Preferences

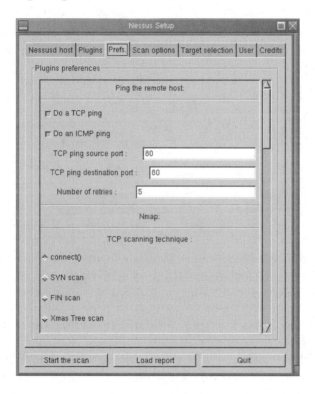

These options are available once you open the Nessus client and connect to a Nessus server. For specific steps on connecting the client to the server, consult the exercise later in this section. Notice that you can configure Nessus to forego using ICMP, and you can configure various Nmap settings. The preferences you configure here will apply to all scans you make using this client. The client will try to impose these settings on all additional servers.

Creating a New Nessus User

Before you can use your Nessus client, you must define a user using /usr/local/ sbin/nessus-adduser, an interactive application that creates users in the ~/.nessus .keys file. Two types of users exist in regard to Nessus:

- **Local** These users are listed as username@127.0.0.1. These users can access Nessus only from the local system.

- **Remote** Users that are allowed to access nessusd remote systems. They will be listed as username@remote-ip-address, where remote-ip-address is the one you specify in the /usr/local/sbin/nessus-adduser program.

Nessus-adduser allows you to add the users who are allowed to connect to the Nessus daemon and conduct scans. The process of adding local and remote users is quite different. Although you use nessus-adduser to add both, when you specify that you want to add a local user, Nessus will create a local key pair for this user. This key pair will be used to authenticate with the local nesssd daemon only.

If you wish to add a remote user, you must first take the following steps:

1. Using useradd or Linuxconf, add the user who will become a remote Nessus user.

2. Launch nessus-useradd and add this same user.

3. Tell nessus-useradd that this user is not a local user.

4. Specify the IP address of the machine from which this user can connect. It is best to specify a single machine, but if you wish, you can specify an entire network. However, most versions of Nessus will automatically map this user account to the one IP address on the network that first makes the connection. Thus, even though you think you have allowed a user named nesussadmin to connect to a nessus daemon from the entire 192.168.3.0 network, if you connect to this daemon from the 192.168.3.75 host, this one host will be the only one that can use the nessusadmin account.

The Rules Database

Whenever you configure a new client in nessus-adduser, you will be asked whether you wish to apply a set of rules on this user. These rules determine the hosts that this user can scan. If the rules database is left blank, then the user can scan all hosts. The following is an example of a rule set that allows a user to scan one host, and nothing more:

```
accept 10.100.100.1/24
default deny
```

The **default deny** entry forbids everything that is not specifically allowed. This particular list is likely too restrictive to be useful. Try the following:

```
accept 10.100.100.0/24
192.168.2.0/24
default deny
```

Now, a user with this rule set applied can scan all hosts in the 10.100.100.0/24 and 192.168.2.0/24 networks. For more information about Nessus, consult the nessus, nessusd, and nessus-adduser man pages, or the FAQ page at www.nessus.org.

SECURITY ALERT!

There may be times that you will have to reconfigure a server, and you may lose the private key of your Nessus server. If this happens, this server's public key that your client uses to connect to this Nessus host will also become invalid. You will know this when your client informs you about a "spoof alert." If this happens, edit or delete the .nessus.keys file in your home directory. When you add a new user to your Nessus host, you can then connect to this host. It will then send you a new public key, and you will be able to authenticate again using public key pairs.

Exercise: Installing Nessus and Conducting a Vulnerability Scan

1. Install Nessus from a tarball or from an RPM using the instructions given earlier.

NOTE

If you install from an RPM, you will not be able to conduct differential and detached scans. If you install Nessus using tarball files, make sure that you specify ./configure **--enable-save-kb --enable-save-sessions** when you install the nessus-core files.

2. Log on locally to the system that will house the Nessus daemon.

3. Start Nessus using either of the following commands:

```
/etc/rc.d/init.d/nessus start
```

or (to manually run nessusd as a daemon):

```
/usr/sbin/nessusd -D
```

NOTE

When installing Nessus, if you see a message informing you that there was an error in loading shared libraries, and that the libnasl.so.0 module can't be found, you have not modified the /etc/ld.so.conf file to contain a reference to /usr/local/lib, and then run ldconfig. Even if you have, try it again. If you wish to stop nessus, issue the following command: **killall -9 nessusd**.

4. Issue the following command to create a local account that can administer the system (you can, of course, specify any user or password you wish):

```
nessusd -P root,password
```

5. You now have established a username and password for a local user. Now, create a username and password for your local system named nessus:

useradd nessus

passwd nessus

```
New UNIX password:
Retype UNIX password:
```

This account is not used by nessusd. However, the nessus-adduser program will sense that this account exists, which will make it easier for you to allow remote clients to use this account.

6. Next, issue the following command:

```
/usr/sbin/nessus-adduser
```

7. When prompted for a username, enter **remotenessus**.

8. Indicate that you want to use the cipher authentication method (the default) by simply pressing **ENTER**.

9. Nessus will ask you if the user you are adding is a local user. Indicate no (the default) by entering **n**, and then press **ENTER**.

10. You will then be asked to provide the IP address for the source host. This IP address should be of the client that will access the computer. If, for example, you are going to access this system from a remote host with the IP address of 10.100.100.1, enter **10.100.100.1**, then press **ENTER**. Note: If you have only one Linux system, enter the IP address of that system.

11. Nessus will then ask you for a one-time password for this user. This password is important, because nessusd and the Nessus client will use this password once to initiate the public key exchange. Once this password is used, it will be discarded in favor of the public keys. Make sure you remember this password. Once you have entered this password, press **ENTER**.

12. Nessus will then ask you to enter rules for the *remotenessus* user. These rules determine exactly which networks and hosts this user will be able to scan. If you leave the rule empty, then no limitations will be applied, and this user account will be able to scan all systems. Leave this rule blank for this user, and press **CTRL + D**.

13. You will be given a chance to review the settings for *remotenessus* user. If they are acceptable, enter **y** to the question "Is that OK?" and press **ENTER**.

14. Once you have added this user, you will receive a "user added" message. If you see any other message, you must add this user again. The chief reason for errors is the failure to use useradd and passwd to add the user to the Linux database. To confirm that you have added this user, enter the following command:

```
/usr/sbin/nessusd -L
```

15. Notice that you can see the remotenessus account you just added. It currently says that the account is based on a user password, rather than a user key. Notice also that it reads remotenessus@x.x.x.x. This means that remotenessus can only be used by that specific IP address. Understand that if the IP address is not the same as the system you are trying to use as a client, you will not be able to connect. Make sure that this account has the proper IP address of the system you will use as a client.

16. Open a nessus client on the machine with the IP address you listed in step 8. If, for example, you wish to use the Linux nessus client, you would enter the following at a command prompt: **nessus &**.

17. You will be prompted to create a password to protect the client against unauthorized use. Enter a password and confirm it, and then you will see the Nessus client main window. You are not currently logged in.

18. Prepare to log in to the remote nessus server. In the Nessus host tab, enter the name or IP address of the host running nessusd. In the Port window, make sure it reads 1241, because you are connecting to a newer server. In the Login field, enter remotenessus and click **Log In**.

19. You will be connected. The best way to tell that you are connected is that the Plug-ins window will appear automatically. If the client hangs after a minute or so, you have failed authentication. Once you are connected, go back to your server and issue the **/usr/sbin/nessusd -L** command again to view the key for the remotenessus user. You will notice that this user now has a user key entry. From now on, you will authenticate using public keys, rather than sending passwords across the network.

20. Now, use your Nessus client to conduct a remote scan. Select **Enable All But Dangerous Plug-Ins**, and then select the **Prefs** tab. Scroll down until you see the Nmap section. Choose the options you feel are appropriate for your situation, and then scroll down further to the FTP login account entries. Enter **anonymous** and an e-mail address here.

21. Scroll down further until you see the imap and POP3 valid account entries. Enter a username and password for each account. Make good guesses, as these will be used on every e-mail server you scan.

22. Click on the **Target Selection** tab and enter a remote server. Make sure that this server is not a critical server, and that you have authorization to scan these servers.

23. Once you have entered this server's host name or IP address, click **Start The Scan**.

24. Nessus will show you a progress screen, similar to that shown in Figure 3.31.

Figure 3.31 Nessus Scanning a System

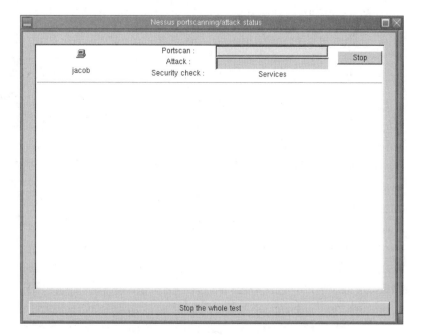

25. After some time, the scan will finish. Depending on the nature of the host you have scanned, you will receive a detailed report explaining what Nessus has found. The report includes a description of the problem, a determination of the severity of the problem, and advice on how to fix it.

Updating Nessus

As with antivirus or IP fingerprinting programs, a scanner is only as good as its database of vulnerabilities. If the Nessus database could never be updated, the application would be worse than useless, because the old information would lull you into a false sense of security. Fortunately, the Nessus project has been quite active, and it has a good record for providing regular plug-in updates. Some of the plug-ins are written by Nessus developers; however, the majority are donated by Nessus users.

The most efficient way to update your Nessus daemon is to issue the following command as long as you have Nessus 1.0 or later:

```
nessus-update-plugins
```

If you wish to update your Nessus plug-ins manually, follow these steps:

1. Go to www.nessus.org and find the downloads page (as of this writing,
    www.nessus.org/plugins).

2. Download the plug-ins. Usually, you can download all of the plug-ins, or
    choose to download only certain plug-ins that interest you.

3. Copy any and all plug-ins to the following directory. The default direc-
    tory is /usr/local/lib/nessus/plugins/. It is possible that you have speci-
    fied a different directory in the /etc/nessus/nessus.conf file.

4. Restart nessus. You can do this by using its system V script
    (/etc/rc.d/init.d/nessus start), or by finding the daemon's PID, and then
    issuing the **kill –HUP** command.

Understanding Differential, Detached, and Continuous Scans

Earlier, you learned about options to specify when compiling the nessus-core
files. These options, **--enable-save-kb** and **--enable-save-sessions**, allow the
Nessus client and server to communicate in a more sophisticated way. Specifically,
the compilation option allows the client to "remember" past sessions and to configure a nessus daemon to conduct a scan all by itself. These capabilities are
respectively called *differential* and *detached* scanning. The ability to save sessions
allows you to begin sessions that have been interrupted. All of these features will
be enabled by default in later versions of Nessus; for now, you must compile
them yourself.

A differential scan is where Nessus can compare its current scan to past scan
results and then provide you with a short list of changes. From this list, you can
identify what daemons have been updated, shut down, or turned on. The two
benefits of a differential scan are that you can quickly identify changes in a network host, and you will not have to generate as much network traffic. The
--enable-save-kb option creates, among other things, an additional tab, KB,
in the Nessus client. Figure 3.32 shows the KB tab.

Figure 3.32 Configuring Nessus to Do a Differential Scan in the KB Tab

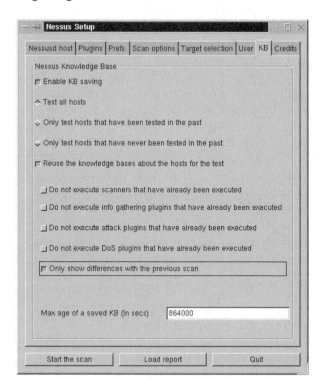

A detached scan allows you to use your client to attach to the Nessus daemon, request a scan, and then disconnect. Normally, if this were to happen, nessusd would cancel the scan. However, if you have enabled the **--enable-save-kb** feature, the scan will continue, and nessusd will then e-mail you the results of the scan. You can also use this feature to have Nessus conduct a new scan after a certain number of hours have passed. Figure 3.33 shows how to configure a properly configured client and server to conduct a detached scan. It is vital that you enter a valid e-mail address; because you will end communication with the server before the scan completes, you will not be able to view the results any other way.

You have likely noticed the Continuous scan option. This allows you to repeat a scan multiple times. You can set the delay between two scans in seconds. Thus, to set a scan to happen daily, you could choose the **Continuous scan** option, and then specify the value of **28800** (eight hours), or **144000** (five days).

For more information about KB saving, consult the following URL: www .nessus.org/doc/kb_saving.html.

Figure 3.33 Configuring the Nessus Client for a Detached Scan

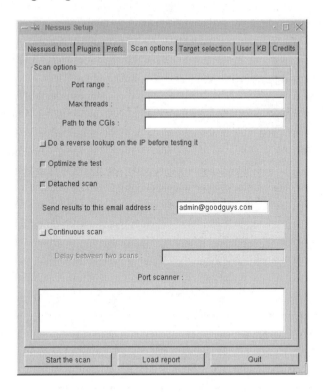

SECURITY ALERT!

Improper use of detached and differential scans can seriously impact
host and network performance. Be very careful when configuring these
options, or you may inadvertently conduct a DoS attack against your
own network.

Exercise: Conducting Detached and Differential Scans with Nessus

1. Make sure that the sendmail daemon is started:

```
/etc/rc.d      /init.d/sendmail start
```

2. Make sure that sendmail is in your path. If you are using the BASH shell, issue the following command:

```
echo $PATH
```

```
lots of output :/usr/sbin/
```

Another way to do this is to just type **which sendmail** and examine the full path to the executable. That path should be in the output of the echo $PATH command.

3. If sendmail is not in your path, enter the following:

```
PATH=$PATH:/usr/sbin
```

4. Now, open your Linux nessus client.

5. Log in to your nessus daemon.

> **NOTE**
>
> Make sure the nessus daemon is compiled to allow detached scans. Use the **/usr/local/sbin/nessusd-d** command to learn more about the daemon's configuration.

6. In the Linux Nessus client, select the plug-ins that you want to use. Configure any plug-ins as necessary.

7. Click on the **Scan options** tab, and select both the **Optimize the test** and **Detached scan** options. You will have to acknowledge that these scans can be dangerous.

8. Enter an e-mail address you can readily check in the **Send results to this email address** section.

9. When you have verified all settings, click **Start The Scan**. After some time, you will receive an e-mail report concerning the scan. If you receive no e-mail report, then the scan did not find any vulnerabilities.

10. Now, you are ready to do a differential scan. First, conduct a full scan of a host.

11. Once this scan has completed, click on the **KB tab** and select the **Enable KB saving**, **Reuse the knowledge bases about all the hosts for the test**, and **Only show differences with the previous scan** buttons.

12. Conduct your scan of the same host again.

13. The scan will not execute any new commands, because you have effectively told Nessus to skip these tests, because you already know about the weaknesses. Now, if you update Nessus and it receives additional plug-ins, only these plug-ins will be used for future scans. Be careful, however, with this setting. If you leave it enabled, Nessus will not conduct these scans on this host, which could lead you into a false sense of security.

14. Disable **KB saving** for now.

15. To enable continuous scans, prepare your scan, and then select the **Scan options** tab. Select the **Continuous scan** button, and then enter an appropriate value, such as 201600 for a weekly scan (every seven days). Next, begin your scan. The initial scan will begin and (eventually) finish, and then it will begin again automatically in seven days, if nessusd is still running and available.

Summary

In this chapter, you learned how to scan your operating system for viruses. You then learned more about how to stop DDoS attacks. Although applications such as Zombie Zapper are not foolproof, they can still help you prepare against such attacks. You should remain current about DDoS attacks and learn more about related tools that can help you recover from this type of security breach. This way, if a system is compromised, you can recover from the event in a graceful way, rather than simply shutting down your system.

You then learned how to scan your system's ports using tools such as Gnome Service Scan and Nmap. The latter program is somewhat more sophisticated, in that it allows you to learn the version of the operating system you are using, the open ports, and the system's TCP sequencing abilities. Nmap is an important tool to understand, because it is used in many other applications, including Cheops and Nessus.

Although not specifically a security application, Cheops enables you to monitor systems on your network, and provides a graphical map. This map is functional, in that you can then right-click on host icons to access these services. Finally, you learned how to use Nessus, a powerful vulnerability scanning tool. Nessus provides you with the ability to update its configuration, and is able to conduct detailed tests of any host on your network.

You now have a thorough understanding of the tools required to lock down and test your system's services. In the next chapter, you will learn more about how to enhance host and network logging so that you can discover if your system has been compromised.

Solutions Fast Track

Scanning for Viruses Using the AntiVir Antivirus Application

☑ Virus scanners will perform the following tasks: check the system's boot record; search directories and subdirectories; automatically delete infected files; save scans into a log file; use an internal scheduler, or an external scheduler, such as at or cron; scan NFS-mounted drives; delete infected files; and move infected files to a central, "quarantine" area of your own choosing.

☑ The AntiVir for Servers binary is a truly impressive command-line virus scanner sold by H+BDEV. It is capable of searching for and deleting macro viruses, boot sector viruses, e-mail viruses, and DDoS daemons.

☑ An antivirus application is only as useful as its virus definition file. Your application should provide you with frequent updates.

Scanning Systems for DDoS Attack Software Using a Zombie Zapper

☑ Attackers wage denial of service (DoS) attacks by first finding and hacking into insecure systems on the Internet. Then, they install programs such as Tribe Flood Network 2000 (Tfn2k), stacheldraht, and others. The compromised systems now have illicit programs installed on them called *zombies*.

☑ Once a zombie is commanded to attack a victim, it will generally continue the attack until it is forced to stop. If you notice large amounts of unknown traffic when you monitor your network or network perimeter, you can use a zombie zapper against the host or hosts generating this traffic.

☑ Limitations of a zombie zapper can include the following: they are programmed to shut down only certain DDoS servers; it may be blocked by a firewall; the malicious user may have changed the password of the illicit server; or the attack server may have spoofed packets.

Scanning System Ports Using the Gnome Service Scan Port Scanner

☑ Systems administrators find port scanners useful when auditing their own systems. Although a simple port scanner such as GSS does not actually test for flaws in binaries and Web applications, a good port scanner can help you isolate which ports are open, and then take any action that is necessary.

☑ Port scanning a machine may set off an alarm for the system's administrator, who might take a dim view of your actions. Unless you have explicit (sometimes, even written) permission from the system administrator, you may cause a serious violation of your security policy.

Using Nmap

☑ Nmap is an advanced Unix-based port scanner. It can be used to audit your network, test your router and switch configurations, test your firewall configurations, and identify the nature of suspicious remote systems.

☑ You can use Nmap as a basic port scanner for a system on your internal network, or you can have it identify the operating system version of a remote system on another firewall-protected network. Nmap is capable of manipulating aspects of TCP to hide its scans from firewalls.

☑ Nmap's "interactive mode" allows you to do two things that you should be aware of as a systems administrator: It can conduct multiple Nmap sessions, and it can disguise the fact that it is running on your system.

Using Nmapfe as a Graphical Front End

☑ The Nmap Front End (NmapFE) provides a well-written, stable GUI that allows you to control almost every aspect of Nmap.

☑ Note that this interface is somewhat unstable, and given to faults that lead to complete crashes (core dumps). This is especially the case in systems that have been upgraded (say, from Red Hat version 7.0 to 7.1).

Using Remote Nmap as a Central Scanning Device

☑ Remote Nmap (Rnmap) enables a client system to connect to a central Nmap server. It is currently in beta, but both the client and the server are quite strong.

☑ Rnmap has the following features: user authentication, a command-line and GUI client, and available encryption (still in beta form). Rnmap is written in the Python scripting language, which means that your Linux system must have Python installed.

Deploying Cheops to Monitor Your Network

☑ Billed as a graphical network neighborhood, Cheops is related to applications such as HP OpenView. Both Cheops and HP OpenView allow you to create a graphical map of the network, and then manage any host on that map. Although Cheops is not nearly as sophisticated, it still allows you to quickly learn which hosts are up on a particular network segment.

☑ Cheops issues network broadcasts, and then processes these replies to discover remote hosts. Some older versions of Cheops use an application called Queso to read the replies of remote systems. Queso is similar to Nmap, although not as sophisticated or as recent. As with Nmap, Queso does use stack fingerprinting to guess the operating system of a remote server.

☑ Cheops is capable of two types of monitoring. First, it can have your Linux system issue simple ping requests to see if a remote host is up. Second, instead of relying on a crude ping request, Cheops allows you to pick a specific service offered by the remote host.

Deploying Nessus to Test Daemon Security

☑ Using vulnerability detection software, you can find out exactly what specific application is listening on that port. A good hacker is well informed concerning the popular servers on the Internet, and can quickly take advantage of a specific daemon that has a security problem. Nessus allows you to proactively scan your system to determine its weaknesses.

☑ The Nessus client allows you to connect to the Nessus daemon, which is usually on a remote server. Several different clients exist, including those for Windows, Macintosh, and Unix/Linux systems.

☑ The Nessus project has been quite active, and has a good record for providing regular plug-in updates.

☑ When you launch the client for the first time, it will take some time to create a public key pair, which will be used to authenticate with any Nessus daemon.

☑ The compilation option allows the client to "remember" past sessions and to configure a nessus daemon to conduct a scan all by itself. These capabilities are respectively called *differential* and *detached* scanning. The ability to save sessions allows you to begin sessions that have been interrupted.

Frequently Asked Questions

The following Frequently Asked Questions, answered by the authors of this book, are designed to both measure your understanding of the concepts presented in this chapter and to assist you with real-life implementation of these concepts. To have your questions about this chapter answered by the author, browse to **www.syngress.com/solutions** and click on the **"Ask the Author"** form.

Q: I have downloaded and compiled AntiVir. However, it says that I am running in "non-key mode," and won't allow me to scan any subdirectories off the /directory. Why not?

A: You need to obtain the license key from www.hbedv.com. You can either purchase a license, or use the private license, if you are qualified. Once you obtain this key, rerun AntiVir. You will see that the "non-key mode" message no longer appears. This key will also allow you to obtain an update every two months. If you do not want to obtain a license, you can still scan each subdirectory manually.

Q: Although I can compile and configure TkAntivir, I can't seem to get it to run. I was able to start it, and saw the "splash screen," but then I saw nothing. What is wrong?

A: Some window manager environments do not support TkAntivir well. Try running TkAntivir in Gnome or KDE. In addition, you need to have sufficient resolution (at least 800 x 600) in order for TkAntivir to run.

Q: The configuration script for TkAntivir crashes every time I run it. What can I do?

A: Make sure that you have the correct libraries and resolution for the program. See the instructions earlier in this chapter, as well as information at the TkAntivir site (www.geiges.de/tkantivir). If your system supports RPM files, try using RPM instead.

Q: Is it legal for me to scan other people's systems using Gnome Service Scan or Nmap?

A: While legal issues are rather complex, it is never acceptable to scan systems that are not your own. You should scan only those systems for which you are directly responsible. You can also scan any system if you have been given explicit permission to do so.

Q: When using Rnmap, I keep getting an "Access is denied message." Why?

A: You must add a user using the **./rnmap–adduser** command. You can receive this message only if Rnmap is running. Otherwise, you would receive a "Can't connect to remote host" message. A common mistake is to assume that the GUI interface will remember the password. This is not the case, and you will have to re-enter the password each time you want to connect to the remote Rnmap server.

Q: I want to enable KB saving sessions for Nessus, but I can't see the KB tab. Which client has this tab?

A: You must manually compile KB and session-saving support. If you installed Nessus using an RPM, these features are not enabled.

## Chapter 4

Implementing an Intrusion Detection System

Solutions in this chapter:

- **Understanding IDS Strategies and Types**
- **Installing Tripwire to Detect File Changes**
- **Updating Tripwire to Account for Legitimate Changes in the OS**
- **Configuring Tripwire to Inform You Concerning Changes**
- **Deploying PortSentry to Act as a Host-Based IDS**
- **Configuring PortSentry to Block Users**
- **Optimizing PortSentry to Sense Attack Types**
- **Installing and Configuring Snort**
- **Running Snort as a Network-Based IDS**
- **Configuring Snort to Log to a Database**
- **Identifying Snort Add-Ons**
- ☑ **Summary**
- ☑ **Solutions Fast Track**
- ☑ **Frequently Asked Questions**

Introduction

Perhaps the best way to ensure system security is to have your system or network report certain changes to you. In this chapter, you will learn more about open source intrusion detection tools that can help you detect activity at the system and network level.

Chances are, your home or place of work has an alarm system. A home alarm is an intrusion detection device. Generally a system device at your home—or at your place of work or in your car—will do the following:

- Accept programming to work reliably when you are away.

- Actively monitor the likely break-in points.

- Use motion sensors to aid in monitoring an empty home.

- Detect an unwanted intruder.

- Send an alert to you or a trusted third party in case of an event.

In regards to computing, an *Intrusion Detection System* (IDS) is any system or set of systems that has the ability to detect a change in the status of your system or network. An IDS can then send you alerts or take appropriate predefined actions to help you protect your network. In the introduction to this book, you learned that an IDS *auditing station* can monitor traffic. An IDS can be something as simple as a network host using a simple application, such as Tcpdump, to learn about the condition of a network, or it can be a more complex system that uses multiple hosts to help capture, process, and analyze traffic. Because an IDS can contain multiple hosts and applications, this chapter often uses the term *IDS application* to refer to a specific IDS element. Generally, an IDS will have the following five elements:

- **An information gathering device** One of the IDS elements must have the ability to capture data. For example, it must be able to detect changes on a hard drive, capture network packets, or read open system files.

- **An internal process monitoring mechanism** The IDS should have the ability to monitor itself and conduct self checks so that it can inform you (or a person you designate) that it is working properly. For example, Tripwire can warn you about a problem by using **cron** to alert you that the database is missing. An IDS such as Snort can inform you about problems by sending messages to the /var/log/messages file.

- **Information storage capability** The IDS must be able to store the network packet information it obtains in a carefully organized way that allows you to store data in an organized manner.

- **A command and control device** The IDS must provide a way for you to easily control its behavior.

- **An analysis device** The IDS should provide you with the ability to search your organized data store using queries and/or applications.

You will see in the following sections how each of these IDS elements is implemented.

Tools & Traps...

False Alarms

If your car alarm system is like most others, it sometimes goes off because it mistakes legitimate activity for a break-in. And, the alarm will usually go off at the most inconvenient time possible. Especially at first, you will find that your IDS will mistake legitimate activity for an attack. Whenever an IDS triggers an alert by mistake, it is said to have generated a *false positive*. Generally, a false positive is caused by any one (or more) of the following:

- The IDS application has been improperly configured so that it reacts to legitimate traffic.

- The type of network traffic has changed, and the IDS is unaware of the change.

- You need to update the IDS application. Sometimes an update means that you have to edit the configuration file. In other cases, you will need to download new plug-ins and files so that the IDS application is able to cope with new types of network data or new signatures.

- It is the nature of the beast. Sometimes, an IDS application just won't be as reliable as you'd like. It is the nature of most IDS applications to make mistakes, because IDS applications are just barely leaving their infancy. Even the most costly and perfectly marketed IDS is bound to generate false positives;

Continued

this problem has nothing to do with the nature of open source applications.

So, as you go about installing IDS applications, you will at first be very pleased that you are logging anything at all. You will be excited that you are receiving alerts about internet Control Message Protocol (ICMP) packets and User Datagram Protocol (UDP) echoes. After a while, however, you will find yourself hoping that you can make all of this information cohere into something useful. At this point, you will begin to tell a true alert from a false positive.

Understanding IDS Strategies and Types

Two general strategies are used when it comes to detecting intrusions:

- **Rule-based IDS applications (also called signature-based)** This is the most common type of IDS, mainly because it is easier to install. After you are able to get the IDS to load all of the signatures properly, you are on your way to establishing an effective IDS. The challenge in regards to a signature-based IDS is making sure that the rules remain current. Similar to an anti-virus application, if you have old signatures, the IDS will not capture and react to the latest attacks.

- **Anomaly-based IDS applications** This type of IDS first spends time gathering a sample of baseline (acceptable) network activity. The IDS stores this information in a database, then responds to traffic that falls outside the accepted baseline of activity. This type of IDS application is generally more challenging to configure, because it is rather difficult to determine exactly what "acceptable" and "normal" is, in regards to network traffic.

Rule-based IDS applications sometimes rely upon the terms *rule* and *signature,* which are used interchangeably. Traditionally, the term *signature* refers to an actual attack that has been identified. Any time, for example, that a port scan occurs, the fact that a number of ports have been scanned in a short period of time comprises a signature. A *rule,* on the other hand, is the piece of code that you use to inform your IDS application about a specific signature. Therefore, a rule enables an IDS to recognize an attack, log it, then send out alerts and/or reconfigure operating system or firewall parameters.

IDS applications do their work either continuously in "real-time," or at certain intervals. *Real-time* intrusion detection is often useful in the following cases:

- You are using a host-based IDS application, and you wish to supplement your host's security.

- Your network has had a history of attacks, and you wish to use your network-based IDS application to trace and/or stop them.

- You have systems that are capable of logging large amounts of traffic.

- You have the time to check all of the logs generated by the IDS.

Continuous intrusion detection may seem to be the only real option, but this is not always the case. This strategy can often provide too much information, and so you may want to enact *interval-based* intrusion detection. Possible times to activate your IDS may include:

- Any time when you are not able to monitor traffic, such as after your regularly scheduled work times and during weekends and holidays.

- At random times during the regular workday. This strategy reduces the amount of log files, yet also gives you an idea of what is happening on your network.

You may also wish to have your IDS application generate new log files after a certain period of time. For example, if you are logging to a database, have the IDS archive its log files and begin a new log file. This way, you can search through a manageable 2MB log file, as opposed to a monstrous 2GB file.

IDS Types

Although there are many different IDS application vendors, two different types of IDS applications exist:

- **Host-based** An IDS application that either scans system logs and open network connections, or that scans the hard disk and then alerts you if an event occurs.

- **Network-based** An IDS application that listens for traffic as it passes across the network.

Host-Based IDS Applications

As you might suspect, a host-based IDS application resides on a single network host and then monitors activity specific to that one host. All host-based IDS applications run as daemons. Two types of host-based IDS applications exist:

- Log analyzers
- System drive analyzers

Log analysis IDS applications generally run as daemons and scan log files in real time. They search for open network connections, and/or monitor the ports on your system. Each time a port is opened, the log analysis IDS application will then listen in to find out what is happening on these ports.

System drive analyzers scan a system's hard drives and other peripherals (removable drives, tape drives, print devices, and so forth) and then create a database. This database contains a record of the "original" condition of the system's hard drives, for example. Then, whenever the drive analyzer detects a change, it can take action by, for example, logging the change or sending an alert.

All host-based IDS applications require some sort of policy file that determines the behavior of the application.

Network-Based IDS Applications

Network-based applications operate at the application through network layers of the Open Systems Interconnection Reference Model (OSI/RM). They have become quite popular, because it is generally considered that they are the easiest to configure, and most network administrators simply like being able to look at all of the network packets as they cross the network. However, after the novelty of seeing the packets wears off, more-seasoned professionals realize that network-based IDS applications tend to generate a great deal of traffic, which few people take the time to properly analyze. Still, network-based IDS applications are extremely helpful when you wish to analyze network traffic.

Although not necessary, using several different hosts when creating a network-based IDS application is often wise. The use of multiple hosts can help ensure that you have enough processing power and storage space to properly capture, store, and analyze traffic. Figure 4.1 shows how a network IDS can break up these duties among several different systems on the network.

The network IDS shown in Figure 4.1 greatly simplifies the flow of information in a network-based IDS. As network traffic is generated, the sensor pulls the packets into the host. Then, the Monitor and Storage host pulls the file that contains the packets from the sensor. The Analyzer/Control station can then either read the packets where they are stored, or it can actually pull selected log files from the Monitor and Storage station.

Figure 4.1 A Sample Intrusion Detection System

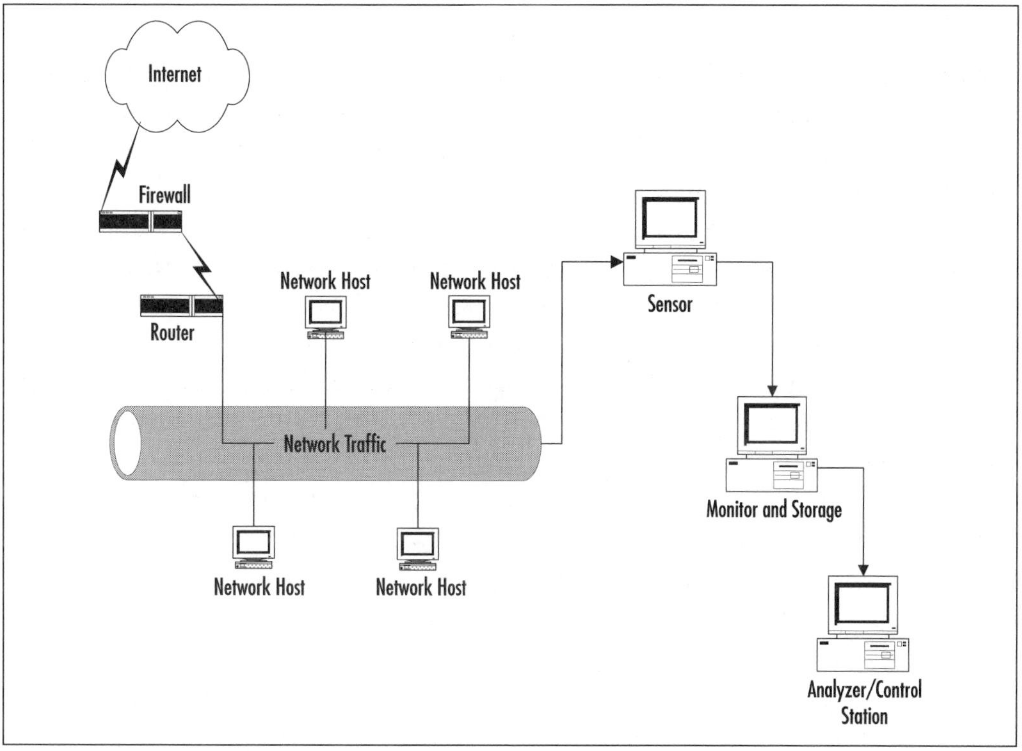

IDS Applications and Fault Tolerance

You may be asking yourself why anyone would use so many systems just to implement an IDS. It is important that your IDS does not have a single point of failure. The use of redundant systems provides fault tolerance and enhanced performance. In regards to fault tolerance, a dedicated system—such as an IDS sensor—will generally fail less often than a system responsible for multiple responsibilities, such as a single system that is responsible for monitoring, storage, and analysis. The principle that applies to computing also applies to mechanical devices, such as engines: The more moving parts you have, the greater the chance that one of these parts will fail. When it comes to computing, distributing tasks among several different machines actually reduces the chance of a problem.

Distributing tasks ensures that if one element fails, then your IDS has not been completely shut down. For example, should the Analyzer/Control station fail, intrusion detection will still occur, because the sensor can still grab packets. If the Monitor and Storage station fails, the IDS will still be able to gather the information. Fixes can be made quickly, and you can concentrate on only one element of the broken IDS, rather than trying to figure out exactly which element has failed.

The information can stay on the Monitor and Storage device, or it can be brought to the Analyzer/Control station. The Monitor and Storage device may have all log files ready to be served up via a Web server. The Analyzer/Control station may be nothing more than a simple Linux host using a Web browser. The administrator at the Analyzer/Control station can then use a Web browser to access the Monitor and Storage device's Web server. Also, network administrators commonly use a program such as Secure Shell (SSH) to open a terminal-based connection and then query the database or log files directly.

Of course, dividing tasks even further between hosts is possible, or simply making one host responsible for all tasks. Ultimately, your management team is responsible for determining the needs for your network. As far as performance is concerned, consider that in many cases, an effective IDS application requires a great deal of processor time in order to work well. Log files require a great deal of hard drive space, especially in busy networks. Thus, simply for the sake of performance, consider using multiple systems to gather, store, and analyze information.

NOTE

Whenever you transfer information between different hosts, make sure that this information is encrypted and authenticated. If you do not do so, a malicious user may be able to "sniff" the network and gather sensitive information about your network. Information can include the passwords used to access systems, as well as the actual log files themselves.

Damage & Defense…

IDS Implementation

Three factors will determine your ability to implement an IDS:

- **Security policy** The very first thing that you should implement is a comprehensive security policy. Your security policy is the first tool necessary to implement any security measure.
- **Cost** Although an open source IDS can be very cost effective, you may not have enough resources available to implement a multiple-host IDS.
- **Support staff** Make sure that you have enough people to properly implement, maintain, and analyze the IDS you wish to implement. It is rather common for an IDS application to log activity, only to have the systems administrators ignore this information because they are too busy to read the logs.

NOTE

Most network-based IDS applications do not work properly in a switched network. Many systems administrators have voiced frustration that their IDSs don't work properly, only to learn that the reason is that the network uses virtual LANS (vlans), which do not broadcast traffic, as does a standard hub-based Ethernet network. You have several options, listed here in order of preference:

- Configure your network switch to allow one port to monitor all traffic, then plug your host into this monitor port.
- Find a location between the switch and the router, and plug in a standard hub.
- Obtain a network-based IDS, such as Ettercap (http://ettercap .sourceforge.net), that helps sniff traffic in switched networks.

The best option is to configure your switch so that it will monitor all traffic. Introducing a new piece of hardware can increase network latency and even introduce security problems, if you do not enforce sufficient physical security.

What Can an IDS Do for Me?

Thus far, you have learned about IDS responsibilities in a general way. An IDS can provide the services presented in Table 4.1.

Table 4.1 Services Provided by an IDS

Service	Description
Traffic identification	An IDS application must always accurately identify the nature of the break-in or the nature of the traffic, including source and destination ports and addresses.
Logging enhancement and threshold enforcement	Most IDS applications require that you establish limits. After a limit (threshold) has been exceeded, the IDS application will then send alerts and/or log behavior. An IDS generally extends your logging capability by placing additional information into a log file or into a database.
Alerting	An IDS often has the ability to send alert messages to the network administrator or responsible party.
System reconfiguration	Many IDS applications provide you with the ability to reconfigure the operating system or a firewall in case of an attack. For example, PortSentry has the ability to automatically update the /etc/hosts.deny file and effectively deny access to any services offered by xinetd.
Drive verification	This offers the ability to take a snapshot of the network or operating system, then send you alerts when an anomalous event occurs.

The following sections describe each of the IDS services in greater detail.

Traffic Identification

Perhaps the most important element of an IDS that logs network traffic is that it can inform you about all details of a packet that enters your network. A host-based IDS can identify the following items:

- **Protocol type** The IDS will inform you about the nature of packets on the network. It will report whether the packet is UDP, TCP, ICMP, and so forth.

- **Origin** The source IP address of the system. Hopefully, this is a source IP address that has not been spoofed.

- **Destination** Where the packet was sent.

- **Source port** If the packet is a UDP or TCP packet, the application will tell you which port the originating host used.

- **Destination port** For UDP and TCP packets, the port on the destination host.

- **Checksums** The checksums that guard the integrity of the transmitted packets.

- **Sequence numbers** If, for example, your network host receives a number of ping packets, the IDS can tell you the order in which they were generated. Understanding the sequence numbers can help you understand the nature of the attack.

- **Packet information** Many IDS applications can delve deep into the packet and analyze its contents.

One of the more useful elements of an IDS is that it can make educated guesses about the nature of traffic. Part of the ability to monitor traffic is the ability for the IDS to suggest that a portion of traffic may constitute a port scan or other network security problem. This can help you take steps to block it by, for example, reconfiguring the firewall or moving a network host.

Logging Enhancement

Logging enhancement is closely related to traffic identification, because most of the time, the additional information discussed earlier is placed in some sort of log file on the local system or on a remote system. Using enhanced logging information, you can conduct *tracebacks*, which give you the ability to learn the source of a network packet. Many times, however, achieving an accurate traceback is not possible, because more experienced hackers are able to spoof IP connections. Be careful: You may think that you have identified and caught a malicious user, but in fact, the person with the suspect IP address and host name may know nothing about the attacks waged against you.

An IDS provides a detailed audit trail. As a security administrator, it is your job to become a forensics expert—you get to slice open a connection log or packet and then view it for suspicious activity. Sometimes, this practice can be quite tedious, but the payoff is that you get peace of mind knowing the exact nature of packets entering your network and network hosts.

An IDS stores its information in several places:

- **System logs** Many IDS applications are configured to send messages directly to pre-existing system log files—such as /var/log/messages and /var/log/security—in Red Hat Linux, either directly or through syslog.

- **Simple text files and directories** Directories and text files that act just like /var/log/messages, but are specifically created by the IDS application. Sometimes, the IDS will create a separate directory for each new host it detects. Each directory could, for example, be named after the IP address of each host. The IDS will then populate the appropriate directory with separate files for each specific protocol used. This way, you can then identify the nature of the traffic on the network.

- **Databases** The most elegant way to store information is in a database. A database generally stores the information in a far more logical way, and it allows the information to be searched efficiently. After the information is stored in a database, it is then possible to port this information to a Web server, which makes it possible to read IDS information from any Web browser or use third-party analysis tools to analyze the gathered data.

Threshold Enforcement

When a threshold is met, an IDS can do several things. It can send the event to a special alert log file, send an alert to a remote system, send an e-mail, or even reconfigure a host or a firewall. Not all IDS applications have this ability, however. Many IDS applications can be configured to inform you about sudden increases in traffic, or if traffic appears threatening. For example, you can configure your IDS to log ICMP traffic into a special database or to inform you via e-mail about a specific login.

File System Integrity Verification

Host-based IDS applications such as Tripwire are able to take a snapshot of your file systems, then compare their later condition to that snapshot. You can then identify whether certain sensitive files have been altered. Such file system verification software is useful for guarding against Trojan horses, which are malicious applications designed to appear as legitimate applications, such as su, ls, and ps.

If you have been able to protect your operating system with an application such as Tripwire, all but the most subtle and sophisticated attempts to substitute a Trojan horse for a legitimate application will fail.

Which IDS Strategy Is Best?

By now, you probably get the idea that no one IDS application or method is "the best." Many different types of IDS applications exist, and as with any other task, you must use the right tool for the right job. Security professionals commonly say that, for example, PortSentry is a bit crude compared to Snort. This is not the case at all. PortSentry is a very useful tool, as long as you use it as intended: It is designed to identify traffic and log it to a central console. It can then send alerts and block traffic. However, it is not designed to detect attacks as they travel across your network. To detect traffic as it passes across your network, you will want a network-based IDS, such as Snort.

Thus, arguing that one application is more useful or sophisticated than another is impractical. Rather, it is appropriate to say that PortSentry is useful when protecting a specific host, and that Snort is useful for detecting problems with network traffic. If you combine PortSentry with Tripwire, you will have a system that informs you of all port scans and file changes.

Thus far, you have learned about the hardware and software necessary to implement an IDS. Don't forget that the "wetware"—the people who implement the IDS—are an essential component to your success. In fact, you and your well-trained support staff are probably the most important part of an IDS. The IDS hardware and software are really nothing more than tools.

Network-Based IDS Applications and Firewalls

No IDS can act as a replacement for a firewall. A firewall is the primary means of establishing perimeter security, as you will see in Chapter 9. A firewall can block and allow traffic, depending upon your wishes. IDS technology is not at all suited for this. The primary function of an IDS is to monitor internal network traffic.

An IDS can, however, act as a supplement to a firewall, because it can help you monitor traffic on the internal network. Sometimes, it may be useful to place an IDS application outside the firewall, or in the DMZ so that you can learn more about the attacks waged against the firewall itself. However, in this case, the IDS is not acting as a firewall in any way. In such cases, your IDS is acting as an attack detection device.

One of the most common strategies is the practice of allowing your IDS application to reconfigure the firewall in case of an attack. For example, the IDS application can communicate with the firewall and ask it to automatically close a port or block a host. This functionality, however, is not readily available in open source firewalls. You will have to create custom scripts to do this, right now.

IDS Applications

Table 4.2 provides a list of common IDS applications: Some of these are not open source IDS applications, but they are listed to give you an idea of what you can choose.

Table 4.2 Common IDS Applications

IDS Product Name	Description
NetProwler (Symantec) www.Symantec.com	A network-based IDS product designed to provide alerts and to work with additional Symantec offerings, such as Enterprise Security Manager (ESM).
RealSecure (Internet Security Systems) www.iss.net	Considered to be one of the first commercial network-based IDS applications.
eTrust Intrusion Detection (Computer Associates) www.cai.com	A popular network-based IDS application, due to its ease of use.
Network Flight Recorder (NFR Security) www.nfr.com	One of the more highly-regarded network-based IDS applications, mainly because its developers have written the code for specific hardware platforms. This IDS application has roots in the open source community.
Snort (open source) www.snort.org	Widely considered to be one of the more flexible and reliable lightweight network-based IDS applications.
Shadow (open source) www.nswc.navy.mil/ISSEC/CID	A collection of Perl scripts and Web pages that can help you log and analyze scanning attacks that have occurred over a long period of time (for example, port scans that have occurred over a period of days or weeks).
Tripwire (Tripwire, Inc., open source) www.tripwire.com	A host-based IDS designed to inform you concerning files that have changed.
Ettercap (open source) http://ettercap.sourceforge.net/	A network-based sniffer designed to work in switched networks.
PortSentry (Psion, Inc.) www.psionic.com/abacus/portsentry and www.psionic.com/download	A host-based IDS application that listens to log files. It detects port scans and responds to them.

Continued

Table 4.2 Continued

IDS Product Name	Description
Hostsentry (Psion, Inc.) www.psionic.com/download	Another host-based IDS application that specifically searches log files for activity. If activity fits a signature, then Hostsentry will send an alert.

Many more IDS applications exist. You can learn more about additional open source IDS applications at the following sites:

- www.securityfocus.com
- http://packetstorm.securify.com
- www.linuxsecurity.com.

General Dependencies for Open Source IDS Applications

Most open source IDS applications require several supporting applications. These often include:

- **Tcpdump** www.tcpdump.org
- **Perl** www.perl.com
- **PreHypertext Processor, or PHP** www.php.net
- **Apache Server** www.apache.org
- **Databases, including PostgreSQL** www.postgresql.org or www.pgsql.com and MySQL www.mysql.com
- **Secure Shell** www.openssh.org
- **Supporting libraries, such as Libnet, Tcl/Tk, and pcap**

The IDS you choose will inform you concerning any additional applications or libraries you require. Now that you have received a rundown of the important IDS elements, you can begin implementing them on your Linux systems.

NOTE

One of the most important things to remember in regards to an IDS is that it should never affect system or network performance. Unless you have a compelling reason, you should not "double up" on a machine by making it, say, a firewall and an IDS application at the same time. An IDS can be an effective *supplement* to a firewall. Just make sure that the IDS resides on a separate system, and you will not encounter any performance problems.

Installing Tripwire to Detect File Changes

Tripwire is one of the most popular applications for determining when a file or directory has been altered. It scans your system's hard drive and creates a database. After its database has been created, Tripwire can conduct regular scans of your hard drive and inform you (via e-mail or a log file) about any changes. Tripwire does not inform you concerning changes as soon as they occur. Rather, Tripwire can be placed into integrity checking mode and will then inform you of any changes to the file. After it is working properly, you can then be confident that you know about any and all changes that have occurred on your hard drive. To use Tripwire, you should follow this process (which is briefly illustrated in Figure 4.2):

1. Install the binaries and configuration files.

2. Edit the /etc/tripwire/twpol.txt file.

3. Run the **/etc/tripwire/twinstall.sh** program, which creates a key pair and then allows you to secure all configuration files.

4. Run Tripwire in database initialization mode. Tripwire will scan your system and use message digests to create signatures for the files you specify. Whenever Tripwire creates its database, it is said to enter *database initialization mode.*

5. You can then set Tripwire to rescan these files and compare their signatures to the signatures stored in the database. This is called *integrity checking mode.* If a file has changed, Tripwire can inform you about the change. By default, you can check a text file. You can, of course, specify additional options, including having Tripwire send you an e-mail informing you of any changes.

Figure 4.2 Using Tripwire

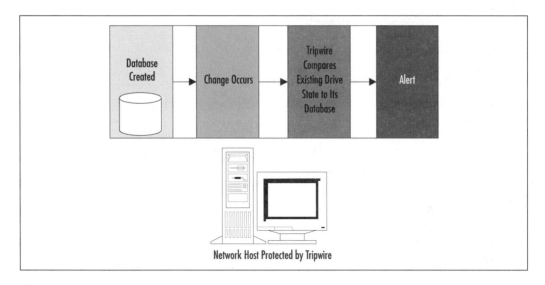

Tripwire Dependencies

Tripwire does not require any specialized daemons or applications. All of the following are standard to most Linux implementations:

- sed
- grep
- awk
- gzip version 2.3 or higher
- tar
- gawk

Availability

You can obtain Tripwire from the following sources:

- At www.tripwire.org
- At http://sourceforge.net/projects/tripwire
- On the accompanying CD (tripwire-2.3-47.i386.tar.gz)

A commercial version is available at the www.tripwire.com site. This site also offers for-fee services for those who can afford to hire consultants to configure Tripwire. The developers of Tripwire wrote the application to work on many platforms, including most Linux flavors (Red Hat, SuSE, Slackware, Caldera, and so forth). You can download Tripwire as a tarball or in the RPM format. As of this writing, the Tripwire site recommends installing the RPM for Linux systems.

Deploying Tripwire

To properly configure Tripwire, you must take the following three steps:

1. Install the Tripwire binaries and configuration files.
2. Configure the Tripwire policy file.
3. Create the database by conducting an initial run of the Tripwire binary.

After you have taken these three steps, you can then run the tripwire binary from cron so that it conducts regular scans.

Tripwire Files

Here is a list of Tripwire files that you will become familiar with as you deploy them in your Linux/Unix systems:

- **/usr/sbin/tripwire** The tripwire binary responsible for reading, creating, and updating the database.

- **/etc/tripwire/twpol.txt** The Tripwire policy configuration file. This file is not the actual file Tripwire uses when it runs. Rather, it contains the instructions that determine what the /etc/tw.pol file will contain.

- **/etc/tw.pol** The signed Tripwire policy file. Tripwire reads this file to determine what it will place into its database.

- **/etc/tripwire/twinstall.sh** The file that signs the /etc/tripwire/ twpol.txt and /etc/tripwire/twcfg.txt files. It also configures password information for Tripwire.

- **/etc/tripwire/twcfg.txt** Configures the environment for the /usr/sbin/tripwire binary. You will usually not need to edit this file.

- **/var/lib/tripwire/hostname.twd** The default location of the Tripwire database file. You can change this location, if you wish. All you have to do is tell the Tripwire binary the location of the database. In fact, storing the database on a different device than the hard drive is a good idea. The first thing a reasonably talented hacker will do after obtaining root is find and erase the database. In the past, many systems administrators would place the database on a write-protected floppy disk. However, many Tripwire databases are very large (over 2 MB), so placing the database onto a more permanent read-only volume—such as a CD—is far more practical. A CD is also more appropriate, because a floppy disk is bound to fail more frequently than a CD.

Tripwire Installation Steps

Figure 4.3 shows the steps to take when installing the Tripwire binary. First, the **rpm –qpil** command lists the contents of the RPM package. Then, when you install Tripwire using the **rpm –ivh** command, you will be informed that you must edit the /etc/trwipwire/twpol.txt file. Then, run the **/etc/tripwire/ twinstall.sh** command to create a key pair and then sign all Tripwire files for the sake of security. Make sure that you do not forget the password you choose, or you will not be able to use Tripwire.

Although installation seems straightforward, make sure to read the configuration information so that you can customize Tripwire to suit your own situation.

Configuring the Tripwire Policy File

The Tripwire policy file, /etc/tripwire.twpol.txt, is configured to read all files found in a Red Hat 7.*x* installation. You can use a simple text editor to customize the file. You have many options available to you. Table 4.3 shows the most important options.

Figure 4.3 Installing Tripwire

Table 4.3 Tripwire Configuration File Examples

Option	Description
/etc/shadow -> $(IgnoreNone);	Any file followed by the **IgnoreNone** argument will be checked by Tripwire's "paranoid mode," which means that any and all changes will be reported to you. You must place a semi-colon after any directory name.
!/proc;	Informs Tripwire to ignore the /proc directory. It is recommended that you not check the integrity of the /proc directory, because it is a virtual file system.

Continued

Table 4.3 Continued

Option	Description
!/~james/Desktop;	This particular setting shows how it is possible to ignore all contents of a subdirectory (in this case, the Desktop subdirectory of the james home directory. The Desktop directory is for the X Window environment, and will likely change often. It is also possible to specify a single file, as opposed to a single directory.
"/home/fred/big file" -> +pingus;	This syntax shows how it is possible to specify a file that has spaces in it.
/etc -> +ug (emailto=james@stanger.com, severity=50);	Allows you to have your system send you an e-mail report in case anything in the /etc/ directory changes. Such options are useful only if you are reasonably sure that you do not want any changes to occur on the /etc/ directory (or whatever directory you wish to specify).
/var/log/messages -> $(Growing);	Tells Tripwire that the it is expected for the /var/log/ messages file to grow in size. However, Tripwire will still inform you if the file gets smaller or is erased.
/etc -> +ug (rulename=etc);	Tells Tripwire to check the /etc directory for basic changes in user and group settings and then organizes any output into a section named etc.

The default file, /etc/tripwire/twpol.txt, contains a rather complex structure that has the following variables, among others:

- **SEC_CRIT** The same as **$(IgnoreNone) –Sha;** which is for files that cannot be changed.

- **SIG_LOW** The same as severity **33;** which is for files of lesser importance.

- **SIG_MED** The same as severity **66;** which is for files of moderate importance.

- **SIG_HI** The same as severity **100;** which is for files of highest importance.

You can change these values at will. For more specific information about the options, consult the Tripwire man page, or read the /usr/doc/tripwire/policyguide.txt file.

If, for example, you have just installed Cheops to monitor your network, include the path to the Cheops binary and databases. Then, after you run Tripwire, you can be reasonably sure that no one has replaced this file with a Trojan. Also, you may not want to scan the entire hard drive. Rather, you may want to concentrate only on certain commonly-used binaries.

You should then use /usr/sbin/twadmin to sign the configuration file you are using. This way, you will be able to test it to see if someone has altered the file without your permission.

Creating the Tripwire Policy File

After you have installed Tripwire and edited the /etc/tripwire/twpol.txt, you are ready to begin the initial scan. Simply run the /etc/tripwire/twinstall.sh script, which should already be executable. It will then create the Tripwire configuration file. The twinstall.sh process will do the following:

- Create site and local host key pairs, which allow you to ensure that your Tripwire files are secure.

- Create the /etc/twpol file, which is what Tripwire will use when it enters database initialization mode.

- Create backup copies of the /etc/twpol.txt file, which you should secure so that no one can alter them.

Database Initialization Mode

After you have created a policy file, you can then enter database initialization mode by using the following command:

```
tripwire --init
```

This command creates the actual Tripwire database, as shown in Figure 4.4.

Figure 4.4 Creating the Tripwire Database

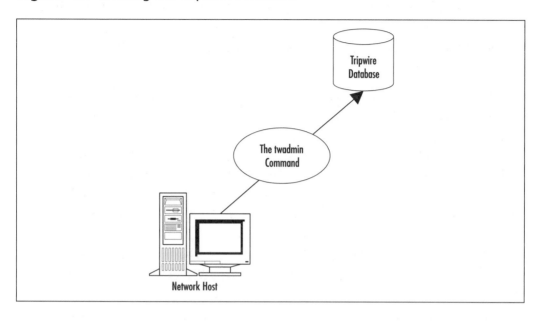

You will then be asked to enter your passphrases. It is possible to specify additional options at the command line, but this is usually not necessary. Tripwire will then default to reading its configuration file (/etc/tripwire/tw.pol). If you wish to use an alternative policy file named altpolfile.pol, you can issue the following command:

```
tripwire --init  --polfile altpolfile.pol
```

For additional information, you can read the tripwire man page, or you can issue the following command:

```
tripwire --help init
```

Depending upon the number of directories and files you specify, creating the database can take a significant period of time. For example, it took over an hour to create the database for an 18GB file on an 850Mhz Pentium III system using the default configuration file. After editing the policy configuration file to check only selected files in the /etc/ directory (such as /etc/passwd, /etc/shadow, and the cron directories), initializing the database took about a minute.

Testing E-Mail Capability

Earlier, you learned how to enter an emailto= entry into the policy configuration file. To ensure that your version of Tripwire can actually send e-mail, issue the following command, making sure to substitute your own e-mail address:

```
tripwire --test --email youraccount@mailhost.com
```

Tripwire will send a simple test message to the account you specify. If you receive the e-mail, you know Tripwire is working.

Integrity Checking Mode

After you have created the database, you can run Tripwire in integrity checking mode. You can either run the command manually or create a cron entry. To start Tripwire in integrity checking mode, issue the following command:

```
tripwire --check
```

It generally takes as much time to check the hard drive as it did to create the database. About the only significant difference between creating the database and checking integrity using the **-check** option is that you will not have to enter a password. If you have configured Tripwire to send an e-mail message by placing an emailto= entry into the /etc/tripwire/twpol.txt file, use the **-M** option:

```
tripwire --check -M
```

To automate the process, create a simple text file named *tripwire* and enter the following text:

```
#!/bin/bash
# Script to run Tripwire every week.


/usr/sbin/tripwire --check -s -M
```

The added option, **-s**, has Tripwire forego sending a report to standard output. You will not need to see this output, because this script will likely be run when you are not logged on. Cron runs as root, so this command will run as long as you use chmod to make it executable, and you place the file into any of the following directories:

- /etc/cron.hourly/
- /etc/cron.daily/

- /etc/cron.weekly/
- /etc/cron.monthly/

You can, of course, create a root-owned crontab file by using the crontab **-e** command as root, or you can create the appropriate file for the /etc/cron.d/ directory.

Specifying a Different Database

If you choose to burn the Tripwire database onto a CD, you will have to specify the location of the database:

```
/usr/sbin/tripwire --check -d /dev/cdrom/hostname.twd  -s -M
```

Reading Reports

If you choose not to mail reports to your e-mail account, you can check them by reading the report files Tripwire generates. Reports are stored in the /var/lib/ tripwire/ directory. If you have not activated e-mail, you can read the report by issuing the following command:

```
/usr/sbin/twprint --print-report -r
    /var/lib/tripwire/report/filename.twr
```

Tripwire will create a separate report for each scan. File names are a combination of the host name and the time the report was generated.

Updating Tripwire to Account for Legitimate Changes in the OS

Eventually, legitimate changes will occur to your operating system. These changes will keep appearing in reports unless you update your database. Database update mode allows you to update the database so that it no longer recognizes any differences between itself and the operating system. Many systems administrators make the rookie mistake of completely rewriting the database by using the following command:

```
twadmin --create-polfile /etc/tripwire/twpol.txt
```

This command is a mistake because it also requires you to re-initialize (in effect, rewrite) the entire database, which can result in lost information, especially if a security breach has occurred. The proper way to update the Tripwire database is to use the following command:

```
tripwire -m u -r /var/lib/tripwire/reportyourreport.twr
```

You will then be placed into "interactive mode," which is where the report will be opened in the vi editor. You can then scroll through the report and determine which events you wish to have Tripwire ignore. As you scroll down the text file, you will see that each change has a checkbox with an X in it. Tripwire, for some reason, calls this the *ballot box*. If you leave the X as is, the event will no longer be reported. If you enter edit mode in vi (just press **Esc** and then the letter **I**), you can erase the X, which means that Tripwire will still report the event.

Updating the Policy

Updating the policy is different than updating the database. sometimes, you may need to update your policy. If, for example, you install a new application, you may want to ensure that these files are protected by Tripwire. To update the policy, you would first edit the policy file (usually /etc/tripwire/twpol.txt) to suit your needs, then issue the following command:

```
tripwire -m p /etc/tripwire/twpol.txt
```

You must use this option to update the /etc/tripwire/twpol.txt file. If you change the policy file by manually editing the file and then use the **twadmin --create-polfile** command to update the file, you will cause inconsistencies in the database that can cause Tripwire to misreport information, even if you re-initialize the database.

NOTE

Skipping the scan of the /proc directory is generally a good idea. Also, because cron is such a powerful daemon, you should consider scanning the cron directories and files in the /etc/ directory. Directories include /etc/cron.d, /etc/cron.daily, /etc/cron.hourly, /etc/cron.monthly, and /etc/cron.weekly. Make sure that you also scan the crontab file.

What Do I Do if I Find a Discrepancy?

If you find that a file has been altered without your permission, you can do the following:

- Edit the file so that it is back to its original configuration.

- Replace the suspect file with a clean copy from a backup or installation media.

- Consider removing the altered system from the network.

- Conduct a full audit of the operating system to ensure that additional changes have not been made.

- Change your system password.

Configuring Tripwire to Inform You Concerning Changes

Now that you have an understanding of the moves required to make Tripwire effective for you, it is time to actually implement the application. As with any Linux/Unix application, you will have to do quite a bit of "tweaking" to make this application suit your needs.

Exercise: Installing Tripwire

1. Obtain the Tripwire RPM file either from the CD that accompanies this book (tripwire-2.3-47.i386.tar.gz—the file looks like a tarball, but it is actually a gzipped RPM), or from www.tripwire.org, or from the other sites discussed earlier in this chapter.

2. Make a copy of the /etc/tripwire/twpol.txt file and call it /etc/tripwire/twpol.orig. You are going to edit the original file, and you want to have the original handy in case something goes wrong.

3. After you are finished installing, open the /etc/tripwire/twpol.txt file and edit it to your needs. We highly recommend that you eliminate all references to files that do not actually belong on your system. We also highly recommend that you use the ! sign to ensure that the /proc directory is not read. Finally, add the following line, which has Tripwire report any and all changes to the /etc/shadow file:

```
/etc/shadow                              -> +pinusgamctdbCMSH
   (emailto=youraccount@youremailserver.com);
```

Make sure that you enter this information all in one line, and that you substitute your own e-mail information.

4. Run the /etc/tripwire/twinstall.sh script and enter the site and local passwords. Write down the passwords here, in case you forget:

Site password: _____

Local password: _____

5. When you are finished, initialize the database using the instructions given earlier in this chapter.

6. Test whether Tripwire can send e-mail using the instructions given earlier in this chapter.

7. After you know that Tripwire is able to send e-mail, test your configuration by adding a new user and changing the password. Unless you add an emailto= value to the /etc/passwd entry, you will have to change the password in order to alter the /etc/shadow file.

8. Issue the following command to have Tripwire perform an integrity check:

```
tripwire --check -M
```

9. After some time, Tripwire will complete its integrity scan. Check your e-mail to view a report. Alternatively, use the **twprint** command:

```
twprint --print-report -r /var/lib/tripwire/report/reportfile.twr
   |less
```

You will see that Tripwire will inform you about the change. Press **q** to quit the **less** command.

10. Run Tripwire again and perform an integrity check. You will see a very similar message.

11. You obviously know about this addition to the /etc/shadow file, and probably do not want to be informed about this change. Issue the following command to update the database:

```
tripwire -m u -r /var/lib/tripwire/report/reportfile.twr
```

Note that the file you specify should be the report from the latest integrity check.

12. You are now in vi, viewing the report. Deselect any file that you wish to continue hearing about. Otherwise, make no changes to the file. If you wish to make a change to the file, press **Esc** then **I** to enter insert mode. When you are finished, press **CTRL**, then **ZZ** to exit.

13. After you have exited, you will be asked for the password to the database. Enter it now.

14. Run Tripwire again in integrity check mode. You will see that any e-mail message you receive no longer contains a detailed reference to the /etc/shadow file. You will, however, see a message informing you about the fact that the file's access time has changed. This is because Tripwire is reading its own scan of the file. The fact that you no longer see information about how the file has been changed means that the database has been updated.

15. If you wish, modify the /etc/tripwire/twpol.txt file and eliminate the access timestamp value (a) from the /etc/shadow entry. The newly edited entry should read as follows:

```
+pinusgmctdbCMSH
```

16. Issue the following command to update the policy file:

```
tripwire -m p /etc/tripwire/twpol.txt
```

17. Run Tripwire in integrity check mode again. You will receive a report that no files have changed.

You now have configured, deployed and updated Tripwire.

Exercise: Securing the Tripwire Database

1. Burn the database to a CD. You can use a CD-RW disk, although this option is far less secure, because in theory someone could modify the data on the CD-RW disk, but in practice that is not easy to do via the network.

2. Modify your **tripwire --check –M** command so that are now reading from the database on the CD.

3. You now can be reasonably sure that your sensitive files and directories are protected.

Exercise: Using Cron to Run Tripwire Automatically

1. As of this writing, Tripwire no longer runs automatically. Configure a cron job so that Tripwire runs every week. Use the simple script discussed earlier in this lesson. If you wish, you can issue the **crontab -e** command and enter the following:

```
5 0 * * * root /usr/bin/tripwire --check -M
```

This command will have Tripwire run daily at five minutes after midnight.

2. Make sure that you specify the correct database file, if you have stored it onto a CD.

3. You may not want Tripwire to send you any messages unless a problem occurs. To make Tripwire remain silent until a problem occurs, add or modify the MAILNOVIOLATIONS line to read as follows:

```
MAILNOVIOLATIONS=false
```

4. Issue the following command:

```
twadmin --create-cfgfile -S /etc/tripwire/site.key
    /etc/tripwire/twcfg.txt
```

Now, you will no longer be notified unless a problem occurs.

5. When you are finished, removing all text-based configuration files is a good idea. Keep backup copies on a floppy disk for future use.

You now have automated Tripwire to run every week. You can, of course, create a crontab that runs this job more often or less often.

Deploying PortSentry to Act as a Host-Based IDS

PortSentry is a host-based IDS application that monitors all open ports. It is an effective tool if you wish to detect TCP and/or UDP port scans, and if you wish to have your host reconfigure itself in case of a port scan. You can also configure PortSentry to do the following:

- **Drop all packets returning to a host using the route command** This is not the preferred option, but if you do not have Ipchains or Ipfwadm support, you will have to use it.

- **Automatically update the /etc/hosts.deny file to block xinetd-based connections** This is useful if all of your system's daemons are started by xinetd.

- **Automatically use Ipchains or ipfwadm to block connections** This is the most comprehensive option, because it will block any and all connections from a host PortSentry has identified as an attacker. You should understand, however, that the 2.4 kernel does not support Ipchains.

- **Log additional connection information** By default, PortSentry logs all of its observations and actions to the /var/log/messages file, and it informs you concerning scans conducted by most popular applications, such as Nmap. This includes most "half-open" SYN scans, as well as the XMAS, NULL, and FIN scans. For more information, read the README files that ship with the product. Because PortSentry acts automatically, it is always revealing to check this file periodically to see what hosts have scanned your system. Of course, monitoring this file is wise, because PortSentry may generate false positives and block a host that you actually wish to allow full access.

PortSentry is not distributed under the GNU General Public License (GPL). However, it is freeware, and you can modify the source code for your own purposes. However, you cannot give this modified source code to anyone else. PortSentry will compile on any standard Linux system that has TCPWrapper and Ipchains or Ipfw support. As mentioned earlier, you can obtain PortSentry from www.psionic.com/abacus/portsentry.

Important PortSentry Files

All of the PortSentry files are located off of the /usr/local/psionic/portsentry/ directory. These files include the following:

- **portsentry** The actual daemon responsible for detecting attacks.

- **portsentry.conf** The configuration file for the entire daemon.

- **portsentry.blocked.stcp** If you configure the portsentry.conf file to block stealth attacks, this file will log systems that have been blocked.

- **portsentry.blocked.tcp** A temporary file that informs you concerning the systems blocked since the last time PortSentry was activated.

- **portsentry.history** Contains detailed information concerning the hosts that have been blocked.

- **portsentry.ignore** Hosts that PortSentry will not respond to. This file is necessary so that you do not forbid access to your own system. Also, some default behavior from systems such as Microsoft Exchange boxes and DNS servers can be mistaken for scans. Cutting off all communication to such systems would be a mistake if they are essential for your job or for normal operation of your operating system.

Installing PortSentry

All files are owned by root, and the program must be started as root, because it places your NIC into promiscuous mode. Generally, an application or daemon must be started as root in order to do this. The /usr/local/psionic/portsentry/ directory must be owned by root, and have "700" permissions. The portsentry.ignore and portsentry.conf files need only have 600 (read and write by owner) permissions.

Configuring PortSentry to Block Users

The /usr/local/psionic/portsentry/portsentry.conf file contains several fields. First, you will find that the default setting has PortSentry bind only to certain ports. Three predefined groups of ports are created for you. You can edit these at will. However, you must have only one pair uncommented at a time. The Advanced Stealth Scan Detection Options determine the port numbers that PortSentry will monitor when you use the **–stcp** option to start PortSentry. By default, PortSentry listens only to ports up to 1023. You can change this setting to read all ports, but vulnerable ports are usually those that reside below 1023, so you probably won't need to alter these settings.

The Dropping Routes section allows you to determine how PortSentry will deny connections. The KILL_ROUTE options allow you to configure various system tools to actually do the work of denying hosts. PortSentry allows you to use only one KILL_ROUTE option, so if you experience any troubles, check that you have not mistakenly uncommented multiple entries. The two most useful KILL_ROUTE options are the following:

- **KILL_ROUTE="/sbin/ipchains -I input -s $TARGET$ -j DENY -l"** Uses Ipchains to identify the attacker (the attacker's host IP address is stored in the $TARGET$ value), then deny all incoming connections from that host. This is the preferred option.

- **KILL_ROUTE="/sbin/route add -host $TARGET$ reject"** Uses the route command to reject all packets emanating from the target host.

After you uncomment either of these entries, PortSentry will do the rest. The KILL_HOSTS_DENY entry allows you to deny connections to any host controlled by xinetd. Two entries exist. For Red Hat 7.0, select the second entry, which appears as follows:

```
KILL_HOSTS_DENY="ALL: $TARGET$ : DENY"
```

As with the KILL_ROUTE entries, after you uncomment these entries, PortSentry will act automatically.

Optimizing PortSentry to Sense Attack Types

There is more than one way to attack a system. Hackers can send UDP packets to scan systems, or they can conduct full TCP scans or only "half-open" scans. As a result, there is more than one way to start PortSentry. You can start PortSentry in various ways, depending upon the types of attacks you wish to detect. For example, if you note that many scanning attacks are being waged using half-open scans, you can use the **-stcp** option, which is discussed shortly. The options that you specify in the portsentry.conf file will also affect how you start PortSentry. For example, if you wish to listen to UDP traffic, you would configure the portsentry.conf file to contain additional references to UDP ports. The startup commands for PortSentry include the following:

- **portsentry -tcp** Starts the program as a standard TCP host-based IDS. PortSentry simply listens to the open TCP ports you specify.

- **portsentry -udp** Starts the program as a standard UDP host-based IDS. PortSentry simply listens to the open UDP ports you specify.

- **portsentry –stcp** Allows PortSentry to listen for stealth TCP scans. The chief difference between this argument and the simple **–tcp** argument is that PortSentry opens up a socket to capture FIN, half-open-connection, and full-connection scans.

- **portsentry –atcp** Configures PortSentry to block all hosts connecting to the ports you specify in portsentry.conf. You must explicitly exclude any hosts that legitimately use the ports listed, or they will be blocked. As you might guess, this feature can result in false positives. One possible result is that you may block yourself from FTP, Web, and e-mail sites as you try to use them.

- **portsentry –sudp** Allows PortSentry to listen for stealth UDP scans, similar to the **–stcp** option.

- **portsentry –audp** Configures PortSentry to become ultra-sensitive to udp scans. Except for the fact that this option has PortSentry bind to UDP ports, it behaves exactly like the **–atcp** argument.

Customize each system that you have depending upon its function and place in your network. For example, if you have any systems residing in a *demilitarized zone* (DMZ)—which is a special network that usually houses DNS, Web, and even e-mail servers—you may wish to use the **–atcp** option so that PortSentry can block scanning hosts.

Exercise: Installing and Configuring PortSentry

1. Obtain PortSentry from www.psionic.com.

2. Place the tarball into the /root/ directory.

3. Untar the file by using the following command:

   ```
   tar –zxvf portsentry-1.0.tar.gz
   ```

4. Change to the portsentry-1.0 directory.

5. The PortSentry installation process asks that you use the **make** command with an option particular to your operating system. To install PortSentry on your Linux system, enter the following command:

   ```
   make linux
   ```

6. **Make** will compile the binaries. Install these binaries into the /usr/local/psionic/portsentry/ directory by issuing the following command:

   ```
   make install
   ```

7. Change to the /usr/local/psionic/portsentry/ directory.

8. Open the portsentry.conf file in your favorite text editor, such as pico or vi.

9. Scroll down to the Port Configuration section and notice that the intermediate setting is not commented out. This means that the TCP and UDP ports listed will be monitored. If you wish, you can add ports to this list. Just make sure that you use a comma to separate ay ports you wish to monitor and that you end the entire list with a quotation mark.

10. Scroll down to the Dropping Routes section. Review the default settings as you pass by.

11. Find the Generic Linux entry, then scroll down to the packet filter options.

12. Find the KILL_ROUTE="/sbin/ipchains -I input -s $TARGET$ -j DENY -l" line, then uncomment it. This entry uses the **ipchains** command to add the attacking host to the Ipchains table. If a host scans your system or even connects to a listed port, PortSentry will cause Ipchains to deny all connections between this host and yours. As a result, your system will not respond to any packets originating from the attacking host, and your system will become a "black hole," as it were. Only uncomment one KILL_ROUTE entry at a time, because PortSentry does not support multiple entries and will crash. If you wish, edit this entry so that it uses Iptables, instead.

13. Scroll down to the TCPWrappers section and comment the first KILL_HOSTS_DENY entry and uncomment the second one that purports to be for New Style systems.

14. Finally, scan down to the Port Banner Section and uncomment the PORT_BANNER line. This entry has PortSentry automatically issue a warning to anyone trying to listen in on your port.

15. After you have edited portsentry.conf, quit the file, making sure to save your changes.

16. Start PortSentry using the following command:

```
portsentry -stcp
```

17. Use the **ps** command to see whether PortSentry has activated:

```
ps aux | grep psioni
root         787  0.0  0.0  1660    24 ?           S     Mar09    0:03
    /usr/local/psioni
```

Note that this command has the **ps** command search all processes, then use **grep** to search for the letters *psioni* in psionic.

18. Now that you have confirmed that PortSentry is running, use a remote host's copy of Nmap to scan your host.

19. The Nmap scan may complete, or it may hang. On the host running PortSentry, test to see if your settings were effective. First, issue the following command to see if the host running Nmap has been added to the /etc/hosts.deny file:

```
cat /etc/hosts.deny
```

20. You should see that your scanning host has been added. However, the /etc/hosts.deny file protects only those daemons started by xinetd. The more comprehensive and powerful way to block remote hosts is the use of Ipchains. The **ipchains** command allows you to implement a packet filter on your Linux system. You will learn more about how to use Ipchains to create a firewall in future chapters. Note, however, that Ipchains is not supported by the 2.4 kernel. You will have to edit the portsentry.conf file to use Iptables. If your system does use Ipchains, PortSentry simply uses this application to automatically configure your host to drop any and all packets coming in from the attacking host. List the packet filtering table to see if your scanning host has been added to the ipchains filtering table:

```
ipchains -L
Chain input (policy ACCEPT):
target      prot opt      source          destination          ports
DENY        all  ----l-    yourhost.yournetwork.com anywhere   n/a
Chain forward (policy ACCEPT):
Chain output (policy ACCEPT):
```

21. This output shows that all incoming traffic from your scanning is denied. Try to use any Web browser, FTP client, or Telnet to access this host. You will be denied. You won't even be able to ping the host.

Exercise: Clearing Ipchains Rules

1. You may want to allow a blocked host to communicate with your system again. Do this by editing the /etc/hosts.deny file and eliminating any reference to the host you have just blocked.

2. Use the following command to eliminate the first Ipchains input entry:

```
ipchains -D input 1
```

3. You may have to delete additional rules in the input chain. If so, you can specify additional rules:

```
ipchains -D input 2
```

4. You can then list all chains again to ensure that you have blocked all traffic. To eliminate any and all entries, use the **flush** command:

```
ipchains -F
```

Exercise: Running an External Command Using PortSentry

Although not always appropriate in all instances, you can configure PortSentry to run an external command. In this example, you will run Nmap against the scanning host. Remember, this may not be the best option, because it is possible that the person who has scanned you has spoofed the connection, and you will be blocking the wrong IP address. The command shown in this exercise is an example of what you can do with PortSentry.

1. Open the /usr/local/psionic/portsentry/portsentry.conf file.

2. Scroll down to the External Command section, and enter the following all on one line:

```
KILL_RUN_CMD="/usr/bin/nmap -O $TARGET$" >>
        /usr/local/psionic/portsentry/scan.txt
```

3. Exit the file and save your changes.

4. Completely kill PortSentry:

```
ps aux | grep psion
[pid info]
kill PID
```

5. Restart PortSentry in standard **tcp** mode. This mode will generate fewer false positives when using an external command.

```
portsentry -tcp
```

6. Make sure that all /etc/hosts.deny and Ipchains entries are eliminated.

7. Conduct a scan from a remote host.

8. After the scan is completed, check Ipchains and the /etc/hosts.deny file to see that PortSentry added the route. Now, check the /usr/local/psionic/portsentry/scan.txt. You will see that your own system has conducted a reverse scan of the attacking host. This exercise has shown a simple Nmap scan, however. Consider what would happen if a malicious user used Nmap to spoof your default gateway. You would be denied access to the rest of your WAN.

9. Issue the following command to continuously read the /var/log/messages file:

```
tail -f /var/log/messages
```

10. Use your scanning host to scan the host with PortSentry enabled.

11. You will see messages from PortSentry informing you of the scan and the actions it has taken. If the scanning host is already added to the Ipchains forward chain and to /etc/hosts.deny, then PortSentry will inform you. If you have restarted PortSentry, then the program will add another entry using Ipchains and TCPWrappers.

12. You need to ensure that PortSentry will start at boot time. You can create your own custom script and place it in the /etc/rc.d/init.d/ directory, or you can simply place it at the bottom of the /etc/rc.d/rc.local file. Now, each time your system boots, PortSentry will start.

Installing and Configuring Snort

Snort, available at www.snort.org, is best suited to detailed log analysis. Like PortSentry, it places your NIC into promiscuous mode. Unlike PortSentry, it captures all traffic on your network segment, as opposed to traffic destined for just one host. Its method of capturing and logging packets is also much more sophisticated, because it can log its findings into remote or local databases. Snort's analysis feature is able to read the contents of the captured packets and then inform you about any attacks waged against your network.

Availability

You can download Snort in various forms, including the following:

- **Binary RPM** A version of Snort that is ready to operate. Generally, however, precompiled versions of Snort have certain features disabled. You also often have to edit various files before Snort will operate correctly. This version is quite convenient, because it will automatically provide startup scripts and plug-ins. However, this distribution format currently has some important limitations, including the fact that the Snort binary does not support database logging.

- **Source RPM** Installs all source files to the same locations as the binary RPM. You must then run **make** against the installation files in order to compile the Snort binary and the supporting files.

- **Tarball** The preferred format because you can specify compile-time options to enable specific database support.

Supporting Libraries

For full functionality, you will need the following libraries:

- **Libpcap** Usually installed by default, this is a library responsible for capturing network packets.

- **A database** In order to use Snort with a database, you will need a database such as PostgreSQL or MySQL. This chapter focuses on PostgreSQL.

- **Libnet** Snort has a feature called *Flex Response*, which enables it to issue third-party commands to help block network traffic after an alert occurs.

In order to use the Flex Response feature, you must have Libnet installed. The Flex Response feature is still experimental, and its use is not recommended.

Understanding Snort Rules

Snort is able to automatically detect attacks based solely upon the rules it uses. Depending upon the rules you specify, Snort can identify various attacks, including the following:

- **Port scans for all hosts, including stealth port scans** This feature is useful even if you have PortSentry installed, because Snort will read the attacks as they come across the network wire before they reach the host.

- **Attacks meant to exploit well-known buffer overflows, such as attacks against older versions of Sendmail that lead to a root compromise** Snort is able to do this because the SMTP-specific rules are able to have Snort capture and then analyze all SMTP-based packets for typical text strings and packets used in such exploits.

- **CGI attacks** Snort can help protect your Web servers from the most commonly-known attacks.

- **Server Message Block (SMB) probes** You can protect your Windows servers by searching for typical attacks, such as brute force, scanning, and dictionary attacks.

- **Operating system fingerprinting** Snort can identify many of the most common tools such as Nmap and Queso.

Snort Variables

For the sake of logging accuracy, you can configure the snort.conf file to recognize the "home" (local) network, as well as any external networks, as well as the network's DNS servers. Typical entries are as follows:

- **var HOME_NET [192.168.1.0/24]** Specifies the 192.168.1.0 network, with a standard class C subnet mask. Snort always uses Classless Internet Domain Routing (CIDR) notation, because it cannot simply assume that all IP addresses use standard Class A, B, and C subnet masks.

You, of course, would substitute your own IP address. It is important that you follow the syntax of this variable exactly. You may have to edit the /etc/snort/snort.conf file so that it uses brackets instead of quotes. If you have many internal networks, you can enter multiple IP addresses: **var HOME_NET [192.168.1.0/24, 10.100.100.1/24]** to ensure that all systems on your network are logged when you place Snort into IDS mode.

- **var EXTERNAL_NET any** This particular example has Snort treat all IP addresses other than 192.168.1.0 as external to its interface. Instead of using the any keyword, you can enter specific network addresses (such as 192.168.2.0 and 192.168.3.0).

- **var DNS_SERVERS [10.100.100.50/24,192.168.2.50/24]** Allows you to determine the DNS servers Snort can use.

Snort Files and Directories

Here is a review of the files and directories used by Snort:

- **/usr/local/snort** The Snort binary, when installed from an RPM package. The binary RPM version is not configured for database support.

- **/usr/local/bin/snort** The binary, when installed from a tarball.

- **/etc/snort/** A directory that contains the Snort configuration file, as well as all Snort rules.

- **/etc/snort/snort.conf** The Snort configuration file, which informs Snort about the nature of the network it is monitoring and which allows you to exclude certain hosts, determine the rules used, and set logging and alerting options.

- **/usr/share/doc/snort-1.7** The documentation directory if you install Snort using the RPM. If you install using a tarball, the documentation will be in the subdirectory where you installed all of the source files.

- **/etc/rc.d/init.d/snortd** The initialization script for snortd. This script comes with the RPM package. You will be editing this script to customize how Snort initializes.

Snort Plug-Ins

It is possible to use several detection plug-ins. You specify the use of plug-ins in the snort.conf file by using preprocessor entries. They include the following:

- **stream** Called the TCP Stream Reassembly plug-in; is able to reconstitute TCP connections between network hosts. This ability is important, because most IDS applications have difficulty tracing extremely slow scans and attacks.

- **defrag** Allows Snort to search and reconstitute IP traffic.

- **http_decode** Tells Snort to listen for packets addressed to ports you specify.

- **portscan** Allows you to specify a separate logging location for port scans.

- **portscan-ignorehosts** Sometimes, you will want to specify hosts that are allowed to conduct scans, or which are allowed to send unusual packets. DNS servers, for example, can send replies that Snort can misunderstand. This plug-in allows you to list such hosts.

- **minfrag** Snort is able to reconstitute attacks that have been broken up into smaller bits using this plug-in.

Sometimes, plug-ins do not require additional arguments. At other times, they require you to specify additional parameters. For example, the stream preprocessor requires that you give a timeout period, which ensures that Snort does not become bogged down. You can then specify the ports to monitor and then set a limit on the maximum number of bytes Snort will capture. Here is an example:

```
preprocessor stream: timeout 4, ports 21 23 80 8080, maxbytes 17000
```

Here are additional entries:

- **preprocessor defrag** Enables the defrag value.

- **preprocessor http_decode: 80 8080** Specifies monitoring of ports 80 and 8080 on the network.

- **preprocessor portscan: $HOME_NET 4 3 /var/log/snort/ portscan.log** Creates a log entry for port scans.

- **preprocessor portscan-ignorehosts: $DNS_SERVERS** Has Snort read the DNS_SERVERS variable entry.

- **preprocessor minfrag: 128** Tells Snort to issue an alert if the value of a fragment is below 128.

Some plug-ins, such as Spade, are also available. As of this writing, the Spade plug-in is still experimental. You can read more about the plug-ins by consulting the Snort documentation in the /usr/share/doc/snort-1.7/ directory.

Starting Snort

You can start Snort in three basic ways. To start Snort as a simple packet sniffer, issue the following command:

```
snort -v
```

This command will log traffic only at the network level. Figure 4.5 shows what Snort reports when it logs a simple ICMP packet sent between two other hosts on the network.

Figure 4.5 Using Snort to View ICMP Packet Information

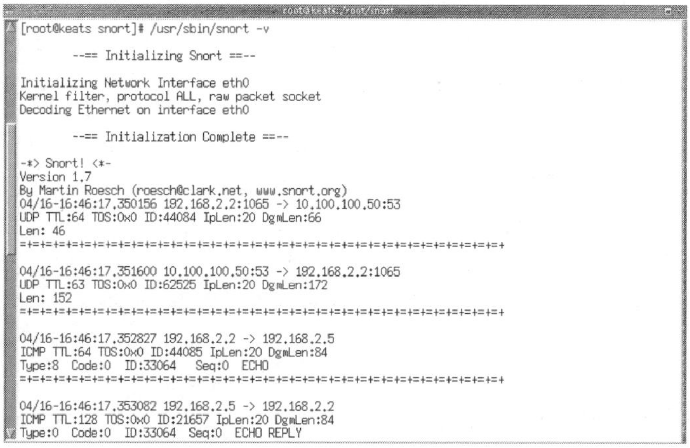

Notice how you are able to read the source and destination information, as well as the nature of the packet (the TTL, the sequence (ID) number, and whether the ICMP packet is an ECHO or ECHO REPLY).

After you end your session, you will receive a message informing you about the total number of packets Snort has been able to capture. See Figure 4.6.

Figure 4.6 A Snort Summary Report

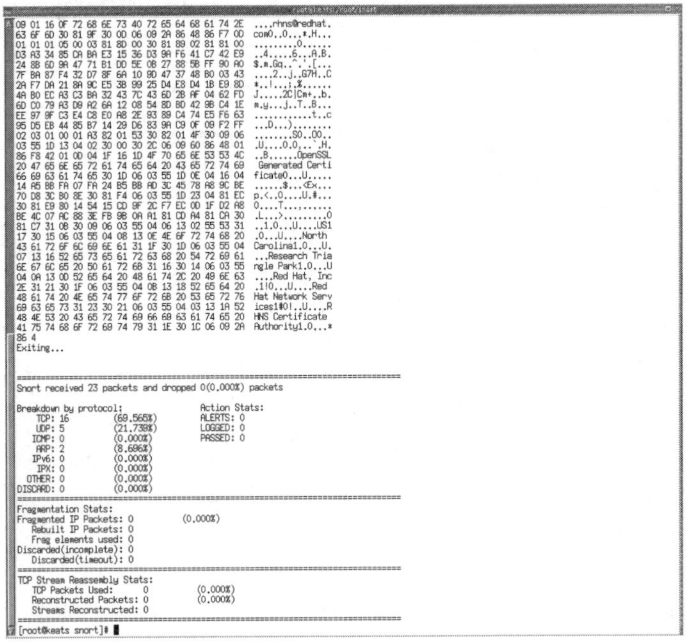

If you use the **–d** option to have Snort capture application-layer data, you will capture additional information. Figure 4.7 shows the additional information Snort finds when it is started as follows:

```
snort -vd
```

Notice that you can now see the host names involved (james and jacob). You also see additional information concerning the exact nature of the ICMP packets being sent back and forth. Figure 4.8 shows Snort capturing a simple HTTP session. Notice how it is able to capture the text "This is james" from the HTML that creates the Web page.

As you can see, Snort can report all information found in an unencrypted packet. Thus far, you have been using Snort as a glorified packet sniffer.

Figure 4.7 Capturing Application-Layer Data with Snort

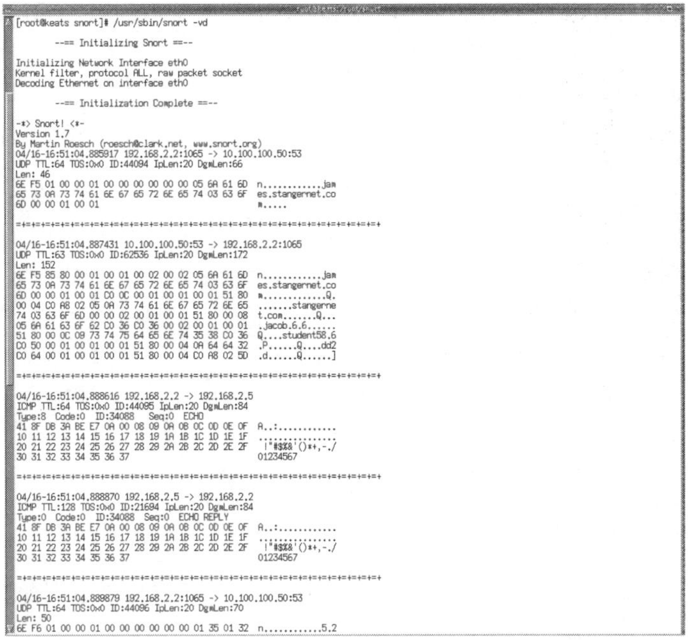

Figure 4.8 Capturing an HTTP Session

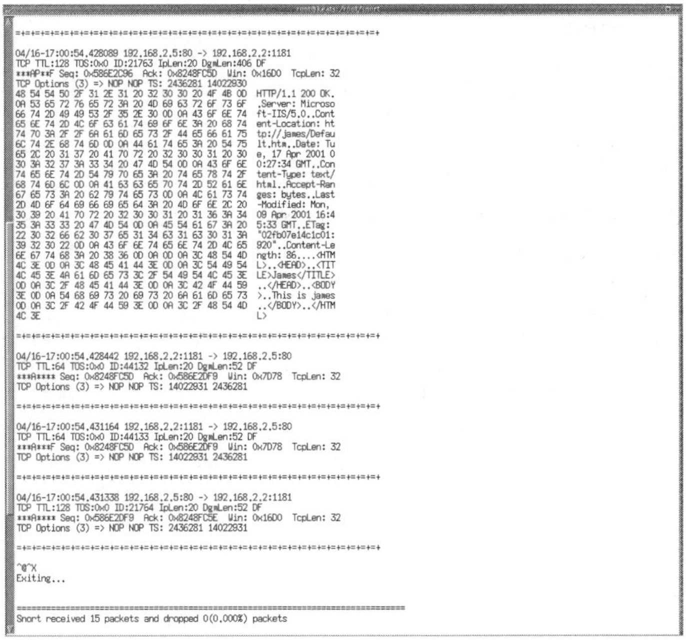

Logging Snort Entries

The next way to use Snort is to have it store what it finds into log files. Issue the following command:

```
/usr/sbin/snort -u snort -g snort -dev -l /var/log/snort -h
    192.168.2.0/24
```

This command starts Snort under a user and group of Snort (the RPM file installation automatically creates these users), then logs all packets to the /var/log/snort directory. You can specify any directory you wish. The **e** option has Snort read data link layer headers, as well. The **–h** command tells Snort that the 192.168.2.0/24 network is the home network and to log all packets relative to the 192.168.2.0 system. You will have to ensure that the /var/log/snort directory exists before you issue this command. All packets will be logged to this directory. Snort will create a directory for each host it detects. Each directory will contain a file that contains the messages specific to that host.

Running Snort as a Network-Based IDS

Thus far, you have seen how to run Snort from the command line so that it captures all traffic. However, the snort.conf file gives you the ability to use Snort as a true IDS because it has Snort use rules and plug-ins. You can also specify more sophisticated home network and logging methods. After you begin using the rules and plug-ins found in snort.conf, it will begin selectively logging traffic. Specifically, it will log only suspicious activity for your home network. The following line has Snort run using the /etc/snort/snort.conf file. The **–D** option has Snort run as a daemon:

```
snort -u snort -g snort -dev -h 192.168.2.0/24 -d -D -i eth0 -c
    /etc/snort/snort.conf
```

This command has snort run in daemon mode (**–D**) and specifies the eth0 interface. The last part of the command specifies the snort.conf file, which if properly configured will enable Snort to log traffic only as it violates the rules it contains. If you use this command, make sure that your snort.conf file is properly edited. For example, you will want to make sure that you specify all subnets for your home network.

Ignoring Hosts

You may want to tell Snort to ignore certain hosts on your network. The two easiest options for configuring Snort to ignore hosts are the following:

- Use Tcpdump-style filters on the command line (not in the /etc/snort/ snort.conf file).

- Use the portscan preprocessor entry in /etc/snort/snort.conf.

When using Tcpdump-style filters, suppose that you wished to monitor all hosts on the network except for the host named *james*. You would specify the following at the command line:

```
snort -u snort -g snort -dev -h 192.168.2.0/24 -d -D -i eth0 -c
    /etc/snort/snort.conf
    ip and not host james
```

For more information, consult Chapter 5, or read the main page for Tcpdump.

As far as using the portscan preprocessor is concerned, specify the hosts that you want to ignore by IP separated only by white space:

```
preprocessor portscan-ignorehosts: $DNS_SERVERS 10.100.100.50/32
    192.168.2.4/32
```

Make sure that you specify 32 for the subnet mask when you wish to block a specific host.

Additional Logging Options: Text files, Tcpdump, and Databases

If you wish to have Snort log all alert activity to a single log file, you can use the following option in the /etc/snort/snort.conf file:

```
output alert_full: /snortlog/snort.log
```

NOTE

The **output alert_full: /snortlog/snort.log** option will not log port scans. The option for logging port scans is always specified by the "preprocessor portscan:" value.

Many applications can read files that are created in Tcpdump format. Snort supports Tcpdump-compatible formats. Using the **–b** option allows you to use applications such as Tcdump and Ethereal to read them later on. To do enable Snort to do this, use the **–b** option to the command line (Make sure you enter this all on one line.):

```
snort -u snort -g snort -dev -h 192.168.2.0/24 -d -D -i eth0 -c
    /etc/snort/snort.conf -b
```

This command does not specify a directory. By default, Snort will place the Tcpdump-readable file into the /var/log/snort/ directory. The file will be named snort-★.log, where the ★ is the month, day, and time the capture was started. To read the file using Snort, issue the following command:

```
snort -dv -r /var/log/snort/packet.log |less
```

Configuring Snort to Log to a Database

The most elegant way to log traffic is to place it into a database. To begin logging to a database, take the following steps:

1. Install a database and ensure that it is running properly. In the upcoming exercise, you will configure PostgreSQL.

2. Create a user, such as *snort*, on the database. Make sure that this user has privileges to insert rows and data into the database.

3. Compile a version of Snort that supports logging to databases. The RPM binary currently does not support database logging.

4. Create a database that will contain the log information.

5. Edit the database so that it has the structure Snort expects. Snort contains files for the PostgreSQL and MySQL databases, as well as others.

6. Edit the /etc/snort/snort.conf file so that Snort logs to your database.

Here is an example of the entry to place into the snort.conf file:

```
output database: log, postgresql, dbname=snort user=snort
    host=localhost password=password
```

All of this information should all be on one line. This line tells Snort to send its data to a database with the log priority. You can also use the alert priority, which gathers all information concerning ping and port scans. The next entry gives the name of the database you have created. The user, host, and password entries tell Snort exactly which host to log to. This example has the database log to a local database, but it is possible to log to a remote database:

```
output database: log, postgresql, dbname=snort user=snort
    host=localhost password=password
```

The commas are extremely important. You place them after the log and database entries. You would, of course, enter your own information. If you were using MySQL, you would enter the following all on one line:

```
output database: log, postgresql, dbname=snort user=snort
    host=databasehost.yournetwork.com password=password
```

Controlling Logging and Alerts

On busy networks, you need to configure Snort to log less information. The following command-line options help you control how much your IDS will log:

- **-A full** The default setting, which issues all alerts found by the plug-ins. The alert contains detailed information about the nature of the perceived attack.

- **-A fast** This option has Snort write only a short description, complete with the source and destination IP addresses and ports and the time the alert occurred. All other information is left out.

- **-A unsock** This option has Snort send alerts to a local Unix socket where third-party applications can obtain the data. A Unix socket is much like a port, except that it is open only to the local host.

- **-A none** This option completely disables logging.

Additional configuration options are available, including the ability to configure Snort to send alerts to Windows systems that have the Server service running. To enable SMB alerts, you will have to configure Snort with the `--enable-smbalerts' option (make sure to use the backtic character first—the key above the Tab key—and then the standard single-quote character). For more information, consult the USAGE and INSTALL files that ship with the application.

Getting Information

Snort is being developed quite rapidly. To learn more about the latest Snort developments, you can consult the following resources:

- **The snort mailing list** Go to www.snort.org and select the mailing list link. This link allows you to sign up for the Snort mailing list, which is very active and usually informative. Both novice and experienced users frequent the list, so chances are you will receive the help you need just by giving adequate information about your system and by asking specific, well-worded questions.

- **The snort user archives page** Go to http://lists.sourceforge.net/mailman/listinfo/snort-users. This archive contains past postings from the Snort mailing list.

Exercise: Installing Snort

1. To begin experimenting with Snort, install it from the RPM, which is on the CD that accompanies this book:

```
rpm -ivh snort-1.7-1.i386.rpm
```

Later, you will install the snort-1.7.tar.gz file, which has the ability to log to databases. The RPM version contains a binary that is not compiled to work with databases.

> **NOTE**
>
> When you install Snort using the RPM, a user and group named Snort will automatically be generated. The /etc/rc.d/init.d/snortd script will also be created. However, you will first need to edit this script before you continue.

2. After Snort is installed, run Snort as a simple sniffer:

```
snort -vde
```

3. If possible, have additional systems ping each other. If you are on a non-switched network, or if your switch is configured to report all traffic to your host, you will see the contents of the packets on your screen.

4. Stop Snort by pressing **CTRL+C.** You will see a report summarizing all of the packets it has captured. Now, issue the following command, substituting the proper values when necessary (Make sure you enter this all on one line.):

```
snort -u snort -g snort -dev -l /var/log/snort -h
    your.ip.address.here /CIDR -i eth0
```

5. Snort will report the captures to both standard output (your screen) and also to the /var/log/snort/ directory. Make sure that you specify your IP address, complete with the proper CIDR notation for your subnet mask. If you are already using eth0, then you do not need to specify it.

6. Generate some traffic on the network. For example, ping several hosts on and off the network or open a Web browser or FTP client. Open a terminal and list the /var/log/snort/ directory. Snort will create a directory for each system logged and will also log to the /var/log/snort/alert file. Change to one of the directories off of the /var/log/snortd/ directory. Notice that this directory contains a message concerning an ICMP echo packet. Snort has logged this packet because it defaults to logging all ICMP traffic, which is a chief tool used in denial of service attacks.

7. Issue the same command again, except this time, log the information to a Tcpdump-readable file.

```
snort -u snort -g snort -dev -h your.ip.address.here/
    CIDR -d -D -i eth0 -b
```

8. After you have created this file, read it using the following command:

```
snort -dv -r /var/log/snort/logfilename.log
```

9. After you learn more about Tcpdump and Ethereal in the next chapter, you will be able to read these files to gather more information about the traffic on your network.

Exercise: Using Snort as an IDS Application

1. Configure Snort to use the /etc/snort/snort.conf file. Doing so will make Snort become a true IDS application. First, edit snort.conf so that all variables match values for your specific network. The RPM process

should accurately guess your system's configuration, but check it to be sure. One problem Snort has is determining the correct CIDR value for the subnet mask. Don't change this value right away, however. It is more likely that you have made some sort of mistake typing in information. Here is a list of values to customize or add (comments are entered to give you an idea of what each entry means):

```
var HOME_NET [192.168.2.0/24,10.100.100.0/24]
    # Add all "home" network IP addresses.
var EXTERNAL_NET any    # A standard entry.
var DNS_SERVERS [10.100.100.50/24]
    # Make all of your DNS servers are listed here.


preprocessor defrag    # A standard entry.
preprocessor http_decode: 80 8080
    # Add the Web ports used on your network.
preprocessor portscan: $HOME_NET 4 3 /var/log/snort/portscan.log
    # A standard entry.
preprocessor portscan-ignorehosts: $DNS_SERVERS
    # A standard entry.
```

2. Review the additional entries. You do not need to make any other changes, because the RPM file installs a default set of rules, which are all in the /etc/snort/ directory.

3. Exit this file, making sure to save your changes.

4. After you have ensured that all of your snort.conf entries are correct, issue the following command, all on one line:

```
snort -u snort -g snort -dev -h your.ip.address.here/
    CIDR -d -D -i eth0 -b -c /etc/snort/snort.conf
```

5. Snort should have entered daemon mode. It should be logging information to all files in the /var/log/snort/ directory. Use the **ps** command to see if Snort is running properly:

```
ps aux | grep snort
```

If you do not see anything, or see only the **grep** command itself, a problem has occurred with either your command line or with the snort.conf file. Carefully review each. Also, consult the documentation that comes with the package to see what elements specific to your system may require changes to these steps.

6. After you have verified that Snort is running, generate some new traffic. For example, use Nmap to scan a system that is not your DNS server and ping a host that is not on your network. Notice that instead of logging all information about all hosts, Snort now logs information relevant to your home network.

7. Check the alert and portscan.log files by opening two terminals and using the **tail –f** command:

```
tail -f /var/log/snort/alert
tail -f /var/log/snort/portscan.log
```

8. Using a port scanner, scan a host on your network. You should see messages to each of these files.

Exercise: Configuring Snort to Log to a Database

1. Stop Snort:

```
killall snort
```

2. Use the following command to make sure that Snort isn't running:

```
ps aux | grep snort
```

3. Make sure that you have PostgreSQL installed on your system. Red Hat Linux, for example, ships with this database. Use the following command to query the RPM database:

```
rpm -qa | grep postgres
postgresql-server-7.0.2-17
postgresql-devel-7.0.2-17
postgresql-7.0.2-17
```

Your versions of Postgres may differ. This is not important.

4. Although you have already installed a version of Snort using the RPM, this version does not support database logging. Obtain the tarball version

from the CD that accompanies this book (snort-1.7.tar.gz), then unzip and untar it:

```
tar -zxvf  snort-1.7.tar.gz
```

5. Change to the snort-1.7 directory. This directory contains all of the source files necessary to compile Snort. Now, issue the following command:

```
./configure
```

This simple command will begin a process that automates the creation of configuration and make files for your specific system. This program will automatically find installed database servers, such as Postgres and MySQL. It will also automatically find the libpcap libraries. If the configuration program fails, you will have to compile Snort using any of the following options:

- **./configure `--with-libpq-libraries=DIR'** If the configuration file can't find the Postgres libraries, use this option. The libraries are often found in the /usr/include/ directory.

- **./configure `--with-libpq-includes=DIR'** The includes are often found in the /usr/include/ directory.

- **./configure `--with-libpcap-includes=DIR'** The libraries are often found in the /usr/lib/ directory.

- **./configure `--with-libpcap-libraries=DIR'** The libraries are often found in the /usr/lib/ directory.

Additional options exist, but these are the ones relevant to database connectivity. For more information, read the README.database and INSTALL files.

6. As Snort configures itself, take note of the messages you see. You should see messages informing you that it has found the database you are using.

NOTE

When using configure options, make sure that you use the backtic character at the beginning of the option and the standard apostrophe at the end. Otherwise, compilation will fail. If you wish, you can combine options: ./configure `--with-libpq-libraries=DIR--with-libpq-includes=DIR':

7. Issue the following commands, one after the other:

```
make

make install
```

8. The tarball version of Snort 1.7 will install the Snort binary into the /usr/local/bin/ directory. Because the /etc/rc.d/init.d/snortd script is still very handy, open it in a text editor and edit the script. This script, like all of the others in this directory, contains sections that start, stop, and restart the daemon. Find the start section. Edit this section so that it reads as follows:

```
daemon /usr/local/bin/snort -dev -D \
        -i $INTERFACE -l /var/log/snort -u snort -g snort -c
            /etc/snort/snort.conf -b
```

9. Exit this file, making sure to save your changes.

10. It is time to configure the database. After you do this, you will edit the /etc/snort/snort.conf file so that Snort logs to the database.

11. Start PostgreSQL:

```
/etc/rc.d/init.d/postgres start
```

12. After PostgreSQL has started, use the /usr/sbin/ntsysv command to make sure that the database will begin each time you reboot. After in ntsysv, place an asterisk next to the **postgresql** command. While you are at it, check to see if snortd is also selected.

13. Exit ntsysv.

14. Become the postgres user:

```
su postgres
```

15. Create a user that can manipulate a database:

```
createuser snort
```

Make sure that you answer Yes to both questions: This user must be able to create databases and create more new users.

16. Create another user, root. This user must also be able to create databases and create more new users.

17. As root, create a database:

```
createdb -h 127.0.0.1 -U snort -W -e snort
```

This command has **createdb** create a database on the local host and allows the user named *snort* to manipulate it. The **-W** command creates a password, and the **-e** option simply has **createdb** echo its processes to you. The last item, **snort**, is the name of the database.

18. Exit the postgres shell:

```
exit
```

19. Change to the Snort source directory created when you unpacked the tarball.

20. Change to the contrib/ directory.

21. This directory contains several different applications and files that supplement Snort's capabilities. Find the create_postgresql file and issue the following command:

```
psql snort < ./create_postgresql
```

22. You will see this script create several tables in the database. You have now created a structure that Snort can log to.

NOTE

PostgreSQL stores its databases in the /var/lib/pgsql/data/base/ directory.

23. Edit the /etc/snort/snort.conf file and add the following command, all on one line:

```
output database: log, postgresql, dbname=snort user=snort
    host=localhost password=yourpassword
```

Make sure that this entry is all on one line. You will, of course, have to enter the appropriate password information. If you have altered any of the steps in this exercise, make sure that this line reflects your changes.

24. Exit this file, making sure to save your changes, then restart snortd:

```
/etc/rc.d/init.d/snortd start
```

25. Use the following command to verify that Snort has started successfully:

```
/etc/rc.d/init.d/snortd status
```

If you receive a message that the subsystem is locked, there is a problem with your syslog.conf configuration. Check the file and make any necessary changes. Remember, the RPM binary does not support logging to databases. Also, this exercise is specific to PostgreSQL. If you have not compiled in database support, or are using a different database, view the README.database file for more information.

26. After you have verified that Snort is operating properly, generate some traffic by using a port scanner. Also, ping several of the hosts.

27. The database you have created earlier is called *snort*. Use the **psql** command to access the snort database:

```
psql snort
```

28. Now, issue the following command to see the tables:

```
\d
```

You will see a list similar to that in Figure 4.9.

Figure 4.9 Viewing the Snort Database

29. You can view the contents of these tables. For example, issue the following SQL command:

```
SELECT* FROM event ;
```

This command chooses all data (*) from the event table. As long as you have generated some traffic, you will see information similar to that shown in Figure 4.10.

Figure 4.10 Viewing the Event Table

```
snort1=# SELECT * FROM event ;
 sid | cid |                                   signature                                    |       timestamp
-----+-----+--------------------------------------------------------------------------------+------------------------
   1 |  32 | IDS162 - PING Nmap2.36BETA                                                     | 2001-04-17 01:42:21-07
   1 |  33 | spp_portscan: PORTSCAN DETECTED from 192.168.2.2 (THRESHOLD 4 connections exceeded in 0 seconds) | 2001-04-17 01:42:21-07
   1 |  34 | IIS - Possible Attempt at NT INETINFO.EXE 100% CPU Utilization                 | 2001-04-17 01:42:21-07
   1 |  35 | Netbus/GabanBus                                                                | 2001-04-17 01:42:21-07
   1 |  36 | spp_portscan: portscan status from 192.168.2.2: 587 connections across 2 hosts: TCP(586), UDP(1) | 2001-04-17 01:44:11-07
   1 |  37 | ICMP Destination Unreachable                                                   | 2001-04-17 01:44:11-07
   1 |  38 | spp_portscan: portscan status from 192.168.2.2: 1 connections across 1 hosts: TCP(0), UDP(1) | 2001-04-17 01:44:42-07
   1 |  39 | spp_portscan: End of portscan from 192.168.2.2: TOTAL time(141s) hosts(2) TCP(586) UDP(2) | 2001-04-17 01:44:48-07
   1 |  40 | ICMP Destination Unreachable                                                   | 2001-04-17 01:46:11-07
   1 |  41 | ICMP Destination Unreachable                                                   | 2001-04-17 01:48:12-07
   1 |  42 | ICMP Destination Unreachable                                                   | 2001-04-17 01:50:12-07
   1 |  43 | ICMP Destination Unreachable                                                   | 2001-04-17 01:52:12-07
   1 |  44 | ICMP Destination Unreachable                                                   | 2001-04-17 01:54:12-07
   1 |  45 | ICMP Destination Unreachable                                                   | 2001-04-17 01:56:12-07
   1 |  46 | ICMP Destination Unreachable                                                   | 2001-04-17 01:58:12-07
   1 |  47 | ICMP Destination Unreachable                                                   | 2001-04-17 02:00:12-07
   1 |  48 | ICMP Destination Unreachable                                                   | 2001-04-17 02:02:12-07
   1 |  49 | ICMP Destination Unreachable                                                   | 2001-04-17 02:04:12-07
   1 |  50 | ICMP Destination Unreachable                                                   | 2001-04-17 02:06:12-07
   1 |  51 | ICMP Destination Unreachable                                                   | 2001-04-17 02:08:12-07
   1 |  52 | ICMP Destination Unreachable                                                   | 2001-04-17 02:10:12-07
   1 |  53 | ICMP Destination Unreachable                                                   | 2001-04-17 02:11:59-07
   1 |  54 | ICMP Destination Unreachable                                                   | 2001-04-17 02:12:04-07
   1 |  55 | ICMP Destination Unreachable                                                   | 2001-04-17 02:12:12-07
snort1=#
```

30. Query the iphdr table:

```
SELECT * FROM iphdr ;
```

This table gives you all IP information concerning your network hosts. See Figure 4.11.

Each table column gives you the IP addresses of the hosts on your network, as well as the hosts that have made suspicious connections to your network. If you are in the X Window environment, resize your terminal so that you can see all of the information.

If Snort has logged a large number of packets, they will go off the screen. Use the up and down arrow keys to scroll through the information. When you are finished viewing a particular table, press **Q** to exit. PostgreSQL also has a history feature, which allows you to scroll up to view previous commands.

31. Now, create SQL queries to obtain only the information you want. Issue the following commands:

```
SELECT * FROM iphdr WHERE cid=1 ;
SELECT * FROM iphdr WHERE cid>4 ;
SELECT * FROM iphdr WHERE cid>=4 ;
```

The first command obtains only the first row in the table. The *cid* value is the "connection id" value, and it is always in sequential order.

Figure 4.11 The iphdr Table

snort1=# SELECT * FROM iphdr ;

sid	cid	ip_src	ip_src0	ip_src1	ip_src2	ip_src3	ip_dst	ip_dst0	ip_dst1	ip_dst2	ip_dst3	ip_ver	ip_hlen	ip_tos	ip_len	ip_id	ip_flags	ip_off	ip_ttl	ip_proto	ip_csum
1	1	1090545852	65	0	104	188	1090545847	65	0	104	183	4	5	0	84	47415	0	0	63	1	28414
1	2	1090545852	65	0	104	188	1090545847	65	0	104	183	4	5	0	84	47416	0	0	63	1	28413
1	3	1090545852	65	0	104	188	1090545847	65	0	104	183	4	5	0	84	47417	0	0	63	1	28412
1	4	1090545852	65	0	104	188	1090545847	65	0	104	183	4	5	0	84	47418	0	0	63	1	28411
1	5	1090545852	65	0	104	188	1090545847	65	0	104	183	4	5	0	84	47419	0	0	63	1	28410
1	6	1090545852	65	0	104	188	1090545847	65	0	104	183	4	5	0	84	47420	0	0	63	1	28409
1	7	1090545852	65	0	104	188	1090545847	65	0	104	183	4	5	0	84	47421	0	0	63	1	28408
1	8	1090545852	65	0	104	188	1090545847	65	0	104	183	4	5	0	84	47422	0	0	63	1	28407
1	9	1090545852	65	0	104	188	1090545847	65	0	104	183	4	5	0	84	47423	0	0	63	1	28406
1	10	1090545852	65	0	104	188	1090545847	65	0	104	183	4	5	0	84	47424	0	0	63	1	28405
1	11	1090545852	65	0	104	188	1090545847	65	0	104	183	4	5	0	84	47425	0	0	63	1	28404
1	12	1090545852	65	0	104	188	1090545847	65	0	104	183	4	5	0	84	47426	0	0	63	1	28403
1	13	1090545852	65	0	104	188	1090545847	65	0	104	183	4	5	0	84	47427	0	0	63	1	28402
1	14	1090545852	65	0	104	188	1090545847	65	0	104	183	4	5	0	84	47428	0	0	63	1	28401
1	15	1090545852	65	0	104	188	1090545847	65	0	104	183	4	5	0	84	47429	0	0	63	1	28400
1	16	1090545852	65	0	104	188	1090545847	65	0	104	183	4	5	0	84	47430	0	0	63	1	28399
1	17	1090545852	65	0	104	188	1090545847	65	0	104	183	4	5	0	84	47431	0	0	63	1	28398
1	18	1090545852	65	0	104	188	1090545847	65	0	104	183	4	5	0	84	47432	0	0	63	1	28397
1	19	1090545852	65	0	104	188	1090545847	65	0	104	183	4	5	0	84	47433	0	0	63	1	28396
1	20	1090545852	65	0	104	188	1090545847	65	0	104	183	4	5	0	84	47434	0	0	63	1	28395
1	21	1090545852	65	0	104	188	1090545847	65	0	104	183	4	5	0	84	47435	0	0	63	1	28394
1	22	1090545852	65	0	104	188	1090545847	65	0	104	183	4	5	0	84	47436	0	0	63	1	28393
1	23	1090545852	65	0	104	188	1090545847	65	0	104	183	4	5	0	84	47437	0	0	63	1	28392
1	24	1090545852	65	0	104	188	1090545847	65	0	104	183	4	5	0	84	47438	0	0	63	1	28391
1	25	1090545852	65	0	104	188	1090545847	65	0	104	183	4	5	0	84	47439	0	0	63	1	28390
1	26	1090545852	65	0	104	188	1090545847	65	0	104	183	4	5	0	84	47440	0	0	63	1	28389
1	27	1090545852	65	0	104	188	1090545847	65	0	104	183	4	5	0	84	47441	0	0	63	1	28388
1	28	1090545852	65	0	104	188	1090545847	65	0	104	183	4	5	0	84	47442	0	0	63	1	28387
1	29	1090545852	65	0	104	188	1090545847	65	0	104	183	4	5	0	84	47443	0	0	63	1	28386
1	30	1090545852	65	0	104	188	1090545847	65	0	104	183	4	5	0	84	47444	0	0	63	1	28385
1	31	1090545852	65	0	104	188	1090545847	65	0	104	183	4	5	0	84	47445	0	0	63	1	28384
1	32	1090545852	65	0	104	188	1090545847	65	0	104	183	4	5	0	84	47446	0	0	63	1	28383
1	33	1090545852	65	0	104	188	1090545847	65	0	104	183	4	5	0	84	47447	0	0	63	1	28382
1	34	1090545852	65	0	104	188	1090545847	65	0	104	183	4	5	0	84	47448	0	0	63	1	28381
1	35	1090545852	65	0	104	188	1090545847	65	0	104	183	4	5	0	84	47449	0	0	63	1	28380
1	36	1090545852	65	0	104	188	1090545847	65	0	104	183	4	5	0	84	47450	0	0	63	1	28379
1	37	1090545852	65	0	104	188	1090545847	65	0	104	183	4	5	0	84	47451	0	0	63	1	28378
1	38	1090545852	65	0	104	188	1090545847	65	0	104	183	4	5	0	84	47452	0	0	63	1	28377
1	39	1090545852	65	0	104	188	1090545847	65	0	104	183	4	5	0	84	47453	0	0	63	1	28376
1	40	1090545852	65	0	104	188	1090545847	65	0	104	183	4	5	0	84	47454	0	0	63	1	28375
1	41	1090545852	65	0	104	188	1090545847	65	0	104	183	4	5	0	84	47455	0	0	63	1	28374
1	42	1090545852	65	0	104	188	1090545847	65	0	104	183	4	5	0	84	47456	0	0	63	1	28373
1	43	1090545852	65	0	104	188	1090545847	65	0	104	183	4	5	0	84	47457	0	0	63	1	28372
1	44	1090545852	65	0	104	188	1090545847	65	0	104	183	4	5	0	84	47458	0	0	63	1	28371
1	45	1090545852	65	0	104	188	1090545847	65	0	104	183	4	5	0	84	47459	0	0	63	1	28370
1	46	1090545852	65	0	104	188	1090545847	65	0	104	183	4	5	0	84	47460	0	0	63	1	28369
1	47	1090545852	65	0	104	188	1090545847	65	0	104	183	4	5	0	84	47461	0	0	63	1	28368
1	48	1090545852	65	0	104	188	1090545847	65	0	104	183	4	5	0	84	47462	0	0	63	1	28367
1	49	1090545852	65	0	104	188	1090545847	65	0	104	183	4	5	0	84	47463	0	0	63	1	28366
1	50	1090545852	65	0	104	188	1090545847	65	0	104	183	4	5	0	84	47465	0	0	63	1	28364
1	51	1090545852	65	0	104	188	1090545847	65	0	104	183	4	5	0	84	47466	0	0	63	1	28363
1	52	1090545852	65	0	104	188	1090545847	65	0	104	183	4	5	0	84	47467	0	0	63	1	28362
1	53	1090545852	65	0	104	188	1090545847	65	0	104	183	4	5	0	84	47468	0	0	63	1	28361
1	54	1090545852	65	0	104	188	1090545847	65	0	104	183	4	5	0	84	47469	0	0	63	1	28360
1	55	1090545852	65	0	104	188	1090545847	65	0	104	183	4	5	0	84	47470	0	0	63	1	28359
1	56	1090545852	65	0	104	188	1090545847	65	0	104	183	4	5	0	84	47471	0	0	63	1	28358
1	57	1090545852	65	0	104	188	1090545847	65	0	104	183	4	5	0	84	47472	0	0	63	1	28357
1	58	1090545852	65	0	104	188	1090545847	65	0	104	183	4	5	0	84	47473	0	0	63	1	28356
1	59	1090545852	65	0	104	188	1090545847	65	0	104	183	4	5	0	84	47474	0	0	63	1	28355
1	60	1090545852	65	0	104	188	1090545847	65	0	104	183	4	5	0	84	47475	0	0	63	1	28354
1	61	1090545852	65	0	104	188	1090545847	65	0	104	183	4	5	0	84	47476	0	0	63	1	28353
1	62	1090545852	65	0	104	188	1090545847	65	0	104	183	4	5	0	84	47477	0	0	63	1	28352
1	63	1090545852	65	0	104	188	1090545847	65	0	104	183	4	5	0	84	47478	0	0	63	1	28351
1	64	1090545852	65	0	104	188	1090545847	65	0	104	183	4	5	0	84	47479	0	0	63	1	28350
1	65	1090545852	65	0	104	188	1090545847	65	0	104	183	4	5	0	84	47480	0	0	63	1	28349
1	66	1090545852	65	0	104	188	1090545847	65	0	104	183	4	5	0	84	47481	0	0	63	1	28348
1	67	1090545852	65	0	104	188	1090545847	65	0	104	183	4	5	0	84	47482	0	0	63	1	28347
1	68	1090545852	65	0	104	188	1090545847	65	0	104	183	4	5	0	84	47483	0	0	63	1	28346
1	69	1090545852	65	0	104	188	1090545847	65	0	104	183	4	5	0	84	47484	0	0	63	1	28345
1	70	1090545852	65	0	104	188	1090545847	65	0	104	183	4	5	0	84	47485	0	0	63	1	28344
1	71	1090545852	65	0	104	188	1090545847	65	0	104	183	4	5	0	84	47486	0	0	63	1	28343
1	72	1090545852	65	0	104	188	1090545847	65	0	104	183	4	5	0	84	47487	0	0	63	1	28342
1	73	1090545852	65	0	104	188	1090545847	65	0	104	183	4	5	0	84	47488	0	0	63	1	28341
1	74	1090545852	65	0	104	188	1090545847	65	0	104	183	4	5	0	84	47489	0	0	63	1	28340
1	75	1090545852	65	0	104	188	1090545847	65	0	104	183	4	5	0	84	47490	0	0	63	1	28339
1	76	1090545852	65	0	104	188	1090545847	65	0	104	183	4	5	0	84	47491	0	0	63	1	28338

--More--

The second command obtains all rows after the fourth. The last command obtains the fourth row, as well as all of the ones above 4.

32. Now, obtain only the IP address information for the sending and receiving host for the first three records:

```
SELECT sid, cid, ip_src0, ip_src1, ip_src2, ip_src3, ip_dst0,
    ip_dst1, ip_dst2, ip_dst3
    FROM iphdr WHERE cid<3 ;
```

This command selects only certain columns from the iphdr table. If your table does not have the first three rows, then find the appropriate cid number and enter it here. Try the additional commands:

```
SELECT sid, cid, ip_src0, ip_src1, ip_src2, ip_src3, ip_dst0,
    ip_dst1, ip_dst2, ip_dst3

    FROM iphdr WHERE cid>30 ;
```

```
SELECT cid, ip_dst1, ip_dst2, ip_dst3 FROM iphdr WHERE cid>40 ;

SELECT sid, cid, ip_src0, ip_src1, ip_src2, ip_src3, ip_dst0,
    ip_dst1, ip_dst2, ip_dst3
    FROM iphdr WHERE cid<32 ;

SELECT cid, ip_dst0, ip_dst1, ip_dst2, ip_dst3 FROM iphdr WHERE
    ip_src0=FIRSTIPFIELD
    and ip_src1=SECONDIPFIELD and ip_src2=THIRDIPFIELD and
    ip_src3=FOURTHIPFIELD ;

SELECT cid, ip_dst0, ip_dst1, ip_dst2, ip_dst3 FROM iphdr
    WHERE ip_src0=
    FIRSTIPFIELD
    and ip_src1= SECONDIPFIELD and ip_src2= THIRDIPFIELD and
    ip_src3<FOURTHIPFIELD ;
```

33. Eventually, you will want to clear your database or trim certain rows. To delete row 31, for example, from the iphdr table, issue the following command:

```
DELETE FROM iphdr WHERE cid=31 ;
```

34. If you wish, issue the following command to delete all rows and column data from the iphdr table:

```
DELETE FROM iphdr ;
```

You now know how to log Snort output to a database, and you can manipulate the data.

Exercise: Querying a Snort Database from a Remote Host

One of the more useful elements of a database is that you can query it from a remote host. To do this, take the following steps:

1. On the system that has the Snort database, use a text editor to open the pg_hba.conf file. On many Red Hat systems, this file is in the /var/lib/pgsql/data/ directory.

2. Once in the database, add the following line at the end of the file:

```
host        snort      192.168.2.10      255.255.255.255          trust
```

This line allows the host with the IP address of 192.168.2.10 to access only the snort database from a remote connection. If, for example, you wished to allow all hosts on the 192.168.2.0 network to access this host, you would modify the line as shown:

```
host        snort      192.168.2.0      255.255.255.0            trust
```

3. Now, from a remote Linux host, issue the following command:

```
psql -h ids.yournetwork.com snort -U snort
```

This command uses the psql client to connect to the remote host named *ids* to access the database named *snort*, using the database user name of *snort*.

4. You will be logged into the remote database, and you can now issue queries just as if you were logged in at the console. This particular form of authentication is not as secure as others, because it relies upon authentication by IP address, and it also allows unencrypted transfer of information. Consult the PostgreSQL Web site (www.postgresql.org) for more information about securing communications. Options include using encrypted passwords and Secure Sockets Layer (SSL). Also, consider using IPsec between the hosts.

Identifying Snort Add-Ons

The following sections include a quick discussion of some applications written to help you read Snort log files. The first, called SnortSnarf, is a collection of Perl scripts designed to read the Snort alert file (/var/log/snort/alert) and then generate HTML output. The program is available either from www.silicondefense.com/software/snortsnarf, or from the src/ directory if you have installed Snort from a tarball.

SnortSnarf

You can configure SnortSnarf in various ways, including the ability to automatically process Nmap log files into HTML. Consult the documentation for more information. In the following short exercise, you will use SnortSnarf to generate an HTML report based on the Snort alert file.

Exercise: Using SnortSnarf to Read Snort Logs

1. Obtain the SnortSnarf file from the CD that accompanies this book (SnortSnarf-041501.1.tar.gz), and unpack it using the **tar –zxvf** command.

2. Change to the SnortSnarf-* directory, where * is the version of the program.

3. Find the snortsnarf.pl file and then open it in a text editor.

4. Some versions of SnortSnarf require that you make a minor change to the code. Find the text that reads snort.alert and change it to read as follows:

   ```
   snort/alert
   ```

5. After you have edited the file, issue the following command, substituting information that is valid for your host and network:

   ```
   ./snortsnarf.pl -d /var/www/html   -homenet x.x.x.x
   ```

6. After some time, the command will complete. Open a browser and access the /var/www/html/index.html page. You will see a page similar to that shown in Figure 4.12.

Analysis Console for Intrusion Databases

Analysis Console for Intrusion Databases (ACID) is a more sophisticated version of SnortSnarf. It connects your PostgreSQL or MySQL database to your Web server, which allows you to conduct searches right from your Web browser. You can download ACID from the following sites:

- www.cert.org/kb/acid

- http://sourceforge.net/projects/acid-mysql

- www.andrew.cmu.edu/~rdanyliw/snort/snortacid.html

Figure 4.12 Viewing SnortSnarf Output

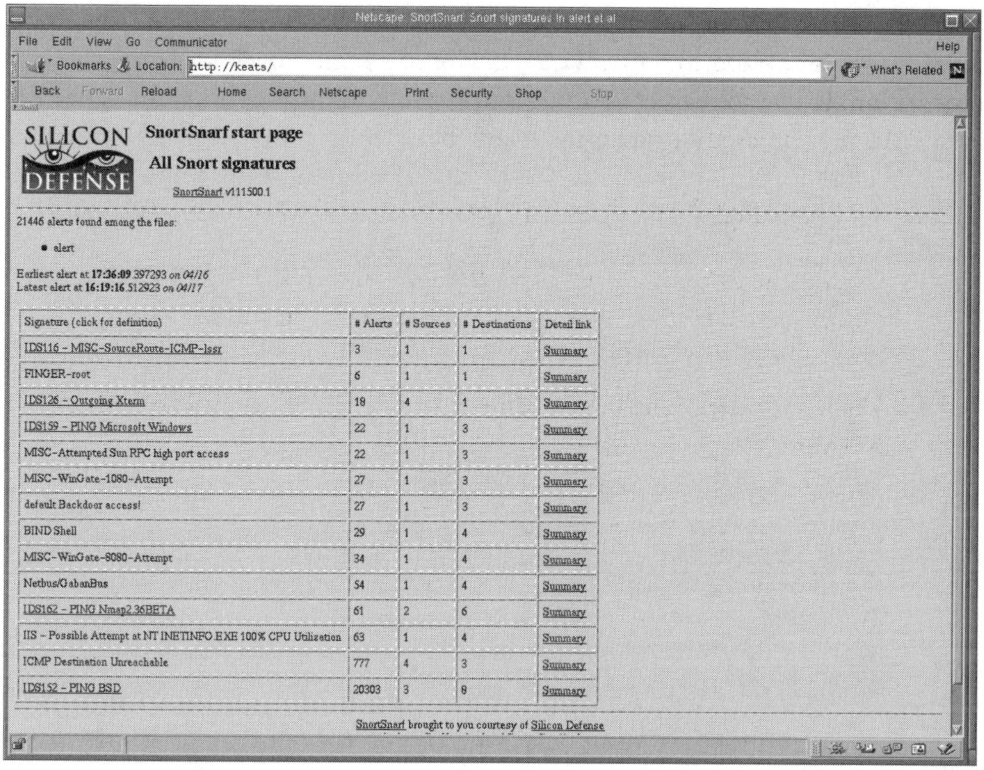

ACID requires the following items, in addition to Snort:

- **Apache Server** www.apache.org
- **PHP version 4** www.php.net
- **The Snort database plug-in** www.incident.org

For more information, consult any one of the ACID home pages.

Summary

In this chapter, you have implemented an IDS on your network. You have installed two host-based IDS applications (Tripwire and PortSentry), as well as a network-based IDS (Snort). Now, you can begin logging and analyzing connections for attacks, and you can proceed with a bit more confidence now that you have implemented some safeguards. Additional IDS applications exist, of course. In time, the open source community will create and adopt even more sophisticated tools to help you make your network more secure.

Several tasks lie ahead. You now get to:

1. Read even more logs than before you read this chapter.

2. Deploy the IDS applications you have read about on systems in your network.

3. Secure your IDS application elements (such as your PostgreSQL database) so that none of these elements can be compromised. For example, if you are logging to a remote database or file, find a way to secure the connection between the two hosts.

4. Monitor network and/or performance to make sure that your IDS is not significantly affecting performance.

So, even though an IDS helps you do your job, it will never be able to do your job for you. The open source community has done a fairly good job keeping current with the latest IDS demands. As the Linux kernel and operating system stabilizes further, chances are that you will be able to implement even more sophisticated solutions.

Solutions Fast Track

Understanding IDS Strategies and Types

☑ An Intrusion Detection System (IDS) is any system or set of systems that has the ability to detect a change in the status of your system or network. Because an IDS can contain multiple hosts and applications, this chapter will often use the term *IDS application* to refer to a specific IDS element.

☑ Two general strategies are used when it comes to detecting intrusions, rule-based IDS applications (also called *signature-based)* and anomaly-based IDS applications.

☑ IDS applications do their work either continuously in real-time, or at certain intervals (interval-based intrusion detection).

☑ Two different types of IDS applications exist: host-based and network-based.

☑ In many cases, an effective IDS application requires a great deal of processor time in order to work well. Log files require a great deal of hard drive space, especially in busy networks. Thus, simply for the sake of performance, consider using multiple systems to gather, store, and analyze information.

☑ Most network-based IDS applications do not work properly in a switched network.

☑ An IDS stores its information in several places: System logs, simple text files and directories, and databases.

☑ An IDS can act as a supplement to a firewall, because it can help you monitor traffic on the internal network. Sometimes it may be useful to place an IDS application outside the firewall, or in the DMZ so that you can learn more about the attacks waged against the firewall itself.

Installing Tripwire to Detect File Changes

☑ Tripwire is one of the most popular applications for determining when a file or directory has been altered. It scans your system's hard drive and creates a database. After its database has been created, Tripwire can conduct regular scans of your hard drive and inform you (via e-mail or a log file) about any changes.

Updating Tripwire to Account for Legitimate Changes in the OS

☑ Eventually, legitimate changes will occur to your operating system. These changes will keep appearing in reports unless you update your database. Database update mode allows you to update the database so that it no longer recognizes any differences between itself and the operating system.

☑ Updating the policy is different than updating the database. It is sometimes necessary to update your policy. If, for example, you install a new application, you may want to ensure that these files are protected by Tripwire.

Configuring Tripwire to Inform You Concerning Changes

☑ As with any Linux/Unix application, you will have to do quite a bit of "tweaking" to make Tripwire suit your needs. Refer back to the Installing Tripwire, Securing the Tripwire Database, and Using Cron to Run Tripwire Automatically Exercises for more information on how to install and use Tripwire.

Deploying PortSentry to Act as a Host-Based IDS

☑ PortSentry is a host-based IDS application that monitors all open ports. It is an effective tool if you wish to detect TCP and/or UDP port scans, and if you wish to have your host reconfigure itself in case of a port scan.

☑ PortSentry will compile on any standard Linux system that has TCPWrapper and Ipchains or Ipfw support.

☑ All of the PortSentry files are located off of the /usr/local/psionic/ portsentry/ directory. All files are owned by root, and the program must be started as root, because it places your NIC into promiscuous mode.

Configuring PortSentry to Block Users

☑ The Advanced Stealth Scan Detection Options determine the port numbers that PortSentry will monitor when you use the **-stcp** option to start PortSentry. By default, PortSentry listens only to ports up to 1023.

☑ The Dropping Routes section allows you to determine how PortSentry will deny connections. The KILL_ROUTE options allow you to configure various system tools to actually do the work of denying hosts.

Optimizing PortSentry to Sense Attack Types

☑ You can start PortSentry in various ways, depending upon the types of attacks you wish to detect. Customize each system that you have depending upon its function and place in your network.

Installing and Configuring Snort

☑ Snort, available at www.snort.org, is best-suited to detailed log analysis. Like PortSentry, it places your NIC into promiscuous mode. It captures all traffic on your network segment, as opposed to traffic destined for just one host.

☑ Snort can log its findings into remote or local databases. Snort's analysis feature is able to read the contents of the captured packets and then inform you about any attacks waged against your network.

☑ Snort is able to automatically detect attacks based solely upon the rules it uses.

☑ You can use several detection plug-ins. Sometimes, plug-ins do not require additional arguments. At other times, they require you to specify additional parameters.

Running Snort as a Network-Based IDS

☑ However, the snort.conf file gives you the ability to use Snort as a true IDS because it has Snort use rules and plug-ins. You can also specify more sophisticated home network and logging methods. After you begin using the rules and plug-ins found in snort.conf, it will begin selectively logging traffic.

Configuring Snort to Log to a Database

☑ On busy networks, it is necessary to configure Snort to log less information. Certain command-line options help you control how much your IDS will log.

☑ Additional configuration options are available, including the ability to configure Snort to send alerts to Windows systems that have the Server service running.

Identifying Snort Add-Ons

☑ SnortSnarf is a collection of Perl scripts designed to read the Snort alert file (/var/log/snort/alert) and then generate HTML output. The program is available from www.silicondefense.com/software/snortsnarf.

Frequently Asked Questions

The following Frequently Asked Questions, answered by the authors of this book, are designed to both measure your understanding of the concepts presented in this chapter and to assist you with real-life implementation of these concepts. To have your questions about this chapter answered by the author, browse to **www.syngress.com/solutions** and click on the **"Ask the Author"** form.

Q: I am trying to configure PortSentry to use both the **ipchains** and **route** command to drop suspect connections. Why doesn't the second command work?

A: Currently, PortSentry allows only one KILL_ROUTE line. If possible, use the Ipchains options. If your kernel doesn't support Ipchains (for example, if you are using the 2.4 kernel), then use the **route** option or work on using Iptables.

Q: I want to use Snort to automatically respond to attacks. How do I do this?

A: Compile Snort with the `--enable-flexresp` option. For more information on actually creating rules, consult the README.FLEXRESP file that comes with the RPM or source tarball.

Q: I have configured Tripwire, but I would like to send e-mail using Qmail rather than Sendmail. What can I do?

A: Open the /etc/tripwire/twcfg.txt and replace the MAILPROGRAM line with a reference to Qmail. You can also use Qmail-specific options to customize how Tripwire messages will be processed.

Q: Why doesn't my copy of Snort grab traffic to and from any other host than my own?

A: Unless you have somehow misconfigured your HOME_NET value (or some other element of the snort.conf file or the command line), you are probably on a switched network. If this is the case, Snort will only be able to capture traffic between the local host and any other that connects with it. In other words, Snort will behave just like a fancy version of PortSentry.

Q: I would rather use MySQL than PostgreSQL. What can I do?

A: Other than some minor changes in the snort.conf file, you simply have to install MySQL and then connect the database. You are in luck when it comes to Snort add-ons, as well, because they all work with either MySQL or PostgreSQL.

Q: What are some additional readings concerning how to implement an IDS?

A: You can choose from quite a few. Here are some of the more popular titles:

- *Network Intrusion Detection: An Analyst's Handbook* (2nd Edition), Stephen Northcutt, Donald McLachlan, and Judy Novak. Indianapolis: New Riders Publishing, 2000. ISBN: 0735710082.

- *Intrusion Detection*, Rebecca Bace. Indianapolis: MacMillan, 2000. ISBN: 1578701856.

- *Intrusion Detection: Network Security Beyond the Firewall*, Terry Escamilla. New York: John Wiley & Sons, 1998. ISBN: 0471290009.

## Chapter 5

Troubleshooting the Network with Sniffers

Solutions in this chapter:

- **Understanding Packet Analysis and TCP Handshakes**

- **Creating Filters Using Tcpdump**

- **Configuring Ethereal to Capture Network Packets**

- **Viewing Network Traffic between Hosts Using EtherApe**

☑ **Summary**

☑ **Solutions Fast Track**

☑ **Frequently Asked Questions**

Introduction

A sniffer, or packet sniffer, is software or hardware that captures network traffic. This traffic can be analyzed to determine problems in a network, such as bottle-necks or performance degradation. It can also confirm hacker attacks against your network systems. If you suspect a system is under attack, you can capture the packets on its interface to identify what types of packets are hitting the system, as well as where the packets originated. Once a problem is determined, an administrator can make network changes to ensure that the network operates efficiently and securely.

Packet sniffers capture packets on a specific interface, or on all interfaces, depending on how you configure the sniffer. By default, they display all traffic captured on the network. However, this usually results in far too much traffic for an administrator to sort through. Therefore, sniffers offer filters that allow you to only capture and display packets that meet particular criteria. For instance, you may only be interested in capturing packets between one client and one server to determine the server's response time, or to determine why a particular client cannot access a server. Sniffers allow you to enter the Internet Protocol (IP) addresses of the client and server, so that only the network traffic between the two IP addresses will be captured and displayed.

This chapter introduces you to three popular open source Linux sniffers:

- **Tcpdump** A command-line network traffic monitoring tool. It has been around for a long time and most graphical sniffers depend on it. Visit the tcpdump public repository at www.tcpdump.org. Tcpdump is shown in Figure 5.1.

- **Ethereal** A graphical network traffic-monitoring tool that is more user friendly than tcpdump. It allows you to view real-time packet captures and uses many tcpdump commands and options for filtering. Once the data is captured, Ethereal allows you to interactively view each packet and its individual headers. Descriptions of the packet headers are sum-marized. It also allows you to view reconstructed TCP streams. It dis-plays real-time traffic, as well as traffic saved to a file. Visit the Ethereal home page at www.ethereal.com. Ethereal is shown in Figure 5.2.

- **EtherApe** A graphical network traffic monitoring tool. Unlike Ethereal, EtherApe displays networking activity graphically by identifying hosts and the links that exist between the hosts. The links are color coded and change constantly as the host connections change. It displays real-time traffic, as well as traffic saved to a file. Visit the EtherApe home page at http://etherape.sourceforge.net. EtherApe is shown in Figure 5.3.

Figure 5.1 Tcpdump

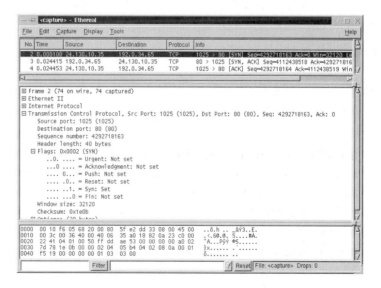

Figure 5.2 Ethereal

When you complete this chapter, you will know how to configure a packet sniffer. These skills will be assumed throughout the rest of this book, as packet sniffing is used regularly to determine network problems and possible security violations. You will capture packets regularly as a security professional.

Figure 5.3 EtherApe

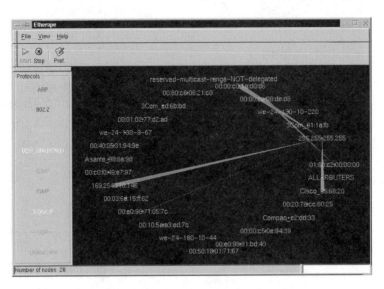

Before you use the individual open source sniffers, you must understand how to read a packet and be able to analyze a Transmission Control Protocol (TCP) connection. Without these skills, you will be unable to analyze the traffic captured by the sniffers.

Understanding Packet Analysis and TCP Handshakes

As you would expect, packet analysis requires an understanding of network packets. This chapter requires you to already understand the seven layers of the Open System Interconnection Reference Model (OSI/RM) and the TCP/IP protocols within each layer. If you are not familiar with the seven layers and their respective TCP/IP protocols, visit the Cisco Press Internetworking Basics document at www.cisco.com/cpress/cc/td/cpress/fund/ith2nd/it2401.htm. For additional Internetworking fundamentals documents, visit www.cisco.com/cpress/cc/td/cpress/fund.

One of the most important tasks for a security administrator is analyzing TCP traffic. It can tell us a great deal about our network connections. It can also identify many denial-of-service (DoS) attacks and man-in-the-middle, or hijacking, attacks. Because TCP is the protocol used for making a connection in TCP/IP, a careful analysis of the connection process can be extremely helpful for all packet analysis.

TCP Handshakes

Whenever two hosts establish a connection on a TCP/IP network, a TCP handshake must occur to establish the session. The handshake consists of rules that the two hosts must follow. All sniffers are capable of viewing any TCP connection establishment and termination, which includes the TCP handshake.

TCP handshakes use special mechanisms, called *flags*, to establish and terminate a connection. Flags are included in the TCP header, and each flag completes a different function in the TCP connection process. The flags used in a TCP connection are listed in Table 5.1. The next section explains how the flags are used in a TCP handshake.

Table 5.1 Flags Used in TCP Connections

Flag	Description
SYN	Synchronize sequence numbers. Used for connection establishment.
FIN	The sender is finished with the connection. Used for connection termination.
RST	Reset the connection.
PSH	Push the data.
ACK	Acknowledgment
URG	Urgent

Establishing a TCP Connection

To open a TCP connection, the TCP header includes different flags. The hosts exchange packets with these flags set to determine who opens the connection and who terminates the connection. The hosts must acknowledge each flag so that each host knows that the connection process is complete. If acknowledgments were not required, it would be much easier for hackers to hijack a TCP connection that was still active, even though the original host already thought it terminated the connection.

There are three steps required to open a TCP connection. These steps are called *the three-way handshake*. This example will be the establishment of a TCP connection between a client and a server.

1. **Client** Sends a SYN flag and the server port number with which it wants to communicate (such as port 80 for a Web server). It also includes the client's Initial Sequence Number (ISN).

2. **Server** Responds with its own SYN flag and ISN to the client's TCP port. It also responds with an ACK flag to acknowledge the client's SYN flag.

3. **Client** Responds with an ACK flag to acknowledge the server's SYN flag.

Once the three-way handshake is complete, a TCP connection is established. The Application layer protocols, such as Hypertext Transfer Protocol (HTTP), can now send data through this TCP connection. The three-way handshake is shown in Figure 5.4.

Figure 5.4 Three-Way Handshake

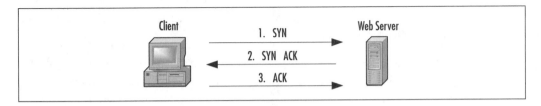

Terminating a TCP Connection

After the session is no longer required, or the data transfer between the hosts is complete, either host may terminate the TCP connection. There are four steps to terminate a TCP connection. Either host can terminate the connection (i.e., the client or the server). In this example, the server will terminate the connection.

1. **Server** Sends a FIN flag to the client. The FIN flag is usually sent in response to the client issuing a **close** command in an application on the server. This is often called an *active close*.

2. **Client** Responds with an ACK flag to acknowledge that the connection will be terminated.

3. **Client** Sends a FIN flag to the server. This is often called a *passive close*.

4. **Server** Responds with an ACK flag to acknowledge that the TCP connection is terminated.

Once both hosts acknowledge the FIN flag from the other host, the TCP connection is terminated. It is possible for data to be sent one way if only one direction has been terminated. However, most applications do not take advantage of this TCP possibility. The TCP termination process is shown in Figure 5.5.

Figure 5.5 Terminating a TCP Connection

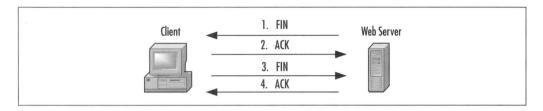

The TCP Flaw

An inherent flaw in TCP was discovered in the mid-1980s that has recently received attention in the media and in security advisories. The problem centers on the Initial Sequence Numbers (ISNs), which are packet numbers used in TCP connections. These numbers are only known by the hosts that are making the connection. The sequence numbers are used to identify legitimate packets and determine which packets are part of a given transmission. The packets that follow contain a sequence number based on the INS. The sequence number changes each time by adding the number of bytes that are transmitted to the other host.

The problem is that *if* the ISNs of a TCP connection are not random, or if they are not random in subsequent TCP sessions, a hacker can guess the ISN. If he or she guesses correctly, the hacker will be able to hijack the session.

Hackers attempting to exploit this vulnerability will have an extremely difficult time. Not only will they need to guess the ISN, but they must identify the vulnerable systems. The actual attack is extremely difficult to implement. However, if a hacker develops tools for this hack and makes it available on the Internet, any person with a modem and not much experience will be able to implement it.

The TCP flaw is 20 years old and is still a concern. As recently as 1996, researchers at AT&T proposed a solution to the Internet Engineering Task Force (IETF). To date, only OpenBSD is considered to have consistently random ISNs. Linux and Solaris would be considered average at performing this task.

Creating Filters Using Tcpdump

Tcpdump is a command-line network traffic-monitoring tool that can capture packets on a network interface and allows administrators to analyze the results. It is maintained by the TCPDUMP Group.

Because tcpdump is a command-line tool, analyzing the results can be difficult. Tcpdump allows you to capture all packets on a given interface, or all interfaces on a system, for analysis. If the interface is not specified, it searches for the lowest interface number, excluding the loopback, and prints the packets for that interface. To filter the packets that tcpdump captures, you can add filters by using options and expressions, which you will learn about in this section.

As stated earlier, tcpdump has been around for a long time, and most graphical sniffers use similar filter specifications. Tcpdump usually installs during standard Linux installations. The tcpdump public repository is located at www.tcpdump.org, and the Red Hat Linux tcpdump Red Hat Package Manager (RPM) can be downloaded at www.redhat.com/apps/download/ (keyword *tcpdump*). For Linux installation, the program must be installed as root, or setuid to root.

Any version of tcpdump will work for the following examples. Version 3.6 and later has additional support for IPv6 and support for Solaris 8. If you require either feature, download version 3.6 or later.

Tcpdump Options

Options are used in tcpdump to filter the amount of packets your system captures. Without them, administrators can be overwhelmed by the number of packets that tcpdump prints. Figure 5.6 displays the printout of 12 packets captured in just .3 milliseconds. All network packets were captured without any filters. Several Address Resolution Protocol (ARP) requests exist, and all packets were captured on the default eth0 interface, since no interface was specified.

Table 5.2 lists many of the tcpdump options that assist in filtering tcpdump captures. For a complete listing, please access the tcpdump man page.

Figure 5.6 Tcpdump Capture without Options or Expressions

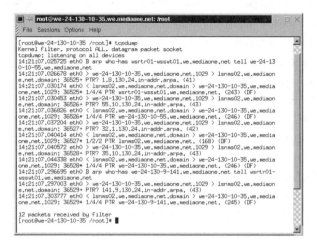

Table 5.2 Tcpdump Options

Option	Description
-a	Display data in ASCII.
-b	Capture packets using the Data Link layer specified. These include the following protocols (see RFC 1340 if you want to list these protocols as decimal values): ip ipv6 802.2 802.3 arp rarp dec lat atalk aarp x25 ipx
-c	Quit tcpdump after a specific number (count) of packets have been captured.
-e	List the link-level header for each packet that is captured.
-F	Instead of listing options and expressions, you can use a file as the input for your filter expression. If a file is used, any expressions you list on the command line will be ignored.

Continued

www.syngress.com

Table 5.2 Continued

Option	Description
-i	Specify the interface you want tcpdump to listen. If the interface is not specified, it searches for the lowest interface number, excluding the loopback, and prints the packets for that interface.
-n	Do not list host names, only list host addresses as numbers (such as IP addresses). This avoids Domain Name System (DNS) lookups.
-nn	Do not list port numbers as service names. The /etc/services file is used for the service names.
-p	Do not enable promiscuous mode for the interface.
-q	Quick output to reduce the amount of protocol information displayed by tcpdump on each line.
-r	Read packet data from a saved file instead of capturing data on an interface.
-t	Do not list the timestamp.
-v	Print out verbose output from the capture. Includes even more data, such as time-to-live (TTL) and type of service data. The –**vv** option will list additional data.
-w	Write the tcpdump packet capture to a file instead of displaying it.
-x	Display the packet information in hexadecimal format.

You can use options to filter out all traffic except for ARP requests and replies. To do this, enter the following:

```
tcpdump -b arp
```

In Figure 5.7, notice that only ARP requests and replies appear. The requests are *arp who-has* entries, and the reply is listed as an *arp reply* entry. There is only one reply (entry number 10) in this capture, but many ARP requests.

In the next example, you will use options to filter out host names, specify your interface, capture only 10 packets, and only capture ARP packets again. To do this, enter the following:

```
tcpdump arp -n -i eth0 -c 10
```

In Figure 5.8, notice that host names no longer appear, and IP addresses and hardware addresses are captured. Notice that most of the ARP requests are broadcasts. Line 4 is an ARP request for the hardware address of 24.130.8.1, which happens to be the default gateway of that system. The ARP reply follows in line 5, which lists the hardware address as 0:10:f6:5:68:20.

Figure 5.7 ARP Filter

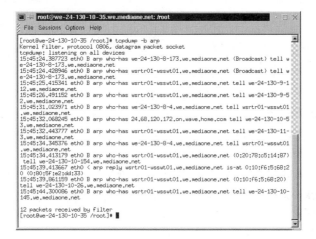

Figure 5.8 ARP Filter with No Host Names, a Specified Interface, and a 10 Count

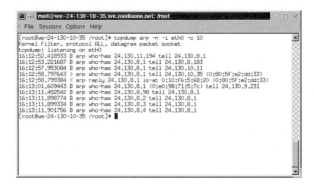

Tcpdump Expressions

The tcpdump options listed in Table 5.2 are important in determining how the data will be printed. Tcpdump *expressions* can determine which network hosts you will capture data from. If you do not specify an expression, all packets on the network between all hosts will be printed. An expression will ensure that only the data you require, such as the IP traffic between your interface and a specific host, will be printed.

Each expression is made up of at least one *primitive*. A primitive is an *id* followed by *qualifiers*. An id is a host name or number, and a qualifier can one of three types, as shown in Table 5.3.

Table 5.3 Three Types of Qualifiers in an Expression

Qualifier	Description
type	Specifies the id as a host, network, or port. The syntax is **host**, **net**, or **port**. For example, you can enter host 24.130.10.35, net 192.168.60, or port 80.
dir	Specifies the direction of traffic you want to capture. By default, traffic in both directions will be captured, which is **src** or **dst**. The directions you can specify are **dst**, **src**, **src and dst**, and **src or dst**. For Data Link layer protocols, such as Serial Line Internet Protocol (SLIP) or Point-to-Point (PPP), use the *inbound* and *outbound* qualifiers to define your direction.
proto	Specifies a protocol to capture. The protocols you can choose from are the following: ether fddi ip arp rarp decnet lat sca moprc mopddl tcp udp

You can combine qualifiers to include several different filters. For example, you can enter the tcpdump command followed by **ether dst 24.130.10.35** or **tcp port 80**. It all depends on how specific you want your search to be. The following examples in Table 5.4 are allowable primitives that you can use. Notice the repetition between the *host*, *ether*, *net* and *port* primitives. For more examples, see the tcpdump man page.

Table 5.4 Allowable Primitives

Primitive	Description
dst host *host*	Captures all packets with the destination IP address (or name) of the specified host.
src host *host*	Captures all packets with the source IP address (or name) of the specified host.

Continued

Table 5.4 Continued

Primitive	Description
host *host*	Captures all packets with the source and destination IP address (or name) of the specified host.
ether dst *ethernet_host*	Captures all packets with the destination Ethernet address (or name from /etc/ethers) of the specified Ethernet host.
ether src *ethernet_host*	Captures all packets with the source Ethernet address (or name from /etc/ethers) of the specified Ethernet host.
ether host *ethernet_host*	Captures all packets with the source and destination Ethernet address (or name from /etc/ethers) of the specified Ethernet host.
dst net *network*	Captures all packets with the destination network address (or name from /etc/networks) of the specified network.
src net *network*	Captures all packets with the source network address (or name from /etc/networks) of the specified network.
net *network*	Captures all packets with the source and destination network address (or name from /etc/networks) of the specified network.
dst port *port*	Captures all packets with the destination port number (or name from /etc/services) of the specified port.
src port *port*	Captures all packets with the source port number (or name from /etc/services) of the specified port.
port *port*	Captures all packets with the source and destination port number (or name from /etc/services) of the specified port.

In the following example, the host we-24-130-10-192.we.mediaone.net will be monitored for all packets with its host name in the source or destination fields. You need to select a host name that you can monitor on your local network. This will not work outside of your network.

I used the hostname of a local workstation. To generate traffic, I pinged the host from my system. In Figure 5.10, you can see an ARP request and reply, the echo request and reply, and Windows Network Basic Input/Output System (NetBIOS) User Datagram Protocol (UDP) packets. As you can see, we are monitoring a Windows host from our Linux system. The tcpdump command entered on the Linux system is:

```
tcpdump host we-24-130-10-192.we.mediaone.net
```

The results are shown in Figure 5.9.

Figure 5.9 Monitoring a Host on a Local Network

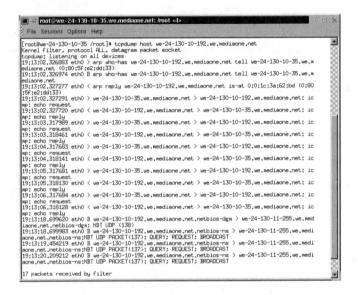

The following primitives listed in Table 5.5 are extremely helpful for identifying specific protocols, broadcasts, and multicasts on a network.

Table 5.5 Additional Primitives

Primitive	Description
tcp udp icmp ip arp rarp decnet	Captures all packets that match the specified protocol.
ether broadcast	Captures all Ethernet broadcast packets.
ip broadcast	Captures all IP broadcast packets. This includes all-one and all-zero broadcasts, as well as broadcasts based on the subnet-directed broadcasts. Helpful for determining

Continued

Table 5.5 Continued

Primitive	Description
	problems with automatic IP address allocations, such as Bootstrap Protocol (BOOTP) and Dynamic Host Configuration Protocol (DHCP).
ether multicast	Captures all Ethernet multicast packets.
ip multicast	Captures all IP multicast packets.

For example, if you believe your system is experiencing a denial-of-service (DoS) attack, you can filter out Internet Control Message Protocol (ICMP) packets to determine if that system is the victim of a ping flood. To filter out ICMP packets that are destined to your system, enter the following command:

```
tcpdump  icmp -n -i eth0
```

The results are shown in Figure 5.10. As you can see, the host names are filtered out, as well as all protocols except for ICMP protocols. This can assist you in determining the source of the ping flood. In this case, the ICMP echo request packets are originating from a host at 24.130.10.192.

Figure 5.10 Determining the Source of a Ping Flood Using Primitives

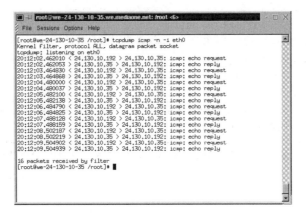

Boolean Operators

You can also use Boolean operators to further specify a filter. Boolean operators are the AND, OR, and NOT operators. For example, you can specify that you want to capture packets between 192.168.60.10 *and* 192.168.60.11. You can also capture packets between bob *or* susan. Finally, you can capture packets between susan and all hosts except for bob by using the *not* operator.

In the next example, you will capture packets between a host and the Web server at www.tcpdump.org by using a Boolean operator. The command is as follows (substitute your host name or IP address):

```
tcpdump –i eth0 host we-24-130-10-35.we.mediaone.net and www.tcpdump.org
```

Only the packets sent between the mediaone.net host and the www.tcpdump .org Web server appear, as shown in Figure 5.11.

Figure 5.11 Capturing Packets between Two Specific Hosts

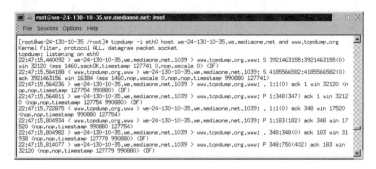

> **NOTE**
>
> The first three packets in Figure 5.12 comprise the TCP three-way hand-shake that establishes the TCP session. After the handshake, the Web page data is downloaded to the client, such as the images and text files that make up the Web page.

To learn more about Boolean operators, please consult the tcpdump man page. You now have enough knowledge to create meaningful filters in tcpdump.

Installing and Using Tcpdump

Your system should already have a version of tcpdump installed. If you require the latest version of tcpdump (for instance, you need bug-free IPv6 support), you should visit the tcpdump repository at www.tcpdump.org and download the latest version. The tcpdump repository is shown in Figure 5.12.

Figure 5.12 Tcpdump Repository

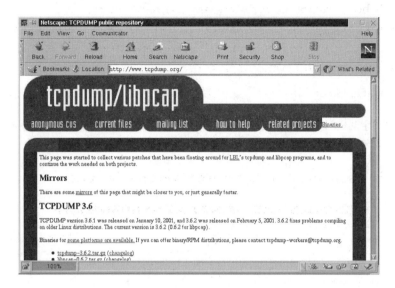

If you are using Red Hat Linux, you can download the latest RPM at www.redhat.com/apps/download and perform a search for keyword *tcpdump*. The latest RPM is usually several versions behind the latest tcpdump repository version. Follow these steps to install tcpdump:

1. Verify that the tcpdump RPM is installed on your system by entering:

```
rpm -qa | grep tcpdump
```

2. If you do not receive a reply, such as tcpdump-3.x-x, then you need to download and install tcpdump.

3. Once you have verified tcpdump is installed, you are ready to capture packets.

4. Capture all the packets on your network by entering:

```
tcpdump
```

5. Press **CTRL+C** and to stop the capture.

NOTE

If no packets appear after you stop the capture, you need to generate packets. For example, you can ping localhost or a server.

6. View the captured packets. It may resemble the following packet, which will be used to describe some of the important features of the packet.

```
23:20:26.356520 eth0 > we-24-130-10-35.we.mediaone.net.1047 >
    www.tcpdump.org.www: S 1722963211:1722963211(0)
```

The first section is the timestamp (23:20:26) followed by milliseconds (.356520). The interface used to capture the packets is eth0. Next, the source host is the we-24-130-10-35.we.mediaone.net. It is sending the packet using its TCP port 1047. It is sending this packet to the destination host www.tcpdump.org. The destination port is port 80, which is identified as *www* in the /etc/services file (the port number or port name can be used). The *S* is a synchronize flag used in a TCP handshake. In this case, it is the first SYN flag sent to the server. Therefore, the ISN for the TCP connection is 1722963211. All sequence numbers for this TCP connection will be based on this ISN. 1722963211:1722953211 is also the starting sequence number and the ending sequence number for this packet. The (0) indicates that no data (in bytes) is sent with this packet. If data had been sent with this packet, the ending sequence number would have increased by the number of bytes sent.

7. Can you find any TCP handshakes in your packet capture? Identify the basic elements of the packets you have captured using the previous step as an example.

8. Next, capture only ARP packets on your network by entering the following:

```
tcpdump -b arp
```

9. Capture ARP packets again, but specify the interface to use (eth0 is used as an example):

```
tcpdump -i eth0 -b arp
```

10. Capture IP packets this time. Print the results with number only (no DNS lookups required) and only capture 12 packets. To accomplish this task, enter:

```
tcpdump -n ip -c 12
```

Your screen may resemble Figure 5.13, depending on your network traffic.

Figure 5.13 Tcpdump Command Using Filters

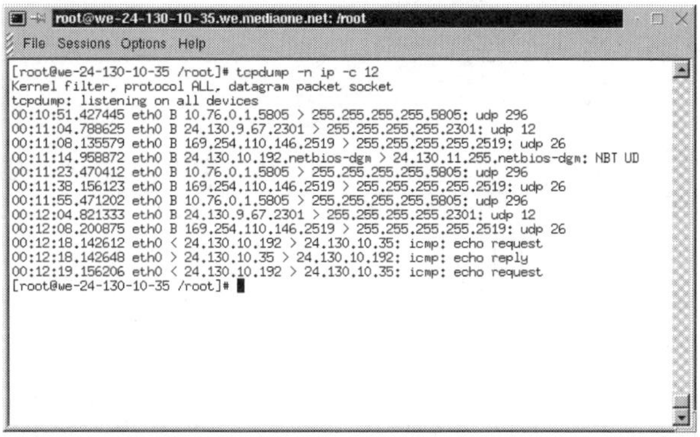

```
root@we-24-130-10-35.we.mediaone.net: /root
File  Sessions  Options  Help
[root@we-24-130-10-35 /root]# tcpdump -n ip -c 12
Kernel filter, protocol ALL, datagram packet socket
tcpdump: listening on all devices
00:10:51.427445 eth0 B 10.76.0.1.5805 > 255.255.255.255.5805: udp 296
00:11:04.788625 eth0 B 24.130.9.67.2301 > 255.255.255.255.2301: udp 12
00:11:08.135579 eth0 B 169.254.110.146.2519 > 255.255.255.255.2519: udp 26
00:11:14.958872 eth0 B 24.130.10.192.netbios-dgm > 24.130.11.255.netbios-dgm: NBT UD
00:11:23.470412 eth0 B 10.76.0.1.5805 > 255.255.255.255.5805: udp 296
00:11:38.156123 eth0 B 169.254.110.146.2519 > 255.255.255.255.2519: udp 26
00:11:55.471202 eth0 B 10.76.0.1.5805 > 255.255.255.255.5805: udp 296
00:12:04.821333 eth0 B 24.130.9.67.2301 > 255.255.255.255.2301: udp 12
00:12:08.200875 eth0 B 169.254.110.146.2519 > 255.255.255.255.2519: udp 26
00:12:18.142612 eth0 < 24.130.10.192 > 24.130.10.35: icmp: echo request
00:12:18.142648 eth0 > 24.130.10.35 > 24.130.10.192: icmp: echo reply
00:12:19.156206 eth0 < 24.130.10.192 > 24.130.10.35: icmp: echo request
[root@we-24-130-10-35 /root]#
```

11. Capture source and destination packets to another host on your network. For example, enter:

    ```
    tcpdump host [hostname]
    ```

12. Capture a specific type of packet on your interface. For example, enter:

    ```
    tcpdump icmp -i eth0
    ```

13. Finally, capture packets between your system and another system, such as a Web server. For example, enter:

    ```
    tcpdump -i eth0 [your_hostname] and www.tcpdump.org
    ```

You have learned the basics of tcpdump. You can apply this knowledge to all sniffer programs because tcpdump is the basis for all sniffers. Because tcpdump is difficult to analyze, and because the file size is flat, many network administrators use graphical sniffers to determine network problems and to troubleshoot possible security threats. The remaining sniffers in this lesson are more user friendly than tcpdump and will simplify the packet analysis process.

Configuring Ethereal to Capture Network Packets

Ethereal is a graphical user interface (GUI) packet sniffer that is much easier to use than tcpdump. It performs the same tasks as tcpdump, but in a user-friendly format. Because Ethereal uses many of the same filters as tcpdump, it is essential that you fully understand the tcpdump commands and filters, as they will be used in Ethereal throughout this chapter and in your daily administrative work.

Ethereal is very flexible because it allows you to read capture files from other programs, such as tcpdump, Network Associate Sniffer Basic and Sniffer Pro, NetXRay (now Sniffer Basic), snoop, atmsnoop, Microsoft Network Monitor, and Lucent/Ascend router debug output. When opening these files, Ethereal automatically determines the file type.

Both Ethereal and tcpdump capture packets using the pcap library (libpcap). Since they both use the pcap library syntax, they can share many of the same commands, such as filtering options and primitives.

Ethereal uses the same screen format as other packet sniffers—if you learn how to use Ethereal, you can apply your knowledge to any GUI sniffer. It divides the screen into three panes. The top pane is used for *packet summary*. It typically shows the summary of many different packets. The middle pane is a *protocol tree*, which displays the OSI/RM layers of the selected packet in the summary pane. The bottom pane is a *hex dump*. The hex dump displays the packet as it looks when traveling across the physical wire. Figure 5.14 displays a random packet capture of a network. Note that the pane sizes are adjustable.

Figure 5.14 Ethereal Panes

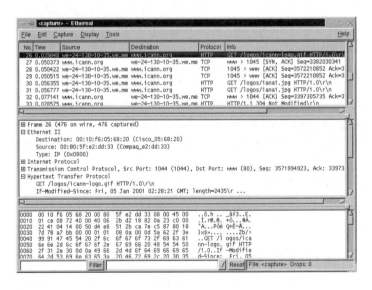

In Figure 5.15, an **HTTP GET** command is listed in the summary pane, which is the top pane. It displays the basic data regarding the packet. In this case, it states that the **HTTP GET** command will download the icann–logo.gif image to the client's Web browser.

Figure 5.15 Hex Code for an HTTP GET Command

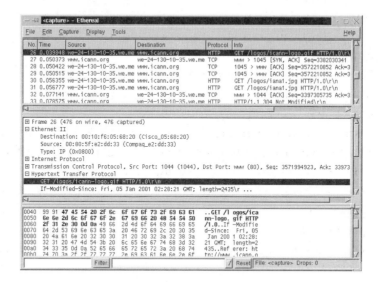

The second pane displays the protocol tree for the packet. Each packet can be expanded by selecting the **+** sign. You can discover a great deal about each packet using the protocol tree, such as the hardware address of your host (Ethernet II Source field) and your default gateway (Ethernet II Destination field), the TCP port number and sequence numbers, and all Application layer activity. Expand each protocol to learn more about the packet.

The third pane displays the hexadecimal format of the packet, which is how it appears when traveling over the wire. If you highlight a line in the protocol tree, the corresponding hex code will appear in the hex pane, as shown in Figure 5.15.

Ethereal Options

Unlike tcpdump, Ethereal options are run before the packet capture occurs (in most cases). The options are run at the command line before the program runs. For example, at the command line you would enter:

```
ethereal [options]
```

The program will run using the options you specify. For example, if you wanted Ethereal to use numbers instead of host names to avoid DNS lookups, you would specify this as an option at the command line *before* the program runs. The Ethereal options are listed in Table 5.6.

Table 5.6 Ethereal Options

Option	Description
-c	Defines the default number of packets to capture.
-f	Defines the filter expression to use for all captures.
-h	Displays the version number and available options.
-i	Defines the interface to use for all captures.
-k	Instructs Ethereal to start the packet capture immediately. If the interface is not defined, Ethereal (similar to tcpdump) uses the lowest number interface (excluding the loopback).
-m	Defines the font for Ethereal text.
-n	Disables names in Ethereal so only numbers will be used. This disables DNS lookups, as well as TCP and UDP port names.
-r	Instructs Ethereal to display a packet capture within a file.
-R	Allows you to apply a packet filter to a file. Any packet that does not apply to the filter is removed from the display.
-s	Defines the default length, in bytes, of each packet capture.
-t	Defines the timestamp format. There are three choices: **Absolute (a)** Actual time and date the packet is captured. **Delta (d)** The time since the last packet was captured. **Relative (r)** The time since the first packet was captured in the current packet capture. By default, the relative timestamp format is used.
-w	Defines the default packet capture filename.

NOTE

When determining the timestamp format to use, consider the purpose of your packet capture. If you are determining the performance response time of a server, the *delta* timestamp is ideal because it will indicate how long it takes a server to respond to a client request. If you are determining a possible attack, you may want to use *absolute* timestamp to document the date and time an attack took place.

Ethereal Filters

Ethereal filters are similar to the filters in tcpdump. The easiest way to apply filters is to open the program using the **ethereal** command at the command line, and then using the GUI to navigate to the filter configuration screen. You can then use the same filters used in tcpdump. The only difference is that you will not enter **tcpdump** before the filter specifications.

Once benefit of Ethereal is that you can easily save your filters and access them as needed for each packet capture you make. You can have multiple filters from which to choose for different needs. For example, one filter might be used for capturing packets between two hosts, while another is used to capture ICMP packets on the network for troubleshooting purposes.

To learn more about filter syntax, please consult the Ethereal and/or tcpdump man page.

Configuring Ethereal and Capturing Packets

The following steps will teach you how to configure Ethereal and capture packets on your network. Your system may already have a version of Ethereal installed. If you require the latest version of Ethereal, you should visit the Ethereal Web site at www.ethereal.com and download the latest version. (This RPM is also available on the CD accompanying this book (ethereal-0.8.9-4.i386.rpm). The Ethereal Web site is shown in Figure 5.16.

Figure 5.16 The Ethereal Download Site

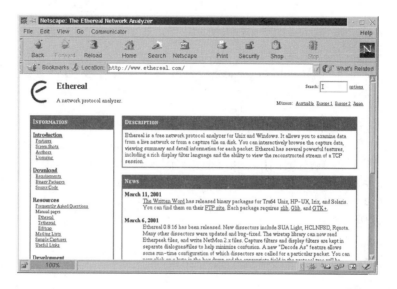

If you are using Red Hat Linux, you can use the files on the CD or download the latest RPM at www.redhat.com/apps/download and perform a search for keyword *ethereal*. The latest RPM is usually several versions behind the latest Ethereal Web site version. To install Ethereal, complete the following steps:

1. Verify that the Ethereal RPM is installed on your system by entering:

   ```
   rpm -qa | grep ethereal
   ```

2. If you do not receive a reply, such as ethereal-8.x-x, you need to download and install Ethereal.

3. Once you have verified that Ethereal is installed, you are ready to capture packets.

4. To add filters to Ethereal, open a command interface and enter:

   ```
   ethereal
   ```

5. Select the **Edit menu**, and choose **Filters**. The Ethereal: Filters screen appears, as shown in Figure 5.17. Since no filters have been configured, the configuration screen is blank.

Figure 5.17 Ethereal Filter Configuration Screen

6. To create a filter that allows only traffic between your host and another host, you must add a filter name and a filter string. For example, to create a filter between your host and the Web server at the ICANN (192.0.34.65), enter the filter name and filter string shown in Figure 5.18. Enter your IP address, not the 24.130.11.35 address listed in Figure 5.18.

Figure 5.18 Creating a Filter between Two Hosts

NOTE

The filter string in Ethereal is the same primitive used in tcpdump. Both Ethereal and tcpdump use libpcap, which allows them to share many of the same filter configurations.

7. This filter will only capture packets with a source or destination address that matches 24.130.11.35 (the IP address of my system) and 192.0.34.65 (the IP address of the ICANN Web server). Please note that we could have also listed the host names (we-24-130-11-35.we.mediaone.net and www.icann.org).

8. After the two fields are complete, click **Save**, and then click **New**. Your filter will appear in the filter field, as shown in Figure 5.19.

Figure 5.19 Completing the Filter Creation Process

9. Click **OK** to return to Ethereal. You can add additional filters, such as an ICMP filter, by repeating the process. Your new filter will appear in the

Ethereal: Filter screen directly beneath the ICANN Web Server Filter. Each new filter will simply be added to the list, as shown in Figure 5.20.

Figure 5.20 Adding Multiple Filters

10. To add the filter to a packet capture, you need to specify the filter. You can do this before or after the packet capture occurs. For example, to apply the filter before the capture, simply select the Capture menu and choose **Start**. The Capture Preference screen appears, as shown in Figure 5.21. Click **Filter** and choose the filter that you want to apply. In Figure 5.21, the ICMP filter was chosen.

Figure 5.21 Ethereal Capture Preferences

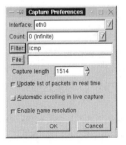

Notice that the **Update list of packets in real time** and **Enable name resolution** check boxes are selected. This ensures that packets are displayed as they are captured (i.e., "live"), instead of displaying them only when the capture is complete. The **Enable name resolution** check box will display host names, as well as protocol names. You can also disable name resolution at the command line by entering **ethereal –n** when you run Ethereal, or by deselecting the **Enable name resolution** check box in the Capture Preferences screen.

11. After you select the desired filter, click **OK** and the capture starts. Packets appear as they are captured so you can analyze the traffic on your network in real time. When you capture several packets, click **Stop**.

12. The packet capture appears in Ethereal. Your screen may resemble Figure 5.22, which shows Router solicitation packets and echo request and replies on the network.

Figure 5.22 Ethereal Packet Capture with Filter Applied

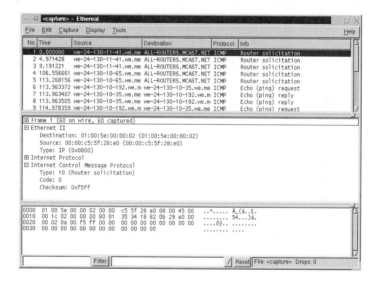

> **NOTE**
>
> Ethereal can take a long time to process packets after you stop the capture. Be patient. You may have to wait up to a minute for the captured packets to display properly. You may lose your capture if you interrupt Ethereal before it displays the packets.

13. Apply the host filter you created in Step 6 to filter only traffic between your host and another host (i.e., a server).

14. Create your own filters and apply them to a packet capture. Use the filter techniques you learned in the tcpdump section, especially the primitives in Tables 5.4 and 5.5.

As you can see, the GUI provided by Ethereal allows administrators to view detailed information about each packet. The protocol tree is especially helpful in determining the purpose of each protocol within the packet. The combination of Ethereal and tcpdump provides administrators with almost all of their sniffer needs on Linux systems.

Viewing Network Traffic between Hosts Using EtherApe

EtherApe is a graphical network traffic-monitoring tool. Unlike Ethereal, EtherApe displays networking activity graphically by identifying hosts and the links that exist between the hosts. The links are color coded and change constantly as the host connections change. It displays real -time traffic, as well as traffic saved to a file. Visit the EtherApe home page at http://etherape.sourceforge.net, shown in Figure 5.23.

Figure 5.23 EtherApe Home Page

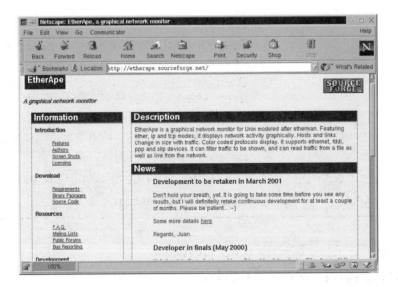

As you can see, EtherApe supports Ethernet, Fiber Distributed Data Interface (FDDI), PPP, and SLIP devices, and is capable of reading network traffic live and from a file. It can also save network traffic and display it later. The program uses GNU Network Object Model Environment (GNOME) libraries for the interface. Similar to tcpdump and Ethereal, EtherApe uses libpcap, the library for packet capturing and filtering.

EtherApe uses the command-line options listed in Table 5.7. Enter these options as needed when you run the program. Use the format:

```
etherape [options]
```

Table 5.7 EtherApe Options

Option	Name	Description
-d	Diagram only	Do not display diagram text.
-f	Filter	Define a specific capture filter.
-F	No fade	Do not allow old links to fade in diagram.
-i	Interface	Define the interface for EtherApe to listen for network traffic.
-L	Link color	Define the color of the diagram links.
-m	Mode	Define the operation mode. You can choose from the following: ethernet fddi ip tcp By default, the lowest level is used for the device.
-n	Numeric	Disables names so that only numbers will be used. This disables DNS lookups, as well as TCP and UDP port names.
-n	Text color	Define the color of the diagram nodes.
-r	Infile	Defines the input file.
-T	Text color	Define the color of the diagram text.
-?	Help	Display help message.

Configuring EtherApe and Viewing Network Traffic

The following steps will teach you how to configure EtherApe and view traffic on your network. Your system may already have a version of EtherApe installed. If you require the latest version of EtherApe, you should visit the EtherApe Web site at http://etherape.source-forge.net and download the latest version.

If you are using Red Hat Linux, you can download the latest RPM at www.redhat.com/apps/download and perform a search for keyword *EtherApe*. (This RPM is also available on the CD accompanying this book: etherape-0.5.6-4.i386.rpm.) To install EtherApe, complete the following steps:

1. Verify that the EtherApe RPM is installed on your system by entering:

    ```
    rpm -qa | grep etherape
    ```

2.   If you do not receive a reply, such as etherape-0.5.x-x, you need to download and install EtherApe.

3. Once you have verified EtherApe is installed, you are ready to capture packets.

4. To open EtherApe, open a command interface and enter:

    ```
    etherape
    ```

5. EtherApe opens and displays the network traffic diagram by default. If you are running Red Hat Linux 7, the diagram text is unreadable. You must select a font in order to read the text. To select a font, click **Preferences** on the EtherApe toolbar. The EtherApe Preference screen appears, as shown in Figure 5.24.

    Figure 5.24 EtherApe Preferences: Choosing a Readable Font (If Necessary)

    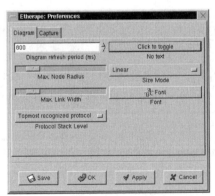

6. Click **Font** and choose a font; for example, Helvetica or Times New Roman. Click **Save** so you will not have to do this again, and then click **OK**.

7. The network traffic diagram now appears with readable network addresses, as shown in Figure 5.25.

Figure 5.25 Ethernet Traffic on EtherApe

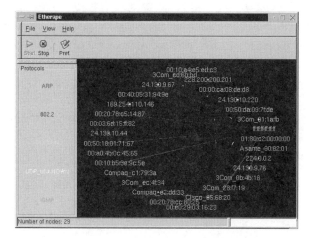

8. By default, EtherApe diagrams the lowest-layer protocols, which are Ethernet protocols. If you are diagramming a busy network, ARP packets may quickly overrun your diagram. To diagram IP traffic instead, exit EtherApe. At the command line, enter:

```
etherape -m ip
```

This command opens EtherApe in IP mode, which will display the IP addresses and host names on your network, as shown in Figure 5.26.

Figure 5.26 EtherApe in IP Mode

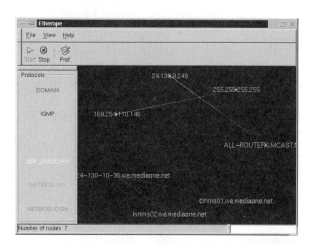

9. Experiment with the filter field by clicking **Preferences** and selecting the **Capture** tab. Using the **Capture filter** field, create an end-to-end IP filter or a port-to-port TCP filter.

As you can see, EtherApe offers a graphical representation of your network traffic. Instead of displaying individual packets, it creates a diagram of network traffic links between hosts. EtherApe used in conjunction with tcpdump, and Ethereal provides a complete toolkit for a network administrator.

Summary

In this chapter, you learned that a *sniffer*, or *packet sniffer*, is software or hardware that captures network traffic. This traffic can be analyzed to determine problems in a network, such as bottlenecks or performance degradation. It can also confirm hacker attacks against your network systems. If you suspect a system is under attack, you can capture the packets on its interface to identify what types of packets are hitting the system, as well as where the packets originated. Once a problem is determined, an administrator can make network changes to ensure that the network operates efficiently and securely.

You learned about three different programs that capture packets using the pcap library (libpcap), as well as the importance of identifying packet functions. For example, you learned about the function of a *TCP handshake*, how to identify one, and its importance on TCP/IP networks.

Tcpdump is a command-line network traffic-monitoring tool that prints out packet headers on a network interface and allows administrators to analyze the results. Because tcpdump is a command-line tool, analyzing the results can be difficult. Options are used in tcpdump to filter the amount of packets your system captures. Without them, administrators can be overwhelmed by the number of packets that tcpdump prints. An expression determines from which network hosts you will capture data. If you do not specify an expression, all packets on the network between all hosts will be printed. An expression will ensure that only the data you require, such as the IP traffic between your interface and a specific host, will be printed.

Ethereal is a graphical user interface (GUI) packet sniffer that is much easier to use than tcpdump. It performs the same tasks as tcpdump, but in a user-friendly format. Ethereal uses the same screen format as other packet sniffers. If you learn how to use Ethereal, you can apply your knowledge to any GUI sniffer. It divides the screen into three panes. The top pane is used for packet summary, and typically shows the summary of many different packets. The middle pane is a protocol tree, which displays the OSI/RM layers of the selected packet in the summary pane. The bottom pane is a hex dump. The hex dump displays the packet as it looks when traveling across the physical wire.

EtherApe is a graphical network traffic-monitoring tool. Unlike Ethereal, EtherApe displays networking activity graphically by identifying hosts and the links that exist between the hosts. The links are color coded and change constantly as the host connections change.

EtherApe used in conjunction with tcpdump and Ethereal provides a complete toolkit for a network administrator. All three packet-capturing tools provide troubleshooting assistance for network problems, and can be used to identify potential security problems on your network. You will use these tools throughout this book, so it is important that you have an understanding of their functionality.

Solutions Fast Track

Understanding Packet Analysis and TCP Handshakes

☑ Analyzing TCP traffic is one of the most important tasks for a security administrator. It can tell you a great deal about your network connections, as well as identify many denial-of-service (DoS) attacks and man-in-the-middle, or hijacking, attacks.

☑ A TCP handshake must occur whenever two hosts establish a connection on a TCP/IP network. This handshake consists of rules that the two hosts must follow.

☑ Special mechanisms, called *flags*, are used to establish and terminate a TCP connection. Flags are included in the TCP header, and each flag completes a different function in the TCP handshake. The flags used are SYN, FIN, RST, PSH, ACK, and URG.

Creating Filters Using Tcpdump

☑ Tcpdump captures packets on a given interface, or on all interfaces on a system, for analysis. It is a command-line tool, which can make it difficult to read.

☑ Tcpdump options allow you to filter the packets that are captured. For example, you can limit the capture to ARP packets or display only IP addresses (not host names).

☑ Tcpdump expressions allow you to specify the hosts from which you will capture packets. For example, an expression will ensure that only the data you require, such as the traffic between your interface and a specific host, will be printed.

Configuring Ethereal to Capture Network Packets

- ☑ Ethereal provides a GUI environment for capturing network packets, which makes it easier for many administrators to use.

- ☑ Ethereal and tcpdump capture packets using the pcap library (libpcap). Since they both use the pcap library (libpcap) syntax, they can share many of the same commands, such as filtering options and primitives.

- ☑ You can easily save Ethereal filters and access them as needed for each packet capture you make. You can have multiple filters from which to choose for different needs.

Viewing Network Traffic between Hosts Using EtherApe

- ☑ EtherApe is a GUI that displays networking activity graphically by identifying hosts and the links that exist between the hosts. It displays real-time traffic, as well as traffic saved to a file.

- ☑ EtherApe also uses the pcap library (libpcap), the library for packet capturing and filtering, which is similar to tcpdump and Ethereal.

- ☑ EtherApe uses options to specify the capture information, such as the interface, link colors, or whether names or numbers will be used.

Frequently Asked Questions

The following Frequently Asked Questions, answered by the authors of this book, are designed to both measure your understanding of the concepts presented in this chapter and to assist you with real-life implementation of these concepts. To have your questions about this chapter answered by the author, browse to **www.syngress.com/solutions** and click on the **"Ask the Author"** form.

Q: How does a sniffer eavesdrop the traffic on a network?

A: Ethernet was designed as a shared network since all systems share the same physical wire. It was designed so that systems would ignore all traffic that was not addressed to a particular system's hardware address. Sniffer, or wiretap, programs turn off this filter, and switch a system's interface into *promiscuous* mode, which then views all packets on the same physical wire.

Q: Now that I can sniff network traffic, how can I stop people from sniffing *my* data?

A: As you have learned, packet sniffing is a powerful tool. It allows malicious hackers to capture packets that contain passwords and usernames. The only way to protect yourself against hackers with packet sniffers is to encrypt your data. Even if hackers capture your encrypted data, they will be unable to decrypt it (unless they are extremely determined).

Q: When I use Ethereal, the only TCP packets I can capture are those to and from my interface. Why?

A: Your network interface card (NIC) probably has not switched to promiscuous mode for the packet capture. Promiscuous mode forces an interface to supply all network packets it sees to a host. Your operating system may be unable to switch your interface to promiscuous mode, or your interface may not support promiscuous mode. If your interface cannot be put into promiscuous mode, you will only see TCP traffic addressed to your interface, link-layer addresses, broadcast and multicast packets. Try another interface for your packet captures.

Q: When I perform a live capture in Linux, Ethereal freezes. Why?

A: This problem was fixed in Ethereal 0.8.2 and later. Ethereal would freeze during a live capture because of the libpcap library. If the network was idle, libpcap was unable to return control to Ethereal, and Ethereal would freeze. Code was added to Ethereal to fix this issue.

Q: When I use EtherApe, the hosts move before I can identify them. How can I keep them on my screen for analysis?

A: You must set the node timeout to zero (0), or else the hosts will disappear after they are finished transmitting their data.

Q: I installed EtherApe, but the diagram host names and addresses are a garbled mess. I can't read anything.

A: You must configure the font. When EtherApe is running, click **Preferences**. In the Diagram tab, click **Font**, and choose a font such as Helvetica or Times New Roman. Make sure you click **Save** so you avoid this problem in the future.

Chapter 6

Network Authentication and Encryption

Solutions in this chapter:

- **Understanding Network Authentication**
- **Creating Authentication and Encryption Solutions**
- **Implementing One-Time Passwords (OTP and OPIE)**
- **Implementing Kerberos Version 5**
- **Using kadmin and Creating Kerberos Client Passwords**
- **Establishing Kerberos Client Trust Relationships with kadmin**
- **Logging On to a Kerberos Host Daemon**

☑ Summary

☑ Solutions Fast Track

☑ Frequently Asked Questions

Introduction

You have seen in previous chapters how the open source community has created powerful sniffing tools. You have seen how they can be used either to administer your network or to attack it. Because these sniffing tools are open source, and because it is relatively easy to place a Linux host on your company network, you need to consider ways to minimize improper use of packet capturing tools. Encryption solutions, such as Secure Shell (SSH) and enhanced authentication schemes such as one-time passwords (OTP) and Kerberos version 5 (v5), are common solutions to this problem. In this chapter, you will learn about how to implement one-time passwords, as well as how to implement Kerberos v5 realms. These will help you reduce sniffing attacks. In future chapters, you will then learn more about how to encrypt transmissions using SSH and IPSec. But, before you do this, it is important to review the concepts of network authentication and how many current implementations leave themselves open to attack.

Understanding Network Authentication

The traditional way to log on to servers is to provide a username and password pair as authentication tokens (credentials). The client first presents these credentials by sending them across the network to a server. The server then compares this information to its own database, then allows or denies access to system resources, depending upon the results of the comparison. Up until about the last ten years, this process had been considered quite effective and secure. Due to the increased sophistication of network tools (as well as hackers that may use them), this traditional practice has become less tenable.

Still, users very commonly authenticate over the Internet using clear text passwords. Increasing amounts of people are working at home and logging on to remote e-mail and File Transfer Protocol (FTP) servers using passwords, all of which are sent in clear text. Such practices can only invite sniffing attacks that can lead to compromised user accounts and network servers.

Even if employees remain behind the firewall, many system services allow clear text authentication, including the following:

- Telnet
- FTP
- Standard Network Information Service (NIS)

With relatively little expertise, an attacker can obtain authentication information quite simply. About ten years ago, most operating system vendors implemented encryption as a way to thwart sniffing attacks.

Attacking Encrypted Protocols

Encrypting the packets certainly seemed to be the answer to sniffing attacks. It stopped all but the most resourceful users from even trying to decrypt such protocols. Within the past five years, however, even encrypted transmissions such as Windows NT Server Message Blocks (SMBs, also known as the Common Internet File System [CIFS]), have become susceptible to attacks, because many versions of SMB/CIFS still send passwords. Although they are encrypted, the passwords are still sent across the network, which is a problem because attacking encrypted protocols has become much easier. Many tools exist that help hackers wage a sniffing attack, which is a type of "man-in-the-middle" attack, where a "sniffing host" that resides in-between two systems captures the information. All the sniffing host operator has to do is place her Network Interface Card (NIC) into promiscuous mode to be able to capture encrypted information (such as passwords and ensuing transmissions passing between hosts). Figure 6.1 shows how a "sniffing host" can sit in-between two systems and obtain encrypted information.

Figure 6.1 Conducting a Man-in-the-Middle Attack

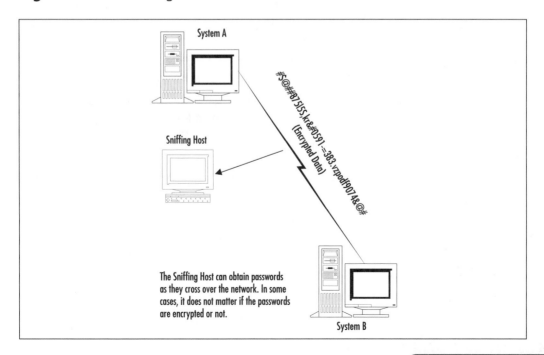

System A

#$@#87$JS$,kr&#0$9).=383.vzpodk90748@#
(Encrypted Data)

Sniffing Host

The Sniffing Host can obtain passwords as they cross over the network. In some cases, it does not matter if the passwords are encrypted or not.

System B

After a hacker obtains encrypted data, he can still act on it. The hacker will need more than a simple packet sniffer, of course. Still, it is now possible to cull passwords and other information from these packets. The specific steps of a man-in-the-middle attack, described in Figure 6.2, apply to encrypted packets as much as they do packets sent in clear text.

Figure 6.2 Steps for Obtaining Network Passwords

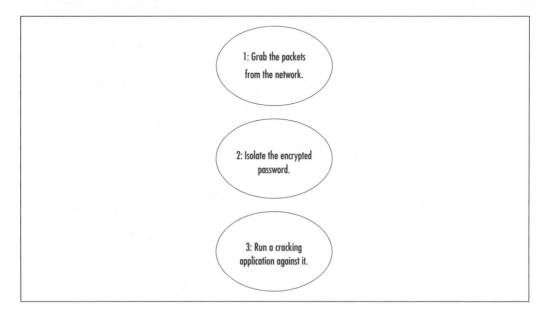

After the packets containing the encrypted passwords are captured, hackers use cracking applications such as L0phtCrack (www.securitysoftwaretech .com/lc3), John the Ripper (http://packetstorm.securify.com), and others. All of these are designed to crack passwords after they are obtained. Some, such as L0phtCrack, are designed to both capture and crack sniffed encrypted passwords. Hackers create or find new resources and use more powerful computers all of the time. In order to secure your network more fully, you should consider finding a strategy that makes it even more difficult to capture and decrypt passwords.

Tools & Traps...

Man-in-the-Middle Attacks

Man-in-the-middle attacks come in several varieties. Sniffing attacks are simply the most popular form. Other man-in-the-middle attacks include the following:

- **Replay** Where the attacker captures network packets, stores them, then resends them out onto the network. Sometimes, an attacker can obtain a login sequence, which can then be used repeatedly to log in.

- **Insertion** When the attacker isolates a data stream and then injects arbitrary packets into it. Most of the time, such attacks are meant to annoy Internet Relay Chat (IRC) and Telnet users, but more sophisticated insertion attacks occur. Some programs are able to insert bogus packets into network transmissions to help evade network-based Intrusion Detection System (IDS) applications. Insertion attacks are not limited to just the network data stream, either. For example, versions of Microsoft Word are susceptible to an attack that allows a malicious user to insert information into a document that can cause Word to execute arbitrary code on the system. For more information, consult the following URL: http://packetstorm.securify.com/0001-exploits/mo2.htm.

Creating Authentication and Encryption Solutions

When it comes to authenticating safely, you have two options:

- Find a way to authenticate without sending passwords across the network. In modern networks, Kerberos is the best way to do this. Kerberos is a scheme that allows hosts to communicate using public keys. It ensures that no passwords whatsoever traverse the network.

- Find a way to discard any password that is sent across the network. The accepted phrase for this strategy is *one-time passwords* (OTP). This strategy requires that the client and the server cooperate to ensure that once a password that traverses the network is used, it is never used again.

You should also understand that it is important to encrypt the transmissions that occur after authentication. Kerberos has the added ability to encrypt transmissions once authentication occurs. The use of OTP, however, does not encrypt subsequent transmissions. OTP is usually much easier to implement than Kerberos, however. Here are some additional ways to encrypt transmissions in addition to avoiding sending passwords across the Internet.

- **Secure Sockets Layer (SSL)** This protocol is designed to provide "on the fly" encryption by inserting a special layer on top of the transport layer of the Open System Interconnection Reference Model (OSI/RM). It uses public and private keys to establish a session that, theoretically at least, is readable only between a client and a server.

- **Secure Shell (SSH)** This protocol encrypts the data stream, and it also allows for authentication using public keys. Using a server (SSHD) and a client (SSH), users can communicate with hosts much like using Telnet. Unlike Telnet, however, SSH is encrypted and allows users to authenticate without having passwords cross the Internet.

- **IPSec (IP Security Architecture)** An add-on to IP that provides encryption and authentication at the network layer of the OSI/RM. This encryption occurs "on the fly" between properly configured systems.

Except for one-time passwords, all of these solutions use public key encryption to try to create a secure data pipe in an open, insecure network.

SECURITY ALERT!

Even protocols such as SSH are not immune to attacks. For example, in 1998 the then-current version of SSH was vulnerable to an attack that allows a malicious user to forge and insert invalid packets into the data stream, resulting in decryption of the data stream. Although the problem was corrected, this example shows that even the most secure protocols can be attacked.

Now that you understand some of the ways to secure network data, let's take a closer look at one-time passwords and Kerberos, the two authentication options discussed earlier.

Implementing One-Time Passwords (OTP and OPIE)

In the Linux world, the most universal way to implement OTP support in your Linux systems is to install the OPIE. For you Andy Griffith fans, OPIE doesn't refer to Ronnie Howard's character. It stands for "one-time passwords in everything." It's not a perfect acronym, but as far as OTP is concerned, OPIE is just about as perfect as you can get. OPIE is based on another, older OTP application named S/Key. What makes OPIE different is that it supports the Message Digest 5 (MD5) algorithm, which has become a de facto standard.

What Files Does OPIE Replace?

Once installed, OPIE automatically secures the use of the substitute user (**su**) application, as well as securing Telnet-based login. In order to do this, OPIE automatically replaces the following applications:

- /bin/su
- /bin/login

By default, OPIE does not enforce OTP whenever you log in interactively. Any user is given the choice of using OTP or the standard login procedure. This is necessary, because the creators of OPIE realized that too many people were locking themselves out of their own systems. Thus, OPIE is not an ideal solution for securing interactive login. However, any Telnet-based connections that come from a remote host will be required to log in using OTP.

OPIE does not currently support OTP for X Window sessions. Therefore, if you allow users to connect to your server through X, you must consider an alternate way to secure these connections (such as SSH or IPSec).

How Does OPIE Work?

OPIE works by generating a list of passwords that can (you guessed it!) be used only once. After a user logs in remotely, OPIE will issue a challenge. This challenge will always contain two elements:

- **Sequence number** A number that begins by default at 499. Each time a user logs in, the count will decrement by one. After the count reaches 0, the systems administrator will have to regenerate the password information using **opiepasswd**.

- **Seed number** A fixed number for each account. Each account gets a completely random number.

After a user enters his name at a remote server's login prompt, OPIE will send these two values over the network to the client's terminal. The user will then enter these two numbers into an OTP generating program, such as **opiepasswd** (for Linux systems) or WinKey (for Windows 9*x*, Me, and 2000 systems).

OPIE will issue a challenge in the following situations:

- **Using Telnet** The login program ensures that Telnet users are always challenged.

- **Using su** Any nonroot user who uses su will always be challenged.

- **Using FTP** If configured, OPIE supports FTP as well.

OPIE Files and Applications

Here is a list of the files that the systems administrator will use:

- **/usr/local/bin/opiepasswd** Used by the administrator to generate passwords for all users.

- **/etc/opiekeys** Contains the usernames and values used for the server's request. The additional information is a hash value of the secret password and the date the password was created. It is vital that you secure this file from all users.

- **/etc/opielocks/** Contains entries of the users who are locked out.

- ***/opieftpd** Allows you to use OTP via FTP, and it is meant as a replacement for the in.ftpd daemon. The asterisk represents the OPIE source code directory, which will vary. You will learn more about **opieftpd** shortly.

- **/etc/opieaccess** Allows the systems administrator to specify certain hosts that do not have to use OTP. This, of course, means that usernames and passwords will traverse the network.

Users can use the following applications to generate responses:

- **/usr/local/bin/opiekey** A command-line Linux utility. For security reasons, OPIE will not allow users to execute this application remotely. Otherwise, passwords will traverse the network.

- **/usr/local/bin/opieinfo** A command-line Linux utility that informs users concerning the next sequence number and seed number they will use. As with **opiekey**, this application will not allow users to execute this application remotely.

- **opie.tk** An X Window application written in tcl/tk that does the same thing as **opiekey**.

- **WinKey** A Windows 2000/NT/Me/9*x* utility that does the same thing as **opiekey**.

Generally, using these applications requires the use of two terminals or windows: one to begin the actual login session and the second to generate the response. Although safeguards are built into these applications, it is vital that you do not first establish an insecure connection, then use these applications.

SECURITY ALERT!

If you install OPIE and then do not run **opiepasswd -c** on each user, these users will not be able to log into your system remotely. You must use this command on the root account, as well. Otherwise, you will only be able to log in to your system interactively. If you try to log in remotely, all accounts will be forced to use OTP. Because you have not yet generated a password list, your OTP implementation will forever forbid you from remotely accessing the system.

---

opiepasswd

Although several options exist when using the **opiepasswd** command, the following is the most important:

```
opiepasswd -c username
```

Any user that you add must already belong to the /etc/passwd and /etc/shadow database. The **opiepasswd** command allows you to create OTP password lists for each user you specify. The **-c** option allows the systems administrator (root) to simply enter the root password, as opposed to entering an OTP password. Then, **opiepasswd** will generate a key for each user. This process involves selecting a private key for each user. Consider using passwords of at least ten characters, although OPIE will use any length. After you have added the user,

OPIE will report information about the user. Those who are truly meticulous will write this key down for each user and store it in a safe place. You will have to use this command against every single user in your system, including the root user.

When the count for a specific user reaches 0, you will have to run **opiepasswd –c** again on the account. Without the **–c** option, you will have to first use **opiekey** to generate a password, then enter the response when adding any user. For more information, consult the **opiepasswd** man page.

SECURITY ALERT!

Do not use the **-c** option remotely, because using it requires passwords to traverse the network. If you must use **opiepasswd** over a network, simply use the **opiepasswd** command. For example, if, as root, you want to change a password for the user named *james*, you would issue the following command:

```
opiepasswd james
```

However, you will have to train your users to never attempt this command while they are using a remote connection. The **opiepasswd** command will not allow it. Still, naïve users may still try to enter passwords. This results in passwords crossing the network, which can erode your network's security.

As soon as the **opiepasswd** command is used against a user, it is then possible for that user to use OTP to log in. However, make sure that you give all users their first passwords, as well as their secret passphrases. If you do not do this, users will not be able to use OPIE. In fact, it is wise to give users at least a small list of passwords so that they can get used to the concept.

Password Format

Each password that is generated will appear similar to the following:

```
KING MORT GEM WASH STAR SING
```

Although this text string appears to be six passwords, it is only one. Inform your users that they should enter these passwords in all caps, just to be consistent. Figure 6.3 shows the addition of a user named *opieuser*.

Figure 6.3 Using opiepasswd to Add a User

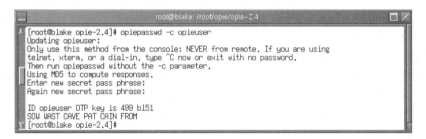

Using opiekey

Any user who receives a request will have to generate a response. The **opiekey** command generates responses. Users will have to find a way to transfer the server's challenge into the opiekey command line. Figure 6.4 shows a use of **opiekey** where the challenge of 498 ke3468 has been entered. **Opiekey** then requires that you enter your secret passphrase, which the administrator must give to the user in a secure manner. The user must exercise extreme caution with this secret key, because if it is made public, anyone with an OTP application could log on to the server.

Figure 6.4 Using opiekey to Compute a Response

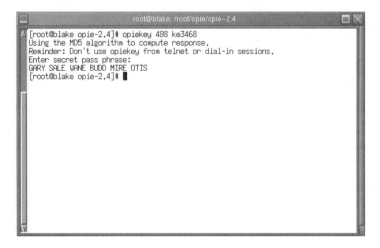

It is vital that you explain to all OPIE users that they cannot reveal their secret keys. If a user reveals his key, then the systems administrator will have to re-create the user's OTP list using a different secret key.

Using opieinfo and opiekey to Generate a List

When the systems administrator creates an OTP password list, the user can use the **opieinfo** command to generate a list of passwords for later use. This way, a user can still log in to a system if an OTP calculator is not available. The following command creates a list of the next five passwords and stores it into a file named opiejames.txt:

```
opiekey -n 5 `opieinfo` > opiejames.txt
```

```
opiekey -n 5 496 ke 7116
492: AGEE NU ORR MIT SALE BOW
493: FUSS SONG MAIL STUB SOIL WARM
494: TENT SMUG JOT WEAN CLAW BIRD
495: BANG SAD OF TORE TALL DUNE
496: ROW PO SPA HEFT CUE QUIT
```

This command works because it first has **opiekey** use the **opieinfo** command to learn about the current sequence and seed number for the user, then print out the next five passwords. You can then e-mail this list to the user, who can then print it out and use it at any terminal. All the user has to do is pay attention to the sequence number given by the server, then enter his secret key and the password. It is really not a problem if a user loses this list, as long as the user does not reveal her secret key.

Installing OPIE

If you are using a mainstream system, such as Red Hat or SuSE, the installation process is simplicity itself. You just do the following in the source directory:

```
./configure
make
make install
```

Configuration Options

The configure script has several different options, although most people will not find them necessary. You can read about them all by issuing the **./configure --help** command. Table 6.1 provides a list of the more important options.

Table 6.1 Configuration Options for OPIE

Option	Description
--enable-access-file=FILENAME	Allows you to create a file that allows hosts to bypass OTP. This file is not installed or supported by default, because it can defeat the purpose of installing OPIE in the first place. Although not necessarily a security hole, this option can cause problems, because once again, passwords will begin to pass over the network.
--bindir=DIR	This option allows you to determine where the OPIE binaries will be placed, if you do not want them in the /bin/ directory.
--disable-user-locking	By default, users will be kicked out after a number of failed logins unless you specify this feature.
--enable-user-locking[=DIR]	Allows you to specify the location of the user locking directory.
--enable-retype	Allows users to retype their secret pass phrases if they make a mistake.
--enable-insecure-override	Allows the use of **opiepasswd** and **opiekey** over a network. As with the --enable-access option, this option can cause security problems.

Installation Options

It is also possible to install only the OPIE clients. This option is useful, because you may want to disable all login options for a particular client system but still allow this system to log in to remote servers. If you wish to install only the client, you can issue the following command after issuing the **./configure** command, complete with any options you desire:

```
make client install
```

This option installs only **opiekey** and **opieinfo**. Or, if you wish to install only the server, you can issue the following command:

```
make server-install
```

You can learn more about configuration features by reading the README and INSTALL files that come with the distribution.

> **NOTE**
>
> The **opiekey** command requires a seed value that is over five digits. If the **opiepasswd -c** command generates a value that is too short, **opiekey** will fail. This often happens after you reinstall OPIE. If you encounter this problem, edit the /etc/opiekeys file and erase the entry of the account having this trouble.

Uninstalling OPIE

Upon installation, OPIE copies the existing /bin/su and /bin/login files su.opie.old and login.opie.old. After installing OPIE, you can use the **make uninstall** command to return the system back to its original state. The OTP versions of su and login will be removed and replaced with the original versions.

However, the **make uninstall** command will work only if the installation went well and if you are in the original directory from which you compiled OPIE. This means that you will have to keep the original installation directory handy in case a problem appears. Relying completely upon an uninstallation program to do the right thing every time is usually unwise, so remember the exact permissions of the original files. In Red Hat Linux, these permissions are as follows:

- /bin/su: -rwsr-xr-x
- /bin/login: -rwsr-xr-x

Exercise: Installing OPIE

1. Create a subdirectory off of your home directory named *opie*.
2. Using a Web browser, download the OPIE 2.4 tarball source code from the CD accompanying this book, or from www.inner.net/opie.
3. After you have obtained the file, place it in the opie directory.
4. Issue the following command:

   ```
   tar -zxv
   ```

5. Change to the source directory (it should be named opie-2.4).

6. Issue the following commands, in order:

```
./configure
make
make install
```

You can tell that things are going well when the ./configure script finishes in a way similar to that shown in Figure 6.5.

Figure 6.5 Installing OPIE

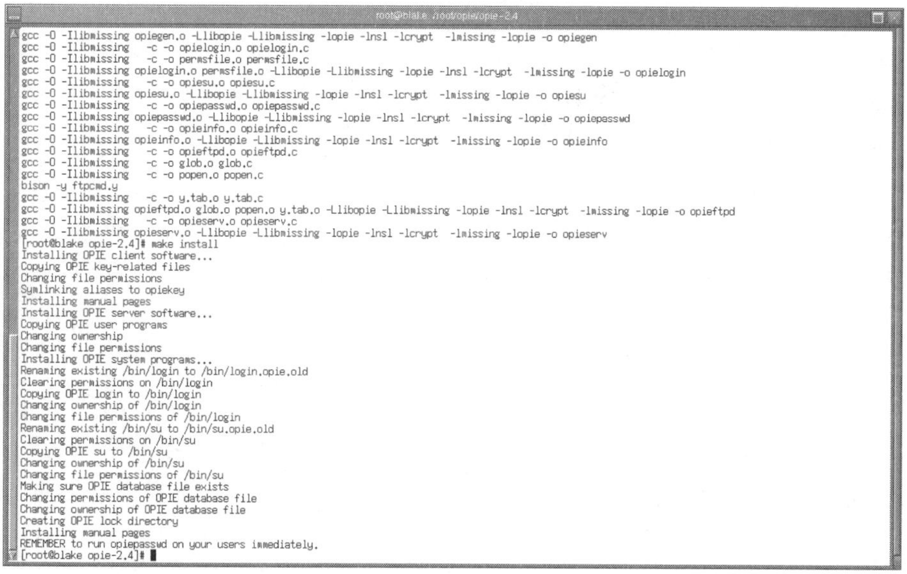

7. After running **make install**, immediately issue the following command:

```
/usr/local/bin/opiepasswd-c root
```

Now, follow the instructions given by the **opiepasswd** command.

8. When **opiepasswd** completes, write down the resulting sequence number, seed number, and password here:

_____

_____

_____

9. After you have added root, you can now access this account from a remote server by using Telnet. But first, create two new users using the **useradd** and **passwd** commands:

```
opieuser1
opieuser2
```

   Make sure that you use the **passwd** command to give these users standard passwords in the /etc/shadow directory.

10. Issue the following commands:

```
/usr/local/bin/opiepasswd-c opieuser1
/usr/local/bin/opiepasswd-c opieuser2
```

11. Now, issue the following command to generate OTP lists for root, opieuser1, and opieuser2:

```
opiekey -n 5 `opieinfo` > otplistroot.txt
opiekey -n 5 `opieinfo opieuser1` > otplistopieuser1.txt
opiekey -n 5 `opieinfo opieuser2` > otplistopieuser2.txt
```

12. You now have a list of the next five challenges OPIE will issue for all of the users you have added, in case they (and you) can't get to an OTP generator such as **opiekey** or **WinKey**. Test your OPIE installation locally. Open another terminal and log in as a normal user. If you are running X, just open another terminal screen and use su to become a nonroot user (if you have a nonroot account named *james*, use the command **su james**). If you are at the command line, press **CTRL+ALT+F2**, or **CTRL+ALT+F3**, then log in as the nonroot user.

13. Now, as a nonroot user in a new terminal, use the **su** command:

```
su
```

14. Notice that instead of the standard password, you are now given a challenge from OPIE.

15. To create a response, get to any terminal and use the **opiekey** command as shown earlier in this chapter. That is, enter the following information, substituting the sequence and seed numbers, as shown:

```
opiekey sequence#  seed#
```

16. The **opiekey** command will respond by asking you your secret password. Enter this password correctly, because **opiekey** will use this secret password with the sequence and seed values to calculate the correct password. Remember, the sequence key will look something like "495," and the seed value will look something like "bl13468." Enter nothing else.

17. When you enter the correct sequence and seed numbers, **opiekey** will respond with a password consisting of several uppercase words. Go back to the terminal and carefully enter this password in all capital letters into the **Response** section in the other terminal, and you will be logged in.

Congratulations. You have installed OPIE on your Linux system. Now, you can install the client portion on a remote server and test your work. See the next exercise for details.

Exercise: Installing the OPIE Client on a Remote Server

1. On another host than the one you used in the previous exercise, create a subdirectory named *opie*. This host will be called the *OPIE client*.

2. Change to the opie subdirectory and obtain the OPIE tarball.

3. Run the following commands:

```
./configure
make
make client install
```

4. Telnet to access the original server that has the full OPIE installation. This server will be called the OPIE server. The copy of OPIE on this server will issue you a challenge (the sequence number and the seed number).

5. Now, open another terminal on the OPIE client and run **opiekey**. Enter the challenge and seed numbers to log in. If you have any questions, follow the instructions given earlier in this chapter.

Exercise: Using opie-tk and Allowing Windows Users to Deploy OPIE

1. It is very likely that you work with users who use the X Window environment, as well as Microsoft Windows systems. Several OTP generators exist that run right from any modern Windows systems. You can even find clients that run in DOS and Windows 3.11, if you want. Linux GUI clients exist, as well. Download the following files from www.inner.net/opie:

   - **winkey.exe** A self-executable zip file, which contains the WinKey application for Windows 2000, NT, 9*x,* and Me. This file is available on the CD that accompanies this book.
   - **opie.tk-v2.3.gz** A tarball containing the opie.tk GUI for Linux. This file is also available on the accompanying CD.

   If you wish, you can also download additional clients, such as those for Macintosh or HP-UX machines.

2. First, let's start with using the opie.tk application. Unzip the application, then run it as follows:

   ```
   ./opie.tk-v2.3
   ```

3. Begin a telnet session with the OPIE server and enter a login name so that you receive a challenge.

4. Enter this challenge into the opie.tk-v2.3 screen and press **Calculate**. You will see a response similar to that shown in Figure 6.6.

   Figure 6.6 The opie.tk Interface after Calculating a Response

   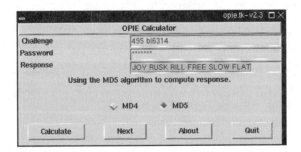

5. Enter this response into the Telnet terminal and log in.

6. Now, unzip the WinKey binary, which is in a self-executing file.

7. Repeat the OPIE login procedure. See Figure 6.7, which shows a user receiving a challenge.

Figure 6.7 Logging On to a Linux System from Windows 2000 Advanced Server

8. Enter the challenge values into the WinKey client and press **Compute**. You can copy and paste these values, if you wish. You will receive a response similar to that shown in Figure 6.8.

Figure 6.8 Using WinKey to Generate a Response

9. Now, enter the response into the client. Sometimes, the Windows screen will allow you to paste the response right into the proper place. Just right-click on the screen. If this doesn't work, just enter the values manually.

10. When you enter the response properly, you will be logged in.

Exercise: Installing opieftpd

1. OPIE does not automatically place the compiled **opieftpd** file into a standard directory, nor does it program xinetd to recognize and use the binary. The compiled binary will be found in the OPIE source code directory of the OPIE server. Copy this file to the /usr/sbin/ directory.

2. Now, create a simple text file named *opieftpd* in the /etc/xinetd.d/ directory and enter the following into it:

```
service ftp
{
        disable = no
        socket_type             = stream
        wait                    = no
        user                    = root
        server                  = /usr/sbin/opieftpd
        server_args             = -l
        log_on_success          += DURATION USERID
        log_on_failure          += USERID
        nice                    = 10
}
```

3. Now, disable the wu-ftpd daemon by editing its file (it should be in the /etc/xinetd.d/ directory) and change the *disable* = value to *yes*. If you have another FTP daemon configured to run from xinetd or any other daemon, disable it now.

4. Restart xinetd:

```
/etc/rc.d/init.d/xinetd restart
```

5. Now, FTP to the OPIE server and enter your name to begin the OPIE login sequence. If you don't see an OTP challenge, then recheck your work.

6. Use any OTP client you wish to generate a response. Make sure that you enter your secret key (password) and sequence/seed numbers accurately.

7. The text you copy in from WinKey, for example, will not echo. Trust that it has been entered and press **ENTER**. You may have to repeat this process a few times in order to get it correct.

8. When you enter the information correctly, you will be logged in. You now have enabled OTP support for the **su** command, as well as for Telnet and FTP.

Implementing Kerberos Version 5

Kerberos has become the premier way to allow network authentication. It provides a central login point for a network that allows single sign-on for the network resources the user is allowed to access. Kerberos v5 is a revolutionary step in network authentication, because it allows you to establish a domain that authenticates not only individual hosts and users, but individual daemons, as well. Using Kerberos, it is possible to centrally control which hosts and users can access the daemons on your network. In this sense, Kerberos is revolutionary. It obviates the use of the Network Information Service (NIS), for example, and is a vast improvement upon it. Both NIS and Kerberos allow you to centrally manage users, but NIS does not encrypt transmissions, and it requires passwords to be given across the network. Microsoft now uses its proprietary version of Kerberos for its Windows 2000 products.

After Kerberos is established on a network, passwords do not ever cross the network, not even in encrypted form. It is also possible to configure Kerberos to encrypt, ensuring communications between authenticated hosts. Kerberos is implemented by a Key Distribution Center (KDC), which holds all of the information that allows Kerberos clients to authenticate; the KDC contains the database that makes single sign-on possible. Whenever you have a system of Kerberos clients authenticating with a KDC, you are said to have a Kerberos "realm," which is shown in Figure 6.9.

Whenever you have a host that joins a Kerberos realm, it is often said to be "Kerberized." Whenever an application is altered to participate in a Kerberos realm, it is also said to be Kerberized. This chapter discusses Kerberos version 5, which is the most current version as of this writing.

Figure 6.9 A Kerberos Realm

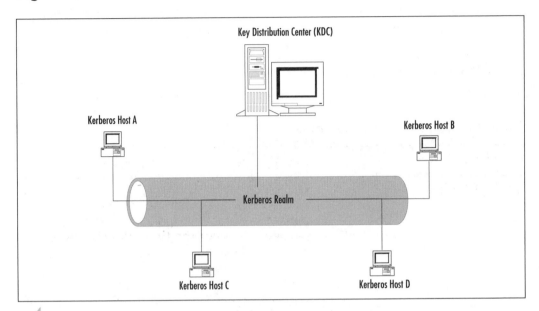

NOTE

Usually, a Kerberos realm is given the same name as the Domain Name System (DNS) name for the company. Thus, a company with the DNS name of yourcompany.com will likely have the Kerberos realm name of YOURCOMPANY.COM. This practice is not absolutely necessary, however. You will see how you can edit a portion of the /etc/krb5.conf file to map dissimilar DNS domain and realm names to each other later in this chapter.

Why Is Kerberos Such a Big Deal?

The KDC's database does not work in the traditional way. Traditionally, a standard user database waited for passwords to be sent across the network, and then the authentication mechanisms would present authentication information (a user-name and a password) to the database, make a comparison, and then access would be granted. In Kerberos, all network information (data about users, services, and hosts) is stored in the Kerberos database. This database contains the public keys of all principals. A principal is the name for any host, service, or user that is allowed to authenticate on a Kerberos network. Any sensitive information, such as passwords, always stays on the KDC and on the client. Using public key cryptography, the KDC and the client establish trust relationships that allow the KDC to then determine exactly which services a host and/or user can access.

Kerberos Terms

Table 6.2 provides the terms used when implementing Kerberos.

Table 6.2 Common Kerberos Terms

Kerberos Element	Description
Key Distribution Center (KDC)	The system that authenticates principals. The KDC is responsible for the storage and transmission of principals on a Kerberized network. Most of the time, the KDC houses the Ticket Granting Server (TGS). The TGS provides a special token called a ticket granting ticket. The KDC also houses the Authentication Server (AS), which grants the actual tickets clients use when accessing hosts and daemons.
Client	A host that is part of a Kerberos realm. A client can house several daemons that can be accessed only if a user has properly authenticated with a KDC.
Ticket Granting Ticket (TGT)	A special access token obtained from the KDC that enables users to obtain additional tickets. Every user on a Kerberos realm must use the **kinit** program to obtain a TGT.
Authentication Server	A server that is responsible for granting tickets to users, hosts, and host daemons (principals). The Authentication Server first communicates with the TGT to ensure that the principal has been authenticated, and it then issues the ticket. In Linux systems, the Authentication Server is housed in the same system as the KDC.
Ticket	Temporary credentials generated when a properly authenticated client accesses network service, such as an FTP server, a printer, or a router. The ticket authenticates a client that wishes to use a remote service in a realm. If a client (Host A) wishes to access

Continued

Table 6.2 Continued

Kerberos Element	Description
	a host in a Kerberos realm (Host B), the KDC will issue a ticket to Host A, which allows access to the service for a certain period of time (hours, by default). A ticket is not generated by **kinit**.
Principal	The equivalent of an entry in the /etc/passwd and /etc/shadow database in a standard Linux system. A principal can be defined as either a user, a host, or a host daemon that runs on hosts, and is comprised of three parts: The primary, the instance, and the realm. See Figure 6.10.
Credential cache/ticket file	Usually a file in the /tmp/ directory that contains your TGT, host, and host daemon keys. Service keys are generated when a client attaches to a Kerberized daemon that is able to authenticate with the KDC.
Keytab (Key table)	A file on a Kerberos client that includes the public keys of the hosts and host daemons that this server can access. Whenever a connection is made, Kerberos checks the contents of the keytab, then checks the current user's credential cache. If these elements are approved, Kerberos will allow access to the remote server. It is vital that you update this file on each client. The file is usually named /etc/krb5.keytab.
Policy	A special limit placed upon a Kerberos principal that determines the amount of time a particular user, host, or host daemon ticket remains valid.

Kerberos Principals

You have already read that a principal consists of a primary (also known as a "root"), an instance, and a realm. Figure 6.10 shows an example of a host principal, which uses all of the three elements of a principal. A host principal always has the word "host" as the primary, then has the name of the host as the instance and the realm name in the realm section. A principal can exist for daemons run by hosts, as well.

Figure 6.10 A Kerberos Principal

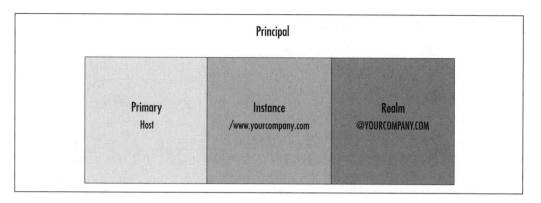

The following is an example of a host daemon principal:

`ftp/www.yourcompany.com@YOURCOMPANY.COM`

This principal recognizes the FTP service for the www.yourcompany.com service. Any user who properly authenticates with the KDC and who is allowed access to this service will then be able to use the FTP service on the www.yourcompany.com host.

Many times, however, a principal does not have an instance. For example, it is possible to create a user principal, which would appear as follows: james@YOURCOMPANY.COM. This principal would allow a user to log on to any host in a Kerberos realm. You can, of course, specify an instance for a user. For example, the following principal would allow login to only the system named www.yourcompany.com: james/www.yourcompany.com @YOURCOMPANY.COM

The Kerberos Authentication Process

The information in the next couple of paragraphs is greatly simplified, but it is more than enough from a system administrator's point of view. When a Kerberos client first obtains a TGT from the KDC, this token does not actually provide access to any particular daemon or network service. It is simply a token that informs other hosts that the KDC has authenticated this host, and that this host and user can request services from other hosts. Because the TGT is signed by the user's password and turned into a hash, the user can use the **kinit** command and his own password to generate the same hash and make a comparison between the two. If the TGT and password match, then a session key is established and a credential cache is created, usually in a file in the /tmp/ directory.

After the credential cache file is populated with the TGT, the host and user can then use this TGT to actually log on to hosts and request services. When it comes time for a user (a principal) to access a host's daemon (such as Kerberos-FTP and rlogin), the user uses his TGT to contact the KDC and ask for an actual ticket, which is the access token for a specific service. If the KDC authenticates this request, the KDC will send a ticket and update the principal's credential cache with information about the service he or she has requested. If the Kerberos database does not contain the service or host name, then access will be denied.

How Information Traverses the Network

When a ticket is transported across the network, it is signed by the user's password, which is entered whenever a Kerberos administrator uses the kadmin program to add a principal to the database. Note that the ticket does not actually contain the password. It is only signed by a password, which creates a hash. Not only that, but Kerberos places a time stamp on this ticket, so that even if someone with a supercomputer were to subject this ticket to a brute force attack and then generate a valid hash, the access token would no longer be valid. The Kerberos version in Red Hat Linux defaults to 8 hours. For this reason, time synchronization on networks and systems that use Kerberos is essential. NTP (Network Time Protocol) may be used for this purpose.

NOTE

For a more exhaustive discussion detailing how Kerberos works, go to http://web.mit.edu/kerberos/www/dialogue.html. This URL will take you to a document entitled "Designing an Authentication System: A Dialogue in Four Scenes." Not only does it explain Kerberos quite well, it is also a well-written parody of a dialogue using the Socratic Method. I know that the document sounds pretty stuffy, but it's an easy read and will help you learn more about exactly why Kerberos was developed and exactly what it does.

However, understand that this document was originally written for Kerberos version 4. The current version of Kerberos is version 5. The chief alterations between Kerberos v4 and Kerberos v5 is that Kerberos v5 uses public key encryption. So, as clearly written as the dialog is, if you don't understand public key cryptography well, then you probably won't understand Kerberos very well.

Creating the Kerberos Database

After installing Kerberos, you will have to create a database where all principals will be stored. You do this by issuing the following command:

```
/usr/kerberos/sbin/kdb5_util create -s
```

This command creates the necessary database files in the /var/kerberos/ krb5kdc/ directory. After you have created the database entries, you then edit the /etc/krb5.conf and /var/kerberos/krb5kdc/kdc.acl files to reflect your Kerberos realm and DNS domain names. You must then add an administrative user, as well as additional principals, to the database.

Using kadmin.local

Because you have a new Kerberos realm, you are presented with a logical conundrum: You need to administer Kerberos, but the **kadmin** command requires that you present a username and a password. However, no administrative user or password exists in the database yet. So, how do you get started? The answer is the **/usr/kerberos/sbin/kadmin.local** command. It does not require a user to first authenticate. As long as you have created the Kerberos database and edited the proper files, you will then be able to use kadmin.local to add an administrative user:

```
/usr/kerberos/sbin/kadmin.local -q "addprinc james/admin"
```

This command has **kadmin.local run** as a one-time command. You can also use **kadmin.local** interactively, which means that you begin a session where you get a special prompt that lets you enter Kerberos-specific commands. You can learn more about **kadmin.local** by reading its man page.

After using **kadmin.local**, Kerberos will have an administrative user, and you can use the kadmin from any host on the network.

SECURITY ALERT!

Because **kadmin.local** does not require extensive authentication, consider the importance of making sure that this system runs no other daemons, and is accessible only via the most stringent security requirements. For example, consider allowing only interactive login and making sure that the computer itself is physically secure.

Using kadmin

The **kadmin** application, also found in the /usr/kerberos/sbin/ directory, is designed to add principals to the Kerberos database. It is much like **kadmin.local**, except you can issue it from any Kerberos client on your realm. **Kadmin** is usually used as an interactive command, as shown in the following sequence:

```
terminal# kadmin
Authenticating as principal james/admin@ YOURNETWORK.COM with password.
Enter password:
kadmin: addprinc james
WARNING: no policy specified for james@ YOURNETWORK.COM; defaulting to
no policy
Principal "james@YOURNETWORK.COM" created.
kadmin: quit
terminal#
```

This example shows a **kadmin** session where the Kerberos administrator, *james/admin*, starts **kadmin**, enters the administrative password, then uses the **addprinc** command to add a user named *james*. This user will then be able to access network daemons and services, as long as the Kerberos administrator takes the additional steps shown in the upcoming example. Notice first that Kerberos automatically adds the realm name. Second, notice that the user james@yournetwork.com is different than the user james/admin@yournetwork .com. This is because the first principal (james@yournetwork.com) has an empty instance, whereas the second (james/admin@yournetwork.com), lists the admin instance, which makes the user an administrative user.

Here is another example:

```
terminal# kadmin
Authenticating as principal root/admin@STANGERNET.COM with password.
Enter password:
kadmin: addprinc -randkey host/www.yournetwork.com
WARNING: no policy specified for host/www.yournetwork.com@
          YOURNETWORK.COM; defaulting to no policy
Principal "host/www.yournetwork.com@YOURNETWORK.COM" created.
kadmin: quit
terminal#
```

This example shows a **kadmin** session where the Kerberos administrator *james/admin* starts **kadmin**, enters the administrative password, then uses the **addprinc –randkey** command to add a host principal named *host/www.yournetwork.com*. The **–randkey** option is unique to host and host daemon principals, because after a principal is created, the password no longer needs to be remembered, because this password will be used to sign tickets for users who are already authenticated. This password is used only to sign tickets. No user will ever have to enter this password. In this case, it is best to let Kerberos create its own difficult password, rather than you taking the time to do so, because you will then have to verify it.

To add a host daemon, you would simply issue the following command from within kadmin:

```
addprinc -randkey ftp/www.yournetwork.com
```

This command adds the ftp daemon for the www.yournetwork.com daemon.

NOTE

For the sake of convenience, you may want to make your administrative user the same name as your login name. Although not the most secure option, doing so means that you don't have to use the following command each time you start **kadmin**:

```
/usr/kerberos/sbin/kadmin -p james/admin
```

Still, it's important that you know this command, because you will need to use it at least once on every host that belongs to your Kerberos network. This is because, as you will see, each client needs to have its keytab file updated by the systems administrator.

Finally, if you are logged into one Kerberos realm named @othercompany.com, and you wish to use Kerberos to log into @yourcompany.com realm, you can issue the following command:

```
/usr/kerberos/sbin/kadmin -p james/admin@YOURCOMPANY.COM
```

This command will also work if you are logging in from the @yourcompany.com realm. Adding the @yourcompany.com is simply redundant in this case, however.

The **kadmin** command also lists, modifies, and deletes principals. To list present Kerberos users from within **kadmin**, enter the following command:

```
kadmin:list_principals
```

```
ftp/blake.yourcompany.com.YOURCOMPANY.COM
```

```
rlogin/wordsworth.YOURCOMPANY.COM
```

```
james.YOURCOMPANY.COM
```

```
sandi.YOURCOMPANY.COM
```

```
host/blake.yourcompany.com.YOURCOMPANY.COM
```

```
kadmin:
```

To delete any principal, you can issue the following command:

```
kadmin: delete_principal user1
```

```
Are you sure you want to delete the principal "user1@YOURCOMPANY.COM"?
(yes/no): yes
```

```
Principal "user1@YOURCOMPANY.COM" deleted.
```

```
Make sure that you have removed this principal from all ACL's before
reusing.
```

```
kadmin:
```

For more information, use the **?** command from within **kadmin** or consult the Kerberos documentation in the /usr/share/krb5*/ directory and the man pages. The asterisk represents the Kerberos version you are using.

Using kadmin on the Client

The **kadmin** command does not simply add and manage principals to the Kerberos realm. It is also used to populate and update the Key table files for each Kerberos host. It is vital that you understand this **kadmin** function, because most of the existing Kerberos documentation skims over this step. This is partially because most people who write about Kerberos do not have the knowledge to actually implement Kerberos, or because they know how to implement Kerberos so well that they just assume that you already know this step. Hopefully, the present discussion will bridge the gap between the overly theoretical and overly technical writers and actually show you how to properly configure Kerberos clients. You will learn more about this shortly. Figure 6.11 shows the gkadmin interface.

Although it is a nice interface, the command-line interface is ideal for updating the /etc/krb5.keytab files on clients.

Figure 6.11 The gkadmin Interface

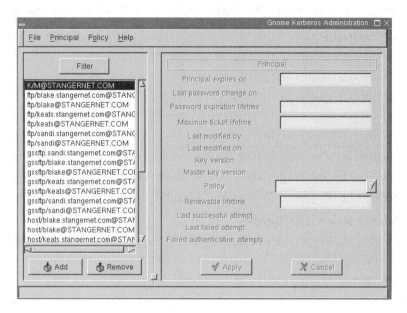

NOTE

If you are running X, you can use the gkadmin GUI utility. Install the gnome-kerberos package for your particular distribution. You can obtain it from www.rpmfind.net, or other sites. It is also available on many distribution CDs, such as the Red Hat Power Tools disk.

Using kadmin and Creating Kerberos Client Passwords

As a Kerberos administrator, you will have to add user principals. The creators of Kerberos (researchers at the Massachusetts Institute of Technology) have recommended client passwords of at least six characters. Passwords should combine upper- and lower-case letters, and they should also include numbers and punctuation marks.

Setting Policies

Kerberos policies are much like standard Unix password policies. They determine password length, whether or not a user's principal will expire at a certain time, when the password will expire, and so forth. Standard principal policy settings include the following:

- **Policy name** When you create a policy, you can name it to help differentiate it from other policies.

- **Minimum password life (in seconds)** How long a user must keep a password before being allowed to change it.

- **Maximum password life (in seconds)** The longest amount of time a user can keep a password.

- **Minimum password length** Sets the number of characters a password must have.

When you add a principal using **kadmin** and do not specify a policy, the default behavior is to establish no policy whatsoever. You can create a policy by using the **addpol** command from within **kadmin**:

```
kadmin: addpol yourdomainpol
kadmin: modpol -maxlife 2/02/2004 -minlength 6 domainpol
```

This policy means that the principal will expire on the second day of February 2004, and that any subsequent password change must be at least six characters long. You can add this policy to a user named *Jacob* by using the **modprinc** command, as follows:

```
modprinc -policy yourdomainpol
```

Using Kinit

The **kinit** command allows a user to obtain a TGT from the KDC. It does not allow a user to get a host or service ticket. A host or service ticket is obtained only when a user is successful logging into the service. Issuing the **kinit** command has the Kerberos client contact the KDC and obtain a TGT, as shown in Figures 6.12 and 6.13.

Figure 6.12 Using the kinit Command

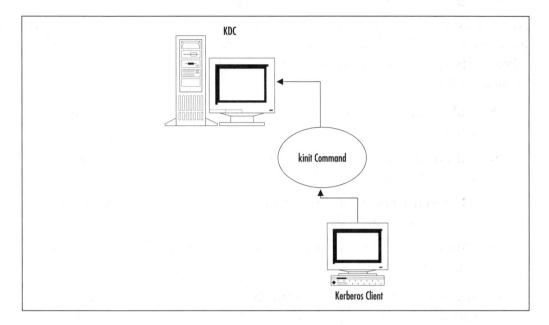

Figure 6.13 Receiving a TGT from the KDC

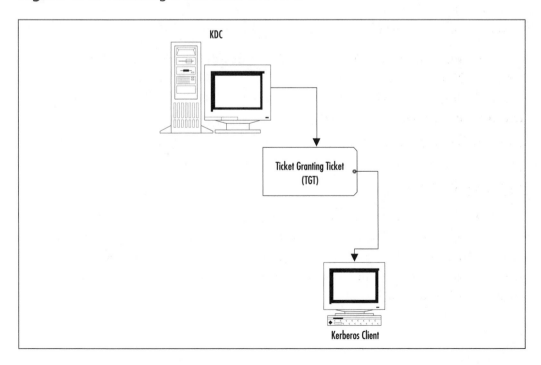

Here is an example of a simple **kinit** session:

```
terminal# /usr/kerberos/bin/kinit
    Password for james@YOURDOMAIN.COM:
terminal#
```

This session has obtained a TGT from the KDC. This credential is usually stored on the local hard disk, usually in the /tmp/ directory. The file is usually in the following format:

```
krb5cc_UID
```

UID is the user identification number of the user who issued the **kinit** command. For example, if you are root, the credential cache file would be krb5cc_0, whereas the user with the UID of 500 would have the credential file named krb5cc_500.

Suppose, however, that your Kerberos name was *james*, and that you wished to obtain your credential, but only had access to a terminal owned by another user named *sandi*. The following command would get you your own TGT:

```
terminal# /usr/kerberos/bin/kinit sandi
Password for sandi@YOURDOMAIN.COM:
```

Now, you have begun your own credential cache, which right now holds only your TGT. For more information about using kinit, consult its man page or the Kerberos workstation documentation in the /usr/share/doc/krb5*/ directory.

The kinit Command and Time Limits

Sometimes you may want to obtain a TGT that is valid for a period shorter than the default (eight hours). Suppose that you know you will use this TGT for only one hour. The following command would make the TGT valid for that period of time:

```
terminal# /usr/kerberos/bin/kinit -l 1h
terminal#
```

Kinit and most Kerberized clients can also forward the tickets they obtain. This means that you can obtain tickets on one host, then have them sent to another. The following command obtains a ticket for the user named *james* in the YOURDOMAIN.COM realm for two hours, then allows you to forward them, as well:

```
terminal# /usr/kerberos/bin/kinit -f -l 1h @YOURDOMAIN.COM
terminal#
```

For additional details concerning how to customize the TGT and tickets obtained from the KDC, consult the man pages for **kinit** and additional clients.

Managing Kerberos Client Credentials

After you run **kinit**, the cache will contain only the TGT. Additional credentials, such as actual tickets to access a daemon such as FTP, will be added only after you access the remote host. This, in addition to properly updating the /etc/krb5.keytab file, is a little-understood part of Kerberos configuration. To list your current credentials, use the following command:

```
terminal# /usr/kerberos/bin/klist
03/21/01 3:05:53 04/21/01 13:05:53
    krbtgt/YOURNETWORK.COM@YOURNETWORK.COM
terminal#
```

This command shows that a TGT has been issued on March 21st for the YOURNEWORK.COM realm. Additional options exist. Consult the klist man page.

The kdestroy Command

When you log off of your system, you should use the **kdestroy** command to eliminate your credential cache. This command erases the /tmp/ krb5cc_UID file. You need to use this command when your TGT and other tickets expire. Many times, a seeming Kerberos problem can be solved by erasing this cache and using **kinit** over again.

NOTE

The gnome-kerberos package ships with the /usr/bin/krb5/krb5 application, shown in Figure 6.14. It is a combination of the **kinit**, **klist**, and **kdestroy** applications, because you can use it to view, delete, and obtain credentials.

Figure 6.14 The krb5 Interface

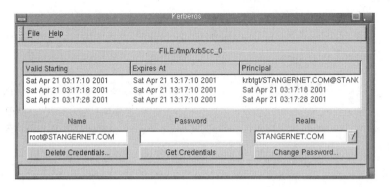

WARNING

Credential caches can grow quite large, and can remain valid long after a user walks away from the terminal. To ensure that your Kerberos realm remains secure, encourage and train users to use **kdestroy** whenever they have finished a session. Otherwise, another user can walk up to the terminal and access network resources.

Exercise: Configuring a KDC

You now have a basic understanding of Kerberos elements. Now, take the following steps to configure a KDC on your Linux system. These steps will allow you to create a Kerberos database, configure the necessary files, and create user, host and host daemon principals.

1. Take the time to plan your DNS domain and Kerberos realm names. If you do not have a proper DNS domain created, take the time to do this now. Enter the following information:

   Planned DNS domain name: _____

   Planned Kerberos realm name: _____

2. Obtain and install Kerberos using the available RPM files. You can download them from www.rpmfind.net. Make sure that you obtain the packages appropriate for your Linux host:

- krb5-libs-*

- krb5-workstation-*

- krb5-server-*

- krb5-devel-*

   The * represents the version appropriate for your Linux host. Also, the krb5-devel package is necessary only if you plan to develop your own Kerberized applications. The 1.2.2-4 versions of these files are on the accompanying CD.

3. Install the packages in the following order:

   - krb5-libs-*

   - krb5-workstation-*

   - krb5-server-*

   - krb5-devel-*

4. Now, edit the /etc/krb5.conf and /var/kerberos/krb5kdc/kadm.acl files so that they reflect your planned Kerberos realm information. If you can, simply substitute your DNS domain and Kerberos realm information for all example.com/EXAMPLE.COM entries. Take special note of the [domain_realm] entries, which map DNS domains to Kerberos realms. This section helps you if your DNS domain is not the same as your Kerberos realm. Properly editing the /etc/krb5.conf file ensures that you will be able to use **kadmin**, **kinit**, and additional commands to access the database on the KDC. You will see how you will have to do much the same thing for each Kerberos client host.

   The /var/kerberos/krb5kdc/kadm5.acl file should appear as follows:

```
*/admin@YOURDOMAIN.COM    *
```

   Now, anyone with the /admin instance has the power to administer all elements of your Kerberos realm.

5. Now that you have installed the correct Kerberos RPM packages and edited the configuration files, create the Kerberos database:

```
/usr/kerberos/sbin/kdb5_util create -s
```

   You will be asked to create and confirm a password. Make sure that you save this password in a save place. The **-s** option creates what is called a "stash file," which contains the password for the Kerberos database. If you don't create this stash file, Kerberos will ask you for the password each time you restart it.

6. Start the kadmin, krb5kdc, and krb24 daemons in the following order:

```
/etc/rc.d/init.d/krb5kdc start
/etc/rc.d/init.d/kadmin start
/etc/rc.d/init.d/krb524 start
```

7. To ensure that these daemons will start at the next reboot, use ntsysv to mark the Kerberos services to start automatically.

8. Now, populate the database you have just created using the **kadmin.local** command:

```
/usr/kerberos/sbin/kadmin.local -q "addprinc
    kerberosadministrator/admin"
```

If you wish to use a name other than kerberosadministrator, substitute your own. However, you must use the /admin instance, because using this instance gives any user you specify the privileges to list, add, modify, and delete users.

9. Check the /var/kerberos/krb5kdc/kdc.conf file and ensure that it reflects the proper realm name.

10. Now that you have created an administrator account and verified all settings, log on using **kadmin** or **gkadmin**:

```
terminal$ /usr/kerberos/sbin/kadmin -p
kerberosadministrator/admin
```

Authenticating as principal kerberosadministrator/admin@ YOURDOMAIN.COM with password kadmin:

If this command fails, check your /var/kerberos/krb5kdc/kadm5.acl file and make sure that it reads as follows:

```
*/admin@YOURDOMAIN.COM   *
```

You will, of course, substitute your own realm information. Make sure that the /etc/krb5.conf file is also correct for your Kerberos realm and DNS information, that your system has proper DNS resolution (both forward and reverse), and that this system is a client to the proper DNS server.

11. After you have been able to obtain a kadmin prompt, enter the fol-
    lowing command:

```
addprinc username
```

   Where *username* is the username you are currently logged in as.

12. When you have added the username *user*, type **quit** to exit **kadmin**.

13. Now, using the username you have just added, use **kinit**.

14. Use klist or krb5 to verify that you can get and list a TGT. Either client
    will show only the TGT, because you have not yet tried to authenticate
    with any of the network hosts. You will obtain actual ticket when you
    log on to remote hosts daemons. If you see a TGT, congratulations. If
    you need to troubleshoot Kerberos further, reread the rest of this chapter
    and consult the Kerberos documentation, which resides in various man
    pages (kerberos, kadmin, kinit, and so forth), as well as /usr/share/doc/
    krb5-server-1.2.2/ and /usr/share/doc/krb5-workstation-1.2.2/
    directories.

Establishing Kerberos Client Trust Relationships with kadmin

A trust relationship in public key cryptography allows two hosts to authenticate
each other and to decrypt information. The only way to establish a trust relationship on the Kerberos client host is to use the **kadmin** command. The systems
administrator must extract parts of the Kerberos database and insert them onto
each client. Figure 6.15 shows the process of updating the /etc/krb5.keytab file
for each client using **kadmin ktadd**.

The administrator must use the **kadmin –ktadd** command on each Kerberos
client that wishes to participate in the Kerberos realm. The process of extracting
records populates the local host's /etc/krb5.keytab file with the hosts and services
that the Kerberos client is allowed to use. The KDC supplies these keys.

The following example shows the **kadmin ktadd –k** command that gives
each client the ability to prove that it has the public keys of the services used. The
/etc/krb5.keytab file contains this information. To update the keytab file of a
Kerberos client (in this example, a host named *wordsworth*), you would go through
the following sequence on the client itself:

```
terminal# /usr/kerberos/sbin/kadmin
Authenticating as principal james/admin@YOURCOMPANY.COM with password.
Enter password:
kadmin:  ktadd -k /etc/krb5.keytab host/keats.yournetwork.com
Entry for principal ftp/keats.yournetwork.com with kvno 6, encryption
type DES cbc mode with CRC-32 added to keytab WRFILE:/etc/krb5.keytab.
Entry for principal host/keats.yournetwork.com with kvno 6, encryption
type Triple DES cbc mode raw added to keytab WRFILE:/etc/krb5.keytab.
kadmin: quit
terminal#
```

Figure 6.15 Establishing Trust Relationships Using the kadmin ktadd Command

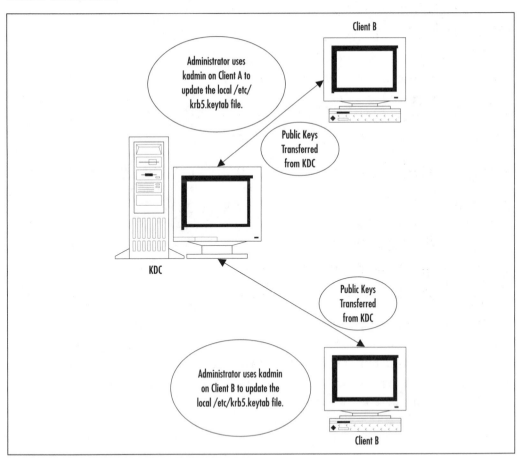

Now, this host has the public key of the *keats* system. It is vital that you give the host principal entry to this client. Otherwise, Kerberos will not be able to compare information to allow the *wordsworth* access to *keats*.

Here is another example that adds the ftp/keats.yournetwork.com principal to the *wordsworth* keytab (/etc/krb5.keytab):

terminal# /usr/kerberos/sbin/kadmin

Authenticating as principal james/admin@YOURCOMPANY.COM with password.

Enter password:

kadmin: ktadd -k /etc/krb5.keytab ftp/keats.yournetwork.com

Entry for principal ftp/keats.yournetwork.com with kvno 6, encryption type DES cbc mode with CRC-32 added to keytab WRFILE:/etc/krb5.keytab.

Entry for principal ftp/keats.yournetwork.com with kvno 6, encryption type Triple DES cbc mode raw added to keytab WRFILE:/etc/krb5.keytab.

kadmin: quit

terminal#

Assuming that the user has run **kinit**, this host can now properly authenticate with *keats* to access the FTP server. You will have to repeat this process to add the host/keats.yournetwork.com entry, as well. Unless you take these two steps, you will not be able to access any daemon on the host named *keats*.

Additional Daemon Principal Names

Generally, you must add a principal to the Kerberos database for each service. For example, to add smtp and pop3 principals for the host named *blake*, you would create the following principals:

- **smtp/blake.yourdomain.com** For a Kerberized SMTP service.
- **pop3/blake.yourdomain.com** For a Kerberized POP3 service.

Remember, the text string "yourdomain" represents your DNS domain. Kerberos does not use the word "domain" to represent its authentication space— it uses the word "realm." Additional Kerberized services exist. Check your xinetd directory (usually /etc/xinetd.d/) for additional service names to add.

Logging On to a Kerberos Host Daemon

Figure 6.16 shows what occurs when a client with a TGT uses a Kerberized FTP client to log on to a Kerberized FTP daemon. Client A, the Kerberized client, first uses its TGT to request a session ticket. The Kerberos KDC checks to see if Client B has a host principal entry, then also checks to see if Client B has a host daemon entry for FTP. Then, the KDC determines that Client A has the proper host and host daemon keys for client B. If all of these credentials match, then client A can connect to client B's FTP server.

Figure 6.16 Accessing a Kerberized Network Daemon

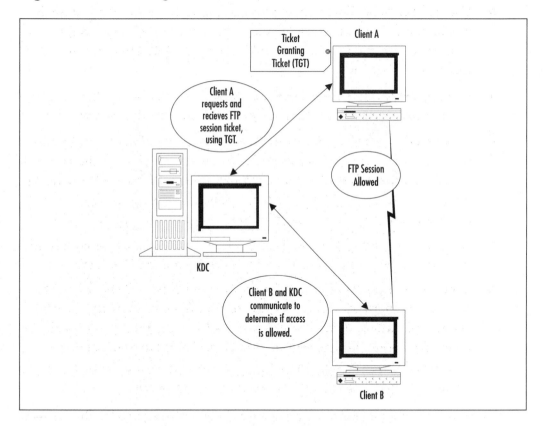

Common Kerberos Client Troubleshooting Issues and Solutions

After you are reasonably sure that your Kerberos setup is correct, consider the following issues:

- **DNS** You will not be able to use Kerberos unless you have a DNS server in place that has flawless forward and reverse zones. Simply having a forward zone or populated /etc/hosts files is not enough to run Kerberos properly.

- **Time skew** The tickets issued by Kerberos are time-sensitive. To help reduce authentication problems, Kerberos will not issue tickets to hosts whose clocks are more than five minutes apart from the KDC. The NTP is designed to ensure that all servers have the same time. The server at www.eecis.udel.edu has additional information about NTP, including network daemons you can install.

- **Old credentials** When you try to administer Kerberos using **kadmin**, it is important to realize that if you make significant changes to the database concerning a user, you will have to use **kdestroy** and then **kinit** to obtain new credentials.

- **Unsupported client applications** Make sure that the application you use actually supports the Kerberos protocol and that the versions match.

- **Unstarted Kerberos client daemons** Check your xinetd configuration on your destination server to ensure that this server has the proper Kerberized daemon started. For example, if you wish to test Kerberos by using your Kerberized FTP client to connect to the server named *james*, make sure that the Kerberized FTP server is started on *james*.

- **Kerberos log files** If you encounter problems, use the **tail –f** command to continuously read the /var/log/kadmind.log and krb5kdc.logfiles.

- **Security concerns** You must configure your Kerberos client hosts to use only Kerberized clients. In order to use Kerberos properly, no other client applications or server daemons should be used on the network, unless they use OTP, encryption, or a similarly secure protocol. For example, if you have just one Telnet daemon open and accepting connections, you still have passwords crossing the network.

For more information about configuring Kerberos clients, consult the documentation in the /usr/share/doc/krb5-workstation-1.2.2/ directory.

Kerberos Client Applications

The Kerberos clients installed with the workstation package are all in the /usr/kerberos/bin/ directory. Here is a description of the more popular ones provided:

- **kpasswd** Kerberos daemon clients can use the **/usr/kerberos/bin/ kpasswd** command to change passwords on the Kerberos KDC.

- **ftp** A Kerberized FTP client.

- **krlogin** A Kerberized rlogin client, which allows you to log in to a remote host without providing a password. This version is an improvement to the standard rlogin, because passwords are not sent in the clear.

- **krsh** A Kerberized rsh client, which allows commands to be executed on the remote host without a password.

- **ksu** Requires that users contact the KDC before being allowed to become root or any other user.

Kerberos Authentication and klogin

After you have created a principal for klogin (klogin/hostname.domainname.com@YOURREALM.COM) and updated the keytab files for all hosts involved, you can configure your host to allow others to access your home directory without divulging your account password. All you need to do is create a hidden file named .k5login in your home directory. The leading dot (.) makes the file hidden. You must then enter the principal of the user whom you wish to allow access. This user must, of course, be defined on the KDC, and the host from which the user is contacting you from must have an updated keytab file, which contains the host and host daemon name for krlogin.

If you wish to add multiple principals to the .k5login file, you can do so by entering each principal on a separate line, as follows:

```
patrick@YOURREALM.COM
```

```
susan@MYREALM.ORG
```

These two entries make it possible for *patrick* and *susan* to access only the home directory (the home directory of the system that contains the .k5login file), and no other area on your machine or any other area on the network. Should you then wish to revoke access to your home directory, simply edit the .k5login file and remove the relevant entry.

Exercise: Configuring a Kerberos Client

In this exercise, you will add user, host, and host daemon principals to your Kerberos realm. This exercise assumes three different systems in the following roles:

- A KDC (host A)

- A Kerberos client running the Kerberized ftp daemon (host B).

- A Kerberos client accessing host B's ftp daemon (host C).

You can, of course, use fewer systems. For example, you can make the Kerberos KDC server offer up its own FTP service and use a remote client to access it.

1. On the KDC (host A), run **kadmin** or **gkadmin** to add the following principals:

```
kerberosuser1
kerberosuser2
host/hosta.yourdomain.com
host/hostb.yourdomain.com
host/hostc.yourdomain.com
ftp/hostb.yourdomain.com
ftp/hostc.yourdomain.com
```

2. Install the krb-libs and krb5-workstation packages on hosts B and C. You do not need to install the server package on every host on the network.

3. As root on hosts B and C, create two users named *kerberosuser1* and *kerberosuser2* using **useradd**, then use the **passwd** command to give each of these users a password:

```
useradd kerberosuser1
useradd kerberosuser2
passwd kerberosuser1
passwd kerberosuser2
```

   If you do not wish to create these local user accounts, you do not have to. However, when it comes time to use **kinit**, you will have to specify the user (such as kerberosuser1 or kerberosuser2) using the **-p** option. Read earlier in this chapter for more information on using **kinit**.

4. Run **kadmin** on hosts B and C. Make sure that you specify the correct administrative user for your KDC. Issue the following commands on both hosts B and C to the local client (not on the Kerberos KDC) from within to populate the local /etc/krb5.keytab file with the principals of the network hosts and daemons you wish to use:

```
ktadd -k /etc/kb5.keytab   kerberosuser1
ktadd -k /etc/kb5.keytab   kerberosuser2
ktadd -k /etc/kb5.keytab   host/hosta.yourdomain.com
ktadd -k /etc/kb5.keytab   host/hostb.yourdomain.com
ktadd -k /etc/kb5.keytab   host/hostc.yourdomain.com
ktadd -k /etc/kb5.keytab   ftp/hostb.yourdomain.com
ktadd -k /etc/kb5.keytab   ftp/hostc.yourdomain.com
```

These commands will transfer information from the KDC to the /etc/krb5.keytab files on both hosts B and C.

5. Now, you need to activate the FTP daemons on the client hosts. This involves editing the /etc/xinetd.d/gssftp file for hosts B and C. Change the *disabled = yes* value to *disabled = no*.

6. Disable any other FTP daemons you may have active. For example, edit the /etc/xinetd.d/wu–ftpd or /etc/xinetd.d/opieftpd so that the disabled entry reads *disabled = yes*.

7. Restart xinetd:

```
/etc/rc.d/init.d/xinetd restart
```

8. Use ping to verify that hosts B and C can access host A.

9. Now, on host B, log on as kerberosuser1 and use /usr/kerberos/bin/kinit to obtain a TGT. Alternatively, log on as any user and specify the Kerberos user (such as kerberosuser1 or kerberosuser2) using the **-p** option.

10. Use /usr/kerberos/bin/klist to view the TGT.

11. Now, use the /usr/kerberos/bin/ftp client to access host c.

12. You will be allowed access. If a problem occurs, open up two terminals on the KDC and use the **tail -f** commands to read the /var/log/kadmind.log and /var/log/krb5kdc.log files to discover the problem. The most common problems are that the proper host and host daemon tickets have not been added either to the KDC, or to the keytabs of hosts B and C.

13. After you have logged on, use /usr/kerberos/bin/klist again to view your credential cache. You will see the host and ftp principal tickets have now been cached. Remember, you are using Kerberos v5, so ignore any Kerberos v4 messages.

Summary

In this chapter, you have been introduced to ways that allow you to avoid sniffing attacks. Encrypting transmissions and ensuring that passwords do not cross the network in plain text are the two strategies. You learned how to implement OTP using OPIE, and then learned how Kerberos allows you to establish a more robust, though involved, authentication scheme. You now know the basic moves to take when implementing OPIE on clients and servers and have been armed with a method for implementing Kerberos. From principal creation to understanding key exchange and credential confirmation, you now know what it takes to implement Kerberos on small networks, as well as enterprise networks that use multiple Kerberos realms.

As you implement Kerberos, you will find that you will have to dedicate additional resources to manage Kerberos principals and secure network daemons. You will also find that it will be necessary to troubleshoot your client/server configuration. Nevertheless, these solutions will help you further secure your network. Now, it is time to learn how to use encryption techniques, such as Secure Shell, to stop sniffing attacks.

Solutions Fast Track

Understanding Network Authentication

☑ Even if employees remain behind the firewall, many system services allow clear text authentication, including Telnet, File Transfer Protocol (FTP), and standard Network Information Service (NIS). Even though transmissions can be encrypted, many tools exist that help hackers wage a *sniffing* attack to capture encrypted information.

☑ After the packets containing the encrypted passwords are captured, hackers use cracking applications such as L0phtCrack, which are designed to both capture and crack sniffed encrypted passwords.

Creating Authentication and Encryption Solutions

☑ To authenticate safely, you have two options: Find a way to authenticate without sending passwords across the network, or find a way to discard any password that is sent across the network. The accepted phrase for this strategy is *one-time passwords* (OTP).

☑ Kerberos has the added ability to encrypt transmissions after authentication occurs. The use of OTP, however, does not encrypt subsequent transmissions. OTP is usually much easier to implement than Kerberos, however.

☑ Other encrypting solutions include Secure Sockets Layer (SSL), Secure Shell (SSH), and IPSec.

Implementing One-Time Passwords (OTP and OPIE)

☑ In the Linux world, the most universal way to implement one-time password (OTP) support in your Linux systems is to install the One-Time Passwords in Everything (OPIE) application. OPIE supports the Message Digest 5 (MD5) algorithm.

☑ By default, OPIE does not enforce OTP whenever you log in interactively. Any user is given the choice of using OTP or the standard login procedure.

☑ Using **opiepasswd** to create OPIE users. As soon as the **opiepasswd** command is used against a user, it is then possible for that user to use OTP to log in. The **opiekey** command generates responses.

☑ When the systems administrator creates an OTP password list, the user can use the **opieinfo** command to generate a list of passwords for later use.

Implementing Kerberos Version 5

☑ Kerberos v5 is a revolutionary step in network authentication, because it allows you to establish a domain that authenticates not only individual hosts and users, but individual daemons, as well. Using Kerberos, you can centrally control which hosts and users can access the daemons on your network.

☑ After Kerberos is established on a network, passwords do not ever cross the network, not even in encrypted form. You can configure Kerberos to encrypt ensuring communications between authenticated hosts.

☑ A principal is the name for any host, service, or user that is allowed to authenticate on a Kerberos network. A principal consists of a primary (also known as a "root"), an instance, and a realm.

☑ The **kadmin** application, also found in the /usr/kerberos/sbin/ directory, is designed to add principals to the Kerberos database. The **kadmin** command also lists, modifies, and deletes principals. It is also used to populate and update the Key table files for each Kerberos host.

Using kadmin and Creating Kerberos Client Passwords

☑ Standard principal policy settings include policy name, minimum password life (in seconds), maximum password life (in seconds), and minimum password length.

☑ You can create a policy by using the **addpol** command from within kadmin.

☑ The **kinit** command allows a user to obtain a ticket granting ticket (TGT) from the Key Distribution Center (KDC). Issuing the **kinit** command has the Kerberos client contact the KDC and obtain a TGT.

☑ After you run kinit, the cache will contain only the TGT. Additional credentials, such as actual tickets to access a daemon such as FTP, will be added only after you access the remote host.

Establishing Kerberos Client Trust Relationships with kadmin

☑ The only way to establish a trust relationship on the Kerberos client host is to use the **kadmin** command.

☑ The administrator must use the **kadmin –ktadd** command on each Kerberos client that wishes to participate in the Kerberos realm. The **kadmin ktadd –k** command gives each client the ability to prove that it has the public keys of the services used.

Logging On to a Kerberos Host Daemon

☑ Client A, the Kerberized client, first uses its TGT to request a session ticket. The Kerberos KDC checks to see if Client B has a host principal entry, then also checks to see if Client B has a host daemon entry for FTP. Then, the KDC determines that Client A has the proper host and host daemon keys for client B. If all of these credentials match, then client A can connect to client B's FTP server.

☑ When you try to administer Kerberos using **kadmin**, it is important to realize that if you make significant changes to the database concerning a user, you will have to use **kdestroy** and then **kinit** to obtain new credentials.

☑ You must configure your Kerberos client hosts to use only Kerberized clients. In order to use Kerberos properly, no other client applications or server daemons should be used on the network, unless they use OTP, encryption, or a similarly secure protocol.

Frequently Asked Questions

The following Frequently Asked Questions, answered by the authors of this book, are designed to both measure your understanding of the concepts presented in this chapter and to assist you with real-life implementation of these concepts. To have your questions about this chapter answered by the author, browse to **www.syngress.com/solutions** and click on the **"Ask the Author"** form.

Q: When using OPIE, don't clients have to log on to the same machine in order to generate the response?

A: No. You can use any OTP generator you wish, as long as you enter the sequence and seed numbers correctly.

Q: If I implement OTP, don't I have to generate a list of passwords and have carry them around with me?

A: Well, yes and no. If users have access to a Linux or Windows computer, they can just use an application such as **opiekey** or **WinKey**. However, if no OTP generator is available, you will then have to find a way for users to access their sequence numbers and seed values. This is when a list becomes handy.

Q: Using OTP means that users don't have to remember passwords, doesn't it?

A: No, not at all. Users still must remember their secret keys, because they use these keys and the server's request to generate a response. The nice thing about OPIE is that passwords do not cross the network.

Q: If I use OTP, usernames still cross the network unencrypted, don't they?

A: This is true unless you use IPsec or SSH. Still, the passwords do not cross the network.

Q: I wish to remove a principal from the keytab of one of my Kerberos clients. How do I do this?

A: Enter kadmin as an administrative user on the Kerberos client (not the KDC) and use the **ketremove** option. For example, if you wanted to remove the principal for the user named *james*, you would do the following:

```
terminal$/usr/kerberos/sbin/kadmin
kadmin: ktremove -p james
kadmin: quit
terminal$
```

Q: How do I create a backup of the Kerberos database? Also, is it possible to create a backup KDC?

A: As for the first part of the question, you can create a backup of the KDC database as follows:

```
/usr/kerberos/sbin/kdb5_util dump keatskerberos
```

You can then read the database using any text editor. Figure 6.17 shows the backup database open in the pico text editor. As far as creating a backup KDC, this is indeed possible and is expected in large networks, or in networks where timely authentication is vital. After all, consider the problems that would occur if users were not able to authenticate. Information for creating a slave KDC is found in the /usr/share/doc/krb5-server*/ directory.

Figure 6.17 Viewing a Kerberos Backup Database

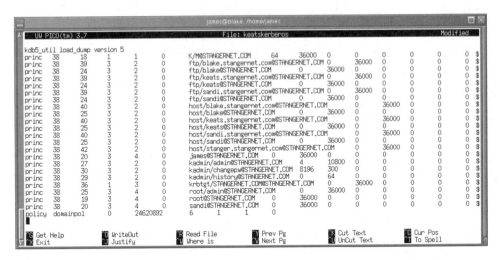

Q: In this chapter, you have discussed both OPIE and Kerberos. I would like to access my Web server from home. Which should I use?

A: If you only have to support one Web server, using Kerberos as a solution would be overkill. Use OPIE along with Secure Shell (SSH), and you will be in great shape.

Q: Can Kerberos authentication cross through firewalls?

A: Yes. As long as you allow your firewall to allow the Kerberos ports, you will have no problem. Table 6.3 provides the most often-used Kerberos ports.

Table 6.3 Kerberos ports

Kerberos Daemon Name	Port	Description
krb5	88/tcp	Used to send TGTs to clients
krb5	88/udp	Used to send TGTs to clients
kerberos_master	751/udp	The port Kerberos uses to issue authentication tickets
kerberos_master	751/tcp	Used to issue authentication tickets
kpasswd	761/tcp	For the Kerberos **kpasswd** command, used by clients to change their passwords on the KDC

Continued

Table 6.3 Continued

Kerberos Daemon Name	Port	Description
kpop	1109/tcp	The standard Pop Kerberos port
krb5_prop	754/tcp	Used by the primary KDC to update backup KDCs
eklogin	2105/tcp	The port for the Kerberos rlogin client that allows encryption
klogin	543/tcp	The standard Kerberized rlogin application for Kerberos version 5
kshell	544/tcp	The port for the Kerberized rsh client
kerberos-adm	749/tcp	The kadmin port

You may have to allow additional ports, depending upon the clients that you wish to support. Consult the /etc/services file for a more comprehensive list.

Q: Does the Linux version of Kerberos support Microsoft's implementation.

A: In a word, no. Microsoft implemented several proprietary extensions to its implementation of the Kerberos protocol.

Q: This chapter has focused on a single-realm implementation. Can you have multiple Kerberos realms?

A: Yes. By editing the /etc/krb5.conf file, you can define multiple realms to further organize realms according to your business needs.

Chapter 7

Avoiding Sniffing Attacks through Encryption

Solutions in this chapter:

- **Understanding Network Encryption**
- **Capturing and Analyzing Unencrypted Network Traffic**
- **Using OpenSSH to Encrypt Network Traffic between Two Hosts**
- **Installing OpenSSH**
- **Configuring SSH**
- **Implementing SSH to Secure Data Transmissions over an Insecure Network**
- **Capturing and Analyzing Encrypted Network Traffic**
- ☑ Summary
- ☑ Solutions Fast Track
- ☑ Frequently Asked Questions

Introduction

You now understand how it is possible to enhance authentication using third-party open source software. You also understand some of the pitfalls involved in deploying such software in various systems. For example, in the last chapter you discovered how to deploy authentication using one-time passwords and Kerberos. These authentication implementations enable systems to verify the identity of a user logging on to them, and the integrity of data.

In this chapter, you will learn about solutions to deploy strong encryption to enhance network security. Encryption ensures data confidentiality by using algorithms to encrypt data before it is sent over a network. The receiving host then decrypts the data to a readable format. The solutions in this chapter combine both authentication and encryption, and include a step-by-step guide to implementing encryption over an insecure network.

Understanding Network Encryption

Network encryption ensures that data sent across a network from one host to another is unreadable to a third party. If a sniffer intercepts the data, it finds the data unusable because the data is encrypted. Therefore, a hacker cannot view any usernames or passwords, and any information sent across the network is safe. The requirement is that all communicating systems must support the same network encryption technique, such as Secure Shell (SSH).

Network encryption is used for any data transfer that requires confidentiality. Since the Internet is a public network, network encryption is essential. E-commerce transactions must ensure confidentiality to protect credit card and personal information. Personal banking Web sites and investment companies often require extremely sensitive information to be sent, such as bank account numbers and tax identification numbers. If these usernames, passwords, and personal information fell into the wrong hands, the information could be used for a front-door attack, since the hacker could pose as a legitimate user.

Rlogin, remote shell (rsh), and Telnet are three notoriously unsafe protocols. They do not use encryption for remote logins or any type of data transmission. For example, if you are an administrator and you want to log in to a system via Telnet, your username and login are sent in clear text. Rsh and rlogin send all data between two hosts in clear text as well (but a password is not required).

If a packet sniffer captured the packets destined for the administrator's system, it would eventually capture the packets containing the username and password, and the attacker could then enter the system as a legitimate user.

Capturing and Analyzing Unencrypted Network Traffic

To view an unencrypted login session, you must capture packets during a login session. In the following steps, you will Telnet into a host and capture the unsecured session with the open source packet sniffer Ethereal.

Note that in order for the following example to work properly, you must have two systems: the Telnet client and the Telnet remote host. All Linux installations include Telnet, so no additional program is required for this example.

1. Verify that Ethereal is installed on your system by entering:

   ```
   rpm -qa | grep ethereal
   ```

2. If you do not receive a reply, you need to download and install Ethereal. Ethereal (ethereal-0.8.9-4.i386.rpm) is included on the CD accompanying this book.

3. Once you have verified that Ethereal is installed, you are ready to capture packets.

4. To add filters to Ethereal without using host names, open a command interface and enter:

   ```
   ethereal -n
   ```

5. Select the **Edit** menu and choose **Filters**. The Ethereal: Filters screen appears. Since no filters have been configured, the configuration screen is blank.

6. To create a filter that allows only traffic between your host and another host, you must add a filter name and a filter string. For example, to create a filter between your host and a host at 24.130.10.35, enter the filter name and filter string shown in Figure 7.1. Please note that your IP addresses will not be the same. You need to select your system's IP address and the IP address of the system you wish to log in to via Telnet.

Figure 7.1 Creating a Filter between Two Hosts

7. After the two fields are complete, you must click **Save**, and then click **New**. Click **OK** to exit the Filter screen.

8. To start a packet capture, simply select the **Capture** menu and choose **Start**. The Capture Preference screen appears. Click **Filter** and choose the "Telnet Login" filter that you created. Click **OK** twice and the capture starts.

9. To generate the Telnet login packets, Telnet into the Telnet host. For example, if you wanted to Telnet to a host at 24.130.10.35, you would enter:

```
telnet 24.130.10.35
```

10. Enter a username and password to log in to the system. If you do not have a username and password on the Telnet host, create a user *telnet* with the password *telnet* on the Telnet host by entering:

```
useradd telnet
```

Create a password for user *telnet* by entering:

```
passwd telnet
Changing password for user telnet
New UNIX password:
Retype new UNIX password:
passwd: all authentication tokens updated successfully
```

11. After you log in as user *telnet* on the Telnet host, exit the Telnet session.

12. Stop the Ethereal packet capture by clicking **Stop**.

13. The packet capture appears in Ethereal. Locate the Telnet data packet that includes the *data: password* field. Your screen will resemble Figure 7.2, which highlights the first password packet.

Figure 7.2 Capturing a Telnet Login Session

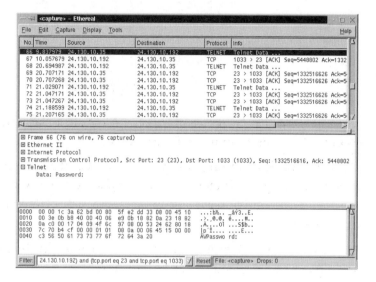

14. Scroll to the second password packet. The password field contains the first character of the *telnet* password. In this case, the character is the letter "t," as shown in Figure 7.3.

Figure 7.3 Identifying the First Character in the Telnet Password

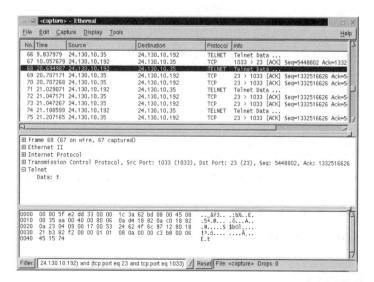

15. Telnet sends each password character as a separate packet. If you continue to scroll down the packet capture and view each Telnet data packet, you will discover the password.

16. An easier way to discover the Telnet password is to follow the TCP stream. To do this, simply select any packet involved in this Telnet connection. It can be a TCP or Telnet packet, as long as it is part of the Telnet session.

17. Once a corresponding packet is selected, select the **Tools** menu and select **Follow TCP Stream**. The contents of the TCP stream appear, as shown in Figure 7.4.

Figure 7.4 Following a TCP Stream to Discover the Username and Password

18. The username and password are displayed in clear text. Please note the echo in the login name. By default, the system distinguishes client keystrokes with brown, and system text as blue. You can see the brown and blue text if you are reading the electronic file on this book's accompanying CD; even if you can't see the brown client text on this printed page, you can see that the packet sniffer has discovered the username and password.

19. Save the packet capture as **unsectel**, and quit Ethereal.

As you can see, it is possible to intercept a login session and discover a user-name and password. In this case, a hacker could now log in to the Telnet host with the same privileges as user *telnet*. *Telnet* is a legitimate user, even though the impersonator is not. The Telnet host is now the victim of a front-door attack.

If network encryption is implemented on the network, the login session will be encrypted. All of the information passed between the two hosts is rendered useless because no application data (such as a Telnet packet) is displayed because it is encrypted, as shown in Figure 7.5.

If the hacker attempts to view the TCP stream to discover the username and password, it will also render useless information, as shown in Figure 7.6.

Figure 7.5 Login Session with Network Encryption

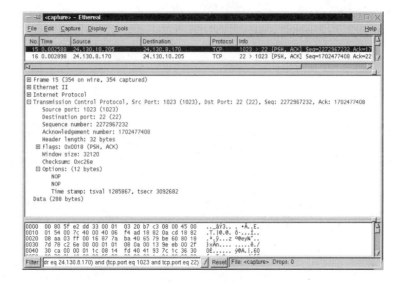

NOTE

Hackers do not capture all Internet traffic in hopes that they will find sensitive information. There is simply too much traffic on the Internet, so this technique would be similar to finding the proverbial needle in a haystack. Instead, they either focus their packet sniffing on one server or client interface, or try to hack into a server that contains the sensitive information they seek. For example, they may attempt to hack into a bank's database server that contains client credit card numbers and per-sonal information. In the steps described in this section, a packet filter was created on the sniffer to focus on the Telnet host.

Figure 7.6 Following a TCP Stream When Network Encryption Is Enabled

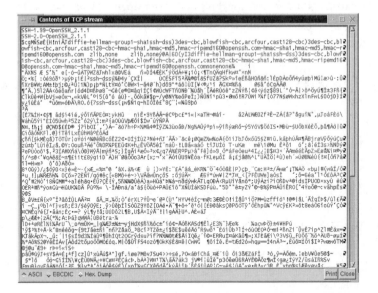

Damage & Defense...

Securing E-Commerce Transactions

If hackers were alerted to an unsecure server, they could capture packets going in and out of the server to gain the data they sought. For example, if an e-commerce server does not use any type of network encryption for transactions, there is a great deal of data to be gained by a hacker. Unfortunately, many small companies or entrepreneurs set up their own Web servers, unaware of potential security problems, and set up simple scripts to process payment forms. Although the transaction takes place, it takes place in an unsecured manner. Every packet may contain valuable information that is very easy to observe over the wire. Secure Sockets Layer (SSL) is ideal for implementing secure e-commerce transactions.

If a hacker intercepts a credit card number, the number may be used or sold. When the Web site customer backtracks to determine where his or her number was stolen, he or she may realize that it occurred shortly after an Internet transaction. This will tarnish the Web site's reputation, since you have lost at least one customer, and eventually put the site out of business. This is particularly troublesome if the Web server is under surveillance by a hacker.

The lesson demonstrated in the following sections demonstrates how to implement an important network encryption system: Open Secure Shell (OpenSSH). This system will ensure that all data transmitted between your hosts is secure, and is useless for hackers.

Using OpenSSH to Encrypt Network Traffic between Two Hosts

OpenSSH (www.openssh.org) is an open source program that encrypts all traffic between hosts using secure shell (SSH). It is a secure replacement for common Internet programs used for remote connectivity, such as Telnet, rlogin, and rsh. Because it encrypts all traffic, it always hides usernames and passwords used for remote logins. After the login occurs, it continues to encrypt all data traffic between the hosts. Open SSH is a free version of the SSH Communications Security Corporation's SSH suite (www.ssh.org). As with most open source software, the tradeoff is that vendor support is not available. Do not confuse OpenSSH with the fee-based SSH suite. The OpenSSH home page is shown in Figure 7.7.

Figure 7.7 OpenSSH Home Page

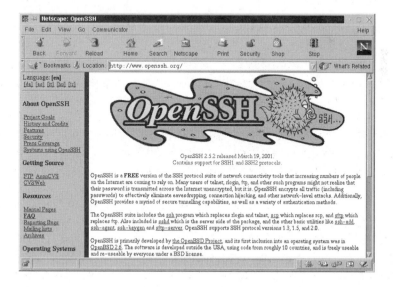

The OpenBSD Project (www.openbsd.org) develops OpenSSH and the Unix operating system, OpenBSD. OpenBSD is a free 4.4BSD-based OS that is designed with security in mind. It uses strong encryption techniques to ward off hackers. OpenBSD claims that the default installation has not experienced a remote hole in over three years. The OpenBSD Project has ported OpenSSH to other operating systems, including Linux, HP-UX, AIX, Irix, SCO, MacOS X, Cygwin, Digital Unix/Tru64/OSF, SNI/Reliant Unix, NeXT, and Solaris. The OpenBSD home page is shown in Figure 7.8.

Figure 7.8 OpenBSD Home Page

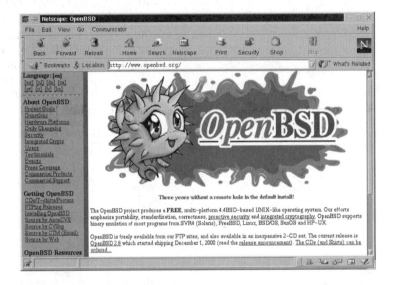

The OpenSSH Suite

OpenSSH is a suite of secure networking connectivity programs. The OpenSSH suite includes the following programs:

- **OpenSSH SSH client (SSH)** Remote login program, used for secure remote logins and session encryption. Secure alternative for rlogin and Telnet.

- **Secure copy program (SCP)** Remote file copy program, used to securely copy files between network hosts. Supports usernames and passwords.

- **Secure file transfer program (SFTP)** Used for secure interactive file transfers. Secure alternative for FTP.

- **OpenSSH SSH daemon (SSHD)** The daemon for SSH.

Many features are included in the OpenSSH suite that ensure secure transmissions across a network, and extend the usefulness of the program. Table 7.1 lists several of the OpenSSH features.

Table 7.1 OpenSSH Features

Feature	Description
Strong Encryption using Triple Data Encryption Standard (3DES) and Blowfish	The 3DES and Blowfish encryption algorithms are patent free in all countries. 3DES is time proven, and Blowfish provides faster encryption by using fast block cipher. Either encryption algorithm can be used. They are applied before authentication to ensure that all usernames and passwords are encrypted, as well as the session data.
Strong Authentication using Public Keys, One-Time Passwords (OTPs) and Kerberos Authentication	Protects against authentication vulnerabilities such as IP and Domain Name System (DNS) spoofing and fake routes. There are four types of authentication methods used with OpenSSH: ■ Public key authentication only ■ Public key-based host authentication along with .rhosts ■ One-time passwords with s/key ■ Kerberos authentication
X11 Forwarding for encrypting X Windows Traffic	Encrypts X Windows traffic between remote systems. Protects against remote xterm snooping and hijacking.
Encrypted Port Forwarding	Allows TCP/IP ports to be forwarded to another system over an encrypted channel. This is ideal for Internet protocols that do not inherently support encryption, such as POP or SMTP.
Agent Forwarding for Single Network Login	A user's authentication keys can be stored on the user's local machine, which becomes the authentication agent. When the user accesses the network from another system, the connection is forwarded to this authentication agent. This prevents the authentication keys from being installed on any network system, and allows the user to securely access the network from any system.
Interoperability	Complies with multiple SSH protocol versions (SSH 1.3, 1.5 and 2.0).

Continued

Table 7.1 Continued

Feature	Description
Data Compression	Allows data compression to occur before data encryption. This is important for networks with slow connections.
Passes Kerberos and Andrew File System (AFS) Tickets to Remote Systems	Allows users to access AFS and Kerberos services by entering their password only one time.

NOTE

OpenSSH 2.0 supports the SSH 1.3, 1.5, and 2.0 protocol. It is important to know that SSH 2.0 does not use the Rivest, Shamir, Adleman (RSA) algorithms, but does support it. Because RSA algorithms still had an effective patent, the SSH 2.0 developers decided to use the Diffie-Hellman (DH) and Digital Signature Algorithm (DSA) algorithms instead. Therefore, if your SSH client and servers use SSH 1.3, 1.5, or 2.0, they will be compatible. Most commercial implementations for Unix, Windows, and others use these versions.

Installing OpenSSH

OpenSSH implementations are significantly different between operating systems because of authentication. In fact, the developers split development into two categories:

- **OpenBSD-based development** Produces secure, clean, and simple OpenSSH code for the OpenBSD operating system.

- **OpenSSH Portability Team** Uses the OpenBSD OpenSSH code to develop portable versions for other operating systems. Each portable version is indicated with a "p" to differentiate it from the OpenBSD version. Portable versions are not released at the same time as the OpenBSD versions. They usually take longer to release, since more time is required for the additional code.

Make sure that you are downloading the specific version for your operating system. To determine if your operating system is supported, visit the Portable OpenSSH Web page at www.openssh.org/portable.html. The download links for each version are located at the bottom of the Web page. Simply scroll down to locate the download site nearest you, and then identify your particular operating system. The OpenSSH installation files required for Linux are included on the CD accompanying this book. The portable OpenSSH Web page is shown in Figure 7.9.

Figure 7.9 Operating Systems Supported by Portable OpenSSH

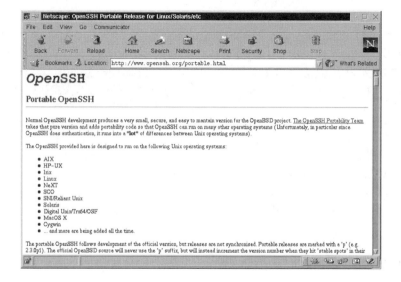

OpenSSH is becoming very popular, and operating systems are now released with OpenSSH installed by default. For example, Red Hat Linux 7 installs OpenSSH 2.1.1p7-1 during the installation process. The following operating systems also include OpenSSH into the base system, as shown in Figure 7.10. These systems include Red Hat, SuSE, Mandrake Linux, FreeBSD, and others.

From the preceding information, you can now determine whether you need to download and install OpenSSH. The examples in this chapter use Red Hat Linux 7. A portable version of OpenSSH has already been created. It is a Red Hat Package Manager (RPM) that is included into the base system of Red Hat Linux 7. These installation files are also located on the CD accompanying this book. Therefore, we are ready to begin configuring OpenSSH after we confirm that OpenSSH is installed.

Figure 7.10 Operating Systems That Incorporate OpenSSH

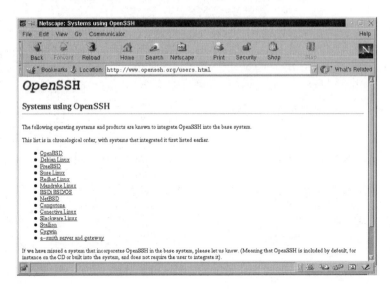

1. To ensure that OpenSSH RPM is installed on your system, enter the following:

    ```
    rpm -qa | grep ssh
    ```

2. You should receive the following response if SSH is installed:

    ```
    openssh-askpass-gnome-2.1.1p4-1

    openssh-clients-2.1.1p4-1

    openssh-2.1.1p4-1

    openssh-server-2.1.1p4-1

    openssh-askpass-2.1.1p4-1
    ```

    If you receive this response, you are ready to configure OpenSSH.

3. If you receive no response, install these files from the accompanying CD, or access www.openssh.org/portable.html to locate a download site nearest you, and download the portable version that matches your operating system. For example, since I am located in Los Angeles, I would locate the Santa Barbara, CA, USA section, and select the "Linux RPMs" link. Then, choose the *RH70/* directory (or equivalent), and download the corresponding RPMs from Step #2. The versions will be higher than the versions incorporated into the Red Hat Linux 7 release, as shown in Figure 7.11.

Figure 7.11 Downloading OpenSSH RPMs for Red Hat Linux 7

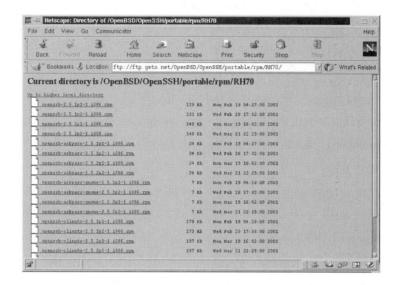

4. Multiple versions will exist for each RPM. Download the latest version of each.

5. Install the RPMs by using the **rpm –i** command. Once installed, you are ready to configure OpenSSH.

Configuring SSH

SSH is the OpenSSH SSH client, and works with the SSHD (SSH daemon). They work together to replace rlogin and rsh. SSH is also a replacement for Telnet. SSH is used to log in to a remote system and execute commands on the remote system. The difference between SSH and Telnet, rlogin, and rsh is that SSH is secure.

At the beginning of this chapter, you used a Telnet connection to log in to a remote host. The entire session was unsecure because all data was sent in clear text, including the username and password. Using the packet sniffer Ethereal, you were able to capture the Telnet session packets and follow the Transmission Control Protocol (TCP) stream. You discovered the username and password used to establish the connection. Since you now have the username, password, and remote host Internet Protocol (IP) address (in this case), you can now log in as the user whose packets you captured.

Using a similar method, you can also capture rlogin and rsh sessions and determine the needed authentication data. For example, because rlogin and rsh use host authentication, you can determine the IP address or fully qualified domain name (FQDN), and the username required to log in to the host. Once the host name and username for authentication are determined, they can be used for IP and Domain Name System (DNS) spoofing.

The SSH client is a replacement for Telnet, rlogin and rsh. It provides a secure data channel between two hosts on a network. These hosts can be untrusted and the network can be unsecured. In order to work, both hosts must support SSH. One host then connects to another host using an encrypted connection. Because the connection is encrypted, any hacker who captures the data will have an extremely difficult time decrypting it.

How SSH Works

The method for implementing SSH combines similar r-command concepts with a private and public key method. In order to understand how SSH works, it is a good idea to understand how the older r-commands work.

Insecure r-command Authentication

The following authentication method is used for r-commands, such as rlogin, rsh, or rcp, in Red Hat Linux 7. For the example, rlogin will be used. Any user logging on to a remote system must have a user account on the remote system. For this example, we will use the account *susan*. If Susan is logged on locally when she connects to a remote host, no password is needed to access the remote host. No password is needed because her account is authenticated by an entry in the .rhosts file located in the remote system's $HOME/susan directory. The .rhosts file must be created in the susan home directory.

The .rhosts file contains the host name and username required for Susan to log in to the system. The host name of Susan's system is we-24-130-10-205.we .mediaone.net, and her username is susan. If her rlogin command matches the entry in the .rhosts file, she is allowed access to the system. No password is required. The .rhosts file is formatted as follows:

```
hostname username
```

The hostname should be the FQDN of the host, not the short host name. For example, use:

```
we-24-130-10-205.we.mediaone.net
```

instead of:

```
we-24-130-10-205
```

The username must be an account on the system. If a user account exists for this username on the system, the user can access *all* user accounts except root.

As mentioned earlier, for Susan to log in remotely, the root user of the remote host must create a .rhosts file in the $HOME/susan directory with her host name and username. For example, if Susan's machine were host name we-24-130-10-205.we.mediaone.net, the root user would enter the following:

```
we-24-130-10-205.we.mediaone.net susan
```

When Susan is ready to access the remote host, she would enter the following rlogin command:

```
rlogin -l susan we-24-130-8-170.we.mediaone.net
```

where *we-24-130-8-170.we.mediaone.net* is the remote host. The **-l** option indicates the account used for the login, which is *susan*.

This method is not secure because the host name and username are sent to the remote host for authentication in clear text. This method opens the remote host to IP spoofing, DNS spoofing, and routing spoofing.

Because of these security vulnerabilities, it is recommended that you disable the r-command utilities. This process was discussed in Chapter 2, "Hardening the Operating System," using the /etc/xinetd.d directory and commenting out the associated text files. The /etc/xinetd.d directory makes it simple to disable services that your system is not using. For example, you can disable the rlogin and rsh services by commenting out the rlogin and rsh entries in the respective file and restarting the service. If the service is commented out, it will not restart. Once disabled, no one can access the machine via the r-command utilities.

1. To disable rlogin, you must edit the /etc/xinetd.d/rlogin file. Open the rlogin file, as shown in Figure 7.12, using vi or an editor of your choice.

2. Comment out the *service login* line by adding a number sign (#) before it:

   ```
   #service login
   ```

3. Write and quit the file.

Figure 7.12 Disabling rlogin Using the /xinetd.d/rlogin File

4. Next, you must restart xinetd by entering:

```
/etc/rc.d/init.d/xinetd restart
Stopping xinetd:                              [ OK }
Starting xinetd:                              [ OK }
```

5. Disable the rsh service using the same method (e.g., edit the /etc/ xinetd.d/rsh and /etc/xinetd.d/rexec files by commenting out the *service shell* line).

NOTE

The rexec service is another r-command tool that provides authentication based on usernames and passwords for remote execution purposes. It is disabled by default.

6. To provide additional security, disable the Telnet service using the same method (e.g., edit the /xinetd.d/telnet file by commenting out the *service telnet* line).

7. Restart xinetd.

You have disabled the remote client programs that send information without encryption. Because these programs are vulnerable to attacks, they should be replaced entirely by SSH. The following sections demonstrate how SSH replaces these programs.

Secure SSH Authentication

SSH is based on public-key cryptography. Versions before SSH 2.0 use RSA-based authentication. Version SSH 2.0 and later use the unpatented DSA instead. Public-key cryptography uses private and public keys to ensure authentication. The private key is only known by the user, and the public key is available to everyone else, such as the remote host.

SSH can create a DSA private/public key pair for a user by using the **ssh-keygen –d** command. In SSH 2.0, the private DSA key is stored in the $HOME/.ssh/id_dsa file. The public key is placed in the $HOME/.ssh/id_dsa.pub file. The public key should be renamed and copied to the $HOME/.ssh/ authorized_keys2 file on the remote system. The authorized_keys2 file contains one public key per line.

> **NOTE**
>
> The $HOME/.ssh/authorized_keys2 file on the remote host is the SSH equivalent to the $HOME/.rhosts file used for the r-commands. Earlier in this chapter, you learned how the .rhosts file is configured to allow a user account to log in remotely using rlogin.

In SSH version 1, RSA authentication is used. An RSA private/public key is created in either OpenSSH version by entering the **ssh-keygen** command without the **–d** option. The private key is stored in the $HOME/.ssh/identity file, and the public key is stored in the $HOME/.ssh/identity.pub file of the user's home directory. The public key should be renamed and copied to the user's home directory on the remote system, to the $HOME/.ssh/authorized_keys file.

SSH offers password authentication if the public-key authentication fails. It also provides password authentication if public-key authentication is not available. This flexibility allows the password to be encrypted and transmitted over the network so that data integrity persists, even if the public-key authentication does not work. Table 7.2 summarizes the locations of the private and public keys used in SSH.

Table 7.2 Public-Key Authentication Locations for SSH

SSH Version 2 Key	Local System Default Location	Remote Host Location
Private key	$HOME/.ssh/id_dsa	Not applicable
Public key	$HOME/.ssh/id_dsa.pub	$HOME/.ssh/authorized_keys2

SSH Version 1 Key	Local System Default Location	Remote Host Location
Private key	$HOME/.ssh/identity	Not applicable
Public key	$HOME/.ssh/identity.pub	$HOME/.ssh/authorized_keys

Other important files used to identify public keys on a system are listed in Table 7.3.

Table 7.3 Additional Files Used in SSH

SSH File	Description
$HOME/.ssh/known_hosts	Lists the public keys for all the hosts to which the user has logged in. The host public keys are listed here if they are not listed in /etc/ssh_known_hosts.
/etc/ssh_known_hosts	Lists the RSA-generated public keys for all the hosts that the system knows. For example, any host that logs in to the system should have its public key listed in this file. Your network administrator should configure this file to list all the user public keys in your company. It should be a world-readable file, with one public key listed per line.
/etc/ssh_known_hosts2	Same as the ssh_known_hosts file, except it lists the DSA-generated public keys for all hosts that the system knows.
$HOME/.ssh/config	Configuration file for each user. Each user can have a specific configuration file (if needed), which is used by the SSH client.
/etc/ssh/ssh_config	Configuration file for the entire system. It is world readable and provides values for users who do not have a configuration file. This file is required for SSHD to start, and is automatically generated upon OpenSSH installation.

Continued

Table 7.3 Continued

SSH File	Description
$HOME/.ssh/rc	Lists commands that will be executed during user login. These commands are run immediately prior to the opening of the user's shell. Used to run any required routines (if needed) before the home directory of the user is accessible. For example, AFS may be needed for the user.
/etc/sshrc	Similar to the $HOME/.ssh/rc file, except it specifies commands that must be run immediately prior to systemwide. It should be world readable.

Implementing SSH to Secure Data Transmissions over an Insecure Network

Before you implement SSH, you need to make sure both the local system and the remote system have SSH installed. It is also a good idea to use SSH 2.0 or later on each system. This ensures that the DSA algorithm is used instead of the RSA algorithm, which is patented in some countries. In the following examples, both systems are running Red Hat Linux 7 with SSH 2.1 installed. Therefore, the DSA algorithm will be used, and no SSH installation is necessary because SSH is built into the operating system.

The **ssh-keygen** command is used to generate and manage SSH authentication keys. To implement SSH, you must first use **ssh-keygen** to create a private and public key on the client using either RSA or DSA authentication. The following steps demonstrate how to implement SSH to securely access a remote system.

1. Create a user on the client system. For example, create the user *dilbert*. Enter:

   ```
   useradd dilbert
   ```

2. Create a password for user dilbert by entering:

   ```
   passwd dilbert
   Changing password for user dilbert
   New UNIX password:
   Retype new UNIX password:
   passwd: all authentication tokens updated successfully
   ```

3. Log on as user *dilbert*.

4. Generate a public and private key (key pair) for dilbert by entering the following command.

```
ssh-keygen -d
```

NOTE

By default, SSH generates an RSA key for SSH 1.3 and 1.5. To generate a DSA key for SSH 2.0, you must specify the **-d** option when generating the key pair.

5. You will receive the following response:

```
Generating DSA parameter and key.
Enter file in which to save the key (/home/dilbert/.ssh/id_dsa):
```

6. Press **ENTER** to save the key to the default directory and filename (/home/dilbert/.ssh/id_dsa). You will then receive the following response:

```
Created directory '/home/dilbert/.ssh'.
Enter passphrase (empty for no passphrase):
```

7. The program requests a passphrase. For this example, do not enter a passphrase. The passphrase is used by 3DES to encrypt the private portion of the private key. A passphrase must be empty for host keys. If you enter a passphrase, do not use simple sentences. Instead, make it at least 10 to 30 characters with numbers, symbols, and letters. Passphrases can later be changed using the **-p** option. Press **ENTER** twice for no passphrase.

SECURITY ALERT!

Passphrases are not recoverable. If you forget your passphrase, a new key must be generated. You must then distribute the new public key to all required systems.

8. The key generator summary will appear:

```
Your identification has been saved in /home/dilbert/.ssh/id_dsa.
Your public key has been saved in /home/dilbert/.ssh/id_dsa.pub.
The key fingerprint is:
ca:3b:f9:80:5a:91:e5:c1:1e:5b:30:02:2f:d5:53:13
        dilbert@we-24-130-10-205.we.mediaone.net
```

9. The entire key-generation process is shown in Figure 7.13.

Figure 7.13 Generating a Private and Public Key Using the ssh-keygen Command

10. You have generated dilbert's private and public keys. View dilbert's private key by entering:

```
cat /home/dilbert/.ssh/id_dsa
```

The private key will resemble Figure 7.14. The private key must always remain secure on the local system.

Figure 7.14 DSA Private Key for User Dilbert

11. View dilbert's public key by entering:

```
cat /home/dilbert/.ssh/id_dsa.pub
```

Dilbert's public key can be distributed freely. Any system with which dilbert needs to communicate securely will need to obtain his public key. Dilbert's public key will resemble Figure 7.15.

Figure 7.15 DSA Public Key for User Dilbert

NOTE

You can rename the public key before you distribute it. For example, you can rename it "dilbert.pub." This is much easier to remember, and will be different from other user public keys created with DSA. You should always rename the public key after you generate a public and private key.

Distributing the Public Key

You must now activate the keys by placing the public key in the proper location on the remote server. The public key can be distributed freely; therefore, you can send it any way you want to the remote host.

For example, VeriSign offers digital ID services for e-mail clients to transmit e-mail securely. The digital ID is basically a public key with ID information embedded. VeriSign automatically posts the user's public key on its Web site. Any user who needs to access a public key for a specific user can download the user's digital ID from the VeriSign Web site at https://digitalid.verisign.com/services/client/index.html.

Figure 7.16 shows the information for downloading the public key (digital ID) for the user George Bush. It is doubtful that this George Bush is the

President of the United States. The U.S. Federal Bureau of Investigations (FBI) would most likely have the President's public key unlisted, which is an option for all VeriSign users. If you needed to transmit e-mail securely with this user, you would download his public key. He would need to download your public key as well. When both of you had each other's public keys, you could transmit data to one another securely.

Figure 7.16 Downloading Pubic Keys from the VeriSign Web Site

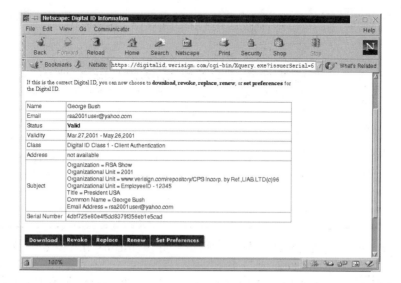

For this demonstration, you will upload dilbert's private key to a Web server. The remote host will then download the public key and activate it. The public key is activated when placed into dilbert's $HOME/.ssh/authorized_keys2 file on the remote system. The following steps demonstrate how to accomplish these tasks.

1. You will upload dilbert's public key to the Apache Web server on your system. Make sure that Apache is installed by entering:

```
rpm -qa | grep apache
```

2. You should receive a response similar to the following if Apache is installed:

```
apache-manual-1.3.12-25
apache-1.3.12-25
apache-devel-1.3.12-25
```

3. If you do not receive a response, you need to download and install Apache.

4. Create a *pubkeys* directory in the default apache root directory by entering the following:

```
mkdir /var/www/html/pubkeys
```

5. Copy and rename dilbert's public key to this Web directory by entering:

```
cp /home/dilbert/.ssh/id_dsa.pub
    /var/www/html/pubkeys/dilbert.pub
```

6. You have uploaded the public key to your local Apache server. Verify it is uploaded by opening a browser, such as lynx or Netscape Navigator, and entering:

```
http://localhost/pubkeys/
```

The directory contents are listed by default. You should see dilbert.pub listed. If not, confirm the root Web directory in Apache and make sure you copied the public key to the correct directory.

7. Remote Host: You need a second system to be the remote host. We will refer to the first system (the one you just configured) as the client. The remote system in this demonstration is a Red Hat Linux 7 system located on the same network. Log in to the remote host as root.

8. Remote Host: You need to create a *dilbert* account. Use the same password from the client system. Enter:

```
useradd dilbert
```

9. Remote Host: Create a password for user dilbert by entering:

```
passwd dilbert
Changing password for user dilbert
New UNIX password:
Retype new UNIX password:
passwd: all authentication tokens updated successfully
```

10. Remote Host: Create a .ssh directory in dilbert's home directory by entering the following command:

```
cd /home/dilbert
mkdir .ssh
```

11. Remote Host: Open a Web browser and access dilbert's public key from the client's Apache server. Enter the URL of host and the *pubkey* directory. For example, if you configured Apache on we-24-130-10-205 .we.mediaone.net, you will enter:

```
http://we-24-130-10-205.we.mediaone.net/pubkey
```

Your browser window will resemble Figure 7.17 in Navigator.

Figure 7.17 Accessing a Public Key from a Web Site

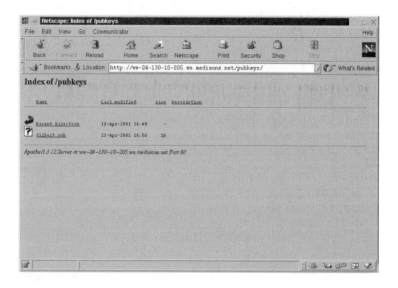

12. Remote Host: Download the public key to the remote host. For example, save it to the root user directory.

13. Remote Host: Next, you need to copy the contents of dilbert's public key file to the /home/dilbert/.ssh/authorized_keys2 file. This file does not currently exist. The simplest way to transfer the public key to this file is to copy `dilbert.pub` and rename it as authorized_keys2. For example, if you downloaded dilbert's public key to the root user directory, you would enter (from the root user directory):

```
cp dilbert.pub  /home/dilbert/.ssh/authorized_keys2
```

The authorized_key2 file lists the public DSA keys that can be used for login by the user. Each public key must be listed as one line in the file. The id_dsa.pub file, when viewed in a text editor, is written as one line. Therefore, it is important that the key is copied as only one line when placed in the authorized_key2 file.

14. Client Host: Physically access the client host.

15. Client Host: Log on as dilbert.

16. Client Host: Log in to the remote host using ssh. If the remote host were we-24-130-8-170.we.mediaone.net, you would enter:

```
ssh we-24-130-8-170.we.mediaone.net
```

17. Client Host: You will receive a message similar to the following:

```
The authenticity of host 'we-24-130-8-170.we.mediaone.net' can't
    be established.
DSA key fingerprint is
9a:e6:64:34:d5:fa:f7:e4:e9:fd:b7:e5:95:b0:1e:40.
Are you sure you want to continue connecting (yes/no)?
```

The message stating "The authenticity of host 'we-24-130-8-170.we.mediaone.net' can't be established" is a standard message that informs you that a trust relationship has not yet been established. This is standard for the first time a trust is established, and is seen on both the commercial and open versions of SSH.

18. Client Host: Enter **Yes** to continue connecting. The following warning message appears, indicating that the remote host's public key is added to the client's $HOME/.ssh/known_hosts file. You will not receive these warnings when you log in to the remote host in the future, as the trust relationship has been established. It is then followed by a prompt (no password is required due to the key pair):

```
Warning: Permanently added 'we-24-130-8-170.we.mediaone
    .net,24.130.8.170' (DSA) to the list of known hosts.
[dilbert@we-24-130-8-170 dilbert]$
```

19. Client Host: You will receive a remote host command prompt for dilbert. All data transmitted between your system and the remote host are encrypted.

20. Client Host: Quit the session by entering the **exit** command.

> **NOTE**
>
> If public key authentication fails, or if you are logged on to the client system as a user other that *dilbert*, ssh will request a password:
>
> ```
> dilbert@we-24-130-8-170.we.mediaone.net's password:
> ```
>
> Dilbert can securely enter his password for the remote host, since he has an account. His username and password will be encrypted via SSH, so the transmission is still secure. If you are asked for a password, you need to retrace your steps. If public key authentication is set up properly, you will not be asked for a password.

Capturing and Analyzing Encyrpted Network Traffic

Now that we have created an SSH connection between two hosts, we need to prove that the session is actually encrypted. To prove this, you will capture packets between the hosts during the SSH session. You will attempt to locate any login data, as well as any session data, and then follow the TCP stream.

1. Log in as root to the SSH remote host.

2. Remote Host: To add filters to Ethereal without using host names, open a command interface and enter:

   ```
   ethereal -n
   ```

3. Remote Host: Select the **Edit** menu and choose **Filters**. The Ethereal: Filters screen appears.

4. Remote Host: To create a filter that allows only traffic between the SSH hosts, you must add a filter name and a filter string. For example, to create a filter between your remote host and a client host at 24.130.10.205, enter the filter name "SSH Login" and filter string shown in Figure 7.18. Please note that your IP addresses will not be the same. You need to select the IP address of your client and remote SSH hosts. After the two fields are complete, you must click **Save**, and then click **New**. Your screen will appear similar to Figure 7.18.

Figure 7.18 Creating a Filter between SSH Two Hosts

5. Remote Host: Click **OK** to exit the Filter screen.

6. Remote Host: To start a packet capture, simply select the **Capture** menu and choose **Start**. The Capture Preference screen appears. Click **Filter** and choose the "SSH Login" filter that you created. Click **OK** twice and the capture starts.

7. Client Host: Physically access the client host and log in as *dilbert*.

8. Client Host: To generate the SSH login packets, log in into the remote SSH host. For example, to log in to the SSH host at 24.130.8.170, you would enter:

    ```
    ssh 24.130.8.170
    ```

9. Client Host: After you log in as user *dilbert* (no password is required because of the public key cryptography) on the remote SSH host, enter a simple command to generate data through the connection. For example, enter:

    ```
    /sbin/ifconfig
    ```

10. Client Host: Exit the SSH session by entering the **exit** command.

11. Remote Host: Physically access the remote host. Stop the Ethereal packet capture by clicking **Stop**.

12. Remote Host: The packet capture appears in Ethereal. Attempt to locate the SSH data packet that includes the data: password field. Recall the easily identifiable data: password field in the Telnet packet from Figure 7.2. You should not be able to find any Application layer data in the capture. Your screen will appear similar to Figure 7.19.

Figure 7.19 Attempting to Locate the SSH Login Session

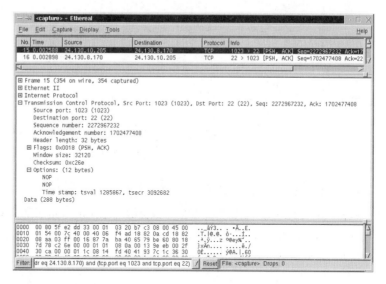

13. Scroll throughout the packet capture. The only information that can be analyzed is the Layer 1 (Physical) through Layer 4 (Transport) of the OSI reference model. We can discover that the SSH remote host is listening and transmitting on TCP port 22. The SSH client is using TCP port 1023. There are no passwords, usernames, or usable data. Figure 7.20 shows the vast array of worthless TCP packets.

Figure 7.20 Packet Capture of SSH Session

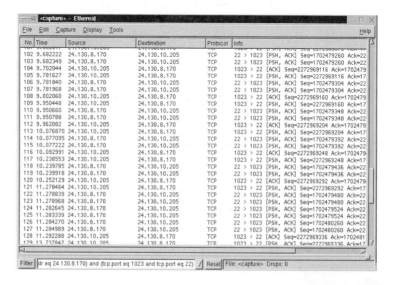

14. An easier way to discover useful data is to follow the TCP stream. To do this, simply select any packet involved in this SSH connection.

15. Once a packet is selected, select the **Tools** menu and select **Follow TCP Stream**. The contents of the TCP stream appear, as shown in Figure 7.21.

Figure 7.21 Following a TCP Stream in SSH

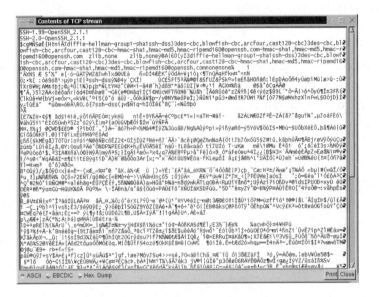

16. The majority of data is encrypted using 3DES (the default symmetric encryption for the session data). The packet sniffer has discovered no useful or usable data by following the TCP stream.

17. Save the packet capture as secssh, and quit Ethereal.

Summary

In this chapter, we discussed network encryption, and why it is essential to the security of your network. Network encryption ensures that data sent across a network from one host to another is secure. If a sniffer intercepts the data, it is unusable because the data is encrypted. Therefore, a hacker cannot view any usernames or passwords, and any information sent across the network, such as confidential data, is safe.

To display the problems associated with unencrypted data transmission, you captured unencrypted network traffic and analyzed it for security vulnerabilities. You learned that rlogin, rsh, and Telnet are three notoriously unsafe protocols. They do not use encryption for remote logins or any type of data transmission. You discovered that Telnet sends each password character as a separate packet. If you continue to scroll down the packet capture and view each Telnet data packet, you will discover the password. An easier way to discover the Telnet password is to follow the TCP stream. The username and password are displayed in clear text, as well as all of the data contained in the transmission.

To solve this problem, you learned how to encrypt network traffic with OpenSSH. OpenSSH (www.openssh.org) is an open source program that encrypts all traffic between hosts. It is a secure replacement for common Internet programs used for remote connectivity, such as Telnet, rlogin, and FTP. Because it encrypts all traffic, it always hides usernames and passwords used for remote logins. After the login occurs, it continues to encrypt all data traffic between the hosts.

You implemented secure data transmissions using OpenSSH over an unsecured network. This required ensuring that OpenSSH was installed on two different hosts. One system was the SSH remote host, and the other was the SSH client. SSH provides authentication by creating a private/public key pair for a user by using the **ssh-keygen** command. In SSH 2.0, the private DSA key is stored in the $HOME/.ssh/id_dsa file. The public key should be copied and stored in the $HOME/.ssh/authorized_keys2 file on the remote system. The authorized_keys2 file contains one public key per line. SSH 2.0 sessions are encrypted using ArcFour, CAST128, Blowfish, or 3DES. Data integrity is ensured using hmac-md5 and hmac-sha1. SSH 2.0 is superior and should be used whenever possible.

Last, you captured an SSH session and analyzed it for security vulnerabilities. The only information that could be analyzed was the Layer 1 (the Physical layer) through Layer 4 (the Transport layer) of the OSI reference model. The login data was unreadable, and the majority of data was encrypted using 3DES (the default symmetric encryption for the session data). The packet sniffer discovered no useful or usable data by following the TCP stream. As you can see, OpenSSH is essential and should be a permanent replacement for Telnet, rsh, and rlogin.

Solutions Fast Track

Understanding Network Encryption

- ☑ Network encryption is used for any data transfer that requires confidentiality. Encryption ensures that data sent across a network from one host to another is unreadable to a third party.

- ☑ Rlogin, remote shell (rsh), and Telnet are three notoriously unsafe protocols. They do not use encryption for remote logins or any type of data transmission. If a malicious hacker captured this traffic, it would display the data, such as usernames or any passwords, in clear text.

Capturing and Analyzing Unencrypted Network Traffic

- ☑ You can capture packets during a Telnet login session using the open source packet sniffer Ethereal. Once the session is captured, you can locate the Telnet data packet that includes the *data: password* field.

- ☑ Another way to discover the Telnet password is to follow the TCP stream. To do this, simply select any packet involved in this Telnet connection, then select the **Tools** menu, and select **Follow TCP Stream** in Ethereal. The username and password are displayed in clear text.

Using OpenSSH to Encrypt Network Traffic between Two Hosts

- ☑ OpenSSH encrypts all traffic between two hosts using Secure Shell (SSH). It is a secure replacement for common Internet programs used for remote connectivity, such as Telnet, rlogin, and rsh.

- ☑ It features strong encryption using Triple Data Encryption Standard (3DES) and Blowfish, as well as strong authentication using public keys, one-time passwords (OTPs), and Kerberos Authentication.

Installing and Configuring Secure Shell on Two Network Hosts

☑ OpenSSH implementations are significantly different between operating systems. The OpenSSH Portability Team uses the OpenBSD OpenSSH code to develop portable versions for other operating systems. You must make sure a specific version exists for your operating system at www.openssh.org.

☑ The method for implementing SSH combines similar r-command concepts with a private and public key method.

☑ SSH can create a DSA private/public key pair for a user by using the **ssh-keygen –d** command. In SSH 2.0, the private DSA key is placed in the *$HOME/.ssh/id_dsa* file. The public key is placed in the *$HOME/.ssh/id_dsa.pub* file. The public key should be renamed and copied to the *$HOME/.ssh/authorized_keys2* file on the remote system.

Implementing SSH to Secure Data Transmissions over an Insecure Network

☑ Both hosts must have SSH installed to transmit data securely, such as the SSH implementation.

☑ You must first use **ssh-keygen** to create a private and public key on each host using either RSA or DSA authentication. Then, distribute the public key to the host with which you wish to communicate, and vice versa.

☑ To establish the connection using SSH, the **ssh** command is used in the format **ssh *remotehost*.** *Remotehost* is the name of the host you will connect to using SSH.

Capturing and Analyzing Encrypted Network Traffic

☑ You can capture packets between two hosts using an SSH session to determine if the data is secure. For example, you can attempt to identify any login data, as well as any session data.

☑ Using Ethereal, or any packet-capturing program, you will find that all Application layer data is encrypted. No passwords, usernames, or usable data is displayed. Following a TCP stream is fruitless. Only the TCP ports are displayed in the capture.

Frequently Asked Questions

The following Frequently Asked Questions, answered by the authors of this book, are designed to both measure your understanding of the concepts presented in this chapter and to assist you with real-life implementation of these concepts. To have your questions about this chapter answered by the author, browse to **www.syngress.com/solutions** and click on the **"Ask the Author"** form.

Q: I am receiving warning messages regarding key lengths. What do these messages mean, and how can I prevent them?

A: The key-length warning messages you see are sent by OpenSSH when it encounters certain defective RSA or DSA keys that are sometimes generated by a bug in the ssh-keygen program (in commercial SSH). These defective keys are Pubkey Authentication keys whose Most Significant Bit (MSB) is not set. Thus, these keys are frequently half as long as advertised (they advertise as full length). The warning messages alert you that OpenSSH has detected this type of defective key.

You can prevent this type of warning message by editing the known_hosts file. Find the entry listing the incorrect key length value (often 1024), and change the entry to list the correct key length value (generally 1023).

Another solution is to simply create new keys. This approach is preferable because even after correction, the modified keys are generally less secure.

Q: Why did I lose support for SSH2 after I upgraded to OpenSSH 2.5.1?

A: When you upgrade OpenSSH versions, your sshd_config or ssh_config programs may incur some modifications. It is advisable to verify the settings in these files whenever you upgrade OpenSSH. If you are upgrading from OpenSSH 2.3.0 to 2.5.1, you can add:

```
HostKey /etc/ssh_host_dsa_key
```

to your sshd_config file. This modification will retain your SSH2 support.

Q: Why does it take so long for SSH to connect with Linux glibc 2.1?

A: The Red Hat Linux 6.1 implementation of glibc offers a universal "IPv6 or IPv4" resolution capability. Although this feature can be convenient, it requires more time to resolve IP addresses from domain names because it must make the IP version determination on a case-by-case basis.

To speed up resolution, you can use the **--with-ipv4-default configure** option. When you enter this option, OpenSSH will resolve only IPv4 addresses. Similarly, you can use the **-6** option to instruct OpenSSH to resolve only IPv6 addresses.

Q: Why does SSHD or "configure" sometimes state they do not have support for RSA or DSA?

A: Your OpenSSH libraries must be constructed to include this support. You can verify that RSA and DSA are supported in your program files by checking internally or by using the RSAref.

Q: The configure file is missing from my distribution, and the **make** command fails when executed. Why?

A: If you receive a missing separator error when the **make** command fails, or you are missing the configure file in your downloaded tar.gz, you probably have the same problem: You may be trying to compile the OpenBSD distribution of OpenSSH on a platform other than the one you used to download it. You must use a portable version of OpenSSH in order to do this without error.

Q: OpenSSH hangs when I exit SSH. Why?

A: Linux and HP-UX systems have been noted to hang when exiting OpenSSH. This bug appears in current OpenSSH versions, and occurs primarily when a background process is active. You can enter **sleep 20&exit** to test for this problem. The man page for your shell should list an option you can use to send a HUP signal to active processes upon exit. Bash users can use the following entry in either /etc/bashrc or ~/.bashrc:

```
shopt -s huponexit
```

## Chapter 8

Creating Virtual Private Networks

Solutions in this chapter:

- Secure Tunneling with VPNs
- Explaining the IP Security Architecture
- Creating a VPN by Using FreeS/WAN

- ☑ Summary
- ☑ Solutions Fast Track
- ☑ Frequently Asked Questions

Introduction

In previous chapters, you have discovered how you can enhance authentication by using third-party open source software, such as Kerberos, "one-time passwords in everything" (OPIE), and the public-key cryptography methods of Open Secure Shell (OpenSSH). You also learned how to employ encryption between hosts by using the application-layer security methods of OpenSSH. In this chapter, you will go a step further to deploy secure authentication and strong encryption at the network layer to establish network security by using virtual private networks (VPNs). VPNs offer certain advantages over other network security protocols, as you will find in this chapter. You will learn about the many solutions provided by VPNs in today's Internet workplace, such as providing secure transmissions between two hosts, routers, or both. We explain the Internet Protocol Security Architecture (IPSec), which is quickly becoming the standard protocol for VPNs. You will finish up the chapter by creating your own VPN by using Free Secure Wide Area Network (FreeS/WAN).

Secure Tunneling with VPNs

A VPN provides a private data network over public telecommunication infrastructures, such as the Internet. It provides both secure authentication and encryption. It creates a data "tunnel" between devices so that all data transmitted between the devices is secure, regardless of what programs the devices are running. After a secure tunnel is established, data can be transmitted securely between the hosts.

Three basic types of VPN solutions exist: telecommuter, router-to-router, and host-to-host. A telecommuter VPN can be used to securely connect a host to a network from any Internet connection and is ideal for traveling workers. A router-to-router VPN is used to create a secure transmission tunnel between two networks, such as two company sites in different locations. A host-to-host VPN creates a secure transmission tunnel between any two hosts. A VPN implementation named FreeS/WAN, which you will implement in this chapter, can provide all three solutions.

Telecommuter VPN Solution

Telecommuters can use VPNs to log in to their company network from home or from the road. Any location with Internet access can be used. The telecommuter must ensure that the laptop, desktop, or handheld system contains VPN client software and the address of the company's VPN server. The telecommuter then accesses the Internet through normal access methods, such as a dial-up, a Digital Subscriber Line (DSL), or a cable network connection. After access to the Internet is achieved, the telecommuter opens a VPN client to log on to the company VPN server—once logged on, the telecommuter has access to the company network. She receives the same user rights and privileges on the company network as if she were physically logged in at a company workstation. If the telecommuter has a fast Internet connection, she will be unable to tell the difference between physically working at the company location and working through the VPN. The VPN concept is shown in Figure 8.1.

Figure 8.1 Telecommuting Using a VPN

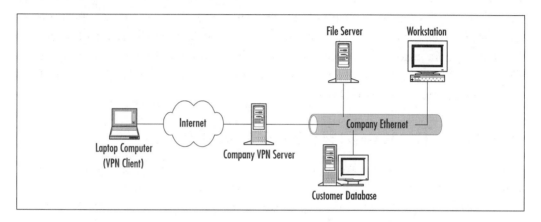

After the VPN tunnel has been established, the telecommuter can run any application as if he were at a company workstation, provided he has the appropriate client. All of these applications will run over the tunnel, and the applications themselves are not required to be secure, because they are transmitted through the VPN tunnel. The VPN tunnel encrypts the data, so any captured data (regardless of the program that generated that data) will be useless. The tunnel concept is displayed in Figure 8.2.

Figure 8.2 Secure Transmission of Data across the Internet Using a VPN Tunnel

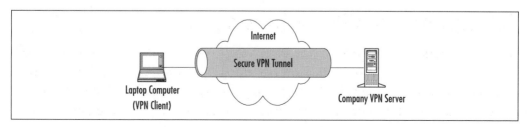

VPNs can also be used by corporate partners. For instance, the customer database displayed in Figure 8.1 could be available for a sales team at another company. The sales team could receive accounts on your network with access to the customer database only.

Router-to-Router VPN Solution

VPNs are a cost-effective way to create a wide area network (WAN) for connecting company satellite offices and corporate offices. In the past, a company leased expensive dedicated lines from phone companies to connect each location. VPNs allow companies to create a router-to-router VPN over the Internet instead.

In order to implement a VPN, you must ensure that each gateway router to your network supports the VPN implementation you choose at each location. These routers are located on the edge of your network and are the end-to-end points for your VPN tunnel. They are responsible for encapsulating the traffic as it leaves the network and removing the capsule as it arrives between your satellite and corporate offices. All router vendors offer VPN functionality. For instance, Cisco offers the Cisco 1600 series of routers that offer a VPN option.

VPNs can connect your corporate networks for a fraction of the cost of leasing dedicated lines. A corporate WAN using VPN-enabled routers is displayed in Figure 8.3.

Figure 8.3 Creating a Corporate Router-to-Router VPN

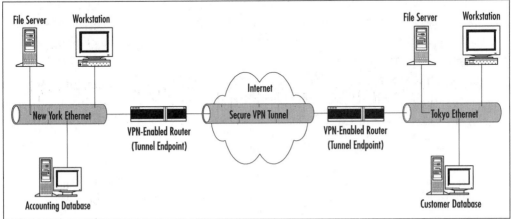

Host-to-Host VPN Solution

VPNs can also securely connect two hosts over the Internet or any unsecured network. Each host is the tunnel endpoint. The only difference is that a separate network does not exist on the other side of the hosts, so no gateway is required with IP forwarding enabled. If you can create a tunnel between two hosts, you can expand your knowledge in an enterprise environment to accommodate both telecommuter and router-to-router VPN solutions. The host-to-host VPN solution is shown in Figure 8.4.

Figure 8.4 Creating a Host-to-Host VPN

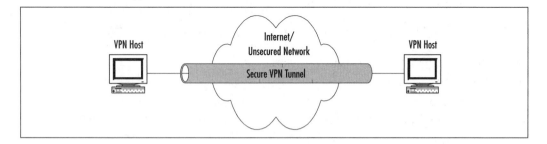

Tunneling Protocols

As mentioned previously, a "tunnel" is created between VPN hosts to ensure that all traffic between them is secure. The tunnel is created with a tunneling protocol. These protocols are responsible for encapsulating a data packet before a host transmits it. After the data is encapsulated, it is sent over the Internet until it arrives at its destination. When it arrives, the capsule is removed, and the data is processed by the destination host.

IP tunneling protocols are particularly powerful because they can transmit foreign protocols over the Internet. For instance, a Novell NetWare host can send an Internetwork Packet Exchange/Sequenced Packet Exchange (IPX/SPX) packet over the Internet by encapsulating it in an IP packet, then transmitting it using Transmission Control Protocol/IP (TCP/IP). When it arrives at its destination, the IP packet is stripped off, and the IPX/SPX packet is processed.

The next generation protocol, IPv6, has a test bed called the 6bone (www.6bone.net). The 6bone is a virtual network that uses IPv6-over–IPv4 tunneling. The IPv6 networks, called *islands,* are connected over the Internet using IPv4 tunnels. The IPv6 packets are encapsulated by an IPv4 packet and sent over the Internet. When they arrive at the destination, the IPv4 packet is removed, and the IPv6 packet is processed on the IPv6 network. The leading VPN tunneling protocols are listed in Table 8.1.

Table 8.1 The Leading VPN Tunneling Protocols

Tunneling Protocol	Description
Point-to-Point Tunneling Protocol (PPTP)	Tunneling protocol developed by Microsoft that is built into the Windows operating system. It is an extension of the Point-to-Point Protocol (PPP) and uses PPP mechanisms for authentication, encryption, and compression. PPTP uses Microsoft Point-to-Point Encryption (MPPE) for encrypting the PPP frames.
Layer 2 Forwarding (L2F)	Tunneling protocol developed by Cisco that is similar to PPTP.
Layer 2 Tunneling Protocol (L2TP)	Tunneling protocol that combines PPTP and L2F. L2TP uses the best mechanisms of each. L2TP is already built into Microsoft Windows 2000 Server and Cisco Internet Operating System (IOS) software for networking and end-to-end hardware products. Like PPTP, L2TP requires that ISPs support it so that it can be used for router-to-router VPNs. This protocol is used in Cisco's "Access VPN" service. L2TP uses IPSec for encryption. L2TP will eventually become the industry standard for VPNs.

Explaining the IP Security Architecture

IP has been a low-cost, efficient protocol for several decades. However, it has always suffered from security vulnerabilities that have required users and businesses to use other methods to ensure data confidentiality across the Internet. A new protocol, IP Security Architecture (IPSec), is designed to add authentication and encryption to IP when needed.

IPSec is an Internet Engineering Task Force (IETF) security protocol that is becoming a standard component of VPN tunneling protocols. As the name suggests, it was designed for IP, and IPSec has gained wide industry support. For instance, Cisco already supports IPSec in its routers and is one of the leading supporters for IPSec standardization. IPSec is currently a proposed standard (Request for Comments [RFC] 2401) within the IETF. The IPSec charter Web page, shown in Figure 8.5, is maintained by the IETF IPSec working group. The URL is www.ietf.org/html.charters/ipsec-charter.html. This site is ideal for monitoring the progress of IPSec and the numerous implementations for the IPSec standard.

Figure 8.5 IETF IPSec Charter

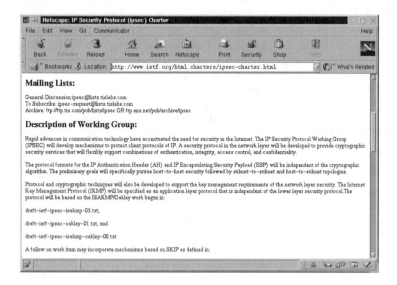

IPSec provides secure authentication and encryption over a network by securing all packets at Layer 3, the network layer, of the Open System Interconnection (OSI) reference model. Layer 3 security is significant because Layer 3 is responsible for IP addressing and routing over the Internet. Security at this layer ensures that everything on the network is secure.

NOTE

Another benefit of IPSec is that it already supports the next generation Internet Protocol, IP version 6 (IPv6). IPSec will be a requirement for IPv6 implementation.

Layer 3 security is in contrast to methods that provide only encryption and authentication to higher-level protocols, such as SSH (you learned about SSH in the last chapter).

Programs such as SSH for remote login, Secure Hypertext Transfer Protocol (SHTTP) and Secure Socket Layer (SSL) for Web applications, and Pretty Good Privacy (PGP) for e-mail secure data between two applications using Layer 4 mechanisms. This method works extremely well but is limited because only the data between the program's associated ports is encrypted. IPSec secures all data, regardless of the program running between the hosts. To demonstrate the limitations of security protocols such as SSH, SHTTP, and SSL, recall the implementation of SSH in the last chapter. First, you captured packets that were unencrypted, shown in Figure 8.6.

Figure 8.6 Unencrypted Packets

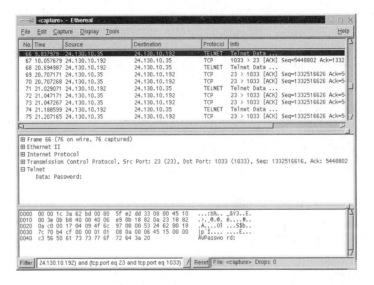

Next, you captured packets between two SSH hosts that used encryption. The application layer data was encrypted, but the Layer 4 (the transport layer) port numbers could be viewed, so you could easily determine the service running. You discovered that the SSH remote host listens and transmits on TCP port 22. The SSH client used TCP port 1023. Figure 8.7 shows the captured SSH traffic. SHTTP and SSL traffic displays in a similar manner when captured, except different port numbers are displayed.

IPSec is different from SSH and other application-based encryption protocols because an IPsec tunnel encrypts data at the Layer 3 (the network layer) so that no transport layer (Layer 4) data is displayed, which reduces security vulnerabilities. Figure 8.8 displays a packet capture of IPSec packets transmitted through a tunnel. Note that the amount of useful information is significantly reduced. For instance,

Figure 8.7 Packet Capture of SSH Session Displaying TCP Port Data

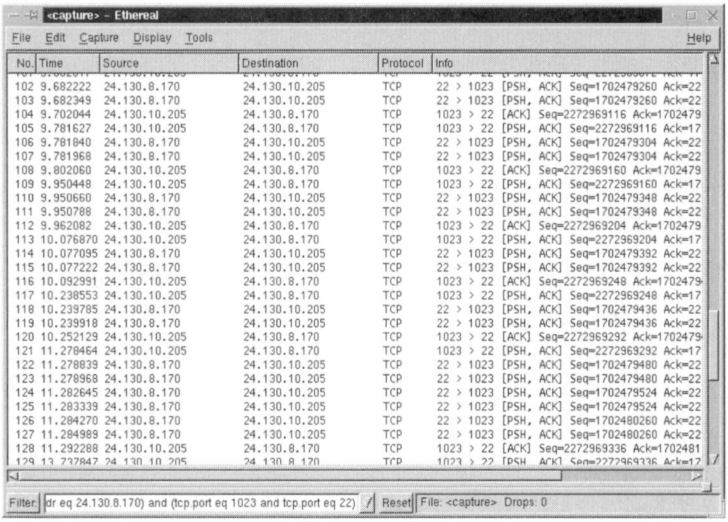

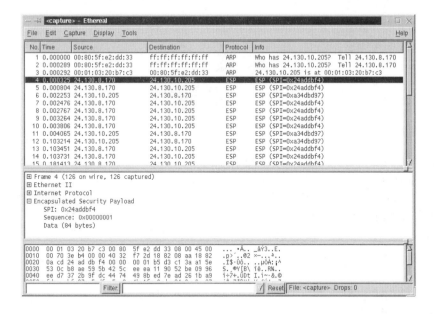

Figure 8.8 Packet Capture of IPSec Session

all transport layer data in the figure is encrypted by an Encapsulating Security Payload (ESP) header, which renders the packet and its contents useless if captured by a hacker. ESP encrypts the packet at the network layer, so even the port information is encrypted. So as you can see, this is an improvement over application-based encryption protocols, such as SSH, which display the transport-layer data.

The packets captured in Figure 8.8 are from a VPN tunnel using IPsec. This tunnel was set up between two hosts (a host-to-host solution), and the tunnel endpoints encrypted all traffic between the two hosts, regardless of the applications running between them. IPsec is used by many VPN implementations. You will learn about these implementations and how they use IPsec in the next section.

Using IPSec with a VPN Tunneling Protocol

IPSec is used as an authentication and encryption standard for VPNs. As you learned in Table 8.1, several tunneling protocols exist, such as PPTP and L2TP. You learned that both PPTP and L2TP are extensions of PPP. One of IPSec's functions within L2TP is to encapsulate the PPP data and encrypt the data at the network layer (Layer 3) of the OSI model. Figures 8.9 through 8.11 display a graphic that displays how IPSec encapsulation works with one type of L2TP implementation.

First of all, a PPP frame is created. This frame contains the IP packet created from the TCP/IP stack on your system with a PPP header attached. It contains data from your system that would normally be sent across the wire. The PPP frame is displayed in Figure 8.9.

Figure 8.9 Starting Out with a PPP Frame

PPP Header	PPP Payload (IP Packet)

Next, the L2TP and User Datagram Protocol (UDP) headers are added to the PPP frame, as shown in Figure 8.10.

Figure 8.10 Adding an L2TP and UDP Header to a PPP Frame

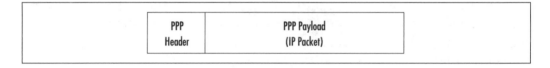

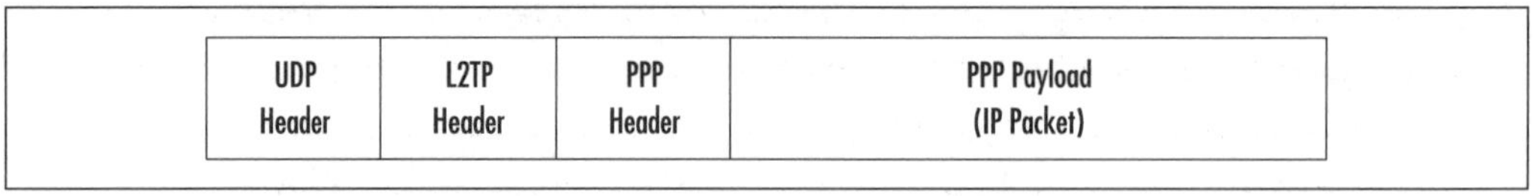

UDP Header	L2TP Header	PPP Header	PPP Payload (IP Packet)

Last, the IPSec encapsulation is implemented. IPSec adds an IPSec ESP header and trailer. It also adds an IPSec Authentication trailer for message authentication and integrity. The L2TP packet is encrypted by IPSec, which uses the encryption keys that were generated form the authentication process.

During this process, the standard IP header is added to the packet. The IP source address is the VPN client (which is sending this packet). The IP destination address is the VPN server that will receive this packet. The IPSec packet is displayed in Figure 8.11.

Figure 8.11 Adding IPSec Mechanisms to an L2TP Packet

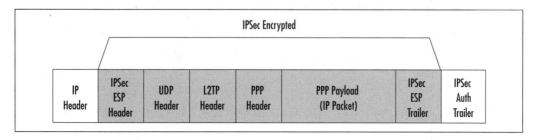

When the packet arrives at the VPN server, the VPN server will strip the IP, IPSec, UDP, L2TP, and PPP headers from the packet to discover the original data sent from the VPN client.

Internet Key Exchange Protocol

IPSec is often used in conjunction with the Internet Key Exchange (IKE) protocol. IKE is a key management protocol standard that enhances IPSec, such as providing a simpler IPSec configuration, flexibility, and more features. IKE is not required to run IPSec, but it enhances the standard.

IKE is a hybrid protocol. It implements three security protocols:

- Internet Security Association and Key Management Protocol (ISAKMP)
- Oakley key exchange
- Skeme key exchange

IKE uses the ISAKMP framework to run the Oakley and Skeme key exchange mechanisms. The combination of these three security protocols provides authentication using digital signature and public key encryption.

IKE allows dynamic authentication of hosts, provides anti-replay services, and can change encryption keys during an IPSec session. It allows IPSec to operate without requiring an administrator to manually configure all of the IPSec security parameters between two hosts, and it negotiates IPSec security associations (SAs) automatically. IKE also allows Certification Authority (CA) support and permits lifetime specifications from IPSec security associations.

To learn more about IKE, read the RFC 2409 proposed standard on the Internet at www.ietf.org/rfc/rfc2409.txt.

Creating a VPN by Using FreeS/WAN

Free Secure WAN (FreeS/WAN) is a Linux VPN implementation that uses IPSec and IKE. IPSec and IKE were discussed in the previous sections and are used to provide secure authentication and encryption of data between two hosts at Layer 3 (network layer) of the OSI model. FreeS/WAN creates a secure VPN tunnel between the hosts. The FreeS/WAN project goal is to provide freely available source code to promote IPSec and allow it to run on many different machines. It also avoids export restrictions and attempts to interoperate with all VPNs that use IPSec. The FreeS/WAN project is based at www.freeswan.org/intro.html (shown in Figure 8.12).

Figure 8.12 Home of the FreeS/WAN Project

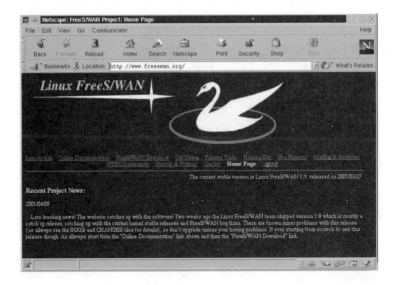

Because FreeS/WAN uses IPSec, it can be implemented on any system that performs IP networking. This includes routers, PCs, laptops, firewalls, and application servers such as Web, mail, and database servers. FreeS/WAN uses three IPSec protocols, shown in Table 8.2.

Table 8.2 IPSec Protocols Used in FreeS/WAN

Protocol	Description
Authentication Header (AH)	Performs authentication at the packet level.
Encapsulating Security Payload (ESP)	Performs encryption as well as authentication.
Internet Key Exchange (IKE)	Performs key exchanges and connection parameter negotiation.

Damage & Defense...

The Need for VPN Interoperability

Interoperability is a major concern with S/WAN and VPNs in general. Currently, almost all firewalls and security software available today offers IPSec support. It is the goal of S/WAN developers for all S/WAN implementations to interoperate, no matter what device they are installed on. This goal is shared by many manufacturers and is spearheaded by the VPN Consortium (VPNC). The VPNC is an international trade association for manufacturers in the VPN market.

The VPNC goal is to show manufacturers where their VPN products interoperate, so that the manufacturers can more easily provide interoperability with other VPN implementations. They also publicize and provide support for testing events for VPN interoperability. By providing a forum for all VPN manufacturers to communicate, the Internet may eventually use one VPN standard, and all vendor VPN products may be able to communicate with one another.

To learn more about VPN interoperability efforts, visit the VPNC Web site at www.vpnc.org.

These IPSec protocols are implemented in FreeS/WAN by using two programs and a variety of scripts, as shown in Table 8.3.

Table 8.3 FreeS/WAN Implementation of IPSec Protocols

FreeS/WAN Implementation	Description
Kernel IPSec (KLIPS)	Performs AH and ESP functions. It also handles packets within the Linux kernel.
Pluto	Performs IKE. Pluto is an IKE daemon.
Variety of scripts	Offers a FreeS/WAN interface for the administrator.

NOTE

In order to add IPSec to the system, FreeS/WAN installs IPSec into the Linux IPv4 TCP/IP stack. This step is necessary because IPSec is not required for IPv4. However, it is required for IPv6.

In the following sections, you will download, install, and configure FreeS/WAN. After you install it, you will capture a variety of unencrypted application packets, then implement FreeS/WAN and ensure that all packets transmitted through the VPN are secure.

Downloading and Unpacking FreeS/WAN

FreeS/WAN is not included with all Red Hat Linux distributions. Many countries have restriction laws that forbid the export or import of strong encryption. Therefore, your version of Red Hat Linux most likely does not include FreeS/WAN.

These installation instructions are written for freeswan-1.9 (this tarball is available on the CD accompanying this book [freeswan-1.9.tar.gz]) and Red Hat Linux 7.0 using the linux-2.2.16 kernel, which will be upgraded to the linux-2.4.3 kernel (this kernel is also included on the CD [linux-2.4.3.tar.gz]). A custom installation of Linux with "everything" was installed.

The program is downloaded as a TAR file that contains the source code and documentation, as well as any patches. To download and install FreeS/WAN complete the following steps:

1. Log in as root.

2. Access the FreeS/WAN download site at www.freeswan.org/ download.html. You can also obtain the necessary files from the CD accompanying this book.

3. Scroll down to the **Latest Release** section, as shown in Figure 8.13.

Figure 8.13 Accessing the Latest Release of FreeS/WAN

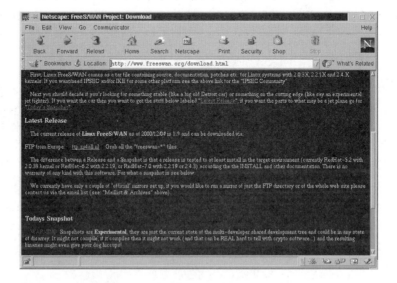

4. In this example, the latest release can be downloaded from Europe via FTP by selecting the **ftp.xs4all.nl** link. Select the corresponding link in your browser.

5. At the FTP site, view the FreeS/WAN files that are listed. For instance, the Europe FTP site is shown in Figure 8.14. You would need to download at least the freeswan-1.9.tar.gz file (your version may differ) to your system. Although not all the files are required to run FreeS/WAN, you

may find them useful. For instance, the RFCs that FreeS/WAN is based are included in the RFCs.tar.gz file. The files you can download are as follows (these files are also located on the CD accompanying this book):

- RFCs.tar.gz
- freeswan-1.9.tar.gz
- freeswan-1.9.tar.gz.sig
- freeswan-sigkey.asc

Figure 8.14 Downloading the FreeS/WAN TAR File(s)

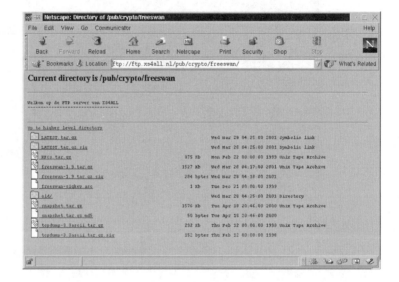

NOTE

You can also access the freeswan-1.9.tar.gz tarball from the supplemental CD included with this book and copy it to your /root directory. This lab is written for version 1.9, which is the version on the CD.

6. Download the FreeS/WAN file(s) to your /root directory.

7. Access the download directory by entering.

```
cd /root
```

> **NOTE**
>
> If you have already compiled your kernel in the past (you have a .config file in your /usr/src/linux directory), then download and unpack the files in your /usr/src/ directory (but not in the *linux* directory).

8. The filename will look like this: freeswan-1.9.tar.gz.

9. In the /root directory, unpack the image by entering:

```
tar -zxvf freeswan-1.9.tar.gz
```

This will create a /root/freeswan-1.9 directory.

 # Compiling the Kernel to Run FreeS/WAN

Now you need to configure the Linux kernel to run FreeS/WAN. The FreeS/WAN code must be added to the kernel. Before you configure FreeS/WAN, you must configure, build, and test a system kernel. This must be done before installing FreeS/WAN because the program uses the results of compiled kernel to make the necessary modifications.

The following tools must be installed before you begin the kernel configuration for FreeS/WAN. If you completed a "Custom" Red Hat Linux installation with "everything" installed, you can skip this warning—all of the required Red Hat Package Manager (RPM) packages are already installed (you may need to update them later in this section).

To check if an RPM is installed, enter **rpm –qa | grep rpm_name**. To install an RPM, enter **rpm –i *rpm_name_version***. Access the RPMs from the Red Hat installation CD /RedHat/RPMS directory, as shown in the following Kernel source code item:

1. **Kernel source code** The Linux kernel source RPM must be installed to configure the kernel. To find out if it is installed, enter **rpm –qa | grep kernel-source**. If you do not receive a reply, access your Red Hat installation CD and install the kernel-source and kernel-headers RPMs (your versions may vary) from the /RedHat/RPMS directory.

2. **Tools** A GNU C compiler RPM must be installed—either *gcc* or *egcs* works. Development tools, including *make* and *patch* must be installed.

3. **Libraries** The *glibc*, *GMP* (required for Pluto's public key calculations), and *ncurses* (if you use menuconfig) RPMs must be installed.

NOTE

The following demonstration is safe and will upgrade your Linux kernel. You will always have the old kernel on your system, so you can switch back if a problem arises. Recompiling the kernel is required to support many new devices in Linux.

If you have already compiled your kernel in the past (you have a .config file in your /usr/src/linux directory), then you can skip this section. Go to the "Configuring FreeS/WAN" section. Please note that you will NOT have to reconfigure the FreeS/WAN Makefile.

4. Revisit www.freeswan.org/download.html (shown in Figure 8.13) to determine if your system's Red Hat Linux version and kernel are supported.

5. For this demonstration, the Linux kernel will be upgraded to linux–2.4.3, and then FreeS/WAN will be compiled.

6. Access the kernel source code from the anonymous FTP site located at ftp://ftp.kernel.org/pub/linux/kernel/.

7. Open the v2.4 directory (or the latest supported by FreeS/WAN) to access the Linux 2.4 kernel versions. Locate the linux–2.4.3.tar.gz file. It is located in the middle of the screen, shown in Figure 8.15.

NOTE

You can also access the linux-2.4.3.tar.gz tarball from the CD included with this book and copy it to your /root directory. This lab is written for Linux 2.4.3, which is the version on the CD.

8. Download the kernel to your home directory, such as /root as shown in Figure 8.16. You can download and unpack the kernel in any directory in which you have permissions, such as your home directory. In this demonstration, the /root directory is used.

Figure 8.15 Locating the linux-2.4.3.tar.gz Kernel

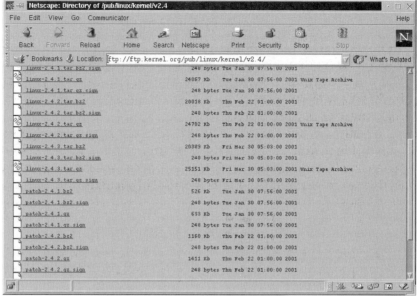

Figure 8.16 Downloading Kernel to Your Home (/root) Directory

9. On your system, access the /root directory by entering the following:

```
cd /root
```

10. Unpack the downloaded kernel by entering the following:

```
gzip -cd linux-2.4.3.tar.gz | tar xvf -
```

   A /root/linux/ directory is created.

11. To remove stale .o files and dependencies, access the new *linux* directory and run the **make mrproper** command. Enter the following commands:

```
cd /root/linux
make mrproper
```

NOTE

View the README file included with the unpacked kernel. The file explains in detail the processes for installing the 2.4 kernel, which are slightly different from previous releases. For instance, the Linux kernel was unpacked in your home directory, not the /usr/src/ directory. In this example, read the /root/linux/README file. This process will also ensure that you do not overwrite your current system kernel.

12. Open the /root/linux/documentation/changes file and see which updated packages are required to run the linux-2.4.3 kernel. For instance, if you are upgrading from linux-2.2.16-22, you will need to upgrade the following packages to these minimum versions:

   ■ util-linux 2.10o

   ■ modutils 2.4.2

   ■ e2fsprogs 1.19

   ■ pppd 2.4.0

   ■ reiserfsprogs 3.x.0j-1

13. Download the required RPMs at the RPM repository (http://rpmfind .net/linux/RPM). These RPMs are also available on the CD accompanying this book.

14. The RPM repository is shown in Figure 8.17. Search for the required RPM by entering its name in the Search field, and clicking the **Search** button.

15. For instance, if you are upgrading from linux-2.2.16.22, you need to download the following RPMs, which are also available on the CD accompanying this book:

   ■ util-linux-2.10s-12.i386.rpm

   ■ modutils-2.4.2-5.i386.rpm

   ■ e2fsprogs-1.19-4.i386.rpm

   ■ ppp-2.4.0-2.i386.rpm

Figure 8.17 Searching for RPMs at the RPM Repository on rpmfind.net

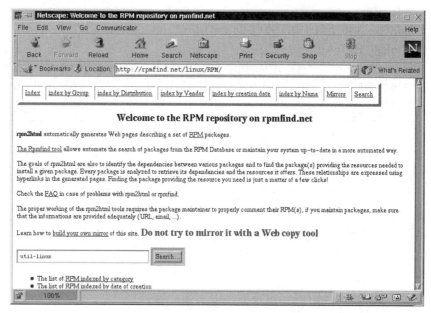

16. Install each RPM using the **rpm –U** command. For instance, to install the RPMs listed in the previous step, you would enter the following:

```
rpm -U util-linux-2.10s-12.i386.rpm
rpm -U modutils-2.4.2-5.i386.rpm
rpm -U e2fsprogs-1.19-4.i386.rpm
rpm -U ppp-2.4.0-2.i386.rpm
```

17. After updating the required RPMs, you are ready to compile the kernel. The easiest way to configure the kernel is to enter X Windows. If you are not already in X Windows, enter the following:

```
startx
```

18. Access the new *linux* directory, which is the required location for this kernel configuration. Enter the following:

```
cd /root/linux
```

19. Open the Linux Kernel Configuration GUI. This program allows you to choose kernel options for your system. Open it by entering the following:

```
make xconfig
```

The Linux Kernel Configuration GUI appears, as shown in Figure 8.18.

Figure 8.18 Configuring the Linux Kernel by Using xconfig

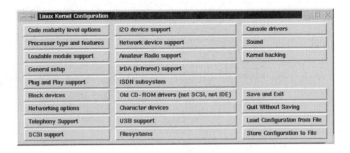

20. Click the **Loadable module support** button.

21. The **Loadable module support** configuration screen appears. Select **Y** for all three options, as shown in Figure 8.19. If they are already selected, then you do not have to change the configuration options.

Figure 8.19 Configuring Loadable Module Support in the Linux Kernel

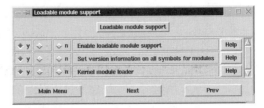

22. Click the **Main Menu** button to return to the Linux Kernel Configuration screen.

23. Select the **Processor type and features** button. In the Processor family drop-down menu, select the process type running on your system. For the first time, modern PC processors are listed, such as the Pentium III and IV, as well as the AMD Athlon/K7. Many times, Linux installs using the i386 processor, even though your system may be

running a more modern processor. Selecting the correct processor type will increase system performance. The **Processor type and features** screen is shown in Figure 8.20.

Figure 8.20 Configuring Processor Type

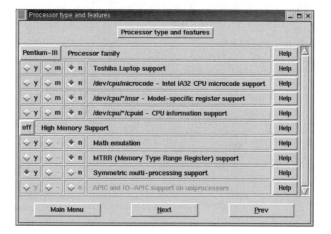

24. Click the **Main Menu** button to return to the Linux Kernel Configuration screen.

25. Click the **Network device support** button and select the **Ethernet (10 or 100Mbit)** option. Select your NIC from the list of available options. The PCI NE2000 and clones support usually works for PCI cards that are not specifically listed. If this is what you require, select **Y**, as shown in Figure 8.21.

Figure 8.21 Selecting the PCI NE2000 and Clones NIC

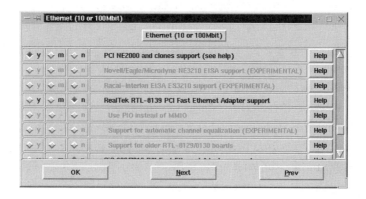

26. Click the **OK** button and then the **Main Menu** button.

27. Make any additional changes required for your system. For instance, if you want printer support, you must activate Parallel port support from the Main Menu and select the **Y** option.

28. Click the **Save and Exit** button. You will receive a message stating "End of Linux kernel configuration." Click the **OK** button.

29. The kernel configurations are saved in the file /root/linux/.config.

30. Continue to run commands from the /root/linux directory.

31. Run the **make dep** command, which finds dependencies between the files. Enter the following:

```
make dep
```

32. Run the **make bzImage** command, which builds a loadable image of the kernel. It compresses the image with bzip. Enter the following:

```
make bzImage
```

33. The bzImage file is created and placed in /linux/arch/i386/boot/ bzImage.

NOTE

At the end of the *make bzImage* process, you may receive a warning (especially if you have installed a large number of kernel options) stating "warning: kernel is too big for standalone boot from floppy." If you receive this warning, you need to copy the image to the hard drive and boot up with lilo.

34. Continue to run commands from the /root/linux directory.

35. Run the command **make install** by entering the following:

```
make install
```

36. Now that you have made a kernel, create the modules by entering the following:

```
make modules
```

37. To install the modules in the proper subdirectories, enter the following:

```
make modules_install
```

38. To boot into the new kernel, you must copy the kernel image to either a floppy disk or to your hard drive. This depends on how you usually boot up Linux.

39. If you use a boot disk, then copy the image to a new floppy disk. The floppy disk must be high density. Then create a boot disk, insert a new HD floppy disk, and enter the following:

```
cp /root/linux/arch/i386/boot/bzImage /dev/fd0
```

Leave the floppy boot disk in your system and reboot the system from the floppy boot disk.

40. If you boot from your hard drive, your system uses lilo. The lilo configurations are specified in /etc/lilo.conf. The lilo.conf file specifies kernel images that are located in the /boot directory. During the installation process, the bzImage file was copied to the /boot directory and renamed *vmlinuz-2.4.3*. It can be named anything you want, as long as you specify the name and location in the lilo.conf file (which you will do in Step 42).

41. To specify your new image in the /etc/lilo.conf file, enter the following:

```
vi /etc/lilo.conf
```

42. Press **I** to insert text. Insert the following text at the end of the file to identify the new kernel image (your entry may vary due to different partitions):

```
image=/boot/vmlinuz-2.4.3
label=linux-2.4.3
read-only
root=/dev/hda5
```

Your lilo.conf file should resemble Figure 8.22.

43. Press **Esc** to exit insert mode. Write and quit the file by entering the following:

```
:wq
```

Figure 8.22 Configuring /etc/lilo.conf to Access the New Kernel Image

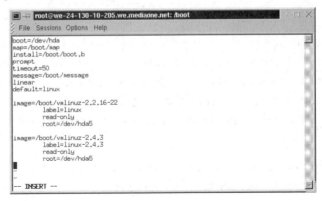

44. To load your lilo.conf changes, enter the following command:

```
lilo
```

You should receive the following response:

```
Added linux *
Added linux-2.4.3
```

45. You are ready to reboot the system and test to see if the new kernel works.

46. Reboot the system.

47. At the lilo prompt, the kernel image labels are presented. If not, select the **TAB** key. Two options will be available to you: the original *linux* kernel and the new linux-2.4.3 kernel you just configured. Select the linux-2.4.3 kernel.

48. The system should boot properly. If you receive errors when booting the new kernel, reboot using the old kernel image and access the /root/ linux/README file. To find out more about kernel configuration commands and troubleshooting problems, visit www.linuxdoc.org/ HOWTO/Kernel-HOWTO.html (be aware, however, that the HOWTO documents are not always up-to-date).

49. Log in as root. You should be successful.

Recompiling FreeS/WAN into the New Kernel

Congratulations! You have successfully created and tested a new kernel image for your system. This will make any troubleshooting of FreeS/WAN much easier, because you know that the compiled kernel works. If you skipped the last section because you compiled your kernel in the past (you have a .config file in your /usr/src/linux directory), then you do *not* have to reconfigure the FreeS/WAN Makefile. Skip to Step 7 in the following demonstration and use /usr/src/freeswan-1.9 instead of the /root/freeswan-1.9 directory for the remainder of the section.

1. Reboot the system and log in to the original kernel as root. *Do not* use the new kernel for the following steps.

2. Access the *freeswan* directory by entering the following (your version may vary):

```
cd root/freeswan-1.9
```

3. Open the /root/freeswan/Makefile by entering the following:

```
vi Makefile
```

4. You need to change the kernel source location where FreeS/WAN looks for the kernel. By default, FreeS/WAN looks in the /usr/src/linux directory. However, you compiled your new kernel in /root/linux. Therefore, you need to change the Makefile to reflect your kernel source location. To change the kernel source location, scroll down the file and locate the following comment:

```
# kernel location, and location of kernel patches in the
distribution
KERNELSRC=/usr/src/linux
```

5. Change the kernel source location by pressing **I** to enter vi's insert mode, then change the location to the following:

```
KERNELSRC=/root/linux
```

   Your file should resemble Figure 8.23.

6. To save and exit the file, press **Esc** and enter the following:

```
:wq
```

Figure 8.23 Changing the FreeS/WAN Makefile Kernel Source Location

```
# kernel location, and location of kernel patches in the distribution
KERNELSRC=/root/linux
DIRIN24=$(KERNELSRC)/net/netlink
FILIN24=$(KERNELSRC)/net/khttpd/main.c
KERNELREL=$(shell { test -f $(FILIN24) && echo 2.3; } || { test -d $(DIRIN22) && echo 2.2
; } )
KCFILE=$(KERNELSRC)/.config
VERFILE=$(KERNELSRC)/include/linux/version.h
PATCHES=klips/patches$(KERNELREL)
# note, some of the patches know the last part of this path
KERNELKLIPS=$(KERNELSRC)/net/ipsec

# kernel make name: zImage for 2.0.xx, bzImage for 2.2.xx and later, and
# different foolishness on the Alpha (what ever happened to standards?)
B=$(shell test -d $(DIRIN22) && echo b)
KERNEL=$(shell if test " `uname -m`" = " alpha" ; then echo boot ; else echo $(B)zImage ;
fi)

# pass pathnames etc. down
SETTINGS=BINDIR=$(PRIVDIR) PUBDIR=$(PUBDIR) PRIVDIR=$(PRIVDIR) \
        REALPRIVDIR=$(REALPRIVDIR) MANTREE=$(MANTREE) \
        DESTDIR=$(DESTDIR) INSTALL="$(INSTALL)"
FULLSET=$(SETTINGS) CONFDIR=$(CONFDIR) RCDIR=$(RCDIR) REALRCDIR=$(REALRCDIR)

# install stuff
INSTALL=install
-- INSERT --
```

7. To add the FreeS/WAN default settings into your Linux kernel's .config file, enter the following command in the /root/freeswan-1.9 directory:

```
cd /root/freeswan-1.9
make oldgo
```

This command installs default FreeS/WAN configurations to the linux-2.4.3 kernel you created. To complete the FreeS/WAN kernel configuration, enter the following in the /root/freeswan-1.9 directory:

```
make kinstall
```

NOTE

When the **make kinstall** command is run from the *freeswan* directory, it performs the same **make** commands that you usually run from the /linux directory to configure and install your kernel. It runs the equivalent **make** commands:

```
make
make install
make modules
make modules_install
```

8. The lilo.conf file already specifies the new kernel image location. However, you can enter the **lilo** command to ensure that it is up-to-date by entering the following:

```
lilo
```

You should receive the following response:

```
Added linux *
Added linux-2.4.3
```

9. You are ready to reboot the system and test whether the new kernel works.

10. Reboot the system into the *new* linux-2.4.3 kernel image.

11. During the reboot, check the messages during boot. You can also check them using *dmesg*. Look for the following:

   ■ Make sure that you are booting into the new kernel.

   ■ Make sure that a message appears for KLIPS initialization.

   ■ Make sure that a start report appears for Pluto.

   ■ Make sure that "ipsec_setup – Starting FreeS/WAN IPsec 1.9" appears.

12. Log in as root.

13. Test the IPSec commands shown in Table 8.4 (just make sure that you get a response).

Table 8.4 Commands to Test if IPSec Is Working

Command	Description
ipsec -version	Shows the FreeS/WAN version, which tests the /usr/local/bin path for IPSec admin commands.
ipsec whac --kstatus	Command used for status information for Pluto.

14. If the FreeS/WAN kernel implementation is successful, you are ready to continue. Please note that you need a second system setup with FreeS/WAN to create a VPN.

15. If you are not successful, please view the Linux FreeS/WAN online documentation at www.freeswan.org/doc.html. It provides a documentation

tree with a troubleshooting section, as shown in Figure 8.24. The specific address is: www.freeswan.org/freeswan_trees/freeswan-1.9/doc/ trouble.html

Figure 8.24 Troubleshooting Tips for Linux FreeS/WAN

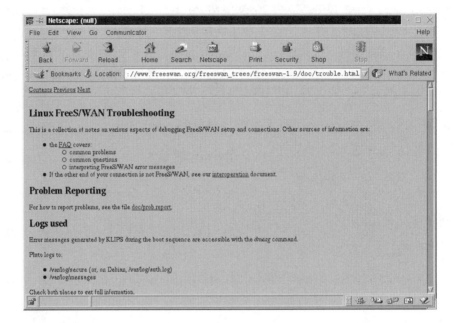

Configuring FreeS/WAN

After you have compiled FreeS/WAN into your Linux kernel and confirmed that IPSec, KLIPS, and Pluto are running, you are ready to configure the program. Any IPSec implementation requires that you first test IP networking on the gateways, or hosts, at each tunnel endpoint. The reason is because IPSec does not work unless a functional IP network is working underneath it.

In this section, you will configure FreeS/WAN between two hosts, which is a host-to-host VPN solution. In an enterprise environment, these hosts would be the VPN gateways into the network. In a telecommuter environment, one host would be the telecommuter, and the other would be the VPN gateway to the company network.

Testing IP Networking

To create a host-to-host VPN solution, both systems must have FreeS/WAN properly installed and tested. Next, you must ensure that IP networking is functioning. For this demonstration, you will also capture HTTP packets between the hosts. This capture will allow you to compare and prove that IPSec is functioning after the tunnel is created between the hosts.

To test IP networking, make sure that each host can ping the others. If successful, access the default Apache Web page on one of the hosts and capture the transmission. View the packet capture to confirm that the packets are not encrypted. This process is documented in the following steps:

1. For this demonstration, we must define our VPN host1 and host2. Write your host1 and host2 in the space provided. From this point forward, the hosts will be referred to as host1 and host2.

    host1 = we-24-130-8-170.we.mediaone.net _____

    host2 = we-24-130-10-205.we.mediaone.net _____

2. Confirm that host1 and host2 are booted into the new kernel that is configured with FreeS/WAN.

3. Confirm that host1 and host2 have FreeS/WAN properly installed and tested.

4. Test connectivity between host1 and host2 using **ping**. For instance, enter the following from host1:

    ```
    ping host2
    ```

    From host2, enter:

    ```
    ping host1
    ```

    You should be successful. If not, troubleshoot your network until you gain connectivity between the two hosts.

5. Host2: Make sure that Apache is installed by entering the following:

    ```
    rpm -qa | grep apache
    ```

6. Host2: You should receive a response similar to the following if Apache is installed:

    ```
    apache-manual-1.3.12-25
    apache-1.3.12-25
    apache-devel-1.3.12-25
    ```

7. Host2: If you do not receive a response, then you need to download and install Apache.

8. Host2: After you confirm that Apache is installed and running, you have completed Apache configuration. This is because host1 will access the default Web site that Apache configures automatically upon installation.

9. Host1: Capture HTTP packets between your Web browser and the Apache Web server on Host2. To accomplish this task, you must first set up a packet capture filter between host1 and host2 using Ethereal. To set up the filter, complete the following steps:

10. Host1: Verify that the Ethereal RPM is installed on the system by entering the following:

```
rpm -qa | grep ethereal
```

11. Host1: If you do not receive a reply, then you need to download and install Ethereal (www.rpmfind.net). You can also install it from your PowerTools CD that is distributed with Red Hat Linux.

12. Host1: After you have verified that Ethereal is installed, you are ready to capture packets.

13. Host1: To add filters to Ethereal without using host names, open a command interface and enter the following:

```
ethereal -n
```

14. Host1: From the **Edit** menu, choose **Filters**. The Ethereal: Filters screen appears. Because no filters have been configured, the configuration screen is blank.

15. Host1: To create a filter that allows only traffic between your host and another host, you must add a filter name and a filter string. For instance, to create a filter between two hosts (host1 and host2), enter the filter name **HTTP Capture** and filter string shown in Figure 8.25. Please note that your IP addresses will not be the same.

16. Host1: After the two fields are complete, you must click the **Save** button and then click the **New** button. Click the **OK** button to exit.

17. Host1: To start a packet capture, simply choose **Start** from the **Capture** menu. The Capture Preference screen appears. Click the **Filter** button and choose the **HTTP Capture** filter that you created. Click the **OK** button twice, and the capture starts.

Figure 8.25 Creating a Filter between Two Hosts

18. Host1: To generate the HTTP packets, open the browser and access the default Web page on the host2 Web server. For instance, enter the following: **http://we–24–130–10–205.we.mediaone.net**.

19. Host1: The default Web page on the host2 Web server appears, as shown in Figure 8.26.

Figure 8.26 Accessing the Default Web Page on the host2 Web Server

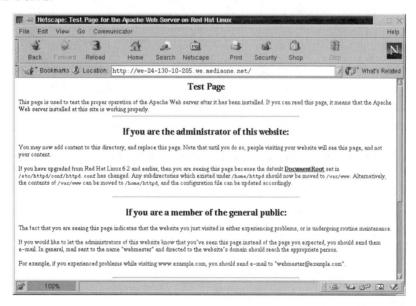

20. Host1: Close the browser.

21. Host1: Stop the Ethereal packet capture by clicking the **Stop** button.

22. Host1: The packet capture appears in Ethereal. The transmission is not encrypted. All application data is displayed, as well as the port numbers. Your screen will resemble Figure 8.27, which highlights the first HTTP packet.

23. Host1: Save the packet capture as *unsecHTTP* and quit Ethereal. A sample *unsecHTTP* file is included on the CD accompanying this book.

Figure 8.27 Capturing an HTTP Session without FreeS/WAN

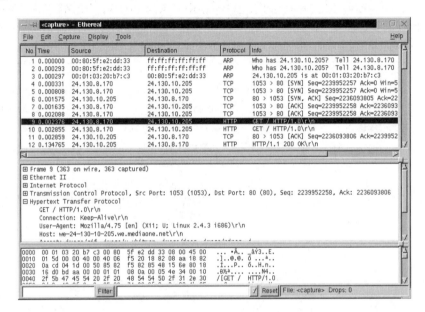

You have successfully tested IP networking between the two VPN hosts. You also captured HTTP packets between the two hosts to prove that a VPN tunnel has not yet been configured. When the VPN tunnel is configured, all traffic between the two hosts will be encrypted, regardless of the applications running between the hosts.

Configuring Public Key Encryption for Secure Authentication of VPN Endpoints

You have tested and confirmed that an HTTP daemon and browser can communication between host1 and host2. *Do not proceed in this chapter until this works.* This proves that the hosts can communicate without IPSec and will make troubleshooting any problems far easier. The next goal will be to have host1 and host2 communicate with the FreeS/WAN IPSec implementation.

For IPSec to work, you have to set up public key encryption. As you learned in Chapter 7, public key encryption uses private and public keys to ensure authentication. The private key is known only by the host, and the public key is available to everyone else, such as all hosts that the system will communicate with.

NOTE

The U.S. patent on the RSA algorithm expired on September 20, 2000. Therefore, RSA is used for the public key encryption in FreeS/WAN and will be incorporated into many additional open source programs as they are developed and new versions are released.

An RSA key pair was created during the FreeS/WAN installation process. The key pair is placed in the /etc/ipsec.secrets file. This file must be kept secure because your private key is listed within it. Only you, the superuser, should have access to this /etc/ipsec.secrets file.

The public key should be placed in the /etc/ipsec.conf file. Because the public key is available to anyone with whom you communicate, security is not as important for the /etc/ipsec.conf file. The private and public key locations for FreeS/WAN are summarized in Table 8.5.

Table 8.5 Location of RSA Key Pair for FreeS/WAN

Key	File Name	Location on Host
Private key Public key	ipsec.secrets	/etc/ipsec.secrets
Public key	ipsec.conf	/etc/ipsec.conf

You will configure these files in the following steps on host1 and host2 so that you can start the tunnel. Complete the following steps to configure your systems for FreeS/WAN. FreeS/WAN and IPSec refer to the VPN endpoints as the "left" and "right" hosts. In this section's demonstration, host1 is left, and host2 is right.

1. Host1: First, you will configure the /etc/ipsec.secrets file, which lists your system's public and private keys. Open the file by entering the following:

```
vi /etc/ipsec.secrets
```

Your file will resemble the one shown in Figure 8.28.

Figure 8.28 Configuring the /etc/ipsec.secrets File

2. Host1: You are using public key authentication, so you need to comment out (#) the line indicating the "Shared secret." To do this, press **I** and comment out the last line in the second paragraph of the file, as follows (your arbitrary character string may vary):

```
# Shared secret (an arbitrary character string, which should be
# both long and hard to guess, enclosed in quotes) for a pair
# of negotiating hosts.
# Must be same on both; generate on one and copy to the other.
# 10.0.0.1 10.12.12.1 : PSK
# "jxmWkkWmm4uV1m4SW3SuUWU1233Wu5S5U3S…"
```

3. Host1: Notice the public and private key listed in the file. Pluto, which is the IKE implementation on FreeS/WAN, uses these keys to authenticate hosts with your system.

4. Host1: Press **ESC**, then write and quit the file by entering the following:

```
:wq
```

IPSec (and FreeS/WAN) use RSA keys by default for authentication between the VPN hosts. Encryption is accomplished by default through 3DES.

5. Host1: Next, you will configure the /etc/ipsec.conf file, which lists the configuration and connection information for IPSec.

6. Host1: Make a backup copy of the /etc/ipsec.conf file and name it **ipsec.conf-backup**. The ipsec.conf file is actually a sample file that you must configure. Enter the following:

```
cp /etc/ipsec.conf /etc/ipsec.conf-backup
```

7. Open the /etc/ipsec.conf file by entering the following:

```
vi /etc/ipsec.conf
```

8. Host1: Your file will resemble the file shown in Figure 8.29 (Figure 8.30, displayed later in this section, displays the remainder of the file, which has three main sections).

Figure 8.29 Configuring the /etc/ipsec.conf File

9. Host1: As you can see in Figure 8.29, /etc/ipsec.conf is the main FreeS/WAN IPSec configuration file, which has three parts. The "basic configuration" and "defaults for subsequent connection descriptions" sections are shown in the figure. The "connection" section is discussed after these two sections are completed.

NOTE

For more information on the configuration options for ipsec.conf, see the following documents:

- www.freeswan.org/freeswan_trees/freeswan-1.9/doc/manpage.d/ipsec.conf.5.html
- man ipsec.conf
- /root/freeswan-1.9/doc/examples

10. Host1: Read the "basic configuration" section as follows. You do not need to make any changes to this section of the file. Additional comments are here for your understanding:

```
# basic configuration
config setup
# THIS SETTING MUST BE CORRECT or almost nothing will work.
# %defaultroute is okay for most simple cases. This defines the
# interfaces that IPsec uses. For instance, you could add
# "ipsec0=eth0" for the interfaces value as well.
interfaces=%defaultroute
# Debug-logging controls: Specifies how much KLIPS and Pluto
# debugging output will be logged. Defaults to "none".
# Enter "none" for (almost) none, "all" for lots.
klipsdebug=none
plutodebug=none
# Plutoload specifies a connection name (identified in the third
# section of this file) that will be loaded into the internal
# database at startup. It does not attempt to start the
# connection until summoned.
plutoload=host-to-host
```

```
# Close down old connection when new one using same
# ID showns up.
uniqueids=yes
```

11. Host1: You must modify the "defaults for subsequent connection descriptions" section. The configurations you enable here will determine how the following "connections" section will behave. Because you are using public key cryptography, you do not require the manual-key testing entries. The section should read as follows (you do not need to enter the comments):

```
# defaults for subsequent connection descriptions
conn %default
# How persistent to be in (re)keying negotiations (0 means
# very).
Keying tries=0
# Indicates that RSA authentication will be used for the VPN
# connection. To generate your public key, open a terminal and
# enter 'ipsec showhostkey'. Copy your public key to the
# leftrsasigkey value. Copy the public key of host2 to the
# rightrsasigkey.
authby=rsasig
leftrsasigkey=
rightrsasigkey=
```

NOTE

The host1 public key is also listed in the /etc/ipsec.secrets file and begins with *#pubkey=0x"* (see Figure 8.28). Only the hexadecimal portion is required, not the *#pubkey="* portion. You can copy the public key from host1 from this file and paste it into the *leftrsasigkey=* value. You may want to use a text editor other than vi to copy and paste the public key.

12. Host1: You must modify the "sample connection" section so that it applies to a host-to-host connection. The connection section is shown in Figure 8.30.

Figure 8.30 Configuring the Connection Section of the
/etc/ipsec.conf File

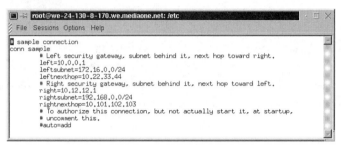

NOTE

If you were configuring VPN gateways for a network, you would enter
the "leftsubnet" and "rightsubnet" options (shown in Figure 8.30). These
options identify the LAN network address that the gateway is attached
to. If you were configuring a VPN involving a telecommuter, you would
identify the subnet on only one side, because the telecommuter has no
gateway, it is a host.

13. Host1: Modify the connection section for a host-to-host VPN solution.
     Modify the section as follows (you do not need to enter the comments):

```
# host-to-host tunnel (no subnets)
# In this demonstration, the hosts talk directly to each other,
# so next-hop settings are not required. The name of this
# connection is "host-to-host."
conn host-to-host
# The left host is the IP address of host1.
left=24.130.8.170
# Next hop to reach the right host — no value required because
# hosts are on the same network.
leftnexthop=
# The right host is the IP address of host2
right=24.130.10.205
# Next hop to reach the left host — no value required because
```

```
# hosts are on the same network.
rightnexthop=
```

14. Host1: Press **Esc**, then write and quit the file by entering the following:

```
:wq
```

15. Host1: Copy the /etc/ipsec.conf file from host1 and transfer it to host2. Doing so will save you a lot of time and effort.

NOTE

If you have security concerns, you can configure the /etc/ipsec.conf file separately on host2. Then, copy the public key of host1 to a text file and name it host1.pub. (A sample *host1.pub* file is included on the CD accompanying this book). The public key is the line in the output of the /etc/ipsec.secrets file that begins with *#pubkey=0x"* (see Figure 8.28). Only the hexadecimal portion is required, not the *#pubkey="* portion. Then transfer the host1.pub file to host2 and place it in the /etc/ipsec.conf file. As usual, authentication of public keys is essential to ensure that you are not tricked into accepting a public key from a hacker. Make sure that you are certain the public key is from host1.

16. Host2: Log in to host2 as root using the FreeS/WAN-enabled kernel.

17. Host2: Make a backup copy of the /etc/ipsec.conf file and name it **ipsec.conf-backup**. The ipsec.conf file is actually a sample file that you must configure. Enter the following:

```
cp /etc/ipsec.conf  /etc/ipsec.conf-backup
```

18. Host2: Replace the host2 /etc/ipsec.conf file with the host1 ipsec.conf file. You need to add only the host2 public key to the *rightrsasigkey=* value, which you will do in the following steps.

19. Host2: Open the /etc/ipsec.secrets file by entering the following:

```
vi /etc/ipsec.secrets
```

20. Host2: Similar to host1, comment out (#) the line indicating the "Shared secret". To do this, press **I** and comment out the last line in the second paragraph of the file, as shown (your arbitrary character string may vary):

```
# Shared secret (an arbitrary character string, which should be
# both long and hard to guess, enclosed in quotes) for a pair
# of negotiating hosts.
# Must be same on both; generate on one and copy to the other.
# 10.0.0.1 10.12.12.1 : PSK
# "jxmWkkWmm4uV1m4SW3SuUWU1233Wu5S5U3S…"
```

21. Host2: Copy the public key of host2. The public key is the line in the output of the /etc/ipsec.secrets file that begins with *#pubkey=0x"*. Only the hexadecimal portion is required, not the *#pubkey="* portion.

22. Host2: Paste the public key of host2 to the /etc/ipsec.conf *rightrsasigkey=* value. You may want to use a text editor other than vi to copy and paste the public key. Both public keys for host1 and host2 should now be listed in the file.

23. Host2: Write and quit both the /etc/ipsec.secrets and the /etc/ipsec.conf file.

24. Host2: Transfer the host2 public key to host1. For instance, copy the public key of host2 to a text file and name it **host1.pub**, (a sample host1.pub file is included on the CD accompanying this book), or copy the /etc/ipsec.conf file to host1. The file will be exactly the same on both hosts, so this method is possible.

25. Host1: Copy the public key of host2 to the /etc/ipsec.conf *rightrsasigkey=* value.

26. Host1 and Host2: The ipsec.conf file on both host1 and host2 should be identical. Figures 8.31 through 8.33 display the completed ipsec.conf file for the host-to-host tunnel for two mediaone.net endpoints. A sample ipsec.conf file is included on the CD accompanying this book.

Figure 8.31 Final Configurations for the "Basic Configuration" Section of the /etc/ipsec.secrets File

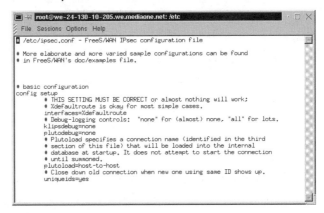

Figure 8.32 Final Configurations for the "Defaults for Subsequent Connection Descriptions" Section of the /etc/ipsec.conf File

Figure 8.33 Final Configurations for the "Connection (Host-to-Host Tunnel)" Section of the /etc/ipsec.conf File

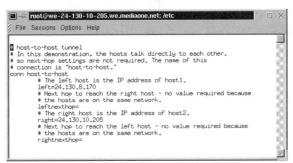

Starting the Tunnel

Congratulations. Both /etc/ipsec.conf and /etc/ipsec.secret files on host1 and host2 are configured with each other's public keys. Now you must create the tunnel. The commands used to start, stop, and maintain the tunnel are IPSec commands. Table 8.6 displays common IPSec commands.

Table 8.6 Common IPSec Commands

Command	Description
ipsec auto --up	Requests Pluto to establish a connection (tunnel) using data stored in its internal database.
ipsec auto --down	Requests Pluto to close a connection (tunnel).
ipsec auto --rereadsecrets	Request Pluto to reread the /etc/ipsec.secrets file.
ipsec look	Lists a minimal amount of debugging information. Main use is to provide a quick look at current connections.
ipsec barf	Lists all debugging information related to IPSec, including encryption and authentication data.
ipsec pluto	The IPSec Key Exchange (IKE) daemon command. The IPSec auto commands are more convenient for establishing and closing IKE connections.
ipsec whack	Provides a control interface for IPSec keying daemons, which is Pluto in FreeS/WAN. The IPSec auto commands are more convenient for establishing and closing IKE connections.
ipsec --help	Most IPSec commands have their own man pages. The *--help* option lists all the IPSec commands.
ipsec --version	Lists the FreeS/WAN version number.
ipsec --copyright	Lists the copyright information.

Most IPSec commands have their own man pages. For a listing, visit www.freeswan.org/freeswan_trees/freeswan-1.9/doc/manpages.html. You can also view the IPSec man page. It lists the associated IPSec commands that have their own man pages.

The following steps will demonstrate how to start the tunnel using IPSec commands:

1. Host1 and Host2: Reboot the systems and make sure that you load the FreeS/WAN-enabled kernel. The reboot loads your "host-to-host" connection that you specified in the /etc/ipsec.conf file into Pluto's internal database at startup. Recall the *plutoload=host-to-host* line.

2. Host1 and Host2: Examine /var/log/messages for any IPSec errors.

3. Host1 and Host2: Check that the following entries exist in /proc/net/ directory:

```
ipsec_version
ipsec_tncfg
ipsec_eroute
ipsec_spi
ipsec_spigrp
```

4. Host1 and Host2: Check for the IPSec virtual interface on the host. Enter the following:

```
cat /proc/net/ipsec_tncfg
```

5. Host1 and Host2: *ipsec0* should be listed. It will point to your physical interface, such as eth0. For instance, it will read as follows:

```
ipsec0 -> eth0 mtu=16260 -> 0
ipsec1 -> NULL mtu=0 -> 0
ipsec2 -> NULL mtu=0 -> 0
ipsec3 -> NULL mtu=0 -> 0
```

The ipsec0 pseudo-device uses the FreeS/WAN eroute utility. This routes all connections through this device and encrypts it before sending it to the underlying physical interface.

6. Host1: On one of the hosts, start the tunnel by entering the following:

```
ipsec auto --up host-to-host
```

where *host-to-host* is the name of the connection you created in the ipsec.conf file.

7. Host1: If no errors are supported, the VPN tunnel should be established. Enter the following command to observe the connection configuration:

    ```
    ipsec look
    ```

8. The response from both ipsec commands should resemble Figure 8.34. If you receive a similar response, your VPN tunnel is established between the hosts.

Figure 8.34 Starting and Confirming the Establishment of a Host-to-Host VPN Tunnel

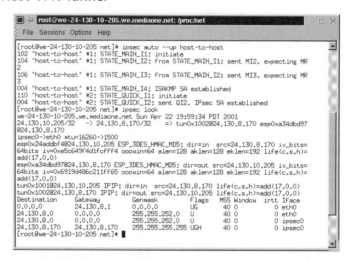

Capturing VPN Tunnel Traffic

To ensure that your VPN is actually encrypting traffic between the hosts, you need to capture packets using the HTTP Capture filter you created in the "Testing IP Networking" section of this chapter. Complete the following steps to prove that the VPN is indeed functioning. Any traffic you send between the hosts will be encrypted.

1. Host1: Open Ethereal without using host names, open a command interface, and enter the following:

    ```
    ethereal -n
    ```

2. Host1: To start a packet capture, simply choose **Start** from the **Capture** menu. The Capture Preference screen appears. Click the **Filter** button

and choose the "HTTP Capture" filter that you created. Click the **OK** button twice, and the capture starts.

3. Host1: To generate the HTTP packets, open the browser and access the default Web page on the host2 Web server. For instance, enter the following:

```
http://we-24-130-10-205.we.mediaone.net
```

4. Host1: The default Web page on the host2 Web server appears.

5. Host1: Close the browser.

6. Host1: Stop the Ethereal packet capture by clicking the **Stop** button.

7. Host1: The packet capture appears in Ethereal. The transmission is encrypted. No application data or port numbers are displayed. Your screen will resemble Figure 8.35, which highlights the first encrypted packet. In this case, ESP uses 3DES for packet encryption and MD5 for packet authentication.

Figure 8.35 Capturing an HTTP Session with a FreeS/WAN Host-to-Host VPN

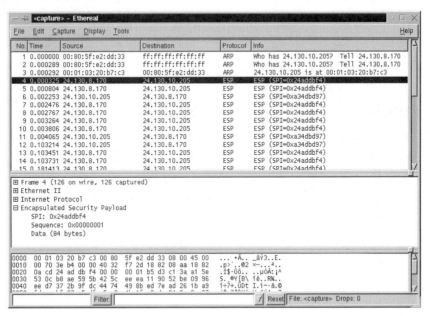

8. Host1: Save the packet capture as **tunntraf** and quit Ethereal. A sample tunntraf file is included on the CD accompanying this book.

You have successfully implemented a VPN host-to-host solution over an unsecured network. You captured HTTP packets between the two hosts to prove that a VPN tunnel has not only been configured, but that it works. When the VPN tunnel is configured, all traffic between the two hosts is encrypted, regardless of the applications running between the hosts.

Closing the VPN Tunnel

To close the VPN tunnel, you must close the connection from *both* endpoints of the tunnel. Even though you started the VPN tunnel from one endpoint, both endpoints must terminate the connection. It can be terminated by completing the following steps:

1. Host1: To close the VPN tunnel from host1, enter the following:

   ```
   ipsec auto --down host-to-host
   ```

2. Host2: To close the VPN tunnel from host2, enter the same command:

   ```
   ipsec auto --down host-to-host
   ```

Summary

In this chapter, you learned how it is possible to deploy secure authentication and strong encryption to establish network security using virtual private networks (VPNs). A VPN provides a private data network over public telecommunication infrastructures, such as the Internet. It provides both secure authentication and encryption. It creates a data tunnel between devices so that all data transmitted between the devices is secure, regardless of what programs the devices are running. There are three basic types of VPN solutions: telecommuter, router-to-router, and host-to-host.

A *tunnel* is created between VPN hosts to ensure that all traffic between them is secure. The tunnel is created with a tunneling protocol. These protocols are responsible for encapsulating a data packet before a host transmits it. After the data is encapsulated, it is sent over the Internet until it arrives at its destination. When it arrives, the capsule is removed and the destination host processes the data.

IPSec is an Internet Engineering Task Force (IETF) security protocol that is becoming a standard component of VPN tunneling protocols. As the name suggests, it was designed for IP, and it has gained wide industry support. IPSec provides secure authentication and encryption over a network by securing all packets at Layer 3—the network layer—of the Open System Interconnection (OSI) model. Layer 3 security is significant because Layer 3 is responsible for IP addressing and routing over the Internet. Security at this layer ensures that everything on the network is secure.

IPSec is often used in conjunction with the Internet Key Exchange (IKE) protocol. IKE is a key management protocol standard that enhances IPSec, such as providing a simpler IPSec configuration, flexibility, and more features. IKE is not required to run IPSec, but it enhances the standard.

Free Secure Wide Area Network (FreeS/WAN) is a Linux VPN implementation that uses IPSec and IKE. IPSec and IKE are used to provide secure authentication and encryption of data between two hosts at Layer 3 (the network layer) of the OSI model. FreeS/WAN creates a secure VPN tunnel between the hosts. It is the goal of S/WAN developers for all S/WAN implementations to interoperate, no matter what device they are installed on. The FreeS/WAN project goal is to provide freely available source code to promote IPSec and allow it to run on many different machines. It also avoids export restrictions.

Last, you learned how to compile FreeS/WAN into a Linux kernel and discovered how to configure and test a host-to-host VPN. You captured the traffic transmitted in the VPN tunnel and realized that it would be useless to a hacker because it is encrypted. When the VPN tunnel is configured, all traffic between the two hosts is encrypted, regardless of the applications running between the hosts.

Solutions Fast Track

Secure Tunneling with VPNs

☑ VPNs provide a private data network over public telecommunication infrastructures, such as the Internet, by providing authentication and encryption through a data "tunnel" between devices. All data transmitted between the devices through the tunnel is secure, regardless of what programs the devices are running.

☑ Telecommuter, router-to-router, and host-to-host are three the basic types of VPN solutions. The solution you choose will depend on your specific needs.

☑ Tunneling protocols are responsible for encapsulating a data packet before a host transmits it. The data is encapsulated and sent over the network to its destination. Upon arrival, the capsule is removed and the data is processed by the destination host. IP tunneling protocols are powerful because they can transmit foreign protocols over the Internet.

Explaining the IP Security Architecture

☑ IPSec is an Internet Engineering Task Force (IETF) security protocol that is becoming a standard component of VPN tunneling protocols.

☑ IPSec secures all packets at Layer 3 (the network layer) of the OSI model by providing secure authentication and encryption over a network. Layer 3 security ensures that everything on the network is secure, such as IP addressing and routing over the Internet, as well as all application data.

Creating a VPN by Using FreeS/WAN

☑ FreeS/WAN is a Linux VPN implementation that uses IPSec and IKE.

☑ IKE is a key management protocol standard that enhances IPSec. It provides enhancements such as simplifying IPSec configuration and adding flexibility and more features. It is not required for IPSec, but is often used in conjunction with it. FreeS/WAN uses Pluto, which is an IKE daemon.

☑ The Authentication Header (AH) performs authentication at the packet level in IPSec. The Encapsulating Security Payload (ESP) performs encryption as well as authentication. FreeS/WAN uses the Kernel IPSec (KLIPS) to perform AH and ESP functions.

Frequently Asked Questions

The following Frequently Asked Questions, answered by the authors of this book, are designed to both measure your understanding of the concepts presented in this chapter and to assist you with real-life implementation of these concepts. To have your questions about this chapter answered by the author, browse to **www.syngress.com/solutions** and click on the **"Ask the Author"** form.

Q: I had great difficulty installing FreeS/WAN. Does a simpler solution exist for an IPSec gateway?

A: The FreeS/WAN program is included in several Linux distributions and various firewall packages. Installation procedures for these products would incorporate FreeS/WAN functionality in your system. Depending on your needs and budget, you may save yourself time and trouble by acquiring FreeS/WAN through one of these alternate sources.

Some available script sets are designed to allow you to manage firewalls that also serve as FreeS/WAN IPSec gateways. You can implement FreeS/WAN through these programs.

Some countries other than the United States have more reasonable encryption laws and thus offer some general-purpose Linux distributions that include FreeS/WAN as well, such as the following:

- **Corel Linux** (the server edition from Canada)
- **Conectiva** (from Brazil)
- **Polish(ed) Linux Distribution** (from Poland)
- **SuSE Linux** (European versions from Germany)
- **Trustix Secure Linux** (from Norway)

You can also use one of the specialized distributions for firewall or router applications. These products offer various alternatives that include FreeS/WAN. Here are a few:

- **Astaro Security Linux** This freeS/WAN configuration is included among the Web-based firewall management tools.
- **Gibraltar** This Debian GNU/Linux-based distribution can be booted from a CD-ROM and can be used without a hard disk.
- **Linux Router Project** This freeS/WAN packaged for LRP is available from the LRP site hosted by Charles Steinkuehler. This distribution can be booted from a floppy disk.

Q: Can FreeS/WAN interoperate with other versions of IPSec?

A: Any IPSec implementations should be able to communicate with others, because the protocols that support IPSec are designed to allow interoperation. However, IPSec protocols are very complex, and therefore difficulties can arise whenever you attempt interoperation with other programs.

Many IPSec implementations can interoperate with Linux FreeS/WAN; FreeS/WAN can even interoperate with previous versions of itself. You can use existing configuration files for newer FreeS/WAN versions in the same series (for example, all versions 1.x). With the impending release of FreeS/WAN 2.0, you will need to use the new configuration files. Table 8.7 lists IPSec implementations that interoperate well with Linux FreeS/WAN.

Table 8.7 IPSec Implementations that Interoperate with FreeS/WAN

Older Versions of FreeS/WAN	PGP Mac and Windows IPSEC Client
OpenBSD	IRE Safenet/SoftPK
FreeBSD	Borderware
NetBSD	Freegate
Cisco Routers	Timestep
Nortel (Bay Networks) Contivity Switch	Shiva/Intel LANrover
Raptor Firewall	Sun Solaris
Gauntlet Firewall GVPN	Sonicwall
Checkpoint Firewall-1	Radguard

Continued

Table 8.7 Continued

Older Versions of FreeS/WAN	PGP Mac and Windows IPSEC Client
F-Secure VPN for Windows	Windows Clients
Watchguard	Windows 2000
Xedia Access Point/QVPN	

Q: When I compile FreeS/WAN, I get the error *gmp.h: No such file or directory.* Why?

A: The gmp.h error occurs if Pluto cannot locate the GNU Multi-Precision (GMP) library. The GMP library enables Pluto to calculate large numbers for public-key encryption operations. Pluto will not compile until the GMP library is installed.

Two RPMs are usually required for GMP installation: libgmp and libgmp-devel. Most distributions provide the GMP library. You can obtain the RPM files from the vendor's site if they are not included on your distribution CD-ROMs.

The GMP home page (www.swox.com/gmp) offers the latest version and information regarding the GMP library.

Q: What type of DES encryption does FreeS/WAN offer?

A: The IPSec standard includes DES support, however DES is not considered adequately secure by the developers of the FreeS/WAN program. Because DES methods are not reliable, FreeS/WAN does not use DES to build connections (at the IPSec level) or to negotiate connections (at the IKE level). FreeS/WAN delivers a higher level of security by using the Triple DES (3DES) algorithm instead.

Q: Which versions of Linux are compatible with FreeS/WAN?

A: FreeS/WAN is designed to run on any CPU that Linux supports. Although most distributions will require some minor adjustments for the specific environment, the program is widely adaptable beyond the Red Hat versions (on which FreeS/WAN is created and tested). As previously discussed in this section, some applications and packages include FreeS/WAN in their distributions. You can visit www.freeswan.org/freeswan_trees/freeswan-1.9/doc/otherdist to consult the FreeS/WAN compatibility document for more information.

## Chapter 9

Implementing a Firewall with Ipchains and Iptables

Solutions in this chapter:

- **Understanding the Need for a Firewall**
- **Deploying IP Forwarding and Masquerading**
- **Configuring Your Firewall to Filter Network Packets**
- **Understanding Tables and Chains in a Linux Firewall**
- **Logging Packets at the Firewall**
- **Configuring a Firewall**
- **Counting Bandwidth Usage**
- **Using and Obtaining Automated Firewall Scripts and Graphical Firewall Utilities**

- ☑ **Summary**
- ☑ **Solutions Fast Track**
- ☑ **Frequently Asked Questions**

Introduction

Thus far, you have seen how to further secure your network by enhancing network authentication and encrypting transmissions. However, even the best authentication and encryption schemes in the world cannot protect a system from scanning attacks, or from applications designed to flood hosts with bogus network packets. Distributed denial-of-service (DDoS) attacks such as those waged by Tribe Flood Network 2000 (TFN2K) and others can instantly flood a network with Internet Control Message Protocol (ICMP), Transmission Control Protocol (TCP), and User Datagram Protocol (UDP) packets, effectively disabling all network hosts. You still need to establish a network perimeter, which means that you need a firewall.

Fortunately, the open source community has excelled in creating firewall software that is ideally suited for networks of any size. Linux natively supports the ability to route and/or filter packets. Modern Linux systems use either Ipchains or Iptables to do this. Ipchains supports Linux kernel versions up to 2.2. If you are using any kernel newer than 2.2 (i.e., the experimental 2.3 kernel, or the stable 2.4 kernel), you must use Iptables. The Iptables package supports packet masquerading and filtering functionality as found in the 2.3 kernel and later. This functionality is known as *netfilter*. Therefore, in order to use Iptables, you must recompile the kernel so that netfilter is installed, and you must also install the Iptables package. RPMs for Ipchains and Iptables can be found on the that accompanies this book. The file names are ipchains–1.3.9–17.i386.rpm and iptables–1.2.1a–1.i386.rpm. You can obtain newer versions from www.rpmfind.net.

NOTE

Ipfwadm is the precursor to both Ipchains and Iptables. Because it is used in older Linux kernels, this chapter does not consider it.

Depending on your kernel version, you can use these applications to configure your Linux system to act as a router, which means that it ensures packets get sent from one network to another. At this level, a Linux router does not examine or filter any traffic. It simply ensures that all traffic addressed to a remote network gets sent to it.

Ipchains and Iptables also allow you to configure your Linux router to masquerade traffic (i.e., to rewrite IP headers so that a packet appears to originate from a certain host), or to examine and block traffic. It is even possible to configure your Linux router to do both. The practice of examining and blocking traffic is often called *packet filtering*. In this chapter, you will learn how to invoke packet filtering on your Linux system.

A packet filter works at the Network layer of the Open System Interconnection Reference Model (OSI/RM). Daemons such as Squid (www.squid-cache.org) also allow you to examine and block traffic. However, Squid is not a packet filter; it is a proxy server, which is designed to operate at the Application layer of the OSI/RM. The primary difference between a packet filtering router (e.g., one created by using Ipchains or Iptables) and a proxy server (e.g., one enabled by Squid) is that a packet filtering router does not inspect network packets as deeply as a proxy server does. However, proxy servers require more system resources in order to process network packets. As a result, a proxy server can sometimes be slow when honoring requests, especially if the machine is not powerful enough. This is why packet filters and proxy servers are both necessary in a network: one (the packet filter) blocks and filters the majority of network traffic, and the proxy server inspects only certain traffic types. You will learn more about Squid in Chapter 10.

In this chapter, you will learn how to configure a system as a simple router and how to implement complex packet filtering so that you can protect your network from various attacks.

Understanding the Need for a Firewall

Regardless of whether you are implementing a packet filter or a proxy server, a firewall provides several services. The most essential Linux firewall functions include:

- **IP address conservation and traffic forwarding** Many firewalls first act as routers so that different networks (i.e., the 192.168.1.1/24 and 10.100.100.0/24 networks) can communicate with each other. Many network administrators use only this function to help create additional subnets. This feature is included as a firewall element simply because it is accomplished using either Ipchains or Iptables. Thus, anyone with only one IP address can create a local area network (LAN) or wide area network (WAN) that has full access to the Internet. You should understand, however, that a firewall does not necessarily have to provide Network Address Translation (NAT). Still, many firewalls (including those provided by Linux and Ipchains/Iptables) allow you to choose this feature.

- **Network differentiation** A firewall is the primary means of creating a boundary between your network and any other network. Because it creates a clear distinction between networks, a firewall helps you manage traffic. A firewall does not necessarily need to be deployed between a trusted, private network and the Internet. Many times, a firewall is deployed within a company network to further differentiate certain company divisions (such as research and development or accounting) from the rest of the network.

- **Protection against denial-of-service (DoS), scanning, and sniffing attacks** A firewall acts as a single point that monitors incoming and outgoing traffic. It is possible for this firewall to limit any traffic that you choose.

- **IP and port filtering** The ability to allow or reject a connection based on IP address and port. Such filtering is likely the most understood function of a firewall. Generally, this type of filtering is usually accomplished by packet filters (i.e., Linux systems that use either Ipchains or Iptables). Packet filtering can become quite complex, because you must always consider that traffic can be filtered according to the source of the packet, as well as the packet's destination. For example, a packet filter can block traffic to your network if it originates from a particular IP address and port.

- **Content filtering** Proxy servers are generally the only types of firewall that manages and controls traffic by inspecting URL and page content. If configured properly, a proxy-oriented firewall can identify and block content that you consider objectionable.

- **Packet redirection** Sometimes, it is necessary for a firewall to send traffic to another port or another host altogether. For example, suppose that you have installed Squid proxy server on a separate host than your firewall. It is likely that you will want to have your firewall automatically forward all traffic sent to ports 80 and 443 (the standard HTTP and HTTPS ports) to your proxy server for additional processing.

- **Enhanced authentication and encryption** A firewall has the ability to authenticate users, and encrypt transmissions between itself and the firewall of another network.

- **Supplemented logging** One of the most important—though commonly ignored—benefits of a firewall is that it allows you to examine all details about network packets that pass through it. You can learn, for example, about port scans and various connections to your system.

A firewall is the most efficient means of reducing scanning threats. In Chapter 4 you learned how network and host-based IDS applications help detect and thwart host scanning. However, an IDS is primarily meant to monitor internal network transmissions, and cannot protect the network as a firewall. This is because a firewall acts as a centralized point that can block or allow incoming and outgoing traffic.

With a firewall in place, you can effectively use one system to protect hundreds of other systems from scanning, sniffing, and DoS attacks. Of course, it is possible to use multiple firewalls in a network, but in general, as soon as you place your network hosts behind an adequately configured firewall, a hacker on the other side of the firewall will have to resort to alternative strategies in order to manipulate internal network hosts.

Building a Personal Firewall

It is possible to use Ipchains or Iptables on a standard client system. You have already seen an example of this in Chapter 4, where PortSentry used Ipchains to block all connections to a host that had illicitly scanned the system. A personal firewall can be helpful in the following situations:

- You have only one system directly connected to the Internet, and don't want to create a router or a firewall as an intervening host.

- You want to log all blocked (or even allowed) traffic, and then read the entries in the /var/log/messages file.

- You want to block certain ports, such as those belonging to X (177 tcp and 177 udp, and tcp ports 6000 and 7100).

- You want to disable all pinging on the host. If you don't want to use Ipchains, you can change the value of /proc/sys/net/ipv4/ icmp_echo_ignore_all to 1 using:

```
echo "1" > /proc/sys/net/ipv4/icmp_echo_ignore_all.
```

When it comes to building any type of firewall, it is important to consider your own situation. The commands you learn in the next section will help you implement the proper solution.

Understanding Packet Filtering Terminology

Table 9.1 provides a list of common terms used when configuring a Linux firewall.

Table 9.1 Common Firewall Terminology

Term	Description
Operating system hardening	Locking down all unnecessary ports and services so that the firewall is as impregnable as possible.
Interface	A network interface card (NIC). Most firewalls have multiple NICs, which you must properly configure in order to filter traffic. Linux refers to the first interface as eth0, the second as eth1, the third as eth2, and so forth.
Multihomed	A host that has at least two interfaces. Generally, one interface is exposed to a public network, and one interface is open only to the trusted network. This way, the router or firewall is able to forward packets on the Internet.
Ingress	Traffic coming into a network host or interface.
Egress	Traffic coming out of a network host or interface.
Rule	An entry in the firewall database that determines how an IP packet will be handled. If an IP packet matches a particular rule, then the packet can, for example, be dropped. However, a firewall can do more than simply drop a packet. A firewall can also forward a packet to another host or port, or it can forward a packet to another rule for processing.
Source IP address	The IP address where a packet was created. A firewall reads this address in a packet to help determine which of its rules apply.
Source port	The port where a packet was created. The source port is almost always associated with the source IP address.
Destination IP address	The IP address of the host to which a packet is addressed. As with the source IP address, a firewall reads this address in a packet to help determine how to apply a rule.
Destination port	The port where the IP packet is supposed to be delivered. The destination port is almost always associated with the destination IP address.

Continued

Table 9.1 Continued

Term	Description
Private IP addresses	In order to conserve IP addresses, the Internet Engineering Task Force (IETF) has established the following IP network addresses as "private." This means that the following networks are meant to be used behind firewalls and routers: 10.0.0.0/8 172.16.0.0/12 192.168.0.0/16 Although it is possible to route these protocols using a Linux router, Internet routers will not forward packets marked with these IP addresses. You will need to masquerade these connections or use NAT/Port Address Translation (NAT/PAT) if you want to forward traffic from private networks to the Internet.
Masquerading	The ability to change a packet's source or destination IP address so that it can be routed to the Internet.

Generally, whenever a packet passes through a firewall, it is compared to its rules. If a packet matches a rule, then the firewall processes the packet. Ipchains gets its name from the fact that it connects each of its rules in an order, much like connecting links in a chain. Whenever a packet enters a chain in Ipchains, it must pass all the way through before the kernel allows it to pass on to the operating system, or pass through to another host. Iptables uses a similar principle, except that it allows you to create specific tables that can be either processed or ignored, making the packet-filtering process quicker and more efficient. Iptables will likely become the standard for some time. Now that you understand some of the basic firewall terms, it is time to learn more about the most common uses of a Linux system in regard to routing and firewalling.

> **NOTE**
>
> Many times, a router can be a completely separate host from the firewall. This is especially the case in medium to large networks, where it is necessary to balance the load between the two. However, routers commonly have features that allow you to program them as a packet filter. Linux is a particularly handy tool because it allows you to do both simple routing and packet filtering.

Choosing a Linux Firewall Machine

Contrary to what you may think, a firewall does not necessarily have to be the most powerful system on your network. It should, however, be a dedicated host, which means that you should not run any other services. The last thing you want to do is configure your firewall to also be a Samba server or print server. Additional services may cause a performance drain, and may open up vulnerabilities as well.

Ideally, a small network would be well served by a typical Pentium III or Pentium IV system with 128MB of RAM and a 500MHz processor. Depending on the amount of traffic the network generates, however, you could get by with a much less powerful system. It is not uncommon to see a network with 25 systems accessing the Internet using a Linux router that is no more powerful than a low-end 300MHz system. A good NIC is vital for firewalls and routers.

Larger businesses, say, those with demands for Web surfing, e-mail retrieval, and additional protocols, may require a more powerful system. Considerations for more powerful systems might include:

- A 1GHZ processor.

- At least 256MB of RAM (512MB of RAM or more may be preferable).

- Quality network interfaces and I/O cards, and possibly RAID 0 for faster data processing. RAID 0 does not provide data redundancy. It does, however, provide you with faster read/write time, which is helpful in regard to a firewall. Although a firewall does not store data as would a database application server, fast I/O is important, because you want the machine to process data as quickly as possible. Fast I/O is especially important if you plan to log extensive amounts of data.

- SCSI hard drives. SCSI systems tend to be faster and longer lasting than their IDE counterparts, thus allowing you a more powerful firewall.

Protecting the Firewall

One of the benefits of having a firewall is that it provides a single point that processes incoming and outgoing traffic. However, consider that a firewall can also provide a central point of attack or failure. A firewall does inform a hacker that a series of networks does exist behind it. If a hacker is able to defeat this one firewall, the entire network would be open to attack. Furthermore, if a hacker were able to somehow disable this host, the entire network would be denied all

Internet services. It is important, therefore, that you take measures to protect your firewall. Consider the following options:

- Limit router and firewall access to interactive login only, and physically secure the system. This way, your firewall is much less susceptible to remote attack. It is still possible, however, that problems in the kernel (e.g., buffer overflows and other programming problems) may occur. Such problems can lead to compromise of the system, even if you have no other services running.

- If remote access is necessary, consider using access only via Secure Shell (SSH), properly configured to use public keys to authenticate. Although SSH is not immune to security threats, it is one of the most popular and secure remote administration tools for Linux firewalls.

- Create a backup host: If your host crashes due to an attack, or simply because of a hard drive failure, you should have an identical system available as a replacement.

- Monitor the host: Use an IDS application to listen in on connections made to your router. Usually, installing an IDS application on a separate host on the network is best. This is called *passive monitoring*, because the remote host does not consume the system resources of the firewall. The IDS application can, for example, send a random ping to the firewall to test whether it is up, and can then inform you if the host is down. Consider using an application such as Cheops, for example.

- Watch for bug reports concerning Ipchains, Iptables, and the Linux kernel. Keeping current about such changes can help you quickly upgrade your system in case a problem is discovered.

Deploying IP Forwarding and Masquerading

IP forwarding is the ability for a Linux system to act as a router. Packets enter the Linux kernel, and are then processed by the operating system. Follow these steps to make your Linux operating system act as a simple IP forwarder:

1. Install at least two NICs into your system. This is necessary, because your Linux system will then be able to service two different networks. You

must, of course, have all of the required cables and hubs to allow systems to use all of the available network hosts.

2. Issue the following command at a terminal:

```
echo "1" > /proc/sys/net/ipv4/ip_forward
```

This command enables IP forwarding on your Linux router. Entering the preceding command into some sort of file that runs whenever the system boots up. This way, if you restart your system, IP forwarding will be enabled by default. You can create your own file, or you can enter it at the bottom of the /etc/rc.d/rc.local file.

3. You can verify whether your system is acting as a router (i.e., IP forwarder) by issuing the following command:

```
cat /proc/sys/net/ipv4/ip_forward
1
host #
```

If it reads 1, then your system is now acting as a router. A value of 0 means that your Linux system is not routing.

The main thing to remember is that a Linux system with simple IP forwarding enabled can route any network address to another. If you are allotted a range of IP addresses from a local or regional Internet registry, you can use a multihomed Linux system to route this set of addresses to another network. For example, if you are allotted the 128.187.22.0/24 block of IP addresses, you can use a Linux router to route this network to the 221.9.3.0 network, or to any other.

NOTE

An Internet registry is the local distribution point for IP addresses. Operating on the authority of the Internet Corporation for Assigned Numbers (ICANN, at www.icann.org), these bodies ensure that IP addresses are meted out properly. If you live in the United States, the American Registry for Internet Numbers (ARIN, at www.arin.net) is the body to contact. European countries obtain IP addresses from the Réseaux IP Européens (RIPE, at www.ripe.net/ripe), and the Asia Pacific region uses the Asia Pacific Network Information Center (APNIC, at www.apnic.net).

However, Internet routers will not forward traffic from private IP addresses (i.e., any network address of 10.0.0.0/8, 172.16.0.0/12, or 192.168.0.0/16). Figure 9.1, for example, shows how traffic from the 10.1.2.0 network and the 192.168.1.0 network can reach all networks, including the 128.187.22.0 network. However, only traffic from the 128.187.22.0 can reach the Internet.

Figure 9.1 A Linux System Configured as a Forwarding Router

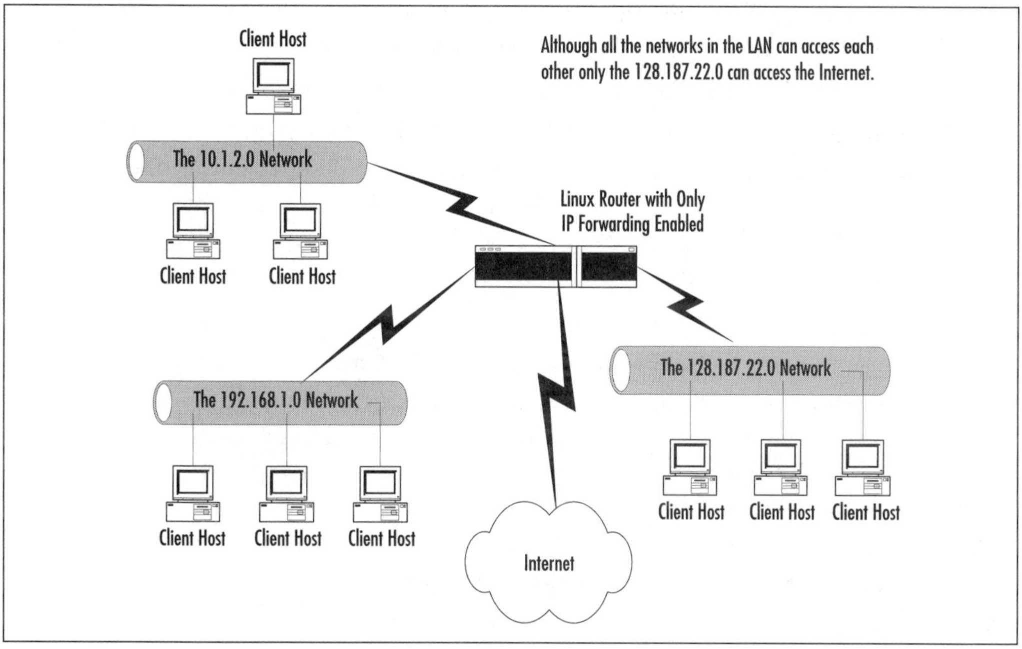

Figure 9.1 shows that traffic from the 10.1.2.0 and 192.168.1.0 networks cannot reach hosts across the Internet, only because the Internet routers will simply drop the traffic. To allow private network addresses to reach the Internet, you need to invoke Ipchains/Iptables-based IP masquerading. However, you have at least two solutions available to you:

- **Place a proxy server on the network that has at least two NICs** This proxy server can be configured to accept requests from the internal network and forward them to the outside network. The first NIC must be internal, because it will receive traffic passing from inside the network. The second NIC must be external, and will pass internal traffic to the outside world, and will also receive outside traffic so that it can be routed to the internal network. Another way of explaining this concept is that the proxy server receives egress traffic (i.e., traffic passing outside of the private IP address networks) and uses an Internet-routable IP address to forward the packets. The proxy server can also receive ingress traffic and translate it so that internal systems can receive it. This option requires the use of an additional software daemon, such as Squid.

■ **Enable IP masquerading** In a Linux router, you can use either Ipchains or Iptables to forward and/or alter the IP headers of packets originating from private IP address networks to pass through Internet routers. Both Ipchains and Iptables do this by processing IP packets through the Linux kernel. As long as the client hosts are configured to use your Linux router as their default gateway, the clients will be able to access any and all Internet services, including ping, traceroute, Telnet, FTP, e-mail (SMTP and POP3), and Web client traffic (ports 80 and 443). This is because the Linux system "mangles" the packets to make them appear as if they originated from a legitimate IP address, and then sends them on their way. You should note that this option is not necessarily secure—IP masquerading leaves all client hosts wide open to attack. If a hacker can attach to your Linux router using Telnet, for example, he or she can then directly access your systems. You will learn about how you can use Ipchains and Iptables to create firewall rules shortly.

We will focus on the second option: Enable IP masquerading.

Masquerading

Masquerading is when your Linux system rewrites the IP headers of a network packet so that the packet appears to originate from a different host. Once the IP header has been rewritten to a nonprivate IP address, it can then be rerouted over the Internet. The practice of rewriting IP packets is colloquially known as *packet mangling*, because it alters the contents of the packet. Masquerading is useful because you can use it to invoke NAT, where one IP address can stand in for several.

As shown in Figure 9.2, masquerading allows the Linux-based system to translate the 10.1.2.0 network in to the Internet-addressable IP address of 66.1.5.0.

Once the private network of 10.1.2.0 is masqueraded as the IP address of 66.1.5.1, all hosts on this network can access the Internet. Depending on the subnet mask used for the 10.1.2.0 network, this means that hundreds and perhaps even thousands of client hosts can be masqueraded under this one IP address.

Figure 9.2 Masquerading the 10.1.2.0 Network as the 66.1.5.1 IP Address

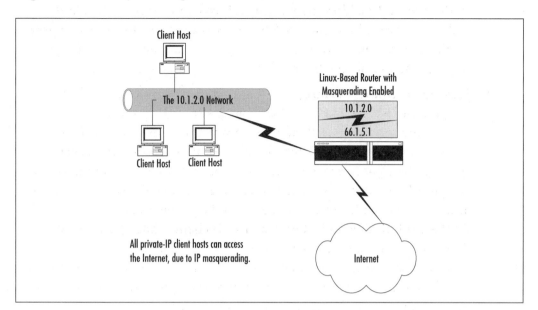

Translating the private to routable Internet address is accomplished by a database stored on the Ipchains/Iptables-based Linux router. The Linux masquerading router keeps this database so that it knows how to "untranslate," as it were, the packets that have been mangled so that they can then be addressed to the local, private network. This process occurs very quickly, although it is important that you have the proper amount of system power to enable the translation database to do its jobs.

NOTE

Ipchains-based NAT is not compatible with Microsoft Point-to-Point Tunneling Protocol (PPTP) VPN clients. Not surprisingly, Microsoft did not follow RFC-defined standards. Not only did they not follow RFCs, but their PPTP is also plagued by a number of design vulnerabilities that affect security. You can, if you want, find workarounds to provide IPSec and VPN support between your Linux system and Microsoft VPN-enabled systems at www.impsec.org/linux/masquerade/ip_masq_vpn.html.

Simple masquerading leaves the network "wide open," meaning that anyone who enters your firewall or router as a default gateway can have full access to all attached networks. Packet filtering is the answer to locking down access to your network. You can learn more about masquerading by reading the NAT-HOWTO file, which can be found on the accompanying CD.

Configuring Your Firewall to Filter Network Packets

Creating packet-filtering rules can become somewhat involved, mainly because you have to spend a great deal of time determining the source and destination IP addresses and ports. You also need to be familiar with how connections are made, managed, and ended. However, there are some simple rules that can help you create a packet filter as soon as possible. As far as outgoing traffic is concerned, you should take the following steps:

1. Configure your Linux firewall to deny all outgoing traffic unless explicitly allowed. This means that your firewall will deny all services to your end users, unless you allow it by creating a rule allowing a specific traffic type.

2. Configure your firewall to allow your internal network to use ports over 1023. Most network clients use these ports to establish connections to network services.

3. Identify the ports of your services to which you want to allow access. If, for example, you want to allow end users to access the Web, you must create a rule allowing all local network hosts to access all remote systems at ports 80 and 443. Likewise, if you want your local clients to use remote POP3 servers, you will have to allow local hosts to use access remote systems at port 110.

As far as incoming traffic is concerned, you have many options. Many systems administrators want to create a firewall that forbids all incoming traffic, except for the TCP and UDP packets necessary when building up and tearing down a network connection. For example, if you want to allow internal clients to allow access to the Web, you will need to allow remote hosts to make connections to your firewall. This involves allowing remote hosts to open up their local ports above 1023 to access your systems at ports above 1023. Therefore, you should take the following steps:

1. Configure your firewall to prohibit all incoming traffic from accessing any services below port 1023. The most secure firewall will not allow any connections to these ports.

2. Forbid all incoming traffic unless it is part of an already established session. In Ipchains, the **-y** option will do this. In Iptables, you would use the **--SYN** option. Each of these options will have the firewall match and discard any incoming packet with the SYN bit set. All other packets with the FIN or ACK bit set will be allowed, because the firewall assumes that these packets are part of an already established session (e.g., an internal user is closing an SMTP or POP3 session with a remote host on the Internet). If you do not add this rule, then it is easier for malicious users to get around your firewall.

3. Disable all incoming ICMP traffic to protect yourself against DoS attacks. This step is optional, of course, because disabling this feature often makes network troubleshooting quite difficult.

4. Disable all forwarding except for networks that require it. The **Ipchains** and **Iptables** commands allow you to masquerade private IP networks. You want to, however, masquerade only certain networks.

5. To enable logging, use the **-l** option in Ipchains, or the **-j** LOG *target* in Iptables.

Damage & Defense…

Customized Packet Filtering

Your firewall configuration needs will be specific to your situation. You need to consider the design of your network, and the services you need to provide. If, for example, you want to allow remote clients to access certain internal hosts, such as a Web server, you can place the Web server outside of the firewall, or you can allow incoming traffic to access port 80. Consider, however, that if you place your Web server behind your firewall, you will have to ensure that this request is then forwarded to a specific internal host. Later in this chapter, you will see how you can manipulate the default INPUT, FORWARD, and OUTPUT chains using Ipchains and Iptables.

Continued

It is common practice to use packet filtering to block the following:

- Incoming and outgoing ICMP packets
- Access to remote POP3 servers
- Access to remote SMTP servers
- Access to the Web, or to certain sites (unproductive or offensive sites)
- Access to additional remote TCP/IP services, such as Telnet, FTP, finger, and so forth

Configuring the Kernel

Most Linux operating systems, such as Red Hat, Slackware, SuSE, and Caldera, support IP forwarding, masquerading, and firewalling by default. However, you may have to reconfigure your kernel in order to provide full functionality. When recompiling the kernel, choose the following option in the Networking section: **Network packet filtering (replaces Ipchains)**. In the 2.2 and earlier kernels, check the following Networking options:

- Network firewalls
- TCP/IP networking
- IP accounting

Packet Accounting

Packet accounting is the ability to summarize protocol usage on an IP network. For example, you can use this feature to list the amount of TCP, ICMP, and IP traffic that passes through your interfaces. Once you have recompiled the kernel and restarted your system, find out if the following file is present in the /proc virtual file system:

```
/proc/net/ip_acct
```

If the file exists, then your kernel supports IP accounting, in addition to all other features. Of course, you may want to check to see if this file exists before taking the time to recompile the kernel.

Understanding Tables and Chains in a Linux Firewall

Iptables derives its name from the three default tables it uses, which are listed in Table 9.2. Each interface on your system can have its packets managed and modified by the chains contained in each of these tables.

Table 9.2 Default Tables and Chains

Table Name	Default Chains	Description
Filter	INPUT FORWARD OUTPUT	Enables you to filter out packets.
Nat	PREROUTING OUTPUT POSTROUTING	Enables masquerading.
Mangle	PREROUTING OUTPUT	Allows you to further "mangle" packets by changing their contents. This feature, for example, allows you to shape packets so that they are ready for certain VPN clients, such as Microsoft PPTP.

Iptables is an extension of Ipchains, because Iptables adds the *nat* and *mangle* tables. Ipchains uses only the three chains listed in the filter table in Table 9.2. Thus, with Ipchains, you have access to only the INPUT, FORWARD, and OUTPUT options. If you want to masquerade using Ipchains, you will use the **--masquerading** option for the FORWARD chain. In Iptables, if you want to filter out packets using, you will use the *filter* table, and if you want to masquerade packets, you will use the *nat* table. In Iptables, if you do not specify a table, it will default to the filter table. Now that you understand tables, it is important to understand the specific chains.

A chain is a series of actions to take on a packet. Whenever you use Ipchains or Iptables to configure a firewall, the proper perspective to adopt is to view all packets from the firewall itself. Even more specifically, you should consider all packets from the perspective of the network interface, the table used, and the specific chains. For example, if you are using the filter table, each interface on your network has three different default chains:

- **INPUT** Contains rules that determine what will be done with all packets that enter this specific interface (i.e., eth0).

- **FORWARD** For the purposes of this chapter, contains rules that determine if a packet will be masqueraded.

- **OUTPUT** Contains rules that determine filtering for packets leaving the interface.

The nat and mangle tables contain two additional chain types. The PREROUTING chain alters packets when they enter the interface. The POSTROUTING chain is used for altering packets when they are ready to leave the host. The POSTROUTING chain is essential to masquerading connections.

Built-In Targets and User-Defined Chains

Ipchains and Iptables use built-in targets to specify the destination of a packet. By far, the most common built-in targets are DROP and ACCEPT. Table 9.3 describes each of these in detail. (Additional targets exist. You can read about them by consulting the Ipchains or Iptables man page.)

Table 9.3 Common Ipchains and Iptables Targets

Target	Description
DROP	The packet is immediately discarded. The target of REJECT is also used.
ACCEPT	Allows the packet to pass through the rest of the chain. By default, all default chains are configured to allow any and all connections.

User-defined chains are often useful if you want to create a large number of rule entries, but do not want a chain to become too long. Chains that become too long can slow down the packet, and are also difficult to read and organize. The following is a sequence where a user defined chain is created, modified, and then invoked:

```
ipchains -N custom

ipchains -A custom -s 0/0 -d 0/0 -p icmp -j REJECT

ipchains -A input -s 0/0 -d 0/0 -j custom
```

This is a trivial example, of course. The **–A** option "appends" a rule, meaning that it is placed at the beginning of a chain. The **–I** option adds the rule to the end of a chain. The user-defined rule of james is created, and then a rule drop-ping all ICMP packets is added to this custom chain. Then, a rule is added to the default input chain that all packets are processed by the custom chain. As a result, any and all ICMP packets will be dropped. If you were to make the mistake of forgetting to have the input chain refer to the chain named custom, then the custom chain would never be read.

In Iptables, the equivalent of the preceding command sequence would be very similar (it is possible, of course, to create user-defined chains that are much more ambitious).

```
ipchains -N custom
ipchains -A custom -s 0/0 -d 0/0 -p icmp -j DROP
ipchains -A input -s 0/0 -d 0/0 -j custom
```

Specifying Interfaces

If no interface is specified, the first interface (usually eth0) is assumed. If you have multiple interfaces, you must specify the interface you want to be added to the chain. Thus, in a multiple-NIC system, when you use the INPUT chain to deny all ICMP traffic, you must specify the interface. If, for example, you have a system with two interfaces that allowed all traffic, you would have to issue the following commands:

```
ipchains -A input -i eth0 -s 0/0 -d 0/0 -p icmp -j REJECT
ipchains -A input -i eth1 -s 0/0 -d 0/0 -p icmp -j REJECT
```

Now, this system will not forward ICMP packets on either the eth0 or the eth1 interface. For Iptables, the commands would be as follows:

```
iptables -A INPUT -i eth0 -s 0/0 -d 0/0 --protocol icmp --icmp-type
    echo-reply -j REJECT
iptables -A INPUT -i eth1 -s 0/0 -d 0/0 --protocol icmp --icmp-type
    echo-reply -j REJECT
```

In both Iptables and Ipchains, the FORWARD chain allows you to specify a source and destination interface. This is because the FORWARD chain is used to masquerade connections. Thus, the **-i** and **-o** options allow you mark packets passing between interfaces.

Setting Policies

Both Ipchains and Iptables default to accepting all connections. The safest option is to set the default policy to first deny all traffic. You can then create rules to explicitly allow certain traffic types. You can change this default stance using the **-P** option. For example, the following Ipchains command changes the default policy of the INPUT chain to deny:

```
ipchains -P input DENY
```

The following command does the same thing in Iptables:

```
iptables -P input DROP
```

To reset the policy to accept, you simply use the ACCEPT target.

Listing Tables and Chains

Once you generate Ipchains or Iptables rules, you can then list them. For example, the following Ipchains command would list all chains and rules:

```
ipchains -L
```

Iptables uses the same command:

```
iptables -L
```

You can, if you want, list specific chains:

```
ipchains -L output
```

Because Iptables allows you to modify three different tables, you can also list specific tables. To list all nat chains, you would issue the following command:

```
iptables -t nat -L
```

The following command would view only the POSTROUTING chain in the nat table:

```
iptables -t nat -L POSTROUTING
```

Consider the following output from the **-L** option in Iptables:

```
iptables -L
Chain INPUT (policy ACCEPT)
target      prot  opt source              destination
custom      icmp --  anywhere            anywhere
```

```
Chain FORWARD (policy ACCEPT)
target      prot opt source              destination

Chain OUTPUT (policy ACCEPT)
target      prot opt source              destination

Chain LD (0 references)
target      prot opt source              destination

Chain custom (1 references)
target      prot opt source              destination
DROP        icmp --  anywhere            anywhere
```

This output shows that the INPUT chain of the filter table contains one rule. This rule does not block ICMP traffic. Rather, it specifies that all ICMP traffic will be handled by the custom chain. The custom chain, listed last, does the actual dropping of all ICMP packets sent to this host.

The following commands allow you to list all of the rules by number:

```
ipchains --line-numbers -L
iptables --line-numbers -L
```

Saving, Flushing, and Restoring Rules

Once you have created rules in Ipchains or Iptables, you can save them using the following commands:

```
/sbin/ipchains-save
/sbin/iptables-save
```

These commands are helpful for two reasons. First, you can save the tables and rules to a text file in order to study them. Second, backing up your rules is important, as it generally takes considerable time to create the "perfect" firewall for your situation, and you should keep a backup in case your firewall configuration somehow gets lost. To save your Iptables information to a text file, for example, you would issue the following command:

```
/sbin/iptables-save > iptables.txt
```

> **NOTE**
>
> You should use a package later than Iptables 1.2.1a or later, because it allows you to use the **ipchains-save** option. Earlier packages did not have it. Red Hat 7.1 and later have a compatible version installed. To install the RPM package on older systems, you need to use the **--nodeps** option:
>
> ```
> rpm -ivh --nodeps iptables-1.2.1a-1.i386.rpm
> ```

To flush any existing rules, you can use the **-F** option:

```
ipchains -F
iptables -F
```

Used without arguments, this command will erase the contents of all rules in Ipchains, and all rules in the filter table of Iptables. To flush a specific chain, you would issue the following command(s):

```
ipchains -F input
iptables -F INPUT
```

> **SECURITY ALERT!**
>
> Many times, the **-F** option is used as a safety measure in firewall scripts. When used at the beginning of a script, it can ensure that the firewall begins its configuration from "ground zero," rather than being appended to an existing firewall configuration.
>
> When creating a firewall script, make sure that you flush all of the necessary chains and tables. Otherwise, you may end up combining your configuration with an existing one, which could lead to connectivity or security problems.

The **-F** option does not delete rules from either the nat or mangle tables in Ipchains, however. To delete information from a specific table, you have to specify the table as follows:

```
iptables -t nat -F
```

The **-F** function does not change a policy from DROP to ACCEPT, either. You must use the **-P** option, discussed earlier.

In case you need to restore your backup information, you can use the following commands:

```
ipchains-restore
iptables-restore
```

For example, to restore the Iptables rules database using the iptables.txt file created earlier, you would issue the following command:

```
/sbin/iptables-restore iptables.txt
```

By default, **Ipchains-restore** will append any restore information to any existing rules. You can use the **-f** option to flush out any existing rules, if you want.

However, the **Iptables-restore** command automatically erases any existing Iptables rules whenever it is used. However, you can use the **-n** option, which appends the contents of the restore file to any existing rules.

Using Ipchains to Masquerade Connections

The Ipchains command has only one table, and three chains (INPUT, FORWARD, and OUTPUT). Using the FORWARD chain and the MASQ target, you can masquerade any IP address you wish. Suppose, for example, that you have a router that connects the 192.168.1.0/24 network and the 10.100.100.0/24 network. Suppose further that this firewall's eth0 interface contains the internet-addressable IP address of 66.1.5.1/8. The following Ipchains command issued on the router would enable both private-IP networks to communicate via the Internet:

```
ipchains -A forward -I eth0 -s 192.168.1.0/24 -j MASQUERADE
ipchains -A forward -I eth0 -s 10.100.100.0/24 -j MASQUERADE
```

This rule specifies that any connection from the 192.168.1.0/24 and 10.100.100.0/24 networks will be masqueraded as 66.1.5.1/8 on eth0. The **-A** option adds the rule to the forward chain, and the **-I** option specifies the eth0 interface. The **-s** option specifies the networks in question.

This particular configuration actually exposes the network. Any remote host would be able to use your masquerading firewall to access your host. The following additions to the FORWARD chain of the filter table ensures that your masquerading router masquerades only for your internal network:

```
ipchains -A forward -s 192.168.1.0/24 -j ACCEPT

ipchains -A forward -d 192.168.1.0/24 -j ACCEPT

ipchains -A forward -s 10.100.100.0/24 -j ACCEPT

ipchains -A forward -d 10.100.100.0/24 -j ACCEPT

ipchains -A forward -j DROP
```

Iptables Masquerading Modules

Many of the protocols you want to use on the Internet, such as FTP or RealAudio, require additional support. Iptables provides several modules that allow masqueraded clients to access these resources. Some of these are described in Table 9.4.

Table 9.4 Ipchains Masquerading Modules

Module	Description
ip_masq_ftp	Module for masquerading FTP connections
ip_masq_raudio	RealAudio
ip_masq_irc	IRC
ip_masq_vdolive	For VDO Live
ip_masq_cuseeme	CU-See-Me

Enabling these options requires that you use the **/sbin/insmod** command. For example, to enable the ip_masq_ftp and ip_masq_raudio modules, you would issue the following command:

```
/sbin/insmod ip_masq_ftp

/sbin/insmod ip_masq_raudio
```

To automate this process, you can place these entries into a script, or into /etc/rc.local.

Using Iptables to Masquerade Connections

Using the same example of the 192.168.1.0/24 network and the 10.100.100.0/24 network connected by the firewall with the IP address of 66.1.5.1/8, you would use the following command:

```
iptables -t nat -A POSTROUTING -d ! 192.168.1.0/22 -j MASQUERADE

iptables -t nat -A POSTROUTING -d ! 10.100.100.0/24 -j MASQUERADE
```

This rule is added to the nat table (-t), and is added to the POSTROUTING chain (-a). The **!** mark tells netfilter/Iptables to masquerade all packets not destined for the internal networks. Specifically, it stipulates that if the packet is not sent to either the 192.168.1.0/22 or 10.100.100.0/24 network, then the packet needs to be modified so that it masquerades as the 66.1.5.1/8 IP address. Consequently, any packet that leaves the interface will be rewritten with the 66.1.5.1/8 address, but packets that stay on the internal network will not be rewritten. The eth0 interface is assumed by default. If, for some reason, you had to specify a different interface that has the Internet-routable address, you would use the **-o** option:

```
iptables -t nat -o eth1 -A POSTROUTING -d ! 192.168.1.0/22
    -j MASQUERADE
iptables -t nat -o eth1 -A POSTROUTING -d ! 10.100.100.0/24
    -j MASQUERADE
```

As with Ipchains, this particular configuration leaves the network wide open. The following additions to the FORWARD chain of the filter table ensure that your masquerading router masquerades only for your internal network:

```
iptables -A FORWARD -s 192.168.1.0/24 -j ACCEPT
iptables -A FORWARD -d 192.168.1.0/24 -j ACCEPT
iptables -A FORWARD -s 10.100.100.0/24 -j ACCEPT
iptables -A FORWARD -d 10.100.100.0/24 -j ACCEPT
iptables -A FORWARD -j DROP
```

Notice the order of these entries. Both Ipchains and Iptables consider rules in strict order, which is why the preceding rules first accept certain packets and then drop all of the rest. If the final entry (iptables -A FORWARD -j DROP) were listed first, then all packets would be denied.

NOTE

Because both Ipchains and Iptables default to allowing any and all input, it is quite easy to create rules that inadvertently allow unwanted traffic to pass through. Some systems administrators prefer to first change the policy of all rules in all tables to deny. Doing so, however, will require you to add explicit rules to all affected chains so that your masquerading will work properly.

Tools & Traps…

Modem Banks: One Way Around Your Firewall

One of the easiest ways to avoid a firewall is to find and exploit improperly configured modem banks. Many times, modems are configured to allow access to all areas of the network, and are often not protected or monitored very closely. As you establish your firewall, consider inspecting any and all systems for modems. You should approach your modem bank with the same care and consideration as you would your firewall.

Even modems not configured to receive incoming calls can be a danger. Consider also that an end user who connects to another network through a modem may be opening up a security breach. For example, suppose that a user has mapped several drives mapped to a file server that contains sensitive information. If an end user connects regularly to a remote dial-up server, it is possible for a malicious user to discover this connection and gain access to the mapped drives, and hence to the sensitive information.

Iptables Modules

Table 9.5 lists some of the most commonly used modules for Iptables.

Table 9.5 Iptables Masquerading Modules

Module	Description
ipt_tables	The module for Iptables support. As with all of these modules, it is possible to compile the kernel so that all of these modules are included.
ipt_LOG	Support for advanced logging, which includes the ability to log only initial bursts of traffic, and capture an certain amount of traffic over a period of time.
ipt_mangle	The IP masquerading module.
ipt_nat	The NAT module.

You can load these modules using **insmod**. Iptables masquerades the FTP, RealAudio, and IRC protocols by default.

Exercise: Masquerading Connections Using Ipchains or Iptables

1. Configure your Linux system with at least two NICs.

2. Enable IP forwarding using the instructions given earlier in this chapter.

3. Using either Ipchains or Iptables, invoke masquerading for your IP addresses using the instructions given earlier in this chapter.

4. Now, configure the FORWARD chain in the filter table (or just the FORWARD chain in Ipchains) so that it will masquerade only your internal hosts.

5. If necessary, load the modules necessary to support FTP, IRC, and additional protocols.

6. You will likely have to adjust your masquerading settings. Make sure that you save your settings using the **/sbin/ipchains-save** command.

Logging Packets at the Firewall

As discussed earlier, the Iptables **-l** option allows you to log matching packets. You can insert **-l** into any rule, as long as you do not interrupt a particular option. For example, the following command logs all matching TCP packets that are rejected:

```
ipchains -I input -i eth0 -p tcp -s 0.0.0.0/0 -y -l -j REJECT
```

However, the following command would be a mistake, because Ipchains would think that **-l** is an argument for the source of a packet:

```
ipchains -I input -i eth0 -p tcp -s -l 0.0.0.0/0 -y -j REJECT
```

Once you establish logging, you can view Ipchains output in the /var/log/ messages file.

Iptables allows you to log packets, as well, but in a much more sophisticated way. This is because Iptables uses the LOG target, which you specify just like DROP or ACCEPT. For example, to reject and also log all initial TCP traffic, you would issue the following two commands:

```
iptables -A INPUT -i eth0 -p tcp -s 0.0.0.0/0 -syn -j LOG
iptables -A INPUT -i eth0 -p tcp -s 0.0.0.0/0 -syn -j DROP
```

As with Iptables, you can view the results of your logging in the /var/log/ messages file.

Setting Log Limits

By default, Iptables will limit logging of packets. The default limit rate is three logging instances an hour. Each time a logging instance starts, only the first five packets will be logged by default. This behavior is meant to ensure that log files do not get too large. You can change the default logging rate by specifying the --limit and --limit-burst flags. The --limit flag allows you to determine the limit rate by second, minute, hour, or day. The --limit-burst figure allows you to determine how many initial packets will be logged. For example, to log ICMP packets at a rate of two per minute, you would issue the following command:

```
iptables -A INPUT -i eth0 -p icmp -s 0.0.0.0/0 --limit 2/min
    --limit-burst 2 -j LOG
```

Notice also that the limit-burst value is set to 2.

SECURITY ALERT!

Be careful not to log too many packets. You will quickly consume hard drive space if you log all packets passing through your firewall interfaces.

Adding and Removing Packet Filtering Rules

Thus far, you have created a masquerading router. However, you have not yet invoked any packet filtering. Following are some examples of packet-filtering rules you may want to create on your system. First, consider the following Ipchains and Iptables commands:

```
ipchains -P input DENY
ipchains -A input -I eth0 -p tcp  -s 0/0 -d 0/0 22 -j ACCEPT
```

Now, consider the equivalent series of Iptables commands:

```
iptables -P INPUT DROP
iptables -P FORWARD DROP
iptables -A FORWARD -i eth0 -p tcp --dport 22 -j ACCEPT
```

These commands effectively prohibit every service from entering your firewall, except for SSH, which uses port 22. No other service can access your network. Notice that Ipchains refers to the input chain in lowercase, whereas Iptables uses the FORWARD chain in uppercase. Iptables always refers to chains in uppercase. In addition, Iptables does not use the INPUT chain for packets destined for the internal network. In Iptables, the INPUT chain refers only to packets destined for the local system. Thus, in Iptables, you should explicitly drop all packets to the INPUT interface, unless you want to allow access to your firewall, say by SSH or another relatively secure administration method. Your firewall will still forward packets on the nat table using the FORWARD, POSTROUTING, and PREROUTING chains.

Notice also that Ipchains uses DENY as a target name, whereas Iptables uses DROP. The difference is in the way source and destination are specified. This difference is actually not necessary; both Ipchains and Iptables can use **-s** and **-d**, or the **--dport** option. When using **--dport** or **--sport**, if you do not specify a source or destination, both Iptables and Ipchains assume the first local interface. The **-I** option in Ipchains specifies a particular interface (in this case, the eth0 interface), whereas in Iptables, the **-I** option specifies the incoming interface.

The preceding configuration is both extremely simple and restrictive. It allows outside hosts to access SSH users to access only SSH, and will not allow any user interactively logged in to the system to check e-mail or any other Internet-based service. This is because the rule is designed to lock down the firewall as much as possible.

ICMP Types

Notice that with Iptables, you can reject specific ICMP types. Table 9.6 explains some of the additional types, including the numbers assigned in RFC 792, which is the document that defines the parameters for all ICMP messages.

Table 9.6 Common ICMP Names and Numbers

Iptables/Ipchains ICMP Message Name	RFC Name and Number	Description
echo-request	8 Echo	The packet sent out by the common **ping** command.
echo-reply	0 Echo Reply	The reply a host gives to the **ping** command.
destination-unreachable	3 Destination Unreachable	Informs an echo request packet that there is a problem reaching the intended host.

Continued

Table 9.6 Continued

Iptables/Ipchains ICMP Message Name	RFC Name and Number	Description
source-quence	4 Source Quench	If a router is too busy and cannot fulfill a client request, it will send back this message to a client.
Redirect	5 Redirect	Sent by a router that has, essentially, discovered a more direct route to the destination than originally found in the network packet sent by the network host.
time-exceeded	11 Time Exceeded	If a datagram is held too long by a router, its time-to-live (TTL) field expires. When this occurs, the router is supposed to send a message back to the host informing it of the drop.
parameter-problem	12 Parameter Problem	Sent by either standard hosts or routers, this message informs other hosts that a packet cannot be processed.

You can learn about additional arguments by typing **iptables –p icmp –h** at any terminal.

A Personal Firewall Example

Suppose that you want to create a personal firewall for a system that you use as a desktop. You would modify the previous Ipchains commands as follows:

```
ipchains -P input DENY
ipchains -A input -I eth0 -p tcp  -s 0/0 -d 0/0 22 -j ACCEPT
```

To create a personal firewall system using Iptables, you would issue the following commands:

```
iptables -P INPUT DROP
iptables -A INPUT -I eth0 -p tcp --dport 22 -j ACCEPT
iptables -A INPUT -I eth0 -p tcp --dport 1023 -j ACCEPT
iptables -A INPUT -I eth0 -p udp --dport 1023 -j ACCEPT
```

The preceding commands allow SSH, but no other service. However, now a user can browse the Web, contact DNS servers, and so forth, and use the system with a reasonable degree of security. This system now cannot even be pinged, which helps to protect it against distributed DoS and ping scanning attacks.

Exercise: Creating a Personal Firewall and Creating a User-Defined Chain

1. Using either Ipchains or Iptables, add the following rules to your INPUT table to create a personal firewall:

   - Deny all incoming ICMP traffic, and make sure the denial is logged

   - Deny all incoming FTP traffic

   - Deny all incoming DNS traffic

   - Deny Telnet

   - Deny SMTP and POP3

2. If you are using Iptables on a standard system with one interface, you would issue the following commands:

```
iptables -A INPUT -s 0/0 -d 0/0 -p icmp -j DROP
iptables -A INPUT -s 0/0 -d 0/0 -p icmp -j LOG
iptables -A INPUT -s 0/0 -d 0/0 -p tcp --dport 20 -j DROP
iptables -A INPUT -s 0/0 -d 0/0 -p tcp --dport 21 -j DROP
iptables -A INPUT -s 0/0 -d 0/0 -p tcp --dport 53 -j DROP
iptables -A INPUT -s 0/0 -d 0/0 -p udp --dport 53 -j DROP
iptables -A INPUT -s 0/0 -d 0/0 -p tcp --dport 21 -j DROP
iptables -A INPUT -s 0/0 -d 0/0 -p tcp --dport 25 -j DROP
iptables -A INPUT -s 0/0 -d 0/0 -p tcp --dport 110 -j DROP
```

   Of course, there is more than one way to do this. For example, you could create a user-defined chain and handle all SMTP and POP3 there:

```
iptables -N icmptraffic
iptables -A icmptraffic -s 0/0 -d 0/0 -p icmp -j DROP
iptables -A icmptraffic -s 0/0 -d 0/0 -p icmp -j LOG
iptables -A INPUT -s 0/0 -d 0/0 -p icmp -j icmp
```

3. List the INPUT chain. If you created a user-defined chain, list this as well.

4. Save your configuration for the sake of backup. If you are using Iptables, use the following command:

```
iptables-save > iptables.txt
```

5. Flush all of the rules you created. If you are using Iptables, issue the following command:

```
iptables -F
```

6. List the INPUT chain (and any other) to verify that you have in fact flushed this chain.

7. Use the iptables-restore (or ipchains-restore) command along with the text file you created to restore your Iptables chains:

```
iptables-restore iptables.txt
```

8. List your tables and chains again to verify that your rules have been restored.

9. Thus far, you have created a personal firewall that starts with a "wide open" policy, and then proceeds to lock down ports. Now, use the **-P** option to block all traffic, and then allow only SSH, or any other protocol(s) of your choice. If, for example, you are using Iptables, issue the following commands:

```
iptables -P INPUT DROP
iptables -A INPUT-p tcp --dport 22 -j ACCEPT
iptables -A INPUT-p tcp --dport 1023: -j ACCEPT
iptables -A INPUT-p udp --dport 1023: -j ACCEPT
```

   You can specify –i eth0, if you wish. However, if you only have one interface, both Ipchains and Iptables will default to using this interface. Remember, you should open up the ephemeral TCP and UDP ports so that you can still do things like checking your e-mail, and so forth. If, of course, you do not want any services open on your network, you could omit the **--dport 22** line altogether.

10. Now, log all traffic that attempts to connect to your system. If you are using Iptables, issue the following command:

```
iptables -A INPUT-p udp --dport 1023: -j LOG
iptables -A INPUT-p tcp --dport 1023: -j LOG
```

This feature may log too much information for your server, depending on your system's activity. Make sure you check your log files regularly.

11. Log all attempts to scan the standard ports for Microsoft networking. If you are using Iptables, issue the following command:

```
iptables -A INPUT-p tcp --multiport  --destination-port
    135,137,138,139 -j LOG
iptables -A INPUT-p udp --multiport  --destination-port
    137,138,139 -j LOG
```

The **--multiport --destination-port** option allows you to specify a range of ports. You can read more about these options in the Iptables man page.

12. If your server needs to support additional protocols, experiment with adding them.

Redirecting Ports in Ipchains and Iptables

Port redirection is where a packet destined for a certain port (say, port 80) is received by an interface, and is then sent to another port. Redirecting ports is common in networks that use proxy servers. To redirect a port in Ipchains to the local system's eth0 interface, you could issue the following command:

```
ipchains -A input -i eth1 -s 0/0 -d 0/0 -p tcp 80 -j REDIRECT 8080
ipchains -A input -i eth1 -s 0/0 -d 0/0 -p tcp 443 -j REDIRECT 8080
```

In Iptables, you must use the REDIRECT target from the nat table:

```
iptables -t nat -A PREROUTING -i eth1 -s 0/0 -d 0/0 -p
    tcp 80 -j REDIRECT /
--to-ports 8080

iptables -t nat -A PREROUTING -i eth1 -s 0/0 -d 0/0 -p
    tcp 443 -j REDIRECT /
--to-ports 8080
```

These rules ensure that any hosts that try to bypass your proxy server by specifying your firewall are redirected to a proxy server on the firewall. Another strategy is to deny all requests to ports 80 and 443, and then make sure that all Web clients are configured to access your proxy server.

Configuring a Firewall

Because your situation will be unique, it is impossible to provide a "cookbook" firewall for you. However, the following is a beginning firewall for a system with three NICs. The NICs have the following IP addresses:

- **Eth0** 207.1.2.3/24
- **Eth1** 192.168.1.1/24
- **Eth2** 10.100.100.1/24

Thus, Eth0 represents the 207.1.2.0/24 network, Eth1 represents the 192.168.1.0/24 network, and Eth2 represents the 10.100.100.0/24 network. The intention is to create a firewall that allows the Eth1 and Eth2 networks to communicate freely with each other, as well as get on to the Internet and use any services (Web, e-mail, FTP, and so forth). However, no one from the Internet should be able to access internal ports below port 1023. Again, this configuration does not spend much time limiting egress (i.e., outbound) traffic. Rather, it focuses on trying to limit ingress (inbound) traffic. Any of the Ipchains or Iptables commands given in the following sections can be entered into any script, or into a directory or file such as /etc/rc.d/init.d/ or /etc/rc.d/rc.local. This way, your rules will be loaded automatically when you reboot your system.

Setting a Proper Foundation

Regardless of whether you are using Ipchains or Iptables, the first thing you will have to do for your firewall is to flush all existing rules using the **-F** option. Then, you need to use the **-P** option to set the firewall policies to deny all connections by default. The subsequent rules you create will then allow the protocols you really want. Then, use the necessary commands to enable forwarding and masquerading, as shown earlier in this chapter. Without this foundation, you will not be able to forward packets at all, and thus firewalling them would be rather superfluous.

Creating Anti-Spoofing Rules

Many times, a hacker will try to use your firewall as a default gateway and try to spoof internal packets. If a firewall's "Internet interface" (i.e., the one that is responsible for addressing packets to the Internet) is not configured to explicitly deny packets from the network, then you are susceptible to this attack. To deny spoofing, you would issue the following commands, depending on what kernel you are using:

```
ipchains -A input -s 192.168.1.0/24 -i eth0 -j deny
ipchains -A input -s 10.100.100.0/24 -i eth0 -j deny


iptables -A FORWARD -s 192.168.1.0/24 -i eth0 -j DROP
iptables -A FORWARD -s 10.100.100.0/24 -i eth0 -j DROP
```

You may want to log all of the attempts, just so you know how often you are attacked:

```
ipchains -A input -s 192.168.1.0/24 -i eth0 -l -j deny
ipchains -A input -s 10.100.100.0/24 -i eth0 -l -j deny
```

The preceding rules are different only in that they specify the **-l** option. In Iptables, create two additional entries to log the traffic:

```
iptables -A FORWARD -s 192.168.1.0/24 -i eth0 -j LOG
iptables -A FORWARD -s 10.100.100.0/24 -i eth0 -j LOG
```

Remember, if you have additional interfaces, you have to add a rule for each. Do not leave one interface open to a spoofing attack. You will be surprised how quickly a hacker can discover this vulnerability.

Allowing TCP

The following is an example of what you can do with your network when it comes to allowing inbound and outbound TCP connections. If you are using Ipchains, issue the following commands to allow TCP connections:

```
ipchains-A input -p tcp -d 192.16.1.0/24 ! 80 -y -b -j ACCEPT
ipchains-A input -p tcp -d 10.100.100.0/24 ! 80 -y -b -j ACCEPT
```

The **-y** option prohibits remote hosts from initiating a connection to any port except port 80. This is because the "!" character reverses the meaning of anything that is immediately in front of it. In this case, only connections meant for port 80 will be allowed; all others will be denied. This may seem strange, but remember, this rule is for the input chain, and many times these rules seem to be the reverse of common sense. The **-b** option "mirrors" the rule, which means that the rule applies to packets going in both directions. This rule allows one rule to do the same thing as repeating the command and reversing the source and destination flags (-s and -d).

If you are using Iptables, issue the following commands:

```
iptables -A FORWARD -m multiport -p tcp -d 192.168.1.0\24
    --dport 25,110, 80, 443, 53 /
! -tcp flags SYN, ACK ACK -j ACCEPT


iptables -A FORWARD -m multiport -p tcp -s 192.168. 1.0\24
    --sport 25,110, 80, 443,53 /
 ! -tcp  flags SYN, ACK ACK -j ACCEPT


iptables -A FORWARD -m multiport -p tcp -d 10.100.100.0\24
    --dport 25,110, 80, 443, 53 ! /
-tcp  flags SYN, ACK ACK -j ACCEPT


iptables -A FORWARD -m multiport -p tcp -s 10.100.100.0\24
    --sport 25,110, 80, 443, 53 ! /
-tcp  flags SYN, ACK ACK -j ACCEPT
```

The preceding rules allow ports to be opened above 1023, as long as they are continuing a connection that has first been established by a host inside of the firewall. You can, of course, add additional ports, according to your needs. The / character is a simple line continuation character that you may have to specify in a script. As with Ipchains, the **!** character reverses the meaning of anything that is in front of it. In this case, it means that any packet that does not have the SYN, SYN ACK, or ACK bit set is accepted.

TCP Connections Initiated from Outside the Firewall

You may want to allow certain outside hosts to initiate a connection to your firewall. If you do, you can issue the following commands:

For Ipchains, you would issue the following:

```
ipchains -A input -p tcp -I eth0 -d 192.168.1.0/24 80 -y -j ACCEPT
```

The difference between this command and those given previously is that this one specifies the interface, as opposed to the IP address.

For outgoing connections, you would issue the following:

```
ipchains -A input -p tcp -i eth0 -d 0/0 -j ACCEPT
```

For Iptables, you would do the following for standard TCP connections:

```
iptables -A FORWARD -m multiport -p tcp -i eth0 -d 192.168.
    1.0/24 80 --syn /
--syn -j  ACCEPT


iptables -A FORWARD -m multiport -p tcp -i eth0
    -d 10.100.100.0/24 80--syn /
--syn -j ACCEPT
```

To allow for outgoing connections, you would issue the following:

```
iptables -A FORWARD -m multiport -p tcp -i eth0 -d 0/0 --syn  -j ACCEPT
iptables -A FORWARD -m multiport -p tcp -i eth1 -d 0/0 --syn -j ACCEPT
iptables -A FORWARD -m multiport -p tcp -i eth2 -d 0/0 --syn -j ACCEPT
```

All other TCP traffic will be locked out.

Firewalling UDP

To filter incoming and outgoing UDP, you would follow many of the same procedures as outlined earlier. However, you should allow both TCP port 53 and UDP port 53, at least at first. Most of the time, DNS uses UDP port 53. However, DNS can use TCP when a request grows too large, so you should account for this by creating explicit rules. For Ipchains, you would do the following to allow incoming connections:

```
ipchains-A input -p udp -i eth0 -d 192.168.1.0/24 53 -j ACCEPT
ipchains-A input -p udp -i eth0 -d 10.100.100.0/24 -j ACCEPT
```

The preceding rule is necessary only if you plan to allow outside users to access your DNS server.

```
ipchains-A input -p udp -i eth0 -d 0/0 -j ACCEPT
```

For Iptables, you would issue the following commands:

```
iptables -A FORWARD -m multiport -p udp -i eth0 -d 192.168.1.0/24 /
--dport  53 -j ACCEPT
iptables -A FORWARD -m multiport -p udp -i eth0 -s 192.168.1.0/24 /
--dport  53 -j ACCEPT
```

Outgoing UDP usually requires that you enable DNS lookups, which are usually at UDP port 53:

```
iptables -A FORWARD -m multiport -p udp -i eth0 -d 0/0 --dport
    53 -j ACCEPT
iptables -A FORWARD -m multiport -p udp -i eth0 -s 0/0 --dport
    53 -j ACCEPT
```

It is possible that your network requires additional ports. For example, if you are running SNMP, you would have to open up ports 160 and 161.

Enhancing Firewall Logs

If you want to log these connections, do the following using Ipchains:

```
ipchains -A input -p tcp -l -j REJECT
ipchains -A input -p udp -l -j REJECT
ipchains -A input -p icmp -l -j REJECT
```

The preceding commands will log any packet that is matched. If you are using Iptables, the equivalent commands are:

```
iptables -A FORWARD -m tcp -p tcp -j LOG
iptables -A FORWARD -m udp -p udp -j LOG
iptables -A FORWARD -m udp -p icmp -j LOG
```

Usually, creating the ideal packet-filtering rules requires some trial and error, as well as research specific to your own situation. For more information about using Ipchains, consult the Ipchains man page, and the Ipchains-HOWTO available at www.linuxdoc.org/HOWTO/IPCHAINS-HOWTO.html#toc1.

For more information about using Iptables, consult the Iptables man page, and the Iptables-HOWTO available at various sites, including www.guenthers.net/doc/howto/en/html/IP-Masquerade-HOWTO.html#toc2. Using the information in this chapter and additional resources, you will be able to create a firewall that blocks known attacks.

Counting Bandwidth Usage

A Linux firewall can inform you about the number of packets it has processed, in addition to blocking and logging attacks. The process of counting packets is often called *packet accounting*. Many companies are very interested in determining how much traffic a department or network has generated. This can help them determine the type of equipment necessary to support the department further. Such information can also help a company determine how much it can bill a client or department. In many situations, the firewall is an ideal place to gather such statistics. If you have the following two networks, these rules will count packets that pass between the two:

```
ipchains -A forward -p icmp -s 192.168.1.0/24 -d 10.100.100.0/24
```

The preceding rule will identify all of the traffic passing from the 192.168.1.0/24 network to the 10.100.100.0/24 network.

If you are using Iptables, you have many additional options. For example, you can identify specific ICMP packets that are forwarded by the firewall:

```
iptables -A FORWARD -m icmp -p icmp -f -j LOG
```

To gather information about a more specific element of ICMP, you could issue the following command:

```
iptables -A FORWARD -m icmp -p icmp --sport echo-request -j LOG
```

This rule will count all icmp echo-request packets (icmp 0). The following command discovers all of the icmp-reply packets that have been forwarded:

```
iptables -A FORWARD -m icmp -p icmp --sport echo-reply -j LOG
```

You are not limited to ICMP packets. If, for example, you wanted to gather information about the HTTP packets being forwarded, you would enter the following:

```
iptables -A FORWARD -p tcp --sport 80,443 -j LOG
```

To determine the amount of HTTP traffic passing between two networks, you would issue the following command:

```
iptables -A FORWARD -s 192.168.1.0/24 -d 10.100.100.0/24 -p tcp
   --sport 80,443  -j LOG
```

Listing and Resetting Counters

To list the counter information, you can issue either of the following commands from a terminal:

```
ipchains -L -v
iptables -L -v
```

You can save this information using the **ipchains-save** and **iptables-save** commands. The following commands reset the counters:

```
ipchains -L -Z
iptables -L -Z
```

Setting Type of Service in a Linux Router

Many routers, including Linux routers using Ipchains or Iptables, are capable of shaping traffic as it passes through. The IP header for all packets has a special field called the Type of Service (ToS) field, which allows you to prioritize traffic as it passes through the router. Using the ToS field, you can make certain types of traffic (e.g., SMTP and POP3) take precedence over others (e.g., SSH and Telnet). Packets that are marked will be treated differently at the router. Setting the ToS field occurs at the Network layer (Layer 3 of the OSI/RM). You can learn more about how ToS works by consulting RFC 1349.

Usually, assigning priority for packets is a secondary concern when configuring a firewall. In some situations, however, you will find it useful for a firewall to "double up" and offer both services. The main reason why you would set the ToS field in network traffic is to cut down on network congestion, especially in networks that have high amounts of traffic.

> **NOTE**
>
> Do not confuse Type of Service (ToS) with Quality of Service (QoS). QoS refers to the ability of physical devices (i.e., switches, routers) to transmit packets according to ToS values found in IP packets. QoS concerns might include whether the packet is delivered via Frame Relay, Asynchronous Transfer Mode (ATM), Ethernet, Synchronous Optical Network (SONET), and so forth. Because ToS refers to the ability to mark certain packets so that they have a higher priority than others do, these markings determine whether they are available for QoS routing.

Service Values

The normal–service value is 0 (or, 0x00 in the actual packet). Table 9.7 lists the four different options available to you when marking a packet.

Table 9.7 ToS Field Options

Service Value	Description
Minimum delay	The minimum delay field reduces the time a datagram takes to get from the router to the host. The minimum delay option is ideal for protocols that require speed when building initial connections, or when transferring control data. Traffic such as the ftp-control port (20), Telnet, and SSH benefits from this setting. Marking this traffic will reduce latency (i.e., the time interval between a request and a reply) at the router. The ToS field bit is 10 (0x10 in the actual packet).
Maximum throughput	This value is appropriate for the ftp-data port (20) and for large file transfers via HTTP. Networks that use the X Windows system to export displays between systems should consider using this bit as well. The ToS field bit is 8 (0x08 in the actual packet). If you anticipate large volume transfers via POP3, you could consider this option as well.
Maximum reliability	Used in an attempt to reduce retransmissions. Sometimes, UDP protocols such as DNS (port 53) and SNMP (ports 161 and 162) are receive this option. However, TCP-based protocols such as SMTP also benefit from this ToS option, because systems can waste bandwidth to keep retransmitting this protocol. The ToS bit value is 4 (0x04 in the actual packet).
Minimum cost	This option is often only implemented by commercial products. The ToS field bit is 2 (0x02 in the actual packet).

It may be useful to consider these four options in terms of common network tasks. Client hosts (i.e., hosts that use X, SSH, FTP, HTTP, and other protocols) may benefit from either maximum throughput or minimum delay settings. Servers generally benefit from maximum throughput, depending on the traffic that they generate.

Setting ToS Values in Ipchains and Iptables

To set ToS values in Ipchains, add the following values to the end of any rule:

```
-t andmask xormask
```

The *andmask* value is usually 01, because this value compares, or "ands" the original TOS value, and then allows you to make a change to the packet. The xormask value can be any of the service values found in Table 9.7 (e.g., 08 for maximizing throughput). This second field is evaluated as an "or" value, meaning that if the value you specify is different from the original value, the one you specify will be set.

For example, to mark the ToS field for maximum throughput for HTTP (port 80) for all packets being sent out to all remote systems, you would do the following:

```
ipchains -A output -s 0.0.0.0/0.0.0.0 -d 0.0.0.0/0.0.0.0 80
   -p 6 -t 01 08
```

The **-p 6** option specifies TCP as the protocol. You would never set a ToS value on a packet that will eventually be dropped. Following are some additional examples of the ToS value being set on additional protocols:

```
ipchains -A output -s 0.0.0.0/0.0.0.0 -d 0.0.0.0/0.0.0.0 21 -p 6 -t 01 04

ipchains -A output -s 0.0.0.0/0.0.0.0 -d 0.0.0.0/0.0.0.0 20 -p 6 -t 01 08

ipchains -A output -s 0.0.0.0/0.0.0.0 -d 0.0.0.0/0.0.0.0 22:22 -p 6 -t 01 10

ipchains -A output -s 0.0.0.0/0.0.0.0 -d 0.0.0.0/0.0.0.0 25:25 -p 6 -t 01 04

ipchains -A output -s 0.0.0.0/0.0.0.0 -d 0.0.0.0/0.0.0.0 53:53 -p 6 -t 01 04

ipchains -A output -s 0.0.0.0/0.0.0.0 -d 0.0.0.0/0.0.0.0 80:80 -p 6 -t 01 08

ipchains -A output -s0.0.0.0/0.0.0.0 -d 0.0.0.0/0.0.0.0 110:110 -p 6 -t 01 08

ipchains -A output -s0.0.0.0/0.0.0.0 -d 0.0.0.0/0.0.0.0 143:143 -p 6 -t 01 04

ipchains -A output -s0.0.0.0/0.0.0.0 -d 0.0.0.0/0.0.0.0 443:443 -p 6 -t 01 04
```

Additional ToS Options in Iptables

Iptables, as you might suspect, adds several options and uses some different terminology. First, you can set your router to either match packets with certain ToS options set, or you can have the router set the actual ToS options. These are two very different things. One allows the router to handle packets with the ToS value already set, whereas the other actually sets the values. To create a rule that matches a ToS field, you would use the **–m** option, complete with its arguments:

```
-m tos --TOS tos_value -j TARGET
```

In the preceding syntax, the tos_value number is any ToS bit found in Table 9.7 (e.g., 08 for maximum throughput). As far as target value is concerned, you can specify any target you wish (ACCEPT, a user-defined chain, and so forth). For example, the following rule accepts packets from port 80 with the ToS value set to 08:

```
iptables -A INPUT -p tcp -m tos 0x08 -j ACCEPT
```

As far as setting ToS values is concerned, you can only set them in the FOR-WARD and OUTPUT chains. The syntax is as follows:

```
-j TOS --set-tos tos_value
```

For example, to set the ToS value to maximum throughput for all outgoing Web traffic, you would do the following:

```
iptables -A OUTPUT -p tcp -m tcp --dport 80 -j TOS --set-tos 0x08
```

Following are some additional examples where Iptables has been used to set ToS fields for various traffic:

```
iptables -A OUTPUT -p tcp -m tcp --dport 21 -j TOS --set-tos 0x04
iptables -A OUTPUT -p tcp -m tcp --dport 20 -j TOS --set-tos 0x08
iptables -A OUTPUT -p tcp -m tcp --dport 22 -j TOS --set-tos 0x010
iptables -A OUTPUT -p tcp -m tcp --dport 25 -j TOS --set-tos 0x04
iptables -A OUTPUT -p tcp -m tcp --dport 53 -j TOS --set-tos 0x04
iptables -A OUTPUT -p tcp -m tcp --dport 80 -j TOS --set-tos 0x08
iptables -A OUTPUT -p tcp -m tcp --dport 110 -j TOS --set-tos 0x08
iptables -A OUTPUT -p tcp -m tcp --dport 143 -j TOS --set-tos 0x04
iptables -A OUTPUT -p tcp -m tcp --dport 443 -j TOS --set-tos 0x04
```

Using and Obtaining Automated Firewall Scripts and Graphical Firewall Utilities

Several attempts have been made to automate the process of creating a firewall in Linux. Similarly, developers are also busy creating GUI applications that make the job easier. Many of these utilities are quite useful, although they are mostly effective in beginning your firewall configuration; you will likely have to customize the rules these applications generate.

The more effective firewall scripts and GUI tools include the following

- **Firestarter** A fairly sophisticated graphical tool that supports both Ipchains and Iptables. It can be used to create a personal firewall, but also supports multihomed systems. Like many automated firewalls, it creates multiple rules to filter out known and expected attacks. You may need to adjust some of these automatic settings. Although Firestarter does support multiple interfaces, it, like most of the open source GUI firewall applications, is best used only as a beginning to a firewall on a multihomed system. You can obtain Firestarter at http://sourceforge.net/projects/firestarter.

- **Mason** A unique product, Mason is designed to first listen in on traffic passing through your firewall, and then generate Ipchains or ipfwadm (the precursor to ipchains and Iptables) rules. As of this writing, Mason does not support Iptables. In spite of this, Mason's approach to rules creation is both unique and sound, as it attempts to create rules based on your network traffic about your firewall needs. You can download this binary at http://users.dhp.com/~whisper/mason. Do not confuse this product with the HTML Mason utilities meant to dynamically generate HTML for Apache Server.

- **Knetfilter** A GUI firewall designed to work with the KDE desktop environment. Although it purports to be stable, it appears to have problems working with common versions of KDE. You can learn more about Knetfilter at http://expansa.sns.it:8080/knetfilter.

- **MonMotha's IPTables Firewall** This is a firewall script, not a GUI interface. It is designed to give you a chance to specify the traffic you want to allow and deny. You must first edit the script and then run it from a command prompt. You can obtain this script at http://mirkk.kurd.nu/~monmotha/firewall/index.php.

- **Firewall Builder** Firewall Builder is in many ways the most ambitious open source GUI tool. It allows you to create rules for multiple interfaces, networks, and hosts. It is also quite unstable on most versions of Red Hat Linux through version 7.1. Learn more about Firewall Builder at http://sourceforge.net/projects/fwbuilder.

- **EasyChains** As of this writing, EasyChains has a ncurses-based GUI, and supports only Ipchains. You can download it at http://sourceforge.net/projects/easychains.

Tools & Traps…

Weighing the Benefits of a Graphical Firewall Utility

As you consider using any of the GUI applications covered in this section, keep is mind the following issues:

- Often, these downloads do not provide public keys or hash values for their code; therefore, before using any of the applications, make sure that you review the source code. If you cannot review the source code yourself, then employ someone to check it, especially if you plan to use it in an enterprise environment.

- Most of these applications are still in beta form, so remember that they often provide limited functionality. Although some, such as Mason, are quite impressive, limitations still persist: As of this writing, Mason does not support Iptables.

- The more advanced GUI applications often require you to upgrade to either the very latest version of a particular window manager, such as KDE or Gnome, or to use an idiosyncratic version or configuration. Consequently, you may have to spend a great deal of time configuring your window manager. Generally, this time could be better spent learning how to use Iptables or Ipchains commands.

Firewall Works in Progress

The following is a partial list of applications being developed at the current time:

- **jb dynFW** (http://sourceforge.net/projects/jbdfw) This project appears to be interested in creating a personal firewall product, as opposed to a multihomed firewall.

- **Heimdall Linuxconf Firewall** (http://sourceforge.net/projects/heimdall) A promising effort, mainly because it proposes to be an add-on to the Linuxconf application.

- **NetFilter-1** (http://sourceforge.net/projects/netfilter-1) If it lives up to its promise, this particular project could produce a truly useful piece of software, because it is trying to mimic the CheckPoint Firewall-1 product. Its "secure logging" feature will employ encryption so that the firewall can log to remote systems without the fear of sniffing attacks.

- **PHP Ipchains project** (http://sourceforge.net/projects/phpchains) The primary strength of this product is that it is based on PHP, which is a truly portable language, and is well supported by Apache Server. Because many other security applications use PHP, this product may allow you to apply skills you have already learned.

- **Positive Control** (http://sourceforge.net/projects/positivecontrol) Not only does this project plan on releasing a GUI, but it also plans on creating a firewall that can detect port scans through *stateful inspection*, which is basically a way for the firewall to maintain and scan its own dynamic database. If this database senses a number of ports that have been scanned in a row, the firewall can take action. Some actions the firewall can take may include automatic firewall reconfiguration and automatic alerts.

 ## Exercise: Using Firestarter to Create a Personal Firewall

1. Make the necessary preparations for your firewall. If you are creating a personal firewall, then you can simply move on to step 2. If you want to use your firewall to masquerade connections, you should understand that Firestarter may not do the best job creating forwarding and nat/masquerading rules, so you may want to create them first. You will see

later in this exercise how you can configure Firestarter to enable masquerading for you.

2. Once you have verified and tested your masquerading (if necessary) copy firestarter-0.7.0-1.i386.rpm from the CD that accompanies this book, or download the latest Firestarter RPM or tarball from http://sourceforge.net/projects/firestarter. The RPM and tarball packages are equivalent. They do not require any special libraries; if you have installed either the Gnome or KDE window managers, you will have no problem.

3. Install Firestarter. If you are using the RPM, you would issue the following command:

```
rpm –ivh firestarter-0.7.0-1.i386.rpm
```

4. Now, start X and enter the following in a terminal:

```
firestarter
```

5. If an existing Ipchains or Iptables configuration exists, you may see the warning shown in Figure 9.3.

   If necessary, click **Yes**. You should note that this warning will also appear if you restart Firestarter. If you are using this wizard on a system that already has masquerading configured, you would click **No** to save this configuration. Firestarter will simply append its configuration to yours.

Figure 9.3 Firestarter Warning

6. When you first launch Firestarter, the configuration wizard, shown in Figure 9.4, should appear automatically.

   If the wizard does not appear, maximize the main interface and go to **Firewall | Run firewall wizard**.

7. Once the wizard begins, click **Next**.

Figure 9.4 The Firestarter Configuration Wizard Initial Screen

8. The Network Device Configuration screen will appear, as shown in Figure 9.5. Select the interface you want to protect, and click **Next**.

   You will notice that in this particular example, the eth0 interface is selected. Firestarter is written well enough so that it will automatically detect all of your interfaces.

Figure 9.5 The Network Device Configuration Screen

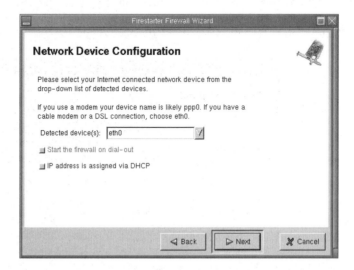

9. The Services Configuration window, shown in Figure 9.6, will appear.

Figure 9.6 The Services Configuration Window

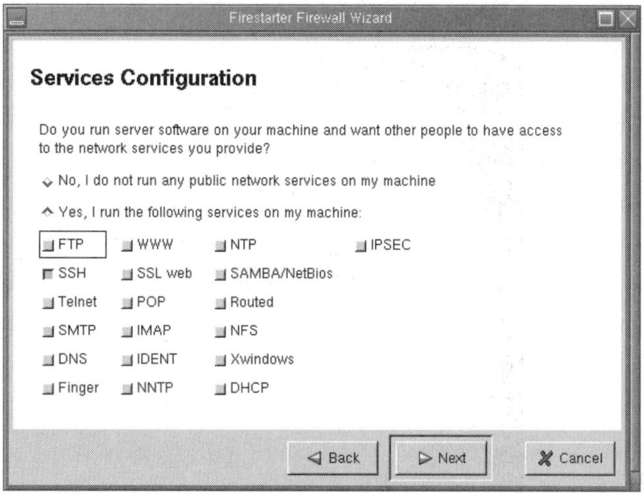

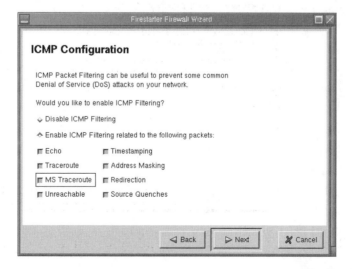

10. Configure the services that you desire. Figure 9.6 shows that only SSH will be allowed to connect to the firewall. Your settings will differ according to your needs. When you are finished selecting the services you want to provide on this interface, click **Next**.

11. The ICMP Configuration screen will appear, as shown in Figure 9.7. By default, Firestarter disables all ICMP filtering, which means that all ICMP packets will be allowed to pass through the firewall. Select

Figure 9.7 The ICMP Configuration Screen

Enable ICMP Filtering, and then select the ICMP packet types that you want to filter. You will notice that in this particular example, no ICMP packets will be allowed to traverse the firewall.

12. When you have selected the ICMP packets you want to block, click **Next**. Firestarter will inform you that it is ready to generate the firewall, as shown in Figure 9.8. Click **Finish** to do so.

Figure 9.8 Completing the Firewall Generation Process in Firestarter

13. The wizard will disappear, and you will see the Firestarter main interface, shown in Figure 9.9.

14. The main interface defaults to the **Firewall hits** tab, which is a graphical logging device. If a packet matches the rules you have generated, it will be instantaneously logged here. From a remote system, generate some traffic that you have blocked. For example, if you have not enabled Telnet support, try to telnet to this system. After enough traffic is generated, you will see the logging screen fill up, as shown in Figure 9.10.

15. Now, select the **Dynamic Rules** tab. From here, you can add rules to those that Firestarter has automatically generated. It is important to understand that Firestarter imposes a fairly strict series of rules. You may need to open up some ports to suit your needs. Following is a brief overview of your options:

   ▪ **Deny all connections from** Allows you to block a specific host. If, for example, you have left the SSH port open to all systems, you

Figure 9.9 The Firestarter Main Interface

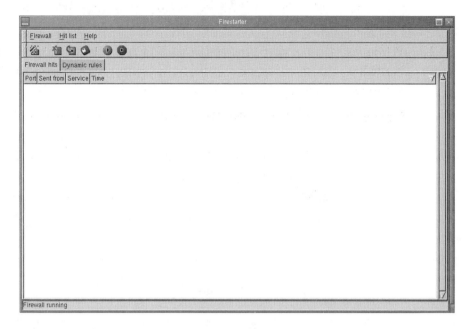

Figure 9.10 Viewing Logged Packet Matches in Firestarter

can specify a host or range of IP addresses here. As with any of the dynamic options, the rules you enter here will override any settings established by either Firestarter or the Firestarter wizard.

- **Allow all connections from** Enables you to allow a host or range of IP addresses full access to your system. Be careful when using this option, because it can expose your firewall to IP spoofing. Remember, it opens all ports on your interface to a remote system.

- **Open service to machine** Allows you to open a specific port or range of ports to a specific host or range of IP addresses.

- **Open service to anyone** Opens a port to all hosts on the network, and any other network. Like the **Allow all connections from** setting, this option is quite powerful, and can reduce your firewall's security. Specifying this option allows any host on your network or on any other to access the port you specify.

You can also add and remove all rules in a particular group, or you can remove all of the dynamic rules you have created.

16. Right-click in the **Allow all connections from** field, and then select **Add new rule**. You will see a dialog box, shown in Figure 9.11, where you can enter either an IP address or a host name. Enter the IP address of a remote host here. Although you can enter a DNS name, it is best if you use an IP address. When you are finished, click **OK**.

Figure 9.11 The Add New Rule Dialog Box

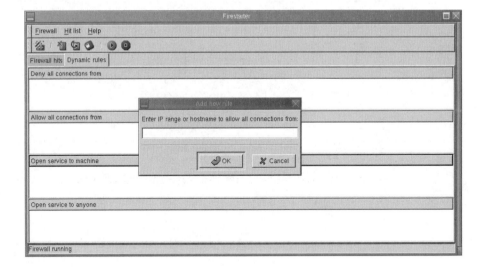

17. You will see that the IP address or host name (if this is what you entered) is entered in the **Allow all connections from** dialog box (Figure 9.12). Test this setting by using the remote client you have specified.

18. Experiment with the additional settings to see how well Firestarter is able to configure the interface to suit your needs.

Figure 9.12 Allowing SSH and Telnet Service to a System Named "keats"

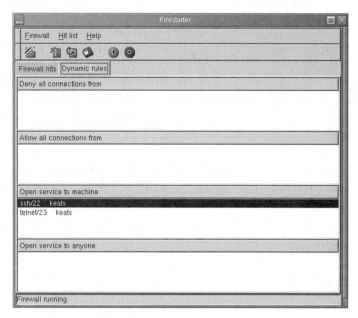

When you have configured Firestarter, open a second terminal and list the chains. If, for example, you are using Iptables, issue the following command:

```
iptables -L
```

19. You will see a list of many different rules, most of which have been added by Firestarter. Consider that some of these rules may not be necessary for your particular situation. Use the **-D** option to delete the rules you do not need. Make sure you test your firewall each time you delete a rule.

20. When you are finished, use the **iptables-save** or **ipchains-save** command to save your rules:

```
ipchains-save > firestarter.chains
iptables-save > firestarter.chains
```

You can then restore your firewall by using the **ipchains-restore** or **iptables-restore** command.

21. It is also possible to save the logs generated by Firestarter. In the main interface, go to **Hit List | Save firewall hit list to file**. You will be asked to enter the name of the text file where the logs will be stored. Do so, and then press **OK**. When you have saved the log file, open it in a text editor. You will see a report that details the connection, including the source IP address, the time of the attempted connection, and the protocol used.

22. When you are finished saving your log, you can clear the log screen and begin logging again.

Exercise: Using Advanced Firestarter Features

1. Go to **Firewall | Preferences** and examine the additional options offered by Firestarter. These include the ability for Firestarter to play a sound whenever a packet matches a rule, starting Firestarter "hidden," so that you do not see the interface, and, the most interesting feature, the one that shows every page in the configuration wizard. You can access this feature by selecting the **Advanced** icon, and then clicking **Show every page in wizard**.

2. When you have done this, restart the wizard. You will then be given additional options, including the ability to create masquerading rules, as shown in Figure 9.13, and the ability to create ToS associations, shown in Figure 9.14.

    This particular page allows you to have Firestarter automatically discover the internal network IP range, which works rather sporadically. In addition, notice that you can also enable specific port forwarding rules. If you do not want to rely on the Autodetect feature, you can specify your own range.

    The ToS configuration feature is effective if you want to give certain services, such as e-mail or the X Windows system, more priority than others have. In this particular example, the choice was made to give priority to server applications, such as FTP, Squid, SSH, SMTP, and POP3. You will, of course, choose the option that best suits you.

    You can choose these settings according to your needs.

3. When you are finished using the wizard, you can then re-edit your settings to create the best firewall for your situation.

Figure 9.13 The IP Masquerade Configuration Screen

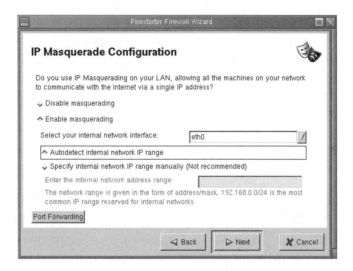

Figure 9.14 The ToS Configuration Screen

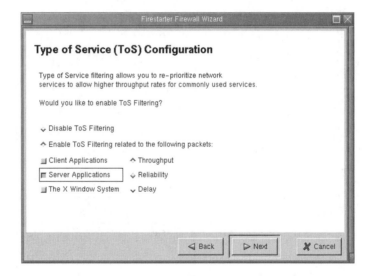

Summary

A firewall is the chief means of establishing a network perimeter. It is vital to separate your own network from all others, as doing so helps you to manage and secure your network hosts. In this chapter, you reviewed concepts essential to firewalling. You have learned about IP forwarding, as well as masquerading and packet filtering. You then used Ipchains and Iptables to create firewall rules.

This chapter also showed you how to enable logging and ToS bits on network traffic, ands how to save, edit, and restore Ipchains and Iptables entries. You were provided with practical advice concerning commands to take, and saw how GUI and automated applications have been created to help build firewalls.

With this information , you now have all of the tools necessary to begin creating your own firewall using either Ipchains or Iptables.

Solutions Fast Track

Understanding the Need for a Firewall

- ☑ Linux natively supports the ability to route and/or filter packets. Modern Linux systems use either *Ipchains* or *Iptables* to do this. Ipchains supports Linux kernel versions up to 2.2. If you are using any kernel newer than 2.2, you must use Iptables. The Iptables package supports packet masquerading and filtering functionality as found in the 2.3 kernel and later. This functionality is known as *netfilter*. Therefore, in order to use Iptables, you must recompile the kernel so that netfilter is installed, and you must install the Iptables package.

- ☑ Ipchains and Iptables also allow you to configure your Linux router to *masquerade* traffic (i.e., to rewrite IP headers so that a packet appears to originate from a certain host), and/or to examine and block traffic. The practice of examining and blocking traffic is often called *packet filtering*.

- ☑ The primary difference between a packet-filtering router (e.g., one created by using Ipchains or Iptables) and a proxy server (e.g., one enabled by Squid) is that a packet-filtering router does not inspect network packets as deeply as a proxy server does. However, proxy servers require more system resources in order to process network packets.

☑ Watch for bug reports concerning Ipchains, Iptables, and the Linux kernel. Keeping current about such changes can help you quickly upgrade your system in case a problem is discovered.

Deploying IP Forwarding and Masquerading

☑ IP forwarding is the ability for a Linux system to act as a router.

☑ A Linux system with simple IP forwarding enabled can route any network address to another. If you are allotted a range of IP addresses from a local or regional Internet registry, you can use a multihomed Linux system to route this set of addresses to another network.

☑ In order to allow private network addresses to reach the Internet, you need to invoke Ipchains/Iptables-based IP masquerading.

☑ In a Linux router, you can use either Ipchains or Iptables to forward and/or alter the IP headers of packets originating from private-IP address networks to pass through Internet routers. Both Ipchains and Iptables do this by processing IP packets through the Linux kernel. You should note that this option is not necessarily secure—IP masquerading leaves all client hosts wide open to attack.

☑ Masquerading is when your Linux system rewrites the IP headers of a network packet so that the packet appears to originate from a different host. The practice of rewriting IP packets is colloquially known as *packet mangling*. Masquerading is useful because you can use it to invoke network address translation (NAT), where one IP address can stand in for several.

☑ Translating the private to routable Internet address is accomplished by a database stored on the Ipchains/Iptables-based Linux router. The Linux masquerading router keeps this database so that it knows how to "untranslate," as it were, the packets that have been mangled so that they can then be addressed to the local, private network.

Configuring Your Firewall to Filter Network Packets

☑ To create packet-filtering rules for outgoing traffic, configure your Linux firewall to deny all outgoing traffic unless explicitly allowed. Where incoming traffic is concerned, you have many options, including to forbid all incoming traffic unless it is part of an already established session, and to disable all forwarding except for networks that require it.

☑ Most Linux operating systems, such as Red Hat, Slackware, SuSE, and Caldera, support IP forwarding, masquerading, and firewalling by default. However, you may have to reconfigure your kernel in order to provide full functionality.

Understanding Tables and Chains in a Linux Firewall

☑ Iptables derives its name from the three default tables it uses: *filter*, *nat*, and *mangle*. Each interface on your system can have its packets managed and modified by the chains contained in each of these tables.

☑ A chain is a series of actions to take on a packet. Whenever you use Ipchains or Iptables to configure a firewall, the proper perspective to adopt is to view all packets from the firewall itself.

☑ If you are using the filter table, each interface on your network has three different default chains: INPUT, FORWARD, and OUTPUT.

☑ Ipchains and Iptables use built-in targets to specify the destination of a packet. By far, the common most built-in targets are DROP and ACCEPT.

Logging Packets at the Firewall

☑ The Iptables **-l** option allows you to log matching packets. You can insert **-l** into any rule, as long as you do not interrupt a particular option. Iptables allows you to log packets in a more sophisticated way because it uses the LOG target, which you specify just like DROP or ACCEPT.

☑ By default, Iptables will limit logging of packets. The default limit rate is three logging instances an hour. This behavior is meant to ensure that log files do not get too large.

☑ An example used in this section uses Ipchains and Iptables commands to add and remove packet-filtering rules, prohibiting every service from entering your firewall, except for Secure Shell (SSH), which uses port 22. This would not allow any user interactively logged in to the system to check e-mail or any other Internet-based service—the rule is restrictive, but is designed to lock down the firewall as much as possible.

☑ With Iptables, you can reject specific ICMP types.

☑ Port redirection in Ipchains and Iptables is where a packet destined for a certain port (say, port 80) is received by an interface, and is then sent to another port, using the REDIRECT target. Redirecting ports is common in networks that use proxy servers.

Configuring a Firewall

☑ Regardless of whether you are using Ipchains or Iptables, the first thing you will have to do for your firewall is to flush all existing rules using the **-F** option. Then, you need to use the **-P** option to set the firewall policies to deny all connections by default. The subsequent rules you create will then allow the protocols you really want. Then, use the necessary commands to enable forwarding and masquerading. Without this foundation, you will not be able to forward packets at all, and thus firewalling them would be superfluous.

☑ Many times, a hacker will try to use your firewall as a default gateway and try to spoof internal packets. If a firewall's "Internet interface" (i.e., the one that is responsible for addressing packets to the Internet) is not configured to explicitly deny packets from the network, then you are susceptible to this attack.

☑ The example describing allowing inbound and outbound TCP connections illustrates that with Ipchains and Iptables, the **!** character reverses the meaning of anything that is in front of it.

☑ Creating the ideal packet-filtering rules requires some trial and error, as well as research specific to your own situation.

Counting Bandwidth Usage

☑ A Linux firewall can inform you about the number of packets it has processed, in addition to blocking and logging attacks. The process of counting packets is often called *packet accounting*.

☑ Many routers, including Linux routers using Ipchains or Iptables, are capable of shaping traffic as it passes through. The IP header for all packets has a special field called the Type of Service (ToS) field, which allows you to prioritize traffic as it passes through the router.

☑ The main reason why you would set the ToS field in network traffic is to cut down on network congestion, especially in networks that have high amounts of traffic.

Using and Obtaining Automated Firewall Scripts and Graphical Firewall Utilities

☑ Several attempts have been made to automate the process of creating a firewall in Linux. Many of these utilities are quite useful, although they are mostly effective in *beginning* your firewall configuration; you will likely have to customize the rules these applications generate.

☑ Most of these applications are still in beta form, so remember that they often provide limited functionality.

☑ Firestarter is a fairly sophisticated graphical tool that supports both Ipchains and Iptables. It can be used to create a personal firewall, but also supports multihomed systems.

☑ Mason is designed to first listen in on traffic passing through your firewall, and then generate Ipchains or ipfwadm (the precursor to ipchains and Iptables) rules.

☑ Firewall Builder is in many ways the most ambitious open source GUI tool. It allows you to create rules for multiple interfaces, networks, and hosts.

Frequently Asked Questions

The following Frequently Asked Questions, answered by the authors of this book, are designed to both measure your understanding of the concepts presented in this chapter and to assist you with real-life implementation of these concepts. To have your questions about this chapter answered by the author, browse to **www.syngress.com/solutions** and click on the **"Ask the Author"** form.

Q: I am using Iptables. Why can't I use the –MASQ target for the INPUT chain?

A: Because Iptables uses a completely different table to do masquerading. In Iptables, the INPUT chain is used for packets that are destined to the firewall system. You must create a rule that specifies the nat table.

Q: I just got used to Ipchains rather than using ipfwadm. Now, I have to get used to using Iptables. Will this ever end?

A: Welcome to the world of the open source community, my friend. It is hoped that Iptables will undergo evolutionary rather than revolutionary changes from now on. Because it is much more sophisticated than Ipchains, and because it will take some time for the 2.5 kernel to become stable enough to become 2.6, it is likely that we will not have to learn a new application any time soon.

Q: I am using Firestarter. It has automatically discovered my interface. However, it seems to block all traffic, even if I specify that I am using SSH and other protocols. What do I do?

A: Manually edit the Iptables chains and remote any offending entries. You can also access the Dynamic rules tab and open up services to specific hosts there. Because Firestarter uses the **-A** option to add a rule, any addition you specify will become an exception to the restrictive rule set created by Firestarter.

Q: Do I have to keep Firestarter running in order for the firewall to be in place?

A: No. However, the Firestarter "Firewall hits" list will not be updated, nor will Firestarter inform you of hits using the sound option. If you establish logging by issuing manual Ipchains or Iptables commands, you can check hits by viewing the /var/log/messages file using the **tail -f** command.

Q: When I use Iptables to list my rules, the listing just hangs, or is very slow. What is going on?

A: One of your rules has disabled DNS lookup. You will find that the same problem will arise if you try to use netstat. Either delete the offending rule, or append a rule that opens up ports above 1023 to access your DNS server at both UDP and TCP port 53.

Q: I am still using a dial-up connection (ppp0). Can I use this dial-up modem to provide access to the rest of my network?

A: Certainly. Just substitute the ppp0 interface for eth0 in many of the examples in this chapter, and you will be up and running in no time.

Q: I have set my default policy to DROP, and now I can't access anything on the network. I have flushed all of the rules, but the policy is still at DROP. What do I do now?

A: Use the **–P** option to change the default policy to ACCEPT.

Q: I am using Ipchains, yet I can't seem to add anything to the INPUT, FORWARD, or OUTPUT chains. Why not?

A: Because Ipchains is case sensitive, and does not use the INPUT, FORWARD, or OUTPUT chains. Specify the input, forward, or output chains, and you will be in good shape. This can be rather confusing, because Iptables is also case specific, and uses the INPUT, FORWARD, and OUTPUT chains.

Q: I have configured masquerading, and have also created several rules that seem to protect my network. However, I used commands different from yours. How come?

A: In Linux, as with all of the Unix community, there is always more than one way to accomplish your goals. This can be liberating, but also rather frustrating. If you are able to get a secure firewall going, congratulations. Now, just remember that you need to test and log your firewall so that you verify that it is helping to protect your network.

Q: Is a Linux firewall ideal for a corporate environment?

A: The answer for this question lies with management, really. Many busy, large environments use Linux routers and firewalls. However, you should ensure that your company's IT and security policies allow the use of Linux systems. You should also test your implementation in an isolated subnet before bringing it into production.

Chapter 10

Deploying the Squid Web Proxy Cache Server

Solutions in this chapter:

- Benefits of Proxy Server Implementation

- Differentiating between a Packet Filter and a Proxy Server

- Implementing the Squid Web Proxy Cache Server

- Configuring Proxy Clients

☑ Summary

☑ Solutions Fast Track

☑ Frequently Asked Questions

507

Introduction

In Chapter 9, "Implementing a Firewall with Ipchains and Iptables," you learned about packet filtering. However, packet filtering is only one way to create a network perimeter. Using proxy cache services, it is possible to filter traffic in a more specific way. In this chapter, you will learn the advantages of using proxy caching on your network, and understand the differences between a packet filter and a proxy server. You will also configure a proxy caching server and a proxy client, and test and troubleshoot a proxy cache server. The proxy cache you will implement in this chapter is called the Squid Web Proxy Cache server.

Benefits of Proxy Server Implementation

A proxy server is an intermediary between hosts on different or separate networks, such as a local area network (LAN) and the Internet. It is used to implement caching for certain services, and for security and administrative control. Proxy servers can implement different functions, such as proxy caching and Network Address Translation (NAT). NAT is technically the function of a network-level gateway, but some vendors include this functionality in their proxy server products as well.

Proxy Caching

Proxy cache servers are implemented at the Application layer and process specific Internet protocols, such as Hypertext Transfer Protocol (HTTP) and File Transfer Protocol (FTP). Rules are set up on the proxy server to determine how a workstation request should be processed.

One of the main tasks of a proxy server is to cache Web pages and FTP files for proxy clients. These types of proxy servers are called *proxy cache servers*. Caching increases the performance of the network by decreasing the amount of data transferred from outside of a local network.

To implement proxy caching, each workstation on the network is configured as a proxy client for a specific service. For example, a Web proxy client would configure his or her browser to acknowledge the proxy server. When the client makes a Web browser request to download a certain Web page, the client's browser makes the request to the proxy server. The proxy server has a cache of recently visited Web pages. This cache contains Web pages that workstations throughout the network have recently downloaded.

The proxy server checks its cache to see if the Web page exists. If the page exists in the cache, then the cached page is sent to the client. If the page does not exist in the cache, the proxy server downloads the client's Web page from the specific Web site, enters it into the cache, and sends the page to the workstation.

To ensure that the Web pages in the proxy cache are not out of date, proxy cache data expires after a preset time. In the Squid program, this setting is called the object *refresh time*. The refresh time ensures that old data is not transferred to the proxy clients.

This process increases network performance because the Web page is immediately downloaded to the client from the proxy server without having to download the Web page from the Internet each time. This speeds up Internet access on the network and saves bandwidth. This seemingly simple operation of adding a small amount of data to a Web cache has a significant impact on browsing speed and bandwidth usage over the network. The Web proxy concept is shown in Figure 10.1.

Figure 10.1 Demonstrating a Proxy Server's Web Caching Function

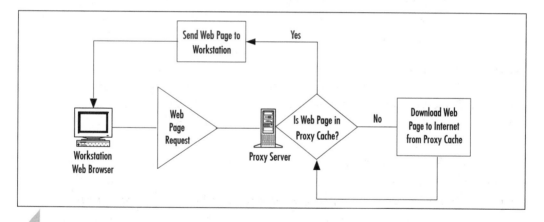

NOTE

One benefit of proxy servers is that the proxy administrator can add rules to filter content. For example, you can filter out Web page requests that contain certain words in the address. If a supervisor from marketing complains that his marketing personnel are spending all of their time looking for other jobs, he could have the administrator create proxy rules to filter out the addresses of popular job search sites, denying all requests for, say, www.needajobfast.com!

NOTE

The correct term for cached content, such as text files, sound files, video clips, etc., is *object*.

Table 10.1 lists the advantages of using a proxy–caching server.

Table 10.1 Benefits of Proxy Caching

Benefit	Description
Reduced bandwidth costs	Internet infrastructure costs are reduced significantly because proxy caching reduces bandwidth usage.
Increased network performance	The network runs faster because less bandwidth is used to access the Internet.
Increased network performance during traffic spikes	Even networks that have a great deal of bandwidth can experience traffic spikes during major events, such as a popular video-streamed broadcast. Caching can help prevent these slow response periods.
Load balancing	Caching servers can cache Web site objects to balance the original Web server's load.
Cache aborted requests	If a user aborts a download, proxy caches can continue to download the object so it will be available to the next user.
Functions when Internet connection is down	If your Internet connection fails, the proxy cache will log the error and send the requested objects (if available, including out-of-date objects) from the cache. The impact of a large-scale Internet outage is reduced.

Network Address Translation

The proxy cache is only one mechanism of a proxy server. Many proxy servers are distributed with the ability to support Network Address Translation (NAT).

NAT allows a company's internal network address to be hidden from the Internet. The company is represented on the Internet as one IP address that is not related to the company's internal IP addresses.

NOTE

NAT is technically the function of a network-level gateway, but many vendors, such as Microsoft, include this functionality in their proxy server products.

Using a proxy server, all Internet-bound traffic within the company is sent to the proxy server. The proxy gives each packet another IP address before transmitting it across the Internet. When the response packet arrives, the proxy server sends it to the appropriate company host who made the initial request. This procedure protects the actual addresses of the internal network from the Internet. Therefore, it is much more difficult for a hacker to attack a system, since the address of the protected system is unknown and is not accessible directly from the Internet. Figure 10.2 shows the NAT process using a proxy server.

Figure 10.2 Demonstrating the Network Address Translation (NAT) Function

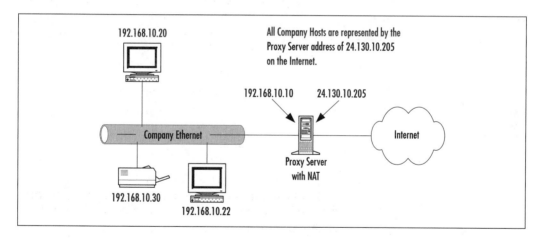

This chapter focuses on the caching services of a proxy server by implementing the Squid Web Proxy Cache service. NAT is presented so you will understand this network-level gateway service that is often added to proxy servers.

Differentiating between a Packet Filter and a Proxy Server

It is common to confuse a packet filter with a proxy server. Both services are placed on the network edge. Both serve as an intermediary between a LAN and the Internet. Both have the capability to filter traffic transmitted in to and out of the network. Both use rules to determine whether certain traffic is allowed to pass through the server or be discarded. So, you may ask, what is the difference?

Basically, a packet filter does not go as deep into a packet as a proxy server. A packet filter analyzes traffic at the Network (Layer 3) and Transport layers (Layer 4) of the Open Systems Interconnection (OSI) reference model. For example, a packet filter determines whether it will allow a certain IP address or IP address range to pass through. If your network is attacked from a consistent range of source IP addresses, you can create a rule to discard all packets that originate from that IP address range. You can also filter traffic by service, or port number. For example, you could create a rule to discard all traffic directed at certain listening ports, such as FTP, rlogin and Telnet traffic, or within a port number range. You can also filter ICMP packets by type/code, which allows you to discard only certain types of ICMP traffic. This is helpful in protecting yourself from common distributed denial-of-service (DDoS) attacks. Because packet filters work at these layers, they are often implemented on routers at the network edge.

A proxy server is capable of analyzing packets at the Application layer (Layer 7) of the OSI model. This allows much more flexibility, because the traffic within one service, such as port 80 (HTTP) traffic, can be filtered. As mentioned earlier, this allows proxy servers to analyze HTTP or FTP traffic, and determine whether the traffic will pass through. If a rule exists that prevents any Web address with "jobs" in it, then any HTTP URL request with "jobs" in it will be discarded. You will implement a Web proxy cache server in the next section. A proxy server is usually installed on an application server at the network edge. Figure 10.3 shows one of the differences between a packet filter and a proxy server.

In this chapter, you will implement a proxy server with Web caching services. The proxy server you will install, configure, and run is the Squid Web Proxy Cache, which is a Unix full-featured Web proxy cache.

Figure 10.3 One of the Differences between a Packet Filter and a Proxy Server

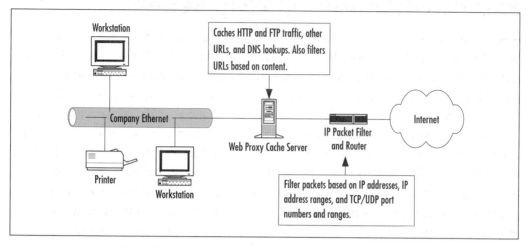

Implementing the Squid Web Proxy Cache Server

The Squid Web Proxy Cache server is a free, Unix open source Web proxy cache. It allows administrators to set up a Web proxy caching service, add access controls (rules), and even cache DNS lookups. The Squid home page is located at www.squid-cache.org, as shown in Figure 10.4.

Figure 10.4 Squid Web Proxy Cache Home Page

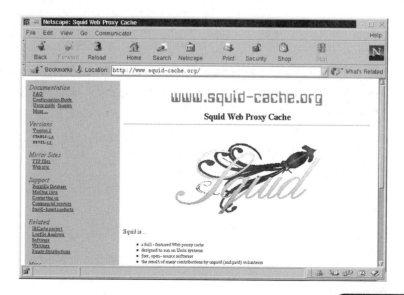

NOTE

It is important to point out that Squid is a Web proxy-caching server only. It does not support other proxy functions, such as NAT or firewall functions.

Squid originated from a program developed by the Harvest project called *cached (Cache Daemon)*. The National Science Foundation (NSF) funds Squid development through the National Laboratory of Network Research (NLANR).

Squid is a Web proxy cache that conforms to the HTTP 1.1 specification. It is used only by proxy clients, such as Web browsers, that access the Internet using HTTP, Gopher, and FTP. Furthermore, it does not handle the majority of Internet protocols. That means that it cannot be used for protocols that support applications such as videoconferencing, newsgroups, RealAudio, or video games such as *Quake*. The main reason for this limitation is that Squid does not support client programs that use UDP. Squid uses UDP for inter-cache communication only.

Any client protocol supported by Squid must be sent as a proxy request in HTTP format. Most browsers support this function, so the following client protocols are supported on most networks that implement Squid:

- FTP

- HTTP

- Secure Sockets Layer (SSL)

- Wide Area Information Server (WAIS)

- Gopher

The protocols will work if you request them using your browser, and if your browser is configured as a proxy client to the Web proxy-cache server. You will accomplish this task later in the chapter.

Squid also supports internal and management protocols. These protocols are used between caches that might exist on different (or the same) proxy-caching servers, or for managing a proxy cache. The supported inter-cache and management protocols are:

- **Internet Cache Protocol (ICP)** Queries other caches for a specific object.

- **Cache Digest** Retrieves an object index from other caches.

- **HTTP** Retrieves objects from other caches.

- **Hypertext Caching Protocol (HTCP)** Currently being added to Squid (not implemented on a wide scale yet).

- **Simple Network Management Protocol (SNMP)** Retrieves information about the proxy cache and sends it to a Network Management Station (NMS) for analysis.

Despite these limitations, Squid is very popular because the Web proxy-cache services are integral to almost all networks connected to the Internet. For example, the products listed in Table 10.2 are based on Squid.

Table 10.2 List of Commercial Products Based on Squid

Product	Description
CacheRaq4	Squid-based proxy cache designed for Linux with a MIPS CPU. Sun Microsystems acquired Cobalt, the creator of this product.
Tsunami	Squid-based proxy cache that runs on Linux. Swell Technologies is the creator of this product.
CacheXpress	Squid-based proxy cache created by Industrial Code and Logic (INDCL). Includes a version for Windows.
Netfilter4.1	A monitoring and traffic management program based on Squid and developed by nXp Technologies.
N2H2	Provides products for filtering solutions. For example, their N2H2 for Microsoft Proxy 2.0 and N2H2 for ISA add enhanced content filtering to these products, and are based on Squid.

These commercial products are supported by their various vendors. Therefore, technical support is available in case you run into any problems. Squid is supported by Visolve.com, which provides free basic support for open source products. These products include Squid, Apache, and Linux itself. Their Web site is located at www.visolve.com. The Squid site contains links to Visolve.com—use their free services at your own risk. The Visolve.com Web site is shown in Figure 10.5.

Figure 10.5 Free Basic Support for Squid and Other Open Source Products at Visolve.com

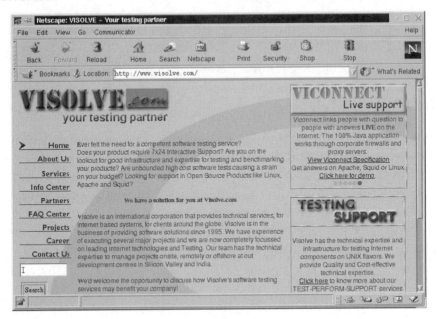

System Requirements Specific to Proxy Caching

By nature, Squid uses certain system resources more than others do. The two main hardware subsystems that Squid (or any other proxy cache) uses heavily and must therefore perform well are the disk random seek time and the amount of system memory.

- **Disk random seek time** When you purchase a disk, the documentation should include a random seek time number. For a proxy cache, make sure this number is as low as possible. The problem is that operating systems try to speed up disk access times using various methods that usually slow the system's performance.

- **Amount of system memory** RAM is also extremely important when using a proxy cache. Squid keeps an in-memory table of its objects in RAM, which should always remain in RAM. If part of the table goes to swap, the performance of Squid is greatly degraded. Squid is one process, so any swapping will slow the program. To give you an idea of the object index size, if you have 16GB of objects stored in your cache, you will require approximately 96MB of RAM for the object index. Ensure you have as much RAM as possible in the system.

Other system requirements, such as CPU speed, are not as important. Processor speed will be noticed during startup when the system must determine the contents of its cache and create the object index. Other than that, a single CPU system usually performs well. A multiprocessor system does not usually make a difference in the proxy cache performance because Squid contains a small portion of threaded code.

Installing Squid

Squid is provided as an RPM package in Red Hat Linux. If you completed a custom installation and installed everything on your Red Hat Linux system, then Squid is already installed. If not, you need to download it at a trusted site, or install it from your Red Hat CD. We have provided version 2.3 on the companion CD (squid2.3.STABLE4-1.i386.rpm). You can also download the source files and compile it. The source code is beneficial because it allows you to turn on some compile-time options that are not included in the binary version. For example, SNMP support is not included in the binary version. If SNMP support is required, you must download and compile the source version of Squid.

The Squid developers only create the source code, but they concentrate on making it as portable as possible. Therefore, other developers are responsible for porting to the different operating systems. The following operating systems have Squid available:

- Linux
- SCO Unix
- BSD/OS
- NetBSD
- MkLinux
- Solaris
- NeXTStep
- OS/2 Warp
- AIX

The location of each of these download sites is available at www.squid-cache .org/platforms.html. This Web site changes as Squid is ported to new operating systems. If your operating system is different from Linux, then download the corresponding version from the site, as shown in Figure 10.6.

Figure 10.6 Downloading Ported Versions of Squid for Multiple Platforms

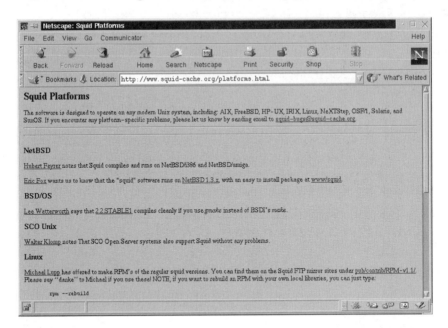

WARNING

When you download binary RPMs, always make sure that you are downloading them from a trusted source. RPMs are installed as root, which means they can do *anything* to your system. They can add new users, reconfigure settings, install new files, and overwrite existing ones. It is possible that an unscrupulous programmer could purposely distribute RPMs meant to exploit and install vulnerabilities into systems. To avoid any security threats, always download your binary RPMs from a trusted source. Most vendor and open source project download sites can be trusted.

You can download binary versions of squid at the Red Hat Web site at www.redhat.com. You can download the Squid development team source code from the Squid site at www.squid-cache.org/Versions/v2/, as shown in Figure 10.7. Make sure you download a stable version of Squid. Any Squid 2.*x* stable version will perform well on your system. Both of the Squid download sites mentioned are trusted.

Figure 10.7 Downloading the Squid Source Version from the Trusted Squid Site

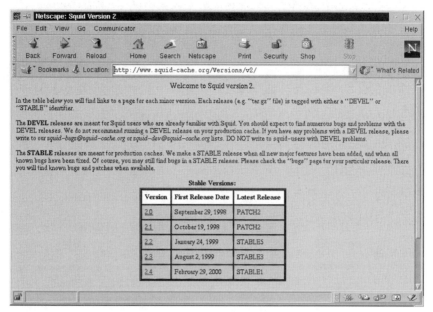

For the following demonstration, we'll use the Red Hat Linux binary RPM included with the Red Hat Linux 7.*x* distribution. For instructions on compiling the Squid source version, visit http://squid-docs.sourceforge.net/latest/html/x366.htm. Complete the following steps to make sure that Squid is installed on your Red Hat Linux system.

1. To ensure the Squid RPM is installed on your system, enter the following:

```
rpm -qa | grep squid
```

2. You should receive the following response if Squid is installed:

```
squid-2.3.STABLE4-1
```

   If you receive this response, you are ready to configure Squid.

3. If you receive no response, access www.redhat.com to click the **Download** link. Perform an RPM search by entering **squid** into the **Find Latest RPMs By Keyword** field. Click **Search**. The latest Squid version provided as an RPM will appear; in this case, it is squid-2.3.STABLE4-1, as shown in Figure 10.8. This RPM is also located on the accompanying CD.

Figure 10.8 Downloading a Squid RPM for Red Hat Linux 7

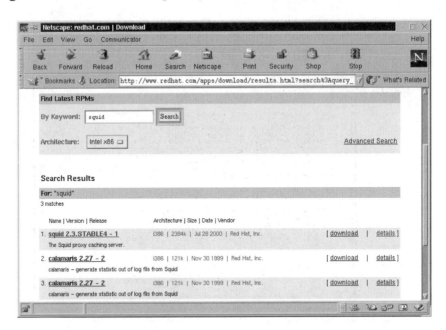

4. Download the latest stable version of Squid.

5. Install the RPM by using the **rpm –i** command. Once installed, you are ready to configure Squid.

Configuring Squid

Once Squid is installed, you must configure it using the /etc/squid/squid.conf file. This file defines the Squid configurations, such as the HTTP port number on which Squid listens for HTTP requests, incoming and outgoing requests, timeout information, and firewall access data. During Squid installation, a /etc/squid/ squid.conf file was created.

The squid.conf file is configured for the Squid configuration default settings and can be used after several changes. You must make changes because squid.conf denies access to all browsers by default. Squid is completely useless until you make changes to the squid.conf.

As it states in the default Squid configuration file, if you do not need to change a default setting, then you do not need to uncomment the setting. The default Squid configuration file, /etc/squid/squid.conf, is shown in Figure 10.9.

Figure 10.9 Configuring Squid with the /etc/squid/squid.conf File

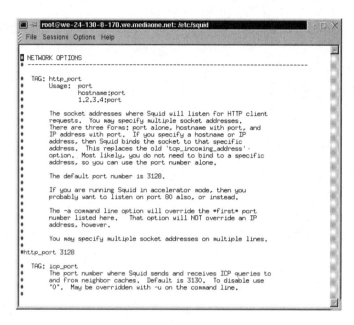

Each configuration option in squid.conf is identified as a *tag*. Each tag is a Squid configuration. For example, the HTTP client request port setting is identified as the http_port tag. We will refer to the squid.conf settings as tags.

In Figure 10.9, the squid.conf file displays the Network Options section. It shows the configuration for the socket address on which Squid will listen for HTTP client requests. The default port number specified, TCP port 3128, is also the default port used by proxy clients to send requests to the proxy cache server. If you change this port on the proxy cache server, you will need to change it on the proxy clients as well.

NOTE

Notice that all of the tags in the squid.conf file are commented out. This means that Squid will use the default settings when no tags are specified. In theory, this file could be empty, and Squid will run the defaults settings just the same. If you specify a tag, then Squid will use that tag instead of the default setting. Also note that a file containing the original default settings of /etc/squid/squid.conf is listed in /etc/squid/squid.conf.default.

The Squid "accelerator mode" mentioned in the http_port description allows Squid to act as a Web server. Squid basically translates client Web requests by changing the destination server and port, and sends the request to a Web server. The response is cached, and Squid sends it to the client. This reduces traffic to the Web server (it "accelerates" the slow Web server) and can protect the Web server through filtering. This chapter will not demonstrate accelerator mode, but you should be aware of it.

The http_port Tag

The http_port tag configures the HTTP port on which Squid listens for proxy clients. By default, Squid does not listen for proxy clients on any ports. Therefore, you have to open at least one port for Squid to work using the http_port tag. The default port is 3128, as shown in Figure 10.9. Port 8080 is also often used for this service. You can configure Squid to listen on both ports by including each number in the http_port tag. In the following steps, you will configure Squid to listen on ports 3128 and 8080 for proxy clients.

1. Open the /etc/squid/squid.conf file by entering:

   ```
   vi /etc/squid/squid.conf
   ```

2. Press **i** to enter Insert mode. Locate the http_port setting:

   ```
   # http_port 3128
   ```

3. Remove the comment (#) and add port 8080 to the setting by entering:

   ```
   http_port 3128 8080
   ```

4. Your http_port tag should resemble Figure 10.10.

   Figure 10.10 Configuring the http_port tag to Listen on Ports 3128 and 8080

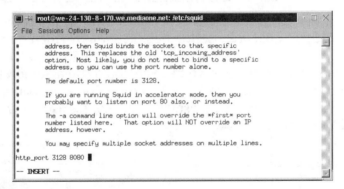

5. Click **Esc** to exit Insert mode. Enter the following to write the file:

    : w

You will configure the squid.conf file further in the next section.

The Cache_dir Tag

The cache_dir tag specifies where the cached data is stored. You can specify different directories for your cache directory by using more than one cache_dir tag in squid.conf. For this demonstration, you will only use one cache directory. Figure 10.11 shows the default settings for the cache_dir tag.

Figure 10.11 Configuring the cache_dir Tag in the squid.conf File

By default, the following cache_dir tag value is presented:

cache_dir ufs /var/spool/squid 100 16 256

The default cach_dir tag is broken down and defined in Table 10.3.

Table 10.3 Defining the Default cache_dir tag in the squid.conf File

Tag Value	Description
cache_dir	Defines the values of the cache directory used for Squid.
ufs	Squid assumes that a Unix file system (ufs) is used for the cache's storage system.
/var/spool/squid	The directory for all cached objects will be /var/spool/squid.
100	The amount of cached data that Squid will store in the caching directory. The default cache size is 100MB.
16	Sets the number of subdirectories to create in the cache. Squid then divides the cached objects into these subdirectories to speed up disk access. For example, Squid will find an object much faster by searching several smaller directories of files, instead of one directory with several hundred thousand objects.
256	Sets the number of second-tier subdirectories to create in the cache. If your cache is extremely large, you may want to increase these values. For this demonstration, and for most implementations, these subdirectory values are sufficient.

You can change these values to meet your particular needs. If you do, remember to remove the comment (#) in front of the tag to activate your changes. If you do not remove the comment, the default values will be used.

For this demonstration, you will use the cache_dir tag default values. The /var/spool/squid caching directory was automatically created when Squid was installed. Verify that the default cache directory exists by completing the following steps:

1. Access the spool directory by entering the following command:

```
cd /var/spool
```

2. List the directory contents to confirm your caching directory exists. Enter:

```
ls
```

3. You should receive a response similar to the following, depending on your system configuration. The squid directory is included.

```
Anacron  cron  lpd  mqueue  rwho  slrnpull  up2date  uucppublic
voice  at  fax  mail  news  samba  squid  ucp  vbox
```

The acl Tag

The acl tag allows you to define an access list. The access list can include client IP addresses, a range of IP addresses, a URL host's IP address, a local socket IP address, or domains. Any access list you define using the acl tag can later be used to allow or deny requests to the cache server. For example, if you define a range of addresses using the acl tag, you can allow any system using an address from this range of IP addresses to use the proxy cache. The acl tag section of the squid.conf file is shown in Figure 10.12.

Figure 10.12 Configuring the acl Tag to Define Access Lists

It is important for you to define access control lists. If you do not, you will not have any definitions to create customized rules. When Squid finds a rule, such as "deny all systems from the IP address range of 192.168.3.1 through 192.168.3.254," it will check that a corresponding acl is created that defines this IP address range.

In this demonstration, you will create an access list that includes the proxy clients that will access your proxy cache server. You will define them by IP address.

1. Open the /etc/squid/squid.conf file by entering (if not already opened):

   ```
   vi /etc/squid/squid.conf
   ```

2. Locate the acl tags defaults section. Press **i** to enter Insert mode.

3. Enter the following acl tags immediately after the acl localhost src 127.0.0.1/255.255.255.255 entry (your addresses will differ depending on your proxy clients):

```
acl proxy_client1 src 24.130.8.227/255.255.252.0
acl proxy_client2 src 24.130.10.205/255.255.252.0
```

4. Your squid.conf file should resemble Figure 10.13.

Figure 10.13 Defining Specific Proxy Clients with the acl Tag

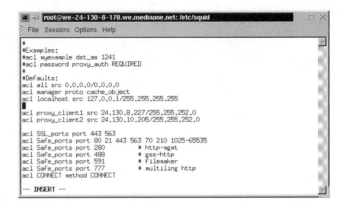

5. Press **Esc** to exit Insert mode. Enter the following to write the file:

```
:w
```

You will configure the squid.conf file further in the next section.

The http_access Tag

The http_access tag permits or denies access to Squid. You can allow or deny all requests. You can also allow or deny requests based on a defined access list. If you remove all of the http_access entries, all requests are allowed by default.

Proxy clients will be unable to use the Squid proxy-caching server until you modify the http_access tags. Please note that some level of access control is recommended, so do not remove all of the http_access tags. The http_access tag section of the squid.conf file is shown in Figure 10.14.

For this demonstration, you will set up a simple access control. You will allow only the systems on your network to use the proxy cache. Each system will be specified by its IP address, as defined in the access control list (acl tag). This system works well for small businesses. To implement access control in a larger organization, you should create classes or users, and then allow or deny these classes. You can place stricter access control after Squid is running by viewing the documentation at www.squid-proxy.org.

Figure 10.14 Configuring the http_access tag to Allow or Deny Squid Requests

NOTE

Squid should never be used without some type of authentication system or access control list. You must restrict Internet users from relaying requests through your Web proxy cache.

To implement access control to your proxy cache, complete the following steps. In this demonstration, there are two proxy clients defined in the acl, proxy_client1 and proxy_client2, that need to use the proxy cache. By default, the localhost can already use the proxy cache.

1. Open the /etc/squid/squid.conf file by entering (if not already opened):

    ```
    vi /etc/squid/squid.conf
    ```

2. Locate the http_access tags. Press **I** to enter Insert mode.

3. Enter the following http_access tags immediately before the http_access deny all entry (your acl names might differ):

```
http_access allow proxy_client1
http_access allow proxy_client2
```

4. Your squid.conf file should resemble Figure 10.15.

   Figure 10.15 Configuring the http_access Tag to Allow Specific Proxy Clients

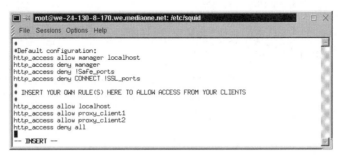

5. Press **Esc** to exit Insert mode. Enter the following to write and quit the file:

```
:wq
```

Always leave the default access control rules, such as http_access deny all, in your squid.conf file. These entries stop people from exploiting your cache. For example, although the last entry states http_access deny all, it still allows incoming requests from the clients you explicitly identify. All other requests will be denied.

The default http_access deny entries in the first part of Figure 10.15 protect your cache from some obscure vulnerabilities. These problems include cache tunneling with SSL CONNECTs, bandwidth loops that consume bandwidth, and other access concerns.

Starting and Testing Squid

You have configured Squid for your network environment. To determine if it is functioning, you must start the Squid service, and then use the Squid client program on the localhost to ensure Web page data is being written to the cache. The Squid client displays data as it is written to the cache, and is extremely helpful in proving the proxy cache is working, and when troubleshooting any problems. Complete the following steps to start and test Squid.

1. Start the Squid proxy cache by entering the following:

   ```
   /etc/rc.d/init.d/squid start
   ```

2. Test that Squid is working by using the Squid client program. Enter:

   ```
   client http://www.squid-cache.org
   ```

3. The data written to the cache is displayed in your terminal, as shown in Figure 10.16. If no data is written, you need to revisit the squid.conf file and determine any incorrect configurations.

Figure 10.16 Testing Squid Using the Squid Client to Witness Web Page Data Written to the Proxy Cache

You have successfully started and tested the Squid Web Proxy Cache server. Now you must configure proxy clients to use the cache. You will learn how to configure a proxy client in Netscape Navigator, Internet Explorer, and Lynx.

Configuring Proxy Clients

A proxy client is a system that uses the services of a Web proxy-caching server. Depending on your network configuration, a client may or may not have to be configured as a proxy client in order to use a Web proxy cache server. For example, some firewalls are configured to forward all port 80 traffic leaving the network to the Web proxy cache server. In this case, the proxy clients do not need manual configuration. In other cases, the client automatically detects the proxy server information on the network and uses it for all Internet access. For this demonstration, you will configure a proxy client to use your Squid Web Proxy Cache.

Configuring a proxy client is far easier than configuring Squid. All proxy client configuration is completed within the browser application. This demonstration will show you how to configure three browsers for a proxy server. One system is a Linux system running Netscape Navigator and Lynx. The other system is a Microsoft Windows Millennium Edition system running Internet Explorer.

NOTE

The proxy clients you configure in this demonstration must be the same proxy clients you added to the /etc/squid/squid.conf file.

Configuring Netscape Navigator and Lynx

In this demonstration, you will configure Netscape Navigator and Lynx on a Linux system. The client configured in the following steps is the proxy_client2 acl entry from the squid.conf file.

Configuring Netscape Navigator

In this section, you will configure the Netscape Navigator browser so it sends all Web requests to the Squid Web Proxy Cache server.

1. Log in to a Linux proxy client that you configured in squid.conf.
2. Start X Windows by entering:

   ```
   startx
   ```

3. Open **Netscape Navigator**.
4. Click the **View** menu, and choose the **Preferences** option.
5. In the **Category** column, expand the **Advanced** tree and click **Proxies**. The proxy configuration window appears. Your screen will resemble Figure 10.17.
6. Click **Manual proxy configuration**. **View** will activate. Click **View**.

Figure 10.17 Configuring a Network Proxy for Netscape Navigator

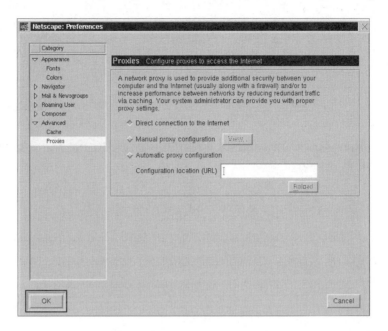

7. You can configure a proxy for each Internet protocol that Netscape supports. Enter the IP address of the Squid Web Proxy Cache server in the HTTP Proxy field. For example, if your Squid system was 24.130.8.170 and you configured Squid to listen for cache request on port 3128, you would enter the values shown in Figure 10.18.

NOTE

Squid supports caching for the additional Internet protocols. For this demonstration, we are only testing Web page caching.

8. Click **OK** twice to return to the browser.

9. In Netscape Navigator, enter the following URL: **www.squid–cache .org**.

10. The Squid home page will appear. If not, your browser proxy settings are incorrectly configured.

Configuring Lynx

In this section, you will configure the Lynx command-line browser so it sends all Web requests to the Squid Web Proxy Cache server. Pico is used in this demonstration to facilitate the search. You can use any text editor you choose.

1. Access the Linux lynx configuration file by entering:

   ```
   pico /etc/linux.cfg
   ```

2. Press **ALT+w** to receive a search prompt. At the search prompt, enter:

   ```
   #http_proxy
   ```

3. Change the http_proxy configuration line from:

   ```
   #http_proxy:http://some.server.dom:port/
   ```

   to

   ```
   http_proxy:http://24.130.8.170:3128
   ```

4. Your screen will resemble Figure 10.19.

   Figure 10.19 Configuring Lynx to Use the Squid Web Proxy Cache

   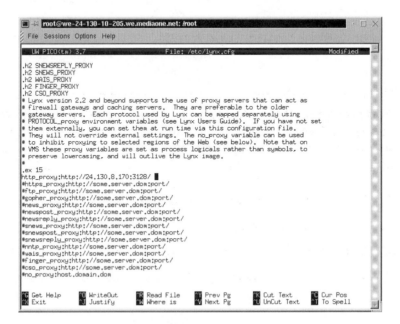

5. Press **ALT+x** to exit the file. When prompted, type **Y** for "Yes" to save the file, and press **ENTER** to write the file.

6. Use Lynx to enter the following URL: **lynx http://www .squid-cache.org**.

7. The Squid home page will appear. If not, your browser proxy settings are incorrectly configured.

Configuring Internet Explorer (Optional)

In this demonstration, you will configure Internet Explorer 5.5 on a Microsoft Windows Millennium Edition system. The client configured in the following steps is the proxy_client1 acl entry from the squid.conf file.

1. Open Internet Explorer.

2. Click the **Tools** menu and choose **Internet Options**.

3. Select the **Connections** tab, and click **LAN Settings**.

4. Deselect **Automatically Detect Setting**.

5. In the Proxy server section, click the **Use a proxy server** check box.

6. In the Address field, enter the IP address of your Squid Web Proxy Cache server.

7. In the Port field, enter **port 8080**.

NOTE

You configured Squid to list on both ports 3128 and 8080 for caching requests. Therefore, you can configure your clients for either port.

---

8. Your LAN Settings window will resemble Figure 10.20.

9. Click **OK** twice to return to the browser.

10. In Internet Explorer, enter the following URL: **www.squid-cache.org**.

11. The Squid home page will appear. If not, your browser proxy settings are incorrectly configured.

Figure 10.20 Configuring Internet Explorer as a Squid Proxy Client

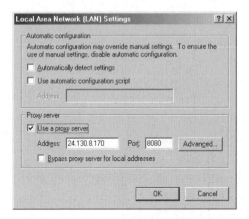

You have successfully implemented the Squid Web Proxy Cache server on a network. You have also configured three different types of proxy clients to use Squid's cache.

Summary

In this chapter, you learned that a proxy server is an intermediary between hosts on a local area network (LAN) and the Internet. It is used to implement caching for certain services, and for security and administrative control. Proxy cache servers are implemented at the Application layer and process specific Internet protocols, such as Hypertext Transfer Protocol (HTTP) and File Transfer Protocol (FTP). Rules are set up on the proxy server to determine how a workstation request should be processed.

Proxy caching increases network performance because a Web page is immediately downloaded to the client from the proxy server without having to download the Web page from the Internet each time. This speeds up Internet access on the network and saves bandwidth. Adding a small amount of data to a Web cache has a significant impact on browsing speed and bandwidth usage, especially in large networks.

You also learned the difference between a packet filter and a proxy server. A packet filter analyzes traffic at the Network (Layer 3) and Transport layers (Layer 4) of the Open System Interconnection (OSI) reference model. It can also filter traffic by service, or port number. A proxy server is capable of analyzing packets at the Application layer (Layer 7) of the OSI model. This allows much more flexibility, because the traffic within one service, such as port 80 (HTTP) traffic, can be filtered.

To learn how a proxy cache works, you implemented the Squid Web Proxy Cache server, which is a free, Unix open source Web proxy cache. Squid is a Web proxy cache that is based on the HTTP 1.1 specification. Squid is used only by proxy clients, such as Web browsers, that access the Internet using HTTP. Any client protocol supported by Squid must be sent as a proxy request in HTTP format. Most browsers support this function, so the following protocols are supported on most networks that implement Squid. The supported client protocols are FTP, HTTP, Secure Sockets Layer (SSL), Wide Area Information Server (WAIS), and Gopher. The protocols will work if you request them using your browser and if your browser is configured as a proxy client to the Web proxy cache server.

Squid also supports internal and management protocols. These protocols are used between caches that might exist on different (or the same) proxy-caching servers, or for managing a proxy cache. The supported inter-cache and management protocols are Internet Cache Protocol (ICP), Cache Digest, HTTP, Hypertext Caching Protocol (HTCP), and Simple Network Management Protocol (SNMP).

The two main hardware subsystems that Squid (or any other proxy cache) uses heavily and must therefore perform well are the disk random seek time and the amount of system memory.

You installed Squid and configured it using the /etc/squid/squid.conf file. The squid.conf file is configured for the Squid configuration default settings and can be used after several changes. You must make changes because squid.conf denies access to all browsers by default. Squid is completely useless until you make changes to the squid.conf. Each configuration option in squid.conf is identified as a *tag*.

The http_port tag configures the HTTP port on which Squid listens for proxy clients. The default port is 3128. The cache_dir tag specifies where the cached data is stored. By default, the cache_dir is located in the /var/spool/squid directory. The acl tag allows you to define an access list. The http_access tag permits or denies access to Squid by using the access lists defined in the acl tags. Proxy clients will be unable to use the Squid proxy-caching server until you modify the http_access tags.

After you configured the squid.conf file, you started and tested Squid. You used the Squid client program on the localhost to ensure that Web page data was written to the cache.

Last, you configured several proxy clients to use the Squid Web Proxy Cache server. The demonstration showed you how to configure three browsers for a proxy server: a Linux system running Netscape Navigator and Lynx, and a Microsoft Windows Millennium Edition system running Internet Explorer.

Solutions Fast Track

Benefits of Proxy Server Implementation

☑ A Web proxy cache server can cache Web pages and FTP files for proxy clients. They can also cache Web sites for load balancing.

☑ Caching increases the performance of the network by decreasing the amount of data transferred from outside of the local network.

☑ Web proxy caching reduces bandwidth costs, increases network performance during normal traffic and spikes, performs load balancing, caches aborted requests, and functions even when a network's Internet connection fails.

Differentiating between a Packet Filter and a Proxy Server

☑ Packet filters analyze traffic at the Network (Layer 3) and Transport layers (Layer 4) of the OSI model. A packet filter can determine whether it will allow a certain IP address or IP address range to pass through, or filter traffic by service, or port number.

☑ A proxy server analyzes packets at the Application layer (Layer 7) of the OSI model. This feature provides flexibility because the traffic within one service, such as port 80 (HTTP) traffic, can be filtered.

Implementing the Squid Web Proxy Cache Server

☑ The Squid Web Proxy Cache server allows administrators to set up a Web proxy caching service, add access controls (rules), and cache DNS lookups.

☑ Client protocols supported by Squid must be sent as a proxy request in HTTP format, and include FTP, HTTP, SSL, WAIS, and Gopher.

☑ Squid is configured using the /etc/squid/squid.conf file, which defines configurations such as the HTTP port number on which Squid listens for HTTP requests, incoming and outgoing requests, timeout information, and firewall access data.

☑ Each configuration option in squid.conf is identified as a *tag*. The http_port tag configures the HTTP port on which Squid listens for proxy clients. The cache_dir tag specifies where the cached data is stored. The acl tag allows you to define an access list. The http_access tag permits or denies access to Squid. Squid will not function until you make changes to the squid.conf file.

Configuring Proxy Clients

☑ Firewalls can be configured to forward all port 80 traffic leaving the network to the Web proxy cache server—clients do not need manual configuration. In other cases, proxy clients automatically detect the proxy server information on the network and use it for all Internet access.

☑ All manual proxy client configurations are completed within the browser application, and it's just a matter of specifying the address of the Web proxy cache server.

Frequently Asked Questions

The following Frequently Asked Questions, answered by the authors of this book, are designed to both measure your understanding of the concepts presented in this chapter and to assist you with real-life implementation of these concepts. To have your questions about this chapter answered by the author, browse to **www.syngress.com/solutions** and click on the **"Ask the Author"** form.

Q: What amount of system resources does Squid require?

A: Squid does not require an extremely fast processor; physical memory is the crucial resource. For high-volume caches, fast disks are important because the bottleneck generally occurs at the disk system. If possible, you should avoid using IDE disks if you want to run Squid.

Q: Does Squid support any security protocols such as HTTPS, SSL, or TLS?

A: Squid offers limited support for secure protocols in that it "tunnels" or relays encrypted bits between clients and servers.

It provides an alternative to the direct SSL connection that a browser generally opens when it encounters an https://–prefixed URL. For HTTPS requests, Squid uses the CONNECT request method to tunnel the request from the browser. The CONNECT method enables tunneling of any connection type through an HTTP proxy. Proxies simply transport bytes between clients and servers, ignoring the connection's contents. This provides secure transmission of the data passed from the browser to the server.

Q: Can I run Squid behind a firewall?

A: Yes. However, if Squid is behind a firewall, it cannot directly access the Internet. Therefore, you must use a parent cache for all connections.

You can dictate which requests to forward to the parent cache outside the firewall by adding the never_direct access list to your squid.conf file. For example, suppose you want all servers to connect through your parent cache except those servers whose names end with safedomain.org. You could add the following code to squid.conf:

```
acl INSIDE dstdomain safedomain.org
never_direct deny INSIDE
```

Any domains that do not match the INSIDE acl will be excluded. If no domains are specified, then the opposite of the last action will occur by default: Essentially, never_direct allow all would be the default rule applied.

Alternatively, you can use IP addresses instead of domain names to specify your internal servers, as shown in the following code:

```
acl INSIDE_IP dst 207.58.100.45/24
never_direct deny INSIDE
```

Consider that when using IP addresses instead of domain names, Squid must first convert URL host names to IP addresses by performing DNS lookups. Your DNS service might be unable to *resolve* external domains.

If you use more than one parent cache and you want to include the never_direct access list in squid.conf, then it is advisable to specify one parent cache as the default, as shown in the following code:

```
cache_peer abc.safedomain.org parent 3128 0 default
```

By using the *default* keyword in the *cache_peer* line, Squid doesn't have to decide which parent cache to use.

Q: I need to configure my cache_dir setting. At what size will my cache directory run Squid most effectively?

A: Administrators generally dedicate a disk partition to the Squid cache. It is advisable to leave some space available rather than using the entire partition, however, because Squid may behave unpredictably if disk space runs out.

Consider a 20GB disk, which will actually yield about 19GB of usable space. If you place and mount a file system on this disk, and then use the *df* program to determine the available space, you will see that some disk space is lost to file system overheads (such as inodes, directory entries, superblocks, etc.). Further consider that Unix generally reserves about 10 percent of disk space. Therefore, after formatting a 20GB disk, you probably have only about 18GB available for your use.

In addition, the Squid swap.state files that reside in each cache directory generally grow until the logs are rotated or Squid is restarted. Therefore, it is advisable to reserve an additional 10 percent for these Squid overheads. The more free space Squid has, the better it performs, so you may want to reserve still more space to allow Squid that freedom. Considering all these factors, a cache_dir setting of 14000 to 16500MB is advisable for a 20GB disk. You can configure your cache_dir setting using the following code:

```
cache_dir ... 16000 16 256
```

Try this conservative setting initially, and then check the disk usage once the cache is full. You can increase the cache_dir setting gradually if you find that you have extra free disk space. You need to decrease your cache size immediately if you receive any "disk full" write errors.

Q: I want to locate the largest objects in my cache. Is there a command I can use to do this?

A: Enter the following command in Squid to return a list of the objects in your cache that are taking up the most space:

```
sort -r -n +4 -5 access.log | awk '{print $5, $7}' | head -25
```

Q: How can I restart Squid with an empty cache?

A: Use the **% squid -k** shutdown command to stop Squid before attempting to restart. There are a couple of methods you can use to restart Squid with a clean cache. The fastest is to overwrite the swap.state files for each cache directory. When using this method, leave a single byte of garbage in the swap.state file. It is ineffective to reduce the file size to zero or delete the file completely. For each cache directory, use the following command:

```
% echo "" > /cache1/swap.state
```

Do not change ownership or permissions on the swap.state files. After you have modified the file for each directory, restart Squid.

Another more time-consuming method for this operation involves recreating all the cache directories. Before doing this, you must move the existing directories to another location, as demonstrated with the following code:

```
% cd /cache1
% mkdir TEMP
% mv ?? swap.state* TEMP
% rm -rf  TEMP &
```

Use the same process for each cache directory. Then issue the **squid -z** command and Squid will create the new directories for you. When you restart Squid, the cache will be clean.

## Chapter 11

Maintaining Firewalls

Solutions in this chapter:

Introduction

Regardless of the type of firewall you deploy, you will have to test and maintain it carefully. You need to actively monitor your firewall so that you can discover scanning attacks, connection attempts, and general weaknesses. Of course, you will have to scan your firewall to ensure that all extraneous ports and daemons are closed. You can use a scanner such as Nessus (www.nessus.org) to do this. However, even an application such as Nessus cannot implement the specific attacks necessary to truly test your firewall. In this chapter, you will learn about how to properly test and log activity. You will be able to verify that the firewall is working, make intelligent changes on demand, and generate useful reports.

This chapter focuses on applications such as Telnet, Netcat, and SendIP, and Nmap to query the firewall. Doing so will help you determine if your firewall is truly protecting your network. Just one accidental omission of a rule can open a hole that could allow a hacker into your network.

You may never know that a hacker has entered your network unless you carefully monitor your firewall logs. Doing so is sometimes an unglamorous, thankless job. However, using applications such as Firedaemon and Fwlogwatch, both of which are profiled in this chapter, you can receive automatic alerts. Fwlogwatch can even automatically reconfigure your firewall for you in case of a scanning attack. Even if you choose to not automatically block traffic, using the testing and logging tools discussed in this chapter you can maintain your firewall so that it is blocking and allowing the right traffic for your business.

Testing Firewalls

Before you can start logging access to your firewall, you need to ensure that you have configured it correctly in the first place. Even if you have extensive experience configuring firewalls, you will have to test your implementation when you first install it. In fact, experienced professionals know that they have to continually test a firewall to ensure that it is properly configured, and that its current configuration protects the network. It is not enough to just check or read the Ipchains/Iptables rules and then think that you have properly tested the firewall. You need to actively send packets and monitor your firewall and internal network to be sure.

Before you learn about applications that can help you test your firewall, you first need to consider some of the actual attacks, problems, and issues to look for. When testing your firewall, consider the following:

- **Internet Protocol (IP) spoofing** Many hackers outside of the firewall try to imitate internal network hosts in order to bypass authentication.

- **Open ports/daemons** Many firewalls and/or routers allow unnecessary ports to remain open, which can expose your firewall to threats unnecessarily.

- **Monitoring system hard drives, RAM, and processors** If your firewall runs out of disk space, or begins to run low on memory, your network may become incapacitated. Check your server's performance regularly using standard tools (*df*, *vmstat*, *top*, and so forth).

- **Suspicious users, logins, and login times** Even if you allow only interactive login at your firewall, monitor it carefully to determine who has logged on. It is vital that you know exactly who is controlling the flow of packets on your network.

- **Check the rules database** One of the common moves by a hacker is to alter the rules database in subtle ways that make it easier for the hacker to gain access to the network. Check your rules and compare them carefully to ensure that no unauthorized changes have occurred.

- **Verify connectivity** After you have configured or reconfigured your firewall, make sure that these changes do not cause problems for management and employees.

- **Remain informed concerning the operating system** Bugs may be discovered in the kernel and/or daemons that you are using. If you do not keep current concerning the tools you are using, you may end up exposing yourself to hackers.

- **Port scans** If you are relatively new to securing firewalls, you will be amazed to find out how many times your firewall will be scanned. Logging all scans can consume an unnecessary amount of hard drive space and processor time. Still, the proper amount of logging will help you remain informed and will help you document scans that may be preludes to an attack.

Following is a more detailed discussion concerning each of these issues.

IP Spoofing

Your firewall should not allow any packets to pass from outside the network into your internal network if the source address is the same as any host in your internal network. Suppose, for example, that your external network interface card (NIC) has the IP address of 128.1.2.3.4/16, and your internal NIC has the address of 192.168.1.0/24. You then need to find a way to test your firewall to see if any traffic is passing through the external interface from, say, the 192.168.1.1 IP address.

If such packets are able to traverse your firewall, then a hacker can configure his or her system to use your firewall as a default gateway and participate on your network. Leaving your packet-filtering firewall open to spoofing attacks largely obviates the reason for having a firewall, so you should take every step to test exactly what your firewall drops and allows. If you require, for example, your end users to have access to the World Wide Web, you will find that it is necessary to allow ephemeral ports (any port over 1023) to access the Internet. However, if you are using private IP addresses (e.g., the 192.168.45.0 network), no system outside of the firewall should ever be able to assume this IP address and access your internal network's ephemeral ports.

Open Ports/Daemons

Your firewall should be as secure as possible. Disable all unused services and configure the used ones with security in mind. If you are running Squid or another proxy server on the firewall, make sure that only this port is open. Daemons such as Telnet, File Transfer Protocol (FTP), Hypertext Transfer Protocol (HTTP) and others should be shut down in almost all situations. In many situations, you may require the ability to remotely administer your firewall. Still, consider disabling all login to the outside interface.

In many situations, it is best to allow only interactive logins at your firewall. This way, you need only secure the firewall's physical security. If you must, use only a relatively secure login application, such as Secure Shell (SSH). You could also consider Kerberos, although this requires you to open several additional ports. Even using one-time passwords (OTP) at the firewall is a solution, although the use of OTP does not encrypt the data that subsequently passes from your system to the router. If you do need to leave certain ports open, be prepared to conduct regular scans of your firewall to test the daemons listening on these ports. As suggested earlier, applications such as Nessus (www.nessus.org) are ideal in this type of situation.

Monitoring System Hard Drives, RAM, and Processors

Firewall logs can consume hard drive space, especially in busy networks. If you configured your firewall to log both accepted incoming and outgoing access, you will find that your log files will grow very large in a short period of time. You may need to cut back on your log settings. However, if you cannot do this, regularly use the **df –h** command to discover the total amount of hard drive space you have left. You could, for example, create a simple crontab entry that sends you this information automatically every Monday at 8:05:

```
5  8  *  *  mon  df -h | mail -s "HDRIVE"
   security.manager@yournetwork.com
```

Of course, keeping the cron daemon enabled on your firewall can present its own problems, because it will require you to ensure that this daemon is not subject to bugs that can cause a security problem. Any daemon, such as Cron, that acts automatically can cause problems if misconfigured, so carefully review all default scripts, and you will be in good shape. It is an additional service, after all. You will have to make the decision yourself.

Following is a quick overview of standard Linux tools that can help you determine if your system is becoming overburdened:

- **vmstat** Informs you about the amount of random RAM and virtual RAM used on the system.

- **top** Used to inform you about the processes that occupy the largest percentage of CPU time. The busiest processes rise to the top of the display. The Gtop and Ktop applications, both available from www.rpmfind.net, are graphical versions that are somewhat easier to use than the original.

Suspicious Users, Logins, and Login Times

Use the **who** and **last** commands to learn about who has logged in to the firewall. In addition, manually check the /etc/passwd and /etc/shadow files to determine if any users have been added. An application such as Tripwire can be extremely helpful if you wish to remain informed about any changes to such files.

Check the Rules Database

Determine if any unauthorized changes have been made to your database. When you first created your firewall, you should have created a backup using either the **ipchains-save** or **iptables-save** commands. Use the **diff** command to compare the two files to see if any changes have occurred. You may also use **md5** to generate fingerprints of the configuration files to see whether any unauthorized changes have been made to them.

Truly talented hackers are interested in entering a network and then controlling it without your knowledge. Accordingly, many will deactivate certain logging rules on your firewall, and then activate them again. If you leave the ipchains or iptables commands on your system, this will be very easy. To at least slow down the hacker, try removing these applications from the system. This way, the hacker will at least be forced to install these applications on your system before he or she can manipulate it. If you have Tripwire installed, you will then be informed of massive changes to the hard drive.

Verify Connectivity with Company Management and End Users

After you install your firewall, check with various managers and employees to ensure that your firewall rules are working properly. You may have to further adjust your firewall to ensure that the right services are available to the company. You may have to inform people about certain services that are no longer available by design. Otherwise, you will receive help desk calls informing you that service has been interrupted.

Employee education is often necessary whenever you make any changes to the firewall. Otherwise, you will receive complaints that the network is "down," when in fact it is behaving according to your design. In order to cut down on ill will and employee frustration, find ways to carefully and tactfully inform employees concerning changes. Consider the following suggestions:

- Contact management and make sure that they understand and agree with the changes you are making.

- Many times, upper management will ask for certain changes and not quite understand how this will affect the end user. Decisions to cut off certain services (e.g., Web traffic, or access to outside Post Office Protocol v3 [POP3] accounts) may negatively affect the company's ability to conduct business, or may cause unnecessary problems with employee morale. Make sure that upper management understands the ramifications of any suggestions they make.

- Warn employees before any changes to the security policy/firewall rules will occur.

- Remind employees that changes have occurred.

- Use e-mail, word of mouth, and employee area bulletin boards to remind people about changes.

Remain Informed Concerning the Operating System

New bugs are found every day in any operating system. It is possible that a bug may be found in Ipchains/Iptables or the kernel that could be exploited. If you do not subscribe to the appropriate mailing lists (see www.cert.org and www.sans.org), you should. It is also likely that the version of Linux you are using has a newsgroup associated with it.

The following are some additional strategies:

- Join mailing lists associated with your operating system.

- Carefully consider upgrades. Update only when you are certain that an upgrade enhances both your system's security and functionality. Do not upgrade simply because an upgrade exists. Just because an upgrade offers a new feature does not mean that this upgrade will allow your system to remain secure. Added features often add complexity to your system, and such changes open a security hole unless you take the time to properly study the changes and alter your system's configuration.

- Network with fellow systems administrators. Share your concerns and solutions with others. You will find that doing so will greatly increase your awareness of the many security solutions that exist.

Port Scans

Ipchains/Iptables-based firewalls are classic examples of packet-filtering firewalls. This type of firewall has traditionally been vulnerable to scanning attacks; they can simply allow scans to occur without informing anyone, because packet filters generally do not pay attention to Transmission Control Protocol (TCP)-based connections. They are interested, rather, in filtering out IP addresses and ports (i.e., they pay attention to the Network layer of the Open System Interconnection Reference Model OSI/RM).

The introduction of log analysis software such as Firelogd and Fwlogdaemon have made it possible to detect and block such scans, all the while sending an alert to the systems administrator. This type of software can help reduce a firewall's exposure to distributed denial-of-service (DDoS) attacks, because it helps the firewall completely drop certain hosts. However, this strategy introduces new problems, because it is possible for attackers to spoof source IP addresses and assume the identity of hosts you trust. The result is that hackers can use your own strategies against you and make your own software conduct a DoS attack against you by blocking your network from its own Domain Name System (DNS) servers, default gateways, and other hosts that you trust implicitly. However, most adjunct software, such as Fwlogwatch, provides ways to exclude trusted hosts from being blocked. You will learn more about this later in this chapter.

NOTE

As long as unencrypted, non-IPsec versions of IPv4 remain the most commonly used version of the Internet Protocol, spoofing will remain a fact of life. If you find that spoofing attacks keep occurring against your network, you can take the following actions:

- Edit the configuration files of your log-watching software and increase thresholds to eliminate false positives.
- Carefully manage any Ipchains/Iptables entries created by your log-scanning software so that sensitive hosts are not blocked.

These strategies are ways that you can mitigate and manage spoofing attacks, as opposed to eliminating them, because until all systems use IPSec or move to IPv6, there is really no way to completely eliminate them. Even when IPSec and/or IPv6 become common, it is likely that hackers will find newer and cleverer ways to spoof these protocols as well.

Using Telnet, Ipchains, Netcat, and SendIP to Probe Your Firewall

Now that you understand what to look for, you can use the following tools to help you:

- **Rule checkers** Although Iptables does not support rule checking, the **ipchains -C** command allows you to check how your existing rule set operates. It will return information as to whether the packet is dropped or accepted. It is up to you to act on this information.

- **Port scanners** A simple port scan can help you determine which ports are left open on your firewall. Using applications such as Telnet and Netcat, you can then determine what daemon is listening behind that port.

- **Packet generators** Using applications such as SendIP, you can generate packets designed to test whether your firewall rules are working properly.

Following is a discussion of some tools that allow you to quickly test your firewall rules.

Ipchains

The **ipchains -C** option allows you to send packets to test whether the rules you have created work properly. Iptables does not have the equivalent, as of this writing. When checking Ipchains rules, you simply place **-C** (make sure you use the uppercase C) in front of the rule. The **--check** and **-C** options, by the way, are equivalent. You will be informed if the packet is blocked. For example, suppose you create the following rule in Ipchains:

```
ipchains -I input -i eth0 -s 0/0 -d 0/0 -p icmp -j DENY
```

To test this rule, you would issue the following command on the same system:

```
ipchains -C input -i eth0 -p icmp -s 0/0 1 -d 0/0 1
```

Ipchains will then inform you that the packet is denied. This tool is handy if you are logged in to the same system as you are testing, and you are becoming familiar with the existing rules and wish to send out packets that test how the rules are working.

Telnet

More universal testing methods exist. The humble Telnet application is still useful when testing a firewall. Do not use it for logging on, however. You can use it to test whether a certain firewall rule is running the way you think it should. For example, suppose that you allow all access but that which is explicitly denied by a rule, and that you have configured the following firewall rule in Iptables:

```
iptables -A INPUT -i eth0 -s 0/0 -p tcp --dport 80 -j LOG
iptables -A INPUT -i eth0 -s 0/0 -p tcp --dport 80 -j REJECT
```

You can use your Telnet client to see whether it is working properly by specifying the port you are blocking and logging:

```
prompt$ telnet firewall.yournetwork.com 80
```

You can then view the log by using the **tail** command to read the file where your system stores kernel messages. For the sake of convenience, use tail's **-f** option so that you can view results as they happen:

```
tail -f /var/log/messages
```

Using Multiple Terminals

If you have logged in to the firewall interactively, it is often useful to open two terminals. You can use the first terminal to issue the **telnet** command, and you can use the second terminal to view the results in the /var/log/messages file. Remember that if you specify more complex logging options, and then send too many packets, the kernel will stop logging traffic after a certain period of time (three logging instances an hour, with only the first five packets logged). If you do not remember this, you may make the mistake of thinking that a certain rule is not working, when in fact it really is.

Netcat

You are not limited to using Telnet. One commonly used firewall testing application is Netcat, available at www.l0pht.com/~weld/netcat/ and packetstorm.security.com. Netcat is quite versatile, and is the self-described "Network Swiss Army Knife." Hackers and systems administrators alike use it as a tool to conduct scans, communicate with open ports, and even transfer information between hosts. Because it is so versatile, it can also be used against you, so if possible, you should install this application only on a client system, rather than on the router. This is because it can be used to open a back door on your system. Still, careful use of the application can allow you to quickly audit your firewall.

Used in the simplest way, Netcat is much like a Telnet client, because it can be used to access any remote host at any port. To connect to the host named firewall.yournetwork.com at port 80, you would issue the following command:

```
./nc firewall.yournetwork.com 80
```

You will then have to press **CTRL+C** to exit the program. If the port is open, you can then enter any command you wish. As far as port 80 is concerned, you can just enter some gibberish once a connection is made, and the Web server will return an error message, which usually includes the name of the Web server. Chances are, the port will not recognize your command, but for the purposes of testing a firewall, you usually want to just see if a port is open and listening. The **netcat –h** command provides a list of all available options, which are listed in Table 11.1 for your reference:

Table 11.1 Netcat Options

Option	Description
-i *value*	Tells Netcat to delay sending packets for a certain number of seconds. For example, to have Netcat wait five seconds between scanning ports, you would specify **-i 5**.
-n	Has Netcat report information using only IP addresses. This option is helpful when conducting ping scans, or if you do not have any DNS support.
-p *value*	A port spoofing option. Allows you to specify the port number of the packet being sent. For example, to have a packet appear as it were sent from port 53 of a host, you would enter **-p 53**.
-r	Allows you to have Netcat scan ports at random, instead of simply one after the other.
-s *value*	Spoofs the source address of a packet. This option does not work on all systems, however.
-u	Netcat defaults to sending TCP packets. This option allows you to send User Datagram Protocol (UDP) packets, instead.
-v	Verbose mode. Reports additional information about the connections you are making. If you specify **-v** twice (**-v -v**), you will receive twice the amount of information.
-w *value*	Sets the time (in seconds) that Netcat will wait at a responding port. This option is often combined with **-z**.
-z	Called "zero-I/O mode," this option has Netcat forbid any i/o from the source system. If you do not use this option, Netcat will

Continued

Table 11.1 Continued

Option	Description
	"hang" indefinitely at a port that responds. This option is mostly applicable when using Netcat as a scanner.
-l	Has Netcat open a listening port. Used with additional options, it is possible to bind a root shell to this listening portlisten mode, which can lead to security problems.

Sample Netcat Commands

To use Netcat in a more sophisticated and helpful way, you must use the following syntax:

```
nc [-options] hostname port[s] [ports]
```

For example, if you wish to scan ports 1 through 1023 of your firewall and ensure that Netcat will not "hang" at any ports, you could issue the following command:

```
./nc -z -w 2 -v -v firewall.yournetwork.com 1-1023
```

The **-z** and **-w 2** options tell Netcat to not bind a port, and to wait only two seconds in case a connection is accidentally made. The two **-v** options place Netcat into ultra verbose mode. It is likely, though, that only certain groups of ports will be open on an unsecured firewall. For example, the following command scans only certain ports and groups of ports:

```
./nc -z -w 2 -v -v firewall.yournetwork.com 20-30, 53, 80, 100-112, 443,
    6000-6050
```

Analysis of Netcat Scan

The preceding scan searches for ports associated with several protocols, including:

- FTP (20 and 21)
- SSH (22)
- Telnet (23)
- DNS (53)
- WWW (both 80 and 443)

- X (ports in the 6000 range)

Figure 11.1 shows the results of a scan against a router that has left several ports open.

This firewall, for example, still allows connections to Simple Mail Transfer

Figure 11.1 Scanning an Open Router

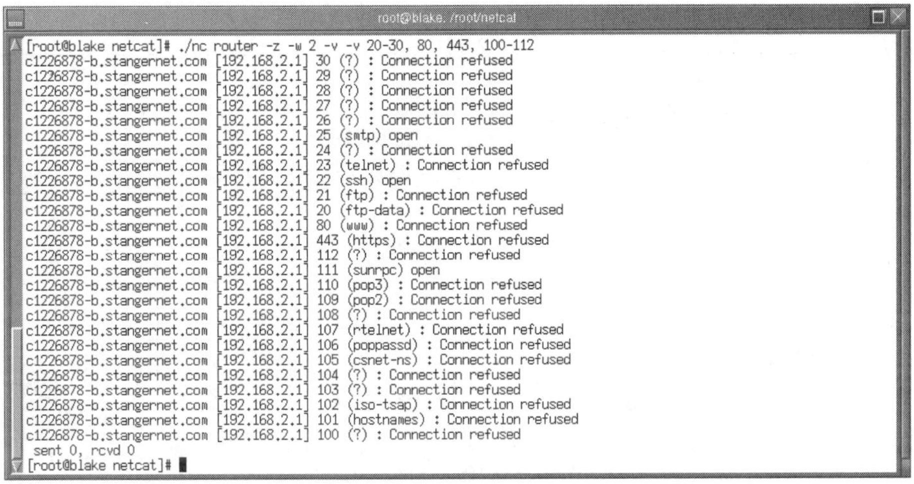

```
root@blake: /root/netcat                                                    □ ×
[root@blake netcat]# ./nc router -z -w 2 -v -v 20-30, 80, 443, 100-112
c1226878-b.stangernet.com [192.168.2.1] 30 (?) : Connection refused
c1226878-b.stangernet.com [192.168.2.1] 29 (?) : Connection refused
c1226878-b.stangernet.com [192.168.2.1] 28 (?) : Connection refused
c1226878-b.stangernet.com [192.168.2.1] 27 (?) : Connection refused
c1226878-b.stangernet.com [192.168.2.1] 26 (?) : Connection refused
c1226878-b.stangernet.com [192.168.2.1] 25 (smtp) open
c1226878-b.stangernet.com [192.168.2.1] 24 (?) : Connection refused
c1226878-b.stangernet.com [192.168.2.1] 23 (telnet) : Connection refused
c1226878-b.stangernet.com [192.168.2.1] 22 (ssh) open
c1226878-b.stangernet.com [192.168.2.1] 21 (ftp) : Connection refused
c1226878-b.stangernet.com [192.168.2.1] 20 (ftp-data) : Connection refused
c1226878-b.stangernet.com [192.168.2.1] 80 (www) : Connection refused
c1226878-b.stangernet.com [192.168.2.1] 443 (https) : Connection refused
c1226878-b.stangernet.com [192.168.2.1] 112 (?) : Connection refused
c1226878-b.stangernet.com [192.168.2.1] 111 (sunrpc) open
c1226878-b.stangernet.com [192.168.2.1] 110 (pop3) : Connection refused
c1226878-b.stangernet.com [192.168.2.1] 109 (pop2) : Connection refused
c1226878-b.stangernet.com [192.168.2.1] 108 (?) : Connection refused
c1226878-b.stangernet.com [192.168.2.1] 107 (rtelnet) : Connection refused
c1226878-b.stangernet.com [192.168.2.1] 106 (poppassd) : Connection refused
c1226878-b.stangernet.com [192.168.2.1] 105 (csnet-ns) : Connection refused
c1226878-b.stangernet.com [192.168.2.1] 104 (?) : Connection refused
c1226878-b.stangernet.com [192.168.2.1] 103 (?) : Connection refused
c1226878-b.stangernet.com [192.168.2.1] 102 (iso-tsap) : Connection refused
c1226878-b.stangernet.com [192.168.2.1] 101 (hostnames) : Connection refused
c1226878-b.stangernet.com [192.168.2.1] 100 (?) : Connection refused
 sent 0, rcvd 0
[root@blake netcat]# ▊
```

Protocol (SMTP), the sunrpc portmapper service (port 111), and X. You can, of course, specify additional ports. For example, the ranges of 20 through 00 and 5900 through 7000 can reveal commonly used ports. Consult your /etc/services file for more ideas.

Additional Netcat Commands

When compiled properly, Netcat can also spoof IP addresses. If you wish to spoof the source IP address, you would use the **–s** option:

```
./nc -s 10.100.100.1 -z -w 2 -v -v firewall.yournetwork.com 20-30, 53,
    80, 100-112, 443, 6000-6050
```

However, you should note that the **–s** option does not work well on some operating systems. Because Netcat defaults to TCP, you can use the **–u** option to send a UDP packet to a port:

UDP Scans

```
./nc -u -w 2 firewall.yournetwork.com 80, 443
```

You will have to press **ENTER** twice to finish the command. Depending on the rules you have set (you will have to explicitly log UDP using either the **-l** option in Ipchains or the **-j** LOG target in Iptables), your firewall will log this traffic.

Testing Source Ports

If you have set a firewall rule to deny a particular source port, you can test it with Netcat. For example, if you have prohibited all hosts from accessing ports 1 through 1023 of an interface, you can test this by issuing the following command:

```
./nc -p 80 -w 2 -v -v firewall.yournetwork.com 1-1023
```

Tools & Traps...

Additional Netcat Features

If you wish to have Netcat open a shell and listen for inbound connections (this is definitely not recommended in most circumstances), you would use the following syntax:

```
nc -l -p port [-options] [hostname] [port]
```

In addition, Netcat ships with several scripts and applications. Some of these are geared toward the hacker community, while others offer quick solutions to common problems. Most of them are less practical than they are interesting. For example, if you want to test port redirection, you can use the webproxy and webrelay applications found in the scripts directory.

You can learn more about using Netcat in this way by reading the README file that comes with the source code. For those who are truly curious about using Netcat to open up listening connections, a patch exists that allows you to authenticate and encrypt traffic that streams between versions of Netcat running on opposite servers. Called *aes-netcat*, you can download it from packetstorm.security.com and other sites.

Testing DNS Connectivity

Many times, you will want to allow UDP and TCP access from and to port 53, in case a domain zone transfer needs to be made. To test whether this port is open, you would issue the following commands:

```
./nc -p 53 -w 2 -v -v firewall.yournetwork.com 53

./nc -u -p 53 -w 2 -v -v firewall.yournetwork.com 53
```

You can also scan a range of ports using Netcat. If, for example, you wished to scan ports 1 through 1023, you would issue the following command:

```
./nc firewall firewall.yournetwork.com 1-1023
```

Exercise: Using Netcat

1. Create a new directory named netcat and change into it. This step is necessary, because the tarball will deposit many different files into the destination directory.

2. Obtain Netcat version 1.10 from the CD that accompanies this book (the file name is nc110.tgz), or from http://packetstorm.securify.com. Just enter **netcat** in the search field. When you save the tarball, save it to the netcat directory.

3. Once you have obtained Netcat and saved it to the netcat directory, untar and unzip it:

```
tar -zxvf nc110.tgz
```

4. Most versions of Linux do well with the following compile option:

```
make generic
```

   However, you may want to read the file named Makefile and see if your operating system is specifically listed.

5. Once you have compiled Netcat, the nc binary will be created in the present directory. Copy it to the /bin/ directory. Or, if you prefer, you can just leave it in the present directory and use **./** in front of the command while it is in the same directory. Now that Netcat is ready to be used, create several firewall rules that log port scans.

6. Open a terminal on your firewall and view the /var/log/messages file:

```
tail -f /var/log/messages
```

7. Now, conduct a sample portscan against your firewall:

```
./nc-w 2 -v -v firewall 1-1023
```

You can now use Netcat to conduct tests against your firewall.

 # SendIP: The Packet Forger

Although Netcat does have the ability to create some packets in certain instances, it is not a true packet generator. SendIP is designed to allow you to create packets of your own choosing. This practice is often called "arbitrary packet generation." SendIP allows you to create your own IP, Internet Control Message Protocol (ICMP), TCP, and UDP packets. For example, you can generate TCP packets with the FIN, ACK, and SYN bits set according to your testing needs. You can obtain SendIP from several sites, including www.earth.li/projectpurple/progs/sendip.html and http://packetstorm.securify.com. RPM and tarball files for version 1.5 can be found on the accompanying CD (sendip-1.5-1.i386.rpm and sendip-1.5.tar.gz).

SendIP Syntax

Although there are many options, SendIP syntax is relatively straightforward:

```
sendip [hostname] -p <type> -d <data> <options>
```

SendIP Options

The **-p** option specifies the protocol you wish to generate, and the **-d** option allows you to enter a random text string. The options, many of which are listed in Table 11.2, allow you to customize the contents of the packets you generate.

Table 11.2 SendIP Options

Option	Description
-p *value*	The option that determines which type of packet SendIP will create. Values include *ip*, *icmp*, *tcp*, and *udp*.
-is	Specifies a source IP address of your own choosing. By default, the "true" IP address of the local host is used.
-id	Specifies the destination IP address for the packet you are generating.

Continued

Table 11.2 Continued

Option	Description
-ih	For customizing the length of the IP header.
-iy	Sets the Type of Service (ToS) field for the packet. Consult the previous chapter for values that you can enter. The default value is to leave all fields blank.
-il	Sets the length of the packet.
-it	Sets the time-to-live (TTL) for the packet you generate. The default value is 255 bytes.
-ip	Tells SendIP to create an IP packet.
-ct *value*	For generating ICMP packet types. The default is echo-request (8), but you can specify any other type by entering **-ct 03**, for example. See the previous chapter or RFC 950.
-us	Specifies the source port for UDP packets. The default is the random port assigned to the packet when it is sent out.
-ud	The destination port of a UDP packet. You must specify a destination port.
-ts	Specifies the source port of a TCP packet. The default is the random port assigned to the packet when it is sent out.
-td	Sets the destination port for the TCP packet. You must specify a destination port.
-tn	Allows you to specify the TCP sequence number. By default, the number will be random.
-tfa	Sets the ACK bit on a TCP packet. By default, the value is not set, unless you use the **-ta** option along with **-tfa**. This is because an ACK packet is used to finish the process of tearing down a connection.
-ta	Allows you to request an acknowledgment packet, which is used to acknowledge that the TCP connection is ready to end.
-tfr	Creates a RESET packet.
-tfs	Alters the packet so that the SYN bit is set.
-tu	Creates a packet with the URGENT pointer set. This pointer begins the process of prioritizing traffic.
-tfu	Sets the URGENT bit in a TCP packet. The default is 0 unless you use the **-tu** option along with **-tfu**. For more information, consult RFC 1122.

Continued

Table 11.2 Continued

Option	Description
-tff	Sets the FIN bit.
-r	Randomizes all options. For example, if you specify IP as the protocol, the **-r** option automatically creates a random sending IP address.

The SendIP man page contains additional options. As you can see, SendIP allows you to forge any part of a TCP session, as well as any element of an IP, UDP, or ICMP packet. SendIP also allows you to forge all elements of IPv6 addresses, and also allows you to forge Routing Information Protocol (RIP) packets.

This tool is useful in regard to firewalls because it allows you to simulate any situation. The **ipchains –C** command has similar functionality. However, you can install SendIP anywhere, whereas many newer kernels do not support Ipchains. Besides, using SendIP, you can spend your time learning only one application.

SECURITY ALERT!

Applications such as SendIP and Netcat are often used in the hacker community. Take care that you do not allow all users on your network to access such applications. In fact, even using Telnet in the way shown previously is not recommended unless you own the systems you are scanning, or you have explicit permission from the operator of the system you are going to scan. Educate your IT personnel that they should use this software very carefully, and that they should never assume that they are allowed to scan or otherwise issue packets to a system that is not their responsibility.

To guard against illicit use of such applications, consider placing a note in your security policy to the effect that only certain users are allowed to access scanning and IP spoofing software for security auditing purposes.

Exercise: Using SendIP to Probe a Firewall

1. The source files do not differ from the RPM. Download SendIP RPM from http://www.earth.li/projectpurple/progs/sendip.html or packetstorm.securify.com.

2. As root, type the following:

```
rpm -ivh sendip-1.5-1.i386.rpm
```

3. Now that you have installed SendIP on this system, it will be known as the "attacking host." You are now going to use SendIP on this attacking host to check your firewall's ability to block spoofed packets coming in from the outside interface. If necessary, review Chapter 9 to learn how to create anti-spoofing rules for your firewall. To check your firewall's configuration, set up a machine outside of your firewall, and then give your firewall's IP address as the default gateway.

4. Suppose that you have only the internal networks of 192.168.2.0/24 and 10.100.100.0/24, and a simple Linux client using the IP address of 192.168.2.37. You wish to test your firewall to see if spoofed traffic from outside the network can get through your firewall to your Linux client. To test this, configure a system on your internal network (say, with the IP address of 192.168.2.37) to use a packet sniffer such as Tcpdump or Ethereal to view all packets on the 192.168.2.0 network. This will be the internal host. If necessary, review Chapter 5 to learn more about packet sniffers.

5. Put the NIC of the internal host into promiscuous mode so that it can capture the spoofed packet you are about to send. Hopefully, the spoofed packet won't get through.

6. Issue the following command from the attacking host to the internal host:

```
sendip 192.168.2.37 -p icmp -is 192.168.2.36
```

7. You have just issued a spoofing attack against your firewall and internal network. Now, stop your capture of packets on your internal host. Were you able to see an echo request from 192.168.2.36? Did the 192.168.2.37 system issue an echo reply? Did you see any DNS traffic that appears to be an attempt to resolve the 192.168.2.37 IP address? If you did, then review your spoofing rules. If you did not, chances are that you have properly configured anti-spoofing on your firewall.

Remember, if you are on a switched network, you will have to configure a packet sniffer on the victim host, and then ping that victim host directly. This is because a switched network does not use broadcasting as does a standard hub-based network.

8. If you have enabled logging for such packets, use the **tail -f** command on your firewall to see if the kernel records capturing the packet.

9. Now, try spoofing with another protocol:

    ```
    sendip 192.168.2.37 -p tcp -ts 2 -td 80 -tn -is 192.168.2.36
    ```

    This command sends a tcp packet with the source port of 2 to the 192.168.2.37 host at port 80. Your firewall should block this packet, because it should not allow packets to privileged ports (ports below 1023) to go into the internal network.

10. When you are reasonably sure that your firewall is blocking spoofed packets, issue the following command from your attacking host:

    ```
    sendip 192.168.2.37 -p tcp -ts 2 -td 80 -tn -is 45.2.5.6
    ```

11. This command does much the same thing, but instead, it creates a packet that has a stronger chance of passing through your firewall. Why? Because this packet apparently originates from the 45.2.5.6 host, which is an IP address that could plausibly originate from the Internet. In addition, at least for the purposes of this exercise, this address does not exist inside your network. However, this packet should not be passed through, either, because it originates from a privileged port and is directed at a privileged port (80) on the destination. Finally, issue the following command:

    ```
    sendip 192.168.2.37 -p tcp -ta 1 -ts 4356 -td 6450 -tn -is
        45.2.5.6
    ```

12. Depending on your firewall configuration, this packet may be allowed to pass through. This is because the ACK bit has been set using the **-ta** option. As a result, the firewall rules may allow it through because it is part of an already-established session. In addition, notice that the source and destination ports are ephemeral, and not well known (below 1023). Consider using additional commands to further test your firewall. Make the necessary changes, without affecting the services that you wish to provide.

Understanding Firewall Logging, Blocking, and Alert Options

You have already seen how you can check the kernel messages for log entries using the **tail –f /var/log/messages** command. However, more elegant ways to capture and view firewall logs exist. Third-party logging applications such as Firewall Log Daemon (Firelogd) and FwLogwatch are available to help you sort and act on the information gathered by the firewall.

Firewall Log Daemon

Firelogd (Firewall Log Daemon) is a relatively simple program that can either be run as an application or (you might have guessed) as a daemon. It does two things:

- It reads the kernel log entries and passes them into a "first in, first out" (FIFO) pipe, which Firelogd can then process.

- Once its buffer is full, it e-mails a report of suspicious traffic to an account of your choosing. You can have it mailed to a local account, or to a remote system of your choice.

The application supports both Ipchains and Iptables. Older versions required you to edit the dmn.h file, and then use the **make** command to compile the application. Now, however, Firelogd supports command-line arguments. You have various options, which are listed in the following sections.

Obtaining Firelogd

You can obtain Firelogd from the CD that accompanies this book. The RPM package is named firelogd-1.3-5.i386.rpm, and it has an accompanying MD5 signature (firelogdmd5sums.txt). You can download more recent versions from www.speakeasy.org/~roux/dmn/ or from http://packetstorm.securify.com. The RPM file is best for Red Hat systems. As of this writing, the tarball format does not have any special features.

Syntax and Configuration Options

The syntax for using Firelogd is as follows:

```
/usr/sbin/firelogd [-dmskh] [-b buffersize] [-e email] [-l log]
    [-t template] [-]
```

If you install Firelogd using the available RPM, you can also start Firelogd by using its startup script (/etc/rc.d/init.d/firelogd). You will have to edit this script to customize it if you wish to change or add any of the options.

Commonly Used Options

Following is a list of the most often-used options.

- **Daemon mode** If used without any options at all, Fwlogwatch runs as a simple application. The **-d** option has firelogd "fork off" and run as a daemon.

- **E-mail destination** The person who receives the e-mail messages. You can specify this either by using the **-e** option, or by editing the /etc/rc.d/init.d/firelogd script that comes with the RPM.

- **Log file** The location of the log file that Firelogd reads from. On Red Hat Linux, for example, this is usually /var/log/messages. You can specify a log file by either using the **-l** option, or by modifying the /etc/rc.d/init.d/firelogd script.

- **Buffer size** Tells Firelogd to wait for x number of entries before mailing them. The default is 10, which means a single e-mail will contain 10 entries. A value of 100 may be a more reasonable number. Using the default, you will receive dozens of e-mails in the case of a simple Nmap scanning attack. Experiment with these settings. If 100 gives you too little information about the nature of traffic at your firewall, then decrease the setting.

- **Template** Firelogd allows you to customize the alert messages. You can have Firelogd send you a great deal of information, or you can configure it to be as sparse as possible. The /etc/firelog.conf file contains the default template.

You can learn more about the additional options by consulting the firelogd man page.

Message Format

The e-mail message you receive will include multiple packet hits giving you the following information:

1. The date and time of the rejected or logged packet.
2. The name of the chain responsible for dropping or logging the packet.

3. The input interface.

4. The packet's TTL.

5. The IP of the firewall host and the number of the port to which the packet was sent (i.e., the destination port).

6. The origin of the IP address. Remember, it is possible to spoof IP addresses.

   Here is an example of a default Firelogd log entry:

```
01:28:37/May-5 ****S* TCP *D* REJECT/input-9 eth0 ***|***** ttl:64
badguy.hackerz.com -> hems(151)
128.37.08.43:4218 -> firewall.goodguys.com:151
```

Output Example

Here is output from a more extended example:

```
prompt# /usr/sbin/firelogd


LOG ENTRY:
April  5 09:53:37 firewall kernel: Packet log: input REJECT eth0 PROTO=6
    45.128.2.3:2748 128.1.2.3.4:3049 L=60 S=0x00 I=0 F=0x4000 T=64 SYN
    (#9)
CONTEXT INFORMATION:
  Time:   April 5 09:53:37
  Msg:    REJECT/input-9
  In:     eth0
  Out:
  Mac:


IP DATAGRAM INFORMATION:
  Source:   45.128.2.3 badguy.badguy.com
  Dest.:    128.1.2.3.4  firewall.goodguys.com
  IPlen:    60
  TOS:    TOS-0x00, PREC-0x00 -> ***|*****
  TTL:    64
  FRAG:   0x4000 -> *D*
```

```
ICMP SPECIFIC DATA:

   Type:

   Code:

   Info:

   Triggering Packet:


TCP SPECIFIC DATA:

   Window:

   Reserved Bits:

   Flags:   SYN -> ****S*


UDP SPECIFIC DATA:

   UDP Datagram length:


TCP/UDP SERVICE PORTS:

   Source Port: 2748(fjippol-polsvr) -> 3049(nsws)
```

In the preceding output, the attacking host's IP address is 45.128.2.3, and the firewall's IP address is 128.1.2.3.4. In this particular example, ICMP logging is not activated on the kernel. However, you can gather information about the nature of the attack by viewing the logs. This is an example of a simple, full TCP scan.

Customizing Messages

You can customize Firelogd messages by editing the /etc/firelogd.conf file and changing the values to suit your own situation. The default file comes with several suggested templates, which are commented out by using the following two words:

```
startcomment

endcomment
```

Firelogd will not read anything within these lines. Firelogd contains three entries. The first, discussed previously, is moderately verbose. The second is described as a "one-liner," and gives information about the time of the scan, as well as the source and destination IP addresses and ports. The final option is quite verbose, informing you about the details of the connection. You can, of course, create your own entry using the syntax described in the /etc/firelogd file. For example, the following sample code records the source IP address and the destination port address, as well as the interface where the traffic occurred. The text "From the firewall at the company" acts as a header for the information.

```
tab From the firewall at the company. nl
tab srcip sp r_dstpt sp in sp
```

The tab, space, and nl entries create tabs, single space, and new lines, respectively. The char srcip field has Firelogd inform you of the source IP address of the packet. The r_dspt field provides the destination port for the packet. Finally, the char in field has Firelogd report the interface. You can, of course, specify your own text and other options. The /etc/firelog.conf file shows you all of the options. Figure 11.2 shows an example of the configuration file.

Figure 11.2 The /etc/firelog.conf File

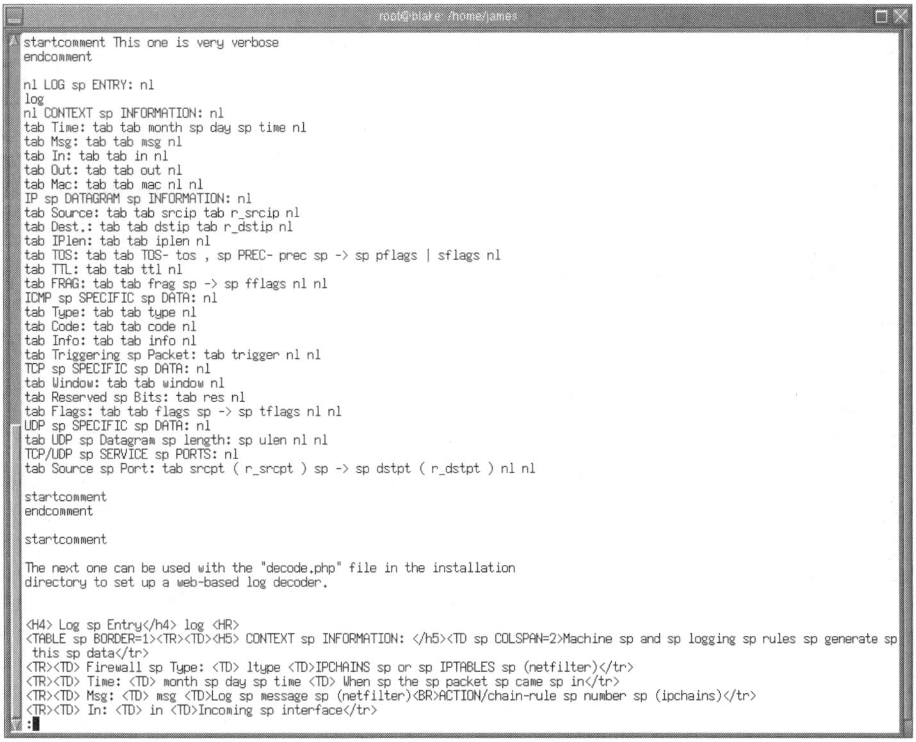

```
root@blake: /home/james
startcomment This one is very verbose
endcomment

nl LOG sp ENTRY: nl
log
nl CONTEXT sp INFORMATION: nl
tab Time: tab tab month sp day sp time nl
tab Msg: tab tab msg nl
tab In: tab tab in nl
tab Out: tab tab out nl
tab Mac: tab tab mac nl nl
IP sp DATAGRAM sp INFORMATION: nl
tab Source: tab tab srcip tab r_srcip nl
tab Dest.: tab tab dstip tab r_dstip nl
tab IPlen: tab tab iplen nl
tab TOS: tab tab TOS- tos , sp PREC- prec sp -> sp pflags | sflags nl
tab TTL: tab tab ttl nl
tab FRAG: tab tab frag sp -> sp fflags nl nl
ICMP sp SPECIFIC sp DATA: nl
tab Type: tab tab type nl
tab Code: tab tab code nl
tab Info: tab tab info nl
tab Triggering sp Packet: tab trigger nl nl
TCP sp SPECIFIC sp DATA: nl
tab Window: tab tab window nl
tab Reserved sp Bits: tab res nl
tab Flags: tab tab flags sp -> sp tflags nl nl
UDP sp SPECIFIC sp DATA: nl
tab UDP sp Datagram sp length: sp ulen nl nl
TCP/UDP sp SERVICE sp PORTS: nl
tab Source sp Port: tab srcpt ( r_srcpt ) sp -> sp dstpt ( r_dstpt ) nl nl

startcomment
endcomment

startcomment

The next one can be used with the "decode.php" file in the installation
directory to set up a web-based log decoder.


<H4> Log sp Entry</h4> log <HR>
<TABLE sp BORDER=1><TR><TD><H5> CONTEXT sp INFORMATION: </h5><TD sp COLSPAN=2>Machine sp and sp logging sp rules sp generate sp
 this sp data</tr>
<TR><TD> Firewall sp Type: <TD> ltype <TD>IPCHAINS sp or sp IPTABLES sp (netfilter)</tr>
<TR><TD> Time: <TD> month sp day sp time <TD> When sp the sp packet sp came sp in</tr>
<TR><TD> Msg: <TD> msg <TD>Log sp message sp (netfilter)<BR>ACTION/chain-rule sp number sp (ipchains)</tr>
<TR><TD> In: <TD> in <TD>Incoming sp interface</tr>
:
```

> **NOTE**
>
> Firelogd simply parses the log files generated by either Ipchains or Iptables. It does not generate the log files themselves. Therefore, you must have logging enabled through Iptables or Ipchains in order for Firelogd to operate properly.

Reading Log Files Generated by Other Firewalls

You can read log files generated by other systems, as well. For example, if you downloaded the /var/log/messages file from a remote system, you can read it with the following command:

```
cat messages | firelogd -
```

The hyphen allows the application to read the command directly from standard input.

Exercise: Configuring and Compiling Firelogd

1. Obtain Firelogd from www.speakeasy.org/~roux/dmn/ or from packetstorm.securify.com. The RPM file is best for Red Hat systems. The tarball does not provide any special configuration options.

2. Install the RPM. Once you install the RPM, the Firelogd will automatically begin running. Stop Firelogd by issuing the following command:

    ```
    /etc/rc.d/init.d/firelogd stop
    ```

3. Issue the following command:

    ```
    /usr/sbin/firelogd
    ```

4. Use a port scanner such as Gnome Service Scan or Nmap to scan your firewall. Remember that the firewall must have logging enabled at the interface you are scanning.

5. You should see output on your screen. You will not receive any e-mail message, because you have not supplied any arguments.

6. Stop Firelogd by pressing **CTRL+C**.

7. Now, prepare firelogd to run as a daemon. Make a copy of the /etc/rc.d/init.d/firelogd initialization script file and name it firelogd.bak. Edit the original so that the entries are as follows:

```
QSIZE=30
# Who is the administrator
MAIL=your_address@yourcompany.com
# Where is the output template
```

   You may have to adjust the QSIZE settings to fit your own situation.

8. Make a copy of the /etc/firelogd.conf in case anything goes wrong, and then edit the original file so that verbose logging is enabled. To do this, first comment out the default log entries, which are immediately below the text that reads "I like the look of the one below." Use the *startcomment* and *endcomment* keywords. Then, uncomment the entry that begins with the text that reads "This one is very verbose," and save the file.

9. Start Firelogd:

```
/etc/rc.d/init.d/firelogd start
```

10. Use Gnome ServiceScan or Nmap to conduct an attack that scans multiple ports of your firewall.

11. View the message using your e-mail client.

12. Re-edit the /etc/firelogd file and comment out the verbose entries and uncomment the entries that are beneath the text that reads "This one is a one-liner." This entry will send terse messages. If you wish, set the QSIZE value to 100, which means that each e-mail Firelogd sends will have 100 entries in it. It also means that Firelogd will not send you alerts as often; the larger the buffer value, the longer it will take to receive a message. Consequently, Firelogd will be less responsive to attacks, and will not inform you as often. However, one longer message is likely easier to read than several shorter messages.

Fwlogwatch

Fwlogwatch, written by Boris Wesslowski, is a logging and reporting mechanism that also allows you to automatically block all traffic that is identified as an attack. Used in conjunction with Firelogd, it helps create a system that continuously keeps you informed concerning port scans and other network events that surpass the thresholds you set. Fwlogwatch is available at the CERT-RUS Web site (http://cert .uni-stuttgart.de/projects/fwlogwatch) and Wesslowski's personal Web site (www.kyb.uni-stuttgart.de/boris/software.shtml). It is available in both tarball and RPM format, and there is no significant difference between the two. The accompanying CD contains both the tarball and RPM versions (fwlogwatch-0.3-bin.tar.gz and fwlogwatch-0.3-1.i386.rpm). Although FwLogwatch is similar to Firelogd, it is far more versatile. You can configure Fwlogwatch to do the following:

- Parse the firewall log file and generate user-friendly HTML reports, which you can read with any Web browser. Fwlogwatch can read log files from any Ipchains or Iptables-enabled system, as well as Cisco firewalls and routers.

- E-mail an alert to you when suspicious activity occurs (e.g., when numerous connection attempts—usually port scans—surpass the threshold you set in /etc/firelogwatch.config, the Fwlogwatch configuration file). As with Fwlogwatch, this option will work only on packets that you decide to log.

- Issue a Windows Messenger Service alert that creates a "pop up" message to a Windows NT or 2000 server of your choice.

- Deliver summary-based e-mail messages informing management of the scans that have occurred.

- Insert Ipchains or Iptables-based rules that block hosts from connecting to your firewall and/or internal network hosts.

- Execute custom-created commands. You can have Fwlogwatch run any script that you wish to create.

Fwlogwatch Modes

Fwlogwatch operates in one of three modes. Table 11.3 describes each.

Table 11.3 Fwlogwatch Modes

Mode	Description
Realtime	Fwlogwatch operates as a daemon and reads the kernel messages file (usually /var/log/messages), waiting for Ipchains/Iptables-generated packets to occur. When the packets surpass the threshold, Fwlogwatch generates an alert. This mode is generally not for generating reports. Several Common

Continued

Table 11.3 Continued

Mode	Description
	Gateway Interface (CGI) scripts are available to help you generate HTML reports.
Interactive	Allows you to have Fwlogwatch read the /var/log/messages file and issue e-mail messages to various destinations. To use this mode, you must uncomment various lines, such as at least one e-mail account, in fwlogwatch.conf (or whatever name you are using). The e-mail messages are formatted according to the information found in the /etc/fwlogwatch.template file. When you start Fwlogwatch in interactive mode, it will parse the /var/log/messages file and then ask you if you wish to send an e-mail message to your recipient.
Log Time	Has Fwlogwatch inform you concerning the total number of entries in the /var/log/messages file. It also includes the first and last entries the kernel makes.

You can also manually generate HTML reports. Figure 11.3 shows the Help menu, which shows all of the command options. You can generate this list by entering **fwlogwatch –h**.

Figure 11.3 Fwlogwatch Command Options

```
[root@c1226878-b fwlogwatch-0.0.27]# ./fwlogwatch -h
fwlogwatch 0.0.27 (C) 2000-12-10 Boris Wesslowski, RUS-CERT
Usage: ./fwlogwatch [options]
Global options:
        -c <file>    specify config file (defaults to /etc/fwlogwatch.config)
        -D           do not differentiate destination IP addresses
        -d           differentiate destination ports
        -f <file>    specify input file (defaults to /var/log/messages)
        -h           this help
        -L           show time of first and last log entry in file
        -l <time>    process recent events only (defaults to off)
        -n           resolve host names
        -p           differentiate protocols
        -S           do not differentiate source IP addresses
        -s           differentiate source ports
        -t           show start and end times
        -V           show version and copyright info
        -v           verbose, specify twice for more info
        -y           differentiate TCP options (SYN/ACK)
        -z           show time interval

Log summary mode (default):
        -m <count>   only show entries with at least so many incidents
        -o <file>    specify output file
        -O <order>   define the sort order (see the man page for details)
        -w           HTML output

Interactive report mode:
        -i <count>   interactive mode with report threshold
        -F <email>   report sender address
                     (defaults to 'root@c1226878-b')
        -T <email>   address of CERT or abuse contact to send report to
        -C <email>   carbon copy recipients
        -I <file>    template file for report
                     (defaults to /etc/fwlogwatch.template)

Realtime response mode:
        -R           realtime response as daemon (default action: log only)
        -a <count>   alert threshold (defaults to 5 entries)
        -l <time>    forget events this old (defaults to 24 hours)
        -k <IP>      add this IP address to the list of known hosts
        -M <email>   send email notifications on incidents
        -B           block host completely with new firewall rule
        -W <host>    send a winpopup alert message to host
        -A <action>  custom action to take when threshold is reached
        -X           activate internal status information web server

[root@c1226878-b fwlogwatch-0.0.27]#
```

You can also consult the fwlogwatch man page for additional details. This chapter will focus on generating reports and configuring Fwlogwatch to send real-time alerts.

Fwlogwatch Options and Generating Reports

Table 11.4 is a list of the more relevant options, if you choose not to use the /etc/fwlogwatch.config file.

Table 11.4 FwLogwatch Options

Option	Description
-c <file>	Allows you to specify your own configuration file. The default is /etc/fwlogwatch.config. If you leave this filename at its default, you will not be able to manually use Fwlogwatch or use CGI scripts to generate automatic reports.
-f <file>	Allows you to read a different kernel log file, rather than the default of /var/log/messages.
-L	Has Fwlogwatch give the time of the first and last log entry.
-l <time>	Allows you to specify only certain events in terms of time. Arguments to the **-l** option include seconds (s), hours (h), minutes (m), days (d), weeks (w), months (m), and years (y). The default is to not have any limit at all, which can result in huge HTML log entries. If, for example, you wished to generate a log file for only the last two days, you would specify **-l 2** at the command line.
-n	Resolves host names in the log file. This can slow performance considerably.
-v	Places Fwlogwatch into verbose mode. Use it twice to obtain more information.
-z	Shows the amount of time between the start of a perceived attack and the end.
-m *value*	Has fwlogwatch ignore all identical packets that number less than the value. The result is that you will receive entries that have a higher uniqueness value. As far as alerting is concerned, you will probably wish to ignore the receipt of multiple packets if they are of only one type. For example, if you wish to ignore all identical packets unless the firewall receives 15 of them, you would specify **-m 15** in the command line.
-s, -d,	Informs you concerning the source and destination ports.

Continued

Table 11.4 Continued

Option	Description
-t	If more than one of the same type of packet is logged, then show the start and end times that they entered the system.
-z	Show the total amount of time that elapses between a series of entries. The series is determined by the threshold.
-y	List all elements of the TCP session.
-p	Informs you concerning all logged protocols (TCP, ICMP, and so forth).
-o	Allows you to specify the location of an output file.
-w	Tells Fwlogwatch that the output file should be in HTML.

Generating Reports

As of this writing, if the /etc/fwlogwatch.config file is present, the Fwlogwatch binary automatically ignores any options you specify at the command line. This poses a problem, because if you wish to manually generate a report, you need to specify command-line options.

> **NOTE**
>
> You will need to rename the /etc/fwlogwatch.conf file to some other name if you wish to use Fwlogwatch to generate HTML reports via CGI or cron.

To solve this problem, rename the /etc/fwlogwatch.config to /etc/fwlogwatch .config.alert. This way, you can still use this file to generate alerts, as discussed later, and still generate manual reports, when necessary. Although many different combinations are available to you, the following command is quite useful:

```
prompt$./fwlogwatch -v -v -s -d -t -z -y -n -p -w -l 2d -o firewall.html
-f /var/log/messages
        Resolving firewall-linux.goodguys.com
        Resolving 10.100.100.1.1 from cache
        Resolving 192.168.2.2 from cache
        Resolving sl-gw8-sj-0-3.sprintlink.net
```

```
Resolving 217.0.54.100

Resolving pD9003664.dip.t-dialin.net

Resolving 192.168.2.2 from cache

Resolving 194.91.224.19

Resolving 10.46.247.251

Resolving pD9003664.dip.t-dialin.net

Resolving adsl-63-206-155-186.dsl.lsan03.pacbell.net

Resolving cpe-24-221-58-193.az.sprintbbd.net

Resolving www.cnn.com

Resolving www.abcnews.com from cache
```

```
prompt$
```

The preceding command has Fwlogwatch read the –f /var/log/messages file and generate a report named firewall.html. The "Resolving . . ." lines indicate that Fwlogwatch has found log entries and is finding the IP address or DNS name for the hosts. Notice that the preceding command reads the firewall entries for the last two days (**-l 2d**), and that it uses the **–w** option to generate an HTML file, instead of a plain text file. Figure 11.4 shows an example of the HTML file, which can be viewed with any Web browser.

Figure 11.4 Viewing an Fwlogwatch HTML File

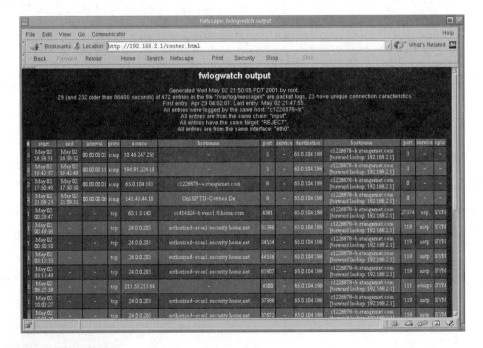

Using Fwlogwatch manually is especially useful if you plan to view log file entries from a remote host, such as another Linux system or a Cisco router. You can obtain the log file, copy it to your home directory, and then issue the preceding command, specifying the log file you wish to read.

As long as you have renamed the /etc/fwlogwatch.config file, you can use cron to have Fwlogwatch automatically create HTML reports and place them in your Apache Server home directory (or any other properly aliased directory).

Exercise: Generating an HTML-Based Firewall Log with Fwlogwatch

1. Make sure that your system is using either Ipchains or Iptables to log packets.

2. Create a user and a group named bw. These groups are necessary to enable Fwlogwatch to run additional processes as a nonroot user.

3. Install the Fwlogwatch RPM. You can, if you wish, copy the fwlogwatch -0.3-1.i386.rpm file from the CD that accompanies this book. The fwlogwatch-0.3-bin.tar.gz file provides the same functionality.

4. Rename the /etc/fwlogwatch.config file to /etc/fwlogwatch .config.alert.

5. Issue the following command to create a simple HTML report:

```
fwlogwatch -v -v -s -d -t -z -y -n -p -w -l 2d -o
      firewallreport.html -f /var/log/messages
```

6. Open the firewallreport.html file in any browser. This report is, of course, portable, allowing anyone (even Windows users) to view it. See Figure 11.5.

Automating Fwlogwatch

Perhaps the most intriguing feature of Fwlogwatch is its ability to automatically configure Ipchains/Iptables and issue alerts. The best way to do this is to edit the three configuration files to suit your needs. The three files you will use are:

- **/etc/fwlogwatch.config (or whatever you rename it to)** The primary configuration file. If you change this filename, then you must use the **-c** option to specify it when starting Fwlogwatch.

Figure 11.5 Viewing a Report in Microsoft Internet Explorer

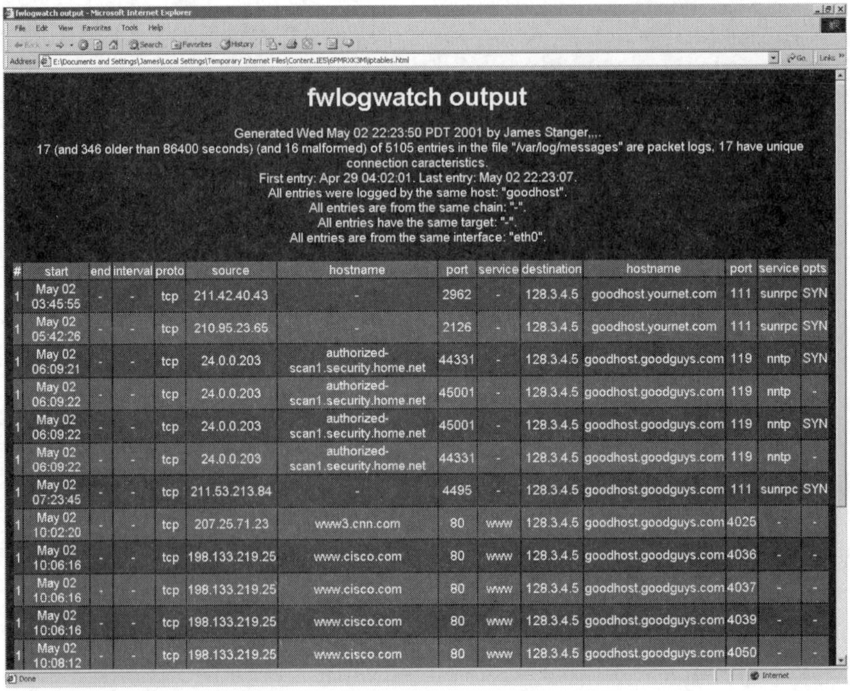

- **/usr/sbin/fwlw_notify** A script that allows you to configure all alerting options, including where e-mail and Samba/Windows "pop up" messages will be sent. Do not confuse these options with the interactive options, which are mutually exclusive. In other words, if you wish to have Fwlogwatch send you alerts, do not configure the interactive mode, which will ask you if you wish to send each report that Fwlogwatch generates.

- **/usr/sbin/fwlw_respond** This script determines Ipchains and Iptables behavior. You do not have to edit this file.

The Fwlogwatch Configuration File

You can customize all Fwlogwatch features by editing the /etc/fwlogwatch .config file (or /etc/fwlogwatch.config.alert, if you have renamed it in order to use the manual option). Figure 11.6 shows the configuration file.

Figure 11.6 The Fwlogwatch Configuration File

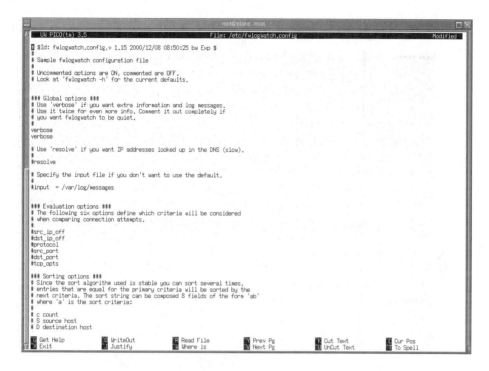

This file allows you to automatically invoke the options listed earlier in Table 11.4. For example, this file allows you to:

- Set verbose logging options.

- Create HTML files.

- Customize the alert threshold.

- Specify a different input file from /var/log/messages.

- Exclude hosts and ports.

- Sort host, protocol, port, and IP entries in the HTML files, as well as configure the files to inform you concerning the time the packets were generated, and the duration of a perceived attack.

- Determine how much of the kernel log file to read (e.g., only two minutes, three days, and so forth).

- Set realtime, interactive, and log times mode options.

- Create a proprietary Web server (not recommended).

If you change any of these values, you will have to restart Fwlogwatch so that it rereads this file.

Setting the Alert Threshold in fwlogwatch.config

It is likely that you will have to experiment with the ideal alert threshold for your firewall. The default value is 10, and you may find it necessary to increase this value significantly (say, to 100) so that you are not overwhelmed by the data you generate.

Understand, however, that if you receive too much data, you may also need to adjust the logging in Iptables/Ipchains.

Excluding Hosts

Fwlogwatch will monitor all entries that pass through the kernel log file (usually /var/log/messages). Fwlogwatch will block any interface—including its own—that violates the alert threshold value. One of the features found in Fwlogwatch is the ability to exclude certain IP addresses and address ranges from alerts and Ipchains/Iptables rules. This is necessary, because anyone with a port scanner that can spoof IP addresses can conduct a port scan on your firewall and specify an IP address important to your network. Such addresses might include the DNS and e-mail servers necessary to keep your business on a paying basis. It is possible to exclude these addresses from Fwlogwatch by opening the configuration file and finding the following lines:

```
known_host =
known_host =
```

Fwlogwatch allows you to get much more granular by using the additional entries shown here:

```
#exclude_src_host        =
#exclude_src_port        =
#exclude_dst_host        =
#exclude_dst_port        =
#include_src_host        =
#include_src_port        =
#include_dst_host        =
#include_dst_port        =
```

These entries allow you to exclude certain source and destination ports, as well as source and destination IP addresses.

Notification Options

To configure Fwlogwatch to notify you about attacks, you must first edit the /etc/fwlogwatch.config file and uncomment the following values:

```
realtime_response
notify
```

Once these values are uncommented, and once you have restarted Fwlogwatch, it will automatically call the /usr/sbin/fwlw_notify file. These files determine who will be informed, and what will be done, respectively. You will have to restart the Fwlogwatch binary for these changes to take effect.

Thankfully, both the fwlw_notify and fwlw_respond files are even easier to understand than fwlogwatch.config. The /usr/sbin/fwlw_notify script, shown in Figure 11.7, allows you to determine who will receive notification messages, and allows you to determine how this notification will occur.

Figure 11.7 The /usr/sbin/fwlw_notify File

```
[root@blake /root]# less /usr/sbin/fwlw_notify
#!/bin/sh
# $Id: fwlw_notify,v 1.3 2001/04/08 11:23:43 bw Exp $
# fwlogwatch realtime notification script

# You can invoke a custom action through this script when fwlogwatch
# issues an alert. A few commented examples are shown below.
# The available arguments (if activated in the configuration, if not the
# fields will contain a '-') are:
# $1 count
# $2 source IP
# $3 destination IP
# $4 protocol
# $5 source port
# $6 destination port


### Use the following lines for email notifications, $EMAIL is the recipient
#
#EMAIL=root@localhost
#
#/bin/echo "fwlogwatch ALERT on $HOSTNAME: $1 packet(s) from $2 to $3" | /bin/mail -s "fwlogwatch ALERT: $1 packet(s) from $2"
  $EMAIL


### Use the following lines for SMB notifications, $SMBHOST is the host the
### alert should appear
#
#SMBHOST=hostname
#
#/bin/echo "fwlogwatch ALERT on $HOSTNAME: $1 packet(s) from $2" | /usr/bin/smbclient -M $SMBHOST


### Use the following line to generate a custom log entry
#
#/usr/bin/logger -p security.alert -t "fwlogwatch ALERT" "$1 packet(s) from $2"


### You may also want to log alerts to a file
#
#NOW=`date +'%Y-%m-%d-%H-%M-%S'`
#/bin/echo "$NOW: $1 packet(s) from $2 to $3" >> /tmp/fwlw.log


### Insert your own ideas here, anything is possible. :-)
/usr/sbin/fwlw_notify (END)
```

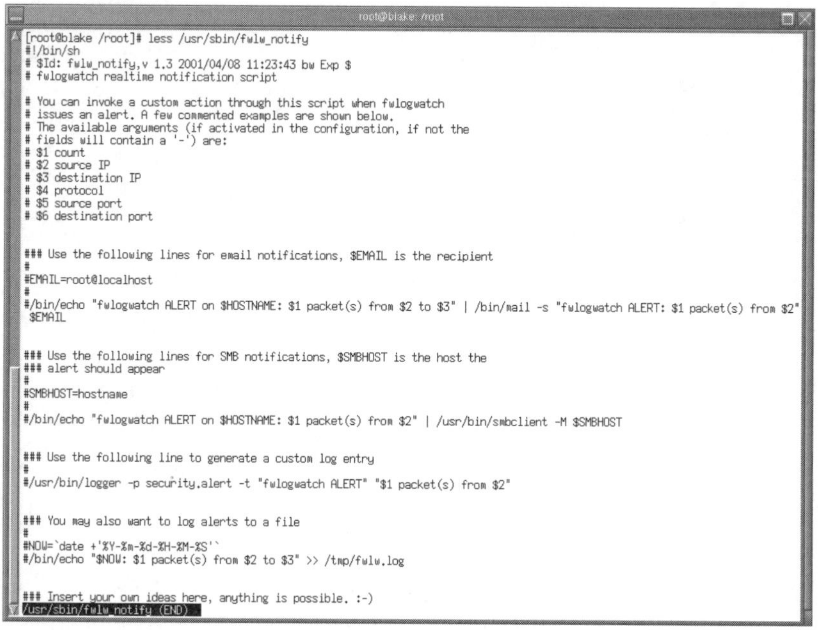

E-Mail Settings

All you have to do is uncomment the lines for any function you wish to enable. Then, enter your own e-mail address in the EMAIL= field. The default setting is for Fwlogwatch to send e-mail to root@localhost. If you are happy with this set-ting, you don't have to edit this line. The next entry to edit determines the actual contents of the e-mail message. By default, the message will contain the following information:

- Number of packets (as indicated by the $1 value)

- The source IP address (as indicated by the $2 value)

- The destination IP address (as indicated by the $2 value)

You can, of course, edit any aspect of the e-mail configuration settings. If, for example, you wish to change the subject heading, edit the quoted line after the -s field. Just make sure that you retain the quotation marks, as they allow you to enter multiple words into one subject line. Figure 11.8 shows an example of an e-mail alert.

Figure 11.8 Viewing E-Mail Alerts Generated by Fwlogwatch

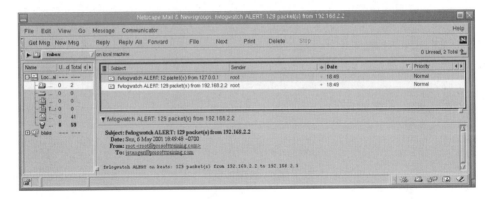

Note that Figure 11.8 actually shows two e-mail messages. The first e-mail message is a result of a log entry that blocks and logs all ICMP traffic. The second message has been generated at the same time. It is an alert informing the systems administrator that the loopback interface (127.0.0.1) has generated an attack. As a result, the loopback interface will be added to the Iptables fwlw user-defined chain, and no traffic will be allowed to pass through it. In many cases, this is not a problem, although it is a false positive. This systems administrator needs to add a rule excluding the local host being blocked.

Windows Pop-Up Messages

Fwlogwatch uses the smbclient application to send messages to remote Windows hosts. All you have to do is uncomment and edit the SMBHOST= line so that a message is sent to a real host, and then uncomment the next line so that a message is sent. For example, to send a pop-up message to a host named *sandi*, you would change the SMBHOST= entry and uncomment the following line:

```
SMBHOST=sandi
/bin/echo "fwlogwatch ALERT on $HOSTNAME: $1 packet(s) from $2" |
    /usr/bin/smbclient -M $SMBHOST
```

You can alter the second line at will. Read the script for additional values to enter. For example, if you wish to be informed of the protocol, you could use the $4 value.

This file also supports the creation of custom log entries through the use of the **logger** command, as well as the creation of a custom log file. Fwlogwatch also allows you to create your own alerting options. If, for example, your Linux system has a paging application installed, you can have your message sent directly to you. Figure 11.9 shows an example of a pop-up message received by a Windows 2000 Advanced Server system.

Figure 11.9 A Windows 2000 Advanced Server "Pop Up" Message

Response Options

To configure Fwlogwatch to actually respond to attacks, edit the /etc/fwlogwatch .config file and uncomment the following values:

```
realtime_response
respond
```

Then, restart Fwlogwatch. The /usr/sbin/fwlw_respond file is quite straightforward. As with /usr/sbin/fwlw_notify, you can edit this file to enter custom commands. You can, for example, have this script load additional scripts and applications that can reconfigure the local system, as well as remote systems. See Figure 11.10.

Figure 11.10 The fwlw_Respond File

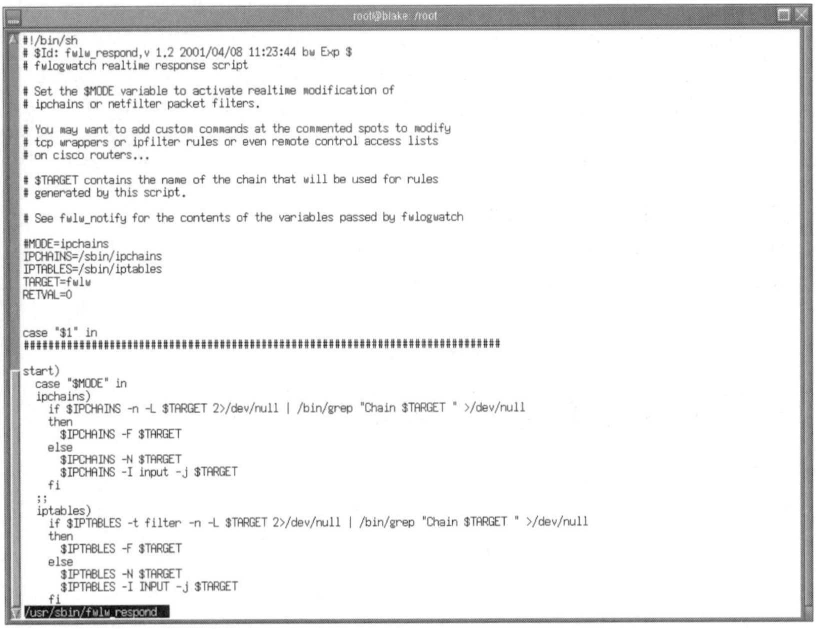

```
#!/bin/sh
# $Id: fwlw_respond,v 1.2 2001/04/08 11:23:44 bw Exp $
# fwlogwatch realtime response script

# Set the $MODE variable to activate realtime modification of
# ipchains or netfilter packet filters.

# You may want to add custom commands at the commented spots to modify
# tcp wrappers or ipfilter rules or even remote control access lists
# on cisco routers...

# $TARGET contains the name of the chain that will be used for rules
# generated by this script.

# See fwlw_notify for the contents of the variables passed by fwlogwatch

#MODE=ipchains
IPCHAINS=/sbin/ipchains
IPTABLES=/sbin/iptables
TARGET=fwlw
RETVAL=0


case "$1" in
#######################################################################

start)
  case "$MODE" in
  ipchains)
    if $IPCHAINS -n -L $TARGET 2>/dev/null | /bin/grep "Chain $TARGET " >/dev/null
    then
      $IPCHAINS -F $TARGET
    else
      $IPCHAINS -N $TARGET
      $IPCHAINS -I input -j $TARGET
    fi
    ;;
  iptables)
    if $IPTABLES -t filter -n -L $TARGET 2>/dev/null | /bin/grep "Chain $TARGET " >/dev/null
    then
      $IPTABLES -F $TARGET
    else
      $IPTABLES -N $TARGET
      $IPTABLES -I INPUT -j $TARGET
    fi
/usr/sbin/fwlw_respond
```

How Hosts Are Blocked

By default, Fwlogwatch creates a user-defined Ipchains or Iptables entry for the specific table and/or chain receiving the traffic. You can, of course, edit the script to alter this behavior, although it works quite efficiently as written.

Fwlogwatch and Root Privileges

Real-time response is protected. Only root can initiate Fwlogwatch to use Ipchains/Iptables blockings or e-mail and Samba-based alerts. Once initiated, Fwlogwatch will then run as the user bw. However, if you only require Fwlogwatch to generate reports, you do not need to run it as root. You must still ensure that Fwlogwatch can read the /var/log/messages file. You can do this by placing the user who will execute Fwlogwatch in the same group as the log file.

> **NOTE**
>
> In regard to Fwlogwatch, alerting and reporting are always two separate things. Do not be surprised that the e-mail message you receive is quite terse. You will learn how to automate reports using CGI scripts later in this chapter.

> **NOTE**
>
> In order to send pop-up messages, your system must have the samba-client package installed. If you are using RPM, the following command will tell you if you have the samba-client package installed:
>
> ```
> rpm -qa | grep samba
> ```
>
> Otherwise, search for the smbclient application. The Samba server is not necessary, and should not be activated at your firewall.

Exercise: Configuring Fwlogwatch to Send Automatic Alerts and Block Users

1. Make sure that you have Iptables/Ipchains entries that your kernel can log. You must have either the –l or –j LOG entries activated on at least one rule.

2. If you have not already, rename your /etc/fwlogwatch.config file to /etc/fwlogwatch.config.alert. The file named /etc/fwlogwatch.config should no longer exist.

    If you do not do this, you will not be able to issue command-line options, nor will you be able to issue alerts.

3. Edit the /etc/fwlogwatch.config.alert file and adjust the following parameters:

    - Enable verbose logging by simply uncommenting both lines that read verbose.

    - Uncomment the resolve option.

    - Enable the times and duration options. The former gives the times of the connections, while the latter gives the entire duration of the session.

    - Uncomment the known_host lines, and enter the IP addresses of your DNS and e-mail servers, as well as others that you do not want to block.

    - Enable the html line so that the daemon generates HTML pages.

- Uncomment the recent value and change it from three days (3d) to one day (1d).

- Uncomment the at_least value to 10 may have to change lower.

- Enable and change the alert_threshold setting to 15.

- Activate the notify and respond values by simply uncommenting them.

4. Edit the /usr/sbin/fwlw_notify file and adjust the following parameters:

- Activate the e-mail and Samba settings.

- Enter an e-mail address that you can check.

- In the Samba settings, alter the HOST=line so that Fwlogwatch sends a message to the correct system. Make sure that your Windows NT/2000 system is configured to receive messages.

5. Review the /usr/sbin/fwlw_respond file, but do not make any changes unless you have a very good idea of what to do.

6. Start Fwlogwatch, making sure you tell it where the configuration file is:

```
/usr/sbin/fwlogwatch -c /etc/fwlogwatch.config.alert
```

7. Now, using Nmap or Gnome ServiceScan, conduct a scan of your firewall so that your activity matches some of the Ipchains/Iptables rules you have created.

8. You will receive e-mail and Samba "pop up" messages informing you that activity has surpassed established thresholds.

Using Fwlogwatch with CGI Scripts

Fwlogwatch ships with two CGI scripts that, with minor modifications, can allow you to check your logs via a Web server. Although it is often important to shut down all services, activating Apache Web server may be a useful and relatively safe exception to this rule. If you have installed the scripts using the RPMP, you can obtain the raw scripts in the /usr/share/doc/fwlogwatch-0.3/ directory. If you have installed the files using a tarball, they will be in the source directory.

The first CGI script is quite simple. It creates an HTML page and tells Fwlogwatch to place all of the events that have occurred within the last hour inside of it. With some modifications, it can create an HTML file in your Apache Server directory. See Figure 11.11.

Figure 11.11 The fwlogsummary.small.cgi File

This file first has the command echoed so that if it is run by Cron, a message will be sent to the systems administrator via e-mail, informing him or her that the command has been executed. The actual command is shown here:

```
/usr/sbin/fwlogwatch -w -l 1h -z -s -d -o
    /var/www/html/fwlogsmallsummary.html
```

You can, of course, alter this script as you wish. For example, if your Web server's HTML directory is located at /home/httpd/html/, you can edit the file accordingly. If you wish to have a more verbose log entry, you can specify **–v –v**. However, this file is meant specifically for a quick rundown of the last hour's traffic.

To automate this file, place the script in the /etc/cron.hourly directory, or create the following crontab owned by root:

```
1 * * * * /fwlogsummary/fwlogsummary.small.cgi
```

When this script executes, you will be able to view the HTML file, as long as you have activated Apache Server. See Figure 11.12.

Figure 11.12 Viewing the Results of the fwlogsummary.small.cgi Script

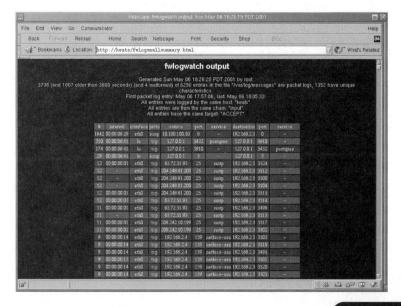

Obtaining More Information

For a more detailed view of the file, use the fwlogsummary.cgi file. Before you use this file, however, edit it so that it has the following characteristics:

- The file should point to a directory supported by your Web server. As of this writing, the fwlogsummary.cgi file defaults to using the /home/httpd/html/ directory, so make sure you specify the correct directory for your Web server. Red Hat 7.1 uses the /var/www/html/ directory, so create a subdirectory named /var/www/html/fwlogdaemon/. Or, you can create an entirely different directory and use an alias. It is up to you. It is important, however, that you create a dedicated directory, because the fwlogsummary.cgi script will create several files inside of it. The most important file is index.html, which contains several links that allow you to view all log entries as defined by the $RECENT value (the default, which you can change, is 1 hour).

- The file should specify the full path of the fwlogwatch binary.

- Remove the line that reads <a href="/cgi-bin/fwlogwatch .cgi">Regenerate summaries now</a>. As of this writing, this feature is not yet supported sufficiently. The edited file is shown in Figure 11.13.

Figure 11.13 The fwlogsummary.cgi File

```
#!/bin/sh
# $Id: fwlogsummary.cgi,v 1.1 2000/10/22 21:08:26 bw Exp $

# You could run this from crontab:
# 30 * * * * /path/fwlogsummary

RECENT="-l 1h"
WEBDIR="/var/www/html/fwlogwatch";
if [ ! -d $WEBDIR ]
then
    mkdir $WEBDIR
fi

if [ -z $1 ]
then
    MESSAGES="-f /var/log/messages"
else
    MESSAGES="-f $1"
fi

/usr/sbin/fwlogwatch $MESSAGES $RECENT -w -t -z -S          -o $WEBDIR/dst.html
/usr/sbin/fwlogwatch $MESSAGES $RECENT -w -t -z      -D     -o $WEBDIR/src.html
/usr/sbin/fwlogwatch $MESSAGES $RECENT -w -t -z             -o $WEBDIR/src_dst.html
/usr/sbin/fwlogwatch $MESSAGES $RECENT -w -t -z    -s       -o $WEBDIR/src_dst_sp.html
/usr/sbin/fwlogwatch $MESSAGES $RECENT -w -t -z         -d  -o $WEBDIR/src_dst_dp.html
/usr/sbin/fwlogwatch $MESSAGES $RECENT -w -t -z    -s -d    -o $WEBDIR/src_dst_sp_dp.html
/usr/sbin/fwlogwatch $MESSAGES $RECENT -w -t -z    -s -d -y -o $WEBDIR/src_dst_sp_dp_op.html
/usr/sbin/fwlogwatch $MESSAGES $RECENT -w -t -z    -s -d -y -n -o $WEBDIR/all.html

cat <<EOF > $WEBDIR/index.html
<html>
<head>
<title>fwlogwatch</title>
</head>
<body text="#000000" bgcolor="#FFFFFF" >
<font face="Arial, Helvetica">
<div align="center">
<h1>fwlogwatch summaries of the last hour</h1>
</div>

<h3>Summary by criteria:</h3>
<a href="src.html">Source IPs only</a><br>
<a href="dst.html">Destination IPs only</a><br>
<a href="src_dst.html">Both IPs</a><br>
<a href="src_dst_sp.html">With source port</a><br>
```

You can make additional trivial changes, such as altering the colors used in the HTML file. Once you have edited the file to your liking, you can place a script in the /etc/cron.hourly file, or create a crontab similar to the one discussed for the fwlogsummary.small.cgi script.

```
1 * * * * /fwlogsummary/fwlogsummary.cgi
```

Viewing the Results

Once you have edited the necessary files, created the necessary directories, and started the daemons (Apache Server and Cron), you can use your Web browser to view the index.html file generated by fwlogwatch.cgi. You will have to specify a directory or alias, but you will not have to specify a filename, because most Web servers present index.html by default. Thus, if your firewall Web server's root directory for HTML pages is /var/www/html/, and you have created a directory named /var/www/html/fwlogwatch/, then you would enter the following URL: http://firewall.goodguys.com/fwlogwatch. Figure 11.14 shows an example for the system named "keats."

Figure 11.14 Viewing the Index Page Generated by fwlogsummary.cgi

If you click on the **All and name resolution** link, for example, you will see a report summary similar to that shown in Figure 11.15.

Figure 11.15 Viewing the All and Name Resolution Page

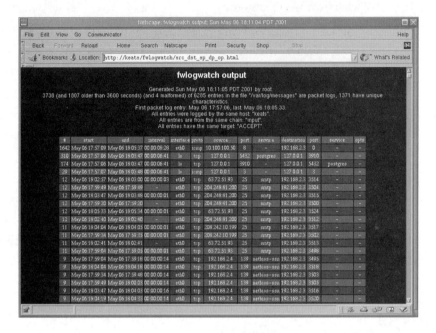

You will see that this particular HTML page is similar to the results of the Fwlogsummary.small.cgi file, except that you will see more hosts listed. The additional links will help you determine what has happened at your firewall.

> **NOTE**
>
> When you capture traffic using the Linux Netscape browser, you may find that it will "hang" for some time before rendering the HTML. You may have to wait for a few minutes to see the Fwlog output. At other times, you may find that the browser has crashed. Lynx, a text-based Web browser, and Windows-based browsers usually do not exhibit this behavior.

Exercise: Using Cron and Fwlogwatch CGI Scripts to Generate an Automatic HTML Report

1. Create the /fwlogsummary directory. This directory will hold your CGI scripts.

2. Find and copy the fwlogsummary.small.cgi and fwlogsummary.cgi scripts to the /fwlogsummary directory.

3. Find the directory that contains your Web server's HTML documents. Create a new subdirectory off of this directory named fwlogwatch. This directory will contain all of the files generated by the fwlogsummary.cgi file.

4. Create another subdirectory off your Web server's HTML document directory named fwlogwatchshort. This directory will contain the results of the fwlogsummary.small.cgi script.

5. Edit the fwlogsummary.small.cgi and fwlogsummary.cgi scripts so that they reflect your environment. For example, make sure that the both scripts refer to the fwlogwatch subdirectory. The fwlogsummary.small.cgi script should specify the fwlogsmallsummary.html file as an output file. This file should go into the fwlogwatchshort directory. Be especially careful to edit the fwlogsummary.cgi file so that it refers to the correct Web server directory, and that it no longer has the <a href="/cgi-bin/fwlogwatch.cgi">Regenerate summaries now</a> link. Read earlier in this chapter for more details.

6. Now, create crontab entries for each script. Make sure that you specify the correct path of the CGI scripts. For example, if you have created the /fwlogsummary directory, you would create the following crontab entries:

```
1 * * * * /fwlogsummary/fwlogsummary.small.cgi
1 * * * * /fwlogsummary/fwlogsummary.cgi
```

You can create these entries by issuing the following command as root:

```
crontab -e
```

You can also create scripts in the /etc/cron.hourly directory, if you wish.

7. Now, after 30 minutes, you will see that these scripts have generated several files. Point your Web browser to your firewall's /fwlogsummary subdirectory, and view the links generated by the fwlogsummary.cgi script.

8. For a more succinct description of the last hour's activities, point your browser at the /fwlogwatchshort directory. You will have to specify the

fwlogsmallsummary.html file, because it is doubtful that your Web browser uses this as a default document. If you wish, you can edit the CGI script to create an index.html file. For the purposes of this exercise, a different name was used to eliminate confusion with the /fwlogsummary directory.

9. Finally, consider the following options:

- If you are using Apache Server, use .htaccess files and htpasswd so that this information is password protected.

- Further secure this directory with Secure Sockets Layer (SSL). You can learn about enabling SSL support with Apache Server at www.openssl.org.

Additional Fwlog Features

Fwlogwatch contains the following features not discussed in this chapter:

- **Sorting** By editing the /etc/fwlogwatch.conf file, you can determine which events are listed first. This is a very useful feature, which allows you to emphasize information that it is important to you.

- **Web server** The Web server offered by Fwlogwatch is not as robust as Apache Server, nor is it as well documented. It is advised that you use Apache Server if you wish to use CGI at all.

 # Obtaining Additional Firewall Logging Tools

Table 11.5 contains an all-too-brief discussion of additional tools available to you.

Table 11.5 Additional Logging Tools

Tool	Description
Ipchains logger	A logging enhancer similar to Fwlogd, but limited to Ipchains. It is especially strong in its ability to log masqueraded connections. Its home page is at http://ipchainslog.sourceforge.net.
LogGrep	This daemon uses the grep utility to read and sort log files. It is limited, as of this writing, to Ipchains. With this utility, you can sort protocol, date, IP port firewall

Continued

Table 11.5 Continued

Tool	Description
	log entries to generate custom log files. Currently, it can also discover port scans, and generate HTML pages. The project's home page is at http://loggrep .sourceforge.net/.
Open Correlation	Although this project has not produced any files as of this writing, this project hopes to create an all-purpose logging daemon that can scan as many different types of log files as possible. Although it is dangerous to mention the word *universal* when discussing anything concerning Linux, this promises to be a helpful tool. The project's home page is at http://sourceforge.net/ projects/opencorrelation/.
Fwlogsum	This application generates HTML-based reports. The developers aim to create a logging utility that is powerful, yet easy to configure. HTML reports are meant to emulate those created by the popular, commercial Checkpoint FW-1 log firewall. The project's home page is at http://fwlogsum.sourceforge.net/.
IP Firewall Accounting (IPFA)	This logging software is meant to enhance IP accounting log information. It allows you to gather the following information: ■ Per month protocol usage ■ User monitoring, as long as identd is enabled on client hosts ■ Binding of IP addresses to MAC addresses You can obtain this software at www.tucows.com, or at http://linuxberg.eunet.fi/conhtml/adm_firewall.html.
Appsend	An application similar to SendIP. However, this application also allows you to simulate additional attacks, such as SYN floods and additional denial-of-service attacks. http://www.tucows.com, or at http://linuxberg .eunet.fi/conhtml/adnload/58289_31510.html.
IPmeter	IPmeter monitors network usage, and is designed to help you bill clients for usage. It generates HTML reports with embedded graphics. You can download it at www.ipmeter.com.
Mrtg	A traffic load monitor that generates HTML reports with embedded graphics. Similar to IPmeter, Mrtg is intended as a network management and monitoring

Continued

Table 11.5 Continued

Tool	Description
	tool, but it can also be very helpful as a security tool, because network management and security management concerns and tools are closely related. You can obtain Mrtg at www.mrtg.org, or at http://ee-staff.ethz .ch/~oetiker/webtools/mrtg/.
Ntop	The a ccompanying CD contains a version of Ntop (ntop-1.3.1-2.i386.rpm) that is compatible with most Linux versions. The latest version is available at www.ntop.org, Ntop is a powerful tool that allows you to identify the nature of all egress and ingress traffic. It is much like the standard top application, in that it gathers information about hosts, and then places the most active hosts at the top of the display. It can be run on a terminal just like the standard top application; you can run it in Web server mode, or as a Web server. This mode supports authentication, thus it allows you to easily limit access to only specific users.

Summary

This chapter focused on ways for you to gain information from your firewall and take action. You read about ways that you can make your firewall aware of port scans, and enhance its reporting and blocking capacity.

It is vital that you make it as easy as possible to read your firewall log files and respond to new threats. Although the premier reason to create a firewall is to selectively allow traffic in and out of a network, the second most important benefit of a firewall is its ability to log traffic. In this chapter, you learned how to test your firewall by conducting limited attacks against it. You also learned how to remain informed concerning scanning attacks and others designed to crash your firewall. You now have the tools and skills required to receive automatic alerts, and have your firewall automatically drop connections to scanning hosts.

It is vital that you maintain your firewall, and with the tools presented in this chapter, you can gather the information required to maintain it intelligently. You now can receive informative alerts, and comprehensive information concerning your firewall. In regard to logging, both Firelogd and Fwlogwatch can be used together to create a comprehensive information system. Of course, new tools are being developed all the time, and you should work to remain informed about new projects, as well as updates to the tools presented in this chapter.

Solutions Fast Track

Testing Firewalls

☑ To disallow IP spoofing, your firewall should not allow any packets to pass from outside the network into your internal network if the source address is the same as any host in your internal network. If you are using private IP addresses, no system outside of the firewall should ever be able to assume this IP address and access your internal network's ephemeral ports.

☑ Disable all unused services and configure the used ones keeping security in mind. If you are running Squid or another proxy server on the firewall, make sure that only this port is open. Daemons such as Telnet, File Transfer Protocol (FTP), Hypertext Transfer Protocol (HTTP), and others should be shut down in almost all situations. In many situations, it is best to allow only interactive logins at your firewall.

☑ Monitor your system hard drives, RAM, and processors. You may need to cut back on your log settings. Standard Linux tools that can help you determine if your system is becoming overburdened are *vmstat* and *top*.

☑ Use the **who** and **last** commands to learn about who has logged in to the firewall.

☑ Check the rules database. Determine if any unauthorized changes have been made to your database. Use the **diff** command to compare the two files to see if any changes have occurred. You may also use **md5** to generate fingerprints of the configuration files to see whether any unauthorized changes have been made to them. If you have Tripwire installed, you will then be informed of massive changes to the hard drive.

☑ Verify connectivity with company management and end users, and remain informed concerning the operating system.

☑ The introduction of log analysis software such as Firelogd and Fwlogdaemon have made it possible to detect and block port scans, all the while sending an alert to the systems administrator. Most adjunct software, such as Fwlogwatch, provides ways to exclude trusted hosts from being blocked.

Using Telnet, Ipchains, Netcat, and SendIP to Probe Your Firewall

☑ Although Iptables does not support rule checking, the **ipchains –C** command allows you to check how your existing rule set operates. It will return information as to whether the packet is dropped or accepted. It is up to you to act on this information. This tool is handy if you are logged in to the same system as you are testing, and you are becoming familiar with the existing rules and wish to send out packets that test how the rules are working.

☑ A simple port scan can help you determine which ports are open on your firewall. Using applications such as Telnet and Netcat, you can then determine what daemon is listening behind that port.

☑ If you have logged in to the firewall interactively, it is often useful to open two terminals. You can use the first terminal to issue the **telnet** command, and you can use the second terminal to view the results in the /var/log/messages file.

☑ When compiled properly, Netcat can also spoof IP addresses. If you have set a firewall rule to deny a particular source port, you can test it with Netcat. Because Netcat is so versatile, it can also be used against you to open a back door on your system. Therefore, if possible, you should install this application only on a client system, rather than on the router.

☑ Although Netcat does have the ability to create some packets in certain instances, it is not a true packet generator. SendIP is designed to allow you to create packets of your own design to test whether your firewall rules are working properly.

☑ SendIP allows you to forge any part of a Transmission Control Protocol (TCP) session, as well as any element of an IP, User Datagram Protocol (UDP), or Internet Control Message Protocol (ICMP) packet. SendIP also allows you to forge all elements of IPv6 addresses, and also allows you to forge Routing Information Protocol (RIP) packets. This tool is useful in regard to firewalls because it allows you to simulate any situation.

Understanding Firewall Logging, Blocking, and Alert Options

☑ Third-party logging applications such as Firewall Log Daemon (Firelogd) and FwLogwatch are available to help you sort and act on the information gathered by the firewall.

☑ Firelogd, which supports both Ipchains and Iptables, can be run either as an application, or as a daemon. It reads the kernel log entries generated by either Ipchains or Iptables and passes them into a "first in, first out" (FIFO) pipe, which Firelogd can then process. Once its buffer is full, it e-mails a report of suspicious traffic to an account of your choosing. You can have it mailed to a local account, or to a remote system of your choice.

☑ Fwlogwatch is a logging and reporting mechanism, similar to Firelogd but far more versatile, that allows you to automatically block all traffic that is identified as an attack. Used in conjunction with Firelogd, it helps create a system that continuously keeps you informed concerning port scans and other network events that surpass the thresholds you set.

☑ The most intriguing feature of Fwlogwatch is its ability to automatically configure Ipchains/Iptables and issue alerts. The best way to do this is to edit the three configuration files to suit your needs: **/etc/ fwlogwatch.config** (or whatever you rename it to), **/usr/sbin/ fwlw_notify**, and **/usr/sbin/fwlw_respond**.

Obtaining Additional Firewall Logging Tools

☑ Additional firewall logging tools include Ipchains logger, LogGrep, Open Correlation, Fwlogsum, IP Firewall Accounting (IPFA), Appsend, Ipmeter, Mrtg, and Ntop.

☑ Ipchains logger is a logging enhancer similar to Fwlogd, but limited to Ipchains. It is especially strong in its ability to log masqueraded connections.

☑ The LogGrep daemon uses the grep utility to read and sort log files. It is limited, as of this writing, to Ipchains. With this utility, you can sort protocol, date, IP port firewall log entries to generate custom log files. Currently, it can also discover port scans, and generates HTML pages.

☑ Ntop is a powerful tool that allows you to identify the nature of all egress and ingress traffic. It is much like the standard top application, in that it gathers information about hosts, and then places the most active hosts at the top of the display. It can be run on a terminal just like the standard top application; you can run it in Web server mode, or as a Web server. This mode supports authentication, thus allowing you to easily limit access to only specific users.

Frequently Asked Questions

The following Frequently Asked Questions, answered by the authors of this book, are designed to both measure your understanding of the concepts presented in this chapter and to assist you with real-life implementation of these concepts. To have your questions about this chapter answered by the author, browse to **www.syngress.com/solutions** and click on the **"Ask the Author"** form.

Q: You mention the use of Nmap as a scanner in this chapter. What other ways can I use Nmap to test my firewall?

A: Use Nmap's "slow scan" feature to map out your firewall's ports. See if your IDS applications and logging daemons such as Firelogd and Fwlogwatch can recognize and report scans that, for example, take five minutes between sending out packets. If you find that you have to set thresholds too low in order to get satisfactory results for slow scans, consider using the Shadow intrusion detection suite (www.nswc.navy.mil/ISSEC/CID).

Q: Some of the solutions, such as using Fwlogwatch, require the use of Cron, while others require the use of a Web server such as Apache. Isn't it a bad idea to use Cron and Web servers on your firewall?

A: Sometimes, it is necessary to run services on your firewall. If you require automated logging, you will either have to use Cron or resort to an internal scheduling application found in one of the applications you use. As long as your system's ports and services are locked down as much as possible, and as long as you keep current concerning the daemons that you do run, you will be both safe and informed. Just to make sure you are on the safe side, use both network-level packet filtering and access control lists (ACLs) in the Web server. If possible, use HTTPS instead of plain HTTP.

Q: I thought packet-filtering routers couldn't detect port scans. Yet, it seems like they now can. Is this a new feature given by Iptables and the 2.4 kernel?

A: No. Packet-filtering routers generally cannot detect port scans. Applications such as Firelogd and Fwlogwatch add this ability.

Q: What command do I use to create entries in the /etc/cron.hourly and/or /etc/cron.daily directories?

A: You simply create a text file in the directory that contains the relevant commands. This file must begin with a "shebang," which appears as follows:

```
#/bin/sh
```

You can then add whatever commands you wish. For example, you can specify the fwlogsummary.cgi file, and it will run hourly or daily, depending on the directory in which it is placed. You do not have to use any of the time fields, as you would if you use the **crontab –e** command. However, if you place a file in the /etc/cron.d/ directory, you will have to use the time fields, just as if you were creating a crontab entry.

Q: Fwlogwatch once created an Iptables rule blocking a host. I have since deleted this entry because I thought it was a false positive. However, I was wrong and I have noticed that this host is constantly scanning my firewall. Why doesn't Fwlogwatch add this host again?

A: Because Fwlogwatch already thinks that it has added the host. You can either add the host to the fwlw chain manually, or restart Fwlogwatch. However, if you restart Fwlogwatch, you will lose any existing blocking rules, so save them before you restart.

Q: I am getting flooded by a huge number of e-mails from Fwlogwatch. What do I do?

A: Increase the alert_threshold value in your Fwlogwatch configuration file. Firelogd allows you to set the threshold as well. If you have installed Firelogd from an RPM, just edit the /etc/rc.d/init.d/firelogd file and increase the QSIZE= value. If you do not have access to this file, then start firelogd with the **–b** *value* option and argument, and specify the buffer size there.

Bastille Log

The following table is provided for logging your Bastille choices. Bastille is simple to use, but it's easy to lose track of the changes you implement. This can be a problem if you are unable to perform a typical operation on the system, or are denied access to a command or service. Many times, it is because you locked down part of the system by mistake, or misjudged the impact of a particular Bastille choice. It is always a good idea to create a hard-copy log of the options you select in Bastille. When you configure Bastille on your systems, use this Bastille log to record the changes you implemented.

Question	Yes	No
Module 1: IPChains.pm		
1. Would you like to run the ipchains script? (Choosing "No" will skip to Module 2.)		
2. Do you need the advanced networking options?		
3. DNS Servers		
4. Public interfaces		
5. TCP services to audit (name or port number)		
6. UDP services to audit (name or port number)—the "Back Orifice" port number on Microsoft clients is listed by default.		
7. ICMP services to audit (name or port number)—an example is the Microsoft "echo-request" service (Microsoft ping and tracert commands).		
8. TCP service names or port numbers to allow on public interfaces (typical workstations should not allow any services).		
9. UDP service names or port numbers to allow on public interfaces (typical workstations should not allow any services).		
10. Force passive mode (i.e., for clients connecting to an FTP server).		
11. TCP services to block (if you force passive mode, you can skip this step).		
12. UDP services to block		
13. ICMP allowed types:		
14. Enable source address verification		

Continued

Question	Yes	No
15. Reject method		
16. Interfaces for DHCP queries		
17. NTP servers to query		
18. ICMP types to disallow outbound		
Module 2: PatchDownload.pm		
1. Would you like to download and install the updated RPMs?		
Module 3: FilePermissions.pm		
1. Would you like to set more restrictive permissions on the administration utilities?		
2. Would you like to disable SUID status for mount/umount?		
3. Would you like to disable SUID status for ping?		
4. Would you like to disable SUID status for dump and restore?		
5. Would you like to disable SUID status for cardctl?		
6. Would you like to disable SUID status for at?		
7. Would you like to disable SUID status for DOSEMU?		
8. Would you like to disable SUID status for news server tools?		
9. Would you like to disable SUID status for printing utilities?		
10. Would you like to disable SUID status for the r-tools?		
11. Would you like to disable SUID status for usernetctl?		
12. Would you like to disable SUID status for traceroute?		
Module 4: AccountSecurity.pm		
1. Would you like to set up a second UID 0 account?		
1a. What should we name the second UID 0 account?		

Continued

Question	Yes	No
2. May we take strong steps to disallow the dangerous r-protocols?		
3. Would you like to enforce password aging?		
4. Would you like to create a nonroot user account?		
4a. What should we name your nonroot account?		
5. Would you like to restrict the use of cron to administrator accounts?		
Module 5: BootSecurity.pm		
1. Would you like to password protect the LILO prompt?		
1a. Enter LILO password, please.		
2. Would you like to reduce the LILO delay time to zero?		
3. Do you ever boot Linux from the hard drive?		
4. Would you like to write the LILO changes to a boot floppy?		
4a. Floppy drive device name		
5. Would you like to disable Ctrl_Alt_Delete rebooting?		
6. Would you like to password protect single-user mode?		
Module 6: SecureInetd.pm		
1. Would you like to modify inetd.conf and /etc/hosts.allow to optimize use of Wrappers?		
2. Would you like to set sshd to accept connections only from a small list of IP addresses?		
2a. IP addresses to accept ssh from:		
3. Would you like to make "Authorized Use" banners?		
Module 7: DisableUserTools.pm		
1. Would you like to disable the compiler?		

Continued

Question	Yes	No
Module 8: ConfigureMiscPAM.pm		
1. Would you like to put limits on system resource usage?		
2. Should we restrict console access to a small group of user accounts?		
2a. What accounts should be able to log in at console?		
Module 9: Logging.pm		
1. Would you like to add additional logging?		
2. Do you have a remote logging host?		
2a. What is the IP address of the machine you want to log to?		
3. Would you like to set up process accounting?		
Module 10: MiscellaneousDaemons.pm		
1. Would you like to disable apmd?		
2. Would you like to deactivate NFS and Samba?		
3. Would you like to disable atd?		
4. Would you like to disable PCMCIA services?		
5. Would you like to disable the DHCP daemon?		
6. Would you like to disable GPM?		
7. Would you like to disable the news server daemon?		
8. Would you like to deactivate the routing daemons?		
9. Would you like to deactivate NIS server and client programs?		
10. Would you like to disable SNMPD?		
Module 11: Sendmail.pm		
1. Do you want to leave sendmail running in daemon mode?		
2. Would you like to run sendmail via cron to process the queue?		
3. Would you like to disable the VRFY and EXPN sendmail commands?		

Continued

Question	Yes	No
Module 12: RemoteAccess.pm		
1. Would you like to download and install SSH?		
Module 13: DNS.pm		
1. Would you like to chroot named and set it to run as a nonroot user?		
2. Would you like to deactivate named, at least for now?		
Module 14: Apache.pm		
1. Would you like to deactivate the Apache Web server?		
2. Would you like to bind the Web server to listen only to the localhost?		
3. Would you like to bind the Web server to a particular interface?		
3a. Address to bind the Web server to:		
4. Would you like to deactivate the following of symbolic links?		
5. Would you like to deactivate server-side includes?		
6. Would you like to disable CGI scripts, at least for now?		
7. Would you like to disable indexes?		
Module 15: Printing.pm		
1. Would you like to disable printing?		
Module 16: FTP.pm		
1. Would you like to disable user privileges on the FTP daemon?		
2. Would you like to disable anonymous download?		

Hack Proofing Linux Fast Track

This Appendix will provide you with a quick, yet comprehensive, review of the most important concepts covered in this book.

❖ Chapter 1 Introduction to Open Source Security

Using the GNU General Public License

☑ The GPL protects the software code, not a corporation or an individual.

☑ Protecting code rather than individuals is a radical change, because it allows code to be improved upon without being made completely proprietary.

☑ Open source code does not necessarily have to be free. For example, companies such as Red Hat and Caldera sell their products, which are based on the open source Linux kernel.

Soft Skills: Coping with Open Source Quirks

☑ As you use open source code, remember that this code may represent a work in progress.

☑ Sometimes, open source code changes radically, forcing you to retrain users. You may find that updates happen irregularly, and that it is sometimes more challenging to update open source code. Furthermore, once you upgrade the code, you may be presented with an application that behaves very differently, or has a radically different interface.

☑ Before installing open source software, make sure that your operating system contains all of the necessary supporting applications and libraries.

Should I Use an RPM or Tarballs?

☑ RPMs sometimes offer convenience. However, precompiled RPMs often do not have all of the features necessary to implement a truly useful product.

☑ Tarballs often require editing of a special file called a *makefile*. However, this is not necessarily all that difficult. It simply requires that you know where your supporting applications and libraries are. Also, most open source software will contain instructions concerning how to edit the makefile. Most well-known operating systems, such as Red Hat Linux and Slackware, do not require makefile modification.

Chapter 1 Continued

☑ RPMs often contain useful startup scripts that are not found elsewhere. Sometimes, it is useful to install the RPM, then the tarball version, and then combine elements from the two for a complete solution.

Obtaining Open Source Software

☑ Sites such as SourceForge (www.sourceforge.com), RPMFind (www.rpmfind.net), and SecurityFocus (www.securityfocus.com) are valuable software sources.

☑ Be especially careful when downloading any source code, regardless of format. Digital signatures can help you determine the author of a package, as well as whether a package has been altered.

☑ The Gnu Privacy Guard (GPG) and Pretty Good Privacy (PGP) packages are available to help you verify signatures. They do not stop the execution of malicious code, however. They simply inform you about the nature of the code's author, and of any changes that may have occurred to the code.

A Brief Encryption Review

☑ Symmetric encryption is the use of one key to encrypt and decrypt information. If a malicious user is able to intercept the key, he or she can then use it to decrypt your secret messages.

☑ Asymmetric encryption uses a mathematically related *key pair* to encrypt and decrypt information. This type of encryption is commonly used on the Internet and on LANs, because it reduces the likelihood that the key can be learned by a malicious user, and aids in authentication.

☑ One-way encryption is the use of an algorithm to encrypt information so that it is, mathematically speaking, impossible to unencrypt. One-way encryption is also used to read a file and then create a *hash* of that file. The resulting hash value is said to be mathematically unrecoverable. Hash code is often used to compare one value to another during the login process: the person logging in enters a username and password, and the authentication mechanism creates a hash of these two values and compares it to the hash values generated from the /etc/passwd and /etc/shadow databases. If the values match, access is allowed.

Chapter 1 Continued

Public Key and Trust Relationships

☑   You must generate a key pair to begin using your public key to authenticate yourself or to encrypt network transmissions.

☑   Establishing a trust relationship involves exchanging public keys. Sometimes, individual users must give public keys. At other times, public keys are exchanged between network hosts.

☑   Never reveal your private key. If your private key is made available to a third party, this person will be able to read all of your encrypted files.

Auditing Procedures

☑   As an auditor, your job is to lock down your network, which means that you must consider the security of each host using tools that allow you to determine changes in files and directories, and who has scanned and accessed your system. You must also monitor network transmission and configure your firewall to establish an effective network perimeter that separates your network from all others.

☑   An Intrusion Detection System (IDS) acts as an auditing host or series of auditing hosts that allow you to monitor and secure data as it passes across the network.

☑   Protecting the network perimeter involves proper firewall and proxy server configuration, logging, and monitoring.

❖ Chapter 2 Hardening the Operating System

Updating the Operating Systems

☑   Operating system releases usually contain software bugs and security vulnerabilities.

☑   Operating system vendors or organizations offer fixes, corrections, and updates to the system. For example, Red Hat offers this material at its Web site, which includes Update Service Packages and the Red Hat Network.

Chapter 2 Continued

☑ You should always ensure your system has the latest necessary upgrades. Many errata and Update Service Packages are not required for every system. You should always read the associated documentation to determine if you need to install it.

Handling Maintenance Issues

☑ After your system goes live, you must always maintain it by making sure the most current patches and errata are installed, which include the fixes, corrections, and updates to the system, as well as the applications running on it.

☑ You should always check the Red Hat site at www.redhat.com/apps/ support/updates.html for the latest errata news.

☑ For example, Red Hat security advisories provide updates that eliminate security vulnerabilities on the system. Red Hat recommends that all administrators download and install the security upgrades to avoid denial-of-service (DoS) and intrusion attacks that can result from these weaknesses.

Manually Disabling Unnecessary Services and Ports

☑ You should always disable vulnerable services and ports on your system that are not used. You are removing risk when you remove unnecessary services.

☑ The /etc/xinetd.d directory makes it simple to disable services that your system is not using. For example, you can disable the FTP and Telnet services by commenting out the FTP and Telnet entries in the respective file and restarting the service. If the service is commented out, it will not restart.

Locking Down Ports

☑ When determining which ports to block on your server, you must first determine which services you require. In most cases, block all ports that are not exclusively required by these services.

☑ To block TCP/UDP services in Linux, you must disable the service that uses the specific port.

Chapter 2 Continued

Hardening the System with Bastille

☑ The Bastille program facilitates the hardening of a Linux system. It saves administrators time from configuring each individual file and program throughout the operating system.

☑ Administrators answer a series of "Yes" and "No" questions through an interactive text-based interface. The program automatically implements the administrators' preferences based on the answers to the questions.

☑ Bastille can download and install RPM updates, apply restrictive permissions on administrator utilities, disable unnecessary services and ports, and much more.

Controlling and Auditing Root Access with Sudo

☑ Sudo (Superuser Do) allows an administrator to give specific users or groups the ability to run certain commands as root or as another user.

☑ Sudo features command logging, command restrictions, centralized administration of multiple systems, and much more.

☑ The **sudo** command is used to execute a command as a superuser or another user. In order to use the **sudo** command, the user must supply a username and password. If a user attempts to run the command via sudo and that user is not entered in the sudoers file, an e-mail is automatically sent to the administrator, indicating that an unauthorized user is accessing the system.

Managing Your Log Files

☑ Logging allows administrators to see who and what has accessed their system. Many helpful Linux log files are located in the /var/log directory.

☑ Linux offers commands that allow administrators to access useful log files. Two commands of interest are *last* and *lastlog*. The message file also offers useful data for determining possible security breaches on your system.

Chapter 2 Continued

☑ The Linux logs should be checked frequently to determine if any security violations have occurred on your system. Logs do not offer solutions, so you must analyze the data and decide how to counteract the attack.

Using Logging Enhancers

☑ Logging enhancers are tools that simplify logging by allowing logging information to be filtered and often displaying logs in simplified formats.

☑ Viewing text-based files with hundreds or thousands of entries can be burdensome, especially if you are only looking for one specific error entry.

☑ Three popular logging services used by administrators are SWATCH, scanlogd, and the next generation of syslogd (syslogd-ng).

❖ Chapter 3 System Scanning and Probing

Scanning for Viruses Using the AntiVir Antivirus Application

☑ Virus scanners will perform the following tasks: check the system's boot record; search directories and subdirectories; automatically delete infected files; save scans into a log file; use an internal scheduler, or an external scheduler, such as at or cron; scan NFS-mounted drives; delete infected files; and move infected files to a central, "quarantine" area of your own choosing.

☑ The AntiVir for Servers binary is a truly impressive command-line virus scanner sold by H+BDEV. It is capable of searching for and deleting macro viruses, boot sector viruses, e-mail viruses, and DDoS daemons.

☑ An antivirus application is only as useful as its virus definition file. Your application should provide you with frequent updates.

Chapter 3 Continued

Scanning Systems for DDoS Attack Software Using a Zombie Zapper

☑ Attackers wage denial of service (DoS) attacks by first finding and hacking into insecure systems on the Internet. Then, they install programs such as Tribe Flood Network 2000 (Tfn2k), stacheldraht, and others. The compromised systems now have illicit programs installed on them called *zombies*.

☑ Once a zombie is commanded to attack a victim, it will generally continue the attack until it is forced to stop. If you notice large amounts of unknown traffic when you monitor your network or network perimeter, you can use a zombie zapper against the host or hosts generating this traffic.

☑ Limitations of a zombie zapper can include the following: they are programmed to shut down only certain DDoS servers; it may be blocked by a firewall; the malicious user may have changed the password of the illicit server; or the attack server may have spoofed packets.

Scanning System Ports Using the Gnome Service Scan Port Scanner

☑ Systems administrators find port scanners useful when auditing their own systems. Although a simple port scanner such as GSS does not actually test for flaws in binaries and Web applications, a good port scanner can help you isolate which ports are open, and then take any action that is necessary.

☑ Port scanning a machine may set off an alarm for the system's administrator, who might take a dim view of your actions. Unless you have explicit (sometimes, even written) permission from the system administrator, you may cause a serious violation of your security policy.

Using Nmap

☑ Nmap is an advanced Unix-based port scanner. It can be used to audit your network, test your router and switch configurations, test your firewall configurations, and identify the nature of suspicious remote systems.

Chapter 3 Continued

☑ You can use Nmap as a basic port scanner for a system on your internal network, or you can have it identify the operating system version of a remote system on another firewall-protected network. Nmap is capable of manipulating aspects of TCP to hide its scans from firewalls.

☑ Nmap's "interactive mode" allows you to do two things that you should be aware of as a systems administrator: It can conduct multiple Nmap sessions, and it can disguise the fact that it is running on your system.

Using Nmapfe as a Graphical Front End

☑ The Nmap Front End (NmapFE) provides a well-written, stable GUI that allows you to control almost every aspect of Nmap.

☑ Note that this interface is somewhat unstable, and given to faults that lead to complete crashes (core dumps). This is especially the case in systems that have been upgraded (say, from Red Hat version 7.0 to 7.1).

Using Remote Nmap as a Central Scanning Device

☑ Remote Nmap (Rnmap) enables a client system to connect to a central Nmap server. It is currently in beta, but both the client and the server are quite strong.

☑ Rnmap has the following features: user authentication, a command-line and GUI client, and available encryption (still in beta form). Rnmap is written in the Python scripting language, which means that your Linux system must have Python installed.

Deploying Cheops to Monitor Your Network

☑ Billed as a graphical network neighborhood, Cheops is related to applications such as HP OpenView. Both Cheops and HP OpenView allow you to create a graphical map of the network, and then manage any host on that map. Although Cheops is not nearly as sophisticated, it still allows you to quickly learn which hosts are up on a particular network segment.

Chapter 3 Continued

☑   Cheops issues network broadcasts, and then processes these replies to discover remote hosts. Some older versions of Cheops use an application called
Queso to read the replies of remote systems. Queso is similar to Nmap,
although not as sophisticated or as recent. As with Nmap, Queso does use
stack fingerprinting to guess the operating system of a remote server.

☑   Cheops is capable of two types of monitoring. First, it can have your Linux
system issue simple ping requests to see if a remote host is up. Second,
instead of relying on a crude ping request, Cheops allows you to pick a
specific service offered by the remote host.

Deploying Nessus to Test Daemon Security

☑   Using vulnerability detection software, you can find out exactly what specific application is listening on that port. A good hacker is well informed
concerning the popular servers on the Internet, and can quickly take advantage of a specific daemon that has a security problem. Nessus allows you to
proactively scan your system to determine its weaknesses.

☑   The Nessus client allows you to connect to the Nessus daemon, which is
usually on a remote server. Several different clients exist, including those for
Windows, Macintosh, and Unix/Linux systems.

☑   The Nessus project has been quite active, and has a good record for
providing regular plug-in updates.

☑   When you launch the client for the first time, it will take some time to
create a public key pair, which will be used to authenticate with any Nessus
daemon.

☑   The compilation option allows the client to "remember" past sessions and to
configure a nessus daemon to conduct a scan all by itself. These capabilities are
respectively called *differential* and *detached* scanning. The ability to save sessions
allows you to begin sessions that have been interrupted.

❖ Chapter 4 Implementing an Intrusion Detection System

Understanding IDS Strategies and Types

☑ An Intrusion Detection System (IDS) is any system or set of systems that has the ability to detect a change in the status of your system or network. Because an IDS can contain multiple hosts and applications, this chapter will often use the term *IDS application* to refer to a specific IDS element.

☑ Two general strategies are used when it comes to detecting intrusions, rule-based IDS applications (also called *signature-based)* and anomaly-based IDS applications.

☑ IDS applications do their work either continuously in real-time, or at certain intervals (interval-based intrusion detection).

☑ Two different types of IDS applications exist: host-based and network-based.

☑ In many cases, an effective IDS application requires a great deal of processor time in order to work well. Log files require a great deal of hard drive space, especially in busy networks. Thus, simply for the sake of performance, consider using multiple systems to gather, store, and analyze information.

☑ Most network-based IDS applications do not work properly in a switched network.

☑ An IDS stores its information in several places: System logs, simple text files and directories, and databases.

☑ An IDS can act as a supplement to a firewall, because it can help you monitor traffic on the internal network. Sometimes it may be useful to place an IDS application outside the firewall, or in the DMZ so that you can learn more about the attacks waged against the firewall itself.

Installing Tripwire to Detect File Changes

☑ Tripwire is one of the most popular applications for determining when a file or directory has been altered. It scans your system's hard drive and creates a database. After its database has been created, Tripwire can conduct regular scans of your hard drive and inform you (via e-mail or a log file) about any changes.

Chapter 4 Continued

Updating Tripwire to Account for Legitimate Changes in the OS

☑ Eventually, legitimate changes will occur to your operating system. These changes will keep appearing in reports unless you update your database. Database update mode allows you to update the database so that it no longer recognizes any differences between itself and the operating system.

☑ Updating the policy is different than updating the database. It is sometimes necessary to update your policy. If, for example, you install a new application, you may want to ensure that these files are protected by Tripwire.

Configuring Tripwire to Inform You Concerning Changes

☑ As with any Linux/Unix application, you will have to do quite a bit of "tweaking" to make Tripwire suit your needs. Refer back to the Installing Tripwire, Securing the Tripwire Database, and Using Cron to Run Tripwire Automatically Exercises for more information on how to install and use Tripwire.

Deploying PortSentry to Act as a Host–Based IDS

☑ PortSentry is a host-based IDS application that monitors all open ports. It is an effective tool if you wish to detect TCP and/or UDP port scans, and if you wish to have your host reconfigure itself in case of a port scan.

☑ PortSentry will compile on any standard Linux system that has TCPWrapper and Ipchains or Ipfw support.

☑ All of the PortSentry files are located off of the /usr/local/psionic/ portsentry/ directory. All files are owned by root, and the program must be started as root, because it places your NIC into promiscuous mode.

Chapter 4 Continued

Configuring PortSentry to Block Users

☑ The Advanced Stealth Scan Detection Options determine the port numbers that PortSentry will monitor when you use the **–stcp** option to start PortSentry. By default, PortSentry listens only to ports up to 1023.

☑ The Dropping Routes section allows you to determine how PortSentry will deny connections. The KILL_ROUTE options allow you to configure various system tools to actually do the work of denying hosts.

Optimizing PortSentry to Sense Attack Types

☑ You can start PortSentry in various ways, depending upon the types of attacks you wish to detect. Customize each system that you have depending upon its function and place in your network.

Installing and Configuring Snort

☑ Snort, available at www.snort.org, is best-suited to detailed log analysis. Like PortSentry, it places your NIC into promiscuous mode. It captures all traffic on your network segment, as opposed to traffic destined for just one host.

☑ Snort can log its findings into remote or local databases. Snort's analysis feature is able to read the contents of the captured packets and then inform you about any attacks waged against your network.

☑ Snort is able to automatically detect attacks based solely upon the rules it uses.

☑ You can use several detection plug-ins. Sometimes, plug-ins do not require additional arguments. At other times, they require you to specify additional parameters.

Running Snort as a Network-Based IDS

☑ However, the snort.conf file gives you the ability to use Snort as a true IDS because it has Snort use rules and plug-ins. You can also specify more sophisticated home network and logging methods. After you begin using the rules and plug-ins found in snort.conf, it will begin selectively logging traffic.

Chapter 4 Continued

Configuring Snort to Log to a Database

☑ On busy networks, it is necessary to configure Snort to log less information. Certain command-line options help you control how much your IDS will log.

☑ Additional configuration options are available, including the ability to configure Snort to send alerts to Windows systems that have the Server service running.

Identifying Snort Add-Ons

☑ SnortSnarf is a collection of Perl scripts designed to read the Snort alert file (/var/log/snort/alert) and then generate HTML output. The program is available from www.silicondefense.com/software/snortsnarf.

❖ Chapter 5 Troubleshooting the Network with Sniffers

Understanding Packet Analysis and TCP Handshakes

☑ Analyzing TCP traffic is one of the most important tasks for a security administrator. It can tell you a great deal about your network connections, as well as identify many denial-of-service (DoS) attacks and man-in-the-middle, or hijacking, attacks.

☑ A TCP handshake must occur whenever two hosts establish a connection on a TCP/IP network. This handshake consists of rules that the two hosts must follow.

☑ Special mechanisms, called *flags*, are used to establish and terminate a TCP connection. Flags are included in the TCP header, and each flag completes a different function in the TCP handshake. The flags used are SYN, FIN, RST, PSH, ACK, and URG.

Chapter 5 Continued

Creating Filters Using Tcpdump

☑ Tcpdump captures packets on a given interface, or on all interfaces on a system, for analysis. It is a command-line tool, which can make it difficult to read.

☑ Tcpdump options allow you to filter the packets that are captured. For example, you can limit the capture to ARP packets or display only IP addresses (not host names).

☑ Tcpdump expressions allow you to specify the hosts from which you will capture packets. For example, an expression will ensure that only the data you require, such as the traffic between your interface and a specific host, will be printed.

Configuring Ethereal to Capture Network Packets

☑ Ethereal provides a GUI environment for capturing network packets, which makes it easier for many administrators to use.

☑ Ethereal and tcpdump capture packets using the pcap library (libpcap). Since they both use the pcap library (libpcap) syntax, they can share many of the same commands, such as filtering options and primitives.

☑ You can easily save Ethereal filters and access them as needed for each packet capture you make. You can have multiple filters from which to choose for different needs.

Viewing Network Traffic between Hosts Using EtherApe

☑ EtherApe is a GUI that displays networking activity graphically by identifying hosts and the links that exist between the hosts. It displays real-time traffic, as well as traffic saved to a file.

☑ EtherApe also uses the pcap library (libpcap), the library for packet capturing and filtering, which is similar to tcpdump and Ethereal.

☑ EtherApe uses options to specify the capture information, such as the interface, link colors, or whether names or numbers will be used.

❖ Chapter 6 Network Authentication and Encryption

Understanding Network Authentication

☑ Even if employees remain behind the firewall, many system services allow clear text authentication, including Telnet, File Transfer Protocol (FTP), and standard Network Information Service (NIS). Even though transmissions can be encrypted, many tools exist that help hackers wage a *sniffing* attack to capture encrypted information.

☑ After the packets containing the encrypted passwords are captured, hackers use cracking applications such as L0phtCrack, which are designed to both capture and crack sniffed encrypted passwords.

Creating Authentication and Encryption Solutions

☑ To authenticate safely, you have two options: Find a way to authenticate without sending passwords across the network, or find a way to discard any password that is sent across the network. The accepted phrase for this strategy is *one-time passwords* (OTP).

☑ Kerberos has the added ability to encrypt transmissions after authentication occurs. The use of OTP, however, does not encrypt subsequent transmissions. OTP is usually much easier to implement than Kerberos, however.

☑ Other encrypting solutions include Secure Sockets Layer (SSL), Secure Shell (SSH), and IPSec.

Implementing One-Time Passwords (OTP and OPIE)

☑ In the Linux world, the most universal way to implement one-time password (OTP) support in your Linux systems is to install the One-Time Passwords in Everything (OPIE) application. OPIE supports the Message Digest 5 (MD5) algorithm.

☑ By default, OPIE does not enforce OTP whenever you log in interactively. Any user is given the choice of using OTP or the standard login procedure.

Chapter 6 Continued

☑ Using **opiepasswd** to create OPIE users. As soon as the **opiepasswd** command is used against a user, it is then possible for that user to use OTP to log in. The **opiekey** command generates responses.

☑ When the systems administrator creates an OTP password list, the user can use the **opieinfo** command to generate a list of passwords for later use.

Implementing Kerberos Version 5

☑ Kerberos v5 is a revolutionary step in network authentication, because it allows you to establish a domain that authenticates not only individual hosts and users, but individual daemons, as well. Using Kerberos, you can centrally control which hosts and users can access the daemons on your network.

☑ After Kerberos is established on a network, passwords do not ever cross the network, not even in encrypted form. You can configure Kerberos to encrypt ensuring communications between authenticated hosts.

☑ A principal is the name for any host, service, or user that is allowed to authenticate on a Kerberos network. A principal consists of a primary (also known as a "root"), an instance, and a realm.

☑ The **kadmin** application, also found in the /usr/kerberos/sbin/ directory, is designed to add principals to the Kerberos database. The **kadmin** command also lists, modifies, and deletes principals. It is also used to populate and update the Key table files for each Kerberos host.

Using kadmin and Creating Kerberos Client Passwords

☑ Standard principal policy settings include policy name, minimum password life (in seconds), maximum password life (in seconds), and minimum password length.

☑ You can create a policy by using the **addpol** command from within kadmin.

Chapter 6 Continued

☑   The **kinit** command allows a user to obtain a ticket granting ticket (TGT) from the Key Distribution Center (KDC). Issuing the **kinit** command has the Kerberos client contact the KDC and obtain a TGT.

☑   After you run kinit, the cache will contain only the TGT. Additional credentials, such as actual tickets to access a daemon such as FTP, will be added only after you access the remote host.

Establishing Kerberos Client Trust Relationships with kadmin

☑   The only way to establish a trust relationship on the Kerberos client host is to use the **kadmin** command.

☑   The administrator must use the **kadmin –ktadd** command on each Kerberos client that wishes to participate in the Kerberos realm. The **kadmin ktadd –k** command gives each client the ability to prove that it has the public keys of the services used.

Logging On to a Kerberos Host Daemon

☑   Client A, the Kerberized client, first uses its TGT to request a session ticket. The Kerberos KDC checks to see if Client B has a host principal entry, then also checks to see if Client B has a host daemon entry for FTP. Then, the KDC determines that Client A has the proper host and host daemon keys for client B. If all of these credentials match, then client A can connect to client B's FTP server.

☑   When you try to administer Kerberos using **kadmin**, it is important to realize that if you make significant changes to the database concerning a user, you will have to use **kdestroy** and then **kinit** to obtain new credentials.

☑   You must configure your Kerberos client hosts to use only Kerberized clients. In order to use Kerberos properly, no other client applications or server daemons should be used on the network, unless they use OTP, encryption, or a similarly secure protocol.

❖ Chapter 7 Avoiding Sniffing Attacks through Encryption

Understanding Network Encryption

☑ Network encryption is used for any data transfer that requires confidentiality. Encryption ensures that data sent across a network from one host to another is unreadable to a third party.

☑ Rlogin, remote shell (rsh), and Telnet are three notoriously unsafe protocols. They do not use encryption for remote logins or any type of data transmission. If a malicious hacker captured this traffic, it would display the data, such as usernames or any passwords, in clear text.

Capturing and Analyzing Unencrypted Network Traffic

☑ You can capture packets during a Telnet login session using the open source packet sniffer Ethereal. Once the session is captured, you can locate the Telnet data packet that includes the *data: password* field.

☑ Another way to discover the Telnet password is to follow the TCP stream. To do this, simply select any packet involved in this Telnet connection, then select the **Tools** menu, and select **Follow TCP Stream** in Ethereal. The username and password are displayed in clear text.

Using OpenSSH to Encrypt Network Traffic between Two Hosts

☑ OpenSSH encrypts all traffic between two hosts using Secure Shell (SSH). It is a secure replacement for common Internet programs used for remote connectivity, such as Telnet, rlogin, and rsh.

☑ It features strong encryption using Triple Data Encryption Standard (3DES) and Blowfish, as well as strong authentication using public keys, one-time passwords (OTPs), and Kerberos Authentication.

Chapter 7 Continued

Installing and Configuring Secure Shell on Two Network Hosts

☑ OpenSSH implementations are significantly different between operating systems. The OpenSSH Portability Team uses the OpenBSD OpenSSH code to develop portable versions for other operating systems. You must make sure a specific version exists for your operating system at www.openssh.org.

☑ The method for implementing SSH combines similar r-command concepts with a private and public key method.

☑ SSH can create a DSA private/public key pair for a user by using the **ssh-keygen –d** command. In SSH 2.0, the private DSA key is placed in the *$HOME/.ssh/id_dsa* file. The public key is placed in the *$HOME/.ssh/id_dsa.pub* file. The public key should be renamed and copied to the *$HOME/.ssh/authorized_keys2* file on the remote system.

Implementing SSH to Secure Data Transmissions over an Insecure Network

☑ Both hosts must have SSH installed to transmit data securely, such as the SSH implementation.

☑ You must first use **ssh-keygen** to create a private and public key on each host using either RSA or DSA authentication. Then, distribute the public key to the host with which you wish to communicate, and vice versa.

☑ To establish the connection using SSH, the **ssh** command is used in the format **ssh *remotehost***. *Remotehost* is the name of the host you will connect to using SSH.

Capturing and Analyzing Encrypted Network Traffic

☑ You can capture packets between two hosts using an SSH session to determine if the data is secure. For example, you can attempt to identify any login data, as well as any session data.

☑ Using Ethereal, or any packet-capturing program, you will find that all Application layer data is encrypted. No passwords, usernames, or usable data

Chapter 7 Continued

is displayed. Following a TCP stream is fruitless. Only the TCP ports are displayed in the capture.

❖ Chapter 8 Creating Virtual Private Networks

Secure Tunneling with VPNs

☑ VPNs provide a private data network over public telecommunication infra-structures, such as the Internet, by providing authentication and encryption through a data "tunnel" between devices. All data transmitted between the devices through the tunnel is secure, regardless of what programs the devices are running.

☑ Telecommuter, router-to-router, and host-to-host are three the basic types of VPN solutions. The solution you choose will depend on your specific needs.

☑ Tunneling protocols are responsible for encapsulating a data packet before a host transmits it. The data is encapsulated and sent over the network to its destination. Upon arrival, the capsule is removed and the data is processed by the destination host. IP tunneling protocols are powerful because they can transmit foreign protocols over the Internet.

Explaining the IP Security Architecture

☑ IPSec is an Internet Engineering Task Force (IETF) security protocol that is becoming a standard component of VPN tunneling protocols.

☑ IPSec secures all packets at Layer 3 (the network layer) of the OSI model by providing secure authentication and encryption over a network. Layer 3 security ensures that everything on the network is secure, such as IP addressing and routing over the Internet, as well as all application data.

Creating a VPN by Using FreeS/WAN

☑ FreeS/WAN is a Linux VPN implementation that uses IPSec and IKE.

☑ IKE is a key management protocol standard that enhances IPSec. It provides enhancements such as simplifying IPSec configuration and adding flexibility

Chapter 8 Continued

and more features. It is not required for IPSec, but is often used in conjunction with it. FreeS/WAN uses Pluto, which is an IKE daemon.

☑ The Authentication Header (AH) performs authentication at the packet level in IPSec. The Encapsulating Security Payload (ESP) performs encryption as well as authentication. FreeS/WAN uses the Kernel IPSec (KLIPS) to perform AH and ESP functions.

❖ Chapter 9 Implementing a Firewall with Ipchains and Iptables

Understanding the Need for a Firewall

☑ Linux natively supports the ability to route and/or filter packets. Modern Linux systems use either *Ipchains* or *Iptables* to do this. Ipchains supports Linux kernel versions up to 2.2. If you are using any kernel newer than 2.2, you must use Iptables. The Iptables package supports packet masquerading and filtering functionality as found in the 2.3 kernel and later. This functionality is known as *netfilter*. Therefore, in order to use Iptables, you must recompile the kernel so that netfilter is installed, and you must install the Iptables package.

☑ Ipchains and Iptables also allow you to configure your Linux router to *masquerade* traffic (i.e., to rewrite IP headers so that a packet appears to originate from a certain host), and/or to examine and block traffic. The practice of examining and blocking traffic is often called *packet filtering*.

☑ The primary difference between a packet-filtering router (e.g., one created by using Ipchains or Iptables) and a proxy server (e.g., one enabled by Squid) is that a packet-filtering router does not inspect network packets as deeply as a proxy server does. However, proxy servers require more system resources in order to process network packets.

☑ Watch for bug reports concerning Ipchains, Iptables, and the Linux kernel. Keeping current about such changes can help you quickly upgrade your system in case a problem is discovered.

Chapter 9 Continued

Deploying IP Forwarding and Masquerading

☑ IP forwarding is the ability for a Linux system to act as a router.

☑ A Linux system with simple IP forwarding enabled can route any network address to another. If you are allotted a range of IP addresses from a local or regional Internet registry, you can use a multihomed Linux system to route this set of addresses to another network.

☑ In order to allow private network addresses to reach the Internet, you need to invoke Ipchains/Iptables-based IP masquerading.

☑ In a Linux router, you can use either Ipchains or Iptables to forward and/or alter the IP headers of packets originating from private-IP address networks to pass through Internet routers. Both Ipchains and Iptables do this by processing IP packets through the Linux kernel. You should note that this option is not necessarily secure—IP masquerading leaves all client hosts wide open to attack.

☑ Masquerading is when your Linux system rewrites the IP headers of a network packet so that the packet appears to originate from a different host. The practice of rewriting IP packets is colloquially known as *packet mangling*. Masquerading is useful because you can use it to invoke network address translation (NAT), where one IP address can stand in for several.

☑ Translating the private to routable Internet address is accomplished by a database stored on the Ipchains/Iptables-based Linux router. The Linux masquerading router keeps this database so that it knows how to "untranslate," as it were, the packets that have been mangled so that they can then be addressed to the local, private network.

Configuring Your Firewall to Filter Network Packets

☑ To create packet-filtering rules for outgoing traffic, configure your Linux firewall to deny all outgoing traffic unless explicitly allowed. Where incoming traffic is concerned, you have many options, including to forbid all incoming traffic unless it is part of an already established session, and to disable all forwarding except for networks that require it.

Chapter 9 Continued

☑ Most Linux operating systems, such as Red Hat, Slackware, SuSE, and Caldera, support IP forwarding, masquerading, and firewalling by default. However, you may have to reconfigure your kernel in order to provide full functionality.

Understanding Tables and Chains in a Linux Firewall

☑ Iptables derives its name from the three default tables it uses: *filter*, *nat*, and *mangle*. Each interface on your system can have its packets managed and modified by the chains contained in each of these tables.

☑ A chain is a series of actions to take on a packet. Whenever you use Ipchains or Iptables to configure a firewall, the proper perspective to adopt is to view all packets from the firewall itself.

☑ If you are using the filter table, each interface on your network has three different default chains: INPUT, FORWARD, and OUTPUT.

☑ Ipchains and Iptables use built-in targets to specify the destination of a packet. By far, the common most built-in targets are DROP and ACCEPT.

Logging Packets at the Firewall

☑ The Iptables **-l** option allows you to log matching packets. You can insert **-l** into any rule, as long as you do not interrupt a particular option. Iptables allows you to log packets in a more sophisticated way because it uses the LOG target, which you specify just like DROP or ACCEPT.

☑ By default, Iptables will limit logging of packets. The default limit rate is three logging instances an hour. This behavior is meant to ensure that log files do not get too large.

☑ An example used in this section uses Ipchains and Iptables commands to add and remove packet-filtering rules, prohibiting every service from entering your firewall, except for Secure Shell (SSH), which uses port 22. This would not allow any user interactively logged in to the system to check e-mail or any other Internet-based service—the rule is restrictive, but is designed to lock down the firewall as much as possible.

☑ With Iptables, you can reject specific ICMP types.

Chapter 9 Continued

☑ Port redirection in Ipchains and Iptables is where a packet destined for a certain port (say, port 80) is received by an interface, and is then sent to another port, using the REDIRECT target. Redirecting ports is common in networks that use proxy servers.

Configuring a Firewall

☑ Regardless of whether you are using Ipchains or Iptables, the first thing you will have to do for your firewall is to flush all existing rules using the **-F** option. Then, you need to use the **-P** option to set the firewall policies to deny all connections by default. The subsequent rules you create will then allow the protocols you really want. Then, use the necessary commands to enable forwarding and masquerading. Without this foundation, you will not be able to forward packets at all, and thus firewalling them would be superfluous.

☑ Many times, a hacker will try to use your firewall as a default gateway and try to spoof internal packets. If a firewall's "Internet interface" (i.e., the one that is responsible for addressing packets to the Internet) is not configured to explicitly deny packets from the network, then you are susceptible to this attack.

☑ The example describing allowing inbound and outbound TCP connections illustrates that with Ipchains and Iptables, the **!** character reverses the meaning of anything that is in front of it.

☑ Creating the ideal packet-filtering rules requires some trial and error, as well as research specific to your own situation.

Counting Bandwidth Usage

☑ A Linux firewall can inform you about the number of packets it has processed, in addition to blocking and logging attacks. The process of counting packets is often called *packet accounting*.

☑ Many routers, including Linux routers using Ipchains or Iptables, are capable of shaping traffic as it passes through. The IP header for all packets has a spe-

Chapter 9 Continued

cial field called the Type of Service (ToS) field, which allows you to prioritize traffic as it passes through the router.

☑ The main reason why you would set the ToS field in network traffic is to cut down on network congestion, especially in networks that have high amounts of traffic.

Using and Obtaining Automated Firewall Scripts and Graphical Firewall Utilities

☑ Several attempts have been made to automate the process of creating a firewall in Linux. Many of these utilities are quite useful, although they are mostly effective in *beginning* your firewall configuration; you will likely have to customize the rules these applications generate.

☑ Most of these applications are still in beta form, so remember that they often provide limited functionality.

☑ Firestarter is a fairly sophisticated graphical tool that supports both Ipchains and Iptables. It can be used to create a personal firewall, but also supports multihomed systems.

☑ Mason is designed to first listen in on traffic passing through your firewall, and then generate Ipchains or ipfwadm (the precursor to ipchains and Iptables) rules.

☑ Firewall Builder is in many ways the most ambitious open source GUI tool. It allows you to create rules for multiple interfaces, networks, and hosts.

❖ Chapter 10 Deploying the Squid Web Proxy Cache Server

Benefits of Proxy Server Implementation

☑ A Web proxy cache server can cache Web pages and FTP files for proxy clients. They can also cache Web sites for load balancing.

Chapter 10 Continued

☑ Caching increases the performance of the network by decreasing the amount of data transferred from outside of the local network.

☑ Web proxy caching reduces bandwidth costs, increases network performance during normal traffic and spikes, performs load balancing, caches aborted requests, and functions even when a network's Internet connection fails.

Differentiating between a Packet Filter and a Proxy Server

☑ Packet filters analyze traffic at the Network (Layer 3) and Transport layers (Layer 4) of the OSI model. A packet filter can determine whether it will allow a certain IP address or IP address range to pass through, or filter traffic by service, or port number.

☑ A proxy server analyzes packets at the Application layer (Layer 7) of the OSI model. This feature provides flexibility because the traffic within one service, such as port 80 (HTTP) traffic, can be filtered.

Implementing the Squid Web Proxy Cache Server

☑ The Squid Web Proxy Cache server allows administrators to set up a Web proxy caching service, add access controls (rules), and cache DNS lookups.

☑ Client protocols supported by Squid must be sent as a proxy request in HTTP format, and include FTP, HTTP, SSL, WAIS, and Gopher.

☑ Squid is configured using the /etc/squid/squid.conf file, which defines configurations such as the HTTP port number on which Squid listens for HTTP requests, incoming and outgoing requests, timeout information, and firewall access data.

☑ Each configuration option in squid.conf is identified as a *tag*. The http_port tag configures the HTTP port on which Squid listens for proxy clients. The cache_dir tag specifies where the cached data is stored. The acl tag allows you to define an access list. The http_access tag permits or denies access to Squid. Squid will not function until you make changes to the squid.conf file.

Chapter 10 Continued

Configuring Proxy Clients

☑ Firewalls can be configured to forward all port 80 traffic leaving the network to the Web proxy cache server—clients do not need manual configuration. In other cases, proxy clients automatically detect the proxy server information on the network and use it for all Internet access.

☑ All manual proxy client configurations are completed within the browser application, and it's just a matter of specifying the address of the Web proxy cache server.

❖ Chapter 11 Maintaining Firewalls

Testing Firewalls

☑ To disallow IP spoofing, your firewall should not allow any packets to pass from outside the network into your internal network if the source address is the same as any host in your internal network. If you are using private IP addresses, no system outside of the firewall should ever be able to assume this IP address and access your internal network's ephemeral ports.

☑ Disable all unused services and configure the used ones keeping security in mind. If you are running Squid or another proxy server on the firewall, make sure that only this port is open. Daemons such as Telnet, File Transfer Protocol (FTP), Hypertext Transfer Protocol (HTTP), and others should be shut down in almost all situations. In many situations, it is best to allow only interactive logins at your firewall.

☑ Monitor your system hard drives, RAM, and processors. You may need to cut back on your log settings. Standard Linux tools that can help you determine if your system is becoming overburdened are *vmstat* and *top*.

☑ Use the **who** and **last** commands to learn about who has logged in to the firewall.

☑ Check the rules database. Determine if any unauthorized changes have been made to your database. Use the **diff** command to compare the two files to see if any changes have occurred. You may also use **md5** to generate fingerprints of the configuration files to see whether any unauthorized changes

Chapter 11 Continued

have been made to them. If you have Tripwire installed, you will then be informed of massive changes to the hard drive.

☑ Verify connectivity with company management and end users, and remain informed concerning the operating system.

☑ The introduction of log analysis software such as Firelogd and Fwlogdaemon have made it possible to detect and block port scans, all the while sending an alert to the systems administrator. Most adjunct software, such as Fwlogwatch, provides ways to exclude trusted hosts from being blocked.

Using Telnet, Ipchains, Netcat, and SendIP to Probe Your Firewall

☑ Although Iptables does not support rule checking, the **ipchains –C** command allows you to check how your existing rule set operates. It will return information as to whether the packet is dropped or accepted. It is up to you to act on this information. This tool is handy if you are logged in to the same system as you are testing, and you are becoming familiar with the existing rules and wish to send out packets that test how the rules are working.

☑ A simple port scan can help you determine which ports are open on your firewall. Using applications such as Telnet and Netcat, you can then determine what daemon is listening behind that port.

☑ If you have logged in to the firewall interactively, it is often useful to open two terminals. You can use the first terminal to issue the **telnet** command, and you can use the second terminal to view the results in the /var/log/messages file.

☑ When compiled properly, Netcat can also spoof IP addresses. If you have set a firewall rule to deny a particular source port, you can test it with Netcat. Because Netcat is so versatile, it can also be used against you to open a back door on your system. Therefore, if possible, you should install this application only on a client system, rather than on the router.

☑ Although Netcat does have the ability to create some packets in certain instances, it is not a true packet generator. SendIP is designed to allow you to create packets of your own design to test whether your firewall rules are working properly.

Chapter 11 Continued

☑   SendIP allows you to forge any part of a Transmission Control Protocol
(TCP) session, as well as any element of an IP, User Datagram Protocol
(UDP), or Internet Control Message Protocol (ICMP) packet. SendIP also
allows you to forge all elements of IPv6 addresses, and also allows you to forge
Routing Information Protocol (RIP) packets. This tool is useful in regard to
firewalls because it allows you to simulate any situation.

Understanding Firewall Logging, Blocking, and Alert Options

☑   Third-party logging applications such as Firewall Log Daemon (Firelogd)
and FwLogwatch are available to help you sort and act on the information
gathered by the firewall.

☑   Firelogd, which supports both Ipchains and Iptables, can be run either as an
application, or as a daemon. It reads the kernel log entries generated by
either Ipchains or Iptables and passes them into a "first in, first out" (FIFO)
pipe, which Firelogd can then process. Once its buffer is full, it e-mails a
report of suspicious traffic to an account of your choosing. You can have it
mailed to a local account, or to a remote system of your choice.

☑   Fwlogwatch is a logging and reporting mechanism, similar to Firelogd but
far more versatile, that allows you to automatically block all traffic that is
identified as an attack. Used in conjunction with Firelogd, it helps create a
system that continuously keeps you informed concerning port scans and
other network events that surpass the thresholds you set.

☑   The most intriguing feature of Fwlogwatch is its ability to automatically
configure Ipchains/Iptables and issue alerts. The best way to do this is to edit
the three configuration files to suit your needs: **/etc/fwlogwatch.config**
(or whatever you rename it to), **/usr/sbin/fwlw_notify**, and
/usr/sbin/fwlw_respond.

Chapter 11 Continued

Obtaining Additional Firewall Logging Tools

☑ Additional firewall logging tools include Ipchains logger, LogGrep, Open Correlation, Fwlogsum, IP Firewall Accounting (IPFA), Appsend, Ipmeter, Mrtg, and Ntop.

☑ Ipchains logger is a logging enhancer similar to Fwlogd, but limited to Ipchains. It is especially strong in its ability to log masqueraded connections.

☑ The LogGrep daemon uses the grep utility to read and sort log files. It is limited, as of this writing, to Ipchains. With this utility, you can sort protocol, date, IP port firewall log entries to generate custom log files. Currently, it can also discover port scans, and generates HTML pages.

☑ Ntop is a powerful tool that allows you to identify the nature of all egress and ingress traffic. It is much like the standard top application, in that it gathers information about hosts, and then places the most active hosts at the top of the display. It can be run on a terminal just like the standard top application; you can run it in Web server mode, or as a Web server. This mode supports authentication, thus allowing you to easily limit access to only specific users.

Index

9000 Regency Parkway, Suite 500
Cary, NC 27512
1-800-COURSES
www.globalknowledge.com

At Global Knowledge, we strive to support the multiplicity of learning styles required by our students to achieve success as technical professionals. We do this because we know our students need different training approaches to achieve success as technical professionals. That's why Global Knowledge has worked with Syngress Publishing in reviewing and recommending this book as a valuable tool for successful mastery of this subject.

As the world's largest independent corporate IT training company, Global Knowledge is uniquely positioned to recommend these books. The first hand expertise we have gained over the past several years from providing instructor-led training to well over a million students worldwide has been captured in book form to enhance your learning experience. We hope the quality of these books demonstrates our commitment to your life-long learning success. Whether you choose to learn through the written word, e-Learning, or instructor-led training, Global Knowledge is committed to providing you the choice of when, where and how you want your IT knowledge and skills to be delivered. For those of you who know Global Knowledge, or those of you who have just found us for the first time, our goal is to be your lifelong partner and help you achieve your professional goals.

Thank you for the opportunity to serve you. We look forward to serving your needs again in the future.

Warmest regards,

Duncan M. Anderson
President and Chief Executive Officer, Global Knowledge

P.S.   Please visit us at our Web site www.globalknowledge.com.

Enter the Global Knowledge
Chrysler PT Cruiser Sweepstakes

This sweepstakes is open only to legal residents of the United States who are Business to Business MIS/IT managers or staff and training decision makers, that are 18 years of age or older at time of entry. Void in Florida & Puerto Rico.

OFFICIAL RULES

No Purchase or Transaction Necessary To Enter or Win, purchasing will not increase your chances of winning.

1. How to Enter: Sweepstakes begins at 12:00:01 AM ET May 1, 2001 and ends 12:59:59 PM ET December 31, 2001 the ("Promotional Period"). There are four ways to enter to win the Global Knowledge PT Cruiser Sweepstakes: Online, at Trade shows, by mail or by purchasing a course or software. Entrants may enter via any of or all methods of entry.

[1] To be automatically entered online, visit our web at www.globalknowledge.com click on the link named Cruiser and complete the registration form in its entirety. All online entries must be received by 12:59:59 PM ET December 31, 2001. Only one online entry per person, per e-mail address. Entrants must be the registered subscriber of the e-mail account by which the entry is made.

[2] At the various trade shows, during the promotional period by scanning your admission badge at our Global Knowledge Booth. All entries must be made no later than the close of the trade shows. Only one admission badge entry per person.

[3] By mail or official entry blank available at participating book stores throughout the promotional period. Complete the official entry blank or hand print your complete name and address and day & evening telephone # on a 3"x5" card, and mail to: Global Knowledge PT Cruiser Sweepstakes, P.O. Box 4012 Grand Rapids, MN 55730-4012. Entries must be postmarked by 12/31/01 and received by 1/07/02. Mechanically reproduced entries will not be accepted. Only one mail in entry per person.

[4] By purchasing a training course or software during the promotional period: online at http://www.globalknowledge.com or by calling 1–800–COURSES, entrants will automatically receive an entry onto the sweepstakes. Only one purchase entry per person.

All entries become the property of the Sponsor and will not be returned. Sponsor is not responsible for stolen, lost, late, misdirected, damaged, incomplete, illegible entries or postage due mail.

2. Drawings: There will be five [5] bonus drawings and one [1] prize will be awarded in each bonus drawing. To be eligible for the bonus drawings, on-line entries, trade show entries and purchase entries must be received as of the dates listed on the entry chart below in order to be eligible for the corresponding bonus drawing. Mail in entries must be postmarked by the last day of the bonus period, except for the month ending 9/30/01 where mail in entries must be postmarked by 10/1/01 and received one day prior to the drawing date indicated on the entry

chart below. Only one bonus prize per person or household for the entire promotion period.
Entries eligible for one bonus drawing will not be included in subsequent bonus drawings.

Bonus Drawings	Month starting/ending 12:00:01 AM ET/11:59:59 PM ET	Drawing Date on or about
1	5/1/01–7/31/01	8/8/01
2	8/1/01–8/31/01	9/11/01
3	9/1/01–9/30/01	10/10/01
4	10/1/01–10/31/01	11/9/01
5	11/1/01–11/30/01	12/11/01

There will also be a grand prize drawing in this sweepstakes. The grand prize drawing will be conducted on January 8, 2002 from all entries received. Bonus winners are eligible to win the Grand prize.

All random sweepstakes drawings will be conducted by Marden-Kane, Inc. an independent judging organization whose decisions are final. All prizes will be awarded. The estimated odds of winning each bonus drawing are 1:60,000, for the first drawing and 1:20,000 for the second, third, fourth and fifth drawings, and the estimated odds of winning the grand prize drawing is 1:100,000. However the actual odds of winning will depend upon the total number of eligible entries received for each bonus drawing and grand prize drawings.

3. Prizes: Grand Prize: One (1) PT Cruiser 2002 model Approx. Retail Value (ARV) $18,000. Winner may elect to receive the cash equivalent in lieu of the car. Bonus Prizes: Five (5), awarded one (1) per bonus period. Up to $1,400.00 in self paced learning products ARV up to $1,400.00 each.

No substitutions, cash equivalents, except as noted, or transfers of the prize will be permitted except at the sole discretion of the Sponsor, who reserves the right to substitute a prize of equal or greater value in the event an offered prize is unavailable for any reason. Winner is responsible for payment of all taxes on the prize, license, registration, title fees, insurance, and for any other expense not specifically described herein. Winner must have and will be required to furnish proof of a valid driver's license. Manufacturers warranties and guarantees apply.

4. Eligibility: This sweepstakes is open only to legal residents of the United States, except Florida and Puerto Rico residents who are Business to Business MIS/IT managers or staff and training decision makers, that are 18 years of age or older at the time of entry. Employees of Global Knowledge Network, Inc and its subsidiaries, advertising and promotion agencies including Marden-Kane, Inc., and immediate families (spouse, parents, children, siblings and their respective spouses) living in the same household as employees of these organizations are ineligible. Sweepstakes is void in Florida and Puerto Rico and is subject to all applicable federal, state and local laws and regulations. By participating, entrants agree to be bound by the official rules and accept decisions of judges as final in all matters relating to this sweepstakes.

5. Notification: Winners will be notified by certified mail, return receipt requested, and may be required to complete and sign an Affidavit of Eligibility/Liability Release and, where legal, a Publicity Release, which must be returned, properly executed, within fourteen (14) days of

664

issuance of prize notification. If these documents are not returned properly executed or are returned from the post office as undeliverable, the prize will be forfeited and awarded to an alternate winner. Entrants agree to the use of their name, voice and photograph/likeness for advertising and promotional purposes for this and similar promotions without additional compensation, except where prohibited by law.

6. <u>Limitation of Liability:</u> By participating in the Sweepstakes, entrants agree to indemnify and hold harmless the Sponsor, Marden-Kane, Inc. their affiliates, subsidiaries and their respective agents, representatives, officers, directors, shareholders and employees (collectively, "Releasees") from any injuries, losses, damages, claims and actions of any kind resulting from or arising from participation in the Sweepstakes or acceptance, possession, use, misuse or nonuse of any prize that may be awarded. Releasees are not responsible for printing or typographical errors in any instant win game related materials; for stolen, lost, late, misdirected, damaged, incomplete, illegible entries; or for transactions, or admissions badge scans that are lost, misdirected, fail to enter into the processing system, or are processed, reported, or transmitted late or incorrectly or are lost for any reason including computer, telephone, paper transfer, human, error; or for electronic, computer, scanning equipment or telephonic malfunction or error, including inability to access the Site. If in the Sponsor's opinion, there is any suspected or actual evidence of electronic or non-electronic tampering with any portion of the game, or if computer virus, bugs, unauthorized intervention, fraud, actions of entrants or technical difficulties or failures compromise or corrupt or affect the administration, integrity, security, fairness, or proper conduct of the sweepstakes the judges reserve the right at their sole discretion to disqualify any individual who tampers with the entry process and void any entries submitted fraudulently, to modify or suspend the Sweepstakes, or to terminate the Sweepstakes and conduct a random drawing to award the prizes using all non-suspect entries received as of the termination date. Should the game be terminated or modified prior to the stated expiration date, notice will be posted on http://www.globalknowledge.com. Any attempt by an entrant or any other individual to deliberately damage any web site or undermine the legitimate operation of the promotion is a violation of criminal and civil laws and should such an attempt be made, the sponsor reserves the right to seek damages and other remedies from any such person to the fullest extent permitted by law. Any attempts by an individual to access the web site via a bot script or other brute force attack or any other unauthorized means will result in the IP address becoming ineligible. Use of automated entry devices or programs is prohibited.

7. <u>Winners List:</u> For the name of the winner visit our web site www.globalknowledge.com on January 31, 2002.

8. <u>Sponsor:</u> Global Knowledge Network, Inc., 9000 Regency Parkway, Cary, NC 27512. Administrator: Marden-Kane, Inc. 36 Maple Place, Manhasset, NY 11030.

GNU GENERAL PUBLIC LICENSE

Version 2, June 1991

Copyright (C) 1989, 1991 Free Software Foundation, Inc.
59 Temple Place - Suite 330, Boston, MA 02111-1307, USA

Everyone is permitted to copy and distribute verbatim copies
of this license document, but changing it is not allowed.

Preamble

The licenses for most software are designed to take away your freedom to share and change it. By contrast, the GNU General Public License is intended to guarantee your freedom to share and change free software—to make sure the software is free for all its users. This General Public License applies to most of the Free Software Foundation's software and to any other program whose authors commit to using it. (Some other Free Software Foundation software is covered by the GNU Library General Public License instead.) You can apply it to your programs, too.

When we speak of free software, we are referring to freedom, not price. Our General Public Licenses are designed to make sure that you have the freedom to distribute copies of free software (and charge for this service if you wish), that you receive source code or can get it if you want it, that you can change the software or use pieces of it in new free programs; and that you know you can do these things.

To protect your rights, we need to make restrictions that forbid anyone to deny you these rights or to ask you to surrender the rights. These restrictions translate to certain responsibilities for you if you distribute copies of the software, or if you modify it.

For example, if you distribute copies of such a program, whether gratis or for a fee, you must give the recipients all the rights that you have. You must make sure that they, too, receive or can get the source code. And you must show them these terms so they know their rights.

We protect your rights with two steps: (1) copyright the software, and (2) offer you this license which gives you legal permission to copy, distribute and/or modify the software.

Also, for each author's protection and ours, we want to make certain that everyone understands that there is no warranty for this free software. If the software is modified by someone else and passed on, we want its recipients to know that what they have is not the original, so that any problems introduced by others will not reflect on the original authors' reputations.

Finally, any free program is threatened constantly by software patents. We wish to avoid the danger that redistributors of a free program will individually obtain patent licenses, in effect making the program proprietary. To prevent this, we have made it clear that any patent must be licensed for everyone's free use or not licensed at all.

The precise terms and conditions for copying, distribution and modification follow.

TERMS AND CONDITIONS FOR COPYING, DISTRIBUTION AND MODIFICATION

0. This License applies to any program or other work which contains a notice placed by the copyright holder saying it may be distributed under the terms of this General Public License. The

"Program", below, refers to any such program or work, and a "work based on the Program" means either the Program or any derivative work under copyright law: that is to say, a work containing the Program or a portion of it, either verbatim or with modifications and/or translated into another language. (Hereinafter, translation is included without limitation in the term "modification".) Each licensee is addressed as "you".

Activities other than copying, distribution and modification are not covered by this License; they are outside its scope. The act of running the Program is not restricted, and the output from the Program is covered only if its contents constitute a work based on the Program (independent of having been made by running the Program). Whether that is true depends on what the Program does.

1. You may copy and distribute verbatim copies of the Program's source code as you receive it, in any medium, provided that you conspicuously and appropriately publish on each copy an appropriate copyright notice and disclaimer of warranty; keep intact all the notices that refer to this License and to the absence of any warranty; and give any other recipients of the Program a copy of this License along with the Program.

You may charge a fee for the physical act of transferring a copy, and you may at your option offer warranty protection in exchange for a fee.

2. You may modify your copy or copies of the Program or any portion of it, thus forming a work based on the Program, and copy and distribute such modifications or work under the terms of Section 1 above, provided that you also meet all of these conditions:

a) You must cause the modified files to carry prominent notices stating that you changed the files and the date of any change.

b) You must cause any work that you distribute or publish, that in whole or in part contains or is derived from the Program or any part thereof, to be licensed as a whole at no charge to all third parties under the terms of this License.

c) If the modified program normally reads commands interactively when run, you must cause it, when started running for such interactive use in the most ordinary way, to print or display an announcement including an appropriate copyright notice and a notice that there is no warranty (or else, saying that you provide a warranty) and that users may redistribute the program under these conditions, and telling the user how to view a copy of this License.

(Exception: if the Program itself is interactive but does not normally print such an announcement, your work based on the Program is not required to print an announcement.)

These requirements apply to the modified work as a whole. If identifiable sections of that work are not derived from the Program, and can be reasonably considered independent and separate works in themselves, then this License, and its terms, do not apply to those sections when you distribute them as separate works. But when you distribute the same sections as part of a whole which is a work based on the Program, the distribution of the whole must be on the terms of this License, whose permissions for other licensees extend to the entire whole, and thus to each and every part regardless of who wrote it.

Thus, it is not the intent of this section to claim rights or contest your rights to work written entirely by you; rather, the intent is to exercise the right to control the distribution of derivative or collective works based on the Program.

In addition, mere aggregation of another work not based on the Program with the Program (or with a work based on the Program) on a volume of a storage or distribution medium does not bring the other work under the scope of this License.

3. You may copy and distribute the Program (or a work based on it, under Section 2) in object code or executable form under the terms of Sections 1 and 2 above provided that you also do one of the following:

a) Accompany it with the complete corresponding machine-readable source code, which must be distributed under the terms of Sections 1 and 2 above on a medium customarily used for software interchange; or,

b) Accompany it with a written offer, valid for at least three years, to give any third party, for a charge no more than your cost of physically performing source distribution, a complete machine-readable copy of the corresponding source code, to be distributed under the terms of Sections 1 and 2 above on a medium customarily used for software interchange; or,

c) Accompany it with the information you received as to the offer to distribute corresponding source code. (This alternative is allowed only for noncommercial distribution and only if you received the program in object code or executable form with such an offer, in accord with Subsection b above.)

The source code for a work means the preferred form of the work for making modifications to it. For an executable work, complete source code means all the source code for all modules it contains, plus any associated interface definition files, plus the scripts used to control compilation and installation of the executable. However, as a special exception, the source code distributed need not include anything that is normally distributed (in either source or binary form) with the major components (compiler, kernel, and so on) of the operating system on which the executable runs, unless that component itself accompanies the executable.

If distribution of executable or object code is made by offering access to copy from a designated place, then offering equivalent access to copy the source code from the same place counts as distribution of the source code, even though third parties are not compelled to copy the source along with the object code.

4. You may not copy, modify, sublicense, or distribute the Program except as expressly provided under this License. Any attempt otherwise to copy, modify, sublicense or distribute the Program is void, and will automatically terminate your rights under this License. However, parties who have received copies, or rights, from you under this License will not have their licenses terminated so long as such parties remain in full compliance.

5. You are not required to accept this License, since you have not signed it. However, nothing else grants you permission to modify or distribute the Program or its derivative works. These actions are prohibited by law if you do not accept this License. Therefore, by modifying or distributing

the Program (or any work based on the Program), you indicate your acceptance of this License to do so, and all its terms and conditions for copying, distributing or modifying the Program or works based on it.

6. Each time you redistribute the Program (or any work based on the Program), the recipient automatically receives a license from the original licensor to copy, distribute or modify the Program subject to these terms and conditions. You may not impose any further restrictions on the recipients' exercise of the rights granted herein. You are not responsible for enforcing compliance by third parties to this License.

7. If, as a consequence of a court judgment or allegation of patent infringement or for any other reason (not limited to patent issues), conditions are imposed on you (whether by court order, agreement or otherwise) that contradict the conditions of this License, they do not excuse you from the conditions of this License. If you cannot distribute so as to satisfy simultaneously your obligations under this License and any other pertinent obligations, then as a consequence you may not distribute the Program at all. For example, if a patent license would not permit royalty-free redistribution of the Program by all those who receive copies directly or indirectly through you, then the only way you could satisfy both it and this License would be to refrain entirely from distribution of the Program.

If any portion of this section is held invalid or unenforceable under any particular circumstance, the balance of the section is intended to apply and the section as a whole is intended to apply in other circumstances.

It is not the purpose of this section to induce you to infringe any patents or other property right claims or to contest validity of any such claims; this section has the sole purpose of protecting the integrity of the free software distribution system, which is implemented by public license practices. Many people have made generous contributions to the wide range of software distributed through that system in reliance on consistent application of that system; it is up to the author/donor to decide if he or she is willing to distribute software through any other system and a licensee cannot impose that choice.

This section is intended to make thoroughly clear what is believed to be a consequence of the rest of this License.

8. If the distribution and/or use of the Program is restricted in certain countries either by patents or by copyrighted interfaces, the original copyright holder who places the Program under this License may add an explicit geographical distribution limitation excluding those countries, so that distribution is permitted only in or among countries not thus excluded. In such case, this License incorporates the limitation as if written in the body of this License.

9. The Free Software Foundation may publish revised and/or new versions of the General Public License from time to time. Such new versions will be similar in spirit to the present version, but may differ in detail to address new problems or concerns.

Each version is given a distinguishing version number. If the Program specifies a version number of this License which applies to it and "any later version", you have the option of following the terms and conditions either of that version or of any later version published by the Free Software

Foundation. If the Program does not specify a version number of this License, you may choose any version ever published by the Free Software Foundation.

10. If you wish to incorporate parts of the Program into other free programs whose distribution conditions are different, write to the author to ask for permission. For software which is copyrighted by the Free Software Foundation, write to the Free Software Foundation; we sometimes make exceptions for this. Our decision will be guided by the two goals of preserving the free status of all derivatives of our free software and of promoting the sharing and reuse of software generally.

NO WARRANTY

11. BECAUSE THE PROGRAM IS LICENSED FREE OF CHARGE, THERE IS NO WARRANTY FOR THE PROGRAM, TO THE EXTENT PERMITTED BY APPLICABLE LAW. EXCEPT WHEN OTHERWISE STATED IN WRITING THE COPYRIGHT HOLDERS AND/OR OTHER PARTIES PROVIDE THE PROGRAM "AS IS" WITHOUT WARRANTY OF ANY KIND, EITHER EXPRESSED OR IMPLIED, INCLUDING, BUT NOT LIMITED TO, THE IMPLIED WARRANTIES OF MERCHANTABILITY AND FITNESS FOR A PARTICULAR PURPOSE. THE ENTIRE RISK AS TO THE QUALITY AND PERFORMANCE OF THE PROGRAM IS WITH YOU. SHOULD THE PROGRAM PROVE DEFECTIVE, YOU ASSUME THE COST OF ALL NECESSARY SERVICING, REPAIR OR CORRECTION.

12. IN NO EVENT UNLESS REQUIRED BY APPLICABLE LAW OR AGREED TO IN WRITING WILL ANY COPYRIGHT HOLDER, OR ANY OTHER PARTY WHO MAY MODIFY AND/OR REDISTRIBUTE THE PROGRAM AS PERMITTED ABOVE, BE LIABLE TO YOU FOR DAMAGES, INCLUDING ANY GENERAL, SPECIAL, INCIDENTAL OR CONSEQUENTIAL DAMAGES ARISING OUT OF THE USE OR INABILITY TO USE THE PROGRAM (INCLUDING BUT NOT LIMITED TO LOSS OF DATA OR DATA BEING RENDERED INACCURATE OR LOSSES SUSTAINED BY YOU OR THIRD PARTIES OR A FAILURE OF THE PROGRAM TO OPERATE WITH ANY OTHER PROGRAMS), EVEN IF SUCH HOLDER OR OTHER PARTY HAS BEEN ADVISED OF THE POSSIBILITY OF SUCH DAMAGES.

END OF TERMS AND CONDITIONS

How to Apply These Terms to Your New Programs

If you develop a new program, and you want it to be of the greatest possible use to the public, the best way to achieve this is to make it free software which everyone can redistribute and change under these terms.

To do so, attach the following notices to the program. It is safest to attach them to the start of each source file to most effectively convey the exclusion of warranty; and each file should have at least the "copyright" line and a pointer to where the full notice is found. and one line to give the program's name and an idea of what it does.

```
Copyright (C) yyyy  name of author

This program is free software; you can redistribute it and/or
modify it under the terms of the GNU General Public License
as published by the Free Software Foundation; either version 2
of the License, or (at your option) any later version.

This program is distributed in the hope that it will be useful,
but WITHOUT ANY WARRANTY; without even the implied warranty of
MERCHANTABILITY or FITNESS FOR A PARTICULAR PURPOSE.  See the
GNU General Public License for more details.

You should have received a copy of the GNU General Public License
along with this program; if not, write to the Free Software
Foundation, Inc., 59 Temple Place - Suite 330, Boston, MA  02111-1307,
USA.
```

Also add information on how to contact you by electronic and paper mail.

If the program is interactive, make it output a short notice like this when it starts in an interactive mode:

```
Gnomovision version 69, Copyright (C) year name of author
Gnomovision comes with ABSOLUTELY NO WARRANTY; for details
type `show w'.  This is free software, and you are welcome
to redistribute it under certain conditions; type `show c' for details.
```

The hypothetical commands `show w' and `show c' should show the appropriate parts of the General Public License. Of course, the commands you use may be called something other than `show w' and `show c'; they could even be mouse-clicks or menu items—whatever suits your program.

You should also get your employer (if you work as a programmer) or your school, if any, to sign a "copyright disclaimer" for the program, if necessary. Here is a sample; alter the names:

```
Yoyodyne, Inc., hereby disclaims all copyright
interest in the program `Gnomovision'
(which makes passes at compilers) written
by James Hacker.

signature of Ty Coon, 1 April 1989
Ty Coon, President of Vice
```

This General Public License does not permit incorporating your program into proprietary programs. If your program is a subroutine library, you may consider it more useful to permit linking proprietary applications with the library. If this is what you want to do, use the GNU Library General Public License instead of this License.

672